American
Amphibious Gunboats
in World War II

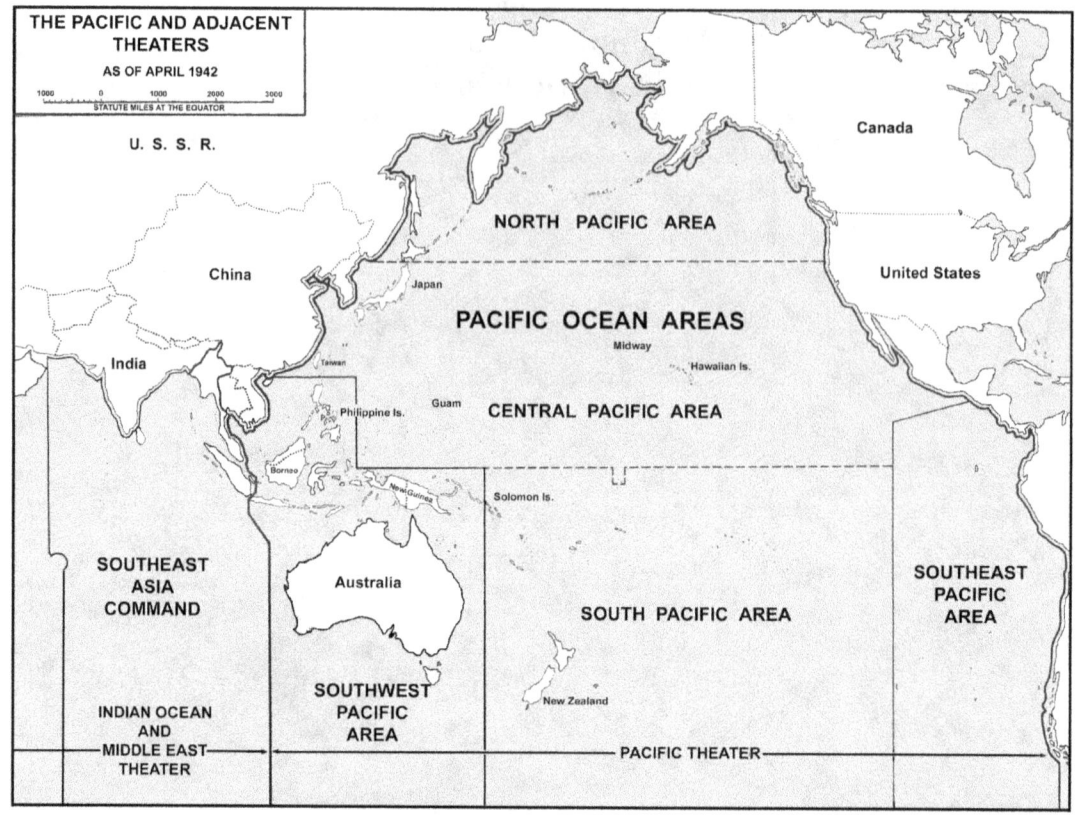

This map of the Pacific Theater and adjacent areas was adapted from map II in Louis Morton's *Strategy and Command: The First Two Years* (*United States Army in World War II* series) (Washington, D.C.: Office of the Chief of Military History, Department of the Army, 1989).

American Amphibious Gunboats in World War II

A History of LCI and LCS(L) Ships in the Pacific

ROBIN L. RIELLY

McFarland & Company, Inc., Publishers
Jefferson, North Carolina, and London

ALSO BY ROBIN L. RIELLY
AND FROM MCFARLAND

*Kamikaze Attacks of World War II:
A Complete History of Japanese Suicide Strikes on American Ships,
by Aircraft and Other Means* (2010; paperback 2012)

LIBRARY OF CONGRESS CATALOGUING-IN-PUBLICATION DATA

Rielly, Robin L.
American amphibious gunboats in World War II : a history
of LCI and LCS(L) ships in the Pacific / Robin L. Rielly.
    p.   cm.
Includes bibliographical references and index.

ISBN 978-0-7864-7422-6
softcover : acid free paper ∞

1. World War, 1939–1945 — Amphibious operations.
2. Amphibious assault ships — United States — History — 20th century.
3. Landing craft — United States — History — 20th century.
4. World War, 1939–1945 — Campaigns — Pacific Area.
5. World War, 1939–1945 — Naval operations, American.
I. Title. II. Title: History of LCI and LCS(L) ships in the Pacific.
D769.45.R48 2013   940.54'5973 — dc23   2013009393

BRITISH LIBRARY CATALOGUING DATA ARE AVAILABLE

© 2013 Robin L. Rielly. All rights reserved

*No part of this book may be reproduced or transmitted in any form
or by any means, electronic or mechanical, including photocopying
or recording, or by any information storage and retrieval system,
without permission in writing from the publisher.*

Cover photo: A line of LCI(R)s fire rockets at Peleliu on 15 September 1944.
The gunboat in the foreground is LCI(R) 77 (NARA 80G 59500)

Manufactured in the United States of America

*McFarland & Company, Inc., Publishers
Box 611, Jefferson, North Carolina 28640
www.mcfarlandpub.com*

For
Allison Shea Rielly

Table of Contents

Preface 1
Introduction 4

1. The Need for a New Weapon 7
2. From Training to Missions 45
3. Operation Cartwheel 73
4. The Central Pacific Campaigns 102
5. The Philippines Retaken — Leyte and Lingayen ... 143
6. The LCS(L)s Arrive 175
7. Iwo Jima 208
8. The Liberation of Borneo 236
9. Okinawa 256
10. Screening the Fleet 288
11. The Radar Picket Line 306
12. War's End and Post-War 329

Glossary 357
Appendix I: LCI Gunboat Flotillas and Commanding Officers 359
Appendix II: Building and Conversion Locations 363
Appendix III: LCS(L) Flotillas and Commanding Officers 365
*Appendix IV: LCI(G), LCI(M), LCI(R), and LCS(L) Ships Damaged
     or Lost in World War II* 368
Appendix V: Awards 370

Notes 372
Bibliography 381
Index 389

Preface

In the grand scale of the conflict that was World War II, the student of history has much to ponder. Most often one's attention is drawn to the major battles and campaigns, centering on the well-known names of admirals and generals. As it concerns naval history, this broad view of major characters and events leaves out an important part of the war, that of the individual ship or unit. In like manner, the capital ships are the objects of much attention as the decisive players in an engagement. Left in the backwater of our memories are the countless thousands of smaller ships and lower ranked officers and men who made great sacrifices and, in many cases, tipped the scales of the battle. This book details the exploits of a group of such naval combatants and their contributions in the Pacific Theater of the war. Collectively I have labeled these ships as the LCI gunboats which include the LCI(G)s, LCI(M)s, LCI(R)s, and LCS(L)s.

Many of these ships were converted in the war zone while others were converted soon after being completed at the builder's yards. Identifying the ships with these designations can be problematic because there was often a delay in changing their official designation from LCI(L) to a (G), (R), or (M) after conversion. In many cases this took several months, even though the physical changes and assignments of the ships had been effected. To avoid confusion, I have used the designations LCI(G), (R), and (M) from the time they were converted and put into use rather than when they officially received that designation.

Another problem with a work such as this is the concern with repetition. Numerous islands were invaded in the Pacific; many were minor adjuncts to major island assaults. In most cases the gunboats operated in a similar manner. They were in action a few days prior to the actual landing of troops, providing close-in fire support for Navy Underwater Demolition Teams and Marine Reconnaissance units. In other cases they accompanied minesweepers, destroying mines cut loose by the ships and providing fire support near shore. When the actual invasion took place, LCI(G)s, (R)s, and M(s), along with the newer LCS(L)s, made their initial runs just prior to the landing of troops and then remained close to the beaches, firing over the heads of troops as they landed. At that point they remained in the area firing on enemy targets identified by the men ashore and working in conjunction with spotter teams placed on board the gunboats. At night they provided harassing fire. As the fighting moved away from the beach, the mortar gunboats with their longer range mortars laid down barrages on enemy positions that direct fire 40mm and 20mm guns could not reach. Many of these were on the reverse slopes of hills and ridges. Toward the end of the war, a longer range rocket came into use and the LCI(R)s were used to great advantage. As the fighting progressed, the need for fire support by the gunboats lessened and they spent much of their time making smoke screens to cover ships from aircraft attacks and salvaging equipment disabled near the beach. In island assault after assault the pattern was basically the same. Therefore, rather than providing an exhaustive list of actions similar in most ways, I have elected to cover those of major importance, as well as those that had unique aspects. While many ships performed courageous and notable tasks in the island invasions, I thought it best to leave out some of the actions to improve readability.

As a result, the story is not "complete" in that many events have been set aside to provide a better view of the big picture. This in no way denigrates the contributions of countless ships and brave crews, but there is a practical limit to how many can be listed. As a result, I believe that the text presents a significant understanding of the ships involved in the actions of the Navy's amphibious forces in the Pacific.

Ranks given are contemporaneous with the event under discussion. Thus Richmond Kelly Turner is described as a Rear Admiral during the invasion of Kwajalein Atoll and, in later events, is described as a Vice Admiral, as those ranks were held at the time the action took place.

Finally, it should be noted that all works must have their limits. The subject of this book is amphibious gunboats that were based on the LCI(L) hull. This included the LCI(G), LCI(R), LCI(M), and the LCS(L). On many missions involving covering the Underwater Demolition Teams (UDT) or in beach assaults, other ships such as the PGMs, PCs, LCS(S)s and others were involved in the battle as well. Barge interdiction usually involved the amphibious gunboats working in conjunction with PT boats. The gunboats were not in the war alone; they were an integral part of a fleet from the largest to the smallest and they played an important role.

This book might give the impression that the LCI gunboats won the war but they had much assistance. However, to write a book covering each and every type of vessel found in the assault or in any of the other duties to which the gunboats were assigned would take many volumes. Accordingly, I have had to limit my work to those four types. Most certainly other ships are mentioned, but the focus in this book is on the LCI gunboats.

The primary documents used in this work show a variety of style. Gunboats may be described as USS or U.S.S. In cases where I cite specific reports, I have not modified them to make them consistent but have placed them in notes exactly as they were written. It should be noted that plurals of the ships at that time were usually written using an apostrophe s, which in today's grammar indicates the possessive. I have also kept these as they were in the original source wherever I have quoted from it. Therefore it is not uncommon to see references in the quoted material to *LCI(G)*'s *345, 346,* etc. It is not clear if this was accepted general usage in the American language at that time, a grammatical error, or if it was simply a form used in Navy reports.

Authors do not operate in a vacuum. The task of finding various materials is daunting and requires the assistance of experts found in each research facility. As the bulk of the research was done at the National Archives in College Park, Maryland, I was able to lean on the staff experts in each of the sections. In the Photographic Section, Holly Reid, Rutha Beamon, Sharon Cully, and Theresa Roy were able to supply their expertise in the search for numerous illustrations, many of which were hidden in various collections. Barry Zerby of the Textual Research Section was frequently able to lead me to material that was otherwise difficult to find.

I must also acknowledge the great and generous assistance of an old friend, who constantly keeps me aware of materials that have escaped my attention. Ron MacKay Jr., who serves as the historian for the LSM-LSMR Association, has made numerous contributions to my attempts to cover gunboat history. His friendship and contributions to my work are most valued.

In our Internet age, various websites have proven valuable for their content as well as providing contacts with individuals interested in naval history. Gary Priolo, of the NavSource.org website, has been most helpful in putting me in contact with a number of individuals who have information on my subject. I am indebted to him for his generous assistance.

In spite of constant checking and re-reading, it is not uncommon for errors to slip through. To avoid mistakes in the text one has to rely on the expertise of friends to double check the manuscript. I am greatly indebted to John Rooney and my wife, Lucille Rielly, who loaned their skills in proofreading the manuscript and offering valuable suggestions and corrections. However, the final responsibility for any work rests with the author.

Introduction

The subject of this work is a class of small United States Navy warships that were developed during World War II to combat specific threats from the Japanese in the Pacific Theater. As the war evolved, the nature, armament, and use for these ships changed to meet new needs in combat.

The conquest of most locations in the Pacific was the result of the actions of a Task Force or Task Group. The number of ships involved in these campaigns usually ran in the hundreds, sometimes over a thousand. In some instances in this work, it would almost seem as though the gunboats were the major factor in the conquest, but this is most certainly not the case. In a typical assault, battleships, cruisers, and destroyers provided heavy bombardment of the landing zone for one day to several days prior to landing day. As this was taking place minesweepers cleared the landing zone waters, with the gunboats following and detonating mines that had been cut loose. If the minesweepers came under fire from shore installations, the gunboats directed fire against them. Following minesweeping, the landing beaches were investigated by Marine reconnaissance units or Underwater Demolition Teams with the gunboats hovering closely offshore to suppress enemy fire directed against the swimmers. As the landings took place, the gunboats preceded the landing craft and then remained inshore for additional cover and call-fire support. In these roles the gunboats generally worked in concert with destroyers. If the firepower of the gunboat was insufficient, the individual boat might fire on the target from a closer range, identifying its position for the destroyer or other ship whose larger guns would then take the target under attack.

Some indication of the number of ships in a given operation may be deduced from the screening chores assigned to the gunboats after the initial landing. They patrolled around the anchorages, preventing attacks by suicide boats, suicide swimmers, and enemy aircraft. When not otherwise engaged they anchored or cruised upwind from anchored ships and provided smoke screens to cover them and thwart enemy air attacks. The variety of uses for the small combatants was large, and they were accomplished with great competence. They seemed to be everywhere at once. Their role was extremely important, particularly for the troops landing on the beaches that had enemy opposition. The presence of the gunboats only a few hundred yards off shore was comforting and added to their safety.

In the early stages of the war in the Pacific it was determined that additional fire support would be advantageous during island assaults. In addition, there was a need to interrupt Japanese inter-island barge traffic, as it had become an important means of transporting Japanese troops and supplies. In mid–1943 consideration was given to converting some of the existing LCI(L), or Landing Craft Infantry(Large), ships to gunboats. With their shallow draft they would be able to get in close to shore to support amphibious assaults and would also pack enough firepower to take on the armored Japanese barges. By the end of the war, 350 of the LCI(L) hulls mounted new and heavier firepower. Some, like the LCS(L), were built as gunboats from the start, while the LCI(G), LCI(R), and LCI(M) were converted from existing LCI(L)s.

The saga of the amphibious gunboats began with the attacks on the Treasury Islands in October 1943 and continued until after the war ended as they performed a variety of duties in the aftermath of the conflict. The early stages of the conflict saw the gunboat conversions put into combat against barge traffic and also to provide support for landings. As the war progressed and new varieties were developed, their tasks included anti-small craft patrol, the laying of smoke-screens, anti-aircraft assignments, and various patrol functions.

With the end of the war, most of the converted LCI gunboats were sent back to the states for scrapping. Some stayed on in the Pacific to aid in minesweeping and various duties in and around Japan, Korea, and China before being sent stateside. The LCS(L)s, built as gunboats from the start, survived to go on to service in various allied fleets, in France, Vietnam, and Japan, as well as other countries. By the 1980s most had been scrapped or sold off, with only one remaining in the Thai Navy. Today, that ship, *LCS(L) 102*, is the last remaining gunboat from World War II and is preserved as a floating museum by The USS Landing Craft Support Museum. Its present location is on the west coast of the United States.

CHAPTER 1

The Need for a New Weapon

War may be considered Darwinian in every sense. The victory is usually to the strongest, and military organizations that fail to adapt to changing situations are eventually defeated. In the midst of World War II, Japanese tactics in the Pacific had caused consternation among the Navy brass, forcing them to rethink the procedures for amphibious assaults. Changes in the manner in which troops were supported as they landed needed to be considered. As American weapons and tactics evolved so did those of the Japanese. In the end, the American adaptations coupled with her great industrial might proved superior, and Japan lost the war.

American adaptations led to the development of four major varieties of gunboat based on the LCI(L) hull: the LCI(G), which mounted additional guns and also rockets, the LCI(R), which was designed to clear the beaches with rockets in preparation for troop landings, the LCI(M), which supported troops ashore with heavy mortar fire and, a final development, the LCS(L)(3) or Landing Craft Support Large Mark 3 which combined many of the features of the first three.

The story of America's amphibious gunboats begins about halfway through the war. In previous wars there had been no need for their service, and it was to take the experience of many amphibious landings on Pacific islands before their need would be recognized. In 1942–1943, with the neutralization of Rabaul as the eventual goal, American forces under Admiral Chester W. Nimitz worked their way up the Solomons chain as General Douglas MacArthur's forces forged ahead on New Guinea and the adjacent islands. The Japanese, who had recognized the danger from American air power in sending their troops on large ships, had changed their tactics accordingly and made increasing use of armed barges to transport them between islands. This became evident during the battle for Guadalcanal from 1942 to 1943, and later after the Battle of the Bismarck Sea from 2 to 4 March 1943. During the latter battle, a Japanese resupply convoy transiting from Rabaul to Lae on New Guinea suffered great losses. Of the eight transports carrying supplies and men destined for Lae and their eight escorting destroyers, all eight transports were sunk as well as four of the destroyers. Supplies destined for the Japanese garrison on Lae were destroyed and the Japanese lost over 3,000 men in the attack. According to Samuel Eliot Morison: "The enemy never again risked a transport larger than a small coaster or barge in waters shadowed by American planes."[1]

The barges in particular posed a special problem. They were shoal draft and could operate in very shallow water. This made it difficult for larger ships to intercept them. PT boats were successful against them, but their light armament and wood hulls made them vulnerable to the enemy's counter-fire. Another type of ship had to be developed, a heavily armed, shoal draft gunboat that could intercept and destroy the barges. The answer was to mount guns on the

LCI(L) ships and send them after the inter-island barge traffic. As a result, the first conversions did not carry rockets, as they were primarily designed to combat barges. The first of the conversions, *LCI(G)s 21, 22, 23,* and *70* were armed with 3"/50 guns, along with 40mm, 20mm and .50 caliber machine guns.

A second major use for armed gunboats came as the landing forces assaulted island after island in the Pacific. As the American forces pushed through the islands they found that their tactics did not always prevent heavy casualties. This became abundantly apparent by the time of the landing on Tarawa in November 1943. It had become a standard procedure to precede each amphibious landing with naval bombardment of the enemy's positions. This did not always work as planned. Japanese defensive positions on the islands frequently consisted of covered trenches and foxholes. Surrounding the interior of a foxhole might be two rows of palm logs fastened together. The roof of such an installation would be built of two layers of palm logs, then sheet metal covered with several feet of earth. When faced with heavy shellfire, the Japanese hunkered down in their well-constructed bunkers and waited it out. Unless the bunker or other installation took a direct hit, it was likely that the defenders would emerge unscathed. Once the gunfire support ended there was usually a short period of time before the landing craft were able to place their troops ashore. This brief period gave the Japanese time to regroup and direct their fire at the assault forces. Japanese strategy at that time was to annihilate the attacking forces on the beach before they could land and consolidate their positions.

The Marine experiences at Tarawa in November 1943 were particularly horrific. Once the capture of Tarawa Atoll had been completed, the performance of the amphibious forces was assessed. Marine Lieutenant Colonel Evans F. Carlson, appointed as a Marine observer and liaison for Colonel David M. Shoup at Tarawa, suggested "that Navy devise an armored boat to carry a gun of 75mm caliber or larger. Boats of this type to be used against shore pill boxes at close ranges (200–700 yards) before assault units approach beach, in order to reduce machine gun and 40mm fire during movement of troops ashore."[2] Fortunately for the Marines and troops which would assault the beaches, such a ship had just come into use, the new LCI(G). Rear Admiral Richmond Kelly Turner, Commander of Task Force 52 at Tarawa, eventually submitted a report to CinCPac, entitled "Lessons Learned at Tarawa." This report, dated 30 November 1944, identified the need for additional fire support of the troops as they began the final assault on an enemy island. He suggested the inclusion of LCI gunboats as important in future amphibious assaults. By that time the gunboat conversions had been in use over a year and had become an obvious addition to all island campaigns.

Early British Close-Support Craft

Although the LCI gunboats and the LCS(L)s provided needed support, they were not the first experiments with close-in support of assault troops. The Royal Navy had already mounted guns and rockets on a variety of small craft. Among the early adaptations was the 195' LCT, the first of which underwent conversion in December 1942. Three varieties of the conversion took place, the LCF (Landing Craft Flak), the LCG (Landing Craft Guns), and the LCT(R) (Landing Craft Tank Rockets). Since they were new weapons, they were considered secret projects and Royal sailors and Marines knew nothing about them until they reported aboard.

Mounted on the first version of the Landing Craft Flak (Mark 3) (*LCF 3-6*) were eight 2 pdr. pompoms and four 20mm guns. A second version (*LCF 7-18*) mounted four 2 pdr. pompoms and eight 20mm guns. Both were designed to defend invading forces against enemy aircraft. They were first used to support the ill-fated raid at Dieppe, France on 19 August 1942, and later at the invasions of Sicily, 9–10 July 1943, and France, on 6 June 1944.

Another conversion of the LCT was the LCG(L). This version was designed to combat shore targets such as pillboxes and gun batteries. It mounted two 4.7" QF naval guns and either two 20mm guns or two 2 pdr. pompoms.

The deadliest shore attack version of the LCT was the LCT(R), described as "one of the more terrifying inventions of the Second World War."[3] Mounted on the deck of the LCT(R) were rocket launchers capable of firing either 792 5-inch rockets in the LCT(2) conversion or 1,064 in the LCT(3) conversion. "According to one authority on Landing Craft, the total salvo of an LCT(R) was equivalent to the combined fire power of 80 light cruisers or 200 destroyers."[4] A pair of 20mm guns rounded out its armament.

Each of the conversions was designed for a specific task. The LCF was tasked with combating German and Italian air attacks, but as the war progressed and Allied air superiority increased, their usefulness diminished. The LCG(L) was an excellent weapon for shore assault as its guns could bear on specific targets and provide support for landings or troops ashore. Although the firepower of the LCT(R) consisted of devastating rockets, they could not be aimed. A rocket had a range of 3,500 yards at a fixed elevation of 45°. The ship had to be pointed in the direction of the target and a ranging rocket had to be fired. Once the proper range had been determined, the entire salvo was launched. It was not as accurate, but its immense barrage made that less than necessary. It would share this characteristic with other rocket bearing gunboats. As devastating as their armed landing ships were, the number of amphibious assaults in the European Theater of war was not that great. Fighting moved quickly inland out of the range of the new gunboats.

Early versions of the LCT conversions ran into design problems, not unusual for ships designed for one purpose and converted under war conditions to another mission. The first of the LCG(L)s were designed so that there was an open space between the bow and the gun decks, with no means of pumping out water that entered the space. On the delivery trip to their base, *LCG(L)s 15 and 16* hit rough weather, shipped water and sank. Modifications were quickly made to the ships and future disasters were thwarted. However, conversions of these ships and others would usually be problematic until the design flaws were worked out.

Although some LCTs were converted for use in the European theater, their use in the Pacific was deemed impractical. Here an LC(F), or Landing Craft Flak, moves toward the French coast for the D-Day invasion on 7 June 1944. This was a British conversion of the LCT(3). NARA 80G 252745.

An LCM(R) with rockets is shown at the Amphibious Training Command, Florida Island, in the Solomon Islands, 24 April 1944. Boats thus equipped were used just prior to the landing of ships. Their rockets cleared away beach obstacles and mines. NARA 80G 270134.

Among the other landing craft armed were the LCM, the LCG(M), the LCVP, the LCS(S) and the LCS(M). These craft provided a variety of support services for the troops as they landed. Rockets mounted on these craft were used to clear beaches of mines and barbed wire, and later for support against enemy troops.

The Development of the LCI Conversions

The beginnings of America's amphibious gunboat conversion took place in early 1943. Under consideration at that time were a number of smaller vessels that might prove adaptable for close-in fire support. Among the ships and craft considered for conversion were:

Vessel	Length	Hull Construction
Landing Craft Support (Small) LCS(S)	36'	Wood
Landing Craft Control (LCC)	56'	Steel
Motor Torpedo Boat (MTB)	80'	Wood
Sub Chaser (SC)	110'	Wood
Landing Craft (Tank) LCT-5	114'	Steel
Patrol Craft Sweeper (PCS)	136'	Wood
Patrol Craft (PC)	173'	Steel

1. The Need for a New Weapon

PC 1078, shown at Albina Engine and Machine Works, Portland, Oregon, on 9 February 1945. The 173 foot PC was considered for conversion into a close-support ship but the necessary changes would have been impractical. NARA 19LCM PC 1078.

A major consideration for the ships was their ability to carry a variety of weapons. The smaller craft were simply not capable of delivering the firepower needed to cover the landings. The wooden hulls on the LCC, MTB, SC, and PCS ruled them out. It was thought they would come off second best in an encounter with an enemy barge and would be too vulnerable to shore fire. The LCT-5, while capable of mounting significant firepower, was simply not seaworthy enough to transit long distances in the Pacific. The small size of the LCC ruled her out and was also a factor in not pursuing conversions of the LCS(S) and MTB. The PC was of significant size but already overloaded. Conversion of her would have required the installation of much more equipment which would prove impractical. The options for a close-in support craft seemed limited.

However, studies by the Bureau of Ships had determined the feasibility of mounting additional guns on the LCI(L)s.

> At the conferences on 18 and 20 May 1943, the Bureau submitted advance prints of a preliminary study of a 153' Support Craft converted from the LCI(L) type. It was emphasized at the time that the scheme was subject to further study and development. The armament shown consisted of two—3"/50 caliber antiaircraft double purpose guns, two—40mm. twin antiaircraft guns (director controlled) and four—20mm. antiaircraft guns.[5]

Subsequent studies revealed the desirability of having a twin 40mm gun forward, making it necessary to eliminate one of the 3"/50 guns in order to ensure stability. Still other armament configurations were considered as additional designs, but the ideas were discarded for reasons of simplification in production and flexibility in ship assignment.

Having determined the desirability of a fire support ship that could operate close-in to the beach and the type of ship to be converted, it was now a question of putting the plan into action.

Within a few months, the Fifth Amphibious Forces gave birth to the first of the LCI(G)s. Captain Roy T. Cowdrey, who served as the Force Maintenance Officer, Service Squadron, South Pacific Force for Admiral William Halsey, developed the plans for mounting additional armament on the LCI(L) ships. The shallow draft of the LCI(L) would allow it to get in close to shore and support the troops as they landed. Japanese barges had an average speed of about six knots and the fourteen knot LCIs could easily catch them. Early LCI(L)s conversions were primarily designed to attack inter-island barge traffic.

The first LCI(L)s to be converted to gunboats came from LCI(L) Groups Thirteen and Fourteen of Flotilla Five. These ships had been active in the Solomons and were sent to Noumea, New Caledonia, for conversion. *LCI(L)s 21* and *22* set out from Flotilla Five's base at Florida Island in the Solomons for Noumea on 26 September 1943 and *LCI(L)s 23* and *70* departed two days later. They returned to Florida Island several weeks later, on 23 October. At Noumea, they came under the experienced hand of Cowdrey who added firepower to the four ships, effectively turning them into gunboats.[6] Mounted on these conversions were:

    1 — 3"/.50 Caliber AA Gun
    1 — 40 M/M Single Air-cooled AA Gun
    4 — 20 M/M AA Gun
    6 — .50 AA Machine Guns[7]

In his letter to BuShips, Cowdrey noted that the additional armament had reduced the stability of the ships and that changes in loading were made. This consisted of recommendations for loading specific tanks with diesel fuel or sea water as ballast. Two of the newly converted gunboats, *LCI(G)s 22* and *23*, were first put into use in the capture of the Treasury Islands on 15 October 1943, and shortly thereafter, during the campaign for Bougainville.

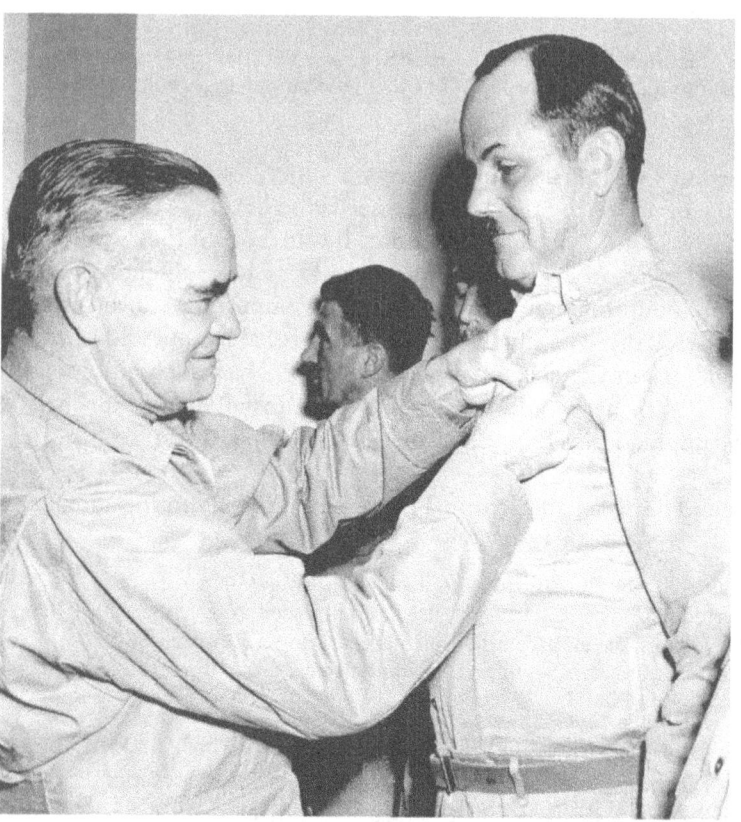

With the value of the new gunboats recognized immediately, a number of conversions took place at several locations. Flotilla Five sent *LCI(L)s 67* and *69* to Noumea for conversion on 10 November 1943 and *LCI(L)s 24* and *68* followed them six days later. They were back with Flotilla Five on 17 December and 28 December respectively. Conversion of other ships in the group continued over the next few months. By mid–1944, Group Thirteen of Flotilla Five would consist solely of gun-

Admiral William Halsey (left), Commander of the South Pacific Force, awards the Legion of Merit to Captain Roy T. Cowdrey for "outstanding service in salvaging damaged ships." Cowdrey was instrumental in converting the LCI(L)s into gunboats. NARA 80G 81392.

boats: *LCI(G)s 21–24, 61,* and *64–70*. They patrolled the waters around Bougainville, the Green Islands, New Ireland, and New Britain, making sure that Japanese barge traffic was kept to a minimum and disrupting the inter-island transport of troops and supplies. In August 1944, *LCI(G)s 23, 64, 65, 68, 69,* and *70* reported to the VII Amphibious Force for the invasion of Morotai.

For the LCI sailors who were on board during the change, the conversion left them with doubts. They recognized that the heavy gun mounted high over the deck would make the ship top heavy and speculated that its presence would "contribute to rougher rides in future storms."[8] For crewmen on the newly converted *LCI(G) 24*, trepidation rose as they approached the testing time for the new armament. Louis V. Plant, a signalman on board the ship, later wrote:

> We don't know if it is going to blow up or if this tub will sink or what. We drop a 50-gallon drum into the water and go out about a thousand yards. The gunners fire the gun and it works. The vibration knocks out the gyrocompass and disturbs a lot of dust in our living quarters, but it works. We miss the barrel by about 100 yards, but practice will improve our marksmanship.[9]

In addition to the new guns, some of the ships were equipped with depth charges, but without sonar gear these were of no use. They were off-loaded at Bougainville.

Converted at Pearl Harbor, beginning in December of 1943, were *LCI(L)s 77–80* and *345–348*. Shortly thereafter, Pearl Harbor converted a second group, consisting of *LCI(L)s 365, 366,* and *437–441*. Also during that month, the San Diego Naval Repair Base converted *LCI(L)s 449–453, 455* and *457* to gunboats. Variations in the armament mounted on these ships was partly based on minor differences of the two main classes of LCI(L), the *1–350 Class* and the *351–1098 Class*. In a letter dated 24 March 1944, Chief of Naval Operations noted armament installations on various LCI(G)s that had been completed by February 1944.

LCI(L) 77–82, 345–348 (Type A)
 2 — 40mm AAG (single)
 3 — 20mm AAG
 6 — cal. .50 AAMG
 10 — 4.5 inch Rocket Launchers, Mark 7 (C.I.T. Type 8)

LCI(L) 365, 366, 437–442 (Type B)
 3 — 40mm AAG (single)
 3 — 20mm AAG
 5 — cal. .50 AAMG
 8 — 4.5 inch Rocket Launchers, Mark 1 Mod 1

LCI(L) 449–453, 455, 457 (Type C)
 2 — 40mm AAG (single)
 4 — 20mm AAG
 6 — cal. .50 AAMG
 10 — 4.5 inch Rocket Launchers, Mark 7 (C.I.T. Type 8)
 2 — Projectors, Mark 22[10]

Gunboats normally used tripod mounted .50 caliber machine guns. However, once suicide boats and swimmers made their appearance, it became obvious that the guns could not depress sufficiently to combat those threats. As a result, gunboat captains acquired additional machine guns. These were set on mounts that were welded onto the rail, allowing the gun to point almost directly down into the water. This gun was mounted on *LCS(L) 48* after several of her companion ships were sunk by suicide boats at Mariveles Harbor in the Philippines. *LCS(L)(3) 48 A Souvenir Photo Booklet* by Robert Amick, circa 1990s, p. 17.

Top: Forward guns on *LCS(L) 8* fire on Mariveles Harbor, 15 February 1945. The two guns shown here are the twin 40mm, which is in the foreground, and the 3"/50 at the bow. The 3"/50 was used on the early LCI(G)s and on a number of LCS(L)s. The twin 40mm was standard on the LCS(L)s and later used on the last LCI(G) conversions. Official U.S. Navy photograph. *Bottom:* Many of the LCS(L) gunboats carried the single 40mm gun at their bow instead of the twin 40mm or 3"/50 gun. This was an interim fit caused by a shortage of twin 40mm guns. Wiring was in place for the twin 40mm gun and, on a few occasions, the swap was made in the war zone. The single 40mm was also mounted on most of the LCI gunboats. This is the bow gun on *LCS(L) 35*. Official U.S. Navy photograph courtesy Charles R. Thomas.

The single 20mm gun could be found on LCI(L)s and LCI gunboats, as well as on the LCS(L)s. This gun is shown on *LCS(L) 35*. Official U.S. Navy photograph courtesy Charles R. Thomas.

LCI(G) 347 is shown underway at Peleliu on 16 September 1944. She was one of the early conversions and saw action in the South Pacific. NARA 19LCM LCI(G) 347 BuAer 257263.

Within the next year, and up until the end of the war, additional conversions took place, each having slightly different arrangements of guns and rockets.

Rocket Development

Rockets as weapons of war date from the early 1200s when the Chinese put them to use against Mongol invaders. However, the Western world did not see them as a viable weapon until the twentieth century. The initial stages of World War II saw the Allied forces attempting to stem Japanese advances throughout the Pacific, and it was not until the first stage of the war against Japan was over that the Americans began to consider the rocket as an offensive weapon. The American organization most responsible for their development and subsequent use in amphibious assaults was the National Defense Research Committee. Working closely with the research group at the California Institute of Technology, the NDRC charged them with the task of developing rockets, explosives, and rocket launchers that might be used against the enemy. Attending a demonstration of the new rockets was one of the Navy's senior officers,

> who immediately suggested the development of a special type of rocket projector for amphibious operations.
> The suggestion was made by Vice-Admiral Wilson Brown, Commander Amphibious Forces, Pacific Fleet, at a demonstration of the Mousetrap and other California Institute rockets. He had assumed that command only a short time before, having previously been the commanding officer of the task force which had made the brilliant raid on Lae and Salamaua some months before. No doubt when he witnessed the rocket demonstration he was thinking of the necessities of his new command, and therefore saw in rockets an opportunity to take care of one of the most critical phases of an amphibious operation.[11]

Based on his previous experience, he saw the mounting of such rockets on amphibious assault craft as the answer to a major problem in amphibious landings. The lapse of time between shore bombardment by larger ships and the actual landing of infantry troops on shore gave the enemy time to regroup. A shallow draft boat or ship was required that could get in close to the shore and continue firing on the enemy positions to keep them off balance as the troops landed. Mounting rockets on shallow draft boats seemed the logical solution. Based on Wilson's suggestions and his description of the Navy's needs, the scientists at CalTech went to work. Within a short space of time they had developed a barrage rocket (BR) based on standard 4.5 inch tubing. Since the immediate plan was to mount them on small boats, the launchers for the rockets were limited to only five feet in length. This was short enough to mount on the Landing Craft Support (Small) or LCS(S) boat that was in existence at the time. The boat was only about thirty-seven feet in length and a rocket launcher could be mounted both port and starboard of the pilot's compartment. The first tests of the rocket carrying LCS(S) took place at San Diego in late July 1944, with the boat successfully delivering rocket fire on the beaches at San Clemente Island, a standard Navy test range.[12]

Word quickly spread about the new rocket boat and the Commander Amphibious Forces, Atlantic Fleet requested a demonstration. This took place at Solomons Island in Chesapeake Bay on 25 August 1942. Apparently the Navy officials were impressed and immediately put in an order for twenty-five pairs of launchers and 3,000 rockets. The invasion of North Africa was imminent and the Navy planned to use them there. As a result, the first amphibious launch of rockets against shore targets was made during the invasion of North Africa at Casablanca on 8 November 1942.

The next amphibian to carry rockets was the DUKW. Engineers of the Second Engineer Special Brigade were convinced that a DUKW carrying rockets was the answer to their prayers.

A DUKW of the Second Engineer Special Brigade shown with rocket launchers mounted at Cairna, Queensland, Australia, on 17 July 1943. The rocket DUKW made its first amphibious assault at Arawe on 15 December 1943. NARA 111-SC 236001.

Work on launchers for the DUKW began at CalTech in November 1942. The first rockets fired by the vehicle took place on 22 January 1943 at nearby Fort Ord. From that point on research on developing better launchers for the DUKW continued, with the final launcher version capable of launching 120 barrage rockets. The success of the rocket DUKW saw the ordering of increasing numbers of rocket launchers for DUKWs as the war progressed. The DUKW would be the first amphibian to fire rockets at the Japanese when it participated in the fight for Satelberg, New Guinea, in early November 1943. However, this was not a beach assault, but rather an inland target fifteen miles from the ocean. The first

Rocket racks are shown installed on one of the first DUKWs to mount them. This photograph was taken at Cairna, Queensland, Australia, on 17 July 1943. NARA 111-SC 236001.

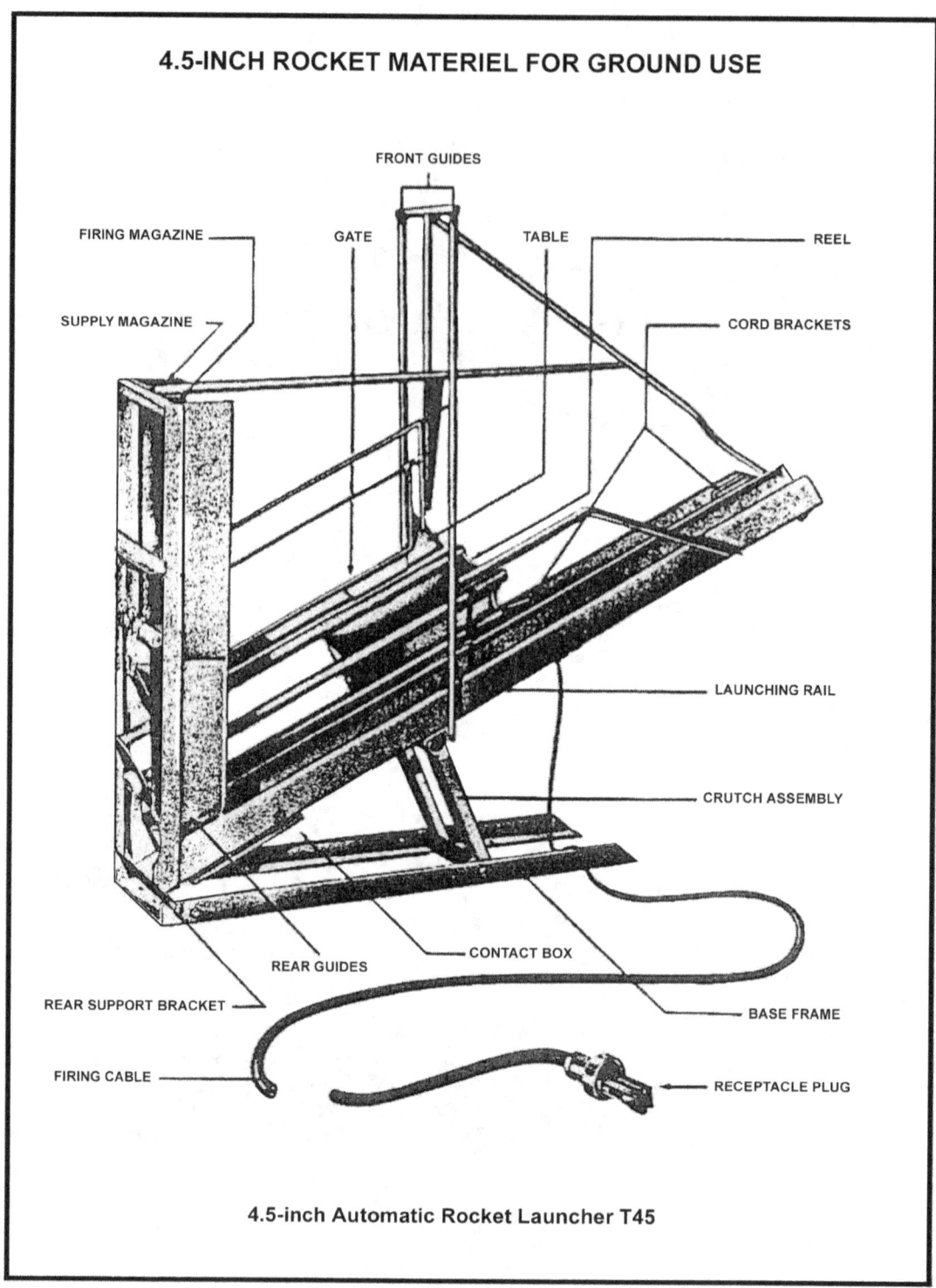

4.5-inch Automatic Rocket Launcher T45

The Mark 7 Rocket Launcher had a simple construction, however, it was not robust as shown by this drawing. It could be quickly fabricated, was adaptable for mounting on all types of craft, and was the primary rocket launcher on the LCI gunboats. War Department Technical Manual TM 9-394, *4.5 Inch Rocket Material for Ground Use* (Washington: DC: War Department, 7 February 1945), p. 12.

amphibious assault involving DUKWs was at Arawe on 15 December 1943 where they were put to use by the Second Engineer Special Brigade as it made its landing.[13] Having proven their worth at Arawe, they were again used on 26 December where they

> supported the landing of the 1st Marine Division and attached troops at Cape Gloucester (Yellow Beach) and Tauali (Green Beach). As at Arawe, the landings were preceded by heavy aerial and naval bombardment including, at Tauali, a close-support rocket barrage from the DUKWs. The effect was so devastating that target areas were completely laid waste and Japanese defenders on the beaches were forced to withdraw into the jungle.[14]

Additional firepower was desired against beach targets, and the scientists at CalTech developed a launcher that could be mounted on the LCM. It consisted of paired rails, each capable of launching a single rocket. With twenty-two such double rails on each side of the cockpit, an LCM could launch a total of eighty-eight rockets.

A further development of the launcher was the Mark 7 Automatic Rocket Launcher which was gravity fed and capable of launching twelve rockets.

The gravity-feed automatic proved to be the most versatile and widely used of all the barrage-rocket launchers. It could be mounted on practically anything—and was. A simple attachment allowed two

In this photograph, taken at Central Rocket School, ATB Fort Pierce, Florida, on 11 April 1944, an instructor stands near a mock up of a Mark 7 rocket launcher used for training. The rockets shown here are the 4.5 inch fin-stabilized barrage rockets (BR) that were in use in the earlier part of the war. Toward the end they were replaced by the 5 inch spin-stabilized rockets which had a greater range. NARA 80G 264471.

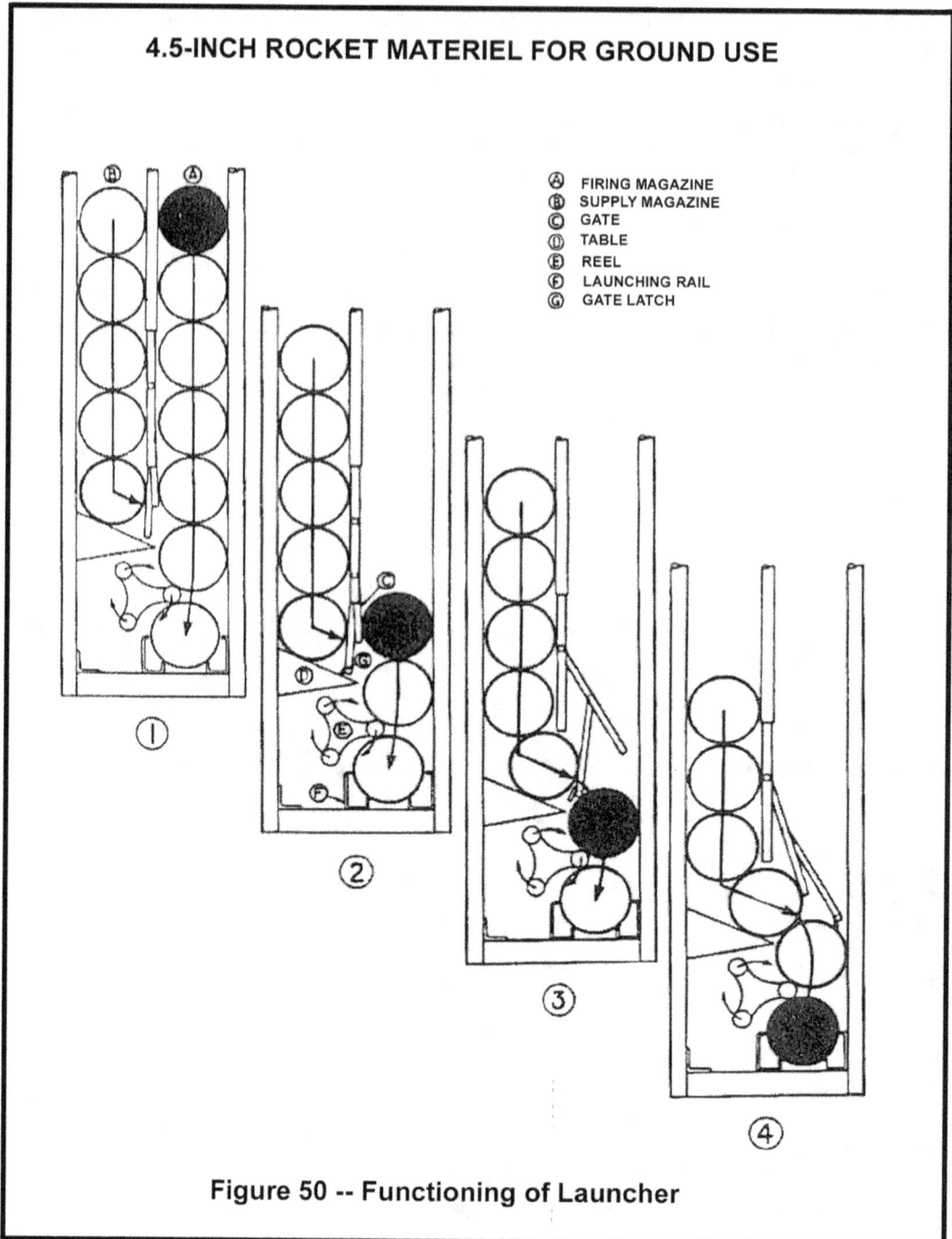

Figure 50 -- Functioning of Launcher

Mark 7 rocket launchers held twelve rockets in two tiers. The sequence for firing the 4.5 inch barrage rockets is shown above. If one of the rockets failed to fire, it would sit in the rack, preventing the others from firing. This was a flaw in the rocket launcher, which needed constant maintenance and repair in the war zone. The fragile nature of the launcher is shown in this diagram. If the frame of the launcher was impacted and thrown out of line, the rockets would fail to feed properly. It was not uncommon for the outboard mounted launchers on the LCI gunboats to suffer damage when they were alongside other ships for transfer of supplies or personnel. War Department Technical Manual TM 9-394, *4.5 Inch Rocket Material for Ground Use* (Washington, DC: War Department, 7 February 1945), p. 96.

to be hung outboard on a jeep. With light blast scoops, twelve could be mounted in the cargo space of a Duck or on a 2½ ton truck. These launchers were mounted on ¾ ton 4 × 4 and 1½-ton 6 × 6 trucks. They were mounted on LCV(P)'s, on LCM's, on LCS's, on LCS(L)(3)'s. They were mounted on PT boats and on LVT(A)'s—the latter the combat version of the amphibious tractor commonly known as the Buffalo. They could have been mounted on rowboats had there been any reason to do so.

In the Pacific, LCI's, with automatic launchers mounted on every available foot of deck and coaming space, came to be used as the standard rocket gunboat for all sizeable amphibious landings.[15]

With the introduction of the rocket carrying DUKW the VII Amphibious Force, under Rear Admiral Daniel Barbey, decided to place the rocket launchers on two LCI(L)s. Thus came about the development of the LCI(R). Barbey reasoned that the use of machine guns against beach defense forces was insufficient. Naval gunfire from the larger ships could not be used for fear of hitting American aircraft operating over the landing area. Rockets were the best answer. The development of these new rocket ships was considered vital as the invasion of Cape Gloucester, New Britain, was imminent. According to Barbey:

Commander Dwight Day, our assistant repair officer, was the man who supplied the answer.
On the decks of the LCI-31 and LCI-34 he installed racks to hold twelve rocket launchers. Each launcher could fire twelve 4.5-inch rockets. Each rocket had a fixed range of about 1200 yards. Since the launchers were in a fixed position, the rockets could only be aimed by heading the ship and hence the launcher in the direction of the target.
The launchers when installed were angled out from zero degrees for the launchers farthest forward, up to three degrees for those farther aft on each side, which gave them a coverage of about three hundred feet.[16]

The conversion of the two LCI(L)s into rocket gunboats was performed from March to April 1943 when the two LCI(L)s were taken to the repair ship *Rigel AR 11* at Efate, New Hebrides, for the installation of 40mm guns on 31 March 1943. After the 40mm guns were installed, the two new rocket gunboats spent several days testing them and training their crews in their use. On 18 April the two moored to *LST 453* at Seeadler Harbor and their rocket launchers were welded in place.[17] The test run for the LCI(R)s would be at Cape Gloucester on 26 December 1943.

Although the rockets mounted on the gunboats were excellent weapons, they frequently proved unreliable. It was not uncommon for launchers to fail. This might occur if the rocket exhaust burned the insulation off the wiring and caused a short circuit. Jams were not uncommon and were likely to occur if the rockets were not loaded properly or if they had been shaken out of position by enemy gunfire or rough weather. Many of the rocket launchers were bent out of shape and rendered inoperable as the gunboats came aside larger ships to replenish supplies and were battered into them by wave action. *LCI(G) 453*, in the attack on Peleliu on 15 September 1944, noted that of 1,008 rockets loaded for the assault, 189 failed to fire. These problems were reported in virtually every amphibious operation, and those of the gunboats of Task Force 79 at Lingayen Gulf in the Philippines were typical. *LCI(G) 451*, part of Task Unit 79.8.2 during the assault on Lingayen on 9 January 1945, reported that 49 of 359 rockets failed to fire due to "hang-ups" in the projectors.[18] *LCI(G) 440*, also at the Lingayen attack reported that: "The failure of two rocket launchers to maintain a live firing circuit is probably due to rockets being loaded too far ahead of time and then subjected to salt spray."[19] On board *LCI(G) 407* 109 rockets fired but others did not. Her CO, Lieutenant (jg) John D. McEnroe, reported that it "was a result of vibrations, caused by 40mm and 20mm fire, which shorted out some of the electric circuits."[20] Captain Theodore W. Rimer, CO of Task Group 79.8, commenting on the action report of *LCI(G) 373*, indicated in his endorsement that less than ten percent of that ship's rockets failed to fire and that the cause was: "Due to the directed procedure of firing rockets in salvos, the heat generated serves to burn away and cause defective firing leads to adjacent unfired banks of rocket launchers."[21]

Commander Dwight H. Day (right) is congratulated by Rear Admiral Albert G. Noble after receiving Silver and Bronze Stars. Day is credited with developing the LCI(R) conversion at the behest of Rear Admiral Daniel E. Barbey. NARA 80G 312798.

Continued development of the rocket produced a new type, the 5 inch spin-stabilized rocket, which first came into use at Iwo Jima and shortly thereafter at Okinawa. It had a range of 5,000 yards compared to the 1,200 yard range of the 4.5 inch fin-stabilized barrage rocket. This solved the problem caused by offshore reefs which kept the rocket gunboats too far from shore to use their rockets during some amphibious assaults. In his letter to the Coordinator of Research and Development, the Chief of the Bureau of Ordnance, Rear Admiral William H. P. Blandy, "requested that a project be ini-

Fixing fuses on board *LCI(R) 708* at Iwo Jima 19 February 1945. The new 5 inch spin-stabilized rockets made their first appearance on LCI gunboats at Iwo Jima. This photograph may be compared with the one showing the 4.5 inch fin-stabilized rocket. NARA 80G 305047.

The 4.5 inch fin-stabilized rocket was the standard for LCI gunboats up until the assault on Iwo Jima at which time the 5 inch spin-stabilized rocket began to appear. LCS(L)s used the 4.5 inch rockets until the end of the war. NARA 80G 257243.

tiated with the National Defense Research Committee for the study and development of rotating rockets using solventless extruded ballistite or its equivalent as a propellant."[22] Blandy noted that CalTech had already made progress in the development of the new type rocket.

Spin-stabilized rockets were mounted on the LCI(R)s of Flotilla Sixteen at Hunter's Point in San Francisco in November 1944. Half of the thirty-six LCI(R)s had six Mk. 51 launchers and the other half Mk. 30 launchers. Flotilla Sixteen, under the command of Lieutenant Commander C. E. Coffin, headed for action at Iwo Jima with the new spin-stabilized rockets.

Mortars

An earlier innovation in naval artillery surfaced during World War II. Mortars had been used on ships by the French and English as early as the 17th Century. At that time they were mounted on purpose built ships known as bomb ketches. Their use continued in more modern navies, and ships with mortars were used during the American Revolution and in the American Civil War. It was only a matter of time before they once again became useful.

Although the development of the LCI(G) and the LCI(R) were strictly Navy innovations, the use of mortars on board ships during World War II and the development of the LCI(M) was a different matter. The Navy, in cooperation with the Army, had experimented with the use of mortars on board landing craft in the European theater in early 1943. The geography of the area and tactical operations demonstrated that they would not be of much use there. In contrast, they might be an ideal weapon to support the many amphibious landings in the Pacific.

Plans to place 4.2 inch mortars on LCI(L)s and LCTs were formulated in early 1942. By 1943 the project was well underway and in "July 1943 a chemical mortar battalion with weapons mounted in landing craft took part in the seaborne assault on Sicily. The battalion was ready to fire from its offshore positions, but the need did not arise."[22]

About the same time at a joint Army-Navy meeting in Hawaii, Colonel George F. Unmacht of the Chemical Warfare Service, presented the idea to Navy officers who found it to their liking. A letter from Colonel Unmacht to Brigadier General Alden H. Waitt, Chief of the Chemical Warfare Service, dated 24 April 1944, noted:

> For many months we have done a great deal of planning with respect to the use of the 4.2 mortar, believing that adequate fire support could be obtained if the mortars were placed in a ship of sufficient size to mount from six to eight mortars with ammunition and personnel. As a result of discussions with the Navy, an LCT(6) was made available, special mortar mounts were built by the Navy, and four mortars fired during the recent Robert's demonstration at Makua. The fire power of these mortars astounded General Richardson and the several hundred, Navy, and Marine officers who witnessed the demonstration. Since the additional tests have been conducted, the mount has been strengthened considerably, and eight mortars have been mounted on the LCT, four firing on the starboard and four on the port.[24]

Apparently the display of firepower from the LCT was impressive. In a post script to his letter, Unmacht noted the reaction of General Burgin, Chief of Artillery, who exclaimed "'Jesus Christ they are still coming down' when 90 shells HE were fired in 1 minute and 12 seconds."[25]

Further experiments were tried using both LCTs and LCI(L)s. By fall of 1944, the Navy was ready to put the experiment into action. An abortive attempt to use mortars mounted on LCTs for the invasion of Saipan in June 1944 had met with disaster. Operational mishaps destroyed the three mortar-equipped LCTs before they could get into the battle. The lack of success in the operation led the Navy to consider other options.

The open well space on the LCT, intended for transporting tanks, made the craft unsuitable for open ocean campaigns. The British had learned this the hard way when several of their early

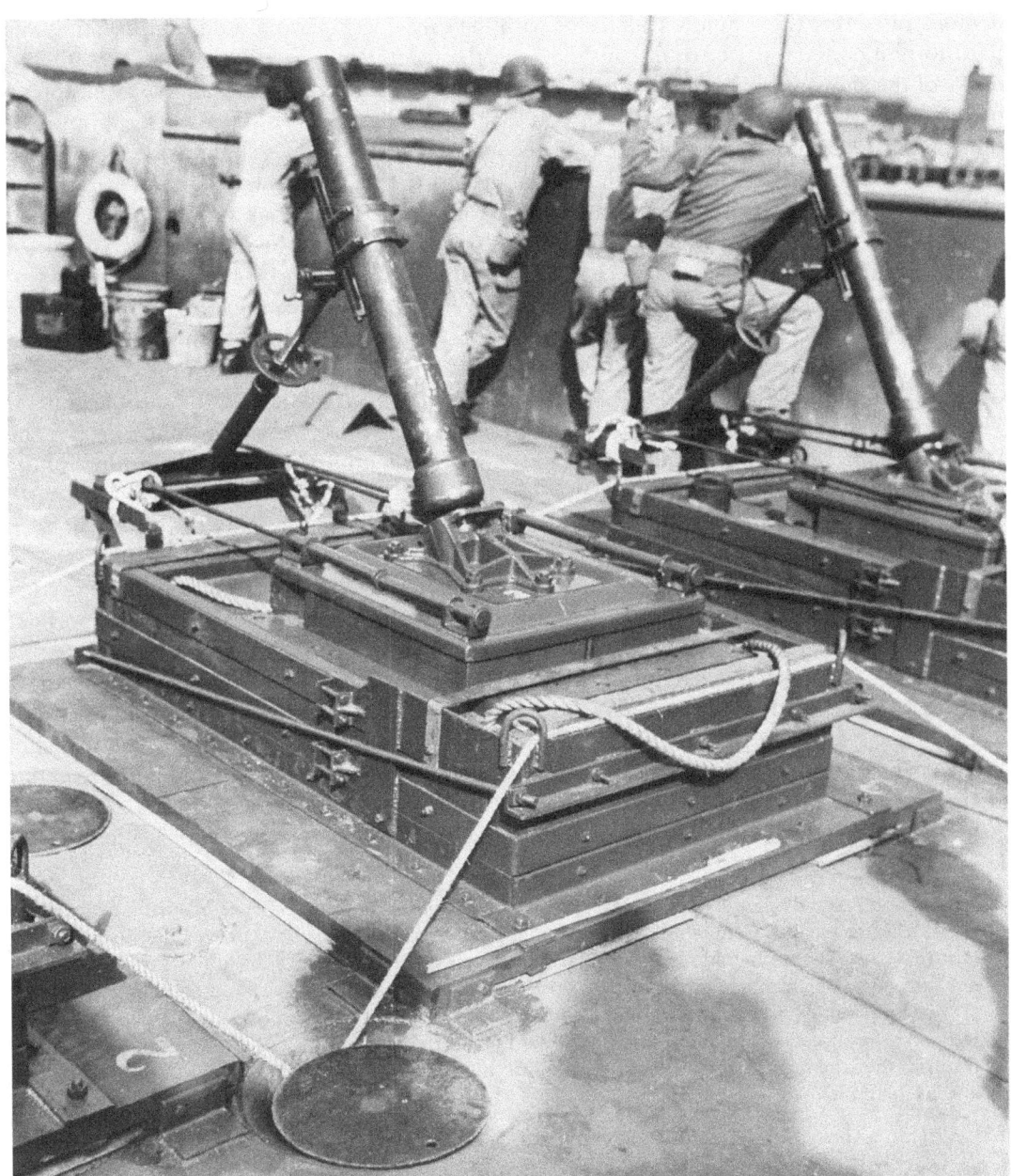

Initial tests mounting the 4.2 inch chemical mortar on LCTs were conducted in June 1944, but the open deck space of the craft made it unsuitable. NARA 80G 307567.

LCT conversions had sunk after hitting rough weather.[26] By this time, the LCI(L) gunboat conversions had proven their worth in carrying extra guns and rockets. A decision was made to mount three of the 4.2 mortars on LCI(L)s. Thus converted, the new gunboat would be designated as the LCI(M).

Four ships from Flotilla 14, Group 40, *LCI(L)s 739, 740, 741,* and *742,* reported to the Navy Yard at Pearl Harbor on 21 July 1944 to undergo conversion to LCI(M)s. On each were mounted three 4.2 chemical mortars. One was mounted forward and two on either side of the ship about amidships. The mortars were fixed and fired over the bow. Earlier tests of the mortars had demonstrated that they could wreak havoc with the ship's deck plating. Additional plating was used to reinforce the deck around and beneath the mortar mounts. To protect the hull and decks of the ships, special mortar mounts had to be devised. These consisted of "a reinforced box to which the standard of the mortar could be bolted. The box was filled with a mixture of sand and sawdust and the base plate was seated on a wooden block which in turn rested on this mixture. A buffer was constructed at the back of the box to take the backlash out of the mortar."[27] The No. 2 crew compartment was converted to a magazine for mortar ammunition designed to hold 1,200 mortar rounds. Sprinkler systems were installed in the magazines as an added safety measure. Work on the mortar ships was finished on 7 August 1944.[28]

Since the mortars were Army weapons, the Navy used Army personnel to man them during the early phases of their use. In this manner *LCI(M) 739*, one of the first of the mortar bearing gunboats, embarked two officers and twenty-five men on 30 July 1944 from the Army's 88th Chemical Mortar Battalion, the 91st Chemical Mortar Company, and the 111th Infantry Regiment. They would man the mortars and eventually train sailors to work them. The following day the LCI(M)s steamed off Oahu and test fired their mortars. The four ships would be the first of the mortar gunboats to see action, participating in the assault on Peleliu and Angaur Islands on 15 September 1944.[29] From that point on they regularly accompanied the other LCI conversions in amphibious assaults

One of the deficiencies noted in the use LCI(G)s and LCI(R)s was that the ships needed time to reload once they had fired their rockets. This was not to be the case with the mortars. Mortars could be fired continuously and their rounds were more destructive than rockets.

Although the mortars were set in specially designed mount boxes, problems did occur. It was not unusual for the support rods and mounts to break. Carrying welding equipment on one of the ships within the group usually proved valuable, as repairs could be made on site. Recommendations in action reports frequently noted that the rate of fire could be increased if the mortars were fitted with water cooling mechanisms.[30]

Further problems with the mounts were noted by Lieutenant (jg) Kenneth L. Bush, CO of *LCI(M) 638* at Okinawa. According to Bush:

> As the mount stands the mortar is not a ship-borne weapon. The simplest type of spring hydraulic recoil counter recoil system would make it so. Mortar ships have, I believe, proved their worth. Future designs should include a mount that can be depended on for the continuous fire wherein lies the principal advantage of the mortar ship as an harassing unit. The makeshift lashings necessary to keep a mortar in action would be considered unsafe for operation on any other Navy weapon. The success of the mortar on ship board is not the result of a satisfactory mount but the result of the ingenuity of the American Sailor and his ability with a piece of line, a pair of pliers and a welding torch.[31]

Within a short time adjustments to the types of fire plans made the weapon more effective. The range of the mortar could be changed by adding additional powder rings. Normally the angle of the mortar could be adjusted to affect the range. This worked well for stationary mortars on land, however, the mortar on the LCI(M) was under continual movement. Four different fire plans were developed during World War II. They were:

1. *Laying a Rolling Barrage Moving at the Same Speed as that of the Ship* was effected by maintaining a constant number of powder rings on all shells. The firing was started at the water's edge and the desired rate of fire was maintained until the barrage had reached its farther limit....
2. *Laying Fire in a Limited Zone* was done by a series of rolling barrages using decreasing increments of powder rings so as to run through the area as in the previous case and then employ a lesser number of rings so that the firing was again started at the beach and rolled inland until the ship reached the limit of its course inshore....
3. *All Firing With the Ship Stopped* is not completely equivalent to land firing since a stopped ship cannot maintain heading and in consequence, moves backward and forward to maintain steer-

ageway and swings to either side of the target. This results in greater dispersion of fire which is not a bad feature when area bombardment is underway but renders pinpoint firing more difficult....

4. *Single Successive Runs* were employed at Iwo Jima. The ships were used in a circle — successively running in toward shore, firing as they went. When they had reached a predetermined distance from shore, they swung out and took position at the end of the line as the next ship went in over the designated course.³²

The LCI(M)s soon proved themselves capable and valuable in island assaults. The 3,200-yard range of the mortars was greater than that of the rockets, and they could reach the reverse slopes where enemy soldiers were protected from rocket and gunfire. From the initial use of four mortar gunboats at Peleliu, forty-five were in operation during the campaign for Okinawa.

Shortly after their introduction, word spread about their effectiveness. Ships that were designed to mount other weapons found that the addition of a mortar or two would be desirable in some situations. Lieutenant (jg) Olin C. Taylor, CO of *LCI(G) 24* at Bougainville, had earlier recommended that LCI gunboats "be allowed two 81MM mortars, one forward and one aft, so that they can shell in areas where only high angle trajectories can reach."³³ Gunboat skippers, ever ready to adapt, would supplement their firepower with whatever they could fit on board. In this manner *LCS(L)s 9* and *10*, operating with Philippine guerrilla forces around Mindanao, each utilized single 81MM mortars in their attacks on enemy positions.

Continual problems with the mortar mounts and beds were of great concern to the unit commanding officers. In addition, the work at some conversion sites was considered inferior to that of others. Lieutenant Commander S. J. Kelley, who served as Commander Task Unit 52.25.2 at Okinawa, noted this problem after his ships had been in action during May of 1945 against enemy emplacements

Colonel George F. Unmacht (center), of the Army's Chemical War Service in Hawaii, is shown viewing a flame thrower demonstration at Schofield Barracks, Oahu, on 23 March 1945. Unmacht was instrumental in pushing for the adoption of the 4.2 inch chemical mortar on Navy ships. NARA 111 SC 231517.

Mortars being loaded on an unidentified LCI(M). The outboard position of the two mortars on each side near the deckhouse exposed the mortar crews to sniper fire and it was recommended that they be shielded or moved to a safer position. This did not happen for the duration of the war. Official U.S. Navy photograph.

near Naha, Okinawa. He wrote, "The usual minor damages were sustained on many base and cradle assemblies. Damages occurred to steel frames, wooden liners, standard supports and tie-rods. Repairs were accomplished by Group Engineering personnel. It is of interest that ships that were converted at PEARL have, for the most part, experienced more of such damages than those converted on the WEST COAST."[34]

One of the downsides for the LCI(M) was the lack of a 40mm bow gun. In order to lighten the weight of the LCI(M), the landing ramps had been removed. This was necessary since the ship would be

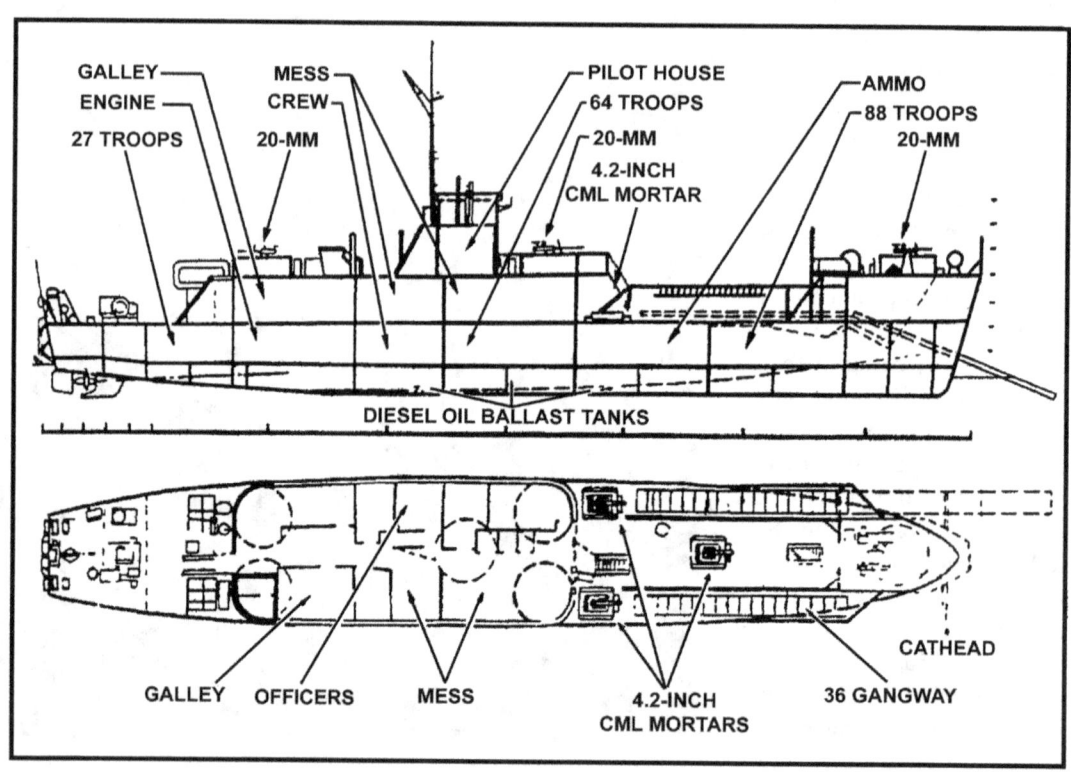

This diagram of an LCI(M) shows the placement of the three mortars. From *Military Review*, November 1946, p. 17.

This photograph shows the conversion of *LCI(G) 803* to the LCI(M) version at San Pedro, California, in December 1944. Visible in this view from the forecastle are the three special beds used for mortar mounts. NARA RG 19 C-LCI(M) 803.

carrying the additional weight of mortar ammunition. It was suggested that by removing the little used forward anchor, anchor winch, cable and engine, along with spare anchor and cable, a savings of 10,229 pounds could be made. The weight of a 40mm gun with its ammunition would be only 9,845 pounds, making the addition of a 40mm bow gun quite feasible.[35] Consideration for this adjustment in armament of the LCI(M) was made in late 1944, and the following year 40mm guns were

LCI(L) 414 being converted to *LCI(G) 414* at George Lawley & Sons Shipyard, Neponsett, Massachusetts. This view shows the installation of gun tub and director on the aft end of the ship. NARA 19LCM LCI(G) 414.

LCI(L)s 414 and *408* being converted to *LCI(G)s* at George Lawley & Sons Shipyard, Neponsett, Massachusetts. This view shows the bow area after the foc'sle had been cleared away. NARA 19LCM LCI(G) 414.

installed on a number of the mortar gunboats. However, shortages of the 40mm in the war zone made it a slow process.

Still another problem with the use of the LCI(L) hull for use as a rocket or mortar platform became quickly evident. The flat bottomed ship had no keel, and maintaining a consistent angle of fire for rockets or mortars proved problematic. In a seaway the ships could easily be pushed off course, making it difficult for them to deliver their missiles on the desired targets. A moderate

By 1945 the value of amphibious gunboats was well known. In addition to the production of the new LCS(L)s, numerous LCI(L)s were under conversion to gunboats. This photograph, taken at Long Beach Naval Shipyard in California, shows ten LCI(L)s undergoing conversion to LCI(G) variants. Also shown are the destroyer *Mustin DD 413* and the escort carrier *Petrof Bay CVE 80.* The one LCI identifiable is *LCI(L) 192*, which is on the port side of *Mustin DD 413*, indicating that the LCI(L)s undergoing conversion were probably from Group 111, Divisions 221 and 222. Their conversion took place from June to July 1945. The ships of Group 111 all carried conversion dates of 15 July 1945. Official U.S. Navy photograph courtesy A. H. Gauthier.

set to the currents off the beaches could push them sideways, requiring constant attention to the helm. In some cases they were unable to deliver their fire on the designated target areas because of this attribute.

A solution to this problem was offered by Ensign Thomas A. Cooke, Commanding Officer of *LCI(M) 659*, based on his experiences at the invasion of Leyte in the Philippines. Cooke recommended that

> due to the fact that a fixed mortar mount which cannot be moved in train is definitely a limiting factor on a mortar ship's operations, especially under conditions of strong current and wind, that future mounts be so constructed as to give a train of at least 90 degrees, if such a mount can be made feasible and practicable. This would considerably increase the versatility and effectiveness of this type of weapon, and would enable a much more accurate bombardment than is possible under present conditions.[36]

There was no modification to the mortar mounts as suggested by Cooke. Although it was a good idea, the modification would have required far more design and production than was possible in the area at that time. The mortar gunboats would continue to do their best with what they had.

The Ultimate Gunboat

The necessity of converting LCI(L) gunboats at forward areas led to a variety of LCI(G), LCI(R) and LCI(M) versions. Each had strong and weak points, however, all had been conversions of ships intended for troop carrying. By mid–May 1943, BuShips noted that preliminary studies for various types of amphibious craft had been undertaken and the most suitable for conversion into a fire support craft was the LCI(L). Various armament configurations had been studied and the final version was to have:

One — 3"/50 caliber double purpose gun
Two — 40mm. twin antiaircraft guns with directors and electric generator
Four — 20mm. antiaircraft guns[37]

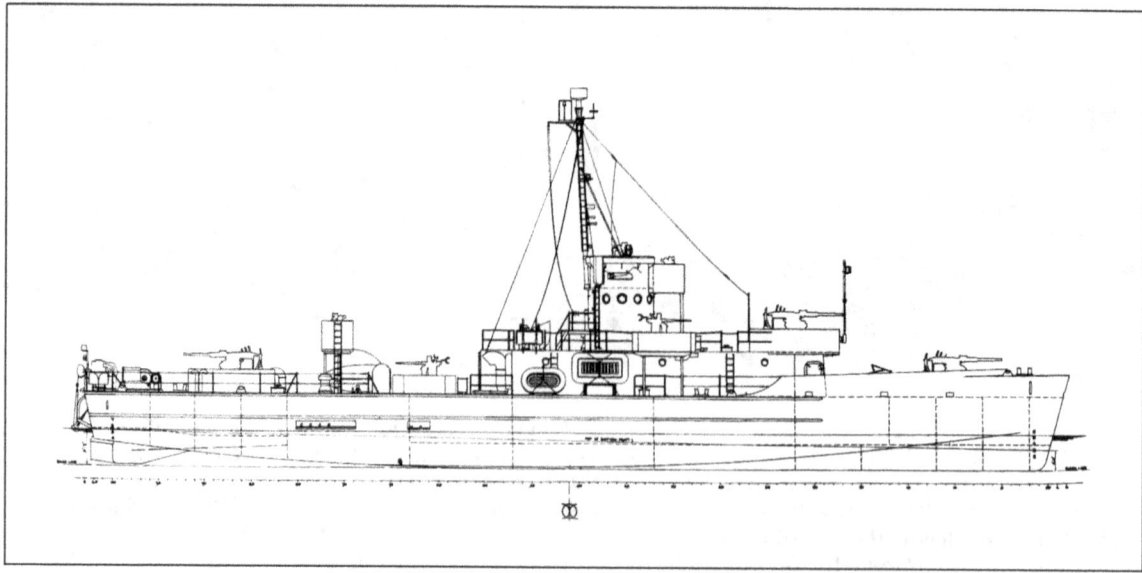

LCS(L)(3) Outboard Profile from Plan No. 1711-111-6 by George Lawley & Son Corporation.

Later changes to the plans would add ten Mk. 7 rocket launchers capable of firing a salvo of 120 rockets. In addition, each of the ships also carried between three and six .50 caliber machine guns. The variation in the number reflected the addition of more of them by individual ship's commanding officers.

Early in 1944, work began on a new series of gunboats using the existing hull form for the LCI(L), but with a greatly modified superstructure. This would become the LCS(L)(3) or Landing Craft Support Large Mark Three. These new gunboats would join their converted sisters during the last year of the Pacific war. Responsibility for the new adaptation fell to the George Lawley & Sons shipyard in Neponset (Boston) Massachusetts.

> LCI(L) plans were ... modified to the LCS(L)(3) type ... by George Lawley & Sons. The gun arrangements were revised; rocket throwers were installed; no landing ramp or bow doors were required: a revised and smaller deck house was installed; the flag ships of both classes were arranged to provide additional officer's quarters and radio and radar equipment.[38]

Initially sixty of the new gunboats were ordered. However, the escalating conversions of gunboats in the Pacific made it obvious that additional LCS(L)s were needed. In a letter from the Supervisor of Shipbuilding in Quincy, MA to the Lawley yard, it was noted that an additional seventy of the new gunboats (hulls 61–130) were authorized for production.[39]

In all, a total of 130 of the LCS(L)(3) ships were built by three yards. George Lawley & Sons built *LCS(L)(3)s 1–25* and *109–130*. The Albina Engine and Machine Works in Portland, Oregon built *LCS(L)(3)s 48–78*, and Commercial Iron Works, also in Portland, built *LCS(L)(3)s 26–47* and *79–108*. The keel for *LCS(L) 1* was laid at Lawley on 28 April 1944 and the ship was launched on 15 May. She was put into commission on 20 June 1944. From keel laying to first commission usually took about two months, although Lawley produced *LCS(L)(3) 118* in only nine days from 28 October to 6 November 1944. Such rapid construction under wartime pressure sometimes led to problems in the ships and LCS(L) commanding officers frequently noted deficiencies with welds on the ships, as well as misaligned engine shafts and faulty bearings.[40]

The ships were produced with three varieties of armament and the only significant difference was in the bow gun. *LCS(L)s 1–10, 26–30, 41–47, 48–50, 58–60* and *79–80* mounted a 3"/50 gun in the bow. *LCS(L)s 11–25, 31–40, 51–57, 61–66, 81–91*, and *109–124* mounted single 40mm guns in the bow, while *LCS(L)s 67–78, 92–108* and *125–130* mounted twin 40mm guns.

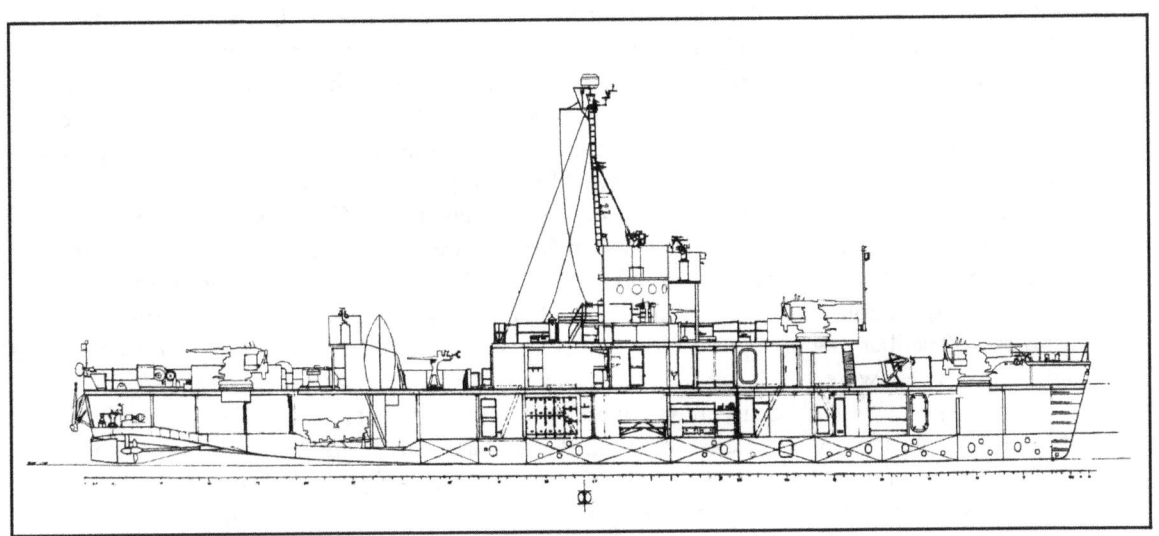

LCS(L)(3) Inboard Profile from Plan No. 1711-III-23 by George Lawley & Son Corporation.

LCS(L) 26 under construction at Commercial Iron Works on 21 July 1944. NARA BS 69622.

The first of the ships produced were destined for the Southwest Pacific and mounted a 3"/50 gun on the bow. Interception and destruction of inter-island barge traffic was one of the primary uses for this variant. A second variant was planned using a twin 40mm as the bow gun. This was considered to be the standard armament for the ship, with the 3"/50 as a special order. By mid–1944, shortages in the production of twin 40mm guns led to an interim arrangement in which a single 40mm gun was mounted on the bow of a number of the LCS(L)s.[41] Ships carrying the single 40mm were wired for twin 40mm guns and Mark 51 gun directors. On at least one occasion an LCS(L) with a damaged single 40mm was able to swap with another damaged LCS(L) and mount a twin 40mm in her bow. This took place at Okinawa.

Immediately behind the number one gun was a set of ten Mk. 7 rocket launchers. One director controlled twin 40mm gun tub was in front of the conning tower and another aft the deck house. A 20mm single was mounted on either side of the conning tower and two more just abaft the deck house. Once the ships reached Pearl Harbor they were usually fitted with at least three .50 caliber machine guns, although some of the LCS(L)s were later found to have as many as six. These were particularly effective against suicide boats and swimmers.

Thomas Lee, who had been a crewman on the destroyer escort *Barber DE 161*, found himself at Fort Pierce, Florida, for additional training. *Barber* was to undergo conversion to a fast transport or APD. After gunnery training at Fort Pierce, Lee was assigned to further training at the amphibious base in Solomons, Maryland. This was in preparation for his new assignment. Lee was to become a member of the first crew for a new ship, the *LCS(L) 31*, which was being completed at Commercial Iron Works in Portland, Oregon. Not sure what he would see when he

LCS(L) 26 is shown under construction at Commercial Iron Works on 21 July 1944. Her keel was laid on 10 July 1944 and she was launched on 13 August 1944. After additional fitting out, she was commissioned on 26 August 1944. NARA BS 69621.

arrived in Portland, Lee's first impression of the LCS(L) was that it was "small, very small, but it had more firepower in a small space — a lot of firepower."[42] *LCS(L) 31* was to serve at Iwo Jima, and later on the radar picket lines at Okinawa where it shot down six kamikazes and was awarded a Presidential Unit Citation. Tom Ryan, who served on *LCS(L) 81* said that "we were so cramped on deck side you could not go more than six feet from a gun ... even the flag man had a machine gun attached to his flag bag."[43] Jim Mallin, QM/3c on *LCS(L) 117* thought that the ships resembled a small destroyer because of their shape and the large number of guns they carried.[44]

The ships were the most heavily armed of the gunboats but did not carry as many rockets as the LCI(R)s or some of the LCI(G)s. As a result they were frequently teamed with LCI(G)s or LCI(R)s during amphibious landings.

Although the first of the LCS(L) ships commissioned, *LCS(L) 1*, was put into service on 20 June 1944, it was used as a training ship at Solomons ATB in Maryland for the duration of the war. It was not until 5 December 1944 that the first of the new gunboats finally appeared in the war zone when *LCS(L)s 26, 27, 48,* and *49* arrived at Humboldt Bay, New Guinea. A few weeks later, on 28 December, they were joined by *LCS(L)s 7, 8, 9, 10, 28, 29, 30,* and *50*. All of these ships mounted 3"/50 guns on their bows.

The first to be used in an assault operation, *LCS(L)s 7, 8, 26, 27, 48,* and *49*, participated in the attack on San Antonio in Zambales Province on the west coast of Luzon in the Philippines.

LCS(L) 50 after completion at Albina Engine & Machine Works, 19 September 1944. Her 3"/50 bow gun is clearly visible. Ships mounting this gun were used in the Philippines, Borneo, and Okinawa. Official U.S. Navy photograph.

From that point on, the new gunboats served alongside the LCI(G)s, LCI(R)s, and LCI(M)s until the end of the war.

Building the Landing Craft

LCI(L)s were produced in a number of yards throughout the United States, including Albina Engine and Machine Works, Portland, Oregon; Brown Shipbuilding Company, Houston, Texas; Commercial Iron Works, Portland, Oregon; Consolidated Steel Corporation, Orange, Texas; Defoe Shipbuilding Company, Bay City, Michigan; Federal Ship Building and

LCS(L) 77, on the left, displays a twin 40mm gun in her bow while *LCS(L) 91*, on the right, has a single 40mm in the Number 1 position. The ships are shown at Astoria, Oregon, on 25 January 1952, just prior to their transfer to the Republic of Korea. Official U.S. Navy photograph.

The keel is layed for *LCI(L) 315* at Port Newark, New Jersey, on 10 August 1942. This was a construction site for Federal Shipbuilding & Drydock Company, a major builder of LCIs during the war. NARA 19LCM-LCI(L) 315.

Dry Dock Company, Port Newark, New Jersey; George Lawley & Sons, Neponset, Massachusetts; New Jersey Shipbuilding Corporation, Barber (Perth Amboy), New Jersey; and New York Shipbuilding Corporation, Camden, New Jersey. Numerous other yards participated in converting the LCI(L)s to gunboats. Only three yards built the LCS(L)s: Albina Engine and Machine Works, Commercial Iron Works, and George Lawley & Sons.

The price for building the ships varied from place to place. Part of the costs had to do with shipping building materials from one location to another. In other cases, the government might require changes to the delivery date, forcing the builders to pay for express shipping and overtime for employees. The average cost for an LCI(L) produced by Albina in mid–1944 was $252,680 and LCS(L)(3)s averaged $315,291.[45] Lawley had initially estimated the cost of an LCS(L) at $275,000, but the government renegotiated the price downward to $263,000. Availability of supplies, shipping, labor contracts and other factors determined the relative costs of the ships at different yards. Although the cost was higher on the West Coast, the ships produced on the East Coast had to make the trip from Boston south through the Panama Canal and then up to San Diego, prior to heading to the war zone. The cost of this trip still made it practical to produce ships on the West Coast, even though they were more expensive. Within six years of their launching, many of the ships were sold off as surplus for a price of about $10,000-$11,000 each. Some were scrapped, while others were put to use in the fishing fleets.

The initial costs for construction of the first vessel built under a contract were usually much higher than the average. Once the process of building was set, additional ships cost less

Left: An alternate construction view of *LCI(L) 315* at Federal Shipbuilding & Drydock Company, Port Newark, New Jersey, on 10 August 1942. NARA 19LCM — LCI(L) 315. *Right:* Construction of *LCI(L) 315* on 12 August 1942. NARA 19LCM — LCI(I) 315.

as the production became more familiar and needed construction equipment and materials were in place. Thus *LCI(L) 1013* required 97,343 hours of direct labor in March 1944, but in May 1944, only 57,380 hours of direct labor was required to produce *LCI(L) 1032*. Direct labor hours for six LCS(L)s built at Albina Engine and Machine Works in September 1944 ran from 98,525 to 78,258 hours, the total hours declining with each ship produced.

Launching a Gunboat

In most cases the launching ceremonies were similar. The Supervisor of Shipbuilding in Portland, Oregon, supervised the building of vessels on the West Coast. He described the process:

> Launching ceremonies were conducted on a modest scale, but were always colorful and were uniformly successful. The launching party usually assembled in the office of the President of the Company, where flowers were presented to the sponsor and her attendants. The party then proceeded to

LCS(L) 48 ready to launch at Albina Engine and Machine Works, Portland, Oregon. Her smooth hull may be compared to later photographs of various LCS(L)s and LCI gunboats. The thin $\frac{3}{16}$ inch hull plating soon took on a deformed look from the constant crashing of ocean waves into their sides. NARA BuShips General Correspondence 1940–1945 LCS(L)(3) Class SS/S1-6 to C-LCS(L)(3) Class 1 S/8.

Opposite, bottom: LCI(L)s 1013 (left) and *1014* (right) under construction at Albina Engine and Machine Works, Portland, Oregon, on 28 January 1944. Various bulkheads are shown installed within the ships' hulls. Albina produced a number of LCI(L)s and LCS(L)s during the war. Many of the LCI(L)s were later converted to gunboats. Naval History and Heritage Command 19-N-61190.

Mrs. A. Allen, wife of the Chief Timekeeper at Albina Engine and Machine Works, Portland, Oregon, christens *LCS(L) 48* on 14 July 1944. NARA RG 19 BuShips General Correspondence 1940–1945.

the launching platform. The launchings were usually scheduled to occur during the lunch hour or between shifts, to permit as many workers as possible to attend and to cause the least interference to production. After the playing of the National Anthem, appropriate remarks were made by the Master of Ceremonies or guest speakers, after which the sponsor, her attendants and distinguished guests were introduced, and a Chaplain or civilian Clergyman offered a prayer. After this, the sponsor took her position at the bow of the vessel, breaking a bottle of champagne

Stern details of *LCS(L) 48* at Albina Engine and Machine Works, Portland, Oregon. NARA BuShips General Correspondence 1940–1945 LCS(L)(3) Class SS/S1-6 to C-LCS(L)(3) Class 1 S/8.

LCS(L) 48 goes down the ways at Albina Engine and Machine Works, Portland, Oregon, on 14 July 1944. NARA RG 19 BuShips General Correspondence 1940–1945.

across the bow just after the vessel started to move, at the same time pronouncing the words of Christening.

After launching, the company usually gave a luncheon for the launching party, at which time a small gift was presented to the sponsor as a remembrance of the occasion.[46]

With the large number of ships produced by the West Coast shipyards, it was difficult to obtain sponsors at times. Larger ships might be sponsored by ladies recommended by the Secretary of the Navy or the Commandant of the regional naval district. Others would be

LCS(L) 48 shortly after her launch on 14 July 1945. NARA RG 19 BuShips General Correspondence 1940–1945.

Commissioning ceremony for *LCS(L) 91* at Commercial Iron Works, Portland, Oregon, 4 January 1945. Official U.S. Navy photograph courtesy Norman H. Wackenhut.

recommended by the Supervisor who depended on recommendations from the shipyard owner. "The majority of the sponsors were selected from the wives and daughters of the yard workmen. The balance were from the families of shipyard officials, Navy personnel, prominent citizens, winners of War Bond contests, etc."[47]

Commissioning ceremonies were held after the ship had been fitted out and was ready to head to sea. The christening of the ship as it headed down the ways in its launching ceremony was the beginning of the end of production. Still to be fitted out were the ship's guns and various other pieces of equipment. This might take from several days to a few weeks. Once the ship was ready to go into action, the official commissioning ceremony took place. As with the christening ceremony, these were fairly standard.

> Commissioning ceremonies were simple, short, and strictly Naval in character. When the Supervisor arrived to commission the vessel, as representative of the District Commandant, the officers and crew were drawn up at quarters. He was accompanied by an official of the Company and they were met at the gangway by the Prospective Commanding Officer. Upon taking his station with the officers and crew, the Supervisor proceeded to read his orders. On completing this, he accepted the vessel on behalf of the U.S. Navy from the contractor's representative, pronounced the vessel in full commission, and ordered the Colors, Jack and Commission Pennant hoisted. The Prospective Commanding Officer was then directed to read his orders, upon completion of which he assumed command, and ordered the watch set, and the starting of the ship's log and the ship's time. A benediction was then pronounced by a Chaplain and the crew dismissed. The ship usually held "open house" for about an hour after commissioning, for guests of the ship's officers and crew, during which time light refreshments were served.[48]

Paint Schemes

Camouflage paint schemes were devised to give the gunboats maximum protection against the enemy wherever possible. This was a more difficult task for amphibious craft as they might be found run up on the beach or far from shore. At the beginning of the war, paint schemes tended to favor the mottled appearance of shallow water. At Okinawa, the excessive air attacks

Some camouflage patterns were designed to give the appearance of shallow water with their mottled paint schemes. In the Pacific these were frequently in shades of green. *LCI(G) 580* is shown in such a camouflage paint pattern just after her conversion in the Chesapeake. Official U.S. Navy photograph.

LCS(L) 58 is shown in San Francisco Bay, probably on her return home after the war. Her paint scheme is designed to give the appearance of a smaller ship and to confuse distance measurements. Official U.S. Navy photograph courtesy of the National Association of USS LCS(L) 1-130.

by the kamikazes brought other camouflage paint schemes into use. This was particularly true for the LCS(L)s on the radar picket lines as they mainly had to be protected from air attack. The LCI gunboats faced similar tasks at Okinawa. Although they were not assigned as radar pickets, they did not run up on the beaches, so camouflage schemes resembling shallow water were not as useful as patterns which broke up the shape of the gunboat or that made it invisible from the air. Various camouflage colors were used during the war in shades of green, brown, blue, gray, and black with the green shades emphasized in the Pacific.

Chapter 2

From Training to Missions

Training the Crews

After being sworn in at various locations throughout the country, new recruits were sent to a number of bases where they were introduced to Navy life. Some of these men, such as Vaughn E. Hampton, enlisted while still minors. Hampton managed to enlist at the age of fourteen and celebrated his fifteenth birthday while going through Amphibious School in San Diego. Eventually his parents found out, after he had been on *LCI(G) 450* for the invasion of Kwajalein Atoll. At Pearl Harbor on 7 April 1944 he was told he was to be discharged because of his age. His paperwork was misplaced and he was reassigned to *Oak Hill LSD 7* before his records caught up with him. He was finally discharged on 14 June 1944.[1] Numerous other under-age boys managed to get past the enlistment officers and join the Navy, as well as the other services. The means to check their ages simply did not exist in the early 1940s.

At the beginning of the war there were four bases that handled most of the training of recruits and those who had finished basic training. The four bases were at Newport, Rhode Island, established in 1883; Great Lakes, Illinois, established in 1911; Norfolk, Virginia, and San Diego, California, both developed in 1917. The rapid expansion of the Navy shortly after the attack on Pearl Harbor saw increased construction at all of the bases, as well as the addition of new ones. The peacetime Navy of 1939 grew from 110,000 men to 3,009,380 in 1945.[2]

The curriculum at the bases included evaluation, physical fitness, introduction to naval customs, traditions and practices, and general training for naval personnel. From that point on, the recruits were sent on to a variety of schools as determined by both their ability and the needs of the Navy. Having completed their advanced schools, they were then sent to one of the Amphibious Training Bases. Among them were the amphibious training bases established at Fort Pierce, Florida; San Diego (Coronado), California; Little Creek, Virginia; and Solomons, Maryland. For the gun crews that served on the gunboats, one of the important bases was at Fort Pierce.

The first of the amphibious training bases was built at Solomons, Maryland. Work on the base began at the end of June 1942. Navy estimates indicated that the base would fulfill its mission of training sailors for the amphibious forces within a year. The immediate mission was the invasion of North Africa. It was thought that once that had been accomplished the base would probably not be needed. Accordingly, construction at the base was viewed as a temporary mission and it was considered usable by August 1942. This led to a number of problems later in the war, as the need for additional training facilities was recognized. Solomons had been constructed in haste, although the buildings were completed in accordance with standard building

Solomons Amphibious Training Base in Maryland was one of the most important bases for the amphibious ships. It trained men for service on the LCI(L)s and LCS(L)s. NARA 80G 203872.

Firefighting was an essential skill for everyone on board ship. Practice in firefighting is shown at Solomons ATB on 23 September 1944. NARA 80G 288608.

practices. The downside of the base was that, since it was assumed to be a temporary facility, there were no sidewalks, recreation areas, gyms, a chapel, theaters, swimming pools, or any other "luxuries" that might be found at a permanent base. Although the location of the base was sufficient for training purposes, the water surrounding it was limited in depth. Larger amphibious ships, such as the LST, could not be beached. They had to be anchored off the base.

John Rooney, who served as a radio man on *LCS(L) 82,* recalled Solomons: "The base sat at the mouth of the Patuxent River along Chesapeake Bay's western shore — sultry, mosquito ridden, swampy — a sort of down-home Guadalcanal without Japs in palm trees."[3]

Liberty was almost non-existent with no real access to the nearby cities of Baltimore and Washington, DC. Solomons itself was a small town and was easily overrun by sailors on liberty. Within a short while, local newspapers ran articles indicating that the base was causing problems for the local populace. On 17 January 1943, *The Baltimore Sun* ran an article not-

Quartermasters training with the sextant on a mock-up of an LCI(L) at Solomons ATB on 7 October 1944. Official U.S. Navy photograph.

ing how the "simple life" of Solomons had changed.[4] *The Calvert Independent* published a poem on 10 June 1943 written by local resident Alberta Woodburn, entitled "Is This 'Solomons' Anymore?"[5] Clearly the presence of the base was having a significant impact on the local population. However, this was to be the case at most locations throughout the country as bases, either newly constructed or long in existence, were swelled by the tide of new military recruits in preparation for numerous campaigns against the enemy.

The resultant impact on the sailors being trained at Solomons was low morale. Stuck on a base in the middle of nowhere under trying conditions made it difficult for the men. Newly commissioned officers had little point of reference and so were a bit less affected by the conditions. In addition, they had the ability to get off the base on more occasions, even though trips to the cities were still a problem. For senior officers the realization that their careers were in decline came with assignment to the amphibious forces. It was considered to be the "Siberia of the Navy" and was also referred to as "Ensign Disposal School." For senior officers it signaled that their careers were over and for new officers, that their futures were bleak.

Many Annapolis midshipmen were enticed into the service at the end of their third year when Commander Edwin Thomas, future Commander of LCS(L) Flotilla 3, Group 8, appeared at Annapolis in search of officer recruits. The amphibious forces were looking for fifty volunteers. Although skeptical, midshipmen soon began to hear rumors that the "volunteers" might find themselves in command of an LCI(L) or LCS(L) or in the position of XO on one of the larger amphibious ships. Further enticements included the possibility that the billet called for the rank of full Lieutenant, meaning a jump of two grades over the normal promotion to Ensign upon graduation from the academy. Fifty volunteers from the class of 1945 made their decision and twelve wound up as commanding officers on LCS(L)s. The other thirty-eight found themselves serving on LSTs and LSMs in various capacities, with a couple becoming skippers on LSTs. Their academic schedule was streamlined and they graduated in June 1944.

Not all of the LCS(L) skippers were without experience. Frank Adams had served on *LCI(L) 69* in the Pacific, participating in patrols at Bougainville. The *69* was then sent to Noumea, New Caledonia, for conversion into a gunboat. Adams found himself heading back to the States where he was eventually assigned command of *LCS(L) 104*, just being completed at the Commercial Iron Works in Portland, Oregon. On 28 February 1945, he stood on the *104*'s deck at the commissioning ceremony and became its new CO.[6]

Lieutenant Commander John H. Morrill, an Annapolis graduate in 1924, had served in the Navy in a number of different capacities. At the outbreak of the war he was in the Philippines commanding a minesweeper. As the Philippines was surrendered to the Japanese, he and seventeen men escaped from Manila Bay in a small boat and made their way to Australia. Back in the United States he requested assignment to the amphibious forces in spite of warnings that it was not a desirable assignment and would hold back his advancement in rank. He rejected the advice and had himself assigned to the command of LCI(L) Flotilla Thirteen and reported to Solomons to take charge of the flotilla.[7]

Trainees at the base spent their time training on LCI(L)s since the newly converted gunboats were basically the same with the exception of armament. *LCI(L)s 569* and *592* were used for training on the base and both LCI and LCS sailors trained on them. In July 1944, the first of the LCS(L)s assigned to the training base arrived and the LCS(L) Training Group was formed. Six LCS(L)s would eventually be assigned to the base for varying lengths of time. Lieutenant Commander H. Heine, Jr. was the CO of the new LCS(L) training Group.[8]

All sailors going through training at Solomons ATB practiced various skills on the LCI(L)s and LCS(L)s that were based there. Practice manning the guns was essential for most. Sailors are shown during gunnery training on board *LCI(L) 1003*. The 20mm gun shown here was found on all the LCS(L)s and LCI(L)s as well as the LCI gunboats. Official U.S. Navy photograph taken 16 October 1944.

Opposite, top: North Platte Canteen. Courtesy Lincoln County Historical Museum. ***Opposite, bottom:*** Citizens of North Platte, Nebraska, showed their patriotism and support of the troops during World War II. On Christmas Day in 1941 they turned the town's train depot into a large dining hall to feed servicemen on the trains passing through. Numerous servicemen were the beneficiaries of their generosity. The canteen was in operation until the end of the war. Similar canteens existed throughout the country during the war. Courtesy Lincoln County Historical Museum.

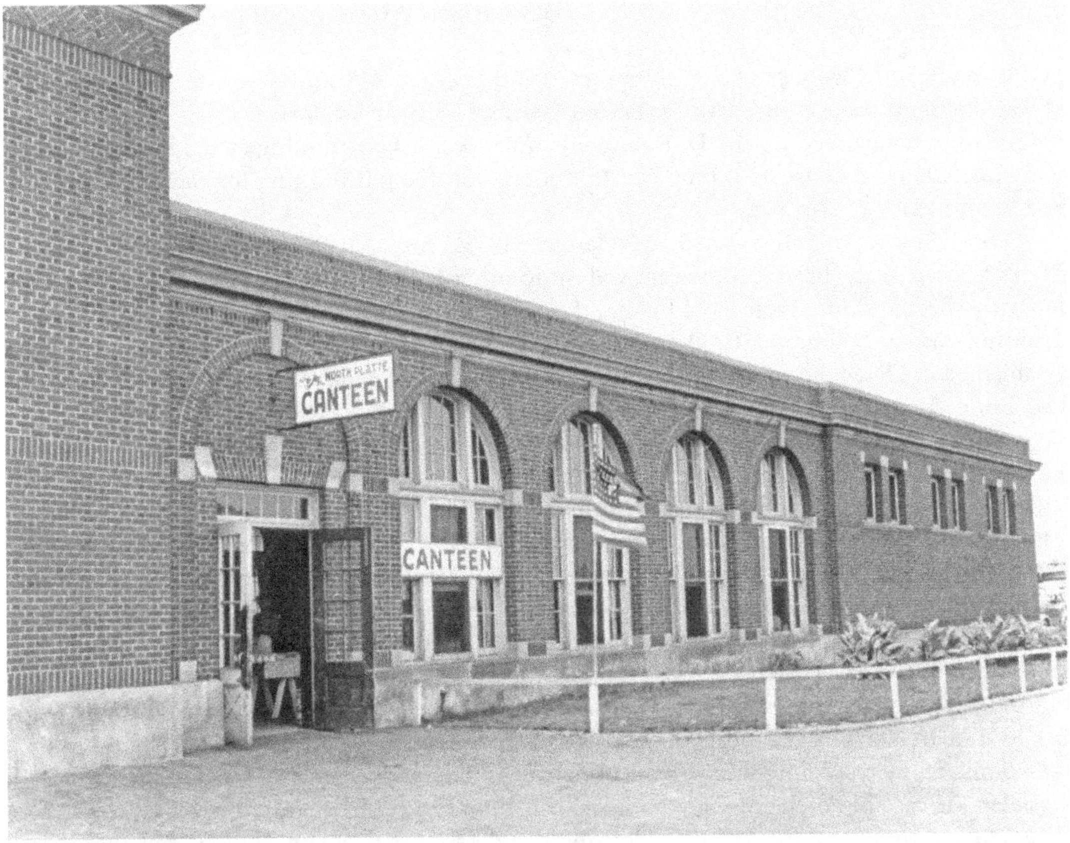
NORTH PLATTE
CANTEEN
CANTEEN

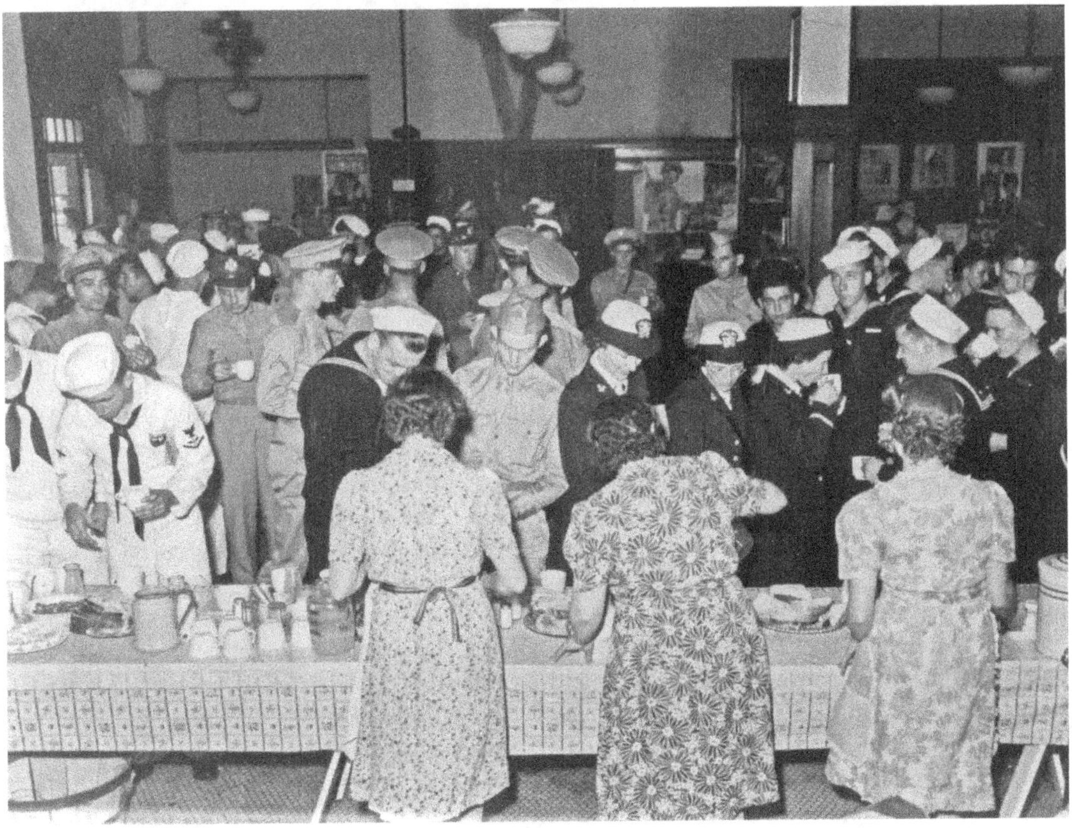

LCS(L)s 1, 5, and 6 were permanently assigned and LCS(L)s 2, 3, and 4 were at the base for use as training ships for approximately six months before heading for the war zone in late February 1945. Crews that served on the LCI gunboats underwent their training at the base, but when their LCI(L)s were converted, they had to undergo on the job training for their new mission and equipment.

Fort Pierce was commissioned on 26 January 1943. From that point on, numerous Gunner's Mates trained at the base and then moved on to other locations to receive additional training for their specific ships. From Fort Pierce, the newly trained men reported to the Amphibious Training Base at Solomons. By 1944 a number of other amphibious training bases had been established at Ocracoke in North Carolina, Panama City, Florida, Morro Bay, California, and Galveston, Texas.

After completing amphibious training at Solomons, crews were sent either to Boston to pick up their ships at the George Lawley & Sons Shipyard or to Portland, Oregon, to get their ships at Albina Engine and Machine Works or Commercial Iron Works. Transportation was usually by bus to Washington, D.C. Some crews were lucky and delayed train schedules gave some a bit of much desired liberty. The trains used for transport varied from jury-rigged transports utilizing freight cars to relatively comfortable regular train cars. Crews transiting the country from Solomons to Portland had the longest ride and, at many stops along the way, they were treated to meals by local groups supporting the war effort. Among them was the famous North Platte Canteen in North Platte, Nebraska. The canteen had been established on 25 December 1941 in an effort by the local people to show their appreciation for the servicemen.

Some of the crews might have some free time in Boston if their ship was not finished. This was also the case in Portland, Oregon. Local inhabitants were frequently quite nice to the servicemen and they were treated well. Nothing could ease the problem of being separated from home and family, but men were kept busy in order to keep them from getting homesick.

Officers and Crew

The number of men on board the gunboats varied. The largest number were on board the LCS(L)s and LCI(G)s, each having a complement of five officers and sixty-five men. LCI(R)s carried three officers and thirty-one men and the LCI(M)s four officers and forty-nine men.[9] The difference in the numbers had much to do with the ship's armament. LCI(G)s and LCS(L)s were the most heavily armed and carried a diversity of weapons, 20mm, 40mm, rockets, and .50 caliber machine guns. The LCI(M)s and LCI(R)s did not have the number of weapons that the others had and thus needed fewer men. Most ships in the U.S. Navy operated at about 85 percent of their assigned crew strength. One of the exceptions was the subs, which always had a full complement.

On each of the gunboats there might have been a different number of officers and men, but they generally shared the same duties. Officers performed supervisory duties. Overall responsibility for the ship fell on the Commanding Officer who made decisions based on orders he received from the Flotilla Commander. He was the supreme authority in all matters relating to the operation of the ship and its crew. Commanding Officers on the gunboats usually held the rank of Lieutenant (jg) or Lieutenant. In a few instances the post was held by an Ensign, although this did not happen often. Second in command was the ship's Executive Officer, who also served as the ship's navigator. The Gunnery Officer was in charge of the weapons systems and the ammunition supply. The Engineering Officer supervised the Motor Machinist's Mates and Firemen, who ran the engines. A Communications Officer kept contact with other ships in the fleet and supervised flag, signal light, and radio communications. On the LCI(G)s and LCS(L)s a sixth officer was also present. He was known as the "Additional Officer" or "First Lieutenant" and might be assigned whatever duties were in need of extra supervision, such as damage control. Ships with smaller crews and fewer officers, such as the LCI(R) and LCI(M), assigned multiple duties to the officers and men where needed. Each of the officers had a senior enlisted man under him who handled the routine duties of supervising the crewmen who were charged with specific tasks.

The day-to-day operation of the ship was handled by the Boatswain (Bosun), Coxswain, and the Seamen. They were the laborers of the ship and were responsible for numerous duties such as steering the ship, docking, anchoring, loading guns, ship maintenance, and whatever jobs needed their attention.

The Boatswain oversaw the conduct of drills and made sure that everyone was in the correct place and familiar with his assigned equipment. Since fire fighting was an important part of training, he made sure that every man knew which fire extinguisher he was assigned to and how to work it. He made daily inspections of the firefighting apparatus, life rafts, life preservers, and other vital equipment. The Boatswain had a great deal of control over the crew and regularly inspected their quarters and all the interior components of the ship. On occasion he would order the compartments aired out, and bedding would be taken topside for a few hours. Clothing lines might be strung through various equipment topside and freshly washed clothes hung to dry. When heavy weather threatened, he saw to it that lifelines were rigged on the ship in case the crew had to work on deck.

Assisting the Engineering Officer was the Chief Motor Machinist's Mate who oversaw the operation of the engine room. He was assisted by a Motor Machinist's Mate and two Firemen who ensured that the engines were supplied with fuel and maintained properly. They were usually referred to as the "Black Gang" and performed the dirty tasks associated with the maintenance of engines. This was a noisy, miserable job. Secured in their engine room compartment, the men were frequently made ill by the smell of diesel oil and stale air. According to Motor Machinist's Mate Edgar De Coursey, who served on *LCS(L) 61*, "it was terrible duty, heavy odor of fuel oil,

LCI gunboats and LCS(L)s not only shared the same hull, they had the same engines. This is the main engine room on an LCS(L) showing the starboard quad engine. The view is looking aft and starboard. Official U.S. Navy photograph.

you had a hard time keeping your food down."[10] The Motor Machinist's Mate on duty could be found at a small desk near the engine room telegraph which was connected to the pilot house. The officer in charge on the conning tower gave the order to the Quartermaster, who in turn transmitted the order to the engine room via the telegraph. The Motor Machinist's Mate on duty signaled back that the order had been received. The Motor Machinist's Mate also maintained the steam generator and the fresh water distillation unit. An Electrician's Mate might be found in the engine room, but he was basically free to attend to any part of the ship that needed his electrical expertise.

The Gunnery Officer oversaw the work of the Fire Directors and the operation of the guns. A gunboat usually had one Fire Control man and seven Gunner's Mates. Assisting in the firing of the guns would be a number of Seamen, who would pass ammunition and load the guns. The Fire Control man operated the Mark 51 gun directors, if the ship was so equipped. These gun directors were located in tubs near the guns. One could be seen on the forward face of the conning tower on the LCS(L), and another in a separate tower aft the deck house. Two men usually occupied the fire control tower. When he was on target, the Fire Control Director closed a key on the gun handles in front of him and fired the gun. The LCS(L)s gun directors provided a distinct advantage, particularly against aircraft. Single 40mm bow guns were manually aimed.

Directly manning the 40mm guns were seven men: a gun captain, a trainer, a pointer, two second loaders and two first loaders. The pointer elevated the gun and the trainer moved the gun from side to side. The gun tubs were filled with ammunition clips, each of which held four rounds. Individual clips held one tracer, one armor piercing round, and two regular rounds. As reloading took place, damage control men working below passed ammunition cans from the ammunition locker. Contained in each can were four ammo clips.

Guns needed continual maintenance. Outside the war zone this might be done at a leisurely pace, but in the war zone under battle conditions, speed was a requisite. In all cases it was not considered wise to break down more than one 40mm gun at a time lest the ship be lacking in defensive capabilities. The ships carried spare barrels which could be switched to allow the dirty one to be cleaned once it cooled down. In some cases water was played on hot barrels to cool them rapidly so that they could be switched. This usually led to warping of the barrel, rendering it useless. Some of the Gunnery Officers learned this the hard way.

Radar men manned the ship's radar. A Radarman and a Radarman Striker took turns standing watch on the screens to identify ships and aircraft in the vicinity. Also on board was a Radar Technician whose skills kept the radar in operation.

The "doctor" on board a gunboat was usually a Pharmacist's Mate. He was tasked with looking after the general health of the crew and would render first aid and diagnose various health problems. If the condition of a crewman was such that his limited skills were not sufficient, he would recommend the transfer of his patient to a shore facility or to a larger ship where a medical doctor might be on board. The Pharmacist's Mate dispensed various medicines and, in conjunction with the Boatswain, supervised the overall cleanliness of the crews. The Pharmacist's Mate might also double in duty as a Yeoman, typing the ship's log, action reports, and other ship's documents which would include the health record of each member of the crew.

Electrician's Mates were responsible for operating and maintaining the electric system of the ship. Highly dependent on the Electrician's Mate was the Communications Officer and his crew, which included the Radioman and Signalman.

While underway, Radiomen maintained a 24-hour listening watch, copying continuous encoded fleet broadcast messages from land-based Naval stations, and passing any relevant traffic to the Communications Officer. In battle conditions, when normal open-sea radio silence was suspended, Radiomen operated short-range voice radios in talk between ships.

Signalmen were trained in the use of the semaphore or blinking light which was used to communicate between ships during periods of radio blackout. Signalmen were also skilled in the use of signaling between ships using flags.

The ship's Quartermaster also had some training in the use of signals in case the Signalman was disabled. Normally the Quartermaster assisted the Executive Officer in navigating with the sextant and maintaining the charts. During periods of general quarters, the Quartermaster was at the ship's wheel or in the emergency steering box situated over the rudder at the aft end of the ship. This position would only be used if the normal steering mechanism was damaged. Steering from the steering box was difficult, particularly due to communications. A Quartermaster Striker might assist the Quartermaster in the performance of his duties and, during general quarters, was assigned to man the engine room telegraph.

The ship's galley was home to the Chief Cook and two assistants. On his shoulders fell the task of feeding the entire crew. In the words of cook Joe Staigar who served on *LCS(L) 61*, "If you were a good cook, most knew you. If a 'so-so' cook, everyone knew you."[11] On an LCS(L) the Chief Cook was allotted $.87 per day per man. However, after the first LCS(L)s were placed in combat in the Philippines, it became apparent that they were subject to extremely hazardous duty, and they were given the same rations allotment as submarines, which also had dangerous assignments. Chopped beef was standard fare which could be cooked in a variety of ways from hamburgers or meatballs to meatloaf and other dishes.

The cook's normal watch involved one day on and one day off, with the cook on watch serving from 0600 to 1900. Hours were not always consistent, since men were unable to eat at regular times because of seasickness and the uncertain routines caused by general quarters during combat conditions. Rough weather might make it impossible for the cook to prepare hot meals and sandwiches might be the best he could produce. Three seamen were routinely assigned a week of mess duty at a time. These assignments were determined by the Boatswain. The men on mess duty assisted with cleaning and preparing vegetables and general galley duties.

The officers' needs were tended to by a Steward's Mate who maintained the officers' quarters and brought their food to them. He had to make the ship's fare look as palatable as possible. Steward's Mates were usually of African-American heritage.

Although Seamen had their assigned duties, which could be varied, some were assigned permanent duty as "Strikers." A "Striker" worked directly under a particular job assignment in order to learn through on the job training in case his skills were needed. Thus a Quartermaster Striker was basically a Quartermaster in training. Strikers worked in other areas as well. Usually the third cook on the ship was a Striker, however, he might have gone through Cook's and Baker's School and would be waiting for the official position of Chief Cook to be available.

Shipboard Life

Life on the amphibious gunboats was difficult and Spartan. The Landing Craft Infantry (Large) and its conversions was designed to get in close to shore and run its bow up on the beach. Prior to landing, the LCI(L) dropped its stern anchor before getting into shallow water. Once run up on the beach and having discharged its cargo, it then used its massive stern winch and anchor to haul itself off the beach. In order to operate in this manner, the ship had to have a flat bottom.

Flat bottom vessels are not comfortable in a seaway. They sit on top of the water and have a pronounced roll as soon as the ocean becomes rough. Originally designed for short missions across the English channel, they were pressed into service to cross the Atlantic and Pacific to transport troops to their landing destinations. Transiting the Pacific from California to Okinawa was not an enjoyable ride. In addition, the LCI(L)s were not that large. Their hull was only 159

Life on board gunboats was a constant series of ship maintenance procedures. Shown here are John Sarsfield on deck and Stanley Wicks on the platform as they chip paint on board *LCS(L) 61* at Saipan Harbor on 12 December 1945.

On board *LCS(L) 61* Peter Panichi and Fred Berter peel potatoes while on KP duty at Yokosuka at the end of the war. Courtesy Robert Blyth.

feet long and they had a beam of just over 23 feet. There was little room for creature comforts. The LCS(L)s, built on the same hull, had virtually the same living space.

The berthing compartments were crowded with pipe racks extending from floor to ceiling, usually about four high. A small foot locker was packed carefully for each man as there was little space available. It would not be unusual for extra ammunition or other supplies to be stowed in various places throughout the ship. The galley was very limited in space and storage of many items was difficult.

One of the great treats for crewmen was ice cream. The LCIs and LCS(L)s did not have the capacity to make ice cream, so they had to depend on the charity of the larger ships. If they had a good relationship with the destroyers or other ships serving alongside them, they might be able to obtain ice cream for the crews. Rescuing a man overboard from a larger vessel was frequently grounds for such a reward.

The small living space left no room for recreation save reading, writing letters home, or card playing, chess, checkers, and shooting dice. Gambling was forbidden, however, the men usually found a way to play when the officers were not around. Many ships kept a mascot and took special care of it. These might range from dogs and cats to monkeys picked up in the Pacific islands.

Ships needed to be kept free of rust and excess paint, so any loose paint was chipped off and new paint applied. Chipping paint was the scourge of crewmen as it was both tedious and difficult.

Officers had quarters that were slightly better, however, they could hardly be compared to a four star hotel. The commanding officer usually had to share his quarters with his executive officer. Included in the small cabin were a couple of chairs and a small writing desk so that the commanding officer could do his paperwork.

Once in the war zone, sleep became a valued commodity. Constant calls to general quarters kept the men from any restful sleep. Even in their off hours such calls guaranteed that they went without rest. On the radar picket stations at Okinawa, any unidentified aircraft were grounds for the GQ klaxon to go off, sending men running for their stations. General quarters could be particularly nerve wracking. Men working below decks could hear guns going off but never knew if they were in immediate danger. With the hatches dogged down they were trapped below if the ship should be hit. The sound of larger guns being fired was one thing, but the sound of 20mm or .50 caliber guns meant that the enemy was close at hand and the ship was in danger. A cutting torch was usually part of the equipment below. The men could use it to cut themselves out if they were in danger of flooding or if the hatches were jammed.

Life on *LCS(L) 61*, which saw action on the radar picket lines at Okinawa, was typical. Normally, the crewmen worked watches of four hours on and were then off duty for eight hours. During their time on watch, some had specific tasks and others had a variety of duties. During the eight hours the men spent off watch, they were expected to do other jobs. The gunners spent their time breaking down guns and cleaning them and making sure that they were in perfect working order. Quartermasters spent time updating the charts and cleaning and painting the inside of the pilothouse. Most of the seamen had a number of chores, including basic ship maintenance. The preferred watch hours were from eight in the morning until noon

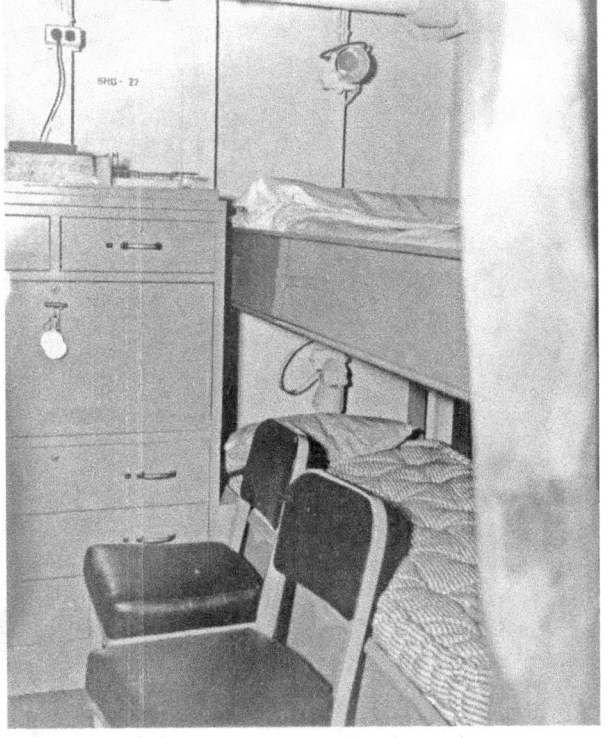

Top: Crew's quarters were similar on both LCI gunboats and LCS(L)s. This is a section of the crew's quarters on an LCS(L), starboard side, looking aft. Official U.S. Navy photograph. *Bottom:* Space on board the gunboats was at a premium. The Commanding Officer shared his cabin with the ship's Executive Officer. This is the Commanding Officer's quarters on an LCS(L). Official U.S. Navy photograph.

and then again from eight in the evening until midnight. That allowed the most normal living conditions. After the eight to midnight watch was over, the crewman could turn in for a regular night's sleep. However, in the war zone, general quarters might sound at any time. If the men were at their battle stations during their normal sleeping time there was no compensation for lost sleep. They simply went back to work. On picket duty around Okinawa, this proved to be difficult, with many of the men called to battle stations at night. In some cases they went without sleep for a couple of days in a row. Sometimes men could barely keep their eyes open on watch after prolonged sessions at general quarters.

Eating accommodations on board the ships were crowded. The mess area was small and only about thirty men at a time could eat. Normal hours for eating were from seven to eight in the morning for breakfast, noon to one for lunch and from four to five in the afternoon for dinner. As men lined up for their turn in the mess hall, those who had the next duty were allowed to go first. Meals usually lasted about fifteen to twenty minutes. One of the breakfast problems centered around the use of the toaster, since there was only one available. Disputes frequently arose over who was next in line to use it. Coffee, the one indis-

Top: On board ship there was occasional leisure time to catch up on the latest scuttlebutt. Crewmen on board *LCI(G) 69* engage in discussion as their ship heads for the invasion of Luzon on 9 January 1945. NARA 80G 472021. *Bottom:* The immediacy of battle left little time for formal meals on board the gunboats. A crewman on *LCI(G) 69* eats at his general quarters station as his ship approaches Luzon on 6 January 1946. A standard, tripod-mounted .50 caliber machine gun is seen over his shoulder. NARA 80G 472034.

pensable item in the work place, was often bad-tasting. If the stainless tanks in which it was made weren't cleaned properly each day, a metallic taste permeated the brew. After finishing their meal, crewmen took their trays up to the next level for cleaning and waste disposal. Once the last meal had been served, the crewmen assigned to their week of mess duty cleaned the area and it was then used for recreation. There the men could play chess, checkers or cards. In card games some men were bigger winners than others, causing occasional fights. Some also indulged in the illegal game of craps. Officers normally avoided the area, leaving it to the crews and Bosun to manage.

Many of the men preferred to sit topside if the weather permitted. There they could relax and enjoy the trip across the Pacific, telling stories of their exploits before the war and their plans for civilian life afterwards. The small library on board the ship provided some reading material, which also helped to break the monotony of the voyage.

The berthing area was confined, with several rows of bunks lined up four high from deck to overhead. Each man had a locker that measured twelve inches wide by eighteen inches deep by four feet high. Clothes had to be rolled carefully in order to fit into these spaces. Under the bottom bunk was a space of several inches where crewmen could stow their shoes. Some of the men with large feet made it through most of the war without proper foot gear. If shoes in their size could not be obtained, they wore an extra pair of socks with rubbers over them. Underneath the mattress bedding on each of the folding pipe berths was a hammock. When a crewman was transferred off the ship, he rolled his mattress and seabag in the hammock and carried it with him to his new

Top: The galleys on the gunboats were of limited size but sufficient to feed the crews. Official U.S. Navy photograph. *Bottom:* The crew's mess area on a gunboat was small in size, with meals staggered at intervals. Once the meal was finished, the area was cleaned and served as a place to play cards and checkers. Official U.S. Navy photograph.

ship. Poor ventilation was a common problem in the berthing area. Although there were fans to move air around, there was no air conditioning. During mild weather, conditions below were bearable, but in the heat of the tropics many men elected to sleep on deck. Crewmen were required to change their sheets regularly, and those who did not received some unpleasant attention from the Bosun.

Tropical heat and the absence of direct threats from the enemy gave this cook on board *LCI(G) 69* the opportunity to do some food preparation on deck, a rare occurrence. The photograph was taken in December 1944. NARA 80G 472022.

The head area on the gunboats measured about ten by fifteen feet. It held two showers, four wash basins, six toilets and a washing machine. On one side a trough type urinal flushed waste water over the side. At certain times during the day the space was quite crowded, but it might also be empty in the evenings. A daily allotment of water determined the availability of showers. If the crew used up the allotment for the day, showers were prohibited. The ship carried distilling equipment that could distill three thousand gallons a day, however, commanding officers were frequently reluctant to deplete more than half the supply of water since it was also used for drinking and cooking. Also, one might never know when the distilling equipment might break down, causing a water shortage. At sea there would be no way to replenish the water.[12]

Race and Service

Service choices for African-Americans during World War II were limited. On the gunboats their primary role was that of Steward's Mate. Duties included cleaning the officers' quarters, making their beds, and serving them meals. It was considered a totally undesirable job by most of the crew. When Steward's Mate Robert Doster on *LCS(L) 35* was transferred off the ship in Shanghai at the end of the war, there was no replacement for him and several seamen were picked to take his place until a new Steward's Mate arrived a few weeks later. Charles Thomas recalled, "It's a duty they detest to a man.... Several of the seamen continue their undesirable steward's duty for several more days until everyone, including the officers, is happy to see a new steward's mate reporting aboard. "[13] Doster was regarded by Thomas as being an intelligent man and had related to him that he wanted to go to college and medical school after the war. He probably would have made a good Pharmacist's Mate, but that avenue of training was not open to African-Americans in general. The attitude of the seamen replacing Doster was understandable. Patriotic young men enlisted to fight for their country, not to become officers' servants.

On board *LCS(L) 61*, StM 1/c Huram McCloud, was a plank owner, having joined the ship's crew on 3 November 1944 at Portland, Oregon, with the rest of the men. McCloud was a quiet man who kept to himself and, in the early days of the ship's Bosun service, was given a difficult time by some of the other crew members. However, the ship's Bosun, Joe Columbus, quickly put an end to the harassment and McCloud's situation became better.[14]

Louis Plant, who served as a Staff Signalman for Flotilla Three under Lieutenant Commander E. P. Stone later wrote his views about the situation. Plant related his observations about life on the destroyer *Terry DD 513* which transported him home after the war. He wrote:

> During this trip home I learned more about the treatment of Negroes. As I believe I have stated before, they were not allowed to be anything but Officer's stewards and mess cooks. On this ship, they were not allowed to sleep in the crews' quarters. They had bunks in the passageways between decks, the pretense being that they had to be up early to prepare our food, they would disturb the crew. However, it was OK to disturb them when walking by their bunks to go on watch. Ridiculous. How these men put up with this situation I shall never know. They were getting shot at just like we were; yet they were treated as being inferior. This was just not right.[15]

Each gunboat had a different story, with some of the African-Americans treated well and, on some ships not well at all. It was long before the civil rights movement and equality was basically non-existent. Relegating a group of men to a minor task was not in the Navy's best interest, however, that was the situation. It was a waste of talent and manpower as numerous Steward's Mates were capable of other roles that would have served the naval effort well.

Gunboat Missions

Assaulting the Beach

One of the primary reasons for development of the LCI gunboats and its later variant, the LCS(L), was close-in fire support of troops as they made their landing. As the assembled landing

A row of LCS(L)s may be seen between the second and third waves of landing craft. After making rocket runs on the beach, the gunboats patrolled close inshore, firing over the heads of the Marines as they landed. Official U.S. Navy photograph.

craft made ready to send their troops and supplies to the enemy shore, the first assault was usually carried out by the amphibious gunboats. In the early campaigns of the war these were either LCI(G)s or LCI(R)s. However, as the war progressed it was not unusual to see a line of LCI(G)s, (R)s, (M)s, and LCS(L)s working side by side to lay down suppressive fire against the enemy-held beach.

It was common practice for the gunboats to head for the beach abreast of one another and, at a distance of several hundred yards, let fly with everything that they had. This first assault included a heavy attack with rockets. After the rockets had been fired, the ships turned broadside in a line and worked over the beaches with their automatic weapons. They then turned and headed back to their departure line, loading rockets as they went. As soon as the rockets were reloaded, they made a second run similar to the first. They then stood by as the landing craft bearing the troops passed through their lines. As the LCVPs and other small craft passed by and landed men on the beaches, the gunboats remained just outside the surf and fired over their heads in order to keep the enemy at bay. Additional LCI(R)s and LCI(M)s might be found covering the flanks of the assault wave.

Barge Interception

American success in aerial attacks, particularly after the Imperial Navy's carrier losses at Midway, made the Japanese increasingly reluctant to transport large numbers of men on troop carriers. The debacles at Guadalcanal in November 1942, and later at the Battle of the Bismarck Sea in March 1943, made this increasingly obvious.

Rabaul blazes fiercely after an attack by U.S. B-25s. In the barge concentration tied up along the waterfront are several Army Type A landing craft. Over 300 tons of war material could be carried by these barges. They could also move personnel in addition to supplies. U.S. War and Navy Departments, *U.S. Army-Navy Journal of Recognition*, No. 7, March 1944, p. 41.

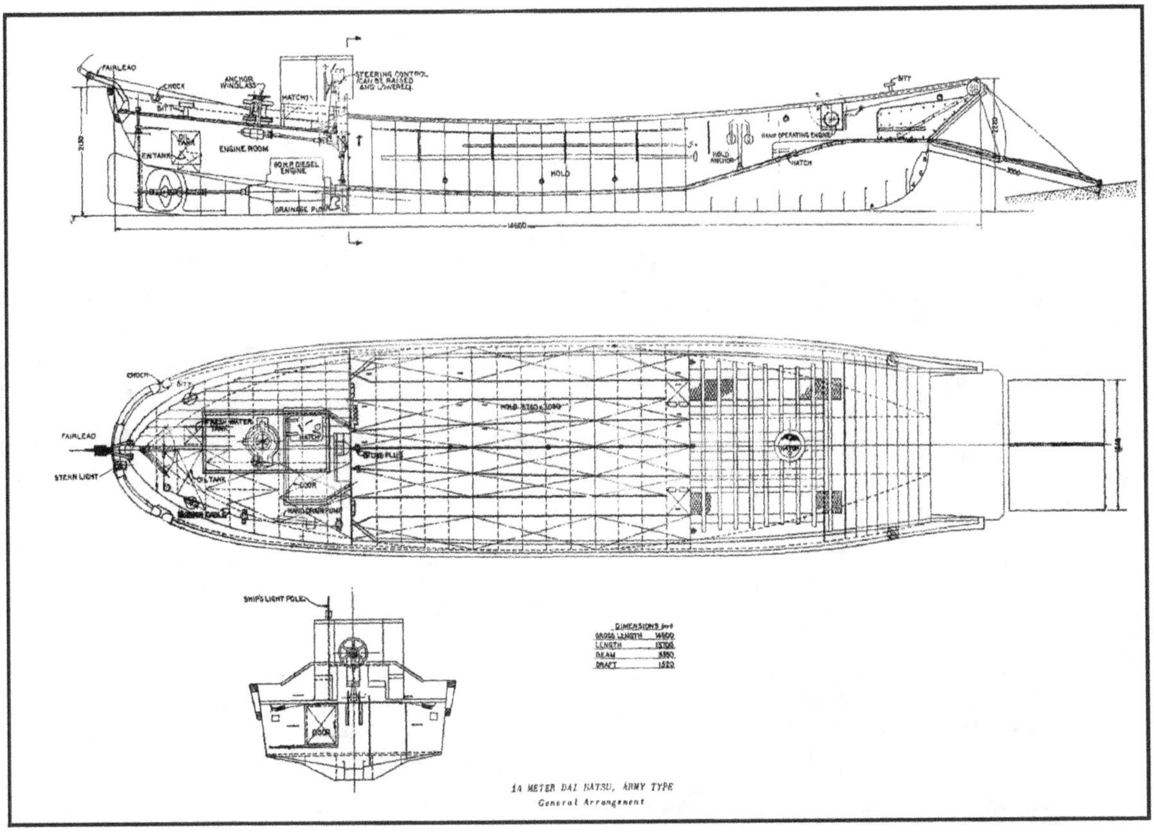

A Japanese 14 meter *Dai Hatsu* Army Type A barge. These were used for transporting men, equipment, and supplies between the islands. Landing craft gunboats were utilized to combat them. U.S. Navy Technical Mission to Japan, *Target Report—Characteristics of Japanese Naval Vessels, Article 10—Landing Craft*, 6 February 1946, p. 23.

A Japanese Navy Type A barge is shown underway on a canal in China.

In mid–November 1942 the Japanese attempted to send a convoy of eleven destroyers and eleven transports under Rear Admiral Raizo Tanaka down the "slot" to reinforce their troops on Guadalcanal. In the midst of the continuing naval battles for the island of Guadalcanal, the transports came under attack on 14 November 1942. Rising to the defense against these troop reinforcements were American Marine and Navy aircraft flying off Henderson Field on Guadalcanal and some from the carrier *Enterprise*. Fifteen Army B-17s from Espiritu

Type A barges were used by both the Japanese Navy and Army. The Navy version had a deckhouse while the Army version did not. The Navy version carried sixty men and that of the Army 100-120. They had a length of forty-nine feet and a beam of eleven and one-half feet. The Army barge shown above was captured and put to use by the American forces. This was a common occurrence in the war zone. NARA 890G 1022361.

Santo joined in the fray. The aircraft took a heavy toll of the transports, sinking seven and destroying the remaining four which had beached themselves on Guadalcanal.

> The Japanese observed that a destroyer screen with fighter cover was not enough to protect feebly armed ships; they must have close support from heavily gunned men-of-war. And they also learned the need of an additional airfield to help protect the "Tokyo Express." The Americans noted how greatly the effectiveness of carrier planes was increased when they were provided with an optional land base.[16]

With such heavy losses the Japanese began to depend increasingly on smaller ships and craft such as barges to supply their forces in the Solomons.

In February 1943 it became necessary for the Japanese to supplement their troop strength in Lae, New Guinea. They planned to transport an additional 6,900 18th Army troops from Rabaul to Lae to reinforce the beleaguered garrison there. The convoy, carrying men and supplies, departed Rabaul at midnight on

The Type B landing craft was one of the smallest Japanese barges, having an overall length of thirty feet and a beam of seven and one-half feet. It was capable of eight to ten knots and carried forty men. U.S. War and Navy Departments, *U.S. Army-Navy Journal of Recognition*, No. 7, March 1944, p. 44.

28 February 1943. Under the overall command of the escort commander, Rear Admiral Masatomi Kimura, the convoy totaled eight transports and eight destroyers. By this time the Japanese had learned not to send ships loaded solely with men or supplies as the loss of either could seriously endanger the invasion attempt. Each transport carried a combination of men and supplies so that if some were lost, any individual ship would be capable of landing men and supplies together, thereby preserving their fighting efficiency. Only one day out of port, the convoy was spotted by American aircraft and tracked from that point on. On 2 March, the Americans and Australians struck. Particularly effective were the B-25s and A-20s of Lieutenant General George C. Kenney's V Air Force. The convoy was under continuous attack from 2 to 4 March. When the Battle of the Bismarck Sea was over, all eight of the Japanese transports and four of the eight destroyers had been sunk. Of the men on the ships only 2,734 were saved.[17] "Thereafter no big ships were risked within range of enemy air power. As had happened in the Solomons, New Guinea began to be supplied by barge."[18] By the spring of 1943, American intelligence estimated that the Japanese had 6,000 barges in service and that this number would increase.[19]

The Japanese Type C barge was heavily armored and diesel powered. It was designed to carry troops and also to support landing operations. It was forty feet long and could make twenty-five knots. U.S. War and Navy Departments, *U.S. Army-Navy Journal of Recognition*, No. 7, March 1944, p. 45.

Barges came in several types and most ranged from

The Japanese Type E barge could be recognized by the aircraft-type propeller on the stern and the round machine-gun tub forward. Here a soldier uses a pole to move the barge away from the others prior to starting the engine. This barge had a flat bottom and could transport about sixty men into very shallow water. It was sixty-three feet long with a beam of nine feet. U.S. War and Navy Departments, *U.S. Army-Navy Journal of Recognition*, No. 7, March 1944, pp. 46–47.

A Japanese Type D barge lands troops near Canton, China, on 12 October 1938. This type of barge was built in several variations ranging from 38 feet to 70 feet. NARA 306-NT-1151-J-4.

The Type F Japanese barge was designed as a small personnel carrier. At a length of twenty-one feet and with a beam of seven feet, it could carry approximately twenty men. It was not armed and the crossbeam could be moved to shift compartment arrangements. U.S. War and Navy Departments, *U.S. Army-Navy Journal of Recognition*, No. 7, March 1944, p. 46.

around fifty to sixty-five feet in length. The larger barges might be armed with two Oerlikon guns and the smaller ones with one or two machine guns. Some barges were as small as thirty feet and were used for the local transportation of troops. The interception and destruction of these barges was of major importance, particularly in the southwest Pacific.

The War Department noted

the barge fleets have turned out to be fine substitutes for cargo vessels and transports, particularly since some sea lanes have been so badly slashed by U.S. air power. To cut down barge losses the Japanese have set up an ingenious short-hop water route. Each leg of the trip, from staging point to staging point, takes a night's sail. The barges usually operate in shallow reef-infested waters inaccessible to U.S. destroyers and PT boats. During the day they remain in hiding, concealed under overhanging trees or are camouflaged on open beaches.

Since 13 Type A barges, each carrying ten tons of supplies, can maintain 20,000 men for a day, the tremendous value of the Japanese barges becomes apparent.[20]

Further reports indicated that

The Japanese Type G landing boat was used to haul reinforcements and supplies once a beachhead was established. It was fifty-two feet long with a beam of thirteen feet. It was unarmed and capable of eight knots. An identifying feature was the small deck house amidships. U.S. War and Navy Departments, *U.S. Army-Navy Journal of Recognition*, No. 7, March 1944, p. 46.

[a] convoy of 73 large barges can move a Japanese infantry regiment and a substantial amount of rations and ammunition a distance of 79 nautical miles 80 land miles, approx per night for several nights, with proper day concealment and fuel supply.... A fleet of 37 large barges seems to be sufficient to transport a Japanese infantry regiment about 34 miles in 36 hours including two nights.[21]

Barges might be used between islands, but might also be used to transport troops from one section of an island to another. This was due to the ever-present and impenetrable jungle on most of the islands. As a result of the dense jungle, most enemy troop concentrations were on the coast where they could easily be supplied. Forcing a supply line through heavy jungle, particularly in mountainous terrain, was well nigh impossible. Constant rain, heat, and humidity made traversing sections of the jungle on these islands extremely difficult, therefore the only practical way to move men was along the coast by boat. This was noted by the Americans in regard to their own troops. "Throughout the campaign on New Guinea, Allied and Japanese forces clung to small enclaves on the coast, leaving the impenetrable hinterland mainly to itself. Because of the dense jungle abruptly rising beyond the shores, 95 percent of the US Army's supply movements in New Guinea had to be made by boat."[22]

Many LCI conversions, as well as the LCS(L)s sent to intercept the barges, mounted a 3"/50 gun for greater effect. This gave them an advantage over the larger barges. Their ability to go into shallow waters allowed them to hunt barges successfully. On such missions they were frequently accompanied by PT boats.

Suicide Boats

By late 1943 the Japanese had recognized that they were in serious danger of losing the war. The island-hopping campaign of the Americans had left their troops isolated on bypassed islands. Additionally, the great losses suffered by their Navy and the air arms of both the Army and Navy had left them vulnerable in many locations. The possibility of defending these island bases by use of aircraft or ships was out of the question as they were now in an inferior position in both areas.

A *Shinyo Type 1 Model 1* suicide boat shown at Nagasaki in the fall of 1945. This particular type was used by the Japanese Navy. Within the bow was an explosive charge that was designed to detonate upon impact with the target. NARA 127-GW-1523-140563.

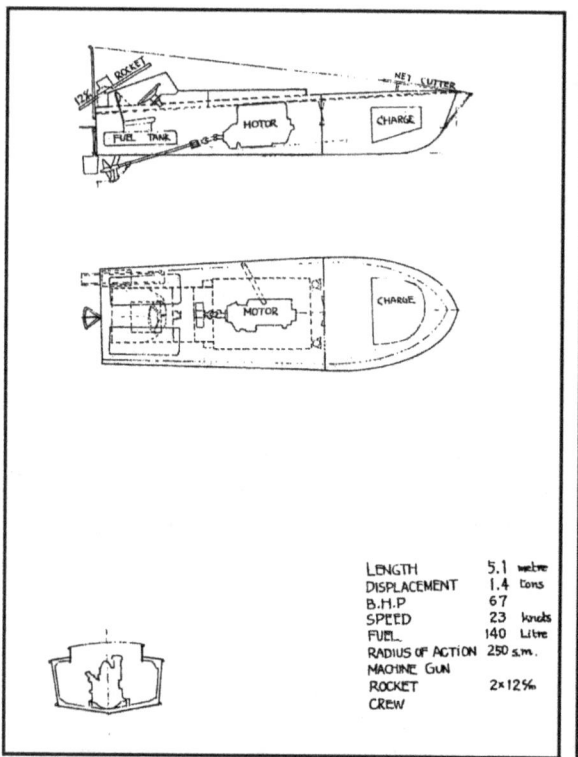 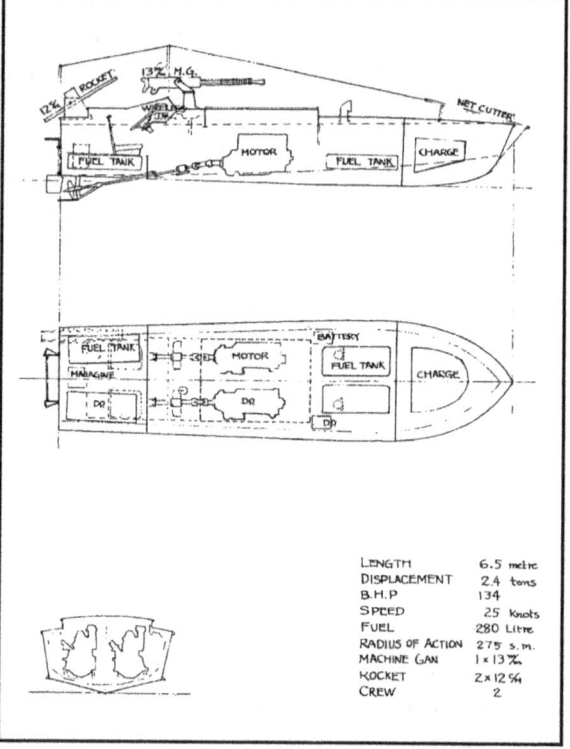

The Japanese Navy employed two types of explosive speedboats, the *Shinyo Type 1 Model 1* and the *Shinyo Type 5*. Both carried a 595 lb. explosive charge in the bow. U.S. Naval Technical Mission to Japan, *Target Report—Japanese Suicide Craft*, 4 September 1945, pp. 11, 14.

How to defend these islands without air or naval support weighed heavily on the mind of Lieutenant General Yoshiaburo Suzuki, Commander-in-Chief of the Army's Shipping Headquarters in Ujina. He determined that local forces would have to bear the brunt of defending the scattered island bases. With few options left, he decided to employ the use of suicide or special attack methods utilizing boats armed with explosives. His views were accepted and Imperial Headquarters directed their Technical Institute to hasten the development of boats that would be suitable for such missions.[23]

Suzuki recommended the following specifications for the suicide boats:

1. Weight to be as light as possible, configuration/size to be suitable for secret storage ashore and carriage by manpower.
2. Operating velocity to exceed 20 nautical miles per hour.
3. Capable of carrying explosive material sufficient in quantity to sink an enemy transport;
4. Number of crew to be up to two; and
5. Capable of being mass-produced.[24]

Work began almost immediately on the design and production of the boats, and the Army had working prototypes cruising Tokyo Bay by June 1944.

Saipan and other bases in the Marianas were seen as crucial to the defense perimeter of Japan. They were considered the inner ring of defense for the home islands. In May 1944, Admiral Soemu Toyoda, newly appointed as Commander in Chief of the Combined Fleet, noted their importance in a dispatch. Toyoda stated: "The war is drawing close to the lines vital to our national defense. The issue of our national existence is unprecedentedly serious...."[25] During the following two months, Saipan, Tinian, Guam, and other islands in the Marianas chain fell into American hands. The loss of these islands was a serious blow to the Japanese and gave added impetus to the production of new special attack weapons and methods.

> Subsequently, the "Sho-Go Military Operations Plan," well-known as Japan's zero-hour battle plan, was finalized for implementation. The "special" combat methods were then formally laid out within the "Guidelines Pertaining to Military Operations Covering Smaller Islands" issued by the Imperial Headquarters. Thus, aided by the spontaneously supportive atmosphere at all levels of military hierarchy, the SBRs [Suicide Boat Regiments] became reality, taking a specific organizational composition of its own.[26]

Within a few months after the production of the prototypes, enough boats had been produced to organize units and send them to their bases. Both Army and Navy suicide boat units were sent to the Philippines, Okinawa, Iwo Jima, Korea, China, and Taiwan. Those stationed in Korea, China, and Taiwan saw no action, as the amphibious assaults were in other areas. Boats assigned to Iwo Jima were quickly destroyed by American air attacks leaving the bulk of the suicide boat operations to the waters around the Philippines and Okinawa.

Although both Army and Navy suicide boats had virtually the same mission, their method of attack differed. For the Navy pilot an attack was sure death, but for the Army pilot there was a chance of escaping to attack again. This distinction had to do with the design of the suicide boats and their method of attack. The Navy boats were known as *Shinyo* (Ocean Shakers) and had 270 kg. (595 lbs.) explosive charges in their bows. At the termination of the attack the *Shinyo* rammed its bow into an enemy ship. The impact detonated the charge and the pilot of the *Shinyo* died in the explosion.

The *Maru-re* mounted two depth charges in the stern area. Early boats mounted them on either side of the pilot, and later models mounted them behind him. The later models carried a heavier payload. During the attack the pilot aimed for the target ship and then swerved away at the last moment, dropping his depth charges alongside the enemy ship. They were timed to explode after a few seconds and blow a hole in the bottom of the ship. If the attack were timed correctly the pilot might make a getaway, but many were caught in the explosion and killed. Still others fell under the fire of the ship as they tried to make good their escape.

Piloting the *Maru-re* might be recruits as young as fifteen or sixteen who had been drafted from high school, while others had a year or two of college or technical school. The primary targets of these small vessels were usually transports and small, lightly armored ships. These craft were limited in their ability to carry fuel and so could only operate close to shore in relatively calm waters.

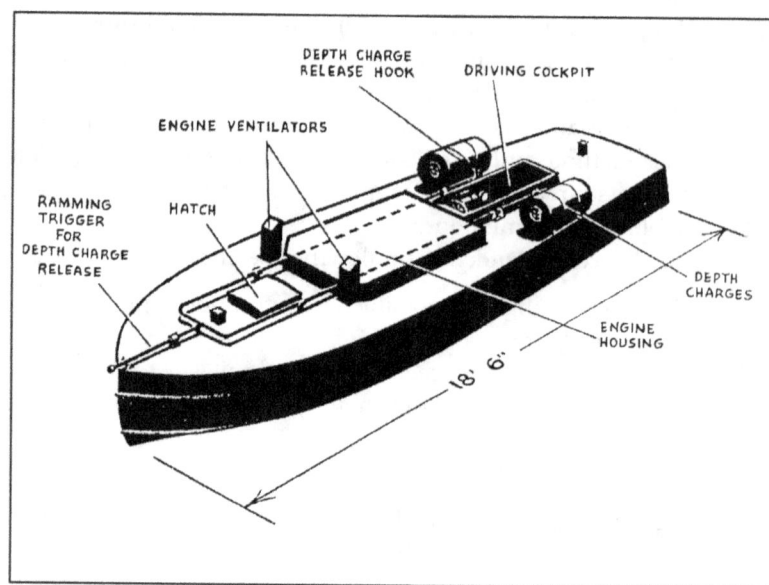

Early *Maru-re* boats had the depth charges mounted alongside the pilot's compartment. The depth charges could be released manually or by ramming the prow into the target ship. Division of Naval Intelligence, ONI 208-J Supplement No. 2, *Far-Eastern Small Craft,* March 1945, p. 31.

Because they were easy targets during the day, their attacks were conducted at night. After reaching the vicinity of their targets, the suicide boats usually operated at a slow speed so as not to give away their presence. Once the target was spotted, they shifted into full speed and made their attack. Many were spotted and destroyed prior to making their final run.

The most successful of the attacks took place in the Philippines. On 10 January 1945, *LCI(M) 974* was sunk by an Army *Maru-re* in Lingayen Gulf. Japanese Navy *Shinyos,* operating from their base on Corregidor, sank *LCS(L)s 7, 26,* and *49* and damaged *LCS(L) 27* at Mariveles Harbor on 16 February 1945. The gunboats were particularly watchful for these enemy speedboats, and hunting them was one of their primary duties. This became increasingly important as time wore on. At Okinawa *LCI(G) 558* was damaged on 29 March 1945 and *LCI(G) 82* was sunk on 4 April 1945. *LCS(L) 37* was put out of commission by suicide boats during the campaign for the island after she was attacked by them twice in two days on 28 and 29 April 1945. Patrolling against the *Shinyo* and *Maru-re* was officially known as "fly-catching." The sailors soon referred to it as "skunk patrol."

Between 10 January 1945 and 4 May 1945, the suicide boats were responsible for sinking seven ships and damaging another sixteen. Only supreme vigilance by sharp-shooting Navy gunners prevented greater losses.

Protecting the UDT and Marine Reconnaissance Units

Prior to each amphibious landing, it was necessary for the Navy's Underwater Demolition Teams to reconnoiter the beaches and determine the best landing areas, as well as to clear away underwater obstacles, both natural and those constructed by the enemy to deter landings. In many landings, particularly the larger ones, the UDT was accompanied by Marine Reconnaissance swimmers. The Marine Recon was required to land and sketch out important objects to be encountered on the beaches and waters near shore, troop locations, enemy weapons, soil samples, and other items of interest to the troops about to land. One Marine usually remained on the LCPR to photograph the beaches as the landing craft made its way along the shore, dropping off and later picking up swimmers. If detected, as they frequently were, the frogmen and Marine Recons were sitting ducks for enemy troops on shore. However, the appearance of an LCI(G) or LCS(L) close-in to shore was usually sufficient to suppress fire. This placed the gunboats in a hazardous position and they frequently came under attack. Covering the work of the underwater demolition teams at Iwo Jima on 17 February 1945 proved to be devastating for the gunboats of Flotilla 3 Group 8 as all twelve were hit, one of which subsequently sank.

Radar Picket Duty

Radar picket duty at Okinawa was considered the most hazardous naval duty of World War II. In order to protect the invasion fleet and its troops at Okinawa, the Navy set up a ring of sixteen radar picket stations around the island. On each station a destroyer, equipped with a fighter director team and special radar, worked in conjunction with the combat air patrol to intercept incoming Japanese aircraft raids. In short order it became necessary to assign extra ships, destroyers, PGMs, LSM(R)s and LCS(L)s to the stations to lend support to the radar picket destroyer. A total of eighty-eight LCS(L)s were assigned to the radar picket stations at Okinawa. Between 12 April and 14 August 1945, two LCS(L) ships were sunk and eight damaged by kamikaze attacks on the RP stations, with casualties of forty-six killed and seventy-four wounded.[27]

Minesweeping

The assault on an island usually required that the prospective invasion site be cleared of mines. The task of the minesweepers put them in constant peril from both the mines that they searched for and the enemy ashore. Most of the minesweeping prior to an invasion was close-in to shore near the landing beaches. This put them directly under the guns of the enemy and made it necessary for them to be given fire support. This was usually done by the LCI gunboats working in conjunction with destroyers and other larger ships off the beach.

Once the mines had been cut

A crewman on board *LCS(L) 28* watches as his ship explodes a mine with gunfire off Tarakan Island, Borneo, on 1 May 1945. Anything from small arms fire to the ship's 40mm gun might be used for this task. Official U.S. Navy photograph.

loose by the minesweepers, the gunboats were responsible for shooting at and destroying them. At the end of the war a serious problem existed in the number of these minefields remaining, and several months were spent working with the minesweepers off the coasts of Japan, Korea, and China to ensure that the waters were safe for peacetime traffic.

Call Fire

Still another mission that put to use the unique qualities of the gunboats was support of specific land operations or "call-fire" missions. To accomplish this task, a ship took on board a fire control officer from the Marine or Army infantry on shore. Using radio communications with his unit ashore, the fire control officer directed the ship's gunners to specific targets in order to aid the ground troops in their attack. Close-in support of the troops in this manner was hazardous with the gunboats continually exposed to enemy fire. LCI(M) ships were particularly useful for this task, as their mortar shells passed over the heads of friendly troops to land on the reverse side of hills where the enemy might be concealed.

Smoke Screens

Most of the ships were equipped to make smoke in order to cover various operations or to protect anchorages. This was a smelly and unpleasant duty and particularly odious when the wind was blowing in the wrong direction. Smoke pots and their fuel were located at the aft end

LCS(L)s 34, 35, and *36* lay smoke to cover anchored ships at Okinawa. Smoke-screening was an important but distasteful task for the gunboat sailors. Official U.S. Navy photograph.

of the ship. It was not unusual for a ship to come off a lengthy patrol and then have to spend the later hours making smoke at the anchorage in order to conceal ships from air attack. Bob Wisner, who served as the Communications Officer on *LCS(L) 37*, complained that after a lengthy period of patrol on the radar picket stations at Okinawa, the ships had to return to the anchorage and make smoke to cover the fleet.[28] This additional task robbed the crews of much-needed rest.

Fire Fighting

Although the earlier LCI(L) conversions had some limited ability to fight fires, the newly designed LCS(L) was far better equipped. A special manifold could be mounted on the foc'sle with a number of outlets capable of pumping large amounts of seawater on a burning ship or shore installation. On many occasions the LCS(L)s came to the aid of other ships and put their fire fighting capabilities to use.

All of the amphibious gunboats based on the LCI(L) hull anchored from the stern. On the stern of each of the LCI(L)s was a large Danforth type anchor attached to a winch. To land troops, the ship headed for the beach and, while still in reasonably deep water, dropped the anchor and continued shoreward until the bow was run up on the beach. This allowed the troops to disembark in shallow water. Once the troops were ashore, the winch was started and hauled the ship backwards off the beach to deeper water. The conversion of the gunboats did not include a change to the anchoring system, so LCI gun-

The special firefighting manifold on the bow of an LCS(L) gave it the ability to assist other ships in need. NARA RG 19 BuShips General Correspondence 1940–1945 C-LCS(L)(3) Class 593 LCS bow pumping system.

boats usually anchored using their stern anchor. A small bow anchor was available and used on some occasions, but the stern anchor had greater holding power. It is interesting to note that the LCS(L)s, built strictly as gunboats and not intended to disembark troops, kept the same anchoring arrangement. This proved useful on a number of occasions as the LCS(L)s were better

equipped to fight fires and, in a number of instances, were run bow first up on to the beach to fight fires near the shore. This method was employed at Iwo Jima as ammunition dumps near the shore were set afire by enemy gunfire and had to be extinguished.

LCS(L) ships had the capability to fight fires, which made them valuable in many situations. Here, *LCS(L) 71* fights a fire at the Marine Barracks in Sasebo, Japan, after the war. *LCS(L) 71* displays a twin 40mm bow gun, the adaptation that began to appear toward the end of the war. The two forward 40mm twins, coupled with the aft 40mm twin, made this variant ideal for antiaircraft support. Official U.S. Navy photograph.

Chapter 3

Operation Cartwheel

By 1942 it had become obvious that Rabaul, on the island of New Britain, would have to be conquered or neutralized. The Japanese had made it one of their most important bases. Situated at Rabaul were the 8th Army Headquarters commanded by General Hitoshi Imamura and the headquarters of the Southeastern Fleet under Admiral Jinichi Kusaka.

General Douglas MacArthur began to consider plans for eliminating its threat. His strategy was known as the Elkton Plan which was developed in three stages, all quite similar. The plan aimed at the eventual capture of Rabaul. Army forces would advance westward along the coast of New Guinea and then across the Vitiaz Strait and Dampier Strait to Cape Gloucester and Cape Merkus on western New Britain. Forces under Admiral William F. Halsey would move westward through the Solomons chain, capturing Guadalcanal, New Georgia and Bougainville. This would complete the encirclement of Rabaul, the final target. However, plans for the assault on Rabaul were not finalized.

At the beginning of 1943, the Army's Chief of Staff, General George C. Marshall, began to consider MacArthur's Elkton Plan. The Joint Chiefs of Staff debated the plan for four months before finally coming to a decision. Part of the problem lay in British pressure to keep the European theater as the focus of Allied effort. MacArthur's plan required the shifting of Army manpower from Europe to the Pacific, a strategy that found little support from the British. A second problem with the plan was that it put MacArthur solely in command of both Army and Navy forces for the capture of Rabaul. This did not sit well with Admiral Ernest King, Chief of Naval Operations. King wished to keep a certain amount of flexibility in the use of naval forces in the Pacific. While he was willing to work with MacArthur, he did not want to see all forces in the southwest Pacific under one command. The point, however, was moot. The capture of Rabaul in 1943 was out of the question; sufficient forces could not be brought to the area. MacArthur's plan quickly morphed into a new operation, code named Cartwheel. The overall strategy was enunciated in the General Headquarters Southwest Pacific Area Warning Instructions #2 of 6 May 1943.

> The general scheme of maneuver is to advance our bomber line towards Rabaul; first by improvement of presently occupied forward bases; secondly, by the occupation and implementation of air bases which can be secured without committing large forces; and then, by the seizure and implementation of successive hostile airdromes.
>
> By destructive air attack soften up and gain air superiority over each attack objective along the two axes of advance. Neutralize with appropriate aviation supporting hostile air bases and destroy hostile naval forces and shipping within range. Prevent reinforcement or supply of objectives under attack. Move land forces forward, covered by air and naval forces, to seize and consolidate each successive objective. Displace aviation forward onto captured airdromes. Repeat this process to succes-

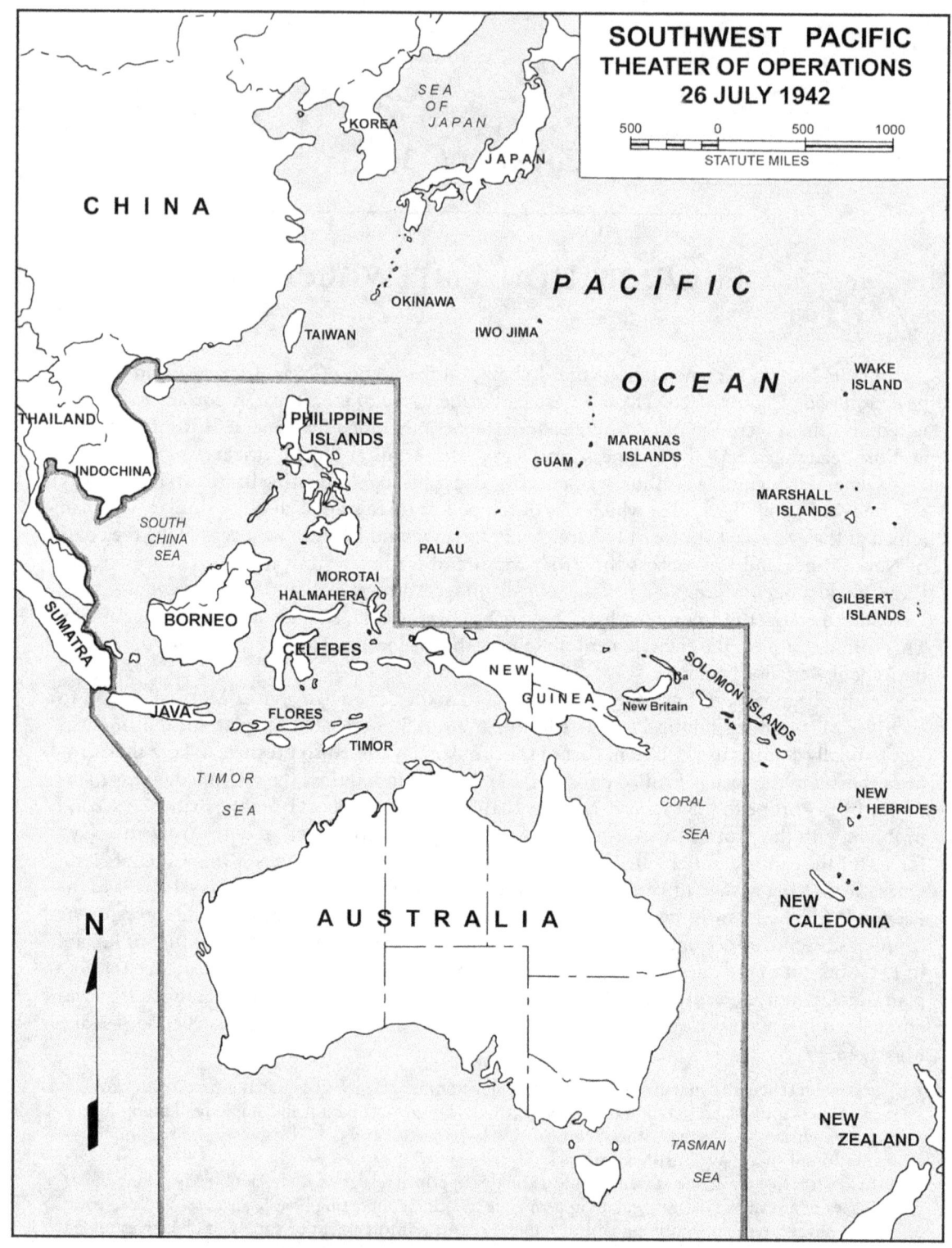

This map is adapted from Major General Hugh J. Casey, Chief Engineer. Office of the Chief Engineer, General Headquarters Army Forces Pacific. Engineers of the Southwest Pacific 1941–1945. Volume I. *Engineers in Theater Operations* (Washington, DC: U.S. Government Printing Office, 1945), facing p. 38.

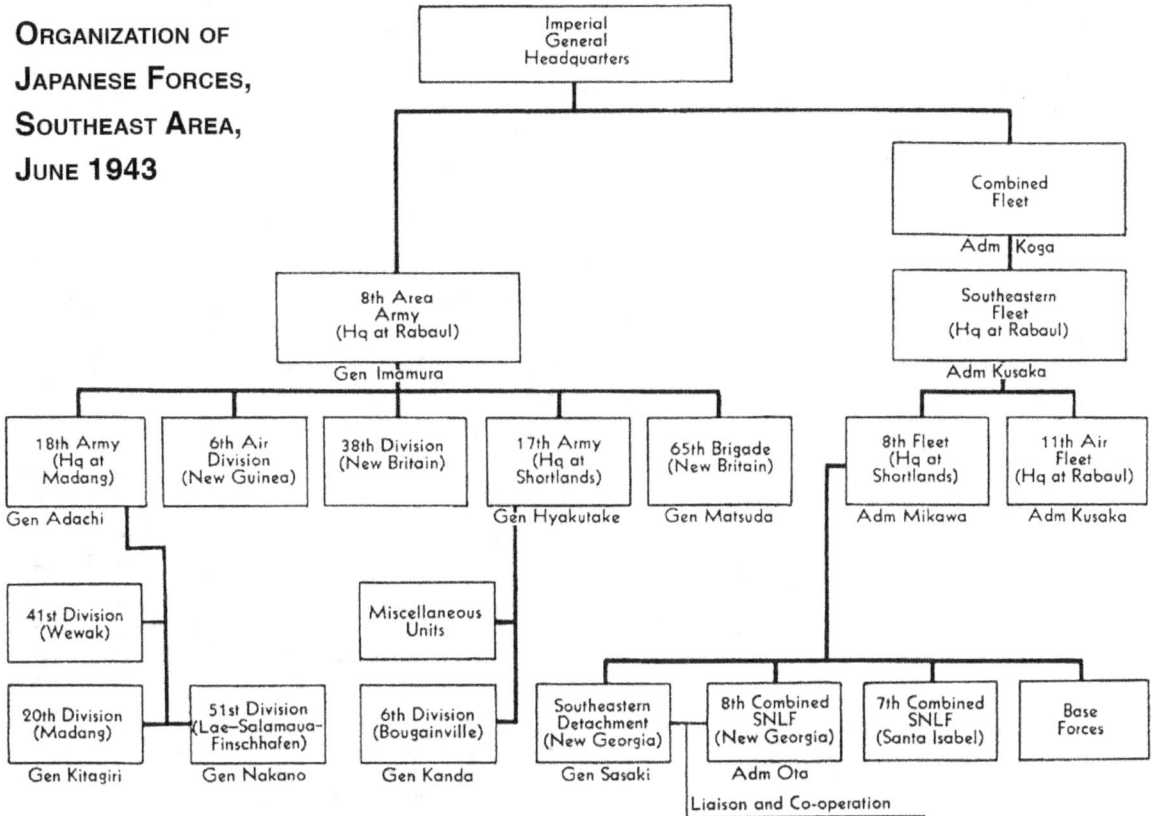

By June 1943, Japanese forces were well established in the Southwest Pacific area. Chart reproduced from John Miller, Jr., *Cartwheel: The Reduction of Rabaul* (Washington, DC: Office of the Chief of Military History, Department of the Army, 1959), p. 33.

sive objectives of immediate attack. The entire movement will be covered by air attack on Japanese air and sea bases along the general perimeter BUKA-RABAUL-KAVIENG-WEWAK, with the objective of denying supply and reinforcement of objectives under attack.[1]

MacArthur's plan had focused on the eventual capture of Rabaul, but at that point in the war, the emphasis was on the European theater, and the Joint Chiefs of Staff did not want to commit the number of Army troops needed to carry out MacArthur's strategy. Allied forces would have to secure bases in the Solomons chain and along the northeastern shores of New Guinea from which to mount an offensive. The struggle for Guadalcanal in the Solomons and Japanese resistance on New Guinea slowed the process. After the capture of Guadalcanal and increasing successes along the coast of New Guinea, as well as the capture of other islands in the Solomons chain, further progress could be made. A final strategy had been worked out, which began with the capture of the Treasury Islands, a diversionary attack on Choiseul Island and, finally, landings on Bougainville. Airfields on Bougainville, along with others in the area, would provide a means by which Rabaul could be attacked. The two major islands in the Treasury group were Mono Island and Stirling Island. Mono Island was larger but mountainous, while the smaller Stirling Island was flat and held the promise of a good air field. Blanche Harbor separated the two islands and was an excellent site for a naval base. From there Navy ships could patrol off Bougainville and American aircraft could attack Japanese bases.

By July 1943 it had been determined that the actual capture of Rabaul would be too costly.

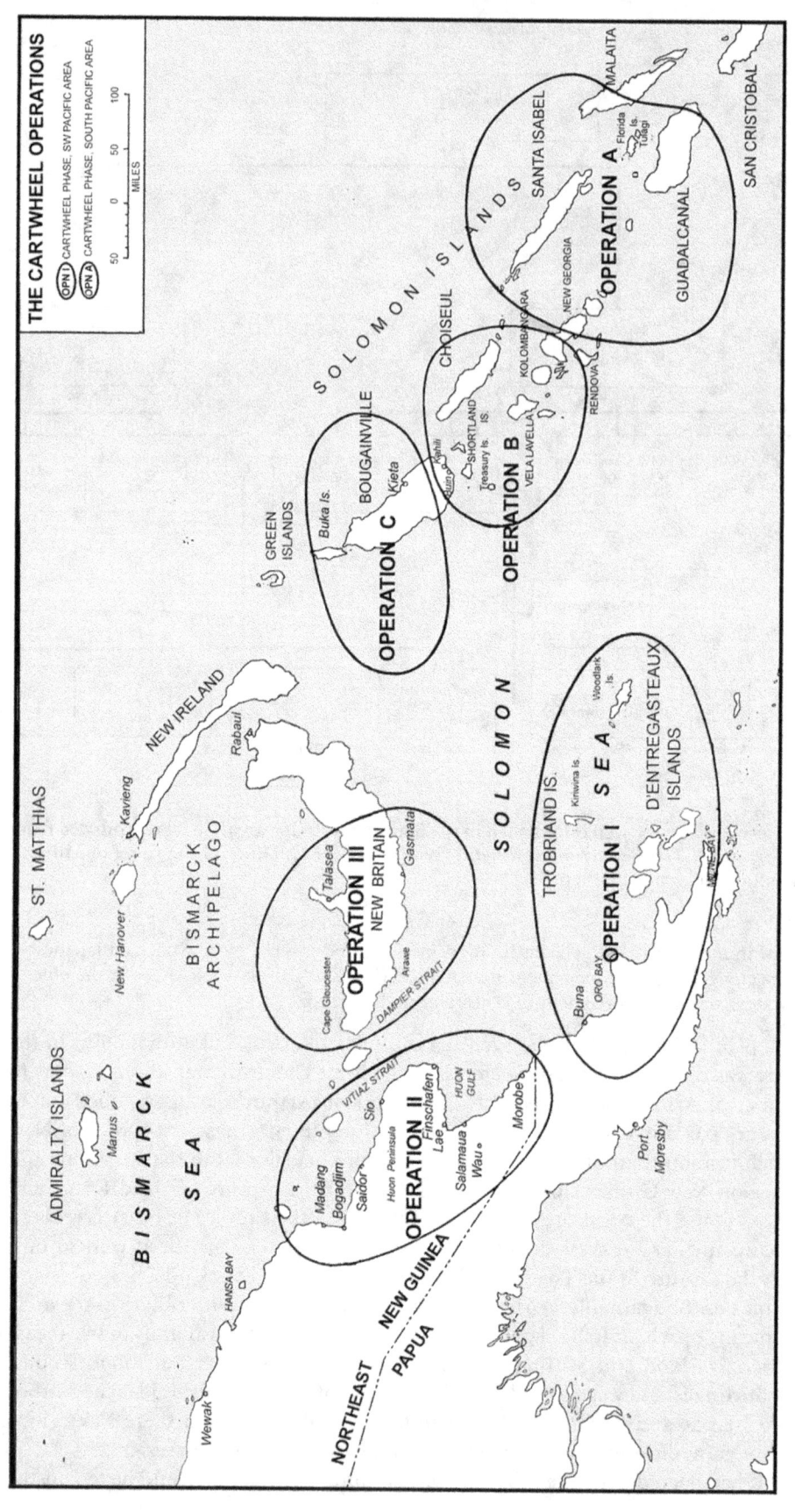

The Cartwheel Operation was designed to surround and neutralize the Japanese base at Rabaul on New Britain. As each island was taken, airfields were built or repaired to serve as new bases from which to attack the Japanese stronghold at Rabaul. Finally, the encirclement of New Britain left the Japanese troops at Rabaul isolated without air or naval protection. It was bypassed using the "island hopping" tactics of the Allied forces. Map redrawn from Map III in Louis Morton's *United States Army in World War II: The War in the Pacific Strategy and Command: The First Two Years* (Washington, DC: Center of Military History United States Army, 1989).

The Joint War Plans Committee had other recommendations for the Joint Chiefs of Staff. They felt that the occupation of western New Britain would commit too many troops to the operation and that this was unwarranted. It would be far better to control Rabaul by cutting it off and destroying its air and naval forces and facilities than it would be to occupy it. Bypassing the Bismarck Archipelago would free the 1st and 2nd Marine Divisions for service elsewhere.[2] Accordingly, the Joint Chiefs of Staff directed MacArthur to neutralize it so that it could be dealt with at lesser expense. This would permit MacArthur's forces to concentrate on the Philippines.

OPERATION CARTWHEEL

Operation Name	Target Date	Target Area
Chronicle	30 June 1943	Woodlark Island
		Kiriwina
Toenails	21 June 1943	Segi Point, New Georgia
	30 June 1943	New Georgia
	30 June 1943	Rendova
	5 July 1943	Zanana, New Georgia
	5 July 1943	Bairoko, New Georgia
	27 August 1943	Arundel Island
Vella Lavella	15 August 1943	Vella Lavella
Postern	5 September 1943	Lae, New Guinea
Goodtime	27 October 1943	Treasury Islands
Blissful	28 October 1943	Choiseul Island
Cherryblossom	1 November 1943	Bougainville
Dexterity	15 December 1943	Arawe, New Britain
	26 December 1943	Cape Gloucester, New Britain
	2 January 1944	Saidor, New Guinea
Admiralty Islands	29 February 1944	
Emirau Island	20 March 1944	

Japanese forces in the Solomons were divided between Army troops and naval forces. The 37,500 Army troops were part of the 17th Army under the overall command of Lieutenant General Seikichi Hyakutake, headquartered in the Shortland Islands. The bulk of Hyakutake's forces, about 25,000 men, were in the Buin-Shortlands area. Enemy presence around Empress Augusta Bay was considered to be light.[3]

On the southern part of Bougainville, Lieutenant General Masatane Kanda's 6th Division with 15,000 men held control at Buin in the south, while the 38th Independent Mixed Brigade had 5,000 stationed at Buka Island in the north. Nearby Kieta Airfield had another 5,000. Special Naval Landing Forces numbering approximately 6,800 men were stationed in the south near Buin, defending the area's two airfields at Kara and Kahil. Offshore islands in the Shortlands also had detachments of men. Ballale Island, for example, was home to a naval airfield.

The estimated 20,000 Navy personnel in the area were under the overall command of Vice Admiral Tomoshige Samejima, Commander of the 8th Fleet. They consisted of the 87th Garrison force near Buka and two units in the south: the 6th Sasebo Special Naval Landing Force and the 7th Kure Landing Force. Rear Admiral Isamu Takeda was in command of the Japanese naval forces centered in southern Bougainville.

The Japanese had stationed only a couple of hundred troops in the Treasury Islands, mostly on Mono Island, with lookouts stationed on Stirling Island. Although Blanche Harbor was about three miles long, it was only about a thousand yards wide, making the use of larger ships, such

LCI(L) 24 loads New Zealand troops at Kukua Beach, Guadalcanal, for the attack on Mono Island. This photograph was taken on 25 October 1943. A few weeks later, on 16 November 1943, she departed for Noumea, New Caledonia, to be converted to a gunboat. NARA 80G 200623.

as destroyers, impractical. Entrance to Blanche Harbor was usually from the west end, with the proposed landing beach (Orange) near the town of Falami, at the eastern end of the harbor. This would require that the assault ships travel about two miles into Blanche Harbor, placing them at risk from enemy gun emplacements on Mono's shore. It would be a good place for the new LCI gunboats to test their abilities. Three additional landing beaches, Purple 1, 2, and 3 were on Stirling Island, although no opposition was expected there.

Task Group 31.1 under Rear Admiral George H. Fort was assigned to attack Mono and Stirling Islands. The destroyers *Cony DD 508*, *Saufley DD 465*, and *Waller DD 466*, minesweepers *Adroit AM 82*, *Conflict AM 85*, and *Daring AM 87*, and *LCI(L)s 24, 61, 67, 69, 222, 330, 334,* and *336* were in the initial landings with a last minute addition were two of the newly converted LCI gunboats, the *22* and the *23*.

From early to mid–October 1943, *LCI(L)s 21, 22, 23,* and *70* had been at Noumea, New Caledonia, being converted into gunboats. The four ships, hereafter referred to as LCI(G)s, barely made it back in time for the operation, arriving at Hutchinson Creek, Florida Island in the Solomons on 23 October. An inspection of *LCI(G) 23*, at that time referred to as an "LCI(L) gunboat," revealed her new armament:

(a) One 3"/50 BLR mounted on platform above and between forward bulwarks; one 40 MM replacing 20 MM on house deck; six 50 cal. machine guns mounted along bulwarks, 3 on each side; the 20MM's formerly mounted on bow and on house deck, relocated on main deck, one on each side of conning station; the two 20MM's on fantail remained.
(b) Radar equipment installed.

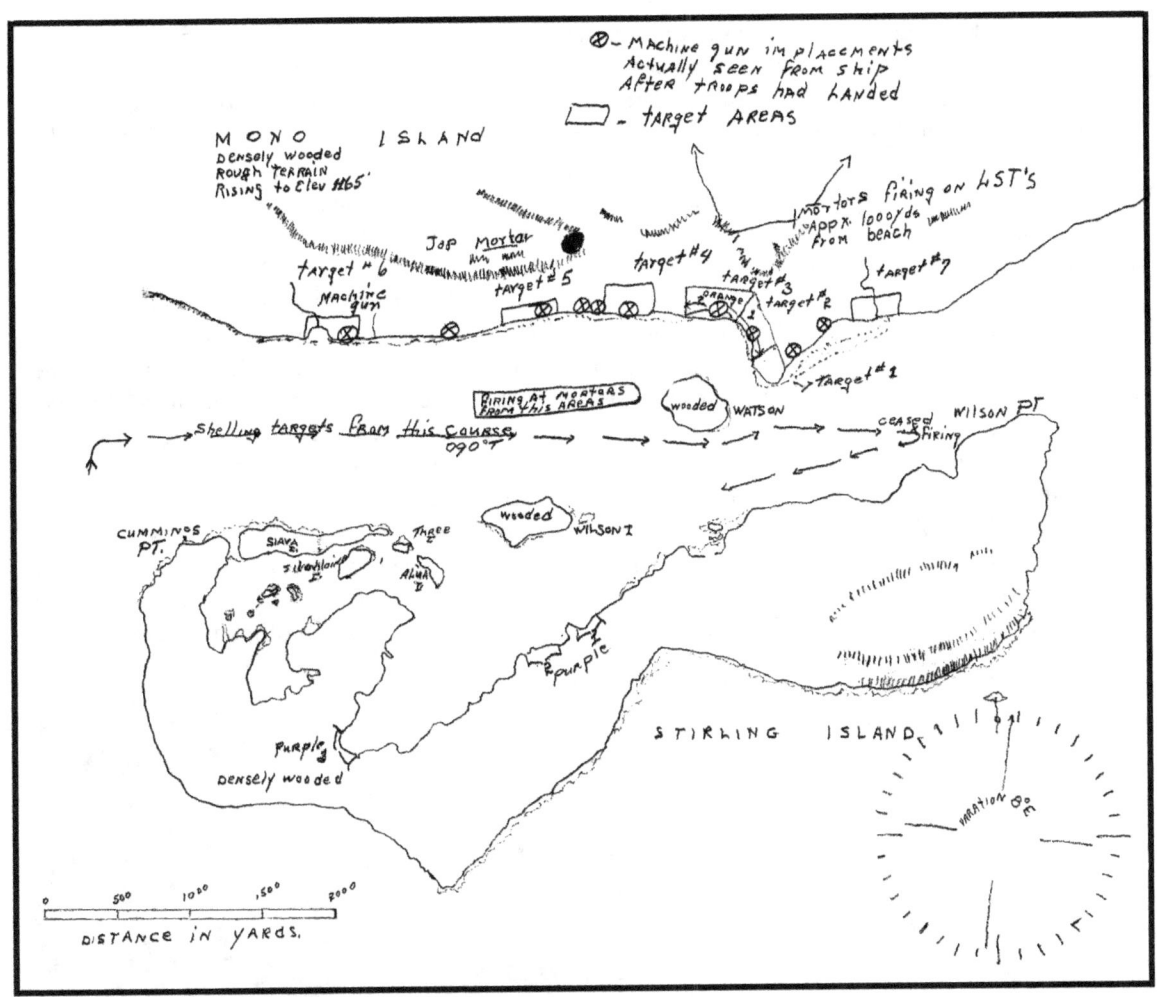

The first use of an LCI gunboat in action and also in an amphibious assault took place in the Treasury Islands on 5 November 1943. *LCI(G)*s *22* and *23* participated in the operation. The above map was taken from the action report of *LCI(G) 22* and shows the target and landing areas. *U.S.S. LCI(L) No. 22, Action Report,* November 5, 1943, Enclosure (A).

(c) Crew complement increased from 23 men and 3 officers, to 45 men and 4 officers. Ship's draft increased 9 inches; speed reduced one knot; troop carrying capacity reduced by 50.[4]

These LCIs would no longer transport troops; their new mission would be to provide close-in fire support as the troop carriers landed soldiers and Marines.

A simultaneous landing at Choiseul Island, to the east of the southernmost tip of Bougainville Island, was planned to divert the attention of the Japanese. Lieutenant Colonel Victor H. Krulak's 2nd Marine Parachute Battalion landed near the village of Voza in the evening of 27 October and immediately began to make its presence known. This made it appear as though the Allied forces were setting up for an attack on their bases in the Shortlands Islands just off the southern tip of Bougainville. As the Japanese prepared to counter the invasion at Choiseul, the main Allied force landed in the Treasury Islands. The major benefit of this maneuver was to keep the Japanese close to their base in the Shortlands, only twenty-two miles away, so that they would not send reinforcements to the Treasuries.

Troops and supplies destined to participate in the attack on the Treasuries had loaded at

Rendova, Guadalcanal, and Vella Lavella in the days preceding the assault. Brigadier R. A. Row of the New Zealand Army commanded the landing force. The landing operation commenced at 0543 on 27 October 1943 with the shelling of the Mono Island beaches by the destroyers. About ten minutes later, *LCI(G)s 22* and *23*, the newly converted gunboats, arrived at the western entrance to Blanche Harbor to lead the LCPs to the beaches. At 0558, the *22* found her first target. Marine raiders had scouted the islands in August and again a few days prior to the landings and identified the locations of machine gun nests on Mono Island. Small in size, they had escaped shelling by the destroyers.

As the landing craft entered Blanche Harbor, *LCI(G) 22* began to pound the gun emplacements along the southern shore of Mono Island with a combination of 3"/50, 40mm, 20mm and .50 caliber fire between 0558 and 0623. Right behind her, *LCI(G) 23* was firing on the targets. No return fire was encountered from the enemy machine guns along the shore. At 0633 the OTC, on *LCI(L) 222*, gave the order for the LCI(L)s to enter the harbor. The landing craft spotted several gun emplacements along the shore and opened fire but received no return fire. As the troops landed, two enemy pill boxes only sixty and eighty yards off the beach opened fire and the LCI(L)s soon put them out of action. Within an hour or two enemy mortars began to zero in on the landing craft and ships. *LCI(L)s 24* and *222* had some near misses from mortar fire. Shortly thereafter, *LST 399* took a mortar hit on her tank deck. The mortars were located at a position of five to seven hundred yards up the mountainside with another about three hun-

Dead Australian soldiers lie on the beach as troops move ashore on Mono Island in the Treasuries. *LCI(L) 24* is beached in the background. It was her last troop delivery prior to being converted to a gunboat. NARA 80G 200633.

dred yards above it. *LCI(G) 22* fired on both and they ceased to operate. Later in the day, at about 1230, *LST 399* again came under mortar fire from positions on the mountainside, and both the *22* and *23* combined their firepower to put them out of action. Charles Ports, first loader on the *23*'s 3"/50, later wrote: "We were close enough to the beach that small arms fire was ricocheting off our structure and on our strafing; one could see bodies falling from the trees."[5] The gunboats secured the beaches and patrolled the harbor, covering LSTs and other vessels operating inshore. The day, however, was not over. The Japanese had been caught off guard by the landings at Mono Island, having assumed that Choisuel and the Shortlands were the primary targets.

Japanese air attacks began around 1520. At 1525 a Zeke dove on *LCI(G) 22* and dropped a small bomb off its starboard quarter. The bomb missed by about fifty yards, and the suddenness of the attack and the plane's position made it difficult for the ship's gunners to get off more than a few rounds of AA fire. Other ships in the area also came under attack. At 1531 *LCI(G) 22* was again a target as a Val dove on her and was taken under fire. The gunboat scored a number of hits on the enemy plane which flew away smoking. The anti-aircraft action was listed as a probable kill for the *22*. Within minutes American aircraft appeared and drove off the attacking Japanese planes. The Treasuries were in Allied hands.

A second echelon, with coverage by *LCI(G)s 21* and *70*, landed more troops and equipment on 30 October and the two gunboats relieved the *22* and *23*, which returned to Guadalcanal. *LCI(G)s 21* and *70* were then assigned to Commander Naval Base Treasury for duty.

With their first combat experience completed, the gunboats assessed their performance. In his action report for the day, Lieutenant B. A. Thirkield, Commanding Officer of the *LCI(G) 23*, recommended:

(a) That support gunboats accompany assault waves all the way to the beach, turning away only in time to avoid beaching themselves. This would provide flank cover for the assault wave to the last possible moment, instead of exposing the flank as occurred in this action when this vessel turned astern of the LCP's at point (A).
(b) That support gunboats, whenever possible, be free of troops, in order that they may retain complete mobility throughout the operation.
(c) That liaison be established between gunboats and shore fire control parties to enable gunboats to provide intelligent supporting fire after landings.[6]

Additional recommendations called for training in the use of the newly installed 3"/50 gun. The ship had been placed in action with little preparation, and prior target practice would have been beneficial. Thirkield's early experience with amphibious gunboats would prove of value to the Navy. At Okinawa he served as LCS(L) Commander Group Nine, Flotilla Three.

Rear Admiral T. S. Wilkinson CTF Thirty-One, in his endorsement to Thirkield's *Action Report of LCI(L) 23*, noted the value of the new gunboats:

1. Forwarded. The LCI(L) 23 along with the LCI(L) 22 were the first two LCI Gunboats to be employed in combat in this area. Both ships proved highly effective as support vessels for this particular operation, and, it is believed, can be gainfully employed in future amphibious operations.
2. As a result of the performance of these two LCI gunboats in this operation four additional LCI's are now being converted to gunboats and will be employed not only as support boats for landing operations but also for supporting PT boats in coordinated anti-barge missions.[7]

Bougainville was the next target of the Allied forces. As a part of the campaign to isolate Rabaul, it was necessary to cut off the Japanese forces residing on Bougainville. Capture of the entire island was not necessary, but the establishment of an air base on the western side of the island was. This landing helped to destroy enemy air potential at Rabaul while bypassing their major troop concentrations. The bypassed Japanese troops could be isolated and confined to the islands by use of continued air and sea patrols. In the matter of sea patrols, PT boats, coupled with LCI(G)s and occasionally destroyers, could keep barge traffic at a minimum and prevent the resupply or reinforcement of the Japanese.

It became obvious to the Japanese that the attack on Bougainville Island was imminent. It began on 1 November 1943. The beaches and terrain on the northeast side of the island were the logical landing place for American forces, however, the area was well-defended. Far too many American troops would be tied up there attempting to oust the Japanese from the island. This was to be a variation of the "island hopping" strategy, with the Americans landing on the western side of the island and establishing a strong perimeter. Airfields and naval bases built inside the perimeter would permit them to attack the Japanese on the eastern and southern parts of the island, as well as Buka Island to the north. Japanese installations at Rabaul would also be within reach. The LCI gunboats, active just to the south at the Treasury Islands, did not take part in the invasion of Bougainville, but mortars mounted on three LCTs were used successfully in the first experiment with these weapons. However, within a short time, the LCI gunboats assumed regular patrol duties operating out of their base at the Treasuries, as well as the base at Puruata Island near Cape Torokina, Bougainville. Their use was crucial in keeping the Japanese from reinforcing their troops via barge and attacking the perimeter of the American lines.

With the invasion of the Treasuries a success, the gunboats turned to routine patrol and escort duties. Additional gunboats were needed and on 16 November, *LCI(L) 24* was ordered to Noumea for conversion.

It had been assumed by the Japanese that the Americans would follow a logical stepping stone pattern toward Rabaul. They anticipated landings first on the Shortland Islands, then at Choiseul Island, and finally on southern Bougainville. Accordingly, their forces were marshaled in the southern part of Bougainville where they expected the landings.

Cape Torokina was on the north end of Empress Augusta Bay with a major concentration of Japanese forces situated to its south. Other Japanese Army units were just off the southern shore on the Shortland Islands. Prior to the landing the airfields on Bougainville, Buka, and Rabaul underwent heavy bombing designed to prevent Japanese air attacks against the invading troops. Bougainville alone had five airfields, all of which could be used against the invasion force. Runways were cratered and grounded aircraft were destroyed in the attack by units of the 5th Air Force flying from New Guinea. Airsols (Air Command Solomons) and Rear Admiral Frederick C. Sherman's TF 38 carriers also participated in these missions. Forces opposing the landing at Cape Torokina were small in number, totaling about 270 in all. A single platoon held Puruata Island in the southern part of Empress Augusta Bay. This became the base for PTs and LCI gunboats.

In what had become standard practice in any landing, cruisers and destroyers from Rear Admiral A. Stanton Merrill's TF 39 spent several days bombarding the landing area in combination with air attacks. It could be said that the 6,421 Marines landing at Cape Torokina simply overwhelmed the 270 Japanese defenders. This was not a reason to celebrate, however, since the bulk of the Japanese forces were not far away. With numerous Japanese units scattered in force through the northern part of the Solomon Islands, it was obvious that the PT boats and the LCI(G)s would have a great deal of work. American, and later Australian forces, held a tenuous hold on the area around Empress Augusta Bay and were primarily interested in maintaining a perimeter around the airfield they had built there. For the Japanese it was a matter of continually launching attacks against the Allied forces in order to prevent both the expansion and operation of the airfield. Supplies for the Japanese forces moved along the coast in barges which were concealed during the day and continued their transport duties at night. Combating them were teams of torpedo boats and LCI(G)s. Air support was available from the airfield on

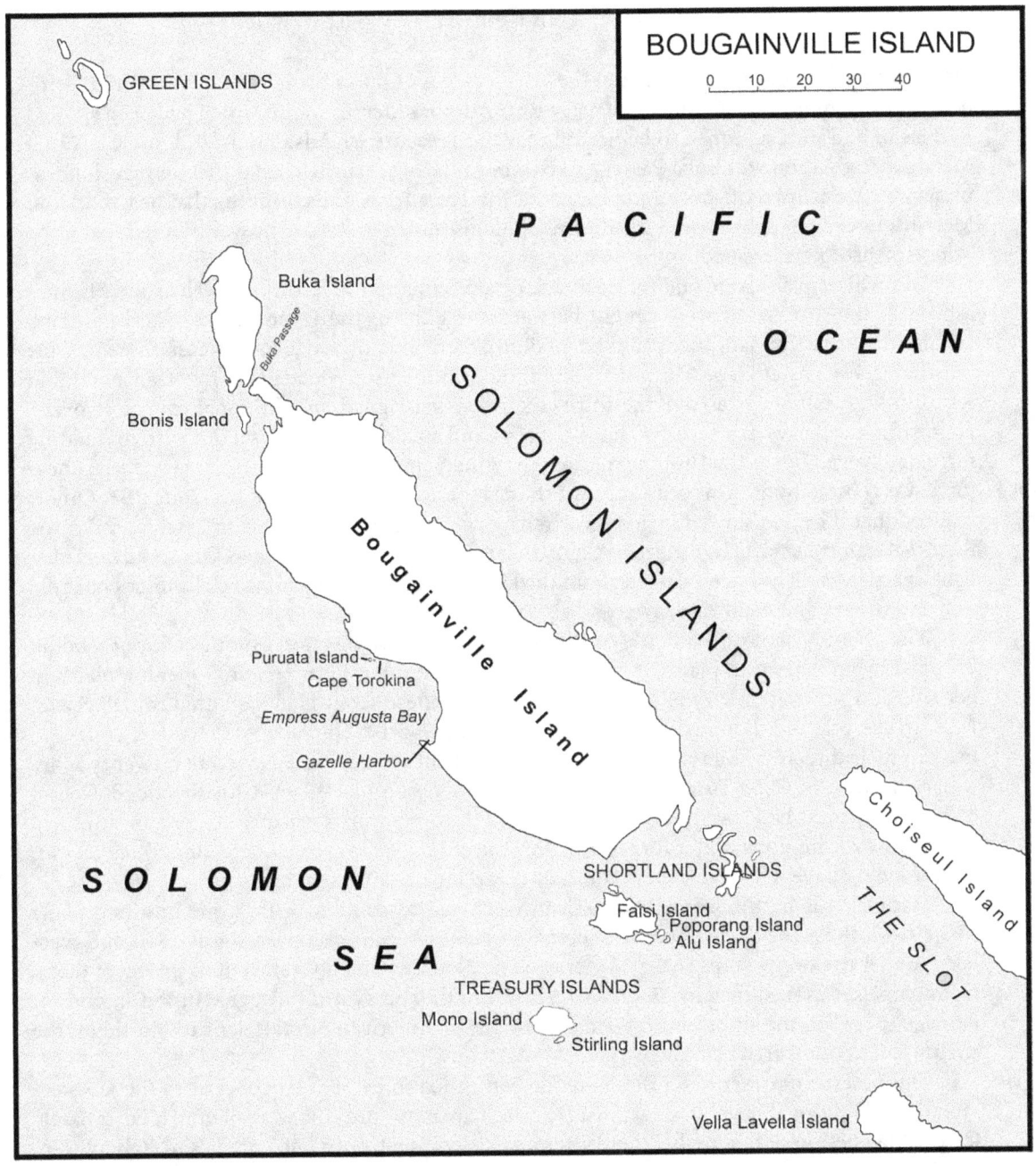

LCI Gunboats were first used in the capture of the Treasury Islands on 5 November 1943. After the Bougainville landings had been made at Cape Torokina in November 1943 the gunboats were active in the area, using Puruata Island as a base. The Treasury Islands were home to another gunboat base. LCI(G)s regularly patrolled the coast of Bougainville and extended their patrols through the Buka Passage and as far as New Ireland and Rabaul in 1944.

Bougainville and Allied fields in other parts of the Solomons. Nighttime support was rendered by night fighters and PBYs flying cover for the gunboats and PTs.

The activity on Bougainville had not gone unnoticed by the Japanese. The Japanese naval force at Rabaul had just been increased by the arrival of Vice Admiral Sentaro Omori whose Cruiser Division 5 had escorted a convoy to the island base. Orders from Fleet Admiral Mineichi Koga, commander of the Combined Fleet at Truk, were sent down to Rabaul, and Vice Admiral

Tomoshige Samejima, Commander of the 8th Fleet, gave Omori his sailing orders. On 31 October, Omori's ships got under way to engage Rear Admiral Merrill's ships which had been spotted in the slot and were assumed to be heading for the Treasury Islands. Omori did not know that Merrill's destination was Buka Passage to bombard the area's airfields and that an invasion was underway. He cruised offshore and headed for the Treasury Islands thinking that he would find Merrill's force there, but missed it entirely. Upon his return to Rabaul he was notified that Cape Torokina had been invaded.

Immediate plans were laid for an attack on the ships still in harbor, as well as the Marines ashore. If the Americans were caught between the guns of the Japanese Navy and its Army ashore, the American landing would be a failure. Samejima organized a counter-force to wipe out the Americans at Cape Torokina. One thousand men were loaded on five transports and sent out with Omori as a covering force. Omori was assigned an additional four destroyers, giving him two heavy cruisers, two light cruisers, and six destroyers. He set out with his landing force on 1 November at 1700 hoping to catch the Americans off guard. Within hours the Japanese force was spotted by an American sub and shortly thereafter was bombed by a lone PBY. Omori realized that if he was slowed by his own transports he would not be able to catch and destroy the American transports in Empress Augusta Bay. They were sent back and Omori advanced at flank speed. Merrill had been alerted about the Japanese force heading his way. His force consisted of four cruisers and eight destroyers.

The opening shot of the Battle of Empress Augusta Bay was not a shot at all, but a bomb dropped by an American plane. It closely missed the heavy cruiser *Haguro*, opening plates in her side and slowing down the Japanese advance. Japanese scout planes spotted minelayers at work in the bay and assumed that they were the transports. The Japanese changed course to head in their direction. Merrill's force intercepted them at 0227 on 2 November, twenty miles west southwest of Cape Torokina, and the battle was soon on. When it finally ended around 0500, the Japanese had lost the cruiser *Sendai* and the destroyer *Hatsukaze*. American ships had suffered hits from guns and a torpedo, with *Denver CL 58*, *Spence DD 512*, and *Foote DD 511* sustaining damage. However, they would undergo repairs and fight again.

With the sea battle over, the American force had to contend with a one hundred plane strike from the airfields at Rabaul. The enemy planes began to appear about 0800 and were taken under fire by the ships and by American and New Zealand aircraft sent to intercept them. Light damage was sustained by *Montpelier CL 57*, but the ships came through without significant damage. Between the ships and the small number of American aircraft sent to aid them, the enemy lost about thirty planes.

The American presence on Bougainville continued to be of great concern to the Japanese at Rabaul. Additional naval raids against the beach areas at Torokina were planned. Fortunately for the Marines on Bougainville, these attempts at sending troops and supplies to Rabaul were continually intercepted by American bombers and fighters, and the potential force was weakened. Finally, aircraft from the carriers *Saratoga CV 3* and *Princeton CV 37* caught the newly assembled Japanese task force at anchor in Rabaul's harbor on 5 November and seriously damaged a number of their ships, including the heavy cruisers *Maya*, *Takao*, and *Atago*, along with the light cruisers *Agano* and *Noshiro*. A follow-up strike on the airfield at Rabaul by Lieutenant General George C. Kenney's B-24 Liberators and P-38 Lightnings found the airfields empty, so they bombed the base's infrastructure. The Japanese aircraft were away on a mission to attack the Americans at Empress Augusta Bay.[8]

LCI(G) 70 had been on patrol off Cape Torokina, Bougainville, and was returning to the Treasury Islands along with *LCT 68* and *PT 167* in the evening of 5 November when the ships came under air attack. At 1915, lookouts on the *70* spotted a flight of twelve Japanese Kate torpedo bombers to starboard. As the formation turned toward the ships, they split into two groups of eight and four aircraft, with the four commencing a run at *LCI(G) 70*. The first Kate was hit by 40mm, 20mm and .50 caliber fire and was in flames as it passed over, crashing into the sea 2,500 yards past the ship. Kate number two met the same fate and the gunboat had two kills within a few minutes. At 1920 the two remaining Kates attacked the ship from opposite angles, and a torpedo dropped by one of them struck the ship between frames 91 and 96. Good luck was with her as the torpedo did not explode. It lodged itself in the engine room where the warhead fell off. This plane was hit repeatedly and crashed close off the starboard quarter. Its companion also made a torpedo run on the ship but its torpedo missed. It was hit by 20mm fire but did not crash. A fifth plane made a run on the ship and was also shot down. *LCI(G) 70* had been a lucky ship. She had dodged three torpedoes, and the one that hit her did not explode. In the action she shot down four enemy planes and damaged two others. One man had been killed and one injured by the entry of the torpedo in the engineering spaces.

Small fires had started in the engine room but they were quickly extinguished. The entry of the torpedo had sheared off the engine controls and the gunboat was dead in the water. Commanding Officer Lieutenant (jg) H. W. Frey ordered the crew to stand by to abandon ship, but subsequent inspections revealed that the torpedo was probably not going to explode. *PT 167* had been fortunate as well. One of the Kates had narrowly missed the ship, clipping the radio antenna as it passed over and crashed nearby. The crew felt a shock but did not realize that their boat had been hit by a torpedo which passed through the bow and kept going. Fortunately the hole was just under the deck and the boat was able to continue operating. A second Kate fell under her guns a few minutes later. Ensign Theodore Berlin, her CO, maneuvered his ship alongside *LCI(G) 70* and transferred most of her crew to *LCT 68*. A skeleton crew remained on board the gunboat and the LCT towed her back to Bougainville. They arrived off Cape Torokina about 0845. The little convoy had shot down six enemy planes and damaged three.

Although *LCI(G) 70* was incapacitated and at anchor off Cape Torokina, her adventures were not over. At dawn on 7 November, her lookouts sighted a barge at a distance of two and

The Nakajima B5N2 Navy Type 97 Carrier Attack Bomber Model 12 was the Japanese Navy's most important torpedo bomber with a top speed of 235 miles per hour at 12,000 feet. It could carry either a 1,764 pound bomb load or a torpedo of the same weight. The Allied code name for this aircraft was "Kate." NARA 80G 427153.

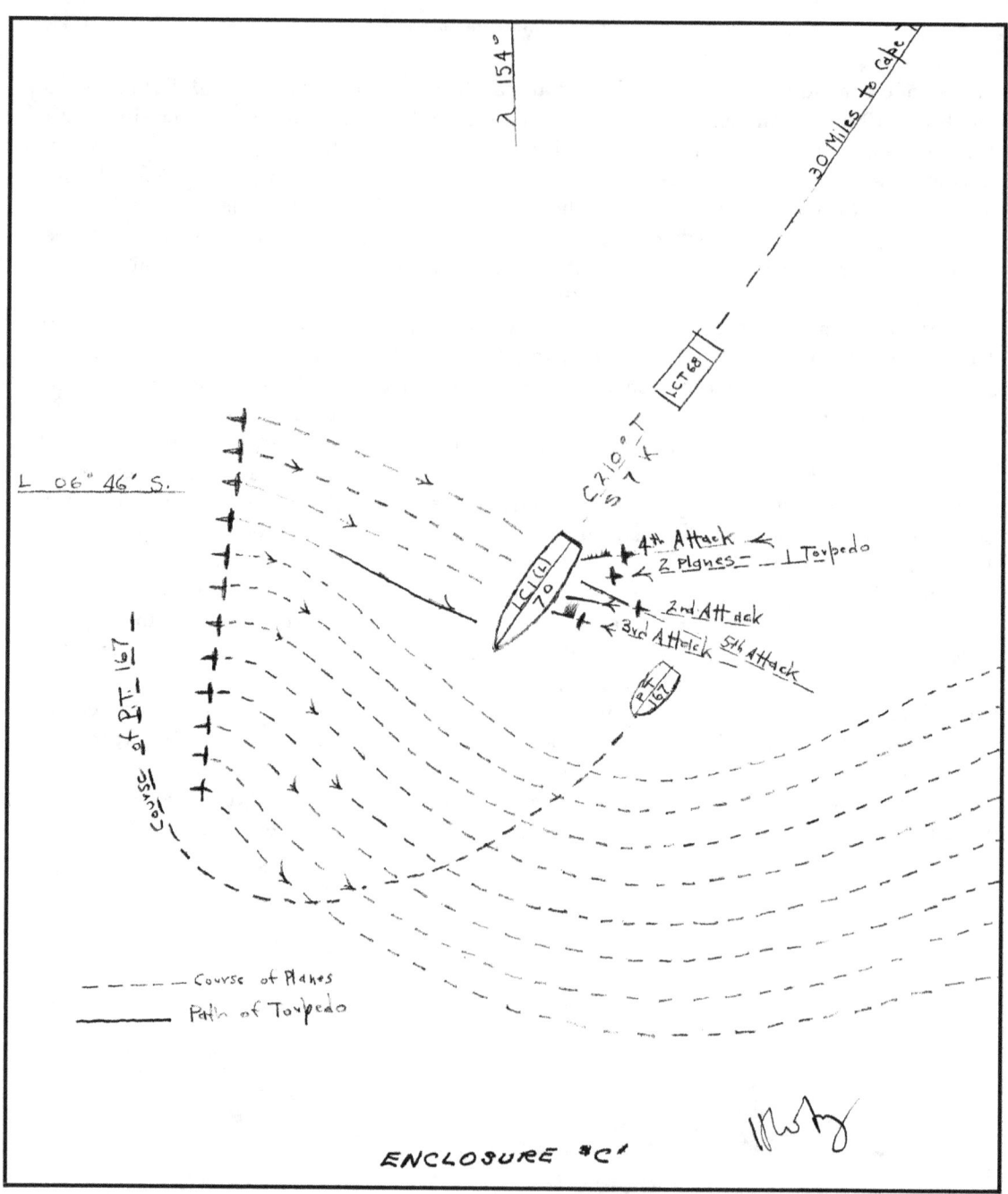

This sketch from the action report of *LCI(G) 70* shows the attack by Japanese aircraft on 5 November 1943. *USS LCI(L) 70 No Serial, Report of Anti-Aircraft Action of 5 November 1943*, 30 November 1943, Enclosure "C."

one-half miles. Unable to determine if it was American or Japanese, the gunboat contacted the PT base at Puruata Island at 0630 and asked that they intercept it. By 0715, two PT boats were attacking the barge and were under fire from its guns. Each time they were in the clear, *LCI(G) 70* fired its 3"/50 gun at the barge in an attempt to knock it out. After a number of near misses the barge drifted out of range. A few hours later two Dauntless dive bombers finally sank it. Lieutenant (jg) Frey reported his frustration. Had the gunboat been operable it would have made short work of the enemy vessel.

On the following day, 8 November, the *70* was again in peril. At 1145 enemy planes were reported in the area and Task Unit 31.5.4, which had been unloading at Cape Torokina, got underway and out of the harbor. At 1215 a group of Vals, Bettys and Lilys were sighted and began to attack the transports. The destroyers took them under fire. At 1225 two Lilys made a bomb run on the gunboat and a nearby PT boat. Its bomb missed *LCI(G) 70*, and the gunboat shot it down about 1,000 yards to port. Although the gunboat escaped unscathed, little more than twelve hours would elapse before the next attack. At 0100 on 9 November, an enemy plane again dropped a bomb which missed the ship. As the *70* fired on the plane, another attacked from astern, dropping a bomb which also missed the ship. The *70* had escaped destruction again.

LCI(G) 22 was on a mission on 20 November when she came under air attack. She had departed from the PT Base with several PT boats for a patrol of the Atsinima Bay area west of Bougainville when they were strafed by two Zekes. One dropped a bomb which missed, but a round from its machine guns hit two of the 40mm clips in the gun tub causing a fire. GM 3/c R. T. Whalon quickly extinguished the fire with a life jacket, saving the ship and its crew from exploding ammunition. Although no one had been killed, eleven men were wounded and the planes escaped undamaged. The *22* headed back to harbor and transferred her wounded.

The Marines held an expanding perimeter at Empress Augusta Bay but faced many threats. In order to protect the right flank of the perimeter, Major General Roy Geiger ordered the 1st Marine Parachute Battalion, under Major Richard Fagan, to join with Company M of the 3rd Raider Battalion and conduct a raid against the Japanese. The landing site was to be ten miles to the south of Cape Torokina and was scheduled for 29 November 1943. The Marines landed at 0325 but soon found themselves the victims of faulty intelligence. They immediately encountered stiff opposition and were forced to withdraw. The Japanese put up a heavy volume of fire and the Marines were pinned down. Geiger requested Navy help and soon had several destroyers pounding the enemy positions as the Marines prepared their withdrawal. A convoy of 27 LCVPs and LCMs headed for the beach area between the May River and the Reini River to pick them up. Accompanying them were *LCI(G)s 21* and *23* and *PT 187*.

At 1555 the gunboats spotted a yellow smoke bomb indicating the Marines' position on the beach, and they turned toward shore. As they were heading in, four Dauntless dive bombers bombed and strafed enemy positions to the northwest of the Marines. A curtain of enemy mortar fire dropped in the water between the beach and the landing boats, driving them off. *LCI(G) 23* positioned herself on their left flank and *LCI(G) 21* positioned herself on their right. Unsure of the Marine and enemy positions, the gunboats held their fire until 1619, at which time they identified targets and used their 3"/50 guns. Mortar rounds fell in front of and abeam of *LCI(G) 21* but did not hit her. At 1640 six more Dauntless dive bombers came over and attacked the enemy positions. The landing craft and gunboats retired to a point two miles off the beach to await reinforcements which arrived at 1740 in the form of the destroyer *Fullam DD 474* and four Corsairs. The destroyer shelled the beach as the aircraft bombed and strafed the enemy. At 1825 the landing craft and the gunboats headed back in with both gunboats firing on the beaches to keep the enemy at bay. The landing craft picked up the Marines and withdrew from the area with the gunboats covering their retreat. *LCI(G) 23* fished a Marine out of the water and then patrolled the area looking for stragglers. *LCI(G) 21* found an LCM towing a damaged LCVP. The gunboats were back at Puruata Island by 2330.

In his endorsement to the action reports of the two gunboats, Rear Admiral T. S. Wilkinson noted:

> The LCI(L) gunboats, converted in the South Pacific according to design by Commander Service Squadron Third Fleet, continue to prove their value as a supporting craft for Amphibious and PT operations in this Area.[9]

Patrols in Empress Augusta Bay continued throughout November and December, with *LCI(G) 22* imperiled again on 11 December. Regular patrols were carried out by the gunboats both to the north and south of their base at Puruata Island off Cape Torokina. While on patrol the night of 11-12 December, they moved in close to shore to investigate unknown targets, possibly three Japanese barges. The sighting proved to be negative but, at 2130, a Japanese float plane passed over the ship at about 1,500 feet. The gunboat held fire and slowed speed so that she didn't leave a wake in the hope that she had not been spotted. To port the sky was dark and cloudy, hiding the plane from sight. To starboard the moon was bright, illuminating the ship. Within minutes, the plane was spotted diving on the ship from dead ahead. The gunboat went to flank speed and opened up with all her guns. The plane dropped a bomb which hit the water about ten feet off her starboard side. Fragments from the blast wounded eleven men in the gun crews. The enemy plane circled around for a second pass. Its next bomb exploded under the ship, shaking it and knocking the crew off their feet. Fire from the *22* hit the plane and its ammunition began to explode. It crashed in flames nearby.

The force of the explosion had damaged the *22* and she began taking water in her #2 troop compartment. Within minutes she was down by the bow. Handy Billies were put to use to slow the flooding as the ship headed back to base at Puruata Island. PT boats came to the rescue and took off the wounded men, and the gunboat began to list to starboard. The gunboat arrived back at Puruata Island at 2250. With her bow settling fast and the ship listing heavily to starboard her skipper, Lieutenant (jg) H. C. Cobb, ran the ship up on the beach on the north side of the island in order to save her. His quick thinking and the work of his crew had saved the *22*.

Even though the ship was under repair, it was still not out of danger. A few days later, on 18 December, while she was anchored off Cape Torokina, she again came under aerial attack. At 0149, two Japanese twin-engine bombers flew over at about 18,000 feet. They dropped a stick of bombs which marched across the water toward the ship. A small anti-personnel bomb hit the ship and wounded one man. Because of the extreme altitude of the planes, the anchored ship was unable to fire on it and was a sitting duck. By the time the raid was over, sixteen enemy aircraft had bombed the area, but none of the larger bombs caused any damage to the *22*. Although the planes had been caught in the searchlights of the shore installations, none of the anti-aircraft guns in the area were able to shoot them down.

The Allied plan had never aimed at capturing the entire island of Bougainville; rather its purpose was to control a section of it. Their perimeter expanded for the first two months, however, it was constantly under attack by Japanese forces seeking to break through. In order to thwart future attacks, the 132nd Infantry planned to advance on the enemy near Mavavia Village, to the east of Cape Torokina. The Navy ships assisted the advance by firing on enemy forces near the shoreline. Ideally suited for this task were the LCI(G) gunboats, and the *24* and *68* were set up as a Task Unit to support the Army's advance on 25 June 1944.

Around 0800 the two gunboats began their shelling of the shore areas which had been identified by Army smoke mortars. For the next forty-five minutes they delivered a variety of gunfire on the beaches and nearby village. Returned enemy mortar fire passed over the ships with no effect. By 0945 the two gunboats had moved to a new position and fired on suspected targets to the north and west of the village. *LCI(G) 68* headed back to Puruata Island at 1030 and the *24* remained in the area for another hour and one-half before returning.

Green Islands

The Allies desired another airstrip closer to their target as they advanced toward Rabaul. The Green Islands, situated approximately thirty-seven miles north northwest of Buka Island, seemed to fit the bill. They were lightly defended by the Japanese and were a suitable location for an airfield. Landing there on 15 February 1944 was the 14th Brigade Group of the 3rd New Zealand Division, supported by U.S. Navy Seabees. LCI(G)s and PTs patrolled nearby islands and atolls, such as Pinipel, during the invasion. Two serviceable Japanese barges were found at Pinipel and destroyed by fire from an LCI(G).

Within a few days the Allied forces had overrun the small contingent of Japanese and begun building a 6,000 foot bomber airstrip that was finished by the end of March. The PTs established a base there for one squadron on Barahun Island, and the LCI(G)s added the area to their patrols.

LCI gunboats and PT boats were assigned to TF 31 while in the Solomons. By February 1944, *LCI(G)s 21, 22, 23, 24, 67, 68, 69* and *70* were operating in the island chain, primarily around the Treasury Islands and in Empress Augusta Bay. Two PT squadrons were based at Cape Torokina on Bougainville and two others at Blanche Harbor, Treasury Islands. Standard missions at that point usually involved two to six PTs, with an LCI(G) along for heavier firepower. In many cases a second LCI(G) would be added to the mission depending on the situation. At Bougainville, as in other locations, the LCI gunboats were frequently teamed with the torpedo boats to combat barges. The PTs could get closer to shore and could also get to the barges faster than the LCI(G)s, but the gunboats had heavier firepower with a longer range. It was an ideal combination. Japanese barge traffic continued to move around the island near shore, usually at night. During the day the barges were camouflaged near shore or up small streams. On 25 February 1944, *LCI(G) 24* teamed with *PTs 245* and *249* for a patrol from Gazelle Harbor to the Jaba River. The gunboat arrived off Matsunkei Village at 2115 and immediately came under fire, but the rounds fell short. Inside Gazelle Harbor tracer fire could be seen as the PTs had discovered some Japanese barges and taken them under fire. The PTs requested that the gunboat fire star shells to illuminate the harbor area. That would provide a better chance of hitting the barges, but the gunboat was too far away to get there quickly. When it finally arrived, it fired eight rounds before its star shell supply ran out. The gunboat headed into Gazelle Harbor at flank speed to assist the PTs and came under fire from shore. *PT 251* had run aground on a reef only 200 yards offshore. Under fire from shore, it was in dire straits and in need of assistance. However, the gunboat could not find it in the dark, and its close proximity to the beach made it difficult for the LCI(G) to get to it. Other PTs came in close but found it impossible to pass a line to it in order to pull it free. *LCI(G) 24* remained nearby waiting for the chance to assist. The PTs spotted barges in a nearby river and took them under fire. The gunboat joined in the attack with its 3"/50 gun. Within ten minutes the Japanese had spotted *LCI(G) 24* and a coastal defense gun, estimated to be 5 inch in size, fired on her. She was bracketed with shells but not hit. Other PTs came under fire from the beach and had to retreat.

Many of the Japanese guns were not fixed in position. To protect their barges the Japanese had a number of mobile field places that could be moved to the scene of a battle such as this. One arrived at the beach and began to fire on *PT 251* which was still grounded on the reef. The first two rounds fired by the artillery piece bracketed the torpedo boat, and the third was right on target. The PT exploded in a ball of fire. Other PTs nearby opened fire on the guns and were then ordered out as the enemy was too well prepared at this point. A sweep of the area the following day picked up three survivors. The patrol had been successful, but it had been costly. Based on the experiences that evening Lieutenant (jg) Olin Taylor, CO of *LCI(G) 24*, concluded in his action report:

A. The Japs have set up temporary M/G posts and heavy gun emplacements along the shore to guard their barge convoys.
B. Usually these guns will not fire unless their barges are moving in the immediate area or; our forces are firing on them. They usually fire irregularly and it makes spotting more difficult.

C. For additional protection to their barge routes it is likely that they are using mobile Army field guns. These can be readily moved along the beach or trails to any position where they need fire-support.[10]

The conversion of LCI(L)s into gunboats continued. *LCI(G) 66* came into existence at Espiritu Santo when her conversion was completed on 1 April 1944. As with previous conversions in the area, she was furnished with a 3"/50 gun forward, a 40mm aft her conning tower mounted on top of the deck house, and eight .50 caliber machine guns. She was designed as a barge destroyer. Her patrols ranged from the base at Sterling Island in the Treasuries to the far northern end of Bougainville.

Gunboats belonging to Group Thirteen, Flotilla Five, continued to patrol the waters around Bougainville, New Ireland, and New Britain until the fall of 1944. Typical of the patrols near Cape Torokina was the one undertaken by *LCI(G)s 23* and *69* from 29 to 31 May 1944. Although the area was nominally under control, it was still possible to find enemy gun emplacements and barge traffic in the area. The two gunboats left their base at Torokina and headed south to Gazelle Harbor. Nearing Marawaka Point they spotted two Type A barges on the beach and attacked them. Several other Japanese barges were near the beach on the north side of the point and they were taken under fire. This was ample justification for fitting the first gunboats with 3"/50 guns. Their firepower was sufficient to destroy such vessels. *LCI(G) 69* led the assault and the *23* followed. Japanese shore batteries, situated a hundred yards inland, began to fire on them and they returned fire. A nearby PBY was contacted and dropped some bombs in the area. The Japanese, under attack from sea and sky, ceased fire. Two barges had been destroyed and several others were damaged. On 31 May the two gunboats were at the nearby Tokissi River to support a troop landing which was uneventful.[11]

Particularly dangerous was the patrol between New Britain and New Ireland. Although the Japanese had been isolated, they had not been defeated and still maintained their combat readiness. A patrol of four gunboats, *LCI(G)s 21, 24, 66*, and *70* set forth from their base at Torokina at 0400 on 1 July 1944. Their mission was similar to others that they had undertaken. Japanese movement through the islands was still possible and primarily dependent on barges. The Japanese forces on New Ireland had been bypassed, and as long as they could be contained on New Ireland, they were no threat. Patrols of this sort usually ran up the coast during the night hours and then retired seaward out of sight during the day. Nighttime raids were most successful as the Japanese could not easily see them coming. In between the nighttime raids the gunboats anchored in the Green Islands.

On 2 July *LCI(G)s 66* and *70* were heading for their station off Dunup Plantation on New Ireland when they picked up a radar contact about a mile and quarter away. At that point they were twenty-six miles west of Chinese Plantation on New Ireland. They headed toward the radar contact to investigate and discovered a barge which they destroyed with gunfire. It was last seen with its decks awash and settling rapidly. The two gunboats continued on to their station near Dunup Plantation, picking up additional radar contacts near shore. As they approached they came under heavy fire from the objects which were assumed to be barges. They returned fire and silenced the guns. Several instances of fire directed against the ships from shore installations occurred a few hours later with the gunboats returning fire and silencing it. The Japanese had been cut off, but they were still a potent fighting force.

About the same time, *LCI(G)s 21* and *24* were on patrol to the north. At 2355 they exchanged fire with the Japanese near Chinese Plantation. A dark object, assumed to be a barge, occupied their attention an hour after midnight and they poured gunfire into it. A large white house south of Dunup Plantation was their next target and their 3"/50 guns caused significant damage to the house. With daylight approaching, the ships moved offshore and out of sight.

At 2103 on 3 July, *21* and *24* were off Chinese Plantation once again. Three barges were sighted at 2155 moving south near the shore and *LCI(G) 21* hit one amidships with 3"/50 fire, breaking the back of the eighty foot long barge. Star shells were fired by *LCI(G) 24* and illuminated three additional Type A barges. Fire from the two gunboats blasted all three and put them out of commission. An hour and one half later the ships were shelling Matakan Plantation. Moving further down the coast to Nakudukudu Bay, they investigated additional objects near shore and came under intense automatic weapons fire. They responded, suppressed the fire, and moved out of the area.

Meanwhile *LCI(G)s 66* and *70* arrived at Dunup Plantation at 2140. They proceeded south, hitting a few targets on the beach and rendezvousing with *LCI(G)s 21* and *24* off Tambaker Point. They then headed south. Daybreak found the four gunboats off Hunter Point where they opened fire on beach targets. A steering failure on *LCI(G) 70*, along with the presence of mines in the area, brought an abrupt halt to their campaign and they had to retreat from the area and

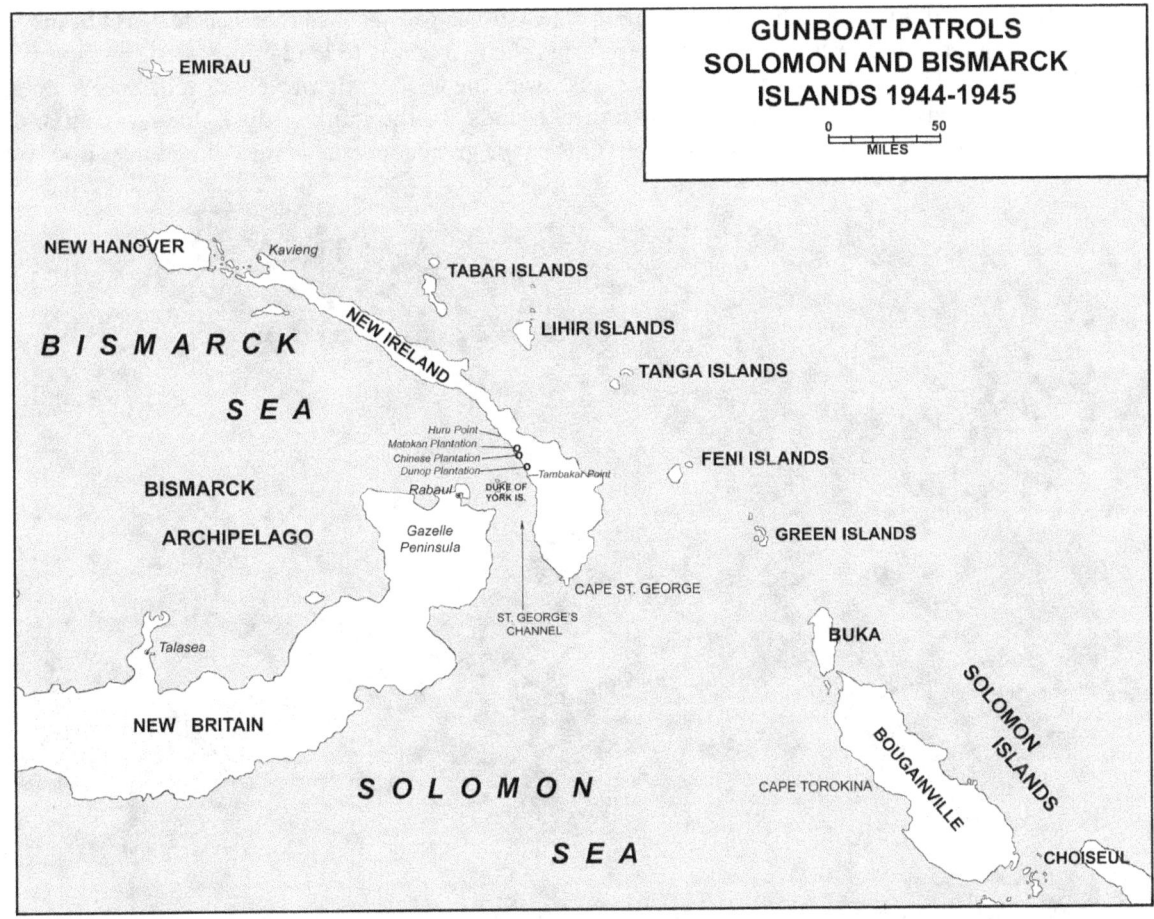

Once Japanese air and sea power at Rabaul had been neutralized, the problem of cut-off Japanese forces on the Solomon and Bismarck islands still remained. In order to keep them from one another and limit their resupply, it was necessary to constantly patrol the waters around the islands. The area between the Japanese base at Rabaul and their forces on New Ireland was of primary importance. LCI gunboats, along with PTs and PGMs, were constantly on patrol in the St. George's Channel. Such patrols usually lasted several days with the ships starting out from their bases at Cape Torokina or in the Treasuries. PT bases in the Green Islands or at Emirau Island were used for layovers or resupply during the days, and patrols usually took place during the night.

head back to their base.[12] Such patrols continued for the duration of the war. Although Choiseul, Bougainville, and the Shortland Islands were bypassed, there was always the potential for problems if the Japanese managed to get supplies to their forces on them.

Not all danger came from shore batteries or barges. On 30 July *LCI(G) 66* was patrolling two miles off the west coast of New Ireland near Huro Point when she was nearly torpedoed. At 0115 her lookouts spotted a torpedo wake as it passed by the ship. Since the gunboats had no sonar or depth charges, they could do little but report the incident to their base. The only possibility they had for destroying an enemy submarine was to catch it on the surface and shell it or call in larger ships or aircraft.

Arawe and Cape Gloucester

The encirclement of Rabaul required advancement along the coast of New Guinea in a northwestward direction. Once a position on New Guinea was reached that was due west of the tip of New Britain, it was necessary to hop across the two straits to land on the western shores of the island. Huon Peninsula lay directly across from the western tip of New Britain, separated by a single body of water and divided by several islands. To the south of the islands was Vitiaz Strait, and to the north was Dampier Strait. One of the great concerns of the Allied forces oper-

Japanese barges were often spotted by aircraft. These camouflaged barges were discovered by airmen flying their 5th Air Force B-25 off the coast of New Britain. In the area between Bougainville, New Britain, and New Ireland, barges fell victim to aircraft, PT boats and LCI gunboats. Aircraft were able to destroy them during the daylight hours, and nighttime hours were left to the gunboats to hunt them. Photograph by 5th U.S. Air Force.

ating on New Guinea was that the two straits might provide an easy access to the Solomon Sea for the Japanese Navy. Such a force might endanger Allied forces ashore and any preliminary landing on New Britain. The purpose of the Allied advance was to acquire airfields that might be used against Rabaul and other Japanese strongholds in the area, as well as against any Japanese naval force transiting the straits.

The Rocket Ships Go into Action

As Allied forces proceeded toward Rabaul along the chain of islands in the Solomons, additional progress was being made along the coast of New Guinea. After the Allies captured Finschafen in New Guinea, they were poised to attack the western end of New Britain in the Cape Gloucester area. As a stepping stone toward Cape Gloucester, the VII Amphibious Force landed the 112th U.S. Cavalry Regimental Combat Team under Brigadier General Cunningham at Arawe on 15 December 1943. The Arawe Islands lay just off Cape Merkus, New Britain, and were at the entrance to a good, but small harbor off Alamut Plantation on a small peninsula. During the landings, rubber boats carrying the troops encountered unexpected fire from the Japanese ashore and many were sunk. Fire from the accompanying destroyer *Shaw DD 373* silenced the enemy guns as further troop landings were attempted. At this point a new weapon came into use, the ship-launched rocket. In this preliminary attempt to use rockets to fire on shore installations prior to a landing, two DUKWs fitted with rockets proved effective against Japanese defenders on shore.[13] Having demonstrated the worth of rockets just prior to the landing phase of the assault, it was only a short time before rockets mounted on LCIs would be put into action.

Although the landing at Arawe had given the Allied forces a foothold on New Britain, it was not of much use. Its airfield was not developed further, as other fields were more useful. It did, however, distract the Japanese forces from the landing at Cape Gloucester.

By early December of 1943, the conversions of LCI(L)s 31 and 34 to rocket ships had been accomplished. According to Vice Admiral Daniel E. Barbey, "The effect of the rocket tryout on a small island near Milne Bay was devastating. The rain forest was cut as with a giant scythe."[14] With this test run, the stage was set for the first use of the LCI(R)s at the invasion of Cape Gloucester, New Britain.

At 0600 on Christmas Day 1944, the LCI(L)s, including the newly converted *31* commanded by Lieutenant (jg) Thomas J. Morrisey) and *34* commanded by Lieutenant (jg) Joseph F. Keefe, got underway from Cape Sudest, New Guinea, to their rendezvous off Buna. Once having assembled at Buna, they departed for Cape Gloucester. Included in the ships gathered for the attack were thirteen destroyers, nine APDs, and three sub-chasers. Overflights of P-47s, P-38s, and P-40s passed over the ships. By late in the day, they had been joined by other destroyers and the cruisers *H. M. A. S. Australia*, *H. M. A. S. Shropshire*, *Nashville CL 43*, and *Phoenix CL 46*, as well as other LCI(L)s. At 0600 on 26 December the invasion began. The landing craft started their trip to the beach after the cruisers and destroyers pounded it in traditional fashion. Over the beach B-25s made a final strafing and bombing attack on enemy positions. *LCI(R) 31* fired 288 4.5 inch rockets at Yellow Beach just ahead of the landing craft. As with all rocket attacks, the volley tore great gaps in the covering foliage and decimated enemy positions near the shoreline. *LCI(R) 34* did not fire during this landing for reasons not covered in the official reports. The two LCI(R)s were designated Task Unit 76.1.33 under Commander Day. The 1st Marine Division under Major General William H. Rupertus landed on the beaches. Green Beach 1 at Tuali was also hit by rocket fire from DUKWs. The pre-landing bombardment by ships, aircraft, and finally the amphibious gunboats, had put an end to any Japanese resistance, which was later determined to be light. The Japanese had thought that the landings were to be further south in

Borgen Bay and had concentrated their troop strength in that area. From this point forward additional LCI(L)s were converted to carry rockets and were be an essential part of any beach assault.

Shortly after the attack on Cape Gloucester, the Associated Press released an article about the new use of rocket gunboats. It read:

> Rockets that swish through the air and disintegrate everything within range of their explosion were used effectively in the allied amphibious operations at Arawe and Cape Gloucester, New Britain, and at Saidor, New Guinea.
>
> American Sixth Army forces landed at Arawe Dec. 15 and at Saidor Jan. 2; marine veterans invaded Cape Gloucester, Dec. 26.
>
> An Army spokesman said today rockets fired from landing craft and small vessels blasted brush and trees along the beach before troops landed, and smashed Japanese gun positions on the Cape Gloucester airstrips before the marines moved in for close fighting.
>
> At Saidor, landing craft and sub-chasers moved in close to the beach, firing rockets directly over the Higgins boats carrying the assault waves. The rockets made a peculiar suction-like sound going overhead. A hundred yards offshore, the concussion from the explosions made pants legs whip against skins of men crouched in the boats.
>
> On land, the rockets were used to blast Japanese from caves and deeply dug pillboxes. In one cave on the first day of Arawe battle, six Japanese were killed in one rocket shot.[15]

To complete the encirclement of Rabaul, the capture of the Admiralty Islands was planned for 1 April 1944. The two main islands in the group, Manus and Los Negros, were suitable for use as air bases. However, their configuration was such that the two islands encompassed a very useful body of water, Seeadler Harbor. Plans were put forth to make this a major naval base that would both cut off Rabaul completely and serve as a major fleet base. Last minute political considerations by MacArthur advanced the invasion date by several days and his orders were to land a "reconnaissance in force" on the islands no later than 29 March. Because of the short notice, the troops had to be carried to the islands on high speed transports and destroyers and landed in small boats. LCI(L)s, LSTs, and slower amphibious ships were left behind. As a result the LCI gunboats were not able to participate, even though their use would have been quite important. The landings took place piecemeal and nearly failed. By a stroke of good luck and poor Japanese strategy, the troops managed to hang on and overcome the resistance.[16]

For the LCI gunboats this would become an important base. Numerous gunboats were converted there or repaired. The Admiralty Islands became a staging area for further campaigns.

Saidor, Toem, Wadke, Biak, Noemfoor

The VI Army established a beachhead at Cape Gloucester but needed an airstrip from which to fly cover for the landing zone. A suitable one existed at Saidor on New Guinea, which was assaulted on 2 January 1944. Again *LCI(R)s 31* and *34* were active in the attack. The next appearance of the rocket gunboats was at Toem, New Guinea. In this landing the newly converted *LCI(R) 73* joined them for the assault on 17 May. The use of the rocket gunboats for call-fire and other missions had not yet been developed. The three rocket gunboats continued to be active in regional landings, participating in the assaults on Wadke on 17 May, Biak, 27 May and Noemfoor Island on 2 July 1944. At this point MacArthur's eyes were on a landing in the Philippines. Numerous LCI gunboats and rocket ships began to assemble at various locations near New Guinea, while others began to undergo conversions that would put them in the first assault waves at Leyte. By the end of September and into early October, most of the LCI(G)s and LCI(R)s headed for the invasion at Leyte. Still others were converted to mount 4.5 inch mortars, which were first used at Peleliu on 15 September 1944. All three gunboat types were active in the invasion at Leyte. The final versions of the LCI gunboats, the LCS(L)s were just being launched and their crews were still in training. They would not appear in the war zone until after the Lingayen landings in early 1945.

Morotai

General MacArthur's forces had advanced along the coast of New Guinea to the Vogelkop Peninsula at the western end of New Guinea. He had to consider both his next step, as well as his final destination. With a landing in the Philippines as his next objective, MacArthur had to find a way to advance his forces toward the Philippines and, at the same time, minimize Japanese interference with those forces. The use of air power from New Guinea against targets in the Philippines was impractical as the distance was too great. In addition, Japanese airfields on the large island of Halmahera might provide the Japanese with bases from which to interfere with American shipping and aircraft. An American airfield was needed part way between the Vogelkop and the island of Mindanao in the Philippines.

The first consideration for a more advanced base was Halmahera, situated about half way between Vogelkop Peninsula and the island of Mindanao. It was quickly ruled out as the Japanese Army force there numbered around 30,000, and the island was large enough that routing them out would take a major effort. The troops there were primarily from the 32nd Division of Lieutenant General Fusataro Teshima's 2nd Army. They were supplemented by the 1st Field Base Unit, the 10th Expeditionary Unit and the 26th Special Base Force. Of the 30,000 Japanese there, only about one-third were actual combat troops. Nonetheless, they could be considered formidable opposition.

Landing on the northernmost coast of Halmahera was considered, however, it would leave the landing forces subject to continual attacks from the Japanese on the island. The situation would be similar to that existing on Bougainville and would be a constant drain on Allied resources. A better choice was the island of Morotai, just fifty miles off the northern tip of Halmahera and lightly defended. The island of Halmahera was placed on the list of islands to be bypassed as MacArthur leapfrogged his forces past a number of Japanese held islands and left the Japanese on them cut off from support. Bombing of the airfields on Halmahera by Army air force planes flying from Sansapor had reduced the number of available Japanese aircraft on the island from 140 to only fifteen. This negated the possibility that an invasion force heading for Morotai would be bombed. The only way for the Japanese to reinforce the small garrison on Morotai would be to transport them fifty miles by barge from Halmahera to Morotai, a dangerous undertaking. Swift PT boats, LCI gunboats, and aircraft would make short work of barges attempting the transit. Morotai would be the next landing.

The island of Morotai is approximately forty-four miles long from north to south and twenty-five miles wide. It is primarily mountainous jungle terrain, suitable for strong defense had the Japanese placed a small number of troops there to defend it. As it stood, there were only about 500 Japanese on the island. They had recently been formed into the 2nd Provisional Raiding Unit, a commando group led by Major Takenobu Kawashima. Of major interest to the Americans was a partly finished airstrip at Pitoe on the southernmost coast of the island. A peninsula, running to the south from the area around Pitoe, was suitable for expansion of the field and would also serve as a good landing point for the invasion. A small harbor was near Pitoe and several small offshore islands would prove usable as bases for gunboats and PTs. Once the airfield was expanded, the island would be a perfect steppingstone to the Philippines. The landing at Pitoe was scheduled for 15 September 1944 at two beaches, Red and White, situated on either side of the airfield.

Assaulting the beach was the 31st Infantry Division under Major General John C. Persons. It consisted of the 124th, 155th, and 167th Infantry Regiments. The 126th Infantry Regiment, 32nd Infantry Division was held in reserve. In addition to these infantry troops were support units of various kinds, bringing the immediate invasion force to around 28,000. To build the airfields and service them, another 28,000 personnel were transported to the island.

Assigned to transport the assault force were various elements of the VII Amphibious Corps, under Rear Admiral Daniel E. Barbey. Barbey would handle the White Attack Group and the Red Attack Group would be under the command of his subordinate, Rear Admiral William M. Fechteler. Three American light cruisers, two British heavy cruisers, and ten destroyers under Rear Admiral R. S. Berkey, would provide heavy fire support. The Japanese airfields on Halmahera, the Celebes, Mindanao, the Palaus, Yap, and Ulithi were bombed continuously during the week preceding the landing at Morotai by aircraft from the 5th Air Force and the fast carriers of the Pacific Fleet. Six days before the assault, Rear Admiral Thomas L. Sprague supplied six escort carriers for anti-submarine patrol. His planes also flew combat air patrols, although the severe bombing of the Japanese airfields during the week gave them little to look at besides the blue seas beneath their wings.

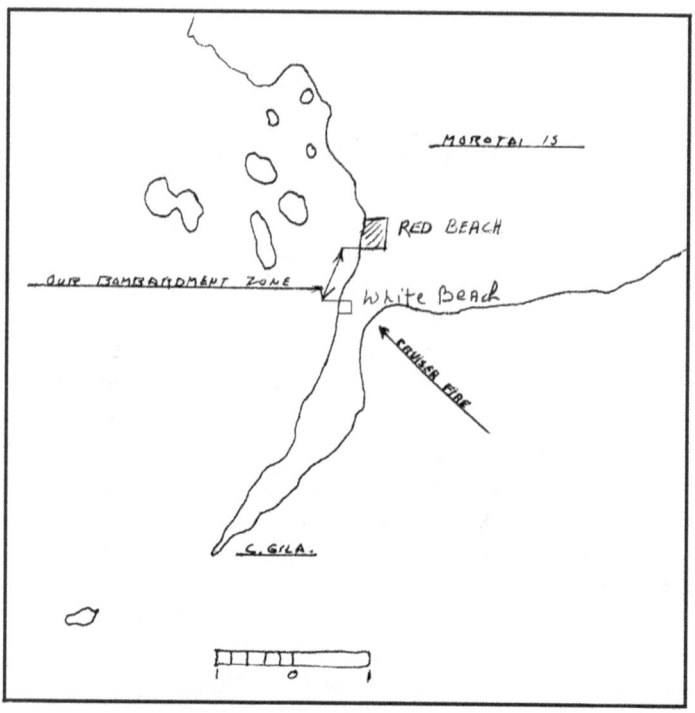

The above sketch from the Action Report of *LCI(G) 65* shows the area attacked by *LCI(G)s 64* and *65* at Morotai on 15 September 1944. USS *LCI(G) 65* No Serial, **Commanding Officer USS *LCI(G) 65* Action Report Morotai Operation,** 18 September 1944, p. 11.

Transporting the troops to Morotai were five APDs, 45 LSTs, 24 LCIs, 20 LCTs, and an LSD. Screening the transports were twenty-four destroyers, four frigates, eleven LCI gunboats, six PCs, four minesweepers, and two PCs.

LCI(G)s 23, 64, 65, and *69* provided close-in fire support for the landing at Red Beach. White Beach was covered by *LCI(G)s 68* and *70*. The troops landed on time, with the gunboats providing ample fire on the beaches to bolster the pre-invasion bombardment of the larger ships. The troops accomplished the landing with no resistance.

Having delivered their troops to the beach, the gunboats turned to coastal patrols. *LCI(G)s 23, 64,* and *65* skirted the coast and checked the nearby islands. Near Cape Wajaboela, about eighteen miles north of the landing beaches, they spotted anti-aircraft fire coming from a village and directed at one of the Navy planes covering the area. They

Opposite, top: The island of Morotai proved to be an ideal location for airfields that could reach the Philippines and other strategic areas. It was taken on 15 September 1944. From Hugh J. Casey, Major General. Engineers of the Southwest Pacific 1941–1945 Volume I, *Engineers in Theater Operations* (Washington DC: U.S. Government Printing Office, 1947), p. 188. *Opposite, bottom:* LCI(G)s 65 and 64 attack the area between White Beach and Red Beach at Morotai, 15 September 1944. National Archives photograph NARA 80G 181441 courtesy Dean Reid.

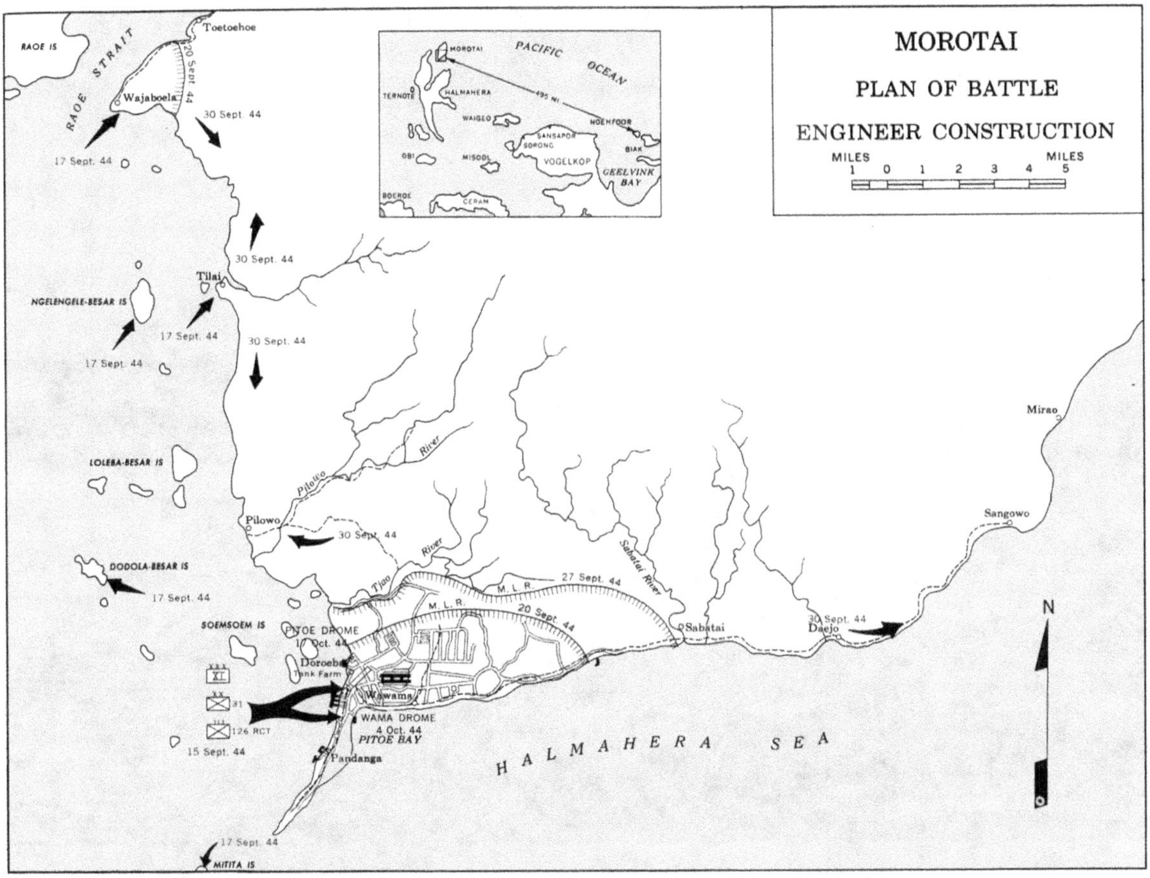
MOROTAI
PLAN OF BATTLE
ENGINEER CONSTRUCTION
MILES 1 0 1 2 3 4 5 MILES
PACIFIC OCEAN
MOROTAI
TERNOTE
HALMAHERA
WAIGEO
NOEMFOOR
BIAK
SANSAPOR
SORONG
VOGELKOP
GEELVINK BAY
OBI
MISOOL
BOEROE
CERAM
RAOE IS
RAOE STRAIT
Toetoehoe
Wajaboela
20 Sept. 44
30 Sept. 44
17 Sept. 44
Tilai
NGELENGELE-BESAR IS
LOLEBA-BESAR IS
Pilowo
Pilowo River
DODOLA-BESAR IS
SOEMSOEM IS
PITOE DROME
17 Oct. 44
Doroeba
Tank Farm
Wawama
WAMA DROME
4 Oct. 44
PITOE BAY
Pandanga
15 Sept. 44
126 RCT
31
Tjao River
M. L. R.
27 Sept. 44
Sabatai River
Sabatai
Daejo
Sangowo
Mirao
N
HALMAHERA SEA
MITITA IS

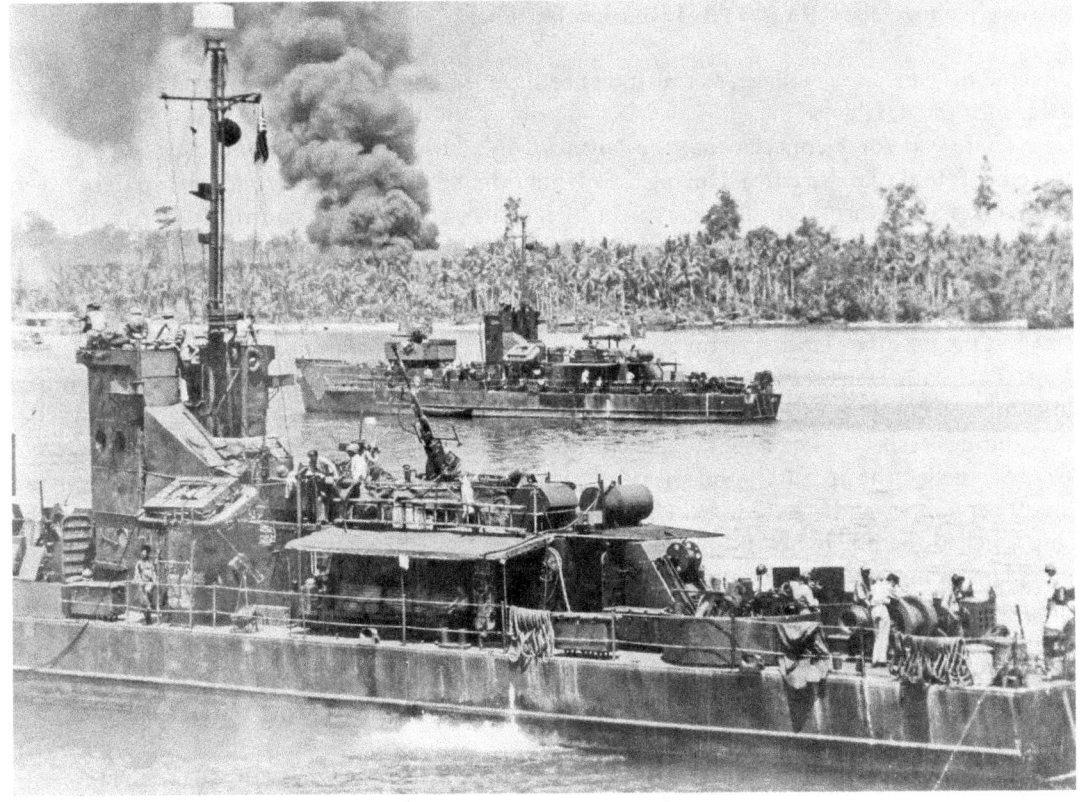

LCI(G)s head for the beach at Morotai on 15 September 1944. *LCI(G) 65* is in the foreground. National Archives photograph NARA 80G 181445 courtesy Dean Reid.

directed their fire at the village, setting it on fire and silencing the gun battery. The area remained ablaze for the next day.[17]

There was some concern that the Japanese on Halmahera might send barges with reinforcements to the landing area. During the night hours, the gunboats patrolled the strait between Halmahera and Morotai until the arrival of PT boats, which would continue the patrols from that point on.

Additional landings were made in the southern area of Morotai. On 17 September an Army assault unit and a radar team landed at Posi Posi to establish a radar station there. *LCI(G) 23* covered them as they landed to no opposition. That same day a similar landing was effected at Cape Tilei with *LCI(G) 70* covering the landing, again with no resistance. On 19 September, uncontested landings were made at Padangi and Cape Sopi with *LCI(G)s 23* and *69* covering the landings respectively. Some evidence of the Japanese was found at Cape Sopi, and *Ringold DD 500* shelled the area for good measure. Another landing at Cape Gorango was completed on 20 September and covered by *LCI(G)s 65* and *70*. Enemy troops were in the area and the ships shelled the jungle behind the landing beaches. The purpose of these landings was to set up radar stations at various locations along the coast. Some minor fighting occurred here between the assault force and the Japanese after the gunboats left the area, and on 23 September *LCI(G) 69* reported to the area to evacuate some wounded Army radar team members.

Nearby Raoe Island seemed to be a good site for another radar installation, and a landing on the southern part was made on 21 September covered by *LCI(G) 69*. Natives on the island greeted the troops and informed them that there were no Japanese on the island.

The U.S. Army did not see the need to chase the few Japanese around the island to eliminate

An LCI(G) fires rockets at Morotai on 15 September 1944. NARA 80G 181442.

them. It was too large an area to cover and the cost far outweighed the effort. The Japanese retreated to the hills and were left in peace until the war ended. With the end of threats from the Japanese on the island, the gunboats returned to Humboldt Bay, New Guinea, departing Morotai on 24 September.

Mapia and Asia Islands

The Mapia Islands lie approximately 130 miles northwest of Biak and 360 miles east southeast of Morotai. Although the war had passed them by, the islands were of value to the American forces as observation posts and weather stations. Their unique position between the Palaus and New Guinea made them valuable in that regard. Additionally, there was no reason to leave them in the hands of the approximately 400 Japanese remaining on the Asia Islands who would be in a position to report any American movements to their own headquarters. Plans to capture the islands corresponded with the invasion of Luzon, which was sure to occupy the efforts of the Japanese and draw them away from the smaller islands to the south.[18]

Overall command of the Task Group 78.14 was held by Captain Lord Ashbourne, D.S.O. Royal Navy in his flagship *H.M.S. Ariadne*. *Ariadne* was an *Abdiel Class* fast minelayer cruiser and had been in action in the Pacific since mid-1944. The close Support Unit TU 78.14.31 was divided into two sections, one to attack Red Beach at Pegun Island in the Mapias and the other to attack White Beach at Igi Island in the Asia group. Gunboats assigned to Red Beach at Pegun Island were *LCI(G)s 567(F) 568, 580,* and *407* under the overall command of Lieutenant Commander J. D. Starkus. *LCI(G)s 461, 439, 462,* and *467* provided supporting fire at White Beach. *LCI(G) 373* had originally been assigned to the assault but damaged a screw and was replaced by *LCI(G) 467*. The Task Group staged from its base at Morotai.

The first group of islands to be invaded was the Mapia Islands. Of the three islands in the group, Pegun was the location of the Japanese main force. Twelve-hundred American troops from the 167th Infantry Regiment, along with several smaller units, landed on Red Beach at Pegun Island on 19 November 1944. Bombardment by the destroyers *Shaw DD 373* and *Caldwell DD 605*, destroyer escort *Willmarth DE 638*, and *PC 1122*, along with that of *Ariadne*, pounded the small island and drove the Japanese off. They waded across the reef to neighboring Bras Island with as much equipment as they could take and were able to offer some light anti-aircraft fire against B-25s that bombed them later in the day.

At 0615 on 15 November the LCI(G)s opened fire on Red Beach on Pegun Island with rocket barrages, 40mm and 20mm fire. The troops landed with no opposition as the bulk of the Japanese force had left earlier for Bras Island. The bodies of thirteen Japanese who had committed suicide were found on Pegun Island. The gunboats then turned their attention to the southernmost tip of Bras and hit it with rockets and automatic weapons fire. They received a few mortar shells in return. Troop landings were made on Bras the following day with the gunboats supplying a standard assault barrage. On 18 November Finaldo was taken and the Mapia Islands were conquered. Light machine gun fire and a few mortar rounds were directed at the gunboats, but their counter fire soon ended the enemy resistance.

The Asia Islands were assaulted on 19 November. Task Unit 78.14.32 gunboats *LCI(G)s 461(F), 462, 467,* and *439* under Lieutenant H. F. Godbout led the assault. Standard rocket barrages and strafing were used against White Beach on Igi Island but the Japanese had withdrawn.[19]

With the end of Operation Cartwheel, American objectives had been obtained. Rabaul was no longer a viable and useful base for the Japanese. Her harbor was filled with the hulks of damaged and sunken ships and her airfields were out of commission. Any aircraft attempting the flight to Rabaul's airfields would have found them cratered. Constant coverage of the area by American aircraft would have resulted in certain death for any Japanese pilot attempting to land. The Japanese high command was forced to abandon its military forces on New Britain as the Allied forces surrounded, cut off, and bypassed the island. Its garrison had to fend for itself without the possibility of launching any offensive action against the Allies who would now move toward other prizes.

The decision to neutralize and bypass Rabaul was a good one. Capture of the island and the elimination of the Japanese defenders would have been exceptionally costly. Several years after the war, Marine Corps historians wrote:

> When the order came for the Japanese to cease fighting, Eighth Area Army had about 57,000 men and Southeast Area Fleet about 34,000 on Gazelle Peninsula, with an additional 7,700 Army and

5,000 Navy troops a night's barge trip away on New Ireland. These men, as part of the amazing display of national discipline evident throughout the Pacific, accepted the Emperor's surrender order without incident.[20]

By the middle of 1944, the United States Navy had developed and put to use two entirely new weapons, the LCI(G) and the LCI(R). Both had proven their worth during Operation Cartwheel and had gone from leading the invasion forces to the beach to bombarding shore installations and destroying barge traffic. Their value having been demonstrated, numerous LCI(L)s would be sent to rear areas for conversion to gunboats and new LCI(L)s back in the states would undergo conversion prior to heading west to the combat zone.

CHAPTER 4

The Central Pacific Campaigns

Early on in the war against Japan it was necessary to develop strategies that would see the eventual defeat of the enemy. As MacArthur advanced across the southern rim of the Pacific through the Solomons and along the coast of New Guinea, equal attention to the central Pacific islands was needed. MacArthur could only advance so far before Japanese forces on numerous

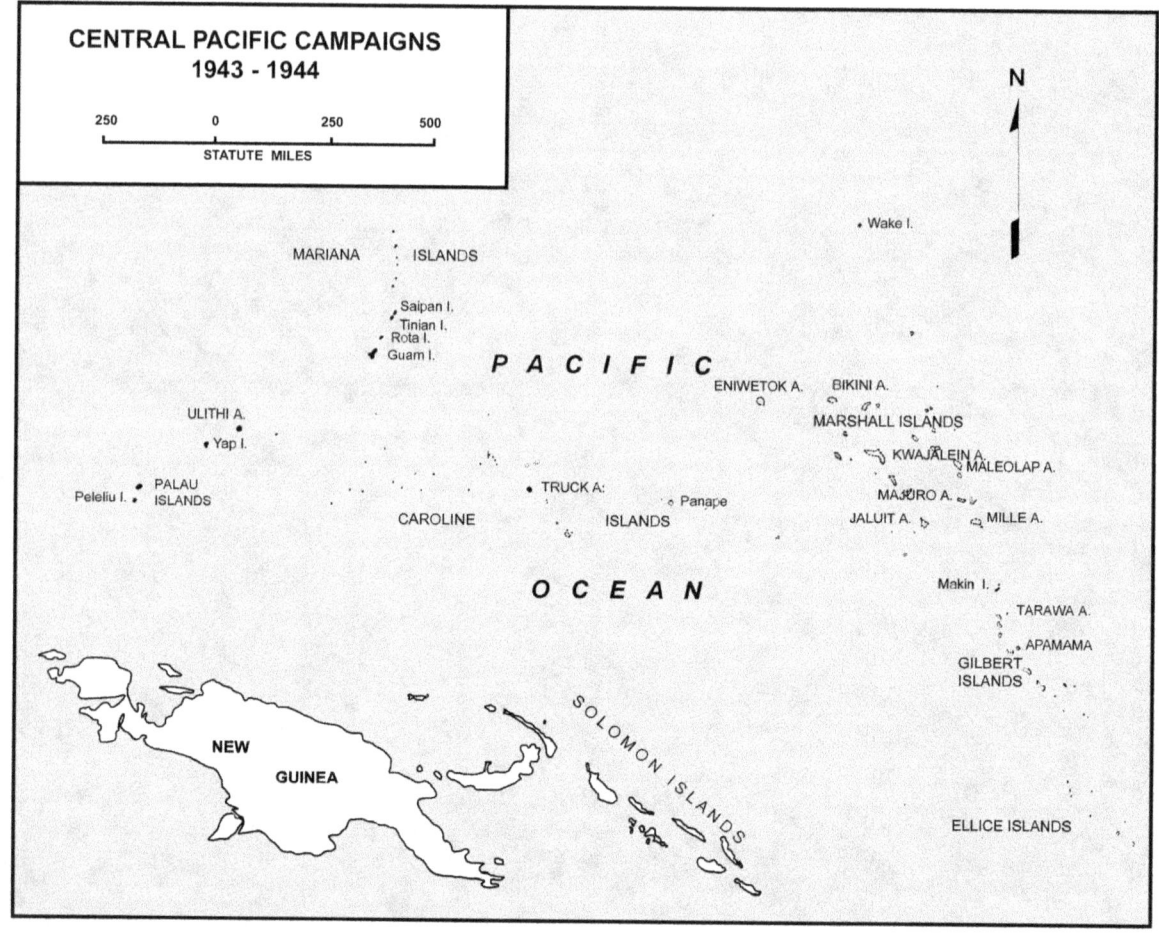

The vast area that had to be covered by American forces is obvious in this map of the Central Pacific Area.

islands throughout the Central Pacific would be able to attack both his flanks and that of the naval forces operating in the Western Pacific. The islands of Micronesia would have to be captured or neutralized. Samuel Eliot Morison noted

> the farther west that America projected her sea power, the more dangerous it became to leave in enemy possession such ample means for flank attacks on Allied lines of communication, and the more urgent it became to capture his airfields and fleet anchorages. Eniwetok, lying a little more than a thousand miles from Saipan, would be worth a dozen Wakes. The Carolines not only included the naval bases of Truk and Palau; they threatened General MacArthur's advance after the Bismarck Barrier was broken. Saipan and Guam in enemy control screened the Philippines; in Allied possession they might bring B-29s within range of Japan. The Marshall's spider web could entangle any westward advance from Pearl Harbor; that of the Gilberts enabled man-made insects to pounce on the America-Australia lifeline.[1]

The key feature of many of these island groups was the presence of airfields or significant harbors from which the Japanese could extend their reach toward American forces. The capture of key bases in each of these areas would ensure American success in the drive westward. Where airfields with lengthy runways existed, these could be used by American aircraft and their capture denied to the enemy. Some of the island airfields could easily be bypassed and neutralized if the aircraft there could be destroyed by American air attacks. The pattern of advancement across the Pacific was designed to accomplish this.

The first of the campaigns was aimed at the Gilbert Islands, with the main targets at Tarawa and Makin. The key island at Makin Atoll was Butaritari. Landing there on 19 November 1943 were 6,472 Army troops from the 165th RCT and a battalion landing team from the 105th Infantry. Both were units of the 27th Division. By 23 November the island had been taken with a loss of only sixty-six dead and 152 wounded. The American Navy fared worse. A turret on the battleship *Mississippi BB 41* blew up killing forty-three and wounding nineteen. Flying air support for the operation were Navy fighters off three carriers under Rear Admiral H. M. Mullinnix's TG 52.3 Air Support Group. They included *Liscome Bay CVE 56*, *Coral Sea CVB 43*, and *Corregidor CVE 58*. *Liscome Bay* was torpedoed by a Japanese submarine on 24 November while operating twenty miles southeast of the atoll. She went to the bottom taking with her fifty-three officers and 591 men, with many more wounded who managed to get off the ship. The Japanese had lost approximately 800, a combination of combat troops and laborers.

By comparison, the battle for Tarawa from 19 to 23 November was among the bloodiest to be fought by the Marines in World War II. The key island in the atoll was Betio where the Japanese had an airfield and their strongest defenses. Surrounding Betio was a reef that extended almost 200–300 yards from the island in some areas. The day of the invasion, 19 November, would see a neap tide during the hours of the actual landings, making it difficult to get the landing craft across the reef. Marines found themselves sitting ducks for the Japanese as they waded ashore. The naval bombardment and air attacks that preceded their landing had pounded the island, but the defenders, dug in deep, had survived. There was no cover as the Marines made their way to shore and many were killed while still in waist deep water. Marine losses at Tarawa totaled 980 dead with 2,101 wounded. Additionally, the Navy lost twenty-nine. The details of the heroic landing and victory at Tarawa have been recounted by numerous historians, and it is not necessary to go into great detail here. The important fact to consider is that the Marines had no close-in fire support as they made their landing, a situation that led to numerous deaths and casualties.

Rear Admiral Richmond K. Turner was an astute observer of the situation and quickly saw the weakness in an American amphibious assault. In his report on "Lessons Learned at Tarawa," written only a week after the end of the battle for Tarawa, Turner advocated better air and submarine reconnaissance of target areas, a greater number of ships that could supply counter-fire against defensive positions, and longer bombardment of the enemy island prior to landing. The LCI gunboats had just come into existence and had been successful in the Treasuries. Turner recommended that they be an integral part of any island assault in future operations, ensuring the conversion of numerous LCI(L)s to gunboat configuration, as well as the completely modified hull that would become the LCS(L). They would be rushed into conversion for the coming assaults in the Marshalls.

The Marshalls

The Marshalls occupied a large area and numerous atolls and islets had to be investigated. Part of the task involved clearing them of any Japanese and surveying them for any possible use as an anchorage or base. The first of the Marshall Islands to be taken was Kwajalein Atoll.

The assault on Kwajalein Atoll had two primary objectives. In the north were the islands of Roi and Namur, connected by a spit of land and a causeway that made them basically one target. In the south the island of Kwajalein was the primary objective. Both were heavily defended, with islands on either side that had to be secured to provide security for the invading forces and positions for artillery to support the landings. Roi-Namur served as the atoll's air base and Kwajalein as the naval base. Just to the north of Kwajalein the Japanese maintained a seaplane base at the island of Ebeye.

Two Task Forces were assigned to the assault on Kwajalein Atoll. The Northern Attack Force (TF 53) under Rear Admiral R. L. Conolly would assault the northern part of Kwajalein Atoll, while the Southern Attack Force (TF 52), under Rear Admiral Richmond K. Turner, was to attack the southern islands of Kwajalein Atoll. Invasion day for Kwajalein Atoll was 31 January 1944.

On 31 January, *LCI(G) 450* was making its run on Ennubirr Island. The noise of the bombardment was so intense that the CO, Lieutenant (jg) Thomas F. Kennedy, Jr., didn't notice when his ship ran aground on a reef as the gunboats were leading the landing craft to shore. In the midst of the attack and grounding, crewmen on the *450* noticed that four LVTs had capsized a few hundred yards astern of the gunboat. Approximately fifty men were in the water being battered by the waves and in danger of being run down by LVTs in the following wave. Lines were thrown to the men and several of them managed to tie the end to a reef buoy, allowing others to hold on. Other lines were thrown to the men and most of them were hauled aboard, severely weakened by their struggle in the rough surf. By 1300 most of the men had been saved but two had drowned. Two more LVTs capsized and three men went under; the rest were dragged on board where emergency facilities had been set up to treat them. Many were suffering from cuts and needed medical care. Because of the efforts of the crew of *LCI(G) 450*, fifty men had been saved. The following day the gunboat was dragged off the reef, but her screws and keel had been damaged. She was towed back to Pearl Harbor for repairs.[2]

Part of Task Force 52, gunboat Support Unit TU 52.8.8 under Lieutenant Commander Theodore Blanchard, departed Maalaea Bay, Maui, Hawaiian Islands, on 14 January 1944 after training in the islands and making preparations for their next assignment. Included in the unit were Division 15 *LCI(G)s 365(F), 438, 439, 440, 441,* and *442.* They arrived off Kwajalein Atoll on 31 January 1944 and prepared for the assault. The first island to feel their power would be Ennylabegan. The assault and landing there were similar to the procedure for most island landings. The gunboats led the landing craft from the line of departure, released rocket salvos, turned out of the boat lanes as the landing craft passed through, and provided covering and call-fire as the troops landed. In some cases there was little or no resistance, and in others the resistance was strong. The interconnectivity of many of the islands in the atolls made it necessary for the ships to keep a vigilant eye on the areas between the islands where Japanese troops might try to escape from one island to the next by wading across the reefs. In like manner, it was also possible for troops and supplies to be brought to an island to reinforce the defenders. Some of the islands were vacant or lightly defended, and others had significant defensive positions and weapons that needed to be eliminated.

The landings on Ennylabegan and Kwajalein saw little return fire at the ships and they suffered no losses. However, after withdrawing from their covering fire runs at Ebeye on 3 February, several of the ships discovered holes in their sides indicating that they had been hit by enemy fire. The most significant was *LCI(G) 442* which counted five holes in her side made by 20mm gunfire, but the damage was slight. Other ships hit that day, but not seriously damaged, were *LCI(G)s 365, 440,* and *441.*

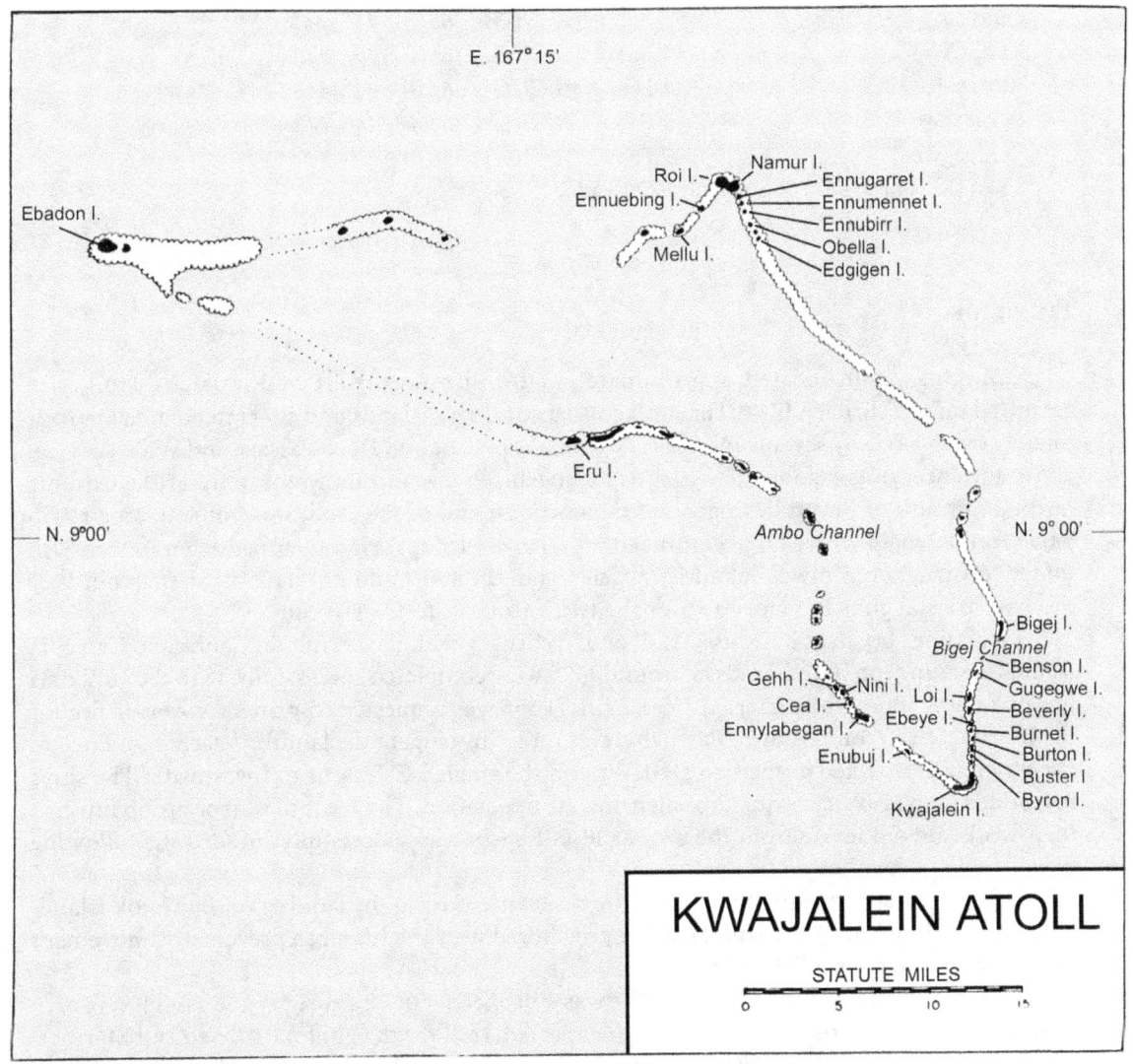

Kwajalein Atoll, the world's largest atoll, is sixty-six miles long and about twenty-two miles wide. It consists of ninety-three small islands of various sizes. The expanse of the atoll was so great that the American forces attacking it had to divide into two task forces, Northern and Southern. Many of the islands were uninhabited and had no known names. As a result, they were only known by the code names assigned to them by the Americans. Names such as Roi, Namur, Ennylabegan and Enubuj stand in contrast to the code names Beverly, Buster, and Burton.

After leaving the Ebeye area, the ships steamed near other islands, strafing suspected enemy locations on Ebeye and Loi Islands in the company of *McKee DD 575*. Firing on Loi had to be halted around 1500 when twenty-five natives appeared on the beach waving white flags. The group consisted of men, women and children, placed in danger by the fighting. The services of the gunboats were no longer needed at Kwajalein and they moved on to Eniwetok Atoll on 15 February.

Southern Kwajalein Atoll	Date	Gunboats Participating
Ennylabegan (X)	31 Jan.	LCI(G)s 365(F), 438, 439, 440, 441, 442
Kwajalein	1 Feb.	LCI(G)s 365(F), 439, 442
Ebeye	3 Feb.	LCI(G)s 365(F)*, 438, 439, 440*, 441*, 442*
Byron		LCI(G)s 365(F), 439, 441, 442
Buster		LCI(G)s 365(F), 439, 441, 442
Loi (XX)	4 Feb.	LCI(G)s 365(F), 441, 442
Burnett (XX)	4 Feb.	LCI(G)s 365(F), 441, 442
Gugegwe	5 Feb.	LCI(G)s 365(F), 441, 442
Gugegwe	5 Feb.	LCI(G)s 438, 439, 440

KEY: (X) Strafed; (XX) Strafed Only; (F) Flagship
*Ship Hit

Eniwetok

Eniwetok Atoll, located approximately 340 miles northwest of Kwajalein Atoll, was assaulted on 17 February 1944. The atoll consists of thirty islands and islets in an area approximately twenty-one by seventeen miles. Two breaks in the atoll, Deep Passage and Wide Passage, allow entrance to its lagoon. The islands of Engebi, Parry, and Eniwetok were at the extreme north and south of the atoll. Engebi, at the northern end of the atoll, was home to an airstrip 4,025 feet in length with a large contingent of Japanese troops. However, her defenses were still under construction. Eniwetok and Parry Islands in the south did not have an airstrip but they did have coastal guns in place to cover the two entrances to the lagoon.

Operations began at Eniwetok Atoll on 17 February with the assault on Canna and Camellia Islands. Landings on both islands at around 1320 were completed successfully, with the gunboats unopposed. A short while later, at 1550, *LCI(G) 365* was requested to provide covering fire for the Joint Beach Reconnaissance Party that was set to investigate the landing beaches on Engebi. Heavy fire was directed at the two DUKWs and the single LCVP sent to investigate. The ships responded with heavy covering fire, silencing the opposition. The reconnaissance group finished their work and withdrew from the area at 1810. Engebi was successfully invaded the following day.

On 19 February the gunboats had little resistance during the landing on Eniwetok Island. Once the landing had been completed, they anchored near the island to prevent any movement of the Japanese troops off the island.

The most difficult battle for gunboats was still ahead. On 22 February the assault on Parry Island would be the most dangerous, yet unexpected, trial for the gunboats. The 22nd Marines, supported by an Army artillery battalion that had been moved to Eniwetok Island, were scheduled to land on the island. As the gunboats maneuvered toward the line of departure at 0805, a message was sent by the Marine Corps attack team that heavy resistance was anticipated on the right flank of the landing beaches. Extra naval gunfire was requested and the Navy complied with the request. The three most aggressive gunboats, *LCI(G)s 365, 440*, and *442*, were assigned to the right flank and additional naval fire from the larger ships was directed at the area.

4. The Central Pacific Campaigns

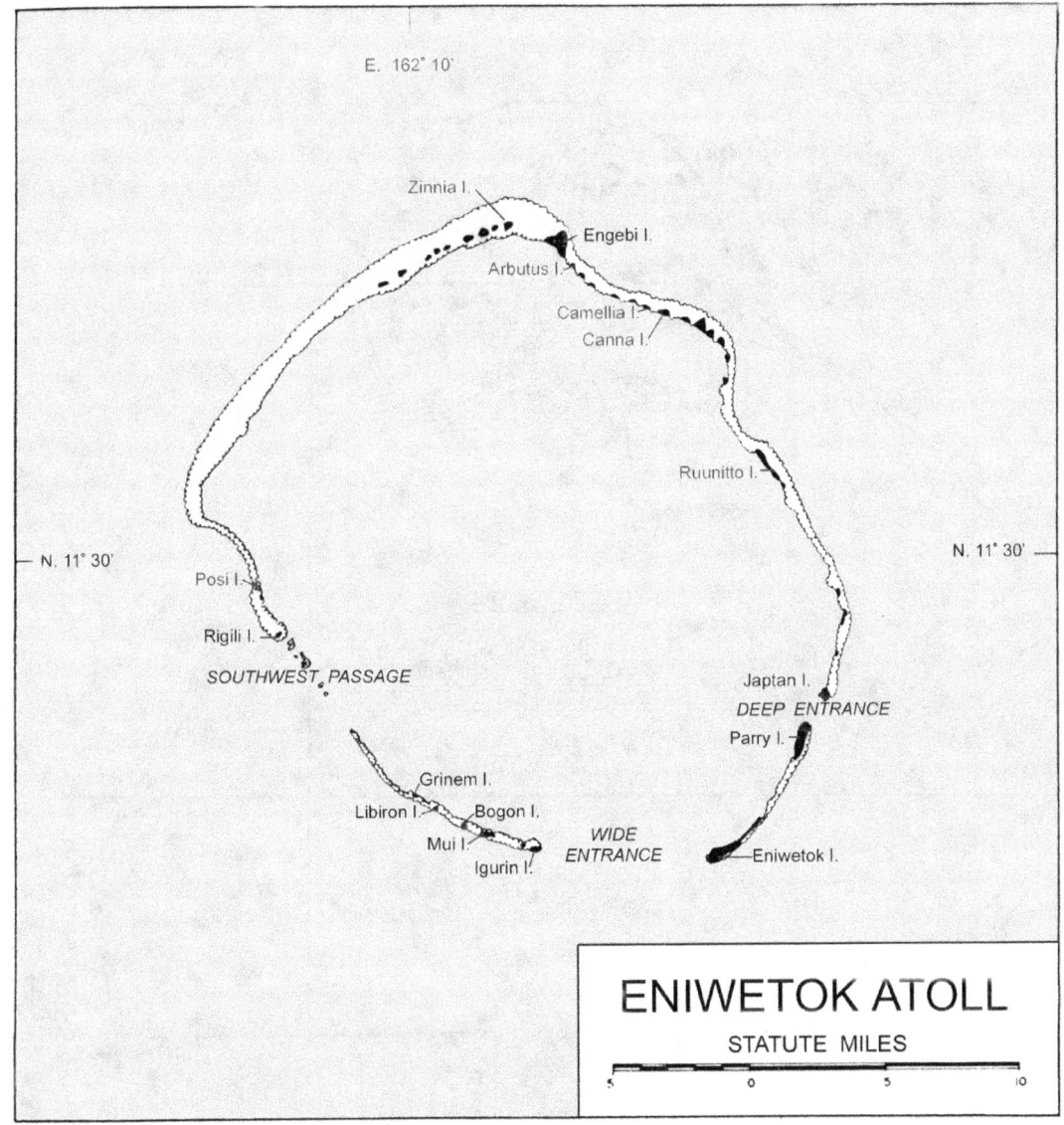

Eniwetok Atoll is approximately twenty-two miles long and seventeen miles wide. It consists of thirty islands of various sizes. Names such as Eniwetok, Ruunitto, and Engebi were well known but other unnamed islands were assigned code names such as Camellia, Posy, and Zinnia.

A major problem existed in this assault as the ships approached the landing beaches from a downwind position. All the smoke and dust from the bombardment blew back toward them, obscuring the target area. As a result, the landing zone was hidden, making it necessary for the destroyers to fire by radar. Their close proximity to the landing beaches placed the three gunboats under the fire of the destroyers, and they were hit by 5 inch shells from the American ships. *LCI(G) 365* took a 5 inch shell in her starboard side amidships. It exploded inside the ship killing and wounding a number of men. *LCI(G) 440* took two shells which killed seven men and wounded forty. At 0855 another destroyer shell hit the fantail of *LCI(G) 442*, killing six and wounding five. Dominick C. Maurone, whose general quarters position was first loader on the boat's 40mm gun, recalled:

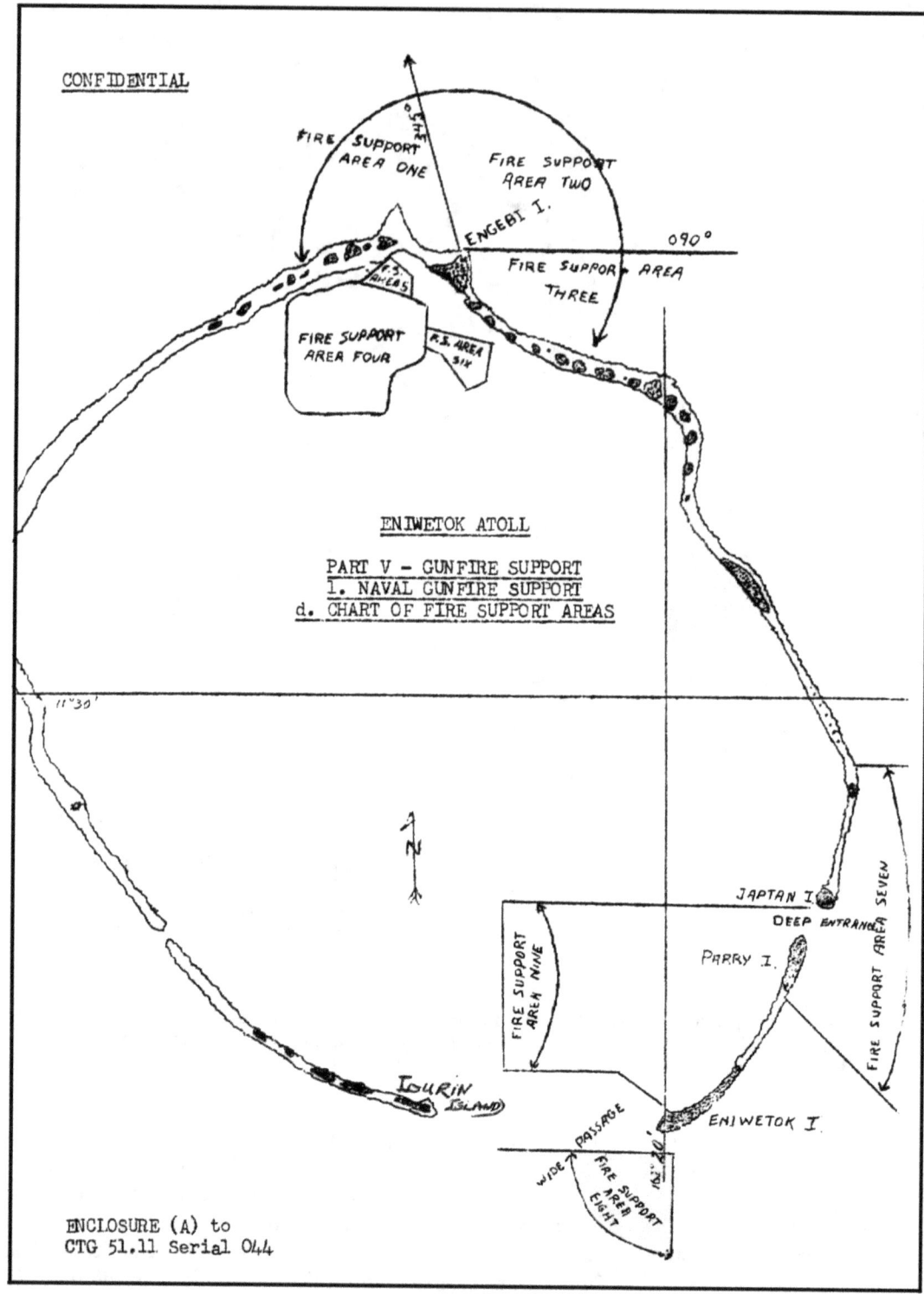

This diagram, taken from the report of the Commander Eniwetok Expeditionary Group, shows the areas of fire support for the conquest of the atoll. Commander Eniwetok Expeditionary Group (Commander Task Group 51.11– Commander Fifth Amphibious Force Group 2, Fifth Amphibious Force) Serial 044, *Eniwetok Operations—Report of,* 7 March 1944, Enclosure (A).

We had just begun to fire on the island when our 40mm gun jammed. I was the first loader on the gun. I had to go beneath the gun to get the shell out that jammed the gun.... While under the gun I heard this large hissing sound, it sounded like rockets going off. I then noticed the second loader of our gun lying on the deck. When I looked at him he was bleeding and had a large gap in his back. I didn't hear anymore firing from our ship and we were under attack.... We were out of action and we were told to take cover. To this day I don't know what made me go to the rear of the gun deck and slide down the ladder to the fan tail while the rest of the crew on the front of the gun deck went down the ladder to the well deck. We were hit with 5" shells. The first one hitting on the front starboard side of the gundeck. The second one hit the ladder going down to the well deck. That day we were carrying some guest Officers who wanted to see what the action looked like up front. The first shell hit the starboard side destroying the 40 mm gun, damaging the conning tower, wounding some of the officers in the conning tower, putting the radio room and steering out of business. While we were drifting out of control we could hear the bullets hitting the winch which sat in the middle of the fantail. Up to that time I was too occupied to feel any fear. Sitting there and praying I was sure as hell scared.... The marines had secured the beachhead and we were able to restart our engines and pull away from the island. We then started to treat our wounded. We were giving morphine to those that were in pain. Our Pharm. Mate was one of the 8 crewmen that was killed.[3]

All three ships were seriously damaged and burning. Their crews commenced fire fighting and soon had the flames under control. The same destroyer fire shot down a Navy observation plane. Later in the day CTG 51.11, Rear Admiral Harry W. Hill, sent the following message to Lieutenant Commander Blanchard and the commanding officers of the three ships:

I AM DEEPLY GRIEVED BY THE DEATH AND INJURIES SUSTAINED IN ACTION BY YOUR FINE MEN. THE GALLANTRY AND CONTEMPTUOUS DISREGARD OF DANGERS DISPLAYED BY ALL LCI(L)S (LCI (L) DIV. 15) ATTACHED TO THIS COMMAND HAS BEEN AN INSPIRATION TO US ALL.[4]

In his comments and recommendations on the operation Captain D. W. Loomis noted, "The use of LCI(L)s for close range support of the leading assault wave, by rocket barrage and 40mm fire, has now become an almost standard procedure in the boat approach phase, since their first employment in atoll landings at RUOTTO-NAMUR and KWAJALEIN."[5]

Night illumination of the targets was deemed desirable as the enemy could not move effectively without cover of darkness. Destroyers normally fired star shells over the area to be illuminated, however they were not able to get into many of the lagoons for fear of running aground. Loomis suggested that it would be a good idea to design a flare rocket which could be fired by the LCI gunboats. Their shallow draft would make it possible for them to get into the shallow waters close to shore and illuminate enemy positions.[6]

Eniwetok Atoll	Date	Gunboats Participating
Camellia	17 Feb.	LCI(G)s 365 (F), 441
Canna	17 Feb.	LCI(G)s 440, 442
Engebi	18 Feb.	LCI(G)s 365 (F) (R), 82, 438, 440, 441, 442
Eniwetok	19 Feb.	LCI(G)s 365(F) (XX) (M), 438 (W), 440, 441 (X), 442 (X)
Parry	22 Feb.	LCI(G)s 365 (F)*, 82, 438, 440* (Z), 441, 442*(Z)

KEY: XX Strafed twice; X Strafed once; W Men wounded; Z Men wounded and killed; M Exploded mine with 40mm fire on 6th shot; R Supported Reconnaissance Party[7]
*Ship hit

The gunboats departed Kwajalein Atoll on 29 February 1944 and headed back to Pearl Harbor for repairs and rest.

On 7 March 1944, a reconnaissance force was sent out from Kwajalein to investigate Wotho, Ujae, and Lae Atolls. The force included *Requisite AM 109, LST 23, LCI(G)s 441* and *345*. On board the LST were Marines from the 1st Battalion, 22nd Regiment. *Callaghan DD 792* was sent along as an escort. Landings were made on all three atolls between 7 and 13 March with slight resistance from a few Japanese on Wotho and Ujae. Once the Japanese realized their plight they committed suicide. The three atolls were explored and the ships went back to base after raising the flag in front of some groups of unfriendly natives.[8]

The Marianas

The war in the Pacific was going well for the Allied forces. Since the initial strike on the American fleet at Pearl Harbor, the American Navy had rebuilt many of the damaged ships and the production of new ships increased with each passing day. McArthur's forces had made significant headway along the coast of New Guinea and Hollandia was in his sights. The Gilbert and Marshall Island groups had fallen to American forces, and the Marianas were considered an important target. From airfields on the islands of Saipan and Tinian, bombers could reach the home islands of Japan. In addition, naval bases on the islands could be developed, giving the Navy an advanced position in the Pacific. The invasion was scheduled for 15 June 1944.

Attacking the Marianas were two task forces organized as TFs 52 and 53. They were both part of Task Force 51 which was the Joint Expeditionary Force under Vice Admiral Richmond K. Turner. The Expeditionary Troops were under the command of Lieutenant General Holland M. Smith USMC. Task Force 52, under Vice Admiral Turner and General Smith, attacked Saipan and Tinian. This assault force consisted of the V Amphibious Corps with the 2nd and 4th Marine Divisions reinforced. Task Force 53, under Rear Admiral Richmond L. Conolly, contained the III Amphibious Corps under Major General Roy S. Geiger. This command held the 3rd Marine Division and the 1st Marine Provisional Brigade. Task Force 53 was to attack Guam.

By the time of the campaign to seize the Marianias, close fire support by LCI gunboats had become a standard practice. However, the reef conditions in these islands posed a particular problem. Because the reefs extended too far offshore, it was feared that it would not be possible for the twenty-four LCI(G)s to get within rocket range on the northern beaches. This would place the landing craft in a particularly perilous position. They would have limited fire support as they approached the beach. Vice Admiral Turner, CTF 51, decided to experiment with other

Lieutenant General Holland M. Smith USMC (left) checks his watch as Vice Admiral Richmond K. Turner looks on. The photograph was taken at H-Hour on D-Day at Saipan, 15 June 1944. NARA 80G 307681.

landing craft. Mortars had been mounted on three LCTs and used successfully at Bougainville in November of 1943. Further tests were made at Pearl Harbor when eight 4.2 inch Army mortars were mounted on the LCT(6) hull. The rate of fire and range of the mortars was thought to be a good supplement to the rocket fire delivered by the LCI(G)s. Rather than heading into the beach, these mortar gunboats could cruise parallel to the beaches and deliver their deadly mortars ahead of the landing craft. The mortars could easily be dismounted from the LCTs and they could then resume regular cargo carrying duties. Rehearsals were held for the invasion of the Marianas, with the LCTs being carried on the decks of LSTs. Heavy weather caused damage and loss of several of the LCTs when their lashings failed and the LCTs went over the side. Short of time, and mindful that the same fate might befall the LCTs on the way to the Marianas, the project was abandoned with the idea that it might be used in some future campaign either with LCTs or LCI(L)s.[9] This proved a valuable experiment, and the mortars eventually found a home on the LCI(L)s. They entered the war at Peleliu in September 1944 as the new LCI(M) gunboat.

Record keepers in the Navy command could not keep up with the rapid conversion of many of the landing craft. It was not unusual for many of the gunboats to keep their initial designation for several months after their conversion. For instance, *LCI(L) 754*, which had been converted to a (G) configuration, was filing her action reports as *LCI(G) 754* at Iwo Jima while she was firing mortars at the enemy on that island. She had already been converted to a mortar gunboat by that time.

Experimenting with various configurations of landing craft used for fire support, Rear Admiral Richmond K. Turner had mortars mounted on six LCTs with the intention of using them for the invasion of Saipan. Operational accidents prevented their use there, but left open for consideration such adaptations in the future. NARA 80G 307495.

Underwater Demolition Team swimmers had been used at Tarawa and Kwajelein, but their technique had not been refined. Pick up of the swimmers was particularly problematic as the small landing craft, usually an LCPR, had to stop to make the pickup. The boat was a difficult target when it was underway, but once it stopped it was an easy target. By the time the Marianas were ready for invasion, new methods had been developed.

> Two men would crouch on a rubber raft that was fastened to the offshore side of the landing craft. One of the men would hold a three-foot length of stiff rope with a loop at each end. The landing craft would approach a swimmer at high speed. Raising his arm, the swimmer would hook his elbow in the loop of the rope held toward him by the man on the raft. This would jerk him alongside the rubber raft, and the second man would boost him aboard.[10]

Task Force 52, under the command of Vice Admiral Turner was involved in the assault on the islands of Saipan and Tinian. Directly under him was the Western Landing Group (TG 52.2) which included the Gunboat Support Group and the Beach Demolition Group. The Gunboat Support Group was designated TU 52.2.3 and was under the command of Commander Michael Malanaphy. It consisted of three LCI Groups: LCI Group Seven under Lieutenant Commander McFadden, contained *LCI(G)*s 77 (GF) *78, 79, 80, 81, 82, 347, 372, 373* (FF), *454, 725* and *726;* LCI Group Nine under Lieutenant Commander Eikel, was comprised of *LCI(G)s 451, 452, 453, 455, 456* (GF), *458, 459, 460, 461, 462,* and *463* and *470*; LCI Group Eight (less Division Fifteen) under Lieutenant Commander Blanchard and consisted of *LCI(G)s 345, 346, 438, 441, 449, 457* (GF).

Saipan

The first island scheduled for conquest was Saipan. Invasion day was set for 15 June 1944. Defending the island were approximately 32,000 Japanese troops, the bulk of which were members of the 31st Army under Lieutenant General Yoshitsugu Saito. Although the Japanese were capable of putting up a strong defense, they were hampered by continued American submarine

LCI(G)s 725 and *726* approach Saipan to fire rockets on 15 June 1944. NARA 80G 253886.

and air attacks on their supply ships. Its western Pacific location placed it well within the extreme limits of Japanese conquest, and they did not realize until late that it would have to be defended. Accordingly, preparations to build up defenses were underway but not complete at the time of the American attack.

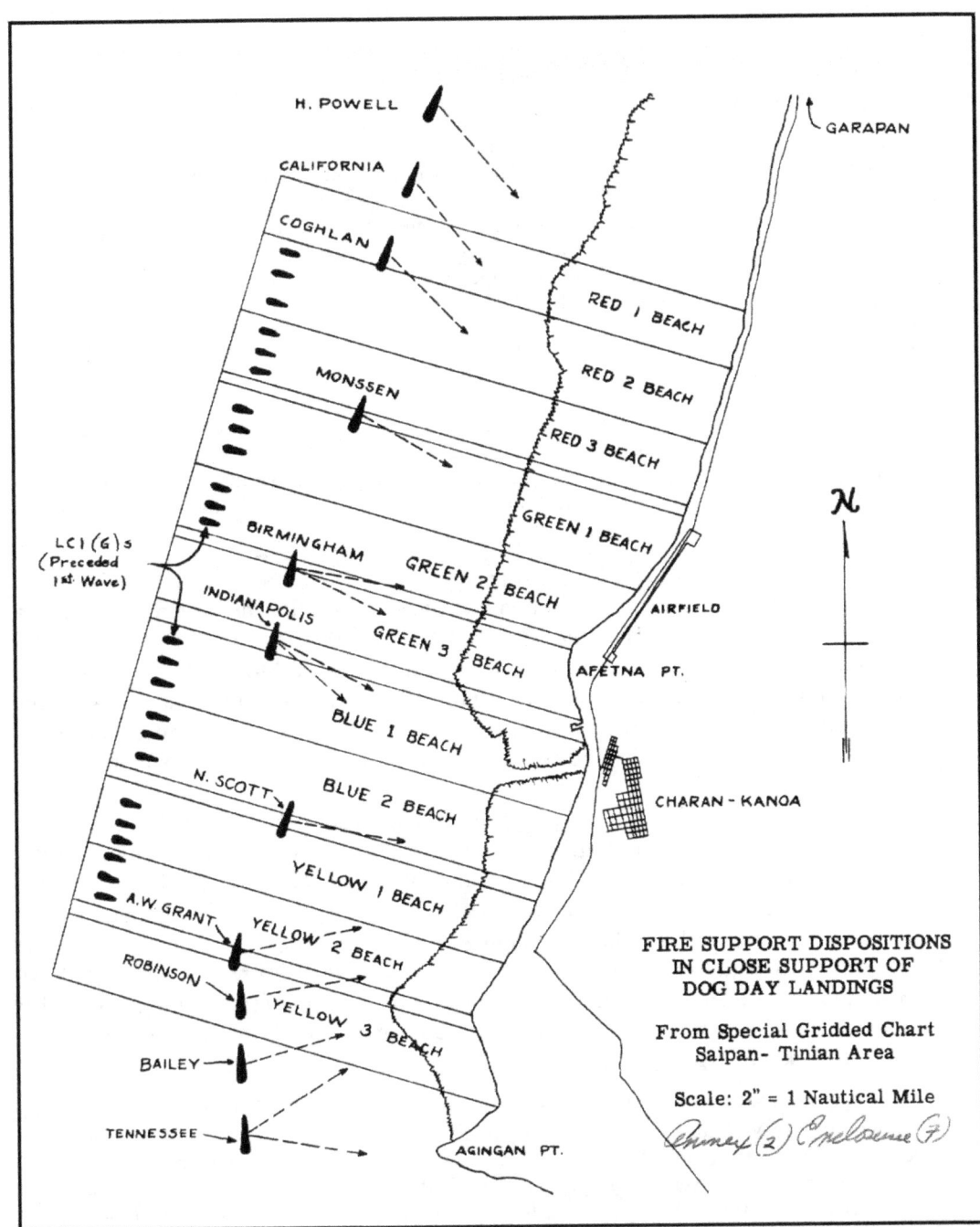

The reefs off the assault beaches at Saipan (shown as a jagged line) prevented the gunboats from getting within rocket range in the northern beach areas and in some of the southern beach areas. Commander Amphibious Forces, Pacific (Commander Joint Expeditionary Force) Serial 00704, *Report of Amphibious Operations for the Capture of the Marianas Islands: Forager Operation, 25 August 1944*, Annex 2 Enclosure (F).

At 0700 on 15 June the LCI gunboats assembled on the line of departure and waited to lead the assault. As they waited, battleships, cruisers, and destroyers bombarded the island with their heavier guns. Heavy strikes on the landing area were made by about 160 carrier based planes prior to the landing, with another seventy-two planes strafing the beaches just as the landing craft touched shore. By 0810 the preliminaries were completed. The gunboats made their attack in typical fashion and then stood by just off shore providing covering fire. However, their fire was not as effective as hoped for. The Commanding General V Amphibious Corps, General Holland Smith, reported:

> LCI(G)'s preceded the boat waves and fired 40mm and rocket barrages onto the beaches. However, the reef off CHARAN-KANOA on all northern beaches and on some southern beaches extended further than the maximum rocket range; this prevented the use of rockets against those beaches. The bombardment enabled our troops to get ashore in effective numbers. But a number of important targets were not destroyed or neutralized. These included enemy mortar and artillery which were able to bear on the beaches from reverse slopes and machine gun and troop positions on the low ground immediately behind the beaches.[11]

LCI(G) 458 reported that the ships in Group Nine, operating off the northern beaches, were hampered in their mission:

> The northern group was held off at least 1800 yards from the beach by an out cropping reef, making rocket fire impossible. The beaches were strongly held by an enemy equipped with light tanks, mortars, machine guns, and artillery. The LCIs were to advance on the beaches just ahead of the first waves of LCTs and by means of their barrage fire hold the enemy down until the initial landings could be made.[12]

Direct Japanese fire on the gunboats was not practical. Any gun battery firing from the shore toward the sea would be quickly spotted and put out of action by the destroyers, cruisers, and battleships. The fire that plagued the gunboats usually came from mortars located on the reverse slopes near shore. These could not be seen and destroyed. Mortar fire came near the gunboats on a number of occasions and, about 0830, *LCI(G) 451* was hit by a mortar round and partially disabled. *LCI(G) 79* reported near mortar misses with shrapnel scattered over her stern. The gunboats completed their mission and withdrew from the immediate area of the assault.

Most of the LCI(G)s converted in 1944 carried rockets in addition to guns. Once they fired their rocket salvo, they depended on 40mm and 20mm fire to suppress the enemy. Unfortunately, this was not always sufficient. An LCI(G) usually mounted a single 40mm gun in the bow and one near the stern. In front of the conning tower were two gun tubs, each holding a 20mm. Two additional tubs were behind the conning tower, also mounting 20mm single guns. This meant that on a direct run to the beach, the LCI(G) could only deliver fire from the single bow-mounted 40mm gun directly ahead and the two 20mm guns in front of the conning tower. They were limited to 40 degrees from dead ahead. Lieutenant (jg) Francis W. Cole Jr., Commanding Officer of *LCI(G) 458* at Saipan, reported:

> In supporting troop landings this ship has never been able to bring more than one or two forty MM guns and no twenty MM guns to bear on the particular sector of beach it is supposed to cover. This is because the bow forty is the only gun which can shoot dead ahead. By turning broadside we can bring two forties and two twenties to bear out of our battery of three forties and four twenties, but are then a large target for the enemy. This deficiency was particularly felt the morning of 18 June when we wanted to head the ship directly for specific targets and bring as many guns to bear as possible.
>
> It is therefore recommended that the forecastle superstructure with its winch be removed and that the bow forty be mounted on the main deck, and that the ramps be removed and the two bow twenties be mounted on the forward ends of the ramp platforms.[13]

The problem noted for the direct fire of the gunboats was remedied later with the introduction of the LCS(L) variant. The LCS(L)s carried a twin 40mm gun just forward of the conn and a bow gun that might be either a 3"/50, a single 40mm, or a twin 40mm gun. Thus the LCS(L) could deliver fire from three or four barrels directly ahead of the ship.

On 18 June, a few days after the landings, enemy barges were sighted off the town of Garapan as they made an attempt to land troops behind the Americans. The LCI(G)s were sent to destroy them. Working in concert, *LCI(G)s 79, 81, 371, 451, 452, 458,* and *460* attacked them. They reported sinking thirteen of the forty-foot-long barges after a gun battle with several.[14] Mortar fire from shore bracketed some of the ships, but none were hit. However, a shell from a 5 inch gun hit *LCI(G) 371*, jamming her rudder. Excellent ship handling by her CO, Lieutenant E. W. Gooding, and covering fire from *LCI(G) 460*, allowed her escape and survival. A week later, at 0220 on 26 June, *LCI(G) 438* sighted two enemy barges near Mutcho Point on Saipan and illuminated them with her signal searchlight. The barges fired on them with 37mm guns and hit the gunboat causing significant damage. At 0230, *LCI(G) 456* sank a barge in the same area, receiving some minor damage from its return fire. Lieutenant Commander T. Blanchard, Commander of LCI(L) Group Eight, led several other gunboats to the area, but no further action occurred.[15]

Enemy troops were still in the area. At 0515 on 4 July, the OD on board *LCI(G) 345* spotted a small boat moving away from Saipan toward Tinian. As the gunboat approached, its occupants were seen to be dropping objects in the water and then hiding in the bottom of the boat to avoid being seen. With all guns trained on the boat, the *345* came alongside and captured four Japanese soldiers who were then taken into custody for interrogation. They had been dropping their rifles, equipment, and grenades over the side before they were captured.

Tinian

With the capture of Saipan completed, it was time to move on to Tinian. The island of Tinian is only ten miles long and about five miles wide. It lies just to the south of Saipan and is separated from that island by a channel three miles wide. The valuable assets of the island were its relatively flat terrain and four operational airfields. Japanese forces on the island numbered about 9,000, about half of which were Army and the other half Navy. The most senior Japanese officer on Tinian was Vice Admiral Kakuji Kakuta, but the Army's operational command was under Colonel Kiyochi Ogata, Commanding Officer of the 50th Infantry Regiment, 29th Army Division. Naval forces were under the direct command of Captain Goichi Oya.

The conquest of Saipan just to the north made Tinian a less important target. However, it still had to be taken. Propaganda leaflets calling on the Japanese to surrender failed to do the trick and American forces prepared to take the island. Isolated from any support or supplies, the Japanese on Tinian could only wait for the attack. With little to hurry about, the American forces were able to take a deliberate approach to the annihilation of the Japanese defenders. Coordinated efforts between the Navy and the Army Air Force slowly weakened the Japanese, and by the time the day of the assault arrived, Tinian's infrastructure had been severely damaged. Air attacks were conducted by planes flying off a fast carrier task group, as well as aircraft from five CVEs and land-based planes from fields on Saipan. The relatively small size of the island, coupled with the large number of aircraft, ensured that very few targets were missed in the aerial assault.

One factor not seen in many landings was the use of shore-based artillery. The closeness of Saipan made it possible to use Army artillery fire from there as part of the pre-landing bombardment. Ninety-six 105mm, twenty-six 155mm howitzers, and twenty-four 155mm guns,

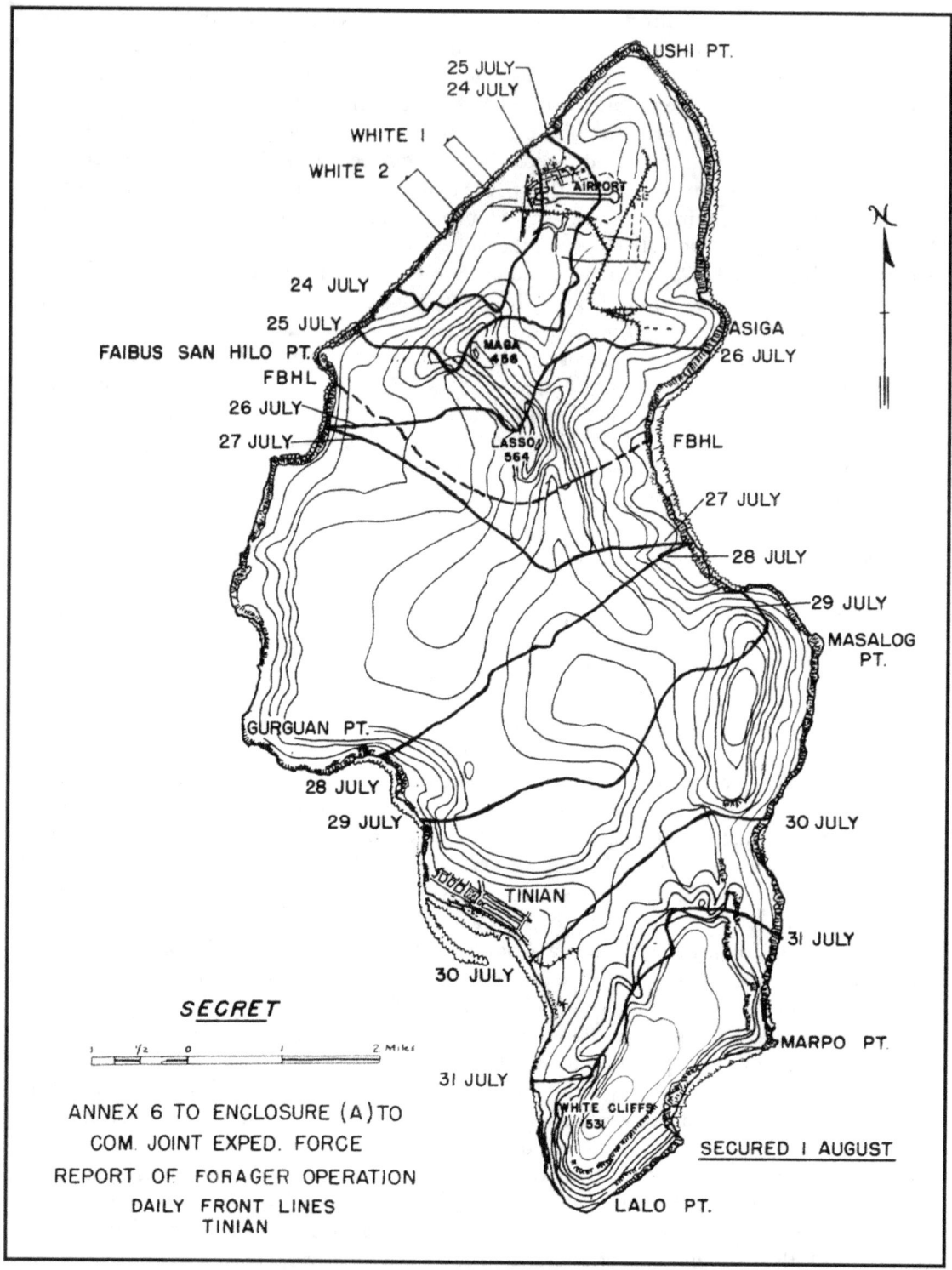

The assault on Tinian took place on 24 July 1944, with twelve LCI gunboats leading the assault on White Beaches 1 and 2. Commander Amphibious Forces, Pacific Fleet (Commander Fifth Amphibious Force, Commander Task Force 51) *Report on Amphibious Operations for the Capture of the Marianas Islands (Forager Operation)*, 25 August 1944, Annex 6 Enclosure (A).

located on the south coast of Saipan participated. D-day was set for 24 July 1944. The 2nd and 4th Marine Divisions, totaling 35,000 men, were scheduled to land. The 27th Army Infantry Division was held in reserve on Saipan.

Disputes arose over which of the beaches at Tinian to use for landing, and the Marine's V Amphibious Corps Reconnaissance Battalion was sent ashore at night in rubber boats to survey the area. Accompanied by UDT swimmers, they identified that the White Beaches were the best landing areas. The mission investigated the Yellow Beaches and White Beach 1 on the night of 10-11 July, and White Beach 2 on the night of 11-12 July.

The plan for using the gunboats to support the landings was outlined in CTF 52's action report for the assault on Tinian. It indicated:

> The LCI(G) support plan generally prescribed the following: 6 LCI(G)'s in WHITE beach ONE boat lane and nine in WHITE beach TWO boat lane, preceded leading LCT wave toward beach and delivered 20 MM and 40 MM and barrage rocket fire on the beaches in close support of the landing. Six LCI(G)'s on the northern flank of WHITE beach ONE boat lane and nine on the southern flank of WHITE beach TWO boat lane, left line of departure at HOW Hour and passed between boat lanes and flanking battleships delivering 20 and 40 MM and rocket fire on flanks of landing beaches at a point 1000 yards from extremities of the beach areas. Flanking LCI(G)'s turned away from landing area, paralleling shoreline on completion of first barrage rocket salvos, reloaded rocket racks and again turned toward shore to deliver second salvos. They continued this until areas were covered to USHI and FAIBUS POINTS respectively. LCI's in the boat lanes turned toward the nearest flanks when the LCT's had passed, and followed the flanking LCI's with fire on the flanks north and south of the landing area.[16]

Gunboats of TU 52.6.7 arrived off the beaches of Tinian at 0625 on 24 July. A strong wind and current from the northeast continually blew them off station, and they frequently had to adjust to keep position. At 0721 they headed toward the beaches firing their 40mm guns, but many of the possible targets ashore were obscured by smoke from the fires started by shelling from the larger ships. Radar equipped *LCI(G) 77* was able to fire her rockets at the appropriate time. Other ships in the group noted her fire and launched their rockets immediately after. Group Nine ships encountered similar problems with obscured targets but still managed to get their rocket salvos off, striking the beach areas. Advancing to within 500 yards of the beach, the gunboats fired on shore targets and then stood by as the LVTs passed through their lines and landed the Marines.

The following morning, at 0635, *LCI(G) 453* received a radio message from CTF 52 to take under fire some specific targets just to the south of the landing beaches. The targets appeared to be several small buildings, and they were hit with a dozen rockets, 508 rounds of 40mm and 1,160 rounds of 20mm fire. Apparently this was enough to support the Marines ashore and the gunboat departed the area.[17] The seven ships of Group Eight followed a similar pattern. When it was over, they reported having launched a total of 1,582 rockets on White Beach 2, along with 8,860 rounds of 40mm and 20,995 rounds of 20mm ammunition.

For the next several days, the gunboats worked in conjunction with the Marines ashore, providing call-fire where needed and firing on Japanese positions. At the end of July and into the first few days of August, the ships lay a few hundred yards off shore. Loudspeakers were used to encourage the Japanese to surrender. Many did, but some committed suicide, and a few were taken prisoner. Group Eight reported that "Marine Headquarters announced that *LCI(G) 457* with Public Address System aboard had talked approximately twenty five hundred (2500) Japanese civilians and soldiers out of the caves to surrender. Only twenty five or thirty personnel remained in caves."[18]

The conquest of the Marianas had taken its toll on American forces, however, for the Japanese, it was a disaster. The United States Strategic Bombing Survey later reported:

The Japanese, for their part, were now faced with a vastly changed strategic situation with American forces strongly emplaced on their inner defense line in a position which gravely threatened their ability to continue hostilities.... Almost unanimously, informed Japanese considered Saipan as the decisive battle of the war and its loss as ending all hope for a Japanese victory.[19]

Guam

The last island conquest in the Marianas was Guam. Originally scheduled for 18 June, the invasion was put off by the Battle of the Philippine Sea, 19 to 20 June, which diverted some of the American naval forces from the Marianas. In addition, the battle for Saipan proved to be more difficult than originally envisioned, and it was determined to increase the size of the landing force on Guam. The Southern Attack Force TF 53, under Rear Admiral Richard Conolly, would land the III Amphibious Corps under Major General Roy S. Geiger. This Corps consisted of the 3rd Marine Division commanded by Major General Alan Turnage and the 1st Provisional Brigade commanded by Brigadier General Lemuel C. Shepherd, Jr. along with the Army's 77th Division under Major General Andrew D. Bruce. This placed a total of 19,000 soldiers and 37,000 Marines on Guam. Opposing them on Guam was the 29th Infantry Division under Lieutenant General Takeshi Takashina. In addition, the 6th Expeditionary Force under Major General Kiyoshi Shigemitsu had 5,100 men. Additional manpower was available, including a 3,000 man naval guard and other miscellaneous units. The total available Japanese fighting force numbered 19,000.

The postponement of the attack on Guam gave additional time for Task Force 53 to choose its targets carefully and deliberately. Using a combination of air and ship attacks, which resulted in the destruction of most of the Japanese artillery on the island, the Task Force significantly weakened Japanese defensive abilities.

The first gunboat casualty connected with the assault on Guam came on 17 June 1944 as *LCI(G) 468* was en route from Kwajalein to Guam as part of Task Group 53.16. Included in the task group were nine LCI(G)s, fifteen LSTs, the landing craft repair ship *ARL 3,* and the net layers *Holly AN 19* and *Aloe AN 6.*

About 1750, as the ships were about 180 miles east of Guam, they came under attack by several Japanese aircraft. The action report of *LCI(G) 468* indicates:

> When the first plane was sighted condition one was set and all guns were ready to fire when the first plane started its run a few seconds later. The first plane came in very low on the beam of the ARL3 which was approximately 800 yards ahead of the LCI(G) 468. This plane dropped a torpedo approximately 700 yards from the ARL3 and turned away going ahead of the formation. At this time another plane appeared from cloud near the point from which the first plane came. Fire was stopped and switched to the second as soon as the second was judged to be in range. At this time tracers were observed coming very near the ship and a few seconds later the ship was hit by fire either from another ship in the formation or from the machine guns of the attacking plane. One wounded officer and man at the after 20 MM guns and one wounded officer on the conning station are believed to have been hit by this fire. It was planned to turn sharply toward the attacking plane to present a smaller target but the casualty on the conning station (bridge) prevented this plan from being carried out. The second plane came within an estimated 150 yards of the LCI(G) 468 and released its torpedo which struck the bow of the ship.... Approximately the forward third of the ship was destroyed.... There was no fire or explosion of ammunition from the torpedo hit and no excessive flooding occurred, with the result that the ship might have remained afloat indefinitely except for threat of further enemy attack and the distance to a friendly base.[20]

Two officers and thirteen men were killed in the attack. In addition the Commanding Officer, Lieutenant (jg) George D. Mayo, and two crewmen were wounded. With a third of the ship

4. The Central Pacific Campaigns

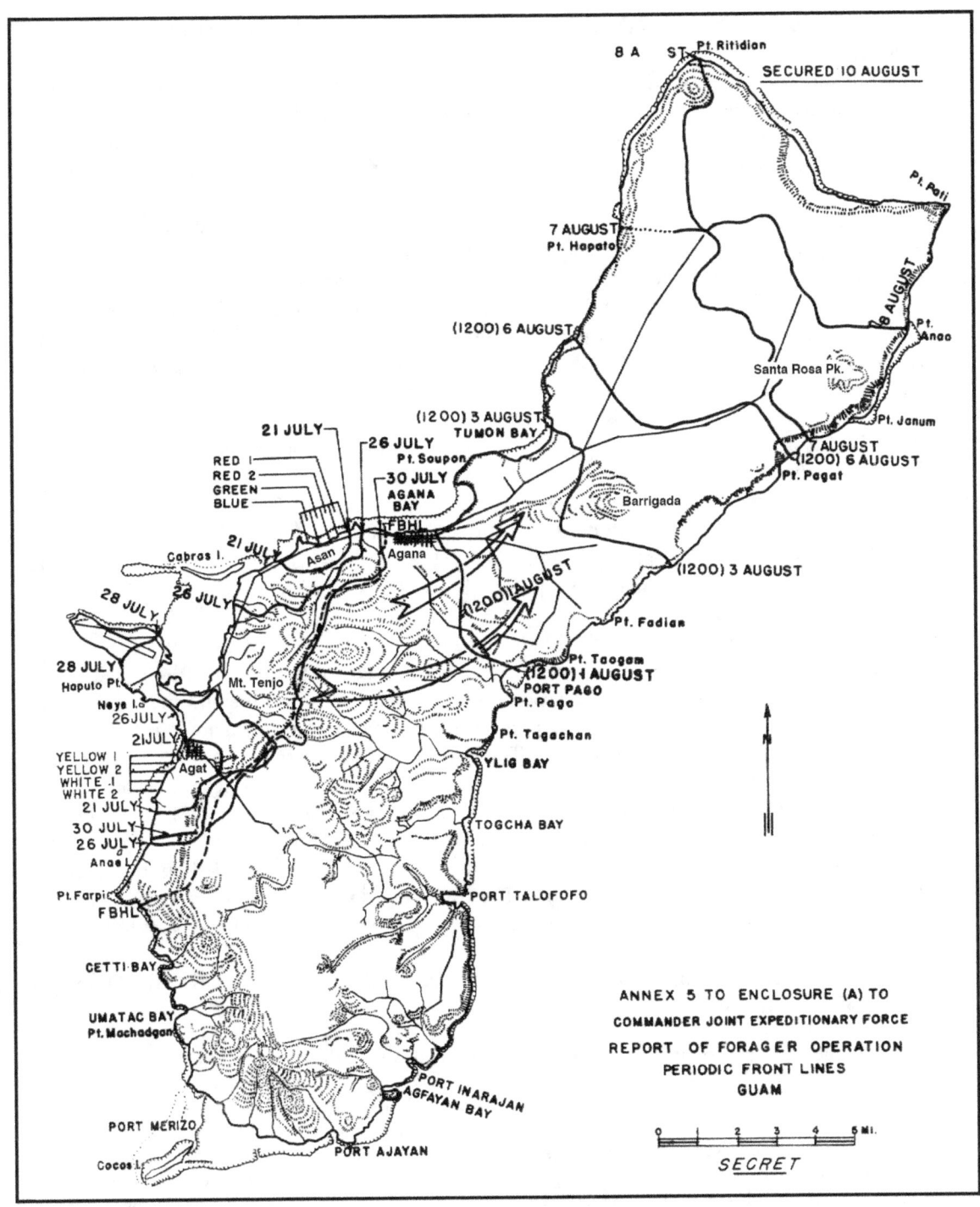

Guam was the last island in the Marianas taken as part of Operation Forager. Originally scheduled for assault on 18 June 1944, the invasion was delayed until 21 July 1944 by the Battle of the Philippine Sea, which took place from 19 to 20 June 1944. Commander Amphibious Forces, Pacific Fleet (Commander Fifth Amphibious Force, Commander Task Force 51) *Report on Amphibious Operations for the Capture of the Marianas Islands (Forager Operation),* 25 August 1944, Annex 5 Enclosure (A).

gone and no safe port nearby, the ship was ordered sunk by gunfire from *Stembel DD 644* the following day.

Prior to the landings, UDTs 3, 4, and 6 conducted underwater reconnaissance of the proposed landing beaches on Guam. They arrived at Guam on board *Dickerson APD 21*, *Kane APD 18*, and *Clemson APD 32* respectively, with UDT 3 arriving on 14 July and teams 4 and 6 arriving on 17 July. Three days were allotted for reconnaissance with four more for demolition of beach obstacles.

Underwater obstacles encountered by the UDT consisted of piles of coral contained in wire mesh and spaced about five feet apart. Once identified, they had to be blasted apart to prevent their interfering with landing craft. Some of this work had to be done at night, but foul weather and heavy rain hampered the nighttime missions during the pre-invasion period. The UDTs used a combination of real and diversionary reconnaissance missions to confuse the enemy. In the case of a diversion, the LCPRs ran in close to shore as if to drop off swimmers, but did not. In all cases, the fire from enemy shore positions was heavy, but the combination of gunboats, destroyers, and cruisers soon put an end to it.

LCI(G)s 469, 471, 472, and 473 were tasked to provide support of the UDTs. Combining forces with the four gunboats were the destroyers *Dewey DD 349* and *MacDonough DD 351* which were replaced part way through the coverage by *Sigsbee DD 502* and *Schroeder DD 501*. The combination of LCI(G)s with destroyers proved so effective in providing covering fire for UDT 3 that additional gunboats were requested for the other teams. Within twenty-four hours of making the request, Lieutenant Commander Blanchard arrived with LCI(G)s 345, 346, 348, 438, 441, 449, 455, and 457.

Problems in working around the islands frequently occurred, as many of the waters were uncharted. At 2000 on 17 July, LCI(G) 348 was covering the operations of UDT 3 off Red Beach 2 when she grounded on a reef. She was soon under mortar and machine gun fire from shore. LCI(G) 471 unsuccessfully attempted to pull her off twice to no avail. Enemy gunfire continued to threaten the two gunboats, and the Task Unit Commander (CO of *Sigsbee*) ordered the crew and officers, along with classified materials, off the ship and to a safer haven on *Sigsbee*. *Sigsbee* and *Schroeder* patrolled nearby to keep away any Japanese attempts to board the ship. Within hours, the cruisers *Wichita CA 45*, *St. Louis CL 49*, and *Minneapolis CA 36* arrived, and their combined fire put an end to any Japanese attempts to shell the stranded gunboat. Under their cover the crew and officers returned. The following day, the tug *Apache ATF 67* arrived from Saipan and pulled the gunboat clear. She was towed back to Saipan for repairs to her bent propeller.[21]

In his report on the operations of UDT 3 at Guam, Lieutenant T. C. Crist, the Officer in Charge of UDT 3, noted:

> One of the most important factors contributing to the success of the Demolition Operation was the fire support furnished, particularly by the LCI(G)'s. They kept the beach covered with such a volume of 40 and 20 MM fire at close range that it seemed almost impossible for the enemy to make extensive attempts to stop the operation. Their fire was accurate (it was often necessary to fire directly over the heads of Demolition personnel working the reef). It is believed that our work would not have been possible without heavy casualties had it not been for this close-in fire support. It is recommended that the LCIs be included in all future pre-assault demolition operations. One difficulty encountered was the problem of keeping the LCIs in proper position and away from foul water during night operations. It is possible that Radar on the LCIs would solve this problem if such installation is practical.
>
> The intensity and accuracy of fire cover during the two days prior to W-day were amazing, considering the fact that while demolition personnel were working within 50 yards of the beach, the beach itself was covered with fire from LCIs, Destroyers, Cruisers, and also from bombing and strafing planes.[22]

On 20 July the area around Agat Bay was covered by *LCI(G)s 437, 442, 474,* and *475.* The work of the UDTs had been finished and there were concerns that the Japanese might attempt to mine or install obstructions to the already cleared areas. The gunboats patrolled off the beach between Alutom Island and Pelagi Rock. Star shells from the cruiser *Honolulu CL 48* illuminated the beaches and gave the gunboats the opportunity to fire on various targets of opportunity.

The assignment for Blanchard's ships at Guam had been the protection of the UDTs. With their task completed, they left Guam and headed back to Saipan for reassignment on 20 July. Other gunboats would cover the invasion.

Numerous obstacles had to be removed by the UDTs prior to the assault on Guam. This map shows the underwater obstacles removed at Asan Beach, Guam, by UDT 3. Officer in Charge Underwater Demolition Team #3 Serial 0022, *Underwater Demolition Team #3—Operation Report*, 18 August 1944. Enclosure (A).

On 21 July the invasion began. Two hours of bombardment by the larger ships was followed by the assault of the LCI gunboats. The area for the landings was at the Red, Green, and Blue beaches near Asan on the western coast of Guam, and the Yellow and White Beaches near Agat which lay six miles to the south. The eighteen LCI(G)s had recently been converted on the West Coast and their armament now included forty-two CIT Type 8 rocket launchers giving each ship the capacity to launch 504 rockets in each salvo. Enough rockets for two salvos were carried by each ship. The northern and southern landing beaches each had nine LCI(G)s to provide close support. The northern beaches off Asan were supported by *LCI(G)s 348, 464, 465, 466, 467, 469, 471, 472* and *473* under Lieutenant Commander William R. McCaleb.

The southern beaches at Agat were supported by LCI(G) Division Fifteen, Group Nine ships under Lieutenant L. Howard Rabenstein, which included *LCI(G)s 365(F), 366, 437, 439, 440, 442, 450, 474* and *475.* The landing assault of the gunboats began shortly after 0801 as they left the line of departure. A total of 4,536 rockets were launched against the beaches, giving the Marines excellent cover as they landed. The number of American Marine lives saved by such a barrage can only be guessed, but it had to be significant.

Lieutenant John F. Auge, CO of *LCI(G) 469* noted:

> By first firing the rockets in launchers set at 30° and then those in launchers set at 45° a barrage was placed upon a strip of beach approximately 250 to 350 yards deep through which it is doubtful if any enemy resistance could exist. The 40MM guns were particularly effective in knocking out visible enemy machine gun emplacements, etc. and in strafing beach together with the 20MM guns.[23]

Continued enemy resistance near the shore led to increased bombardment by the LCI gunboats. Mortar fire was a particular problem, one that was hard to combat as the mortars were fired from the reverse sides of hills. Most of it seemed to be aimed at the LVT(A)s which were near the beaches, with four of them suffering direct hits. Ninety minutes after the landings at Agat, *LCI(G) 365* was hit by a 75mm shell, killing six of her men and wounding eighteen. Return fire from the area around Pelagi Rock and Bangi Point was directed at the gunboats. One of the guns was located in a cave north of the beach, and another was thought to be on top of the bluff. *LCI(G) 437* reported some near misses from what appeared to be three inch shells which showered her with water and shrapnel. Fire was directed at the area near Pelagi Rock and the nearby town of Agat until the counter-fire ceased.

Word was received that the commander of TU 54.4.6, Lieutenant L. Howard Rabenstein, had been injured in the attack on *LCI(G) 365* and Lieutenant Schenck from *LCI(G) 439* assumed command of the task unit. *LCI(G)s 439, 440, 442, 450, 474,* and *475* withdrew from the boat lanes at 0850 and strafed the beaches between Alutom Island and Bangi Point with 40mm and 20mm guns. Bombardment of the area continued until 0944 when the gunboats withdrew from the area to regroup.

For several days after the landings, continued call-fire missions and nighttime attacks on the enemy's positions were completed. *LCI(G)s 465, 466,* and *467* fired salvos of rockets onto Anigua Beach and strafed the area in support of Marine positions in the area. Apparently their work was quite effective, as in the afternoon of 27 July the ships received the following message which had been sent from the Headquarters of the Third Marine Division to CTG 53.1:

> DURING THE NIGHTS OF 25 AND 26 JULY LCI GUN BOAT FIRING INTO OUR LEFT FRONT PRODUCED SECURITY FOR OUR DIVISION LEFT FLANK BY DENYING THE AGANA-ASAN ROAD TO THE ENEMY X LT HAYDEN LIAISON OFFICER ON GUNBOATS REPORTS ROCKETS ST 5 LARGE FIRES AND CAUSED TWO EXPOSIONS IN TARGET AREA 605 WX AND 585 C X THIS DESTRUCTION OF ENEMY SUPPLIES COMBINED WITH CLOSE SUPPORT OF 3RD BATTALION HAS PROVED TO BE OF GREAT ASSISTANCE IN OUR ASSAULT X PLEASE PASS THANKS TO RESPONSIBLE NAVAL SUPPORT.[24]

Although the landings had been completed, the gunboats still found themselves in peril. *LCI(G) 465*, lying to off Adalup Point, suffered a close miss when a fragmentation bomb exploded twenty yards off her starboard quarter, wounding three of her men and puncturing her hull in twelve places. Apparently the bomb came from a TBF Avenger. A group of these had been bombing the ridge east of Adelup Point. After dropping their bombs on the enemy positions, they circled seaward for another run. It was thought that this bomb had become stuck and fell off as the plane was overhead near the ship.

On 24 July, *LCI(G)s 366, 439, 440, 442, 450, 474,* and *475* headed into the south side of Orote and fired on enemy positions. Counter-fire from shore resulted in two of the ships, *366* and *439*, sustaining heavy damage and a number of casualties. Both were hit by 75mm gunfire. Two days later, *LCI(G) 437* was cruising in the same area and came under fire but escaped without damage.

On 28 July *LCI(G) 469* was cruising near Adelup Point to pick up a man from *LCI(G) 466* when she came under shore fire at 1805. Her lookouts first noticed shells falling in the water near some beached LSTs, and within a few minutes she was bracketed by enemy artillery shells. Shrapnel hit her deck but no one was injured. *LCI(G)s 466, 469, 471, 472,* and *473* formed a line and approached Agana Town, opening fire with 20mm and 40mm guns. Fortunately a Marine liaison officer was aboard *LCI(G) 473* and helped to coordinate the fire which suppressed the attack. As soon as the gunboats ceased firing, the shore fire returned. CTG 53.16 ordered the ships to head seaward to escape the threat as it seemed too difficult to pinpoint the source.[25] Additional support was requested by the Marines ashore. On 30 July *LCI(G) 437* took on board a Marine Corps fire support team from the V Phib Corps Artillery. The fire support team found targets on shore in Apra Harbor, and the ship fired on them with 40mm fire from a distance of 650 yards. Two machine gun nests had been discovered there and were slowing the Marine's advance. Difficulties in communication with the shore observers precluded the use of rockets since the Marines location was not obvious.

Although assaults on the beach were usually conducted with landing boats carrying Marines or Army troops, there were often variations to the pattern. On 31 July five amphibious tanks moored alongside *LCI(G) 437* and requested assistance. They were about to attempt an over-the-reef landing near the cliffs in Apra Harbor. Covering fire from the gunboats was requested and agreed upon. At 1000 the tanks headed for shore near the base of the cliff as the gunboats fired into suspected enemy positions with 40mm fire. The gunboats hit beach targets with four salvos of five rockets each. Once the tanks reached the reef, the gunboats ceased firing and stood by in case they were needed. The tanks landed safely and the gunboats retired from the area at 1033.

The possibility of a Japanese counter-attack was relayed to the fleet by Marine intelligence. They had been alerted by natives of Guam and requested that an area be attacked by the gunboats. On 3 August *LCI(G)*s *471, 472,* and *473* strafed the area on the eastern side of Tumon Bay. After their strafing attack, the gunboats sent five hundred rockets over the cliffs into the suspect area and then stayed in the area until the next day in case they were needed. With the campaign for Guam under control, not all of the gunboats were needed. On 4 August *LCI(G)*s *464, 465, 467,* and *472* left Guam and on 12 July *LCI(G)*s *437* and *442* were detached and headed for Pearl Harbor.

Although the island had been captured, there were still pockets of Japanese ready to fight. On 11 August *LCI(G)*s *466* and *469* were on patrol off the Ritidian Point-Pat Point area. On shore a Marine patrol had been ambushed and cut off from their unit. After being signaled by semaphore, the *466* sent a dinghy ashore to evacuate three casualties. One of the Marines had already died and the ship's boat was too small to get through the heavy surf. A Japanese flat-bottomed collapsible boat was spotted nearby on the beach and pressed into service. Both wounded Marines were removed and the ship sent food and water to the remainder of the Marine patrol. The wounded Marines were transferred to *Solace AH 5.*

The following day saw a patrol from the 22nd Marine Pac Howitzer Division ambushed and in need of assistance in the same area. The commanding officer of the patrol had been killed and the remaining men scattered. Two of the patrol were evacuated by *LCI(G) 469.*

From mid–August until the end of the month, the gunboats patrolled the area around Ritidian Point and the surrounding area in northern Guam. Here and there enemy resistance was encountered, with the ships strafing enemy locations. On 16 August *LCI(G)*s *466* and *474* went after some Japanese snipers operating between LaFac and Anao points. It is not clear what the Japanese hoped to accomplish by using rifle fire against the gunboats, but they were out-ranged and outgunned when they did. Both gunboats unleashed 40mm and 20mm fire and some rockets in the areas from which the fire emanated and it was silenced. It was not clear if the enemy had been killed or had taken cover in some of the many caves in the area. Occasionally small numbers of Japanese would appear on the beach and surrender.

LCI(G) 469 took a Marine liaison officer on board for a call-fire mission. En route to the area she grounded on Luminao Reef as she was returning to Apra Harbor. One man went over the side, possibly to inspect the situation and did not surface. His body was recovered the next afternoon. Attempts to get the gunboat off the reef were unsuccessful until she was pulled off by a tug on 3 September. Her commanding officer was found to be at fault and was relieved of command.

Rescue of wounded men was a task occasionally assigned to the gunboats. Their combination of fire power and shallow draft made it possible to do the pickup and evacuation. At 0600 on 13 September *LCI(G) 466* made contact with Marines ashore who had a sick man to evacuate. The gunboat sent its small boat ashore with some food for the Marines. The boat was in peril as a number of Japanese soldiers appeared on top of a nearby ridge. Concerned that the Japanese might fire on their boat as it made its way back, the gunboat unleashed a torrent of 40mm and 20mm gunfire on the Japanese with the Marines acting as spotters. By 0730 the

Japanese had either been killed or driven away, and the boat made its way back to the *466* carrying the sick Marine.

At about 1630 lookouts on the gunboat spotted smoke ashore, possibly from a cooking fire. After checking to see if there were Marines in the area and receiving a negative reply, the gunboat sent a rocket barrage into the area followed by 40mm and 20mm gunfire with indeterminate results. It didn't matter much as the purpose of the fire was simply to deliver harassing fire on the enemy.[26] Such fire was designed to deny the enemy rest and to hopefully cause casualties.

By September most of the Japanese had been driven to the northeast coast of Guam. The month was spent attempting to get them to surrender. Japanese language interpreters, along with captured Japanese, were put on some of the gunboats and loudspeakers were installed on them to entice stragglers. They were guaranteed safety if they would show themselves on the beach and allow themselves to be picked up. Many took advantage of the offer but others refused.

The loudspeaker set up on the gunboat was a temporary installation. It had a limited range depending on wind direction and the terrain. With favorable wind and terrain it might be heard at a range of 500 yards. The jungle could absorb the sound and cut the range in half, so the only Japanese able to hear the surrender call were those relatively near the beaches.

On Thursday, 7 September, about 1,300 leaflets printed in Japanese were dropped in the area known to hold Japanese stragglers. Its English translation stated:

1. On Guam all organized Japanese resistance has ceased. American troops control the entire island. The Japanese Army and Navy troops fought gallantly, but now it is futile to continue hostilities.
2. American troops do not want to kill unarmed soldiers and Navy personnel, civilians, women and children. Many Jap Officers, enlisted men and civilians have already surrendered. They are living in a nice camp. They have plenty of food, water and tobacco. They have received new clothing. They have had the same medical treatment as American troops.
3. They have said you, also, would like to surrender. Therefore we have a plan which gives you an opportunity to surrender. It is as follows:
   (1) Today and tomorrow American forces have been ordered not to fire on any Japanese in the coastal area between Lafac Point and Pago Point. We guarantee you will not be fired on by patrols, by planes, or by gun boats.
   (2) Tomorrow a gun boat will move along the shore between Lafac Point and Pago Point to pick you up from the beaches. This ship will have a banner on saying "SURRENDER."
   (3) When you see this ship, you are to walk out from the beaches into the water and wait to be picked up. You will not carry any sort of weapon on you and must have your hands raised above your head.
   (4) If you do not take this opportunity tomorrow of joining comrades who have surrendered, we shall blast you from the land, sea, and air till we have killed all of you.[27]

From 8 to 20 September, *LCI(G) 471* was designated as the "surrender ship" and cruised from Ritidian Point to Fadian Point. After additional warnings many Japanese still did not surrender. They were fired on and killed by 20mm and 40mm fire after refusing the offer. *LCI(G) 471* captured approximately one hundred Japanese during this period. Of the group, three were found to be Korean women. They had probably been forced into service by the Japanese as "comfort women." There were also a couple of other women and a few children. Not all of the remainder were Army soldiers; some were also laborers. By the end of September there were still stragglers from the Japanese forces being encountered, but the need for the gunboats had ended.[28] They were reassigned in small groups and sent to other areas where their services would be needed.

Instrumental in the surrender process were captured Japanese who agreed to act as interpreters and to talk to their compatriots about surrender. Junzo Niitsuma, a 2nd Class Petty

Officer from the Japanese Navy, was notable among them. Niitsuma had been treated well by his American captors on board *LCI(G) 471* and was considered to be a "trustee." On numerous occasions he went ashore to meet with individuals or small groups to negotiate their surrender. In time, one or two other Japanese "trustees" accompanied him. Their missions were usually successful, owing in large part to the condition of the Japanese ashore. Many of those surrendering had been without sufficient food or medical care for some time and were in poor physical condition. In one case, a group of Japanese was seriously considering surrender due to their lack of food. However, the day prior to their surrender they discovered a cache of food left behind by American Marines. Bolstered by the food supply, they decided to remain ashore and fight. Others refused to surrender because they were convinced they would be killed.

As the gunboats patrolled the inshore areas seeking the surrender of Japanese, they were wary of not giving the appearance of deception. On the other hand, they had to have credibility. Japanese stragglers were given at least five opportunities to surrender with the admonition that they would be killed if they did not. In several cases it was necessary to fire on Japanese who obviously would not surrender.

Getting the surrendering Japanese from shore to the gunboats was frequently a difficult task. The gunboats could only come to the edge of the reef which might lay a couple of hundred yards from the beach. Their method would be to drop their stern anchor farther out and then slowly approach the edge of the reef. Once there, a small boat would be lowered and taken across the reef to shore. Strong currents and breaking surf frequently complicated the transport and, on many occasions, Americans had to swim ashore with a line and life preservers to drag the Japanese back across the reefs. The weakened condition of many of the Japanese made it necessary for them to be assisted in most cases. The process was detailed in the Marines' action report:

> The Northeast coast of Guam is almost entirely surrounded by coral reef. Much of the terrain opposite the beach is sheer cliff, numerous caves and precipitous ridges characterize the beach area. Because of the character of the terrain, evacuation of Japanese was difficult and hazardous.
>
> The evacuation was accomplished by putting into the water a two-man dinghy, which then went to the edge of the reef. The sailor in the dinghy would then throw a reef line to the Japanese on the reef and the Japanese would be pulled out to the dinghy. This system worked in six instances. In four other instances (including the 3 Jap women) it was necessary for a swimmer to swim in across the reef with a line and life jacket, then swim back across the reef with the prisoner. Three prisoners were evacuated in this manner by Lt. (jg) Charles E. Crandall, USNR and the fourth by PFC John R. Brice, C Company, 1st Battalion, 3d Mar. Interrogation of the prisoners and location of their surrender indicated that the following concentration of Japanese remained along the northeast coast of Guam:
> (1) Five officers and 200 men in vicinity of target square 548 Love.
> (2) One officer and forty men in 648 Queen.
> (3) Forty disorganized laborers in the vicinity of 853 Love.[29]

Not all went well for the Japanese trustees as they worked to obtain the surrender of their countrymen. They were working for the Americans and, as such, were considered traitors. On 19 September the trustees returned to the *471* at 0820. They "reported they were chased by an officer who threatened to cut their heads off with his sword."[30] By the end of September, *LCI(G) 471* had obtained the surrender of about one hundred Japanese.

The gunboats had performed excellently at Guam. Lieutenant W. G. Carbury, commanding officer of UDT Four, later wrote:

> The one big lesson learned from the near perfect Guam U. D. T. operation was the very successful application of LCI(G) fire support. It was strongly recommended by the participating Teams 3 and 4, that this coverage be employed where at all possible. The LCI(G)'s 40 mm. guns can effectively spray the beach preceding the teams going in and then stand ready to fire over or flank the personnel in

the water should any machine gun or snipers open up. The DD's and CL's in turn support the LCI(G)'s.[31]

The capture of the Marianas, in particular Saipan and Tinian, gave the United States important air bases from which they could attack the home islands of Japan. Before the fighting on the island concluded, the 6,000 foot Isley Field runway was operational and handling 150 fighters. Their primary mission was the support of troops still fighting in the Marianas. Within a short time after the conquest of the Marianas, development of the runways to accommodate B-29s was well underway, and the islands became the primary base for attacks on the home islands of Japan.

An additional and unexpected result of the taking of the Marianas was the effect on the Tojo cabinet in Japan. The United States Strategic Bombing Survey concluded:

> Announcing the fall of Saipan to the nation, General Tojo, the one man most responsible for his country's entry into war, said: "Japan has come to face an unprecedentedly great national crisis." On 18 July, the Tojo cabinet, which had guided the destinies of Japan since pre–Pearl Harbor days, was forced from office to be succeeded by a government charged with giving "fundamental reconsideration" to the problem of continuing the war.[32]

Caroline Islands, The Palaus

Having taken the Gilberts, Marshalls, and Marianas islands, the next logical step in the advances for the Central Pacific forces were the islands of the central and western Carolines. These included the Palaus, Yap, and Ulithi Islands. This was the last extension of Japanese power in the area. Possession of the islands would give the American forces a solid line of defense, stretching across the Pacific from north to south, and would also provide an excellent forward base at Ulithi which would serve the fleets. The campaign to capture the western Carolines ran from July through September 1944. Enemy air attacks were considered to be less of a problem than the possibility of submarine attacks on American ships in the area. Although Ulithi was considered to be lightly defended, it was thought that the Japanese had 38,000 troops in the Palaus and 10,000 on Yap.

Beginning in March 1944, the fast carriers had begun air attacks on the Palau Islands with such intensity that Japanese air capability was almost non-existent and her shipping in the area was brought to a virtual standstill. Between the last week in August and the first week of September 1944, B-24 Liberators, flying from bases in the Southwest Pacific, conducted nine air attacks on Peleliu, further damaging its infrastructure. Just prior to the landings in the Palaus, additional air attacks were completed against Iwo Jima, Chichi Jima, Mindanao, Luzon, and the Visayas to suppress the enemy's ability to launch air attacks against the landing forces at the Palaus.

Japanese strength in the Palaus was centered on the largest island in the group, Babelthuap. The original garrison of 5,000 had been bolstered in May 1944 with the arrival of the 14th Infantry Division under Lieutenant General Sadae Inoue. The troops there numbered about 25,000. Inoue had his headquarters at Koror Island which lay directly south of the larger island of Babelthuap. Communications between all of the islands in the Palaus was excellent, with cables laid underwater between the islands so that Inoue could be made aware of the situation on any of them. The islands were ringed by a coral reef, and resupply or reinforcement between the islands was easily accomplished by barge. Screening against barge traffic occupied much of the gunboat's time in the Palaus.

Babelthuap's use to the Americans was limited, but this was not the case for the two islands in the southern end of the island group, Peleliu and Angaur. Not as heavily defended as Babelthuap, the two islands were flatter and better suited to the building of airstrips. An existing airstrip on Peleliu was an inviting prize. As a result, it was decided to bypass Babelthuap and land only on Peleliu and Angaur. Air attacks suppressed Japanese forces on Babelthuap, and patrols in the passages between Babelthuap and the other islands to the south prevented the Japanese from moving troops south. Much of this patrolling involved the use of the LCI gunboats and over the succeeding several months, involved them in action as the Japanese on Babelthuap attempted to strike at them.

Most of the island landings in the Pacific followed a similar pattern, with Marine reconnaissance units going ashore in rubber boats several days prior to the landing to identify enemy positions and strength. A few days prior to the landing, underwater demolition teams investigated the inshore waters, identifying features of the bottom and destroying obstacles placed in the water by the enemy. In the case of Peleliu, this was different. Japanese defense in the beach area was considered too heavy for the recon Marines to penetrate safely. UDT reconnaissance of the beaches was only for one day, and their work involved the landing beaches, not what lay beyond. A three day bombardment of the beaches was completed but was not sufficient to suppress Japanese forces.

Japanese defense strategy had evolved by mid–July 1944. Realizing that most of their holdings in the Pacific involved small islands and that the American advance would involve amphibious assaults, they devised new tactics. Each American landing had followed a similar pattern. For a month or two prior to the landing heavy ships bombarded targets on the island and made numerous airstrikes in the region designed to eliminate any air opposition to the landing. Several days prior to the actual invasion naval gunfire from larger ships blanketed the areas near and behind the landing beaches. Additional American air sorties sought out and bombed enemy positions near the beaches and behind them to prevent a build-up of forces or defenses. Just prior to

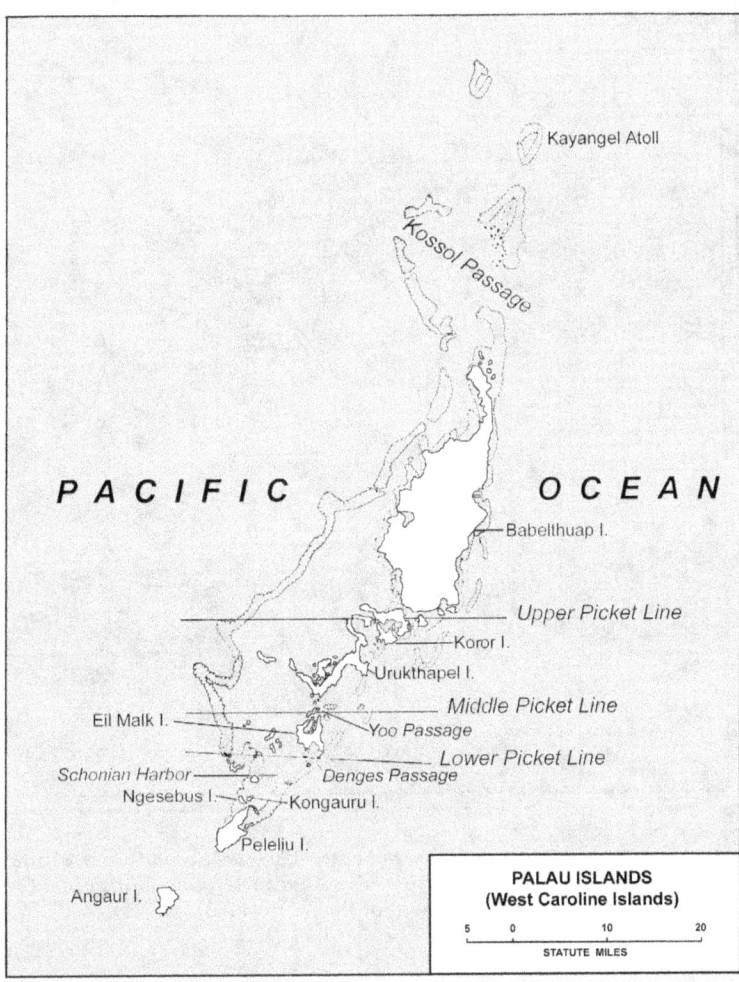

Once the islands of Angaur and Peleliu had been secured, a major problem existed with Japanese forces on the northern islands. Although they had been bombed and shelled repeatedly by American aircraft and ships, they had not lost any of their fighting strength. They continually attempted to infiltrate their forces to the south. In order to prevent the resupply of men and equipment, three picket lines were set up between the islands to prevent barge traffic from moving south. LCI gunboats were assigned the task and were continually in peril.

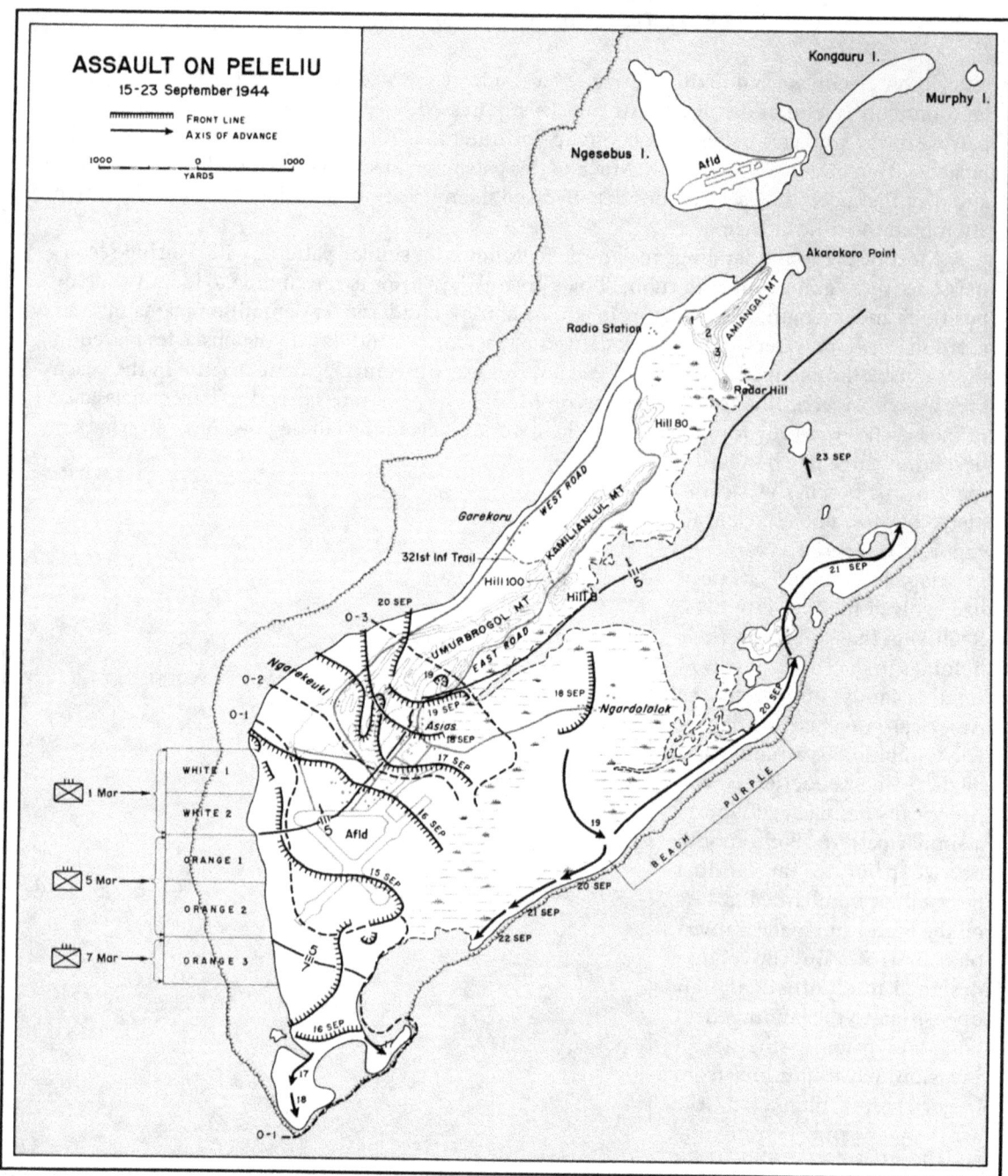

Landing beaches at Peleliu, 15 September 1944. From Robert Ross Smith, *United States Army in World War II: The War in the Pacific: The Approach to the Philippines* (Washington, DC: Office of the Chief of Military History, Department of the Army, 1953), map IX.

the invasion, Underwater Demolition Teams scouted the beaches and cleared obstacles. Minesweepers cleared the area in front of landing beaches in preparation for the landing craft. The assault began in the morning with additional heavy gunfire aimed at Japanese positions, followed by another air strike. Just preceding the landing craft was a line of amphibious gunboats covering the beaches and the area just behind the beaches with rocket and gun fire.

As a result of their experiences in prior invasions in mid–July 1944, the Japanese changed their strategy. Fortifications were built underground with just the gun ports above ground. There were few blockhouses or pillboxes for the enemy to spot. Since the islands were the remnants of ancient volcanoes and built up coral, they were usually honeycombed with caves. As a result, the Japanese built their command posts and a network of connecting tunnels underground. The mouths of caves that faced the ocean were used for gun emplacements carefully hidden behind underbrush and difficult, if not impossible, to spot from the air. Many of the caves were vulnerable to armor piercing shells, but the Navy saved them for engagement with the Japanese Navy and did not use them against shore targets. No longer would the Japanese oppose the Americans at the invasion beach; they would mount defenses near the beaches that would slow down the assault. However, their main line of defense was at sufficient distance from the landing beaches so as not to be destroyed by naval gunfire. The position of their guns was hidden from direct and aerial observation by use of caves and undergrowth. Forces were held in reserve to counterattack the Americans as the opportunity arose.

At Peleliu the lack of American knowledge of the terrain was of great benefit to the Japanese. Maps of the island were sadly out of date and inaccurate. Aircraft and submarine reconnaissance of the island failed to reveal the existence of a thirty foot high ridge on the left flank of the landing beaches. On the extreme right, a small island overlooked the landing beaches. Colonel Kunio Nakagawa, commander of the Japanese 2nd Infantry Regiment on Peleliu, had constructed gun emplacements on both flanks that were capable of delivering a deadly cross-fire on the landing zone. Although the ridge had been denuded of foliage by the naval bombardment and the rocket barrages, the Japanese guns were still in place but not evident.

It was a matter of pride among the amphibious forces that the rocket barrage preceding the landing would ensure that there were no Japanese alive in the landing zone to oppose the Marines and soldiers. In many cases, the rocket barrage killed few Japanese; they simply were not there. Rather than oppose the massive force of American naval gunfire and aircraft bombardment, the Japanese chose defenses inland that were well thought out and provided adequate protection for the Japanese. It was a classic case of adapt or perish.

Landing on the beaches at Peleliu was the 1st Marine Division under Major General Rupertus, with the Army's 81st Division under Major General Paul J. Mueller held in reserve. An overconfident Major General Rupertus informed the press on board that the conquest of Peleliu should only take about four days. Facing them on Peleliu were Nakagawa's 5,300 men, supplemented by another 5,000 support troops. Nakagawa had the advantage of an immense cave system within the Umurbrogol Mountain ridges. Interconnecting tunnels led from one cave to another, and the Japanese could stay there indefinitely as they slowly bled the Marines. This was the first time during the war that this new tactic was used, and it proved to be a useful model for Lieutenant General Tadamichi Kuribayashi as he prepared to defend Iwo Jima several months later.

Eighteen LCI(G)s carrying rockets were active in the attack on Peleliu. They included Group Nine *LCI(G)s 77(GF), 78, 79, 81, 82, 347, 454, 725* and *726* comprising Unit 1 under Lieutenant Commander J. F. McFadden. Unit 2 consisted of *LCI(G)s 452, 453, 455, 456, 458 (GF), 459, 460, 463,* and *470* under the command of Lieutenant Commander Robert Eikel. A second group of nine LCI(G)s under Lieutenant Commander E. L. Yates was in Group 39. It was comprised of *LCI(G)s 396, 397, 404, 405, 406, 727, 728, 729,* and *730 (F)*.

The assault forces attacking Peleliu had a new weapon in their arsenal, the LCI(M). On 16 September the mortar gunboats *LCI(G) 739, 740, 741,* and *742*, under the command of Lieutenant Commander M. J. Lindemann, were added to the Group Nine ships. Plans to mount the Army's 4.2 chemical mortar on Navy ships had been ongoing since early 1943. After experiments with LCVPs and LCTs, the Navy finally settled on converting the LCI(L) to carry three of the mortars. The first ships converted were from Flotilla 14, Group 10. They were *LCI(L)s 739, 740,*

741, and *742*. All four of the ships had been built at Commercial Iron Works in Portland, Oregon, and were commissioned in March and April 1944. After shakedown cruises and training at San Diego, they reported to Pearl Harbor for additional training. While there they were converted to LCI(M)s in late July 1944.

Rehearsals for the assault had taken place at Tetere, Guadalcanal Island, on 1 September, and the mortar gunboats had their first real practice using their new mortars in conjunction with other gunboats. The four mortar gunboats, under Lieutenant Commander Lindemann, were then assigned to Flotilla 14 Group 40 for the attack on Peleliu. Beginning on 16 September, they were assigned Flotilla 13 Group 9.

The gunboats formed up at the line of departure at 0720 on 15 September. At 0749 *Hazlewood DD 531* gave the flag signal to begin the assault and the LCI(G)s and LCI(M)s headed toward the beaches. The assault on Peleliu had begun. At 2,000 yards the gunboats opened fire with their 40mm guns and fired their first salvo of rockets about 1,000 yards off the beach. Having sent their salvo of rockets at the Japanese, they then resumed gunfire as the LCTs passed ahead of them. By 0823 the LCTs were too close to shore for the gunboats to safely fire without hitting them and they ceased fire. Mortar fire from the Japanese was a major problem, with many of the gunboats reporting near misses. *LCI(G) 79* was hit by an armor-piercing shell estimated to be 37mm, which hit near her port-after hatch and passed into the gunboat. Minor damage to the ship occurred with no casualties. The Marines on the beaches were particularly vulnerable to this kind of fire until they secured areas inland. Several of their tanks were hit by mortars and set ablaze.

Private Robert Leckie, of the First Marine Division, observed first-hand the attack of the LCI(G)s at Peleliu. He later wrote: "Slender rocket ships and destroyers were running close-in to shore, as graceful as thoroughbred horses. When the rocket ships discharged their dread salvos there came a terrible roaring noise, like the introduction of hot steel into water, and the air above them would be darkened by flights of missiles."[33]

Their first mortar attacks by LCI(M)s took place at Peleliu from 15 to 16 September 1944 and from 17 to 20 September at Angaur. *LCI(M) 739* reported delivering 1,300 rounds of high explosive mortar rounds on Peleliu and later sent another 834 rounds against Angaur Island.[34] The mortar ships would again be in action at Iwo Jima and Okinawa, but their debut had been a huge success.

Islands to the north of Peleliu held Japanese garrisons that might be sent to reinforce their position on Peleliu. To prevent resupply and reinforcement, a nightly picket station was in place beginning on 16 September. This usually included four LCI(G)s and one or two destroyers patrolling the eastern reef between Ngargersiul and Gorokottan Islands. Destroyers had the capability to provide star shell illumination to the area to help spot any barges attempting to make the run. The first of these supply attempts was made during the night of 22-23 September. The destroyers and gunboats fired on the barges with indeterminate results.

Call-fire was supplied by the ships as needed. On 17 September, *LCI(G) 453* received a call from Marines ashore to assist them against enemy positions. Lieutenant (jg) John H. Terry, CO of *LCI(G) 453* reported:

> As we approached the designated area a yellow smoke grenade was fired by our troops to mark their front line, and we were in radio contact with them through Lieut. Comdr. Eikel. At 1625 we proceeded toward the beach at the designated target area. At 1636 the decks were cleared and ranging rockets fired, our troops ashore "spotting" the rocket ranging shots and reporting via radio that they were on the target; immediately the report was received the entire salvo of rockets was fired. As the target was several hundred yards inshore from the beach it was necessary for us to approach to the very edge of the reef in order to get within proper range. At 1639 we had swung to port to proceed off the reef and opened fire on the target area with the bow and starboard guns. At 1643 ceased fire

Zero hour at Peleliu, 15 September 1944. A line of rocket gunboats are seen in the distance providing rocket fire against Japanese positions as the landing boats prepare to deliver troops to shore. NARA 80G 46642.

and proceeded away from the reef. Two days later the LCI(G) 459 on a similar mission in the same area hit a mine and sank rapidly.[35]

At 1000 the following day, *LCI(G) 452* stood off the Umurbrogol Ridge to provide support for the Marines. She fired a salvo of rockets into the foothills of the mountain. Later in the day, at 1705, she came back for another rocket barrage. Sniper fire from shore plagued the gunboat, but she soon fired her salvo of rockets. This time the result was a large explosion and fire which continued burning until the next day.

The following morning at 1120 on 19 September, *LCI(G)s 458* and *459* were off White Beach One to provide rocket support for the troops ashore. The CO of *LCI(G) 458*, Lieutenant (jg) Francis W. Cole Jr., was observing the mission of *LCI(G) 459* through his field glasses. The *459* was just off the reef and slowly coming into position for her rocket salvo when she disappeared in a large explosion. It was not clear if she had been hit by an artillery round fired from shore or had struck a mine. Smoke and debris shot several hundred feet in the air. When the smoke cleared, the gunboat was seen to be severely damaged amidships and low in the water. *LCI(G) 458* immediately went to her aid. As she approached the stricken ship, it was obvious that it was probably damaged beyond repair. There was a hole ten feet in circumference in her starboard side and she had a forty-five degree list. A number of her men were in the water and the *458* began picking them up. Three crewmen from the *458*, Seamen Arthur L. Davies, James Bricker, and Albert L. Rice, went aboard the sinking ship and searched through it looking for survivors.

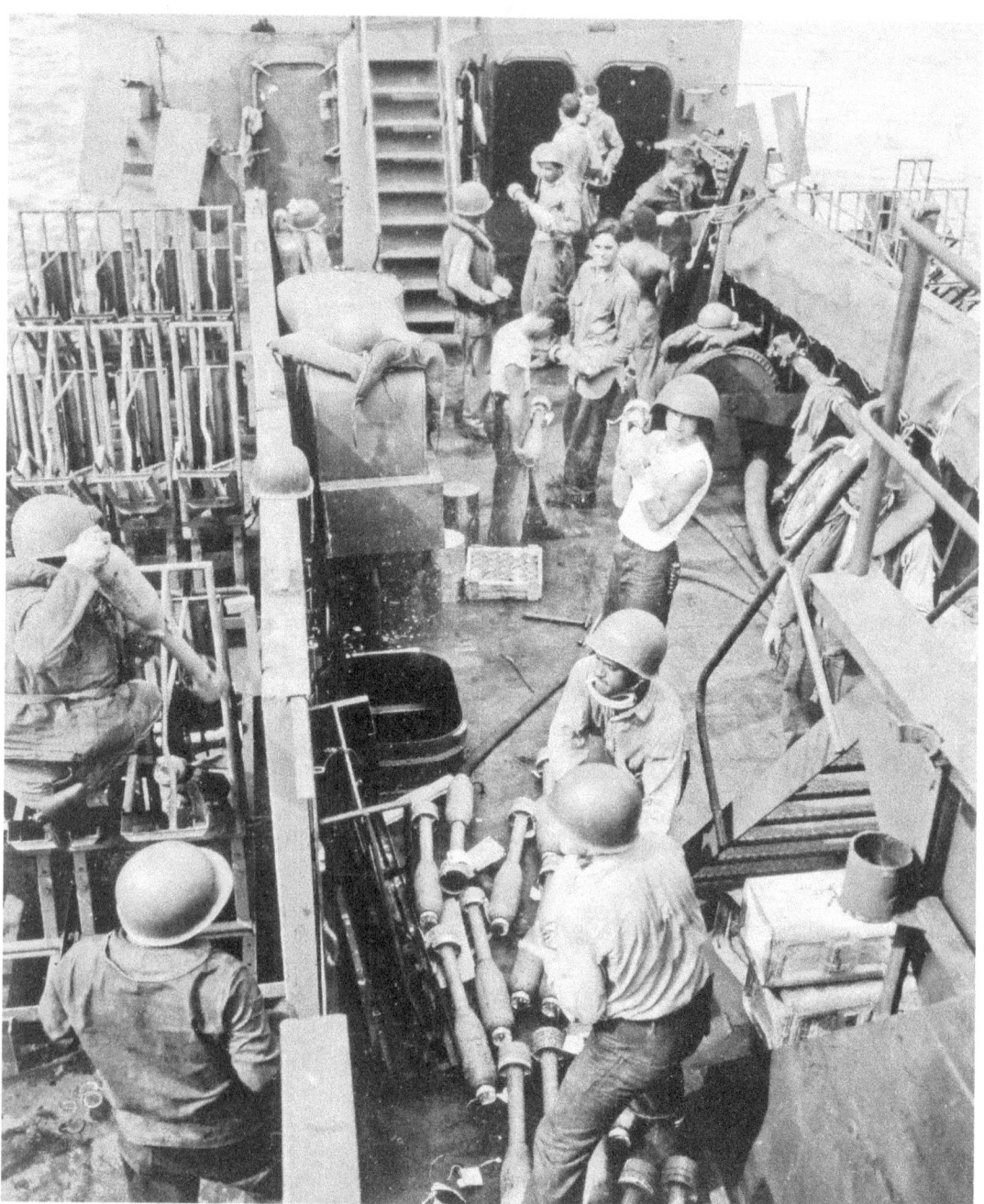

Loading rockets on *LCI(G) 456* at Peleliu on 19 September 1944. NARA 80G 257599.

They left the ship safely after not finding any. Within minutes the ship lurched sharply to port and went under bow first. All the men from the gunboat were saved, including a Marine officer and two Marine non-commissioned officers who had been serving as liaison with the Marines ashore.[36] Among the injured were nine men, including the Commanding Officer, Lieutenant (jg) J. R. Rann, and the Commander of LCI Group Nine, Lieutenant Commander Robert Eikel.

A short while later, at 1400, call-fire was requested again. *LCI(G)*s *82* and *456* headed toward shore to fire their rockets with *456* in the lead. *LCI(G) 82* spotted a mine dead ahead

A line of LCI(R)s fire rockets at Peleliu on 15 September 1944. The gunboat in the foreground is *LCI(R) 77*. NARA 80G 59500.

between the two ships. No sooner had *LCI(G) 456* unleashed her rockets than the mine exploded. Fortunately neither ship was damaged and the two were ordered out of the area because of the threat from mines. Having already lost one gunboat, the Navy was not inclined to lose a second. Nine men on *456* had slight wounds but none were serious.

By 20 September the fighting had moved far enough inland so as to be out of rocket range. In order to reach the targets, the ships would have to enter the shallow waters where they had encountered mines. The Marines were on their own.[37]

Overnight between 23 and 24 September, the Japanese attempted to bring ammunition to their troops on Peleliu with barges. The LCI(G)s on patrol discovered them and quickly took them under fire. Destroyers cruising nearby picked up on the location of the barges as the gunboats scored 40mm hits on them and finished them off, closing in on the reef in spite of the danger from mines. By the end of the action thirteen barges had been sunk in the lagoon midway between Ngargersiul and Gorokottan Islands. Most of them had exploded when hit, indicating that they had heavy supplies of ammunition on board. The following night the Japanese attempted to send a couple of barges again, and one was caught in the channel off Gorokottan Island and sunk while the other escaped. Patrols around the island continued until the end of the war, preventing supply of the remaining forces on the island and movement between the islands.

Damage by friendly fire was always a possibility. On 2 November, *LCI(G) 406* was on picket duty when she was strafed by an American plane. Sixty holes in her hull were the result, along with a good deal of equipment damage.

Reefs extending off shore at Peleliu prevented the LCL(R)s from getting as close as they planned. This diminished the effect of their rocket coverage. NARA 80G 283746.

An important task for the LCI gunboats was the supply of "call-fire" to support troops who had already landed. This was usually accomplished by taking on board an observer from the infantry unit to coordinate efforts. Here a U.S. Marine observer on board *LCI(G) 456* looks for targets on Peleliu on 19 September 1944. NARA 80G 257561.

Additional Army units were brought in to reinforce the Marines who had suffered heavy casualties. Army and Marine units continued to attack the Japanese on the Umurbrogol Ridge for several weeks. Finally on 25 October, Colonel Nakagawa, following the traditions of his military caste, committed suicide. Two days later the final remnants of the Japanese fighting force on the island had been eliminated. Small groups of Japanese managed to evade the Americans on Peleliu and kept hidden in the northern part of the island awaiting the chance to attack. They held out until April 1947 when they finally surrendered.

Angaur

Angaur, to the south of Peleliu, was invaded on 17 September. Landing there was the Army's 81st Division 321 and 322 Regimental Combat Teams. One Japanese battalion, under the command of Major Ushio Goto, defended Angaur. Although he was not a senior office, Goto understood the process by which he could cause the most damage to the American invaders. The landing beaches to the south of the island and the waters just off them were perfect for mining, a task which the Japanese had undertaken. Land on the island was flat in the southern and central areas, gradually rising to an elevated plateau in the northwest area known as Ramuldo Hill. The center of the irregularly-shaped plateau was hollow, giving it the appearance of an old volcano. Both the interior and exterior walls of the plateau were filled with caves that were perfect gun emplacements. Fire from the guns facing outward could blanket the entire island, including the landing beaches. The interior of the plateau was also covered with caves so that any American force attempting to assault one side would come under fire from guns hidden in caves on the opposite side of the depression. Landing beaches were situated on the northeast and southeast sections of the island, away from the guns of Goto's forces which had retired to Ramuldo Hill.

Two days prior to the landing, Rear Admiral Blandy decided to probe the enemy's defenses. Into the breach he sent *LCI(G)s 404* and *728*. Accompanying them was the destroyer *Fullam DD 474* which had damaged one screw on the way to the islands. On 15 September, the three ships ran close to shore while firing on suspected Japanese gun emplacements. Return fire from the shore was minimal and soon ended. Goto's men realized that their defenses were being probed and held back fire. Thinking they had destroyed enemy gun emplacements the commanding officer of *LCI(G) 728* reported back that they had silenced the enemy forces near the beach. Not convinced, Blandy sent them back the following day to check again, this time accompanying them in his command ship *Fremont APA 44*. At this point the Japanese revealed some of their defenses when they directed mortar fire at Blandy's ship. It was not hit.[38]

The landings were made unopposed after a five day bombardment by Navy ships. The gunboats of TU 32.6.5 under Commander John H. Morrill participated in the pre-landing assault. LCI Unit Able, under command of Lieutenant Commander Lindeman, consisting of *LCI(M)s 739, 740 (F), 741, 742* and *LCI(G)s 396* and *397*, attacked Red Beach. Unit Baker, under Commander Morrill, which was comprised of *LCI(G)s 404, 405, 406, 727, 728, 729,* and *730 (FF)*, attacked Blue Beach. The standard rocket and mortar fire was delivered on the beaches prior to the landing of the troops, but the gunboats soon realized that they were in minefields. The best they could do at that point was to put out markers by each mine to indicate its presence. Minesweeping in the beach area had not been an option, as coral heads near the beaches would have snagged the minesweepers' equipment.

After the initial landing, the gunboats worked in concert with the troops ashore. They remained just behind them as they advanced along the beaches and provided call-fire as needed. Major Goto's 1,600 man battalion had withdrawn to Ramuldo Hill in the northern part of the

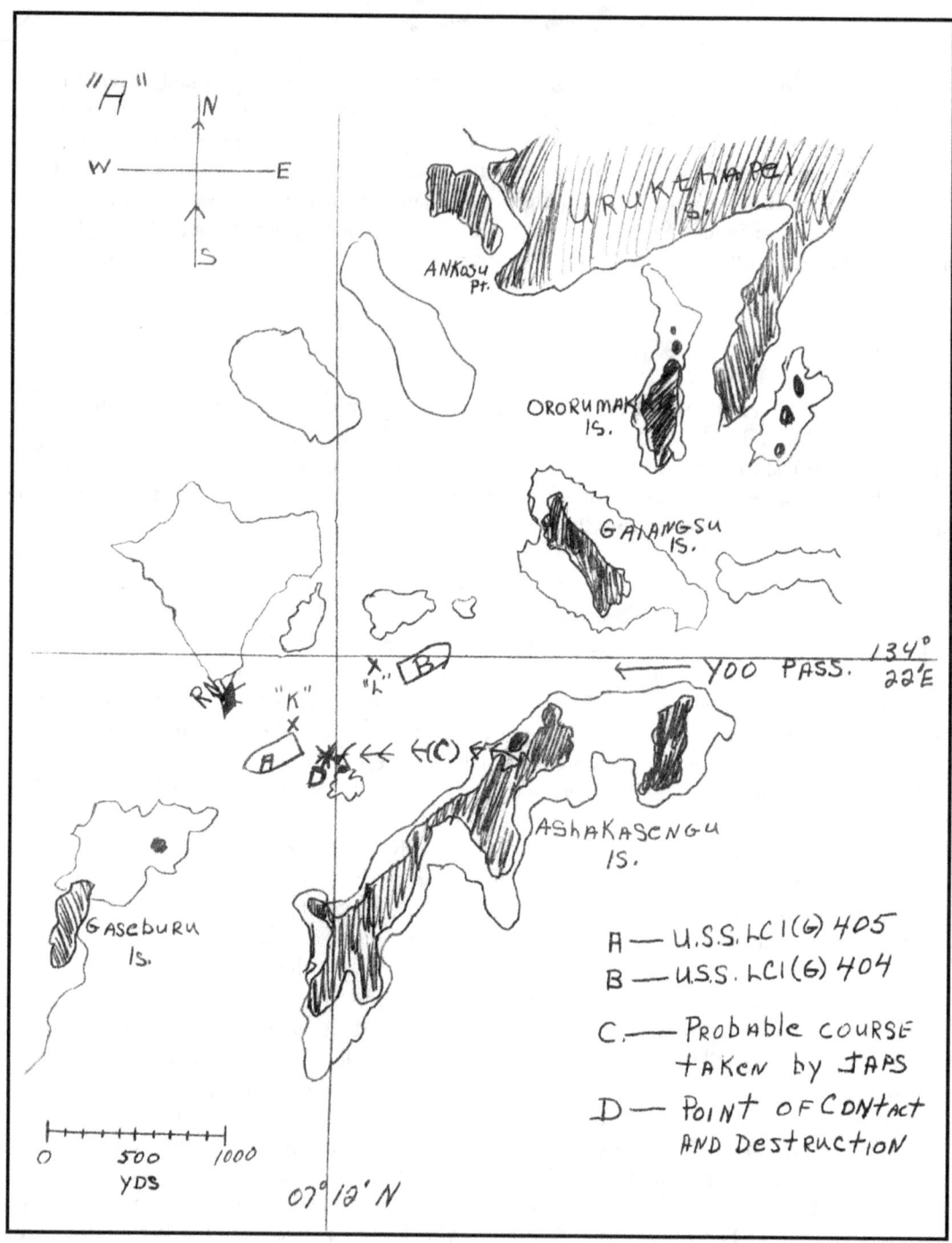

Constant patrols were needed to keep the Japanese away from Peleliu. This duty was performed by the LCI gunboats and, at the end, LCI(L)s. *USS LCI(G) 405* No Serial, *Action Report—Report of Action Morning 24 December 1944*, 15 February 1945, Enclosure "A."

island where they held out until 23 October. As the final stages of the battle on Angaur were taking place, Army engineers were busy constructing an airfield. It became operational on 15 October and served as a base for B-24 Liberators by 21 October.

The taking of Peleliu and Angaur was complete. Angaur, separated from Peleliu by seven miles of water and lying outside of the reef system that encircled most of the Palaus, was fairly secure once the initial conquest had been made. The lack of a significant Japanese force there, along with its small and relatively flat size, made it easier to conquer. Holding it was not a problem, as Japanese reinforcements from the north had too many obstacles to overcome in reaching it.

Peleliu, by comparison, was larger and a bit more difficult to control. Once the Japanese force there had been defeated, there was a constant threat from the north. The Japanese forces on Babelthuap and other islands to the north of Peleliu were still in good condition and ready to cause trouble for the Americans on Peleliu. A large part of the problem came from the number of islands separating Peleliu and Babelthuap, many of which contained Japanese soldiers who could advance further south to raid Peleliu.

To the north of Babelthuap lay Kossol Passage, a large area surrounded by reefs that provided shelter and an anchorage for many Navy ships. Constant patrols of the passage were necessary to ensure that the Japanese did not attempt to attack anchored ships. Inside the reef to the south were numerous islands and good anchorages for American ships. The problem lay in getting to them, as many of the inlets to the inner lagoons had been heavily mined. Of particular value was Schonian Harbor just to the north of Peleliu, which was well-sheltered and close to the island. In order to protect ships anchored there and Pelelilu itself, three picket lines were set up. They were known as the upper, middle, and lower picket lines. The entrance to Schonian Harbor was at Denges Passage, and the middle picket line ran from the ocean to the east, through the passage, and across the lagoon to the reefs on the western side. The upper picket line extended through Yoo Passage to the north. Islands in the area were controlled by the Japanese who attacked the pickets at every opportunity.

LCI Flotilla Thirteen under Commander Morrill was assigned to keep the Japanese north of Peleliu away from the Americans on the island. Morrill had been instrumental in devising strategies to patrol the waters north of Peleliu and had worked well with the Army command under Major General Paul J. Mueller. On 17 October the Navy forces in the Palaus received a new commanding officer, Rear Admiral John W. Reeves. Morrill was called into a conference with his new boss and General Mueller. Mueller announced that he was giving Morrill one hundred Army men for his gunboats to be used at his discretion. The LCI(G)s were also to receive one 4.2 mortar each for an amplification of their armament. Reeves was apparently a realistic commander. He recognized what Flotilla Thirteen under Morrill had been doing and requested a tour north of Peleliu to better understand the situation the gunboats faced. At 0700 the following morning, he went aboard *LCI(G) 730* for his tour. Morrill took him to the areas north of Peleliu and fired on suspected enemy positions. Admiral Reeves was able to judge the situation himself as the gunboat dodged return fire.

Within three days Reeves had devised a plan. He wanted a three-mile buffer zone between the Army forces on Peleliu and the enemy forces on the northern islands. In that area there were to be no Japanese. Morrill set about devising a plan. The Army troops would be used on any islands suspected of harboring Japanese. Working in conjunction with the gunboats, they were to reconnoiter each island, identify any Japanese there, and assist in destroying them. The three picket lines set up by Morrill were manned continuously to prevent further infiltration.[39]

Suicide Swimmers

A new threat arose in the waters off Peleliu. Around 0100 in the morning of 17 November, suicide swimmers made an in-force attack on the ships in Schonian Harbor. Lookouts on board Commander Morrill's flotilla flagship, *LCI(G) 730*, spotted something unusual in the water and searchlights were turned on. Dick Arnold, Quartermaster on *LCI(G) 730*, described the scene:

There were dozens of Kamikaze swimmers in the water, all wearing yellow caps (we found out the significance of that later). They all had grappling hooks and bamboo poles and some of them were pushing rafts of bamboo loaded with explosives.

Their objective was two-fold; to board the ships silently and kill the crew (whom they assumed would be sleeping) and to place the five hundred pound bombs under the sterns of the LCIs and blow them up. All of the swimmers had large sashes tightly bound around their waists to protect them from the blast of the bomb going off.

The problem was that many of the kamikaze swimmers were too close to the boats for our 20mm and .30 caliber guns to be leveled at them.

Our shouts brought the entire crew topside and everyone started shooting at the swimmers with their .45's. It was like shooting clay pigeons. Those further away were dispatched with the machine guns. We also had to be careful not to hit any of the other LCIs close to us.

In the middle of this chaos, one Japanese had managed to hide behind our LCVP, which was tied to the stern. When all the swimmers had been killed or driven off, we discovered this lone Japanese. The "old man," Captain Morrill (John Henry) yelled "hold fire" and we brought him on board.[40]

Robert F. Heath, a crewman on board *LCI(G) 404*, heard an explosion in Schonian Harbor and then heard the reports of the attack. His ship immediately headed for the scene, but by the time they reached the area, the action was over. He noted: "these swimmers are dangerous. There are reports of them climbing up LCI anchor housings and stabbing unsuspecting crew members. I would rather be moving all the time when we are close to Jap held islands at night time. With this latest information we are strengthening our watches even though we have never had problems with watches not being alert."[41]

By 25 November 1944 organized Japanese resistance on Peleliu had ceased. LCI gunboats found themselves patrolling off the island to prevent the escape of any Japanese stragglers and to prevent any Japanese from sneaking troops onto the island. However, they were not out of danger. *LCI(G) 397* had participated in the assault on Angaur Island on 17 December and had participated in the occupation of Ulithi. Following that, she was sent to the Palaus to perform patrol and picket duties in Kossol Passage. A flagship for LCI Group 19, she was part of a six ship mission beginning on 28 November 1944. Their assignment was to patrol the circumference of Eil Malk Island, intercepting and destroying any enemy ships and personnel they encountered. *LCI(G) 397* was anchored near the island the night of 5 December. The weather had turned sour, with intermittent rain and drizzle which blocked out the moon. In all, it was a perfect night for enemy action. Lieutenant James C. Carlton, the CO of *LCI(G) 397*, reported

> at 2120 the OOD noticed a phosphorescent glow about 75 yards bearing 005 degrees relative, the ship's heading about 025 degrees True. Binocular inspection by the OOD proved the phosphorescent glow to be steady in intensity and to be closing the ship. At 2141 the OOD phones the gun captain on the bow 40 MM and asked if they could see anything in the water about 50 to 100 yards ahead of the ship, bearing approximately 005 degrees relative. The answer to this query came back negative. At 2142, not satisfied with this answer, the OOD immediately turned the 12" blinker light on the area and illuminated three swimmers in the water about 30 feet from the bow, bearing about 010 degrees relative. At 2143 the OOD immediately gave the general order to all guns that could bear to fire upon and destroy the swimmers and at the same time brought the ship to General Quarters. 2143. The first person to open fire was the OOD who immediately destroyed one swimmer with a .30 cal. Rifle. The Quartermaster Third Class on watch accounted for another. By this time, seconds later there were so many guns firing that it was not definitely determined who accounted for the third originally in sight off the starboard bow.[42]

It was suspected that there might have been three additional swimmers in the water, but they could not be found. The men had been pushing a wooden raft about 2 × 3 feet in size and it was thought that it might contain explosives. It was taken under fire by 20mm and 40mm guns but proved to be a float with no demolitions attached. Lieutenant Carlton believed that the explosives had already been detached from the raft and that the swimmers were guiding it towards the gunboat. At 2248 the sound of an incoming round was heard, and a small caliber shell exploded about one hundred yards off the ship's port beam. The action raised the concerns about further attacks, and the ship raised anchor and moved to another spot 1,000 yards away.

LCI(G) 405 underwent a similar experience the night of 24 December. She was anchored by her stern anchor in Yoo Passage at 0430 when the OOD and men on watch discovered five Japanese swimmers approaching her port quarter with a 5 × 10 foot raft. On board the raft was a demolition charge estimated to be 12 × 14 inches in size. *LCI(G) 405* was one of many gunboats that had "acquired" additional firepower that could depress sufficiently to combat targets close to the boat. Mounted on her fantail was a .30 caliber machine gun. General quarters was sounded and the men on watch opened up with the .30 caliber machine gun and small arms fire. Three of the swimmers were hit with the first bursts, but two managed to escape by swimming underwater. Unfortunately for them, they surfaced to additional gunfire which killed them. *LCI(G) 405*'s CO, Lieutenant (jg) A. C. Timmons, recommended that ships in the area anchor with their bow anchors, as it would permit them to get underway faster in case of attack.[43]

The continued stealth attacks by the Japanese caused changes in the manner in which the crews were prepared. Virtually all men, particularly those on watch, were issued .45 caliber pistols along with rifles and machine guns. They were directed to fire at anything in the water that moved and alert the remainder of the crew to any possible attack. Since the ships were anchored and their guns could not depress sufficiently to cover the area near the ship, it was necessary to use small arms. In this manner, many such attacks by swimmers were thwarted. However, an attack on *LCI(G) 404* during the night of 8 January was successful. Anchored in Yoo Passage on a dark and rainy night, the gunboat came under attack from an estimated forty swimmers. Most were killed by gunfire, but one managed to set a bomb under the stern of the ship before he was killed. It exploded and disabled the gunboat. She was hauled back to Schonian Harbor for repairs. Her skipper was relieved of duty shortly thereafter.

A similar attack occurred on 12 January 1945 when *LCI(L) 732* was covering the east side of Yoo Passage with *LCI(G)s 405* and *729* on the east. The gunboats were at anchor and in position to cover one another. It was expected that the *732* was more likely to be a target than the two gunboats as she lay closer to the island of Garameyaosu, giving the enemy more cover to attack her.

It was a dark, rainy night, just the sort of conditions needed for a suicide mission to succeed. Two twelve foot row boats, each carrying five Japanese soldiers armed with grenades and rifles, left shore. At 2235 the two boats were spotted by the gunboat's search light at a distance of 350 yards and taken under fire by her automatic weapons. Both boats were destroyed and the shore near them was strafed heavily in case any of the Japanese had made it to shore. The following morning a badly shot up boat was found drifting in Yoo Passage with some Japanese clothing, a sheath knife, some detonators and hand grenade. These were turned over to naval intelligence.[44]

The Palaus were never completely safe. Sporadic enemy attacks continued to plague the gunboats. At 1130 on 18 January 1945, *LCI(G) 396* was heading out of Yoo Passage when she spotted a mine and took it under fire southeast of Ngarmediu Point on Urukthapel Island. Lookouts were stationed to spot any others in the area. At 1155 the gunboat struck another mine which went off underneath the ship amidships on the starboard side. The ship lurched to port under the blast. The Officer of the Deck, Lieutenant (jg) W. B. Townsend, and the signalman were blown out of the conning tower and down on to the gun deck. The CO of the ship, Lieutenant J. Peil, went forward to check damage and saw that the forward part of the ship had been ripped free and was settling to starboard. Oil fires on the water engulfed the forward part of the ship and it broke off and sank. Crewmen extinguished fires on board the ship and a small boat was put over to rescue men who had been blown overboard. *LCI(G) 728* came immediately to her aid and began to tow her out to sea. *LCI(G)s 729, 732*, and *730* arrived to assist. Enemy shore batteries opened up with what appeared to be five or six inch guns. To cover the gunboats, *LCI(G)s 729* and *730* made smoke and returned fire as the damaged vessel was towed out to sea and away from shore batteries. Air support in the form of several Marine Corsairs arrived from the field on Peleliu and silenced the enemy battery. Four men were killed, three missing and presumed dead, and fifty wounded.

Changes in the command structure of the Palaus took place in late January and saw a number of the gunboats reassigned to the coming invasion of the Philippines or sent back to rear bases for repairs. Replacing them were LCI(L)s with untrained commanding officers. Whereas the gunboat skippers knew how to handle the Japanese and had 40mm guns, rockets, and mortars to combat them, the new ships lacked their firepower or experience. The situation grew steadily worse. Commander Morrill later wrote: "At any time after April of 45, Japanese General Sadae Inooue could have retaken Peleliu and Angaur. He did not choose to do so, apparently because the war was winding down in his homeland Japan. Instead, he made raids on our ships and the Peleliu Garrison."[45]

Enemy swimmers continued to be a problem. At 0240 on 17 April 1945, *LCI(G) 456* was anchored in Schonian Harbor, along with fifteen other LCIs and two PGMs, when four Japanese on a bamboo raft tried to approach her. The raft was about three by eight feet, and secured in the middle was a demolition charge. Once sighted by the ship's searchlight, the four Japanese dove overboard and tried to swim away. Two were definitely killed by rifle fire and it was thought that the other two were killed as well. The raft and its demolition charge were sunk near the gunboat.

At the end of April 1945, Commander M. B. Brown, Commander LCI(L) Flotilla Thirteen, reported:

> During the month of April the LCI Picket Line has been subjected to more enemy attacks than during any previous month. During April the LCI Force was fired on by shore installations fourteen times, was attacked by three parties of swimmers, and destroyed 17 enemy mines. This increased enemy activity is indicative that the enemy is probably releasing mortar and light field weapons from BABELTHUAP to the south and has changed his tactics temporarily from suicide swimmers attack with demolition charges to organized and controlled gunfire against our picket ships. Increased heavy shore bombardments and air strikes by our forces against enemy areas of activity have been used as countermeasures against the enemy, in addition to harassing mortar and automatic weapon fire from our pickets.[46]

A new device was added to the patrol gunboats in the form of a sixty-inch searchlight which was installed on *LCI(L) 733*. This replaced the former twelve-inch light and was able to illuminate the entire Yoo Passage area from a distance far enough from shore to prevent attacks on it by Japanese mortars. A noticeable decline in the number of mortar, artillery, and swimmer attacks was noted during May, however, sporadic attacks against the gunboats and LCI(L)s continued until the end of the war. There was no letting down of the guard for the LCIs.

Such activities picked up again in June and continued through July. In the midst of enemy action against the gunboats, there were a number of Japanese who indicated their willingness to surrender, usually in groups of two or three. They would take rafts or small boats out to areas near the gunboats and wave white flags. On occasion their comrades from shore unsuccessfully tried to kill them with mortar fire. Here and there the gunboats destroyed small craft or were fired upon by mortars or artillery, but the war was in its final weeks. The end of the war on 14 August did not signal the end of hostilities at Peleliu. Although the accord had been reached in Imperial Headquarters, it took several days to filter down to the far-flung commands that had been bypassed and isolated. Mortar fire still continued to be directed at Japanese personnel surrendering as late as 16 August. By direction, the gunboats ceased to fire on any Japanese spotted in the area. Finally, on 29 August, two Japanese landing craft with Colonel Nakagawa

Colonel Tokuchi Tada (left) studies terms of surrender as Lieutenant General Sadae Inoue (center) watches. Seated at the end of the table is Brigadier General Ford O. Rogers, USMC. The surrender took place on 3 September 1945 on board *Amick DE 168*. NARA 80G 338573.

and nine other Japanese, came alongside *LCI(L) 737* off Abappaomogan to deliver a message from General Inoue to the American Commander. It read:

> From Sadae Inoue Commanding General Japanese Forces to F. O. Rogers Commanding General American Forces X I am going to send my representative off the coast of Airai intending to confer with your forces at 1300 Tokyo time Tomorrow 30 August X This military messenger shall wait for your answer aboard ship which this message is sent X Signed Sadae Inoue Commanding General Japanese Forces.' Colonel Nakagawa also had in his possession a sealed envelope addressed to the Commanding General American Forces which was delivered the following morning. At 0027(K) the following message was received from Island Command, Peleliu, for relay to the Japanese envoy: 'For Lieut General Inoue X Members of my staff will meet in conference with your representatives at 1300 Tokyo time 30 August in accordance with your proposal X Signed F. O. Rogers Commanding General. Upon receipt of this message the Japanese were allowed to return to their base.[47]

The hostilities at Peleliu had ended.

On 2 September 1945, Lieutenant General Inoue's party boarded the destroyer escort *Amick DE 168* and formally surrendered the Palau Islands.

Present during August 1945 at the Palaus were *LCI(G)*s *406, 566, 729,* and *730,* along with *LCI(L)*s *396, 550, 731–737, 820, 821, 866–872, 874, 875, 973, 991, 1066, 1067* and *1073.* The bulk of the patrolling had been carried out, not by gunboats, but by LCI(L)s. With the end of the war, some were sent on to assist in landing Marines in China and others headed home. On 3 November 1945, *LCI(L)s 869, 870, 871, 874,* and *875* headed for Guam. Although the war was over, there was still work to be done. Many of the LCIs of Flotilla Thirteen remained in the area of the Palaus to sweep mines from the passages and harbors, finally departing for Pearl Harbor on 18 November 1945.

CHAPTER 5

The Philippines Retaken — Leyte and Lingayen

Up until early 1944 the choice of targets for the Americans had been relatively straight forward. In the Central Pacific Area, naval forces under the direction of Admiral Chester Nimitz forged ahead taking one island after another, their choice determined by naval considerations and strategy. In like manner, the Southwest Pacific Area under General Douglas MacArthur had a relatively logical choice of targets. The extermination of Japanese forces along the northern coast of New Guinea and the subsequent neutralization of the Japanese base at Rabaul were primary concerns. At some point the two forces would come together and determine where the next strike would take place. It was obvious that the ultimate goal was a landing on the home islands of Japan, and Okinawa was seen as the logical steppingstone. How to approach Okinawa was another matter. Two schools of thought contended. The Navy asserted that Taiwan was the better target. Once having captured Taiwan, the sea lanes between the southwest Pacific and Japan proper would be cut. In addition, Allied troops could land in China and begin to expel the Japanese from Chiang Kai-Shek's territory as they worked their way northward toward Japan. An invasion of Japan might be launched from Chinese territory at some point. At the very least, the occupation of China would give the Allies numerous air and naval bases from which to conduct operations against the Philippines, Okinawa, and Japan.

A second school of thought, as proposed by General MacArthur, involved the recapture of the Philippines. Most saw this as partly strategic and partly political. Navy planners held that there was no strategic reason for fighting through the jungles of the numerous islands of the Philippines as it would simply waste time and manpower. MacArthur's interest was seen as primarily ego-driven and politically motivated. Although he had vowed to return to the Philippines, this was not necessarily the plan of the Joint Chiefs of Staff.

Meetings of the Joint Chiefs of Staff had earlier pondered this problem and on 2 March 1944, they

> announced to the commanders in the Pacific that the "first major objective" of strategy in the Pacific was to be "the vital Luzon, Formosa, China Coast Area." A tentative target date of 15 February 1945 was set for the occupation of Formosa, with the possibility that Luzon would be taken instead on the same date "should such operations prove necessary prior to the move on Formosa [Taiwan]." Decision between the two was deferred. It was this absence of a decision that caused protracted and sometimes heated discussion during the succeeding months of 1944.[1]

By late May, the conclusion had been reached that once the Marianas had been taken, Taiwan would be the next logical step. However, MacArthur had already advanced a timetable for the

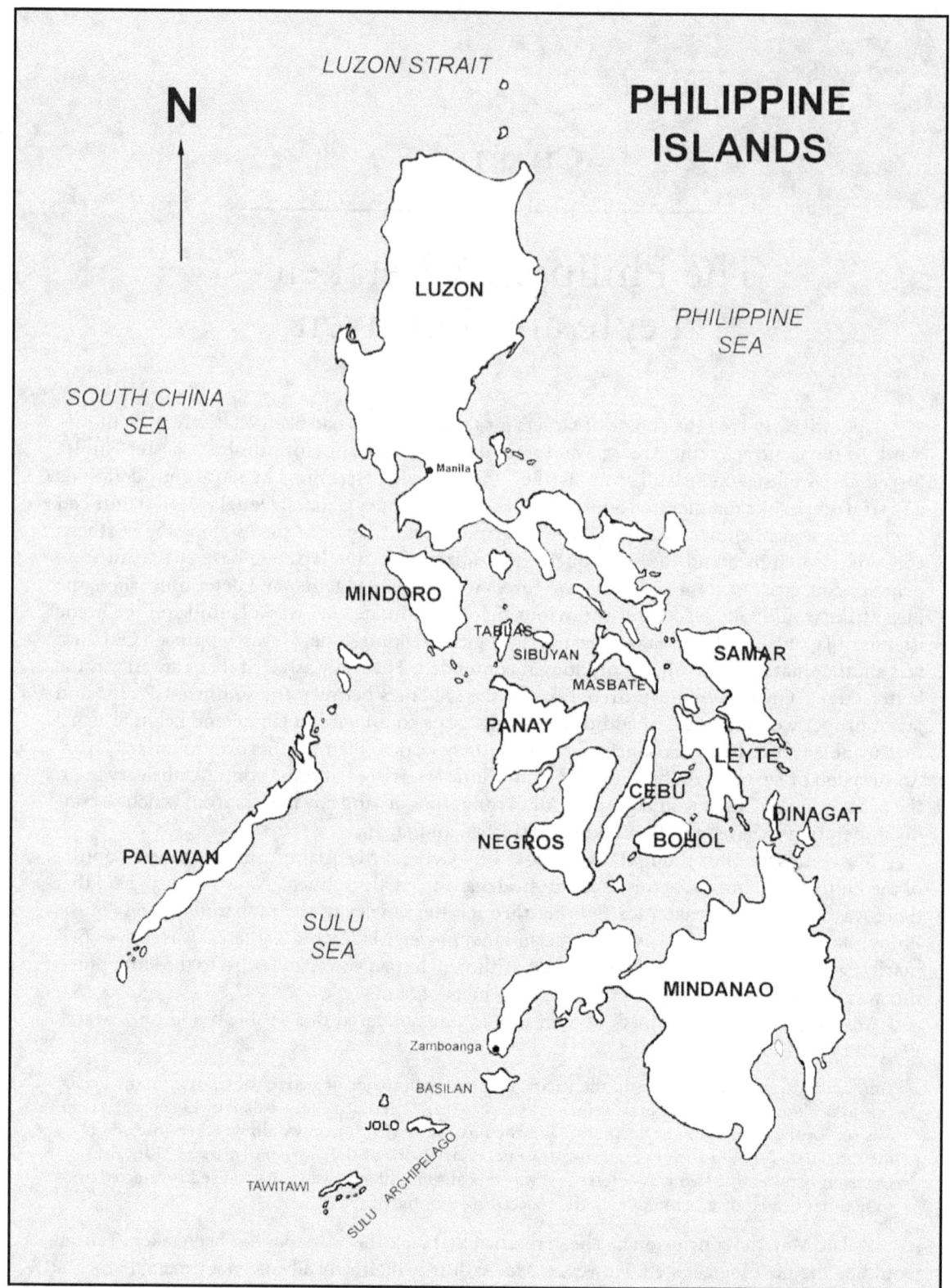

The Philippines consist of 7,083 islands, many of which are less than one square mile in area.

5. The Philippines Retaken — Leyte and Lingayen

Southwest Pacific Area which included: "21 May — Wadke; 1 June — Biak; 1 August — Northern Vogelkop; 15 September — Halmahera; 15 November — Mindanao."[2] Inasmuch as the landings at Wadke had already been accomplished ahead of schedule, MacArthur felt that his timetable was reasonable. The Joint Chiefs were not sure if some of the operations proposed by MacArthur were necessary and that perhaps other options might be more beneficial to the overall strategy. To gain further insight into the problem, they wanted to consult with both MacArthur and Nimitz about the possible course of the war in the Pacific. MacArthur asserted that the taking of Taiwan was not a viable alternative without land-based air support, a situation only possible if Luzon were taken first. He denied that the return to the Philippines had any political considerations attached to it and that his desire to mount an offensive to take the Philippines was based solely on strategic considerations. That having been noted, General MacArthur also allowed that the Japanese would reap a propaganda benefit in the Philippines if we were to bypass them, also noting that they were American territory. The debate went back and forth, and eventually MacArthur met with President Roosevelt in Honolulu to present his views. Also present were Admirals Nimitz and Raymond A. Spruance, along with Vice Admiral Richmond K. Turner. Admiral Ernest King had just left the island, leaving Nimitz to present his views. No firm conclusion came out of the meeting, with Roosevelt leaning toward MacArthur's plan, but the Joint Chiefs still had to study the matter further. It was not settled until 3 October when MacArthur was given the go-ahead to take Luzon. The date set for the return to Luzon was 20 December 1944, but MacArthur was already preparing for a toehold in the Philippines at Leyte Island.

The Philippines consist of 7,083 islands of various sizes, most of which are less than one square mile in size. Luzon and Mindanao are the two largest. Leyte, Panay, Negros, Samar, Bohol, Mindoro, Cebu, Palawan, and Masbate round out the larger islands, many of which were occupied by the Japanese because of their strategic position or the value of their resources. Some would prove of great strategic value to the American forces, but others would be taken simply to free them of Japanese domination.

PHILIPPINE OPERATIONS

Location	Code Name	D-Day
Leyte	King II	17 October 1944
Mindoro	Love III	15 December 1944
Lingayen	Mike I	9 January 1945
Nasugbu	Mike VI	31 January 1945
Palawan	Victor III	28 February 1945
Zamboanga	Victor IV	10 March 1945
Panay and West Negros	Victor I	18 March 1945
Cebu	Victor II	26 March 1945
Bohol		11 April 1945
Southeast Negros		26 April 1945
Mindanao	Victor V	17 April 1945

Return to the Philippines — Leyte Gulf

The initial landings in the Philippines took place at Leyte Gulf on the northeastern side of Leyte Island on 20 October 1944. Numerous LCI gunboats were involved in the assault.

Many of the LCI(G)s were recent conversions and mounted twenty-four 4.5 inch rocket launchers. On 4 October 1944, *LCI(G)s 366, 372, 373, 439, 440, 451(F), 461, 462, 464, 465, 467, 472,* and *475* of TU 79.6.22 arrived at Manus Island for conversion. The Group Commander,

Lieutenant Frank R. Giliberty, reported that "Twenty four rocket launchers were placed aboard. The two ramps and cat heads were removed. The launchers were welded in 3 banks of four on port and starboard side. Some 40 MM ammunition was removed. More 40 MM HEI was brought aboard as well as 500 complete rockets."[3]

In order to secure the entrance to Leyte Gulf for the invasion fleet, several islands had to be liberated from Japanese forces. These included the large island of Dinagat at the southern entrance to Leyte Gulf and the smaller islands of Homonhon, Calicoan, and Suluan which were on the northern side of the entrance to Leyte Gulf. Between Dinagat and the island of Leyte lay Surigao Strait. At the southernmost tip of Leyte Island was Panaon Island, which stood across the strait to the west of Dinagat. Japanese installations were at each of these locations and would

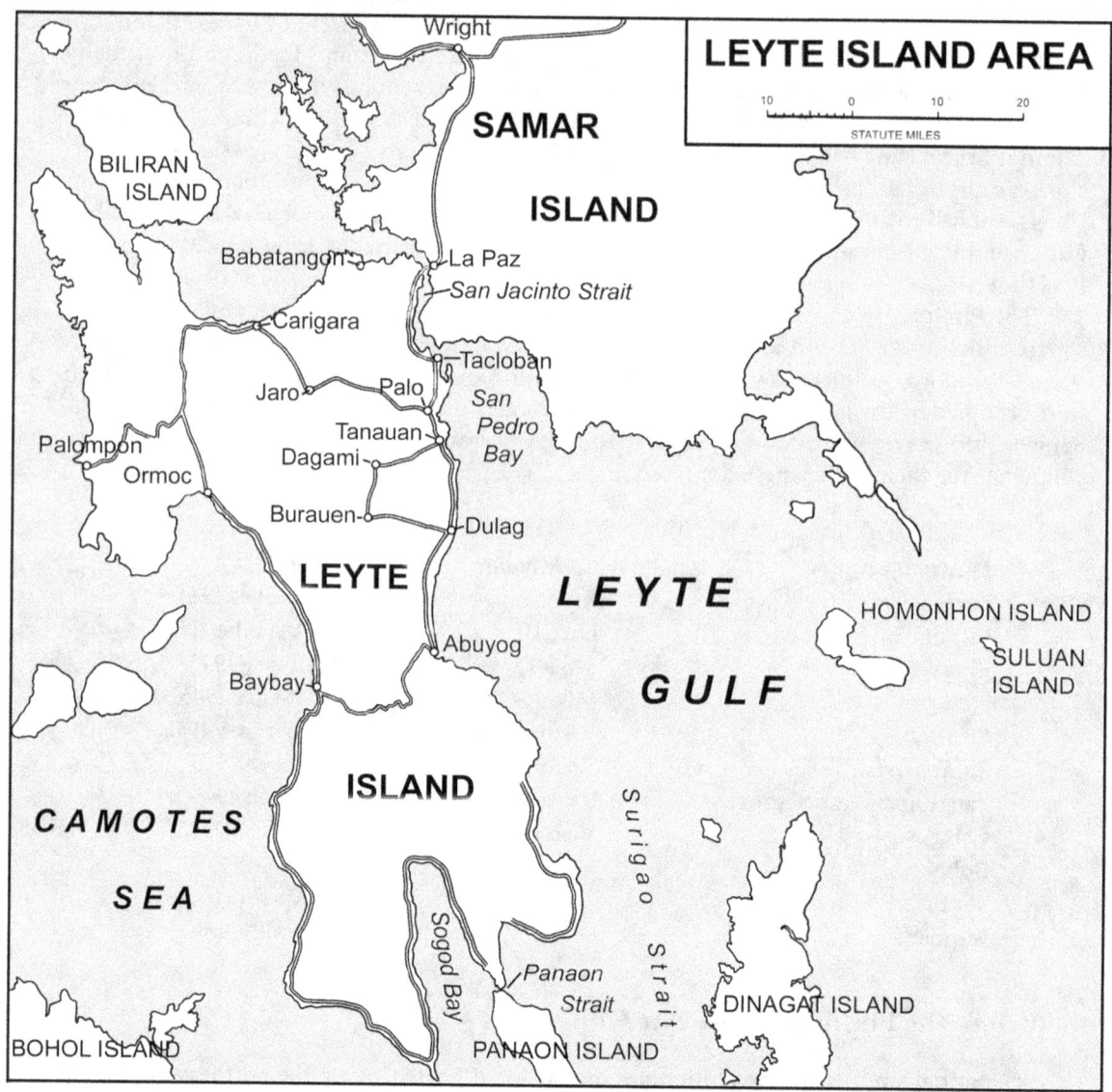

The initial landings on Leyte Island took place on 20 October 1944 in two places on the eastern coast of the island. The Northern Attack Force landed the Army's X Corps in the area between Tacloban and Palo, while the Southern Attack Force landed the XXIV Corps near Dulag. Once sufficient control had been established in the eastern part of the island, the Army's 77th Division landed at Ormoc on 7 December.

be able to monitor the American invasion force and keep the Japanese on Leyte informed of their actions. Accordingly, the Japanese had to be driven off these islands.

Assigned to take the island of Suluan was the 6th Ranger Infantry Battalion, commanded by Lieutenant Colonel H. A. Mucci and supported by the Dinagat Attack Group under Rear Admiral Arthur D. Struble. Company D of the Ranger Battalion landed at 0820 on 17 October with no opposition from the Japanese. A shell from *Denver CL 58* had hit the lighthouse in which the Japanese unit was stationed and had driven them out. The Rangers made short work of them, killing thirty-two.

Dinagat Island was next on the list, but conditions were worsening. In the face of increasing wind and sea, it was impossible to re-embark the Rangers. The LCP(R)s sent to remove them from the island were swamped in the face of sixty knot winds, and their withdrawal was postponed until the next day. Sea conditions were still difficult, but the Rangers made it off the island and were transported to Dinagat where they made an unopposed landing at Desolation Point, the northernmost tip of the island. Filipino guerrillas, led by Captain Hemingway, had driven the Japanese out of the area, and the Rangers had little to do but confiscate Japanese materials for American intelligence.[4] The landing on Homonhon Island on 18 October was similar. The Rangers once again found themselves unopposed, leaving them little to do but forage for intelligence material.

Panaon Island was scheduled to be attacked simultaneously with the main landings on Leyte Island. Task Unit 78.3.5, consisting of *LCI(G)s 68* and *70*, along with *LCI(R)s 31* and *342* and *PCs 1122* and *1133*, furnished fire support for the landing at Green Beach on Panaon, with the two PCs also acting as control vessels. The landing of the 21st Infantry Regiment was slowed by coral reefs. At 0747, the scheduled pre-landing bombardment and the close-in fire support of the gunboats were called off. There were no Japanese forces in the area, only friendly Filipino natives. The following day, 21 October, saw an enemy air attack by one Japanese Army fighter. On 22 October the gunboats were directed to destroy a nearby Japanese radio station at Malitbog. *LCI(G)s 68* and *79* fired on the building containing the station, driving twenty-eight Japanese into the guns of Filipino guerrillas who killed them.

On 24 October, the task unit received news of the approaching Japanese Task Force heading through Surigao Strait. They were ordered to remain close to shore near Sogod Bay. PT boats, working in conjunction with the task group, were scheduled to attack the Japanese force as it transited Surigao Strait. During this encounter, the LCI gunboats were active in relaying messages between the various PT boats while they attacked the Japanese during the night of 24–25 October. The two PCs were directed to hide near shore off Timba and Calipian Point. They observed parts of the battle near them and on 25 October were ordered back to the main assault area near Red Beach in San Pedro Bay.[5]

Northern Attack Force

The invasion at Leyte Island involved two distinct areas. As a result, the invasion force and its covering ships were divided into two units. The Northern Attack Force TF 78, under Rear Admiral Daniel E. Barbey, was responsible for White and Red Beaches between the towns of San Ricardo and Palo. Fire support ships under Rear Admiral G. L. Weyler bombarded the beaches. They included the battleships *West Virginia BB 48*, *Maryland BB 46*, *Mississippi BB 41*, destroyers *Aulick DD 569*, *Cony DD 508*, and *Sigourney DD 643*. They were bolstered by Rear Admiral R. S. Berkey's Close Covering Forces which included the cruisers *Phoenix CL 46*, *Boise CL 47*, *HMAS Australia*, *HMAS Shropshire*, and seven destroyers. Barbey led the invasion against Red Beach and Rear Admiral W. M. Fechteler led his forces against White Beach just to the north. Further north of this area was the peninsula holding the airstrip, and the town of Tacloban lay just across the bay. Landing on the White Beaches were the 5th, 7th, and 12th Cavalry Regiments of the 1st Cavalry Division, with the 8th Regiment held in reserve. Their goal was to capture Leyte Valley.

Tacloban Airfield was an important target. The division's 2nd Brigade, under Brigadier General Hugh F. Hoffman, was assigned to land and immediately capture the airfield. It headed northwest and captured the airfield and the entirety of Cataisan Peninsula on which it was located. Other units of the 7th Cavalry would "push inland, capture San Jose and a bridge across the Burayan River northwest of the town, and seize a beachhead line a thousand yards from White Beach. Cataisan Peninsula would then be sealed off."[6]

Flying bombing and strafing missions over all of the landing beaches were aircraft from the seventeen escort carriers under Rear Admiral Thomas L. Sprague. Landing day saw little air action, but this was to change. Between 25 and 26 October, seven of the jeep carriers were hit by kamikazes. One of them, *St. Lo CVE 63*, was sunk by the newly instituted kamikaze corps. Japanese air attacks on the assembled invasion fleet would make the airfield at Tacloban exceedingly important. Even though it was in poor condition and not completed, American fighters from the carriers used it as a landing spot to refuel. Many crashed on the field, and still others were patched together, refueled, and sent back into the air to fight the Japanese. The field operated under emergency condition for nearly a week. But on 27 October, the 9th Fighter Squadron, 49th Air Group began flying their thirty-four P-38 Lightnings off the field. By mid–November, there were two groups operating P-38s at Tacloban. This was an important step, as the fighters could challenge any Japanese aircraft sent to attack the ships and the men ashore. Unfortunately, the airfield at Dulag was not in as good condition. Although it was captured on 21 October, it did not become operational until 21 November when the 475th Fighter Squadron arrived.

The situation for the amphibious gunboats and their sister ships, the LCI(L)s, was always perilous. Lieutenant (jg) Edward H. Laylin, Commanding Officer of *LCI(L) 1064*, wrote:

> When we first steamed into Leyte Gulf, through Surigao Strait, all seemed pretty quiet. It was an interesting sight to sit at anchor, after our first arrival, and watch the battlewagons and cruisers pour tons of explosives into the Japanese positions on the shore. They kept it up with almost monotonous regularity, and there didn't seem to be any appreciable return fire. We had no planes in the area, but then the Japs didn't either, so it was just a fight with guns, ship-borne and ashore. That relative quiet lasted for about two days. Then came the deluge. We still had no planes except for a few Wildcats from escort carriers outside the gulf, but the Japanese had a lot, a mighty big lot, too. For about three of four days they made life mighty tough for us, coming over at all hours of the day and night, and keeping us from sleeping or eating or indulging in any of the usual affairs of life. One morning, a nice clear warm peaceful day it was too, they came over "in force" and really made life miserable for us. We were at battle stations just about all that day and that night, and had real good shots at Japanese planes. I think we could legitimately take credit for one or two, but the general confusion was so great that nobody bothered to "credit" any planes to anybody in particular. The main point was that there were at least 25 shot down in flames over the harbor. The Wildcats got a few, but most of them were victims of anti-aircraft fire from the ships in the bay.[7]

As H-Hour approached (1000) on 20 October, the gunboats prepared to make their rocket runs on the beaches. *LCI(G) 72*, as part of TU 78.1.8 (LCI(R)s *71, 72, 73, 74, 331(F)*), was assigned to a position inside the left side of the Red Beach boat lane. Her mission, as that of the other rocket gunboats, was to fire a barrage of rockets on to Red Beach, timing the launch of the rockets so that they would cover an area extending to a depth of 800 yards from the water line. She formed up with the other gunboats and began her rocket run at 0940 proceeding toward shore. Enemy shells landed around her, missing her by a close margin. She fired back with her 40mm gun but to no avail and, at 0950 and 0951, fired ranging rockets toward the beach. As the second range rocket was fired, the ship was hit by two shells from Japanese batteries. Nonetheless, she was able to complete her mission, firing twelve salvos of rockets on the beach before slowing to allow the LCVPs to pass through on the way in. Once they had passed, the gunboat turned to port and strafed the left side of Red Beach. Her mission completed, *LCI(G) 72* lay to and assessed her damage. She had been hit on the portside with her hull and pilot house sustaining damage. Eight men had been wounded. *LCI(G) 331* had taken a hit from a 3 inch shell on her port bulwark, causing minor damage and wounding one man. In addition, *LCI(G) 71* sustained casualties and damage at 0950 when she was hit by a mortar round on her starboard side; eight rocket launchers were knocked out. A few minutes later, her pilot house was struck by a 75mm shell, followed by an additional strike from a shell which passed through her starboard bow and exited her port side. Many of the gunboats were saved from serious damage by their light construction. They were designed as troop transports, not warships. Artillery shells frequently passed right through their thin skins without exploding.

On board *LCI(G) 568*, Joe Dumenigo, who served as pointer on the 40mm bow gun during general quarters, recalled the effect of the rocket salvos. According to Dumenigo, "it looked like an inferno."[8]

The CO of *LCI(G) 72*, Lieutenant (jg) J. F. Dray, was concerned that pre-landing bombardment of the beach by the larger ships was inadequate. In his action report he wrote:

> It was noticed from the station of this ship at the line of departure that the prelanding naval air bombardment of Red Beach seemed highly inadequate. The gun fire of BB's, DD's, etc. appeared to be directed entirely at White Beach and at the area to the right of Red Beach. As a result very few shells landed on Red Beach where the assault wave was put ashore. It is believed that had the beach been heavier bombarded and that had the bombardment continued as the Rocket Ships closed the beach the damage and casualties on the Rocket Ships would not have occurred.[9]

During the Battle off Samar, the unfinished Tacloban strip provided refuge for Navy fighters from the beleaguered escort carriers that could not make it back to their ships. At Tacloban they landed under difficult conditions, refueled, and headed back to the battle. This FM-2 Hellcat had a rough landing. NARA 342 FH 4A 40839.

Tacloban airstrip was located on Cataisan Point, a spit of land just to the north of the town of San Jose and across the water from the town of Tacloban. This photograph, taken during late October 1944, shows the airstrip from the north looking south. NARA 80G 102183.

After the landing had been completed, Rear Admiral Daniel E. Barbey, Commander Task Force 78, reported that: "Eleven LCI(R) delivered about 5500 4.5 barrage rockets along RED and WHITE Beaches between 0955 and 1000 (H-hour). This rocket barrage was the best and most effective observed to date in the Southwest Pacific Area. Each ship covered about 400 yards of beach."[10]

Southern Attack Force

The Southern Attack Force was under the command of Vice Admiral T. S. Wilkinson. It would land the 7th and 96th Divisions of the XXIV Corps on the beaches between the town of San Jose on the northern end of Orange Beach 2, as well as the area between the town of Dulag and Yellow Beach 1 near the mouth of the Daguitan River on the south. The beaches from north to south were: Orange 2, 1, Blue 2, 1, Violet 2, 1, and Yellow 2, 1. Dulag was an important site because, like Tacloban, it had an airstrip. The landing of the 96th Division under Major General J. O. Bradley was supported by the ships of Rear Admiral F. B. Royal's TG 79.2. The gunboats of TU 79.7.2, *LCI(G)s 461, 462, 464, 472*, covered the landing at Orange Beach 2, *LCI(G)s 439, 440, 467* Orange Beach 1, *LCI(G)s 366, 451, 475* Blue Beach 2, and *LCI(G)s, 373, 372,* and *465* Blue Beach 1. Supporting their flanks were *LCI(M)s 658, 659, 660* and *754*. Heavier firepower in Wilkinson's Task Force 79 included the battleships *Tennessee BB 43, California BB 44, Pennsylvania BB 38*, along with six cruisers and thirteen destroyers.

Landing zones at Leyte had been reconnoitered by UDTs 3, 4, 5, 6, 8, 9, and 10. Unfortunately, the storm that swept through the area during the time they were investigating the beaches made it impossible to provide the close-in fire support from the gunboats that usually took place. As a result, many of the teams suffered losses, but they still managed to get the job done. Previous experiences with air support made the UDTs reject it as there was too great a danger of bombs dropping in the water.

While the destroyers and APDs were able to fire on the beaches, they were not in the best position to do so, and the UDTs suffered. Numerous casualties were taken during the survey phase of their work. The CO of UDT 10, Lieutenant Commander A. O. Choate Jr., reported:

> Covering destroyers remained approximately three thousand, five hundred (3500) to four thousand (4000) yards off shore instead of inside the three thousand yard line as planned. Four thousand (4000) yards seems to be more than the maximum accurate range of 40mm guns. During operation a great many shorts were observed in the water, some landing as much as three hundred yards from the beach. One destroyer, when asked for 40MM support in one sector, informed the Underwater Demolition Team commander that he was outside 40MM range.[11]

To which Lieutenant Commander J. B. Eaton, Jr., commanding officer of UDT 9, added:

> Past operations show that best possible fire-support can be gained by using LCI's within 500 to 1,000 yards of the beach, firing continued fire from all 40 and 20 MM weapons. For this sort of support it is recommended that three (3) or four (4) LCI's be used for each Team.[12]

Casualties suffered by the UDTs at Leyte were directly laid to the absence of LCI gunboat support. Rear Admiral R. L. Conolly, Commander Task Group 79.1, which was Attack Group "Able," would later recommend that:

> LCI gunboats be used extensively and habitually to render close support and coverage of the underwater demolition teams. The success of landing on hostile beaches often depends on the accurate reconnaissance and successful beach preparation by the demolition teams. Experience has shown that the LCI gunboats have saved many lives and are of inestimable value as close-inshore fire-support units in keeping down mortar, machine gun and rifle fire.[13]

The landings at Leyte included significant use of mortars on board the amphibious gunboats. Since they were an unfamiliar weapon for the Navy men, each LCI(M) had an Army detachment on board that was in charge of firing them. It was not certain how useful the mortars would be. In his action report, Lieutenant (jg) Philip P. Marvin, CO of *LCI(M) 660*, noted: "As this was the first attempt at supporting amphibious operations with mortar fire from a ship, [in actuality Peleliu was the first] assumptions were difficult to make. The effectiveness and accuracy of the mortar fire had not been fully determined. However, it was assumed that the shelling of the beach by mortars would assist in preventing the enemy from making any sort of counter strike against the landing waves."[14] He later noted that "The performance of the 4.2 Army mortars aboard an LCI proved to be highly useful and effective. This was a time where a unit of the Navy and the Army had to work together as one team and the cooperation and work of both branches was highly satisfactory.[15]

The mortars proved to be effective weapons. Direct fire by 20mm and 40mm guns could only reach so far and could not hit targets on the reverse sides of the hills. Rockets could not do this, and their range was much less than that of the mortars which had a range of 3,200 yards. That gave them the ability to reach farther inland than the 4.5 inch barrage rockets carried by the gunboats, which had a range of about 1,200 yards. Mortar fire could be sustained for at least a half hour, but mortar tubes could become overheated and set off powder rings if the tubes were used to fire an excessive number of rounds. The maximum rate of fire for a mortar was twenty rounds per minute for five minutes. After that the barrel was too hot to continue and had to be cooled down. It was thought that the addition of a water jacket might extend the firing time and some experiments were undertaken. Water jackets could be made on board the ships by fabricating them from metal buckets. Lieutenant Commander Carl F. Robinson, Commander LCI(M) Group 18, reported that one of the ships in his group, *LCI(M) 1056*, had been fitted with an experimental water jacket for the invasion of Leyte. This had been designed by Robinson and Major R. H. Skinner of the Army. Robinson described the water jacket as follows:

> The jackets were made from regular water buckets. The bottom of the bucket was cut out and covers were made for the tops out of twelve (12) gauge sheet metal and welded on to the bucket. The jackets were fitted around the lower part of the barrel just above the base cap. They were held in place by a screw collar 1¼" wide. A one half inch (½") hose connection was installed at the top and bottom of the jacket. Water was run in at the bottom and out of the top so as to make sure that jacket would contain water at all times and would not run out in case water supply failed; in which case the jacket would still act as a cooler to some extent by radiating steam out through top outlet. The facilities and equipment aboard for making and properly installing these jackets was very limited but upon completion jackets appeared to be quite substantial and to warrant a trial.[16]

The water jacket seemed to work up to a point, but the rapid firing loosened its fittings and it had to be removed. The principle of cooling the mortar tubes seemed to be viable, but more work would have to be made in the design of the water jackets. An additional problem noted by Robinson was the lack of splinter shields to protect the gunners on the outboard mortars. As the mortar gunboats were configured, there was no protection for the gun crews manning these weapons. The addition of a 40mm gun to the ship's armament was also recommended, as once mortar fire targets had been covered, the 40mm might be used effectively against pill boxes and other targets ashore. The 383rd Infantry Regiment landed on Orange and Blue Beaches and headed north to secure the heights around Labiranan Head, while the 382nd landed and drove inland. The 381st Infantry Regiment was held in reserve and landed later.

Just to the south, on Violet and Yellow Beaches, the 32nd Infantry Regiment and 184th Infantry Regiment of the 7th Infantry Division prepared to hit the beaches. The 17th Infantry Regiment was the reserve for this section, and the 3rd Battalion, 17th Infantry Regiment was to land at Yellow 1, the southernmost beach. This battalion, first held in reserve, would be responsible for covering the left flank of the 184th Infantry Regiment as it drove inland to capture Dulag Airfield. Providing close-in fire support for Violet and Yellow Beaches were the gunboats of TU 79.7.1 under Lieutenant Commander Robert S. Rickabaugh, which included *LCI(G)s 365, 407, 422, 442, 558–561, 564, 565, 567, 568, 580, 676, 751, 752, 975*, and *1055. LCI(M)s 1056–1059* were assigned to work the beaches over with mortar fire prior to the rocket assault by the LCI(G)s. *LCI(L) 564* was assigned to the area to perform salvage work as needed.

Lieutenant Stewart W. Hellman watched the shore bombardment from his ship, *Knox APA 46*. He got on board a landing craft to make the trip to the PC that was serving as the control boat for *Knox*'s landing craft. At 0900 troops from *Knox* headed for Violet Beach 2. He marveled at the close-in fire support supplied by the gunboats:

> As the little gunboats reached a position closer in to the shore they opened up with their rapid fire weapons. The din was terrific. The destroyers, too, had increased the tempo of their fire until the sound was deafening and we could only make signs to each other on the bridge. This was American firepower at its peak.... But the final blast was yet to come. The gunboats were now approaching the beach and with a mighty "swoosh," that defies description, they discharged their rockets. If hell hadn't broken loose before it certainly it had now. With a thunderous clap thousands of rockets blanketed practically every square inch on and behind the beaches. Violet Two was for a moment a solid sheet of blinding and exploding flame. This was the force of War operating against the force of nature and there was no doubt of the outcome. What a moment before had been green was now ashen. What a moment before was growing was now scorched. What had been lush jungle and a place of concealment was now a barren, tangled, smoking, dust covered waste. Seeing it was to understand why nothing could live in its path. The "swoosh" of the rockets, their scream in flight and the blaze of fire as they struck with their terrible power will live long in the memory of those who witnessed it.[17]

Fire directed at the gunboats reflected an adaptation of the Japanese to the assault of the rocket gunboats. As the ships provided rocket fire for the immediate landing zone, it was noted that a number of mortar and artillery shells were bracketing the gunboats. Aware that the Americans were using the rocket ships, the Japanese had moved their anti-ship guns and mortars back from the beach so that they were out of range. Although they could not be reached by rockets, they were still within range of the mortars.[18]

Occasional air attacks plagued the gunboats and the invasion force. At 0630 on 20 October, an enemy air attack developed over the landing fleet but it was beaten off. The ships had sufficient firepower, and they also had air support from the escort carriers off-shore. Some of the ships, such as the LCI(M)s, did not bother to fire, as their 20mm guns could not reach the aircraft. Only the 40mm guns on the (G)s and (R)s could do the job. *LCI(G) 580* was strafed and had nine men wounded, one of whom died.

Labiranan Head, located inland to the north of Orange 2 Beach, was an elevated area that overlooked the landing zone, a perfect place for enemy guns. It needed to be neutralized. At 0915 the four mortar gunboats of TU 79.6.21, *LCI(M)s, 658, 659, 660,* and *754* under Lieutenant Commander G. W. Hannett, were sent just offshore to bombard the landing area at Orange Beach 2 with mortar fire. Beginning at 0915, the four LCI(M)s each fired 120 4.2 mortar rounds on the northernmost landing beach, Orange Beach 2. Following that, the four turned north and unleashed their firepower on the town of San Jose and then targeted Labiranan Head. The lack of return fire by the enemy was seen as an indication of the effectiveness of the mortar ships' fire, which had been extensive. By mid-afternoon, each of the LCI(M)s had fired in excess of 1,150 mortar rounds on San Jose, Libiranan Head, Catmon Hill, and the

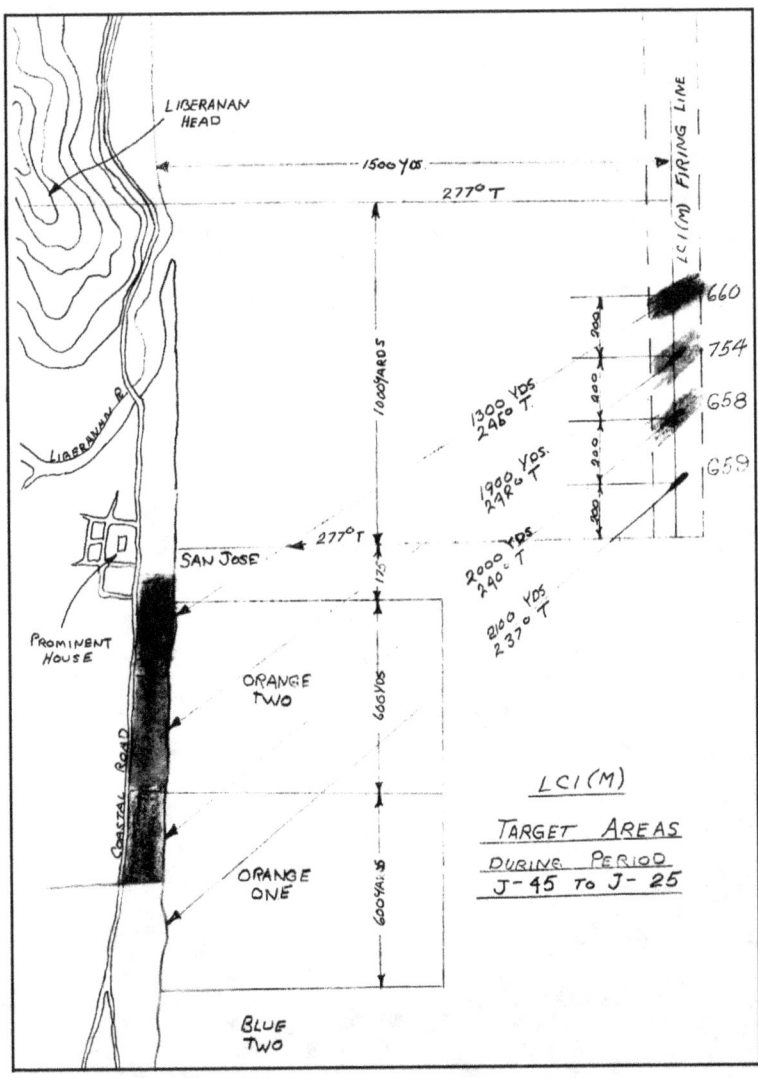

Plan for the mortar attack on Orange 1 and 2 Beaches, San Jose, Leyte Island, 20 October 1945. After the initial assault, the mortar gunboats were assigned to deliver fire on the reverse sides of Liberanan Head. Commander Task Unit 79.6.21 Commander LCI(L) Group 17 Serial 114, *Action Report*, 4 November 1945, Enclosure (A).

surrounding area. Some of the most vital targets for the mortar gunboats were the reverse slopes of Liberanan Head and Catmon Hill, which could not be reached by rockets or direct naval gunfire. Mortars and artillery pieces were firing on the invasion ships from those locations.

After the mortar gunboats had finished their assault, it was time for the LCI(G)s to unleash their rockets just prior to the landing. The order to land came at 0930.

Lieutenant (jg) W.P. Henricks, CO of *LCI(G) 372* reported that the

> [r]ocket barrage was most effective yet seen by originator. First salvo of ranging rockets was fired at 1000 yard radar range from trees on beach (100 yards behind waterline) and all hit the beach approximately 10 yards inland from waterline. Rocket salvos were spaced over interval while ship moved ahead 400 yards. All rocket fired hit beach including ranging shots. From information received subsequently from Army officers, rocket salvos were extremely effective in neutralizing beach area. Casualties to landing personnel were observed from this ship to be much lighter than in previous operations where volume of rocket fire was smaller.[19]

Hendricks was also concerned with the close proximity of the LCI(R) to the beach. His ship delivered its rockets and then moved to within one hundred yards from the beach to use their 40mm and 20mm guns effectively. This was ideal for targeting enemy positions but left the rocket gunboat little room to maneuver if it were fired on by the enemy. He asserted that the closest approach should be 200 to 250 yards, ensuring both good target acquisition and maneuvering room.[20] Additional fire was directed at Liberanan Head by *LCI(G)s 461, 462, 464,* and *472* after they had unleashed their rocket barrage on Orange Beach Two.

Landing craft streak toward the beach during the landing at Leyte, Philippines, on 20 October 1944. In the bottom right hand side of the picture, a row of LCI gunboats may be seen. They are partly obscured by smoke from their rocket fire. Official U.S. Navy photograph.

Some return fire was taken from shore. *LCI(G) 422* was struck by an unidentified shell at 0950 as she fired her first salvo of rockets. Early casualties were unknown as the rocket barrage was underway. Once the rockets had been fired, she turned to port and began strafing the beach with her starboard guns. Normally the 40mm bow gun would have fired also, but the shell had pierced the gun tub and set off some of the 40mm ammunition, killing two men and wounding four. The entire 40mm gun crew in the bow had been put out of commission. The dead and wounded were transferred to *Appalachian AGC-1* for treatment and burial.[21]

The effectiveness of rocket fire was summed up by Lieutenant Carlton W. Hartness, CO of *LCI(G) 475*. In his action report he stated:

> The spacing of salvo fire for the rockets made it possible to cover an area 200 yards wide and 500 yards deep. The thirteen LCI(G)'s in our group each fired in this manner thus covering a beach area 2600 yards long. The troops landing in this reported that they found no living Japanese in this area and met no enemy resistance till they were 500 yards inland, thus showing that rocket fire had completely cleaned out the area in which they fell, from the point at which last salvo or rockets were fired (450 Yards off beach) to a point 100 yards off beach.[22]

Task Force 78, the Northern Attack Force, landed on the northern beaches at Leyte.

Although there was little return fire from the enemy as the ships made their initial rocket runs, resistance picked up as the gunboats made their right hand turns to strafe the beach. Machine gun, mortar, and artillery fire began to show up near them. As they were retiring from the beach area, they noticed that there was a mortar barrage with rounds falling about 1,200 yards from the beach. The gunboats had to pass through it in order to escape, and it lasted until they were about 1,500 yards offshore. Fortunately, there were no hits on the gunboats. The only casualty was an LVT which took a direct hit from a mortar round while it was only twenty yards off the starboard beam of *LCI(G) 568*. Numerous casualties were suffered by the LVT.[23]

Assistance from Philippine natives was not unusual. They were eager to have the Japanese defeated and their islands returned to their control. On 21 October, *LCI(G) 462* was anchored 300 yards north of San Roque off Catamon Head and spent the morning hours strafing the area with her 40mm and 20mm guns. At 1435, she picked up three Philippine natives who were eager to inform them as to the Japanese locations. Apparently there was a line of trenches just behind the beach, with sand mounds in front, in which the Japanese had taken shelter. Based on the information, the gunboat fired on four low mounds of sand. The Filipinos felt sure that the Japanese in that area had been killed. They were sent on to CTU 79.6.22 for further debriefing.[24]

The gunboats found themselves in a variety of situations at Leyte. On 24 October, the fleet tug *Sonoma ATO 12* was tied up to the merchant ship *Augustus Thomas* and *LCI(L) 1065* in San Pedro Bay, when the ships came under attack by four Sally bombers at 0839. One of them was damaged by gunfire from the ships and crashed into the LCI(L) which burst into flames and began taking on water. *Sonoma* cast off and was about to escape when, at 0845, another plane crashed into her. She began to take on water and was quickly aided by *LCI(R)s 71, 72, 331, 337* and *Chickasaw ATF 83* which put out her fires. Twenty-seven men from *Sonoma* were brought aboard *LCI(R) 72* for medical treatment as the tug was beginning to sink. An additional twenty were taken on board *LCI(R) 337*. *Sonoma*'s records and registered publications were transferred to *LCI(R) 72*. *Sonoma* was towed into shallow water off Dio Island and settled on the bottom where she was stripped of valuable gear.

On the northeastern side of Leyte Island lay San Juanico Strait, separating Leyte and Samar. There were concerns that the Japanese might be able to transit the strait and bring supplies and reinforcements to their troops by landing in the area or by taking them through the strait. It was decided that the capture of both shores along the strait would secure the area and prevent Japanese reinforcements and supplies from being landed there. The towns of Babatangon and Guintiguian on Leyte and La Paz on Samar were the targets.

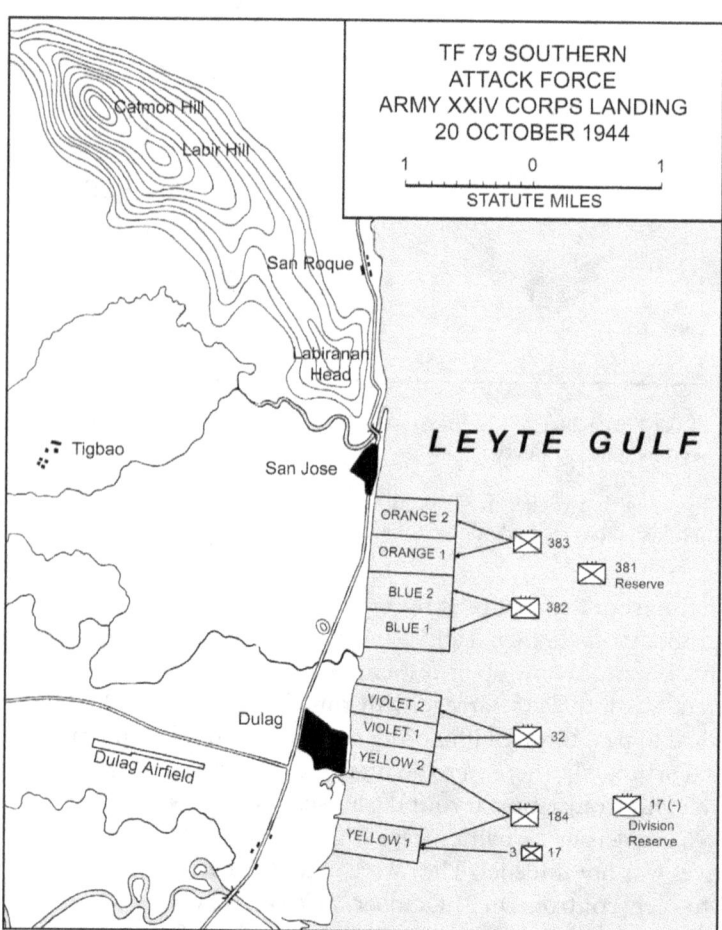

Task Force 79, the Southern Attack Force, landed its troops on the southern beaches at Leyte.

On 24 October *LCI(G) 23*, with three other gunboats and some LCMs, found herself at the northeastern tip of Leyte in Opong Bay off the town of Babatangon. Their mission was to deliver the 1st Squadron of the 7th Cavalry from Tacloban to the area, landing their men and supplies. Eager natives assisted in the unloading of the ships and it seemed as though the mission was a simple one. The men of *LCI(G) 23* and *LCI(R) 338* were near a concrete wharf enjoying the scenery when a Zeke came out of the clouds and dropped two bombs which scored a near miss on the gunboats. Men scrambled for their general quarters positions and the gunboat prepared to get away from the wharf and underway. A Val appeared from behind the hills, strafing the ships and dropping two bombs, one of which hit the stern of one of the LCI(G)s. The gunboats went alongside and assisted in tending to the wounded. A crewman on one of the gunboats recalled:

> We cast off from the wharf and pulled alongside the blasted ship. Lines made her fast to us and hose was broken out for the fire below decks. Astern on the starboard deck three denimed sailors lay crumpled, their blood clotting on the blue painted metal. The entire crew of the 3" 50 rifle had been wounded on the LCI 23. One sailor had fallen out of position to the main deck where he sprawled with horrible limpness, his face hidden by a chalky hand.
>
> At the 40mm gun position a sailor still sat in the trainer's seat, blood running down his face, his dazed eyes fixed on the loader's body huddled under the steel tractor seat at the left of the gun. There was a large jagged hole in the loader's back. A bomb fragment had hit him full in the chest.[25]

It had been a costly attack for *LCI(G) 23*. She suffered ten crewmen dead and three officers and twenty-one enlisted men wounded. Her crew tied her up close to shore where she was camouflaged with palm fronds and tree branches. Eventually she was towed back to Hollandia and repaired.

On 25 October, *LCI(G) 752* was lying to in Tacloban Harbor at 1243 when she came under attack by several Japanese dive bombers escorted by one fighter. Her gunners put up some heavy anti-aircraft fire and the bombs missed her. An hour later several more planes attacked her from astern. This was a weak spot for the LCI gunboats, and the plane dropped a 500 lb. bomb which narrowly missed the stern of the boat and exploded underwater. The blast bent her shafts, jammed her right rudder, and took a chunk from the left. The hull had a large dent from the stern to frame 84 and she began taking on water. Fortunately *Achilles ARL 41* was nearby and the gunboat was towed to her for emergency repairs.[26] A few days later, on 27 October, *LCI(G) 752* was anchored in San Pedro Bay when she was attacked by a Hamp. The plane dropped a bomb about thirty yards off her starboard beam, loosened her plating, bent some deck plates and opened her seams. She developed some leaks but they were repaired in short order.

When not actively strafing shore targets or patrolling various areas, the ships frequently were involved in laying smoke screens to protect larger ships from air attack. Overnight between 25 and 26 October, *LCI(G) 568* had the task of covering the area near her with smoke. This caused additional problems, as the smoke obscured vision and resulted in a collision between several of the gunboats.

Rescue work was a normal part of any Navy ship's tasks. On 25 October the battle off Samar Island kept a number of them busy. *LCI(G) 340* received a message from CTG 78.2 at 1736 on 25 October to proceed, along with *LCI(R)s 34, 71, 341, 357*, and *PCs 111* and *625*, to rescue survivors. *Gambier Bay CVE 73* and *Johnston DD 557* had gone down in the battle and there were men to rescue. The first survivor picked up at 1700 on 26 October was Japanese. He was placed under guard, strip-searched, given medical attention, and fed. On 27 October a survivor from *Gambier Bay* was found and taken aboard. At 0156 seven life rafts were found lashed together. About 110 survivors from *Gambier Bay* were clinging to them. Some were badly wounded and all needed dry clothing, food, and water. Feeding everyone strained the ship's facilities, but they were accommodated. More survivors from *Johnston* were located at 0856 on a life raft the next morning. *LCI(G) 340* took on board another fifteen men, most of whom were badly wounded. With a full load of rescued men, the gunboat left for Leyte where the prisoner was turned over to *AGC 9* and the survivors to *LST 226* and *PCE 852*.[27]

LCI(G) 342 had the ability to put to use her newly-installed firefighting equipment. On 27 October, the freighter *Benjamin Ide Wheeler* was crashed by a twin engine bomber at 1845 as she lay at anchor in San Pedro Bay. *Wheeler*'s hold was full of gasoline, and she was soon ablaze and in danger of exploding. *LCI(G) 342* went to her aid, placed her bow against the side of the burning ship, and played four streams of water against her side and into her hold. In short order she replaced the water with foam, which seemed a better choice since the flames were being fed by the gasoline. Her efforts were later joined by *Cable ARS 19*, and by 0130 of the next morning the fires were under control. The freighter suffered two dead and three wounded. It was noted that the crew of the freighter made little effort to fight the fire.[28]

Many of the ships used San Pedro Bay and the surrounding area as an anchorage as it afforded better protection from the sea's action. However, the close proximity of the airfield at Tacloban made it less than safe. Numerous enemy raids occurred over the area with frequent attacks on the ships and the aircraft ashore.

When a number of LCI(L)s were converted to LCI(R)s, they were equipped with special firefighting equipment. This proved useful in many cases but dangerous in others. At 1900 on 31 October, *LCI(G)s 337, 338, 340, LCI(R)s 34, 71, 72, 74, 341,* and two other gunboats beached near the airfield and spent several hours fighting fires in aircraft and a gasoline dump. Continued explosions of fifty gallon drums of oil plagued their efforts, but in the end the fires were under control. When they tried to retract from the beach several hours later, they were unable to leave due to a receding tide. They had to wait until the following morning to get off the beach.

Other problems were evident in the practice of beaching ships to fight fires ashore. Enemy aircraft were active in the area and the beached ships were sitting ducks for an air attack. Only the dark of the night prevented them from being attacked. The two ships left ashore during the following day were subject to such attacks, one in which a Japanese plane dropped a stick of bombs that missed by only a few hundred yards.

Commanding officers of the rocket gunboats equipped with firefighting equipment noted some very specific problems in using these ships for firefighting, beached or otherwise. It was the practice of the rocket gunboats to keep some of their launchers loaded for possible call-fire missions. When ordered to fight a fire, they had to pull alongside a burning ship with their rockets exposed to flames. When *LCI(R) 71* went to the aid of an LCI(L), her canvas rocket launcher covers caught fire and had to be extinguished. Fortunately, none of the rockets exploded. It was considered impossible to be prepared for rocket call-fire missions and firefighting at the same time. The presence of the rocket launchers on the side landing ramps made it difficult to run hoses effectively; they were frequently caught on the launchers and it took time to move them about effectively. When coming alongside a ship to fight fires, the launchers were easily bent by contact with the ship. Once the launchers were bent even a little, they could not fire their rockets. Attempts to straighten them were usually unsuccessful. The last consideration was the ammunition carried by a rocket gunboat. In addition to the normal load, the LCI(R) had another fifty-five tons of ammunition aboard. Of this amount, the Number 2 hold in the forward part of the ship usually held from 1,100 to 1,400 high explosive rockets.

The weight of the additional ammunition in the hold made it a little more difficult to beach, as it increased the forward draft of the ship. When beached to fight a fire, the firefighting team had difficulty getting ashore. In order to mount the rocket launchers, the landing ramps had been removed. Once the LCI(R) had beached, the water at the bow area would be at least 5 feet 3 inches deep. Firefighting crews had to manually lower a ladder to climb off, and often had to swim before they could get to water shallow enough to work. This proved problematic, as it was time-consuming and dangerous.[29] What had seemed a good idea at first proved to be more of a burden. It was a success in spite of the ships' configuration, not because of it.

On 3 November Tacloban Airfield was attacked and several aircraft were set afire. At 0325 *LCI(R)s 337* and *342*, along with another gunboat, were ordered to the beach off the airstrip to assist in firefighting. They beached at 0500 and found three aircraft aflame. While the majority of the crews remained at general quarters, fire hoses were run ashore to combat the fires in two of them, the third being too far apart from the other aircraft to be a threat. As they fought the fires, a Rufe flew down the length of the field and dropped small anti-personnel bombs, followed by a fighter that strafed the field. The three ships, silhouetted by the fires, made fine targets and three more fighters attempted to bomb them. Men engaged in firefighting found themselves covered in dirt and debris from the nearby bomb explosions. One of the aircraft was brought down by antiaircraft fire from the field. By about 0600 the fires were under control and the LCI(R)s retracted from the beach. But it was not a peaceful departure, as additional enemy aircraft attacked the area. Several were shot down by Army fighters. The gunboats were then ordered to assist fighting a fire on a nearby Liberty ship. Firefighting duties in the area continued as the constant air attacks on the field set aircraft ablaze, along with supply and gas dumps.[30]

Kamikaze action continued. On 12 November *LCI(G) 751* was on screen in San Pedro Bay. Three Hamps came out of the east over the island of Samar and made their attack. On board *LCI(G) 751*, SM 3/c Harold Hoover picked them up at a range of five miles and sounded the alarm. The gunboat and a nearby destroyer took them under fire. Anchored nearby were about twenty cargo ships. One plane passed over the gunboat and crashed into *Alexander Majors* after taking some hits from the gunboat's 40mm guns. The Liberty ship had two men killed and fifteen wounded. *Thomas Nelson* and *Matthew P. Deady* were also crashed by kamikazes, with the worst damage done to *Thomas Nelson*. The plane that hit her penetrated her deck and its bomb went off inside, killing 133 men and wounding eighty-eight. Many of these were Army troops waiting to disembark at Dulag. *Matthew P. Deady* had minor damage and no casualties. Nearby, *LCI(M)1056* was tied up to the repair ship *Achilles ARL 41* when a third kamikaze crashed into both of them. The gunboat escaped with minor damage and no casualties, but *Achilles* suffered thirty-three dead and twenty-eight wounded.

LCI(G)s 422, 559, 560, 751, 1058, and *1059* were steaming in a column toward an anchorage in San Pedro Bay when four Zekes and a Val appeared from the south and west, heading for the anchored transports. All gunboats opened up with 20mm and 40mm fire. One Zeke, hit by several ships, lost a wing and crashed in the water. The Val was shot down close aboard one of the Liberty ships. Another Zeke passed over the gunboats and had a wing shot off; however, it still managed a crash into troop carrier *Jeremiah M. Daily*. Killed in the attack were 106 men, with forty-three others wounded. As with the crash on *Thomas Nelson*, many of the killed and wounded were Army troops waiting to land. Several other cargo carriers and troop ships were hit that day, and the gunboats shot down a number of would-be kamikazes.

LCI(G) 558 experienced a dawn air attack on 23 October. She was anchored 200 yards off Dulag when a Zeke made a pass on her, dropping its bomb. Fortunately it was a dud. The Zeke circled around for a strafing run on the gunboat which took it under fire. Forty and 20mm rounds struck the plane in the fuselage near the engine and cockpit area. It is probable that the pilot was wounded by these shots. The plane lost power and went down to the south of the ship. The pilot's body was later recovered. *LCI(G) 558* was credited with one Japanese plane shot down. Two days later the gunboat was making smoke early in the morning when an enemy plane dropped a bomb near the transports that the gunboat was screening. It hit the water and exploded fifty yards off the port quarter of the *558*, wounding one man slightly. The transports were spared and the plane was driven off by gunfire from the ships in the bay. *LCI(G) 558* seemed to be in the midst of the action almost every day. On 26 October, a high flying formation of Japanese aircraft commanded the attention of many of the ships, taking their attention away from an attack that came in at a low altitude. One Zeke headed for a PT tender and was taken under fire by *LCI(G) 558* whose 40mm fire set it ablaze. It crashed into the bay short of its target. A second Zeke was hit by its gunfire, giving the *558* its second kill in the space of a few days. Continued attacks over the next couple of weeks would give the ship's gunners ample opportunity to practice their skill, but she had no additional enemy planes to her credit during that time.[31]

Gunboats fulfilled a number of roles during the war, including the supplying of Filipino guerrilla forces and the retrieval of Americans behind enemy lines. *LCI(G) 558* became the sole ship in Task Unit 78.2.31 in mid–November 1944 when orders were delivered to its commanding officer, Lieutenant (jg) Harold S. Lewis, stating "Commanding General Sixth Army desires to land 20 tons of supplies on the southeast coast of Samar. This command desires to evacuate a number of survivors, approximately six now under the care of guerrilla forces."[32] Apparently, several American pilots and air crews were safely in the hands of the guerrillas and two tasks might be accomplished by the gunboat.

Following orders, *LCI(G) 558* beached at Leyte and took on supplies for the guerrillas, as well as some passengers. Accompanying them to deal with the guerrillas were Lieutenant Colonel Smith and Lieutenants Charles Hall and James Johns, all from A.U.S., along with five allied war correspondents to record the mission. The gunboat was loaded with guests and supplies and left Leyte at 1504 on 14 November 1944. She headed for Homonhan Island, arriving at dusk. Currents in the area were running at four knots, and the gunboat finally made it to open seas at 0300 on 15 November. The gunboat was essentially on its own and navigating by radar, but the night provided coverage. Before dawn broke, the *558* made it safely into Napla Bay north of Andis Island. A rain storm erupted around dawn and the ship was able to slip undetected into an anchorage near the island. Guerrillas waiting for the ship to appear did not discover her until daybreak when she was visible. They quickly covered her with coconut branches so that she was well disguised and unloaded the supply of food, rifles, mortars, ammunition, clothing, and medical supplies in the space of two hours.

Later in the day, as the ship sat camouflaged only 150 yards off Punta Maria, Samar, the survivors were brought aboard. Two naval pilots and four enlisted men were in relatively good condition, having survived naval battles against the Japanese on 26 October 1944. At 1830 that evening, the gunboat weighed anchor and headed back to San Pedro Bay, arriving at 0910 the following morning. Her passengers were off-loaded and transferred to *Fremont APA 44*.[33]

The landings at Leyte had been successful, but the ships there continued to be plagued by Japanese air attacks. An attack by two Zekes at 1215 on 28 November resulted in damage to *Oak Ridge ARD 19*. Eugene Reed, SM 3/c, was the lookout on duty on board *LCI(G) 751* when he spotted the first plane coming in at a distance of five miles. The ship turned to meet the aircraft head on and began firing at a range of three miles. It passed eight hundred yards across the gunboat's bow as the *751* scored a number of hits on the plane. Other ships fired on the plane and the combined fire caused it to waver. It seemed obvious that it would pass over the ARD, but at the last moment it crashed into the floating drydock's starboard quarter. A second Zeke passed directly over the ship and was hit by several rounds, but it circled the drydock and then flew off.

The landings on the eastern side of Leyte Island at Dulag and the area around Tacloban had been successful. A beachhead had been established, troops had moved inland and were in pursuit of the Japanese, and airfields at Tacloban and Dulag were made operational. By mid–November, it was time to expand the plan. A landing at Ormoc, almost due west of an area just north of Dulag, was the next target. Capture of this area would prevent the Japanese from reinforcing their units and allow the Americans to attack them from the rear. Chosen to land there on 7 December 1944 was the Army's 77th Infantry Division under Major General A. D. Bruce. Transporting them to the attack would be the Ormoc Attack Group TG 78.3, under the command of Rear Admiral A. D. Struble. The Task Group consisted of eight APDs, twenty-seven LCIs, twelve LSMs and four LSTs to move men and supplies. Supporting the landings and providing fire support for the trip from Dulag to Ormoc were twelve destroyers. Prior to the landing, the area was to be swept by nine AM minesweepers. *LCI(R)s 31, 71, 73, 331* and *342* provided covering fire for the actual landing. Two sub-chasers, *SCs 726* and *731*, acted as guides for the landing craft. An ATR tug was on hand to assist any landing craft that became stuck on the beach. Air cover, including bombing and strafing the beaches was a joint venture by the Army and Marine Corps.

The attack force staged at Tacloban in San Pedro Bay on 6 December 1944 and headed south. Their route took them around the southern tip of Leyte Island, through Suragao Strait, then north into the Camotes Sea to Ormoc Bay. During the trip from Dulag to Ormoc there was little enemy presence. Destroyers and LCI(R)s bombarded the beaches and the troops landed without much opposition. The attention of the Japanese had been diverted to the south where they were combating the American's 7th Division which was driving northward up the coast. Once the landings had been completed the Japanese air attacks began. Opposing them were Army and Marine fighters, but the number of attacking aircraft was overwhelming. In spite of many Japanese aircraft being shot down, the newly instituted kamikazes took their toll. By the time the task group made it back to San Pedro Bay, *Mahan DD 364* and *Ward APD 16* had been sunk by Japanese air attacks. Two other ships, *Liddle APD 60* and *Lamson DD 367* sustained serious damage. *LSM 318* was crashed by a kamikaze at 1525, and *LST 737* was crashed by another at 1619. Army P-38s and Marine Corsairs took their toll and shot down numerous planes, but the Japanese still managed to get through.

On the morning of 7 December the landing craft were ready to head to the two landing beaches planned for the assault. Task Unit 78.3.7, with the CTU on board *SC 726*, included LCI(R)s *31, 71, 73, 331*. The rocket gunboats covered the landing beaches with their standard rocket barrage, but there was no opposition. Planning for the assault had placed the landing beaches about ten miles south of the Japanese troop concentration. A major concern for the attacking force was the presence of a large number of enemy aircraft. The convoy and landing force was under frequent attack during the day on 7 December, suffering fourteen different air raids. Damaged in these kamikaze attacks were *Kephart APD 61, Liddle APD 60, Lamson DD 366, Mahan DD 364,* and *LST 737. LCI(R) 331* spotted two incoming Zekes near the landing area at 1215 and took them under fire. She shot down one and was credited with an assist on the second which crashed into the sea.

Resupply of Ormoc was a continuing problem. The large number of operational Japanese airfields in the area gave rise to continued air attacks, many of them utilizing kamikaze tactics. Navy, Marine, and Army Air Force pilots would have their hands full until the Japanese air bases were neutralized.

The Taking of Mindoro Island

With a foothold firmly established in the Philippines through the landings on Leyte Island, the Army's next major target was Luzon and its capital, Manila. However, the Japanese had numerous airfields on the island and any invasion force was sure to feel the wrath of both the Japanese Army and Navy aviators. On Luzon alone, the Japanese had at least twenty-eight airfields, with an additional four on Panay, and six on Negros.[34] Any invasion fleet heading for Luzon would be seriously damaged by air attacks before they reached the beaches. The major problem for the American forces was the lack of air power in the area. The airfields at Tacloban and Dulag were not fully developed by the beginning of December 1944, and occupation of Mindoro would give the Americans additional airfields at San Jose in the southwest corner of the island. Four airstrips existed there but were not in use. They could be quickly improved and would serve as a base for fighters covering the invasion fleet bound for Luzon.

The Regimental Combat Team of the 24th Infantry Division and the 503rd Parachute Regiment landed at San Augustin near the town of San Jose on Mindoro Island on 15 December. Both units were under the command of Brigadier General William C. Dunckel. They numbered

American infantrymen are shown getting information about Japanese activity from a Filipino native near San Jose, Mindoro, after their landing. Such cooperation from the people of the Philippines was common and aided in the effort against the Japanese. U.S. Army Signal Corps photograph.

over 16,500 men, with 5,000 to follow. A token force of several hundred Japanese near San Jose was their opposition. Their main threat came from Japanese aircraft flying off the fields on Luzon, Panay, and Negros.

The Visayan Attack Force, under Rear Admiral Arthur D. Struble, consisted of three parts: the Mindoro Attack Group under Struble; the Close Covering Group under Rear Admiral Berkey; and the Motor Torpedo Boat Group under Lieutenant Commander N. Burt Davis. Included in the Mindoro Attack Group were the LCI gunboats *LCI(G)s 64, 68, 69, 70.* The Inshore Support Unit (TU 78.3.7) included *LCI(R)s 34, 230(F), 337, 338, 342* and *LCI(D) 228.* They left the line of departure and laid a rocket barrage on the beach at 0740. The landing at San Jose was uneventful, with sporadic air attacks on the landing ships and covering force. The gunboats delivered their barrage and then attempted to clear the area. An offshore wind, a common problem, complicated matters. As soon as the first rockets hit, the wind carried the smoke toward the LCI(R)s and made it impossible to determine the effectiveness of the barrage. The smoke was so thick that *LCI(R) 342* ran into an LCI(L) which was heading for the beach, damaging its bow and landing ramp. Normally the gunboats followed up a rocket barrage by strafing the area with their 40mm guns, but the smoke obscured targets ashore and prevented their firing on suspected enemy targets. *LCI(R) 337* reported that the best she could do was fire on some tree clumps to the right of the landing beaches.[35]

At 0845 seven Japanese Army Tonys attempted crash dives on the LSTs and managed to hit two of them. At 0852 a single engine fighter made a run on one of the LCI(R)s which was

P-38 Lightnings of the 36th Fighter Squadron, 8th Fighter Group are lined up on the airfield at San Jose, Mindoro Island, 20 December 1944. They were instrumental in destroying the remaining Japanese air forces in the Philippines and covered the landings at Lingayen Gulf. NARA 111-SC-A30104.

in the company of two LCI(G)s just off the beach. *LCI(R)337* scored some .50 caliber hits on the plane and it began to waver. Other gunboats took the plane under fire as it headed for an LST, and it was shot down between *LCI(R) 337* and the LST.

The airfields at Mindoro were quickly developed and supplied air cover for the landings at Lingayen on 9 January 1945. Supply ships transiting from Leyte Gulf to Mindoro were continually plagued by kamikaze and conventional Japanese air attacks until the threat was eliminated in early January 1945.

Lingayen — 9 January 1945

The largest and most heavily-defended of the Philippine Islands was the island of Luzon. There, in addition to the island nation's capital of Manila, were numerous airfields and the largest concentration of Japanese military personnel in the islands. They numbered 293,000 and were divided into three main regions.

The largest force consisted of the Army's Shobu Group under General Tomoyuki Yamashita. It was divided into four infantry and one tank division, plus the Tsuda Detachment and elements of the 4th Air Army, a total of 152,000 men. Yamashita's force controlled the northern and central part of the island.

In the middle of the island, centered on Clark Field and the Bataan Peninsula, was the Kembu Group under Major General Rikichi Tsukada. His 30,000 troops were made up of the 1st Raiding Group, 2nd Mobile Infantry, 39th Infantry, and elements of the 4th Air Army. An additional 15,000 naval combat and service troops were also in the area.

From Manila down to the end of the Bicol Peninsula, Lieutenant General Shizuo Yoko-

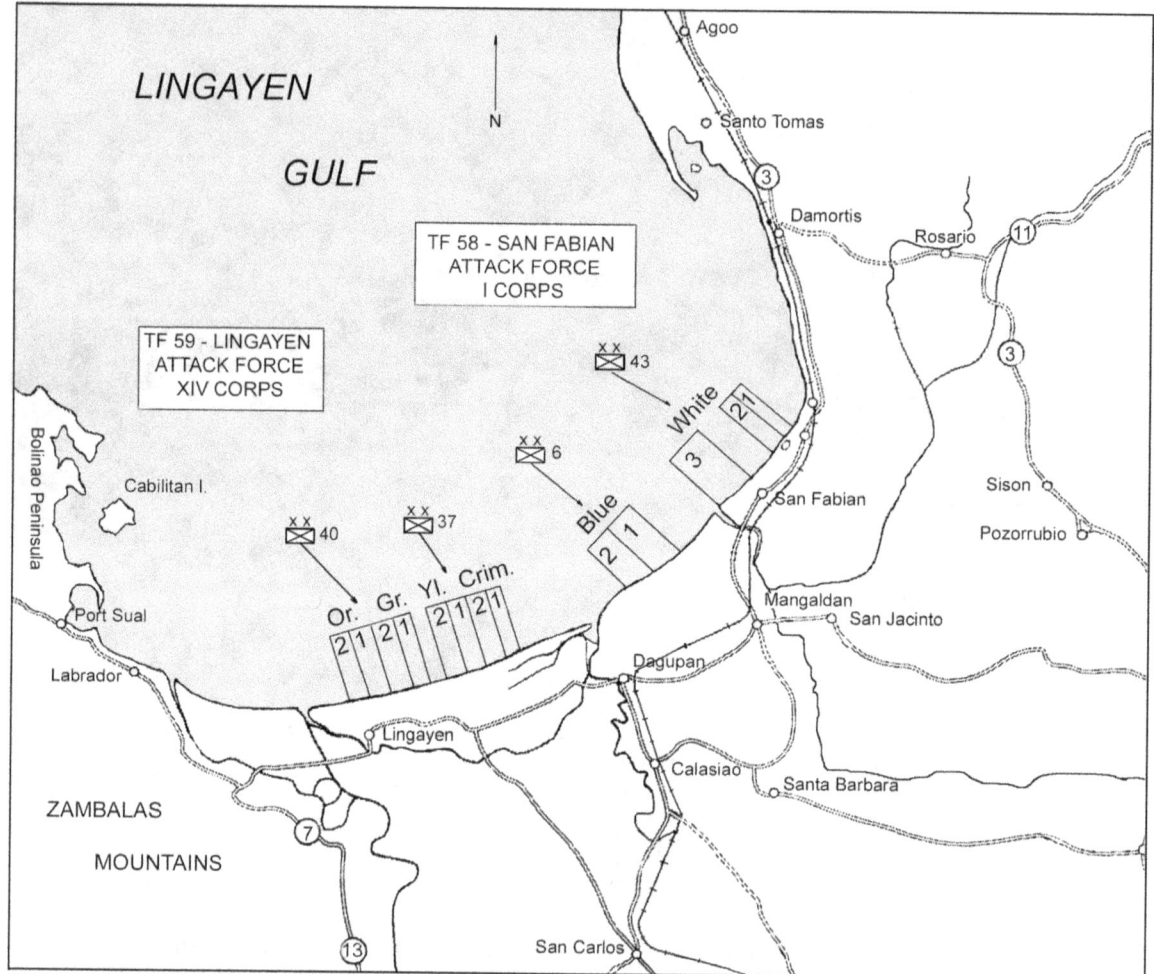

The assault at Lingayen Gulf involved two separate task forces, TFs 78 and 79. Landing on 9 January 1945 were the 6th, 37th, 43rd, and 40th Army Infantry Divisions. LCI gunboats were active in covering the UDT operations prior to the landing, as well as the landing itself.

yama's Shimbu Group held control. Under Yokoyama were 80,000 troops that included the 8th and 105th Army Divisions and elements of the 4th Air Army. The Manila Defense Force under Rear Admiral Sanji Iwabuchi added another 16,000 men to the total.[36]

The attack at Lingayen put American forces in direct conflict with Yamashita's forces. The overall plan was to land at Lingayen and then drive south to link up with American divisions that would drive northward from Manila.

U.S. Navy estimates of the strength of the Japanese placed the number at 224,500, noting that in the area near the Lingayen landing beaches

> were an estimated 35,000 troops, including two divisions, a mixed brigade, and an armored unit of at least one battalion. An examination of the beaches after our landing indicated that no determined defense of the beaches had been contemplated.... It was evident, however, that the enemy intended to hold all the hill country to the north and east of our beaches and had constructed many gun emplacement and other defenses throughout this area.[37]

The Japanese had twenty-eight air bases on Luzon, most lying in the central part of the island, although two were located on the southern end of Bicol Peninsula at Legaspi and Bulan.

Lieutenant (jg) Homer Roesti (in helmet), checks on members of his crew who were wounded in an attack by Japanese aircraft on 3 January 1945. NARA 80G 472019.

They were not expected to mount a major air offensive against the invasion, as American air attacks carried out by the 5th and 13th Air Forces and the carriers of the Third Fleet had taken their toll on Japanese air power. Approximately 700 Japanese aircraft had been destroyed in raids on Japanese fields on Luzon, Taiwan, and Okinawa. American aircraft flew off fields newly-won on Mindoro, Leyte, Morotai, Sansapor, Palau, and Saipan, and air cover over the invasion force was potent. Japanese air attacks were scattered and consisted of a few aircraft in single raids.

Japanese naval attacks on the invasion fleet were deemed unlikely. After the Second Battle of the Philippines, the Americans controlled the area to the east of the Philippines. The carriers of the Third Fleet roamed far and wide and were a serious threat to any Japanese ships attempting to intercept the invasion force. That, coupled with the ever growing effect of the American submarine fleet, made a Japanese naval intervention unlikely.

The trip to Lingayen was not without its perils. Task Group 77.6 departed San Pedro Bay, Leyte, on 2 January and headed for Lingayen to cover the activities of the Minesweeping and

Hydrographic Group. It included *LCI(G)s 64, 65, 68, 69,* and *70*. Along the way it suffered heavy air attacks. On 5 January, on board *LCI(G) 69*, CO Homer R. Roesti watched as a kamikaze headed toward his ship. Fire from the *69* and *LCI(G) 64* hit home and the Japanese plane splashed in the water. Other attacks took place, and by the end of the action *LCI(G) 69* had suffered six casualties from shrapnel.

Other ships en route to the invasion site came under attack on 7 January. At 1830 *LCI(G) 567* was strafed by one Japanese plane and bombed by another. Fortunately there were no injuries and the bomb missed the ship. *LCI(G) 580*, astern of the *567*, took the plane under fire as it passed by the column of ships and was fired on by *LCI(G)s 564* and *568* and *LCI(L) 676*. One plane was shot down and the other escaped after being hit several times.

Preliminaries

The assault on any beach was never a simple matter. Prior to the landing of troops, extensive surveys were needed to determine the best location for the assault beaches, the depth of water off the beaches, currents, surf conditions, location of obstacles and mines, and the clearing of these obstacles. This work was performed under great peril by the minesweepers and the Underwater Demolition Teams. Tasked as the Inshore Cover Unit TU 77.2.8 for the preliminary activities at Lingayen, were *LCI(G)s 64, 65, 68, 69,* and *70*, all of which mounted 3"/50s as their main gun. The remainder of the TU consisted of *LCI(G)s 442, 558, 559, 560,* and *751*, which had three 40mm guns, four 20mm guns, and rockets. Overall command of the task unit was held by Lieutenant Commander Robert S. Rickabaugh. Dividing the TU into two separate sections allowed Rickabaugh to directly command the ships covering the Lingayen area with *LCI(G)s 64, 68, 558, 559,* and *751*. Covering the San Fabian area were *LCI(G)s 65, 69(GF), 70, 422,* and *560* under Lieutenant Commander Holmes. UDT operations were conducted on 7 January with reports indicating that there were no obstacles or mines in the beach area.

LINGAYEN AREA — TF 79

UDT Team	Transport	Beaches	Fire Support
UDT 9	Belknap APD 34 Sands APD 13	Orange, Green	LCI(G)s 64, 558, 559
UDT 15	Blessman APD 48	Orange, Green	LCI(G) 64, 558, 559
UDT 5	Humphries APD 12 Overton APD 23	Yellow, Crimson	LCI(G)s 68, 751

SAN FABIAN AREA — TF 78

UDT Team	Transport	Beaches	Fire Support
UDT 10	Rathburne APD 25 Clemson APD 31	Blue	LCI(G)s 69, 560
UDT 8	G. E. Badger APD 126 Dickerson APD 21	White	LCI(G)s 65, 70, 422
UDT 14	Bull APD 78	White	LCI(G) 65, 70, 422[38]

On 5 January *LCI(G) 70* had finished performing her screening duties for the hydrographic ships when she came under attack by Japanese aircraft. A Zeke made a crash dive on her at 1974, coming in from her stern. It clipped off her mast before plowing into her 3"/50 gun tub, effectively knocking it out of commission. She suffered six dead and nine wounded but was still able to participate in the landings, although without the use of her main gun.

The covering plan for the UDT was to have a half-hour barrage of the landing beaches executed by the heavy ships in the fire support group. Following that, they would remain underway in the area and provide additional fire support as needed. The gunboats provided close-in fire support. They moved to positions 600 yards from the beach and kept up a heavy strafing attack on the beaches to one hundred yards past the waterline while the frogmen were at work.

Difficult conditions faced both the frogmen and their supporting gunboats on 7 January. Heavy swells and a strong undertow hampered their work, and it was only through great effort that they were able to complete their mission. They were harassed by sniper fire as they did their surveys, but the close-in fire support of the gunboats suppressed the enemy sufficiently. Unfortunately, the gunboats' fire was not as accurate as all would have hoped. Heavy swells rocked the flat bottomed boats and made it difficult for them to hit targets as effectively as they might have. More than a few rounds fell in the water near the swimmers but none were wounded. Additional fire was supplied by the APDs whose heavier hulls and design made for a more stable firing platform. Larger warships such as *West Virginia BB 48*, *Laffey DD 724*, and the survey ship *Sumner AGS 5* added their firepower to the mix, but their shells were aimed at larger targets behind the immediate beach line.

Fire support stations for coverage of landing beaches Crimson, Yellow, Green, and Orange at Lingayen during UDT activity on 7 January 1945. Commander Task Unit 79.7.1 (Commander LCI(G) Group 16), Serial 017, *Action Report for Luzon Operation 24 December 1944 to 23 January 1945*, Enclosure Baker.

LCI(G) 559 was off the Green and Orange Beaches supporting UDT 9. Prior to beginning her mission her CO, Lieutenant (jg) J. M. Horner, had decided to establish a given allowance per hour for each of his guns, based on his existing ammunition supply. This proved to be a relatively slow rate of fire, which under most conditions might be acceptable. As she approached the beach, enemy machine gun fire erupted in front of the bow of the LCP(R) carrying the UDT which was only fifty yards ahead. This sudden attack changed his philosophy on the rate of fire, with the gunboat sending a heavy barrage of 40mm and 20mm toward the suspected enemy gun emplacement.[39]

LCI(G) 558, cruising nearby, noted the presence of houses, warehouses, and two large buildings about one hundred yards off the beach. The town of Lingayen had its capitol building in this area as well. At 1330 incoming fire from the enemy emanated from a warehouse, and the gunboat directed 40mm fire on the warehouse, silencing the guns there. More gunfire erupted from the right hand side of the capitol building, and several gunboats directed their fire to the building and soon neutralized the enemy emplacements. The next enemy fire came from the second story of a nearby schoolhouse. Gunboat fire penetrated every window on the second floor, as well as the edge of the roof where suspected enemy snipers were located. To make sure that all opposition was quelled, every hut and house in the area was shelled, allowing UDT 9 to complete its work by 1623. The frogmen were picked up by their LCP(R) and left the area.[40]

On 8 January the UDT operations had ceased and the gunboats were able to pursue other targets. *LCI(G)s 64, 68, 70, 422, 558, 559, 560,* and *751* of TU 77.6.14, under Lieutenant Commander Rickabaugh, lay to in Lingayen Gulf as larger ships bombarded targets ashore. *LCI(G) 558* picked up a blip on her radar that indicated a small object two miles off her port bow. She headed to the object and found a converted fishing boat carrying a supply of airplane tires to the port at San Fernando. Two Japanese were in charge of the boat, along with twelve Filipinos who had been pressed into service. Apparently the boat had been targeted by a

Fire support stations for coverage of landing beaches White and Blue at Lingayen during UDT activity on 7 January 1945. Commander Task Unit 79.7.1 (Commander LCI(G) Group 16), Serial 017, *Action Report for Luzon Operation 24 December 1944 to 23 January 1945*, Enclosure Charlie.

destroyer earlier in the day and presumed sunk. The Filipinos were taken on board and treated as enemy combatants, but the Japanese refused to get on board and were killed as the gunboat pulled away.[41]

Finally a target just right for the gunboat's abilities was discovered. A group of enemy barges and small freighters had been discovered near shore a mile south of Poro Point. The gunboats formed a column and headed in their direction. At a range of 2,000 yards, the first of the gunboats opened fire then turned right and ran broadside to the targets until they were out of range. The entire line proceeded in this practice until the target ships were left in ruin. Fire from one of the gunboats ignited an ammunition dump on shore and it exploded.

Invasion Day — 9 January 1945

The invasion force scheduled to land at Lingayen was divided into two Task Forces, TF 78 and TF 79. Task Force 78, The San Fabian Attack Force, was under the command of Vice Admiral Daniel E. Barbey. It was to deliver the Army's I Corps under Major General I. P. Swift, to the White and Blue Beaches. The I Corps consisted of the 6th and 43rd Divisions. The 6th Division was commanded by Major General E. D. Patrick and the 43rd by Major General L. F. Wing.

Task Force 79, The Lingayen Attack Force, under the command of Vice Admiral T. S. Wilkinson was due to land the Army's XIV Corps, which was commanded by Major General O. W. Griswold. The XIV Corps consisted of the 37th and 40th Divisions. The 37th was commanded by Major General R. S. Beightler and the 40th by Major General Rapp Brush.

White Beach

Task Force 78, the San Fabian Attack Force, was assigned to land the Army's I Corps on beaches White 1, 2, 3 and Blue 1 and 2. Landing on White Beach 1 was the 1st BLT, 172nd RCT. White Beach 2 was assaulted by the 169th RCT and White Beach 3 by the 103rd RCT. All units were part of the 43rd Infantry Division I Corps. The gunboats reported to the line of departure at 0800 and were soon underway. The mortar gunboats *LCI(M)s 359, 362, 431* were in position for their barrage at 0845 and began their bombardment of beach positions on White Beach 1 and to its left. Running along the coast in that location were railroad tracks, and the mortars from the ships were on target. Two hills just behind the beach area were in their target area, and the mortar boats laid another barrage on both the forward and reverse sides of the hills. *LCI(M) 359* reported delivering 167 rounds of high explosives and white phosphorous on the first hill and another 115 rounds of high explosive on the second. The other two mortar ships delivered similar barrages. By 0942, their slow speed of only three knots had carried them to within 1,000 yards of the beach, and they turned off to await call-fire orders. As with most assaults by rockets and mortars, the ships' commanding officers reported that the target was so obscured by smoke and dust that it was almost impossible to correctly find targets or determine the effectiveness of their fire. In many cases radar would have solved the problem, and the ships continually mentioned the need for radar in their action reports. The best they could do was to take fixes on various shore points or depend on larger ships' radar as a guide.

Leading the landing craft to the White Beaches were *LCI(G)s 31, 73, 342,* and *LCI(R)s 72* and *331.* They were to provide rocket fire on the beaches in advance of the LVTs carrying elements of the 43rd Infantry Reinforced. Reports indicated a line of trenches and pill boxes near the beach that were expected to offer heavy resistance to the landing. Beginning at 0857 the rocket ships left the line of departure and began firing 40mm guns at 0913. Their first rocket salvos went shoreward at 0921. *LCI(G) 342* spotted a sandbar dead ahead as she was in the middle of her run. Unfazed by its presence, her CO, Lieutenant (jg) James A. Hynes, ran his ship forward and completed firing his rockets until he grounded on the bar. He deemed it more important to support the troops landing in front of him. Fortunately the ship's slow speed allowed him to back off the bar once his firing was completed. All ships at White Beach reported misfires with their rockets because of wiring problems. However, the overwhelming majority of the rockets did fire, with only about five percent failures reported. Occasional Japanese aircraft passed over the area, but most were shot down by ships' fire or American aircraft. The consolidation of the airfields on islands already captured had given the fleet at Lingayen excellent air cover.

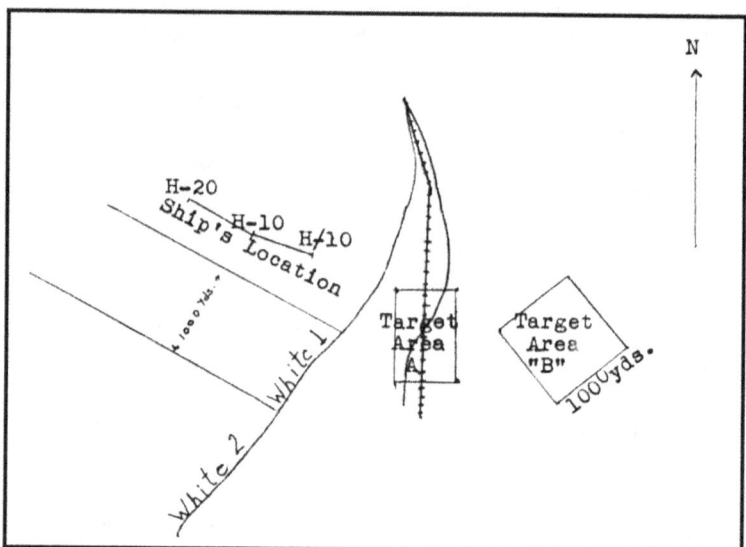

This is the assault course for *LCI(M) 431* at the White Beach flank during the landing at Lingayen. In many beach assaults the LCI(M)s were used on the flanks because of their longer range weapons and their ability to reach the reverse slopes of hills. *U.S.S. LCI(M) 432 Serial 01, Action Report—Lingayen Operation,* 15 January 1945, Enclosure (A).

Blue Beaches

The Blue Beaches, just to the south, were to be the landing sites of elements of the 6th Infantry Division I Corps. Blue Beach 1 was assigned to the 1st RCT and Blue Beach 2 to the 20th RCT. TU 78.5.8 under Lieutenant Commander A. M. Holmes, composed of *LCI(G)*s 64, 69 *LCI(R)*s 225, 226, 230, 337, 338, and *341*, supplied close-in fire support for the landing.

The gunboats were at the line of departure at 0900 and got underway for their rocket runs. The LCI(G)s were on the flanks with the rocket ships in the center. At 0925 the fourth of the ranging rockets hit the beach and was followed shortly thereafter by eight salvos of forty-four rockets from each of the LCI(R)s. *LCI(R) 226* noted a number of five inch shells hitting the water twenty-five to one hundred yards off her bow, seriously imperiling the advancing LVTs. Her CO, Lieutenant (jg) W. L. Harned, ordered the engines backed and gave the order to strafe the beach with all available guns. One 40mm, three 20mm and four .50 caliber guns opened up on suspected enemy locations for a full minute. The boat waves passed by and landed safely. It was just this kind of enemy opposition that doomed many Marines and soldiers in the early days of the war. It called for advances in close-in fire support, which led to the development of the amphibious gunboats. Had it not been for their presence, the LVTs would have been sitting ducks. By the time the gunboats had finished firing off their rocket salvos, they were within 300 yards of the beach.

On board *LCI(G) 226*, Signalman Arden Lee Hunt recorded his experiences as the attack on Lingayen's Blue Beaches developed:

> We all went to General Quarters at 0500 in the morning. It is not dawn yet. All the Can's and Cruisers opened up as soon as it was light enough. There was also three battle ships firing, the first I have seen overseas. They sure could throw the shells in.

5. The Philippines Retaken — Leyte and Lingayen

We were to lay back until 0900, then proceed to the beach and fire our 528 rockets. Before this we had an air attack. We came very close to hitting one zero. They hit a destroyer with a bomb. We, the convoy, shot down several of their planes. One plane crashed dived on a ship setting it afire. Don't know how many were killed. We went in at 0900. We could now hear the battle ships shells singing by over our heads.

We were about 200 yd. from the beach when we started letting the rockets go. About that time there was a big explosion and water shot way up about 100 feet off our stern. About ten seconds later there was another about 100 feet on our port beam. By now we were so scared we were laying on the deck. Then the big one came. It hit just a little over 10 feet from our port bow, spraying us all with water. The boys were really scared now. By now we had launched all the rockets and were backing away from the beach like hell, with engines all wide open. Two more shells hit close off our starboard beam on the way out.

We were never so glad to leave a beach.[42]

The landing beaches assigned to the I Corps lay to the east of the Dagupan River and were designated as Blue 1 and 2, White 3, and White 2 and 1 respectively. Beaches assigned to the XIV Corps to the west of the Dagupan River were Crimson Beaches 1 and 2, Yellow Beaches 1 and 2, and Green Beaches 1 and 2. At the farthest western extreme were Orange Beaches 1 and 2. Army historians described the beaches facing the XIV Corps thus: "In peacetime one would have considered the shore line a beautiful swimming beach, a magnificent strand of firm sand stretching eastward almost nine miles from the mouth of the Calmay River to the mouth of the Dagupan."[43]

Although the beauty of the beaches was notable, a six to ten foot surf had kicked up by 10 January, promising a less than ideal landing for the troops and their supplies. The 43rd Infantry Division was scheduled to land on the three White Beaches. However, conditions on White Beach 3 were poor and it proved unusable. LSTs found themselves too far from the shore for efficient unloading. White Beaches 1 and 2 were much better, affording the landing ships the ability to get in close to shore. With this change in planning, White Beaches 1 and 2 soon became overcrowded, adding to congestion in the area. The downside to White Beaches 1 and 2 were their close proximity to Japanese forces, who soon took them under attack. Fire from the LCI(G)s, which were just off shore ended the threat from these enemy troops.

With the initial landings completed, the gunboats turned to routine patrols and harassment of targets ashore. Laying smoke and screening for the anchored transports was standard duty. Beginning on 10 January 1945, a new threat arose with the appearance of suicide boats and suicide swimmers.

Port Sual on the southwest end of the landing beaches, was home to the Japanese 12th Fishing Boat Battalion. This unit consisted of nearly seventy *Maru-re* suicide boats. Under command of Captain Isao Takahashi, the battalion had lost thirty boats in previous encounters but was still capable of inflicting much damage. During the evening of 9-10 January, three companies, under Second Lieutenants Hayashi, Uemura, and Tahara, led the entire force out into the Lingayen Gulf in search of prey.

LCI(M) 974 supplied mortar fire in the area of Yellow and Crimson Beaches during the landing on 9 January. She had no requests for call-fire for the remainder of the day and prepared for her nighttime assignment of laying a smoke screen to cover the transport. She was anchored to seaward of the anchorage when, at 0400 in the morning, one of the *Maru-re*'s dropped its depth charges next to her hull. The explosion tore a hole in her bottom and she went under in six minutes. The combined crew of Navy sailors and Army mortar men took many casualties, and all but a few of the men were uninjured.

The suicide boats swarmed through the anchorage. The close quarters of the anchored boats and poor visibility from the smoke were excellent conditions for the *Maru-re*. *Philip DD 498*, *Robinson DD 562*, and *Leutze DD 481* were underway and fired on a number of the boats with some success. However, the crowded anchorage made it difficult to fire for fear of hitting friendly ships. In addition, their guns could not depress sufficiently to hit the suicide boats when they were close to the ship.

At 0325 *LST 925* was attacked by two boats, one from port and one from starboard. She was severely damaged, and it took three days of repairs before she was able to land her troops and cargo. *War Hawk AP 168* was hit at 0410. The explosion of the depth charges tore a twenty-five foot hole in her side and killed sixty-one of her crew. She was severely damaged, but her crew patched her together and she survived. The destroyer *Robinson*, attempting to catch some of the boats, had a close call at 0414 when a *Maru-re* dropped its charges near her, but the ship was not damaged.

The LSTs were prime targets. *LST 610* was anchored when she was struck at 0436. The explosion damaged one of her engines and she had difficulty the following day when she tried to beach and discharge her cargo. *LST 1028* came to the aid of *LST 925* after she had been hit and soon was a victim of the suicide boats as well. At 0441, as she was anchored near the *925*, she was able to open fire on the boat, but it got in too close to her for her guns to depress sufficiently and it dropped its depth charges. The pilot of the *Maru-re* was able to get away before the explosion, however, he was caught by the LST's gunners and killed in a crossfire. *LST 548* was attacked at 0524 but was not damaged seriously.

At 0430 *LCI(G) 365* was alerted by the explosion that sank *LCI(M) 974*. She could hear gunfire from other ships in the area but had no knowledge of what was transpiring. At 0443 her lookouts spotted a *Maru-re* off her port beam but did not recognize it for what it was. Ships were wary of firing too quickly on small craft, as there were a number of small boats operating in the area that were from American ships. After several challenges with no response, the order was given to take the craft under fire with the aft 20mm gun. Hits were scored on the suicide boat, but the 20mm jammed after only firing forty-eight rounds. As a result the suicide boat made it to her side and dropped its charges. Lieutenant (jg) John M. Hoctor, CO of the *365*, was on the conn when the blast occurred. He was injured in the attack when the binnacle tore loose and struck him. No one was killed and only three men had minor injuries. Handy billys were rigged to pump out the water which was rapidly filling the hold, however, they could not keep up with the inflow of water and the ship began to list heavily to port. The lines leading to the sea chest intakes had been ruptured, causing water to flood her engine room. *LCI(G)s 442* and *662* came to her aid and began to tow her toward the beach. A Chrysler suction pump was supplied by *LCI(G) 442*, but it was still not sufficient. Ammunition and heavy equipment was transferred to the starboard side to help in righting the ship. *Hidatsa ATF 102* came on the scene with additional pumps. A half hour later the *365* was safe, however her damage was so extensive that she was out of the war. Her crew and ammunition were transferred to *LCI(G) 442*. A skeleton crew remained on board for the long tow back to Pearl Harbor.[44]

The following morning, at 0720, lookouts on *LCI(G) 559* spotted a Japanese swimmer in a life jacket. He was covered with oil and they suspected that he was a pilot or crewman on one of the suicide boats from the earlier attack. Their attempts to entice him on board were to no avail. He slipped out of his life jacket and dove underwater. He never surfaced, apparently preferring death to capture.[45]

In addition to the suicide boats, the ships also had to be on the lookout for suicide swimmers. Japanese soldiers tied explosives to their bodies or pushed explosives on small rafts. Their plan was to get close enough to the ships to set them off.

In his report on the Lingayen Operation, Vice Admiral Theodore S. Wilkinson reported:

> In attacks by hand placed charges miscellaneous small boats were used. These boats depended upon stealth rather than speed in their approach. They have been described as about 18 feet long and "looked like an ordinary rowboat with an outboard motor" or "like a wherry with an outboard

motor." ... One boat was reported to be in the form of a small catamaran with an outboard motor. In this case the resulting explosion was of such intensity that it was evident that the charge must have been of such size that it could not have been carried by the catamaran but must have been suspended beneath. In two instances the Japs were seen to roll a spherical mine-like object about two feet in diameter over the gunwale as the boat reached the ship's side.... The success of these attacks by small boats can be attributed mainly to the lack of alertness and readiness for action by the ships at anchor. Attack by PT boats was anticipated but infiltration by small, quiet, low powered boats caught those on watch unprepared.... Most boats when first seen were so close that machine guns mounted on the ship could not be brought to bear. Corrective measures are obvious, in special watches, portable machine-guns, hand grenades.[46]

Had Admiral Wilkinson known what lay ahead in regard to suicide boats, he would have begun some rapid revision of ship tactics. The disasters at Mariveles and Nasugbu were only weeks away.

Crimson Beach 1–2

Beaches on the southern section of Lingayen Gulf were Crimson 1, 2, Yellow 1, 2, Green 1, 2, and Orange 1 and 2 lying from north to south respectively. The Lingayen Attack Force TF 79 landed the Army's XIV Corps there.

Crimson Beaches 1 and 2 were assaulted by the 129th RCT of the 37th Infantry Division. Yellow Beaches 1 and 2 were taken by the 148th RCR of the 37th Infantry Division. Units of the 40th Infantry Division landed on the Green and Orange Beaches, the 160th RCT on Green 1 and 2, and the 185th RCT on Orange 1 and 2.

The initial assault began at 0826 with the LCI gunboats leaving the line of departure. After firing four rocket salvos, the gunboats lay to and allowed the LVTs to pass. They retired to the left of the beaches to provide call-fire as Army troops advanced along the beach. Participating in this mission were *LCI(G)s 565, 567, 568, 580*, and three mortar gunboats. They strafed the beach about 600 yards ahead of the 129th RCT as it advanced north along the beach.

Lieutenant (jg) Charles J. Macres, CO of *LCI(G) 560*, noted the relative uselessness of both .30 and .50 caliber fire in repelling air attacks. Even the 20mm gun had a range limited enough so that the only danger from these small caliber guns was to other ships in the fleet. He further recommended that ships should "secure all 50 caliber guns not mounted forward on rocket—mortar ships as they approach beach. Some of this small caliber fire is an absolute menace to our own ships."[47]

Green-Orange

Army landings at beaches designated as Green and Orange were supported by gunboats from Flotilla Fourteen under Captain T. W. Rimer's TU 79.8.2. Under Rimer were two units, TU 79.87.2, consisting of thirteen *LCI(G)s, 366, 372, 373, 439, 440, 451(F), 461, 462, 464, 465, 467, 472,* and *475* under Lieutenant Frank R. Giliberty and TU 79.8.1 comprised of *LCI(M)s 659, 660(GF), 658, 754, 755,* and *975* under Lieutenant Commander G. W. Hannett. Two *LCI(L)s, 598* and *738*, performed salvage and firefighting duties under Captain T. W. Rimer, who held overall command of TU 79.8.2. *LCI(G) 462*, part of TU 79.8.2 with her companions, attacked the beach directly in front of the provincial capitol building.

On 10 January *LCI(G)s 440, 461, 465, 467,* and *475*, after supporting the landing of the 40th Infantry Division on Orange Beach One, were ordered to strafe the Cabalitian Bay area while seeking out and destroying any small boats visible. Their first rockets were sent shoreward at 1645 along with 40mm and 20mm fire. The attack destroyed some small boats and a number of houses near the water. Friendly natives reported the absence of Japanese in the area.

Getting the mortar boats on line for the assault proved difficult as the larger fire-support ships were in the area, making it necessary for the LCI(M)s to zig-zag through their line to get to the line of departure. At 0730, while the mortar boats were about 4,000 yards off the beach, a kamikaze attacked and crashed on *Columbia CL 56*. Numerous ships in the area fired at the plane, and a 20mm shell from one landed on the deck of *LCI(M) 975*, wounding four of the crew and one of the officers. The group's doctor was on board *LCI(M) 658* and the men were brought there for medical aid. Having delivered the wounded safely, the *975* went back to her assignment.

The mortar ships accompanied the LCI(G)s as they left the line of departure at 0845 and began firing their mortars fifteen minutes later. They had to slow their progress, as the landing craft were slower and could not keep up. The mortar gunboats finished their run at a distance of 300 yards from the beach as the landing craft passed through their lines. Since their mortars had a long range, they continued to fire them after the troops landed. The order came to lift their firing range to positions one thousand yards inland, and they continued to fire until fifteen minutes after the landing. From that point on their mortar fire was coordinated with the advances of the 185th RCT as it moved westward along the beach.

By late in the evening the mortar ships were in the area off the Agno River. The next afternoon, around 1245, they received a message from the 185th RCT to fire on a grid containing a large contingent of Japanese infantry. Reports indicated that their mortars had been successful in killing many of the enemy and forcing them to retreat from the area.

Later in the day, at 1310, the mortar gunboats joined forces with other gunboats and were sent on a search and destroy mission in the area around Salamanca Island. There they shelled suspected enemy positions including boats, houses, caves, and brush piles. They then entered Salamanca Bay and found numerous small boats on the beach and some suspected enemy positions. These were taken under fire with mortars and rockets and left on fire.

The mortar ships used at Lingayen lacked 40mm bow guns, and it was recommended by Lieutenant Commander Hannett that one be mounted on the LCI(M)s to increase the usefulness of the ship.[48] A number of the mortar gunboats had Army personnel on board to fire the 4.2 mortars. On 12 January the mortar personnel were landed on shore to join their Army comrades. Rocket gunboats in the assault had some problems. The units reported that rocket firing only had a 77 percent successful firing rate, primarily due to electrical malfunctions. With their primary mission completed, most of the gunboats departed for Leyte on 18 January 1945.

CHAPTER 6

The LCS(L)s Arrive

The newly-designed and built LCS(L)(3) ships were late entering the war. Much of the fighting across the Pacific had already taken place prior to their first entrance into the war zone at Hollandia, New Guinea, on 5 December 1944. Arriving at Humboldt Bay were the first ships of what would become Flotilla One, the *LCS(L)s 26, 27, 48,* and *49*. By mid–January, *LCS(L)s 9, 10, 28, 29, 30,* and *50* had joined them and were running constant patrols in Humboldt Bay under the direction of their commander on board *LC(FF) 778*. Their primary duty there was anti-submarine patrol, although their lack of depth charges made this a somewhat unrealistic task. Their first chance at actual combat would come in the Philippines.

Departing Hollandia for the Philippines on 10 January were *LCS(L)s 7, 8, 26, 27,* and *48*. *LCS(L)s 28, 29, 30,* and *50* departed on 24 January. Remaining behind, but following soon after, were *9* and *10*, whose exploits in the Philippines would be unique.

Once having arrived in the Philippines, the LCS(L)s were assigned to Task Unit 78.3.8, which included *LCS(L)s 7, 8, 26, 27, 28, 48,* and *49*, along with *LCI(R)s 225, 226, 337, 338, 340,* and *341*. The area around San Antonio in Zambalas Province on the western coast of Luzon was of interest to the high command, and the task unit was assigned to fire support for the landing of 30,000 troops of the XI Corps, 8th Army under Major General C. P. Hall. Information had been received that the Japanese had left the area, and the gunboats were told to hold fire rather than obliterating everything on the landing beaches as they normally did. The landing craft with their troops hit the beaches at 0832 on 29 January 1945 and were greeted by Philippine natives waving an American flag. A similar unopposed landing was made at Grande Island in Subic Bay. Subsequent landings would not prove so easy. The next targets would be Corregidor, Bataan Peninsula, and Manila Bay.

Nasugbu

To the south of Manila Bay was the area around Nasugbu Point. In order to secure the southern flank of the operations around Manila Bay it was necessary to land troops ashore at Nasugbu. In addition, numerous suicide boats had been located in the area and were a threat to transports.

The troops of the 11th Airborne Division under Major General J. M. Swing were scheduled to land at Nasugbu on 31 January 1945. Escorting them to the beaches and landing them would be Rear Admiral Fechteler's Group 8 ships from the VII Amphibious Corps. The part of that force supplying direct fire support for the landing was Task Unit 78.2.6 under Commander

D. H. Day. It consisted of *LCI(R)s 34, 73(F), 74, 331, LCI(G)s 407, 442, 558, 561, 580, 751,* and TU 78.2.4, consisting of *LCI(M)s 359, 362, 431,* and *755.*

Bombardment by the gunboats preceded the landing. The landing beaches were inside two points of land, Nasugbu Point and San Diego Point, an area that could provide enfilading fire directed at the landing forces. Beginning at 0715 *LCI(R)s 34, 73,* and *LCI(G)s 558,* and *751* delivered rocket barrages on suspected enemy gun positions in those areas. This was followed at 0730 by a mortar barrage from *LCI(M)s 359, 362, 431,* and *755*. Backing up the mortar ships were two LCI(G)s.

The line of departure formed at 0800 and was led by four LCI(R)s flanked by two LCI(G)s on either side. At 0811 the gunboats hit the landing zone with a rocket barrage, and the landing craft passed through and delivered their human cargo to the beach. Enemy mortar and machine gun fire was directed at the beaches from Wawa Village, and at 0915 *LCI(G)s 558* and *442* were detailed to suppress the fire, which they did within a half hour. Identification of enemy pillboxes and gun emplacements continued throughout the day with the gunboats firing on and destroying enemy emplacements.

One could never be sure who or what was on the water. In the afternoon, *LCI(G) 561* was ordered to investigate a native outrigger with five people on board. Close investigation revealed that it was an Army intelligence officer, Major Vanderpool, the Central Luzon Intelligence Coordinator. He was accompanied by four Filipino guerrillas. The gunboat gave them a lift to the Army headquarters on the beach, dodging machine gun and mortar fire on the way in.

Suicide boats were known to be operating in the area. Fourteen gunboats were anchored in an arc around the landing beaches to protect the LSTs. Destroyers and destroyer escorts on the outer screen encountered several suicide boats and destroyed them. These boats were from the Japanese Army's 19th Liaison Boat Battalion which was stationed in nearby Binubusan. Just before midnight on 31 January, they left their base and headed for the anchored invasion fleet at Nasugbu. The first to spot the suicide boats was *PC 1129.* She notified the destroyer *Lough DE 586* of their presence and was told to investigate. She was soon surrounded by the suicide boats and under attack. These were Japanese Army *Maru-re* which carried two depth charges on racks at the rear of the boat. Earl O. Griffis, Sr., a cook on board *PC 1129,* had just finished baking bread and went on deck for some fresh air when the explosion went off, blowing him back to the fantail. The blast holed the ship near the engine room and it soon listed and went under. Only one man died in the attack; *Lough* picked up the sixty-three survivors. The destroyer spotted a number of the *Maru-re* in

Crewmen on *LCI(G) 442's* port 40mm gun fire on a Japanese machine gun nest near Nasugbu, Philippine Islands. NARA 80G 273136.

the water around her and sank six, effectively ending the suicide boat attack that night. None had penetrated to the inner screen of gunboats to get at the transports.

The following day, the destroyers *Claxton DD 571* and *Russell DD 414*, along with *LCI(G)s 73, 442*, and *558*, were sent into Talin and Matabungay Bays to search out and destroy suspected enemy suicide boat bases. Heavy foliage covered the area and it was difficult to determine what might be hidden there. Some sites were obvious and the gunboats had some limited success. They destroyed two probable suicide boats and three outriggers and strafed suspected locations. Continued patrols by gunboats, destroyers, and PT boats put an end to the scourge of the suicide boats in the area.

Commander Task Unit 78.2.6, Commander D. H. Day, reported the strategy for screening against the suicide boats at Nasugbu:

(a) LCIs were anchored in line at short stay, 500 yards apart. It is not believed possible to be sure of seeing a small low craft at distances exceeding 250 yards. Surface radar cannot be relied on especially in a crowded anchorage.
(b) Crews were at condition II, ready to go to general quarters at first contact. All binoculars were in use and small arms were issued out and ready.
(c) Signal searchlights had color screens removed and were manned. Destroyers had reported that craft were extremely hard to see and gunners were frequently blinded by their own tracers. Instructions were therefore issued for ship making contact to immediately illuminate target and keep searchlight trained on as a guide to gunners and other vessels. It is reported that the small suicide craft have little if any return fire, so use of searchlight does not have its usual danger.
(d) Heavy emphasis is laid on alertness. Vessels were reminded of the usual tactics of suicide craft,

A round from *LCI(G) 442*'s port 40mm gun may be seen heading for a target at Talin Point, Nasugbu, Philippine Islands. NARA 80G 273135.

to approach from several directions at once, and all hands were warned against the tendency of ships not engaged, to watch the shooting of other ships and forget their own immediate area.[1]

Although Day's recommendations would have good and bad points, its timing was a bit too soon for the information to filter down to other gunboat units. The disaster at Mariveles Harbor was only days away.

Disaster at Mariveles

The capital of the Philippines, Manila, was an important goal for the American forces. At the entrance to Manila Bay was the island of Corregidor and the Bataan Peninsula, the scene of an inglorious defeat for the Americans only three years earlier.

The 151st Regimental Combat Team under Major General Chase, along with the 3rd Battalion 34th Infantry, was assigned to assault the area around Mariveles Harbor and secure the southern extremity of Bataan Peninsula. Their landing was scheduled for 15 February 1945 and would be covered by TU 78.3.8 under the command of Captain Rae Arison, who served as Commodore of the task unit. It consisted of *LCS(L)s 7, 8, 26, 27, 48, 49* and *LCI(R)s 225, 226, 337, 338, 340, 341* and two PCs.

Two days of minesweeping in the bay preceded the actual assault. On 15 February 1945, firing on shore targets by cruisers and destroyers commenced at 0840. Forty-five minutes later the area was attacked by American bombers. The gunboat task unit had moved into Mariveles Bay at 0825 on 15 February 1945 and fired on Gordo Point with its automatic weapons. Then they launched rockets at Caracol Point. They cruised the bay area looking for targets of opportunity but found little enemy resistance. The line of departure formed and the gunboats made their first run at the landing beaches at 0947. An enemy gun fired on the gunboats from their left flank and was destroyed by fire from an accompanying destroyer. The first wave of landing craft left the line of departure at 0950 and was on the beach ten minutes later.

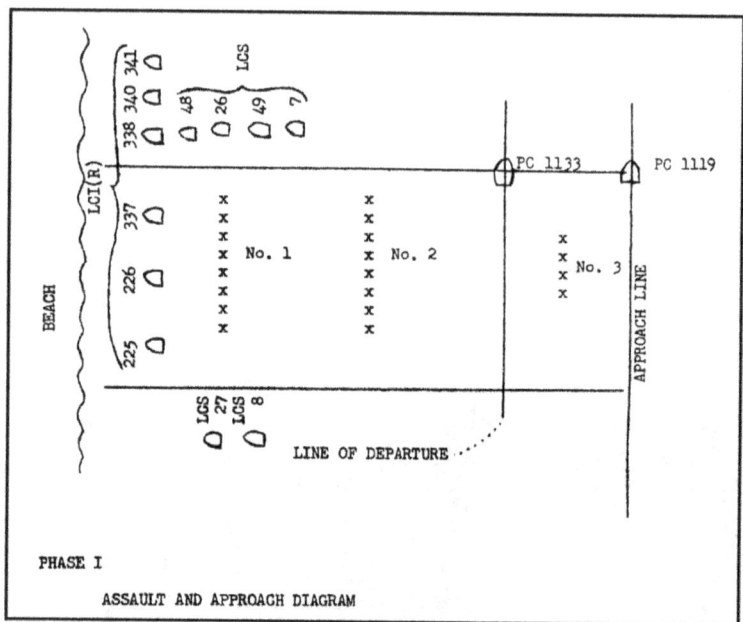

At 1037 *LSM 169* was underway nearby. She struck a mine and her CO, Lieutenant (jg) Paul C. Himelright, gave the order to abandon ship. The fires on the LSM were out of control; men were overboard and other ships moved in to assist. An ocean rescue tug in

This chart shows the assault diagram for the landing of the 151st RCT on the beach at Mariveles Harbor. This was the first assault action for the LCS(L)s. The LCI(R)s were assigned to clear the beaches in front of the assault and the LCS(L)s, with their heavier firepower, were assigned targets on the flanks of the assault force. Unfortunately, several LCS(L)s were lost to suicide boats later that evening. LCS(L) Flotilla One Serial 03, *Action Report USS LCI (L) 778* Flagship, 23 February 1945, Enclosure (A).

the area fought the fires with *LCS(L) 48* standing by. The gunboat and *PC 1133* picked up survivors. *LCS(L) 48* picked up thirteen and delivered to them *LST 667*, which was serving the area as a hospital ship. *LSM 169* stayed afloat, but she was decommissioned a year later and then scuttled.

The LCS(L)s were ordered to anchor across the mouth of Mariveles Harbor on a line stretching from Gorda Point to Cockines Point after the day's action had ended. Their mission was to act as a screen for the landing craft that had deposited their men ashore earlier in the day. Six LSTs were beached at the town of Mariveles, with several LSMs and another LST anchored in the harbor. The six LCI(R)s were anchored in the bay on the western side, leaving the LCS(L)s in the most exposed position. It was thought that the heavier firepower of the LCS(L)s could hold off any attempts to get at the ships in the harbor.

As dusk fell, approximately forty-one Japanese Navy *Shinyo* suicide boats left their caves on Corregidor to seek out and attack American ships at Mariveles Bay, only four miles from Corregidor. Although the numbers of *Shinyo* at Corregidor had been steadily reduced over the preceding month, a number had survived. They were protected in their caves and immune to all but direct hits by naval gunfire or air attack. Lieutenant Yoshihisa Matsueda was in command of the thirty-three *Shinyo* of his 12th *Shinyo-tai* Unit. Eight more of the craft were from the 9th *Shinyo-tai* Unit commanded by Lieutenant (jg) Kenjiro Nakajima. An additional group of thirty-three *Shinyo*, under Lieutenant Commander Shoichi Oyamada, set out from Corregidor, but not all headed for Mariveles. They sought other targets and headed for Subic Bay, but eight of them peeled off from the group and joined in the attack at Mariveles Bay.

The first ships they encountered were the six LCS(L)s anchored across the mouth of the bay. *LCS(L) 7*, under the command of Lieutenant Franklin L. Elder, was the first gunboat hit. At 0305 two boats slammed into her and blew gaping holes in her sides. Within minutes she

As an oceangoing tug fights fires on board *LSM 169* at Mariveles Bay, Philippine Islands, *LCS(L) 48* stands by ready to assist. *LSM 169* struck a mine on 15 February 1945. The LSM was saved, but she had two men killed in action. *LCS(L) 48* picked up thirteen survivors who had been in the water and transferred them to *LST 667*, which was serving as a hospital ship during the invasion. Official U.S. Navy photograph.

This tunnel on Corregidor housed Imperial Navy *Shinyo* boats that were used to counter the American assault on the Manila Bay area. NARA 111-SC 263698.

went to the bottom. Anchored nearby was *LCS(L) 49*. Claude Haddock S 1/c was on watch and saw the attack. He wakened the commanding officer, Lieutenant Harry W. Smith, who sounded general quarters. Unfortunately, it was too late and the *49* was hit only moments later. Within minutes a second *Shinyo* crashed into her port side. The ship quickly exploded, rolled over, and went under. Haddock and other crewmen went over the side and managed to paddle ashore.[2] *LCS(L) 49* suffered twenty-four dead or missing in action and twenty-two wounded.

Still another LCS(L) was attacked at the same time as the *49*. *LCS(L) 26* was struck by *Shinyo* on both port and starboard sides and began taking on water almost immediately. Fires raged below decks and men died attempting to escape the fires below. Dean Bell S 2/c was in the crew's compartment and watched two men burn to death attempting to escape up the ladder. With water up to his chest, he finally braved the flames to go topside. The heat of the flames on the handrail had made them too hot to hold and the flesh on his hands was burned away as he made it to the deck. Bell's injuries made it impossible to tie the strings on his lifejacket. He jumped in the water and was aided by shipmates and finally reached shore along with a number of the crew. By the time they reached shore, their ship had vanished beneath the waters of Mariveles Bay. For Bell the war was over. He would spend time on a hospital ship and then in Navy hospitals before the doctors declared him fit for discharge.

LCS(L) 27 managed to get under way and fight through the swarm of suicide boats. However, after destroying three of the attackers, a forth struck her port side amidships. Her CO, Lieutenant Risley Lawrence, saved his ship by running it up on the beach so that it could not sink. *LCS(L) 27*'s Engineering Officer, Lieutenant (jg) Harry G. Meister, later wrote:

> The Commanding Officer had meantime called the engineering officer to ask if damage was too great to allow beaching of the ship. The engineering officer reported that ship was taking water fast on port side in both engine room and generator room but that it could be attempted on one quad

Three Imperial Navy *Shinyo* suicide boats are shown on tracks leading from their cave to the water on Corregidor. A series of caves may be seen in the cliffside. This made it difficult to eradicate the boats with air or naval attack, but left them vulnerable to disaster if one caught fire in the tunnel. This photograph was taken on 27 February 1945. NARA 111-SC-263697.

of the main engine. Fires in numbers two and three holds were reported also but were subsequently brought under control. Speed was then made standard and ship was put on course toward the west side of Mariveles Harbor. As ship neared beach, a small boat was observed to be closing on the starboard side. It was engaged by 20mm fire on that side and sunk. At approximately 0340 Item this vessel grounded at standard speed having reached a port list of approximately 25 degrees.[3]

LCS(L) 48 served as the flagship of Captain Rae E. Arison, Commanding Officer of LCS(L) Flotilla One. One of his staff officers, Lieutenant (jg) L. Richard Rhame, later described the pandemonium that struck when the suicide boats attacked:

Suddenly, the stillness of the early morning was shattered by a blinding flash! Simultaneously, multiple explosions erupted all along the line of stationary LCS(L)s. The morning sky was aglow with deadly pyrotechnics: bursting shells, fiery streaks of ricocheting tracers piercing the darkness from all directions. Burning oil transformed Mariveles Bay into a blazing sea of flames.... The staccato firing from the .50 caliber machine guns from the LCS(L)s echoed amidst the din of the battle. The larger guns could not be angled down sufficiently to be effective against the surface-level invaders. Voice messages from the ships of the fleet outside the harbor flooded the Communications Center of the USS LCS(L) 48. The "glamour ships" at sea were not positioned to offer assistance — a destroyer, firing illumination shells over the harbor in its efforts to be helpful, was ordered by Commodore Arison to cease such activity as it was being used by the attackers to zero in on their targets with greater accuracy.[4]

This *Shinyo*, on tracks outside its cave on Corregidor, was part of the 9th Suicide Unit under Lieutenant (jg) Kenjiro Nakajima. The forward hatch of the vessel may be seen lying on the ground next to it. Commander Task Force SEVENTY-EIGHT Serial 0907, *Action Reports, MARIVELES–CORREGIDOR Operation, 12–16 February 1945,* Enclosure (G).

Arison immediately ordered the ships to get underway. *LCS(L) 48* had been fortunate in that it had left the line of anchored ships at 2300 hours on 15 February to aid a nearby damaged LSM that had begun to drag anchor. Her return resulted in her anchoring inside the line and saved her from the initial attack. Also escaping the wrath of the suicide boats was *LCS(L) 8*. By morning the extent of the disaster was obvious. *LCS(L)s 7, 26,* and *49* had gone to the bottom and *LCS(L) 27* was grounded on the beach with severe damage. It would be the singular worst disaster of the war for the LCS(L)s. Signalman Arden Lee Hunt on *LCI(G) 226* wrote that it was "one of the most awful sights that I shall never forget as long as I live."[5]

The debacle at Mariveles had not gone unnoticed by the higher command. In his action report for the incident, Vice Admiral Daniel E. Barbey was critical of how the Mariveles operation had been handled. He stated:

2. There was considerable information to indicate the probability of attack by Jap suicide boats on any ships left in MARIVELES Harbor during the night following the landing. It would therefore appear that normal prudence would have indicated the need to withdraw and return the following morning for completion of unloading. There is nothing to indicate any compelling reasons to retain the ships at the beachhead during the night.
3. It is noted that the LCS's which were assigned to protect MARIVELES Harbor from any small craft attempting to enter during the night were anchored across the harbor entrance. Anchored ships could hardly be called an effective screen. Furthermore, the gunboats as a group were not alert.[6]

The disaster did not stop the war and the campaign had to continue. As the sun rose on 16 February, the remaining ships of Task Unit 78.3.8 prepared to bombard Corregidor in preparation for the landing of Army paratroopers. At 1016 they attacked the landing beaches and nearby slopes with rockets, 3"/50 and automatic weapons. Mortar and enemy gunfire emanated from caves on the left flank of the landing ships. The heavier 3"/50 bow guns of the remaining *LCS(L)s 8* and *48* came into use and fired into the caves, silencing the opposition.

The LCI(R)s came under fire from the right flank, with three inch fire directed at them from Caballo Island. *LCI(R) 226* was hit in a number of places on her hull and deck house by small caliber fire but suffered no substantial damage. *LCI(R) 338* took

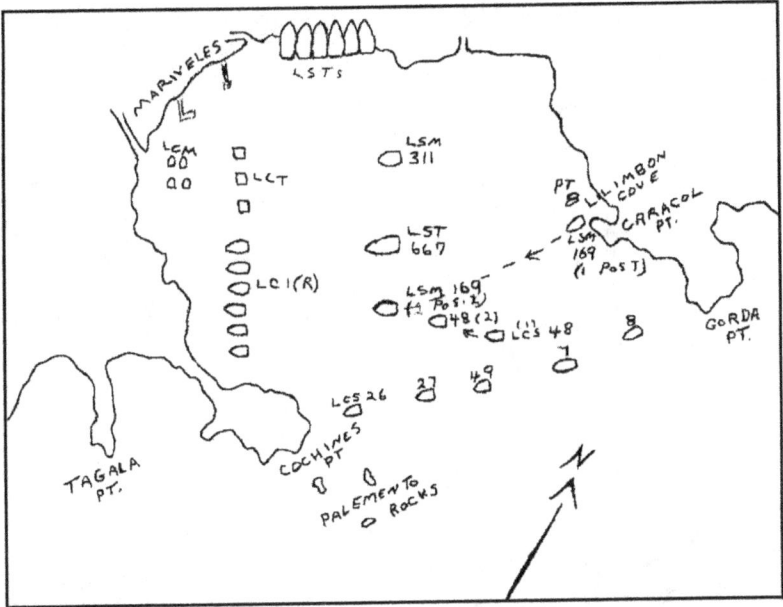

Mariveles Harbor was the scene of a deadly attack on the LCS(L) ships on 16 February 1945. Sunk in the attack were *LCS(L)s 7, 26,* and *49.* In addition, *LCS(L) 27* was badly damaged. Commander Task Unit 78.3.8 Serial 04, *Action Report—Special—Suicide Boat Attack Mariveles, P.I.— 16 February 1945,* 25 February 1945, p. 31.

four 3 inch shell hits in her hull, one just below the water line as she was in the middle of launching her rocket barrages. One of the shells landed only three feet from a fully-loaded rocket launcher, but fortunately none of the rockets exploded. Many were destroyed by shrapnel from the shell. Two of her men were killed and four wounded. *LCI(R) 340* had her mast shot off above her conning tower. An enemy shell burrowed through the pilot house on *LCI(R) 341,* damaging her engine telegraph, but she remained on station. The LCTs passed through the gunboat lines and made their landings. With the landing completed, the task for the ships was ended and at 1700 they formed up and headed for Subic Bay.

Casualties on board the LCS(L)s were difficult to determine. At least four men were known dead and twenty-three wounded, but the actual toll was higher. The total casualties for *LCI(R)s 267, 338,* and *341* were four dead and twenty-six injured.

Across the bay lay Carabao Island (formerly Fort Frank). Its capture was necessitated by its location rather than its concentration of Japanese, who had already withdrawn. The landing there followed the standard procedure of rocket assault preceding the landing of troops. However, the narrow width of the island, from 100–300 yards, made it necessary for the rocket gunboats to fire their salvos from a stationary position. Movement forward during firing, the standard assault practice, would have placed rocket barrages past the island and into the water behind it. At 0918, the gunboats fired their rockets. Heavier ships and aircraft had already destroyed the island, but prudence dictated that close-in fire support be supplied as the troops landed unopposed.

Lubang Island, lying about twenty-five miles southwest of Nasugbu, was taken on 1 March 1945. The Lubang Island Attack Unit consisted of six LCI(L)s, one LSM, one destroyer, one destroyer escort and *LCI(R)s 225, 226, 340,* and *341.* Its target was Port Tilik which lay on the eastern shore of the island. Landing there were elements of the 24th Infantry Division.

The destroyer and the destroyer escort provided some shore bombardment accompanied

LCS(L) 8 stands by off Corregidor as Army paratroopers from the 503rd Parachute Infantry Regiment drop onto the island. The tail of the aircraft that carried them may be seen in the upper right of the photograph. The gunboats and PT boats rescued a number of paratroopers who were blown past the island and landed in the water. Official U.S. Navy photograph.

by an air strike. As the gunboats prepared for their initial run, the rocket barrage was called off and the troops landed unopposed.

Palawan

Once Leyte and Luzon had been invaded, the next island in MacArthur's sights was Palawan. The island was occupied by approximately 2,700 Japanese troops, with the majority centered in the middle of the island near the city of Puerta Princessa.

The importance of the island to American forces was its location. Capture of the island would put the naval forces in range of the oil rich island of Borneo and its aircraft in range of Indo-China. Further, it would allow an easier interdiction of Japanese shipping heading from Borneo and Indo-China to Japan. The date for its invasion and seizure was 28 February 1945. Covering and Support Group (TG 74.2) under Rear Admiral R. S. Riggs protected the convoy on its way to the target area. The firepower of light cruisers *Denver CL 58*, *Montpelier CL 57*, and *Cleveland CL 55*, along with the destroyers *Fletcher DD 445*, *O'Bannon DD 450*, *Jenkins DD 447*, and *Abbot DD 629*, ensured their safety on the trip to the island. Once the landing was imminent, the covering force of amphibious gunboats took over. The Close Support Unit, under Commander D. H. Day, included *LCI(R)s 71, 72, 74, 224, 230(F), 331, 342, LCI(M)s 359(M), 362(M), 431(M) and LCS(L)s 28, 29, 30, and 50*.

At 0815 *LCI(R)s 71, 72, 74, 230(F), 331, and LCS(L)s 28, 29, 30, and 50* left the departure line and began their rocket run, followed by strafing with 3"/50 and 40mm fire. No counterfire was taken, and the landing craft deposited troops on the beach. The remaining gunboats were held in reserve and sent to investigate various sections of the shoreline, including a couple of inlets and coves. One of the major concerns was the threat of suicide boats, however, the few that were found had been destroyed by the Japanese in their retreat. Little resistance was encountered by the ground forces until 2 March when the first serious encounters took place in the foothills outside the city.

The operational Japanese airstrip nearby had been constructed using about 150 American prisoners. Prior to the landing of the American forces, they had been herded into a cave and burned alive. Their remains were recovered and given proper burials. The incentive to go after the Japanese with no quarter given was amplified by discoveries such as these.

The gunboats had little to do except screen the transports against suicide boat attacks during the night hours. Finally after several unproductive days of exploring the area and screening, they headed back to Mangarin Bay, Mindoro, on 3 March.

Victor I — Panay

The first of the Visayas to come under attack by the Americans was Panay. It had been occupied by the Japanese since April 1942. They had landed at Iloilo and quickly driven off the Philippine garrison. It took to the hills and was never subdued by the Japanese and remained in the mountains in the center of the island. By early 1945 the Japanese had determined to vacate the island and move their forces to other positions, but continued American air attacks prevented their leaving. Approximately 2,500 Japanese remained on the island, only 1,100 of whom were regular infantry. The rest consisted of 400 civilians and 1,000 airfield service troops. An important feature of the area around Iloilo was four functioning airfields, San Fernando, Santa Barbara, and Mandurriao in the south, and Loctugan in the north.[7]

The 40th Infantry Division under Major General Rapp Brush led the attacking force. Naval forces were from Task Group 74.3 Amphibious Group 9 under Rear Admiral Arthur D. Struble. The gunboat section providing close-in fire support consisted of *LCI(R)s 72, 74, 224, 331, LCI(M) 359*, and two sub-chasers. The ships were designated as TU 78.3.6 and covered the landing area which lay about twelve miles from Iloilo. As the hour approached for invasion on 16 March, it was discovered that Japanese had withdrawn inland and only friendly Filipino natives were in the area. The planned rocket and gunfire assault by the gunboats was called off and they were sent on minesweeping duty in the Guimaras Strait between Panay and Negros for a couple of days. One of the valuable infrastructure assets in the area was the bridge over Tigbauan Bay. There was concern that the Japanese might attempt to destroy it. *LCI(M) 359* conducted harassing fire in the area to keep the Japanese away. *LCI(R) 331*, also assigned in the area for mine destruction along with *LCI(R) 225*, was called on to go to the aid of a PBM that had lost one engine and landed in the area. It towed the aircraft back to Tigbauan. Later in the day on 25 March, *LCI(M) 359* found two Japanese barges on the beach. After getting permission from CTU 78.3.6, it took them under fire and put them out of commission.

Victor II — Cebu and Negros Oriental

General Macarthur had determined that the next islands to fall under control of the Americans would be those in the Southern Visayas group. The operation, designated as Victor II, included the islands of Cebu, Bohol, and the southern part of Negros. The Americal Division, under the command of Major General William H. Arnold, was assigned to the capture. Task Group 78.2 under Captain Albert T. Sprague, provided naval support for the landings.

Panay, Negros, Bohol, and Cebu were among the most developed and wealthy areas of the Philippine Visayas group. Contained in the island group were two cities, Iloilo on Panay, and Cebu City on Cebu. They were considered to be the second and third in population and importance throughout the island empire.

The island of Cebu contained Cebu City, the second largest industrial center in the Philippines. It was home to a significant Japanese Army force determined to protect its valuable asset. Invasion day was set for 26 March 1945, and rehearsals for the campaign were held at Hinunangan Bay, Leyte.

Two regiments of the Americal Division were set to land near Talisay, which lay just to the west of Cebu City. The invasion force, with Captain A. T. Sprague on board the 327 foot USCG cutter *Spencer*, set sail from Hinunangan Bay, Leyte, at 1753 on 24 March, escorted by numerous warships from Rear Admiral R. S. Berkey's Covering and Support Group. Berkey was on board *H.M.A.S. Hobart*. The close Support Unit was led by Commander D. H. Day with five LCI(R)s and four LCS(L)s. Designated as TU 78.2.6, the gunboats included *LCS(L)s 28, 29, 30, 50* and *LCI(R)s 225, 230(F), 340, 341,* and *342*.

At 0200 on 26 March the minesweepers began working over the area near the landing beaches in the harbor, covered by *LCS(L)s 29* and *30*. That task finished, the gunboats formed up with the other gunboats at the line of departure at 0800. They preceded the landing boats to the beach, unleashing a rocket barrage and strafing the shore with 3"/50 and 40mm fire. Following that, they patrolled the flanks of the landing area in support of troop movements. Opposition to the troops was light and the gunboats saw little action.

In the evenings of 26 and 27 March, the gunboats "anchored in a semicircle around landing beaches to form a protective screen around landing craft, in order to protect them from attacks by suicide boats."[8] It is interesting to note that only a month earlier the same strategy had proven disastrous at Mariveles Bay. One can only assume that this was known to Commander Day and that a vigilant watch was kept by the ships of TU 78.2.6 to prevent a recurrence of the disaster.

A group of guerrillas were to be picked up twenty miles to the south, and *LCS(L) 29* along with *LCI(R) 340*, escorted four LCI(L)s to pick them up and move them to a new area. Further minesweeping duties to the north occupied *LCS(L)s 30* and *50* during this time. Cebu Harbor received some attention from *LCS(L) 28* and *LCI(R) 230* from 0845 to 1600.

The eastern shores of Negros lay just across Tanon Strait. Two gunboats, *LCI(R) 225* and *LCS(L) 29*, were assigned to escort elements of the Americal Division to their landing near Dumaguete Point on the southeastern shore. The objective in the area was the seizure of Dumaguete Airfield. There was no enemy resistance, and the troops landed safely with the gunboats standing by offshore in case they were needed.

An LCS(L) (left) and an LCI(R) (center) lead the landing craft ashore as the Americal Division assaults the beach at Cebu City, Philippines, on 26 March 1945. Official U.S. Navy photograph.

At noon, military installations on nearby Cauit Island in Cebu Harbor were worked over by *LCS(L) 28* and *LCI(R) 230* in preparation for landing a company of infantry at 1420.

Concerns over the timing of the covering fire from the gunboats was noted in the action report filed by the task unit commander, Commander D. H. Day. According to Day, the CO of *LCS(L) 28* Lieutenant R. H. Bost remarked that

> too much time took place between end of rocket barrage and first wave landing. Interval was about two minutes at this landing. It is not practicable to reduce it much further and the remaining time should be filled up with automatic weapon fire until troops actually land. It is desirable that the beachhead be kept under naval fire until the infantry can open up with their own small arms.[9]

This was a valid observation on the part of Bost. One of the reasons for the development and use of the gunboats was to cut down the available time for the enemy to regroup once naval gunfire had blanketed the landing area. That was to be accomplished by close-in fire support, first with rockets and then with gunfire.

A final landing, albeit a minor one, occurred at the town of Campostela, about fifteen miles to the north of Cebu City on 20 April. *LCS(L)s 29* and *30(F)* accompanied elements of the Americal Division as they landed. In early afternoon *LCS(L) 30* was asked to provide call-fire against an enemy troop concentration near the city. An Army L-1 observation plane flew over, directed the rocket fire and then identified targets for the ship's 3"/50 and 40mm guns.

A series of landings on several islands took place over the next month on Western Negros (29 March), Legaspi (1 April), Bohol (11 April), and Southern and Eastern Negros (26 April). Small Japanese forces existed on these islands, many of which were under regular attack from Philippine guerrillas. Some, such as Lieutenant Colonel Satyoshi Oie's 800 man force on Southern Negros, simply retreated to the center of the island where they held out until the end of the war.

Victor V — Mindanao

One of the last remaining strongholds of the Japanese was the island of Mindanao. The operation to clear the Japanese off the island and put it in American hands was code named "Victor V." The plan had four objectives:

(a) Lift the Headquarters Xth Corps from LEYTE and land as later directed.
(b) Lift the 24th Infantry Division and reinforcing elements from MINDORO, landing in assault in the MALABANG Area on R-Day.
(c) Lift the 31st Infantry Division from MOROTAI, and land them on R-5 Day in the assault on PARANG or administratively, as later developments dictated.
(d) Cooperate in subsequent shore-to-shore movements and minor operations as requested.[10]

The attack was executed by Task Group 78.2., the Victor V Attack Group, commanded by Rear Admiral A. G. Noble. It consisted of 137 ships, the largest of which were the cruisers *Montpelier CL 57*, *Denver CL 58*, and *Cleveland CL 55*, along with destroyers *Conway DD 507*, *Eaton*

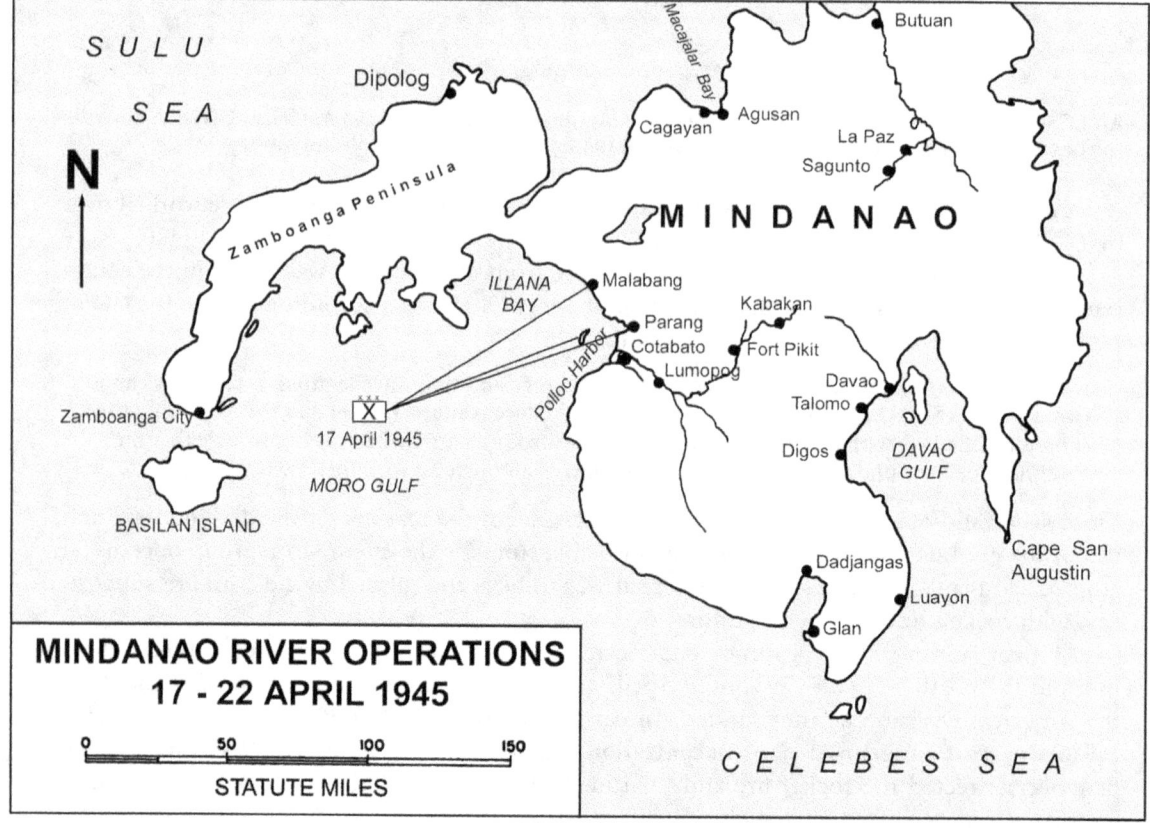

LCS(L)s and LCI gunboats were in constant action around the island of Mindanao. One small group of gunboats was also used to support Army troops as they moved inland along the Mindanao River to Fort Pikit. The gunboats went up the river to the fort to supply heavier firepower against the Japanese.

DD 510, Stevens DD 479, Young DD 580, Sigourney DD 643, and *Cony DD 508.* Numerous intermediate and smaller ships rounded out the number, including the Close Support Unit TU 78.2.12 under Captain Rae E. Arison. It was comprised of three LCS(L)s, six LCI(G)s, and nine LCI(R)s. The amphibious gunboats supplied covering fire for the minesweepers and the landing force. Landing on the shores of Mindanao were the 49,711 men of the Xth Corps, Eighth Army. It consisted of the Army's Xth Corps under Major General Franklin C. Sibert, the 24th Infantry Division (Reinforced), under Major General Roscoe B. Woodruff, and the 31st Infantry Division (Reinforced) under Major General Clarence A. Martin.

The eastern shore of Mindanao in the area of the coast near Illana Bay was scheduled for invasion on 17 April 1945. Ibus Island, off the town of Malabang, and the town of Parang on Polloc Harbor were the targets. Assigned to cover the landings were the gunboats of Task Unit 78.2.12 which consisted of *LCI(FF) 778, LCS(L)s 28, 43, 50, LCI(R)s 71(GF), 72, 74, 226, 337, 338, 340–342, LCI(G)s 21, 22, 24, 61, 66, 67,* and *PGMs 4–6,* and *8.*

The ships departed their base area at Mangarin Bay, Mindoro, on 14 April and reformed off Mindanao on 16 April. The invasion of the western coast of Mindanao at Ilana Bay began on 17 April as elements of the Army's X Corps landed at several locations between Malabang and Parang and in Polloc Harbor. At 0825 a small boat carrying Philippine guerrillas and flying an American flag pulled alongside *LCI(G) 778.* The guerrillas furnished intelligence indicating that the area around Malabang was free of Japanese but that there was a concentration of them to the south near the town of Parang. The landing area there was bombarded by cruisers, destroyers, and amphibious gunboats, but there was no opposition as the troops landed. With the absence of serious opposition, it was determined to move the schedule ahead.

A key part of the operation was the use of the Mindanao River to advance troop-carrying LCMs of the 533rd Engineer, Boat and Shore Regiment to the center of the island, in conjunction with land advances along Route 1 to the center of the island. It was thought that the rapid advance up the river would surprise the Japanese and lead to the successful elimination of Japanese power on the island.[11] The infantry would proceed inland toward Fort Pikit which lay at the intersection of Route 1 and the Mindanao River. Route 1 ran southward along the western coast, passed through Malabang and Parang, and then turned inland toward Fort Pikit. The fort lay on the Pulangi River which emptied into the Mindanao River just to its south. This area was near the important highway junction of Routes 3 and 1 which ran from there to Digos and then to Davao on the east coast of Mindanao. The Army's 19th Infantry would follow Route 1 to the fort. In a conference on the USS *Wasatch AGC-9,* held on 18 April 1945, it was requested that a small flotilla of gunboats accompany the Army's 533rd Engineer, Boat and Shore Regiment, under Lieutenant Colonel Robert Amory, up the Mindanao River to support Army efforts and meet up with the Army units as they headed down Route 1 to assault Fort Pikit.

Assigned to the operation was Task Unit 78.2.12, consisting of *LCI(G)s 61* and *66,* and *PGMs 4, 5, 6,* and *8* under the command of Captain Rae E. Arison. The plan was for the task group to assemble at Cotabato and proceed upriver to the fort. Captured Japanese prisoners provided some basic information about the nature of the Japanese forces which were thought to be in "disorganized retreat."[12]

Captain Rae E. Arison, Commander LCS(L) Flotilla One, in a relaxed moment at the Officers' Club in Subic Bay, Philippine Islands, in mid–1945. Courtesy Robert J. Amick.

Lieutenant (jg) Nail of Spokane, Washington, and Lieutenant O'Neal of Peoria, Illinois, officers on *LCI(G) 66*, question a Japanese prisoner before moving up the Mindanao River in support of the 24th Division. NARA 111-SC 262942.

Communications were problematic, and the unit did not leave the Cotabato area until 19 April after receiving orders from Lieutenant Colonel Robert Amory. He directed them to reach the town of Paidu Palangi by nightfall. Unfortunately, this was not to be the case. The river channel narrowed and the less maneuverable 160 foot LCI(G)s had difficulty making their way around the river bends. The 110 foot PGMs did not have this problem and wound up in the lead. By nightfall the convoy had reached only twenty miles upriver and had to stop for the night. Troops of the 21st Infantry on board LCMs accompanied the gunboats. *LCI(G) 66* experienced mechanical problems and had to anchor, leaving *LCI(G) 61* to proceed upriver with the PGMs. The winding river caused some of the ships to anchor above a bend in the river and some below. A mistake in identification saw the ships briefly exchange .50 caliber gunfire, but there were no injuries.

An LCM came downstream with a message from Lieutenant Colonel Amory that the firepower from at least one 3 inch gun would be needed to take Fort Pikit the following day. The ships headed upriver with the LCMs leading the PGMs and *LCI(G) 61*. *LCI(G) 66*'s mechanical problems prevented her from traveling further. In short order, *PGM 5* struck a log and was disabled, leaving the LCMs, *PGMs 4, 6,* and *8,* and *LCI(G) 61* to continue. They anchored at Inogog after catching up with advanced units of the Army engineers. After a brief meeting it was determined that two of the *PGMs, 4* and *6,* would lead the assault craft with the *LCI(G) 61* and *PGM*

8 covering the rear flank. All four of the gunboats mounted 3"/50 guns, so they would be able to fulfill the mission as requested by Lieutenant Colonel Amory.

A force of about 500 Japanese was known to be covering the river at Balumis just below the fort. As the gunboats rounded the bend and came into view of the Japanese, they opened up with 3"/50 fire, scattering the enemy troops. It was later discovered that the fire from the gunboats had driven off the Japanese, and Fort Pikit was open to the American forces. Had the gunboats not been in position, it was estimated that there would have been serious resistance, causing a great loss of life among both Japanese and American forces. Surveys of the river beyond the fort were taken by men on board the LCMs, and it was determined that further progress of the gunboats was not possible. They eventually returned downstream and resumed normal duties in deeper water. Lessons learned from the experience revealed that since the rivers were small, winding, and uncharted, it would be advisable to have LCMs precede the larger ships to take soundings. Going upstream was not too difficult, as the combination of the ship's normal speed and the speed of the current against her made steering relatively easy. However, going downstream was particularly difficult. Although the ship's navigators knew from previous experience where the shoals were, they had to maintain speed greater than the current carrying them downstream in order to maintain steerage. This situation caused *PGM 6* to run aground as the ships headed downriver. It took two days to set her free.

LCI(G)s 61 and *66* remained at anchor below the bridge downstream from Fort Pikit. The PGMs headed downstream on 23 April but their 10 foot 10 inch draft caused them to run aground, effectively blocking the channel. A lack of rain caused the river to drop, and the gunboats were advised to wait for a storm to deepen the river before heading downstream. By 27 April, the LCI(G)s found themselves anchored in a little over six feet of water. That left them little chance of maneuvering downstream without getting grounded, even though they drew only about 6 feet 6 inches aft and 4 feet 9 inches forward. It was decided that the ships should be anchored by their stern anchors instead of the smaller bow anchor so that they would be headed downstream. They were assisted in turning by an LCM. By 4 May the river had begun to rise and the LCMs went downstream to take soundings. Finally, on 5 May the gunboats headed downstream, with four LCMs to assist them if they ran aground. *LCI(G) 66* soon went aground at Piugug Market and was pulled free by the LCMs. The following day, after careening off riverbanks, bouncing over shoals, and side-swiping an LCM, the gunboats reached open water and headed to Parang Harbor. For the sailors onboard, their inland mission had been a learning experience and they were glad to be in open water again.

As the fighting progressed across the island of Mindanao, the Army became concerned about Japanese threats to the resupply of American forces in the region. The landing of an additional 1,000 troops from the Army, along with 1,500 tons of supplies, had been made at Digos on Davao Gulf on 4 May. Various enemy bases existed in the region around the entrances to Sarangani Bay and Davao Gulf, including suicide boat and PT boat bases. Task Unit 78.3.6 was sent to take care of the threats. It consisted of *LCI(G)s 21, 24,* and *LCI(R) 226,* and *PGMs 4, 6,* and *8,* backed up by *Flusser DD 368* and *Key DE 348*. They arrived in Taloma Bay south of Davao on 11 May 1945 and began to patrol the area. Captain Arison arrived on the morning of 11 May and took over duties as S.O.P.A in Davao Gulf. *Howard DMS 7* shelled a suspected suicide boat base at Maputian Point on Samal Island on 12 May, putting an end to threats in that area. Continued work was necessary to contain the threat from suicide boats and torpedo boats. Support for their efforts was supplied by *PT boats 332, 334, 336, 340, 342,* and *343* from Squadron 24 under the command of Lieutenant Edgar D. Hogland. The PTs and the gunboats joined forces in a series of raids on enemy PT boats in the northeast part of Davao Gulf near Piso Point on 15 May. Close-in work by the PTs had spotted a Japanese PT base hidden up a small creek and well-camouflaged. The Japanese PTs had already taken their toll on American shipping, sinking the Army *FS 225* during the night of 10-11 May. The Army Air Force supplied a B-24 to bomb the area, and *PTs 335* and *343* undertook the destruction of the six enemy PT boats and a nearby ammunition dump. The enemy boats were reported to be about seventy feet long and painted dark green. They blended in well with their background and were hard to spot even at relatively close range. As the American PTs were destroying their enemy counterparts, *LCI(G) 21* found a fifty foot long boat near the shore and destroyed it, along with some pill boxes. Shortly thereafter it fired on an oil dump at Pangasinan Point, leaving it in flames. Later in the day, *LCI(G)s 21* and *22* teamed with *PTs 106* and *341* off Piso Point. Heavier firepower was supplied by *Key DE 348*. *PT 106* cruised within 400 yards of the beach in an attempt to draw enemy fire. The ruse was successful and the PT beat a hasty retreat to the safety of *Key*, where Lieutenant Hogland, who had been on board the *106*, identified the enemy's position so that *Key* could fire on it. The destroyer escort pounded the area with 252 rounds of 5 inch and 1,072 rounds of 40mm fire, setting it ablaze. *LCI(G)s 21* and *22* then closed to within 400 yards of the beach and added to the carnage. At this point four Navy Mitchell B-25 bombers hit the area and, as a final blow, *Flusser DD 368* fired 384 rounds of 5 inch shells. The combined work of the ships and aircraft left the area ablaze and severely weakened enemy capabilities. They continued their attacks on the Japanese from 14 to 21 May 1945.

Macajalar Bay in the northern part of Mindanao Island, was assaulted by the 108th Regi-

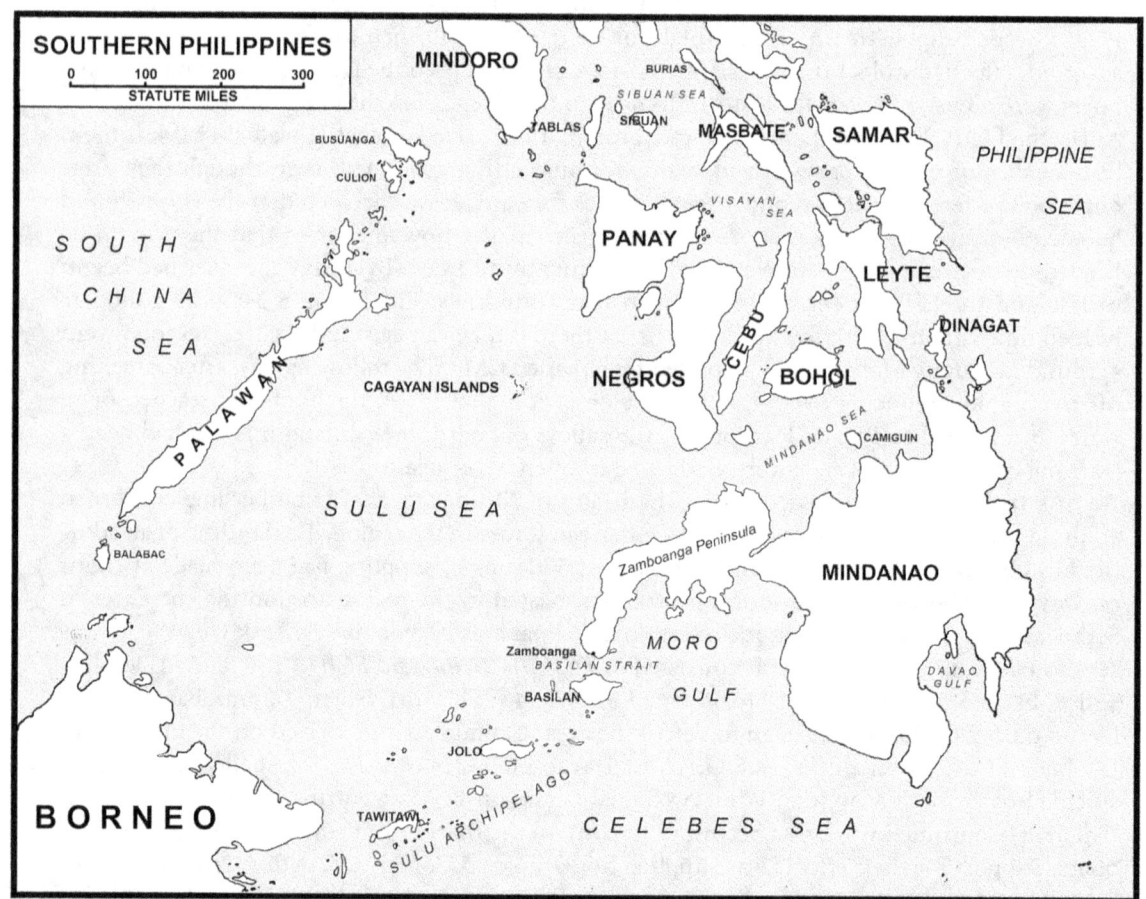

LCS(L)s and LCI gunboats were active in the southern Philippines during the last stages of the war. As other gunboats were involved in the campaign for Okinawa, numerous others were active in the attacks on Borneo, Palawan, and Mindanao to the south.

mental Combat Team, 40th Infantry Division on 10 May 1945. *LCS(L)s 30, 42, 79,* and *80* covered the landing. Standard rocket and gunfire preceded the landing, but there was no return fire or opposition to the landing.

Continued concerns over security in the area around Davao Gulf and Sarangani Bay led to additional landings in early June 1945. These landings were made on 1, 3, and 5 June at Luayon, Balut Island, and Cape San Augustin respectively. Each of the landing areas was considered to have Japanese troops in the area who might cause problems for American supply lines. The 162nd Regimental Combat Team landed its 275 officers and men at each location, cleaned out the enemy, and then moved on to the next assault. Of primary concern were the estimated forty to sixty radio stations operating in each location. *Flusser DD 368* and *Leland E. Thomas DE 420* provided heavy gunfire to soften up the area, and *LCI(G)s 21, 24,* and *LCI(R) 226* led the assault waves. Additional support was furnished by a few LCM gunboats, PT boats and a strike by bombers from the 13th Air Force. The only area with significant resistance was at Balut Island which was first attacked on 3 June. A secondary landing had to be made nearby in order to quash the resistance and destroy the island's radio station.

Mindanao had been a difficult campaign for the Army but had presented some interesting options for the gunboats.

Victor IV — Zamboanga

On the western side of Mindanao Island across Moro Gulf, a large peninsula extends southward ending in the city of Zamboanga at its southern extremity. Just to the south, across the Basilan Straits is Basilan Island. The target for 10 March 1945 was the city of Zamboanga. The 41st Infantry Division under Major General Jens A. Doe made a landing there. Several days of minesweeping in the area off the city and in Basilan Straits was performed by Task Unit 78.1.5, consisting of *YMSs 6, 8, 9, 46, 50, 52, 68(F), 71, 340, 365,* and *481.* The ships of TU 78.1.3, which included *LCS(L)s 28(F), 29, 30, 41–43,* and *50,* along with *LCI(R)s 225, 226, 337, 340, 341, LCI(M)s 362, 431,* and *LCI(D)s 227* and *228,* covered their landing. Ken Krayer RT 2/c was on board *LCS(L) 28* for the Zamboanga assault. He later wrote:

> Anytime you think you have a nasty job to do you can always find someone who has it worse. The minesweeps have one nasty job to do. They're small, mostly wooden craft usually with one deck gun and two 20mm's. They must trail paravanes on cables behind them in an effort to cut the cables anchoring mines in such a way that they float to the surface.... They could get caught two ways. Either fire from the beach from guns or mortars, or if they are fired at and try to get out of the area they could pull a mine into their fantail with their own paravanes. Or they could just plain run into a mine with their hull. None of this made for pleasant thoughts. The Japs loved two things — mines and mortars. Our job was to escort the sweeps and give them close gunfire support should they need it, so we trailed behind them by several thousand yards. We also tended to any mines the sweeps cut loose. We usually shot them with our 20mms. They either exploded when hit, or sank. I preferred the sinkers myself — but they were far less picturesque.[13]

March 9 would prove to be a typical day for minesweepers and gunboats. Covering four YMSs were *LCS(L)s 41, 42, 43,* and *50.* As the sweepers worked an area 300 yards off the beach near Caldera Point and the town of Zamboanga at 0920, the gunboats came under fire. *LCS(L) 43* found herself bracketed by enemy mortar fire near San Mateo Point. Minesweeping operations were halted and the gunboats made four runs on the beach delivering rockets, 3"/50, and automatic weapons fire. After resuming minesweeping operations, *LCS(L)s 41, 42,* and *43* spotted machine gun nests off Great Santa Cruz island and destroyed them. Action of this sort continued throughout the day, preparing the landing beaches for the infantry boats.

Fire support of a heavier nature was furnished by the Cruiser Covering Group consisting of cruisers *Phoenix CL 46* and *Boise CL 47*, under Rear Admiral Berkey. They worked alongside the destroyers *Nicholas DD 449*, *Taylor DD 468*, *Jenkins DD 447*, *Abbot DD 629*, and *Fletcher DD 445*. Screening the transports were eight destroyers and two destroyer escorts under the command of Captain R. H. Smith. Rear Admiral Forrest B. Royal had overall command of the campaign.

Japanese resistance to the assault was expected to be significant, with an estimated 8,300 Japanese troops in the area around the city of Zamboanga. The Japanese were ready and were well-entrenched in defensive positions near the town. As with all Japanese defenses at this stage of the war, they would not seriously oppose the landing but would hold their force in reserve until the Americans moved off the beach. This enabled them to avoid the fierce bombardment of the naval ships and aircraft as they worked over the landing beaches.

On 1 March the XIII Army Air Force began bombing the area, with additional and continuous bombing starting on 8 March. Marine Air Groups 12, 14, and 32 provided close support strafing and bombing for the 41st Division troops as they advanced against the enemy. Wherever possible the gunboats of Captain Arison's TU 78.1.3 were on hand to supply call fire on any targets in the vicinity of the beaches, while the heavier firepower of the larger ships could be utilized against targets farther inland.

One day prior to the invasion the ships began working over the landing zones with gunfire.

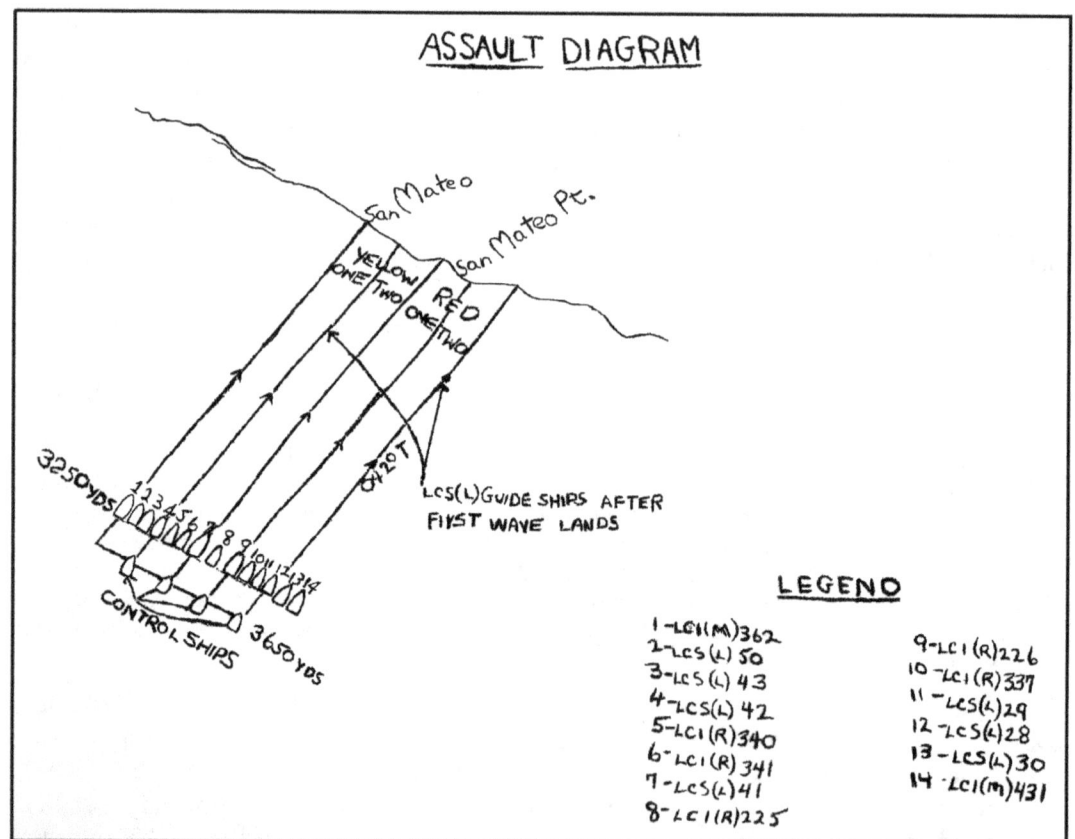

This is the assault diagram for the landing at Zamboanga on 10 March 1945. LCI(M)s 361 and 432 were on both flanks with three LCS(L)s just inboard and the LCI(R)s in the center positions. Commander Task Unit 78.1.3 Serial 014, *Action Report, Zamboanga Operation*, 16 March 1945, Enclosure (A).

6. The LCS(L)s Arrive

On 10 March 1945, the landing craft were ready for the invasion. The LCS(L)s, LCI(M)s, and LCI(R)s made their run on the beaches with 3"/50 caliber and 40mm fire at 0850 and then delivered their rocket barrage and mortar fire at 0908 as they led the LVTs to the beach near San Mateo Point. Following the landings they supported the flanks, suppressing mortar and automatic weapons fire from the enemy.[14] Gavilan Point on the right flank of the landing beaches was of interest, and *LCI(M) 431* reported giving particular attention to the area prior to moving its fire inland. The landing beaches were about three miles northwest of the town of Zamboanga and just three miles from the Japanese airstrip at Calarian.

Within an hour, Japanese fire began to plague the ships. *LCS(L) 50* reported "being rained by mortar fire and *LCS(L)(3) 42* reported that the LCI(L)s which were disembarking troops were being shelled."[15] The situation for the gunboats continued to deteriorate and, at 1340, the ships were ordered out of the area as the mortar fire was intensifying. On 11 March spotter planes located the source of the mortar and artillery fire. The cruiser *Boise*'s fire was on target and the enemy shelling decreased immensely.

Across Basilan Strait lay Basilan Island. The strait had already been swept prior to the landing at Zamboanga, and Basilan was next on the list. Assigned to fire support of the landing on 16 March were *LCS(L)s 41(FF), 42, 43, LCI(R)s 226, 337, LCI(M)s 362, 431, SC 741* and the destroyers *Waller, Robinson* and *Saufley*. Landing on Basilan Island was Company F (reinforced) 162nd Regiment, 41st Division. Standard assault procedures were followed by the gunboats, but shoals prevented the LCMs from landing on shore and they had to be diverted to a local pier several hundred yards to the right of the landing beaches. Fortunately, there was no resistance. However, the village of Semut lay in the path of the shell

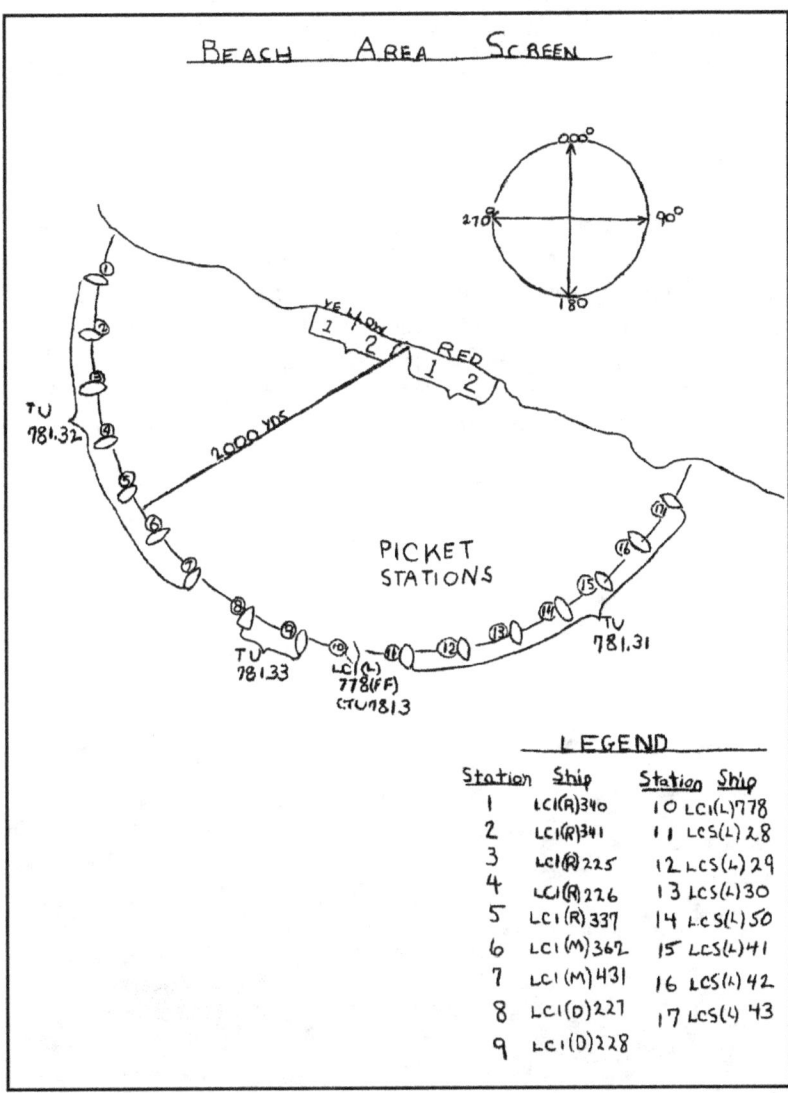

Once the landing craft had delivered the troops ashore, the gunboats maintained a close-in position in order to deliver fire on targets of opportunity and to assist troop movements ashore. Commander Task Unit 78.1.3 Serial 014, *Action Report, Zamboanga Operation*, 16 March 1945, Enclosure (B).

fire and there was collateral damage. Envoys from the natives ashore approached the ships and asked for assistance as there were a number of casualties among the citizens. Seventeen had died and there were fifty-four with serious injuries. Reports from local guerrilla forces indicated that the Japanese had withdrawn their small force from the coastal area at least eight to ten days prior to the assault and had never actually been in the village of Semut.[16] *LCI(L) 778* reported to the area bringing medics and supplies, and the villagers were given aid. The gunboats patrolled the areas offshore that night and continued screening and support activities in the area for the next few days before being ordered back to Tacloban, Leyte.

Having secured the tip of Zamboanga peninsula, the Navy began moving down the Sulu Archipelago heading toward Borneo. The value in these islands lay in their close proximity to Borneo which was still to be conquered. The construction of airstrips on islands in the various groups would place Allied aircraft less than one hundred miles from targets on the big island. Naval installations in the Sulu Archipelago would serve as staging areas for the conquest of Borneo. Capture of the islands of Sanga Sanga on 2 March and Jolo on 9 April placed the Allies in position for the attack on Borneo.

Working with Guerrilla Forces

One of the more unusual occurrences of World War II was the formation of Task Group 70.4 and its operations aiding the Philippine guerrillas in the southern areas of the Philippines. As originally constituted, the Task Group consisted of *LCS(L)*s *9* and *10* and *LCI(L)*s *361* and *363* under the command of Lieutenant Albert C. Eldridge.[17] Organized on 24 January 1945, the main focus of the Task Group was the support and supply of Philippine guerrillas on and around the southern island of Mindanao. On 14 April 1945, *LCI(L) 361* sustained damage and her duties in the task group were taken over by *LCI(L) 429* for a couple of weeks.

LCS(L) 9, shown here, and *LCS(L) 10* were both built at the George Lawley & Sons Shipyard near Boston, Massachusetts. The two were among the first of their class and mounted a 3"/50 gun in the bow.

LCS(L)s 9 and 10 were among the first group of LCS(L)s completed during the war. Both were built at the George Lawley & Sons Shipyard near Boston, Massachusetts. They each mounted a 3"/50 gun in the bow, and additional armament included two twin 40mm guns, four 20mm guns, rocket racks for 4.5 inch rockets, a .50 caliber machine gun, and an 80mm mortar. The two LCI(L)s carried their standard armament of five 20mm guns and two .50 caliber machine guns. Added to their firepower was an 80mm mortar. With the addition of the mortars, the ships had an enhanced ability to attack shore installations where needed. These mortars were not usually found on the ships but had been acquired locally in order to enhance their capabilities. The actual formation of the task group and the inclusion of the two LCS(L)s was one of those random occurrences of the war. *LCS(L) 9*, commanded by Lieutenant Donovan R. Ellis, and *LCS(L) 10*, commanded by Lieutenant Albert C. Eldridge, were a part of LCS(L) Flotilla One, under the command of Captain Ray E. Arison. Arison, a stickler for rules and regulations, was regular U.S. Navy and had just been reassigned to the amphibious forces. The informality and lack of adherence to strict regulations by the officers and men of the amphibious forces grated on him. After several incidents involving the *LCS(L)s 9* and *10*, he decided to teach them a lesson by leaving them behind in disgrace as the rest of the Flotilla's Group 1 ships headed from Hollandia, New Guinea, to the action at Leyte. Shortly thereafter, the two gunboats were ordered to escort a convoy north to Leyte, thus ending their exile from the group. They arrived in the Philippines and, still on the flotilla commander's list, were given an alternate duty, that

LCS(L) 9 crew shortly after the war. Official U.S. Navy photograph.

of supplying guerrilla forces on Mindanao. The forces up to that point had been supplied by submarine, a practice which limited the amount of material they could receive. With a strong American presence in the Philippines, it was possible to use surface craft for supply.

The Philippine guerrilla forces on Mindanao were under the command of Colonel Wendell W. Fertig. Fertig had been a reserve officer and was called to active duty in 1941. When the capture of Corregidor by the Japanese became imminent, Fertig was assigned to Mindanao. His primary assignment there was to take command of the Army engineers as they constructed airfields on the island. When Mindanao fell in May 1942, Fertig was loathe to surrender. Instead, he headed for the jungle to continue resistance against the Japanese. By February 1943 he had established contact with MacArthur's headquarters in Australia, and shortly thereafter, his guerrilla forces began to receive shipments of supplies brought in by submarine. These submarine shipments ceased in December 1944, just in time for surface deliveries to begin. It was to this role that the two LCS(L)s and two LCI(L)s were assigned. From 3 February 1945 to late May 1945, Task Group 70.4 completed thirteen missions.

The first mission began on 3 February 1945 when the ships left their base at Tacloban on San Pedro Bay, Leyte Gulf, and landed about 100 tons of supplies at Mambajao on Camiguin Island and the towns of Iligan and Misamis on the north coast of Mindanao. After delivering supplies, they met with numerous Philippine guerrilla commanders including Colonel Fertig. An added expert in the mix was Commander Charles "Chick" Parsons whose work in organizing the submarine supply of the guerrilla bands had given him a great deal of expertise in the matters facing Task Group 70.4. His advice to the new commander of the task group was described later when Eldridge wrote his ship's history:

> While we were waiting for darkness and the return run to Leyte, the skipper and Comdr. Charles (Chick, Chico) Parsons talked of this and that. Parsons had been the mentor of the previous work by sub and was starting us off on the right foot by giving advice now and then as to what had been done previously and how we might best work with the guerrillas. He had a background as large as all out-doors in Filipino affairs before the war and exploits as long as your arm in spying activities against the Japs in Manila.[18]

It was during this trip that Eldridge conferred with Parsons, leading to the first raids against Japanese installations. Their conversation went as follows:

> "I 'magine there're quite a few Nips 'round here, Commander."
> "Helluva lot of 'em right close."
> "Right over there — across the strait."
> "Mmmm. Doesn't appear more than twenty miles. Wonder how much hot water we'd get into, going over to say hello."
> "Can't say. They have quite a few men, and are building barges in Talisayan."
> "No, that's not the kind of hot water I mean. I mean we have no orders to go running over here and there shooting people up. And someone back in Tolosa might not like my straying from the path on the first run."
> "You're right. Some few can cause a lot of trouble. But there's a mighty nice concentration of them there."
> "Think we could get at them?"
> "They're right on the coast."
> "Mmmm. Like to take a trip? Let's go look at a chart and see what kind of water there is down there."
>
> That was the start of our favorite pastime. On the first bombardment by the Nine and Ten we knocked out barrels and barrels of fuel oil and gasoline, burned up the huts the Nips lived in.... We won or spurs by crippling barge traffic in the area when the fuel was destroyed. We were credited enthusiastically, but slightly optimistically by Filipino reports with killing 600.[19]

Information about their successful raid filtered back to Vice Admiral T. C. Kincaid. Pleased with their success, he authorized them to conduct such raids on future missions whenever practical.

No such opportunity presented itself on the next mission. On 10 February the ships delivered 120 tons of material to guerrilla forces at the port of Sibonga on Cebu Island. However, the third mission saw the ships landing another 120 tons of supplies at Bais on Negros Island. Since the port was safely in guerrilla hands, the two LCS(L)s proceeded to the nearby town of Dumaguete and fired on the electric plant and other Japanese occupied buildings. Guerrilla observers indicated which were held by the Japanese and which were occupied by Filipino civilians. In addition to the structures, three Japanese motor launches and seven fuel dumps were set afire and presumed destroyed. From Dumaguete the LCS(L)s cruised north to the town of Sibulan and supplied supporting fire for guerrillas who were successful in taking the town from the Japanese. Their adventures over for the time being, the gunboats returned to Bais to escort the LCI(L)s back to San Pedro Bay.[20] Mission number four departed San Pedro Bay on 22 February 1945 with Colonel Fertig on board. The ships unloaded 120 tons of supplies at Claver, Mindanao, and the colonel met with the local regimental commander to discuss pressing matters. No action against enemy forces was undertaken on this mission. However, on mission number five, the gunboats shelled a Japanese-occupied sugar preparation area at San Carlos on Negros Island as the LCI(L)s unloaded supplies nearby at Toledo, Cebu. Fifty Japanese soldiers were caught in the devastating gunfire and gave their lives for their cause. Also destroyed was an enemy barge loaded with fuel. Their business completed at Toledo, the LCI(L)s headed to their next delivery at Milagros, Masbate, unloaded sixty tons of material, and embarked Major Donato's 230 man strong guerrilla force.

What followed was a classic use of the LCS(L) gunboats. At Dimasalang, Masbate, the guerrillas staged an amphibious landing with the *9* and *10* supplying shore bombardment, along with a couple of Marine Air Group 12 Corsairs which bombed Japanese positions. Donato's force accounted for 120 Japanese dead and the ships' fire killed eleven others. Fifty tons of Japanese ammunition went up in smoke and numerous small arms and souvenirs were liberated from the ruins. With another successful mission under their belts, the ships returned to their base at Tacloban on San Pedro Bay.[21] Frank P. Muth, a crewman on board the *LCS(L) 9*, later described the task group's experience with the guerrillas. He wrote:

> At this time I would like to explain how the Guerrilla troops operated. They would have an American officer and American Sergeant in charge of a group. Most of them had no uniforms or shoes, a lot of them were barefoot. We would take supplies to their base where they were training. We supplied them with rifles, machine guns, and different types of ammunitions. A lot of times the L.C.I.s were loaded down with clothes and shoes to take to them. The ramps had barrels of oil and gasoline in some places, were we would drop the barrels of oil and gasoline in some places and the Guerrillas would swim with them to shore.[22]

The sixth mission departed San Pedro Bay on 9 March 1945. Their destination was San Carlos, Negros Island, where they delivered supplies and fired on targets under attack by the guerrillas. As a result of their fire, two Japanese Type A barges were destroyed, along with a fuel dump and miscellaneous Japanese structures. The seventh mission, beginning on 16 March 1945, was a very active one. The task group split into two units with *LCS(L) 9* and an LCI(L) heading for the east coast of Mindanao where it embarked the headquarters company of Colonel Fertig and transported it to Iligan. *LCS(L) 10*, accompanied by the other LCI(L), proceeded to Mambajao on Camiguin Island where it left the LCI(L) to await further orders. The *10* then headed for Loay on Bohol Island, arriving there on 16 March. After conferring with local guerrilla forces at Loay, the gunboat proceeded west about ten miles to Baclayon, Bohol, where it provided shore bombardment for a guerrilla force attempting to run the Japanese out of the town. Once their shore bombardment was completed for the day, observers on *LCS(L) 10* spotted a Japanese lugger at anchor nearby. They cut its mooring line and made it a prize of war, turning it over to the guerrillas the following day for their use. The next day saw the gunboat again bombarding

The crew of *LCS(L) 10* fires white phosphorus shells from their 80mm trench mortar at Japanese forces in support of Philippine guerrilla operations at Dimasalang, Masbate Island, 1–4 March 1945. During this mission, guerrilla forces under Major Donato captured enemy equipment and killed 120 Japanese. Fire from the ships accounted for another eleven dead enemy soldiers. NARA 80G 259133.

shore targets in support of the Philippine forces before heading back to a rendezvous with the other ships in the task group. *LCS(L) 9* and the LCI(L) accompanying it had disembarked Colonel Fertig's headquarters company at Mambajao and then moved to Lagonglong on Macajalar Bay, Mindanao, where they embarked 380 guerrillas for transport to their next targets. This included the towns of Talisayan, Lipata, Sipalong, and Bugdan on Mindanao, which were closely located to one another. At this point, the other half of the task group returned from Bohol and joined up with them. Guerrilla landings and the combined fire of the task group accounted for the destruction of numerous Japanese ammunition dumps and facilities. Casualty counts included 145 Japanese dead and six captured, with six of the guerrillas sustaining wounds. Two useable trucks, a good supply of rifles, rice, radios, tools and fuel, along with Japanese defense and other plans, were captured. An added bonus was the capture of two Japanese steel barges which proved useful to the Philippine forces. These were towed to Mambajao, Camiguin Island for repair. Another successful mission completed, the task group headed back to their base at Tacloban, Leyte.[23]

Continued exposure to and interaction with Philippine guerrillas had changed the crews of the *9* and *10*. Where once they adhered strictly to U.S. Navy practices, they had apparently "gone native." Ken Krayer, on board *LCS(L) 28*, recalled encountering the two ships after they returned to Tacloban from their campaign at Zamboanga on 15 March 1945:

Philippine guerrilla operations at Dimasalang, Masbate Island, 1–4 March 1945 resulted in the capture of a great deal of enemy equipment. Guerrilla forces, led by Major Donato, display captured equipment. *LCI(L) 1074* is beached behind the guerrillas and *LCS(L) 9* may be seen offshore. NARA 80G 259134.

> We were dumb struck when we saw them. They had palm trees, plants, parrots, and monkeys on board. They looked like a zoo. They had been operating with the Filipinos so long they were beginning to look like the Philippine Navy. We heard they had some sickness problems and the Medics went on board — inspected — then told them to get rid of the birds and animals. This was all scuttlebutt, but it made sense to me.[24]

The eighth mission, beginning on 26 March 1945, had two stages. The ships again split into two divisions carrying supplies and moving guerrilla forces during the first phase. After completing the initial phase of delivering supplies and embarking guerrilla troops, the ships headed for Masbate City, where they supported a guerrilla assault on several hundred Japanese troops holed up in the city. A narrow channel leading into the harbor at Masbate City caused problems as the ships had to proceed single file, making them a target for Japanese small arms fire. A problem in the reversing gear of the *9* caused it to run aground near shore, making it an easy target. *LCS(L) 10* came alongside and both ships exchanged fire with the Japanese. Fortunately this happened during an incoming tide and the *10* was able to pull the *9* off the bar and tow her back to base. The raid was deemed a success with one Japanese airplane captured intact and many Japanese killed.

Mission nine began on 4 April 1945. The task group left their base and headed for Mambajao to retrieve the two barges they had left for repair. They towed them to Iligan and unloaded their supplies there. One hundred fifty guerrillas came aboard and were transported a few miles down the coast to a landing beach about five miles below Dipolog. Another one hundred were picked

Philippine guerrillas unload supplies from *LCI(L) 363* at Gingoog, Mindanao, as *LCS(L) 10* stands by. The photograph was taken during Mission Nine, which took place between 4 and 10 April 1945. The ships moved guerrillas and their equipment from one location to another. When not engaged in moving and supplying guerrillas, the ships frequently attacked Japanese positions in the nearby islands. NARA 80G 31883.

Philippine guerrillas unload rice from *LCI(L) 361* at Gingoog, Mindanao, on 20 May 1945. NARA 80G 259554.

up at Claver, Mindanao, by *LCI(L) 361* and *LCS(L) 9*, and more supplies were unloaded at Gingoog by *LCI(L) 363*, accompanied by *LCS(L) 10*. The unloading area was too shallow for the LCI(L), a problem which was quickly solved by the guerrillas as they lashed together several small boats and made a rudimentary causeway for the task. With the job of delivering supplies finished, Major Paul Marshall and his 220 man 110th Guerrilla Division embarked on *LCI(L) 363*. At this point, both LCI(L)s were loaded with guerrilla forces which were then transported to a beach below Bilaa Point, Mindanao, and set ashore. The LCS(L)s then proceeded to attack various Japanese installations at Cabadbaran, Buenavista, and several other places before

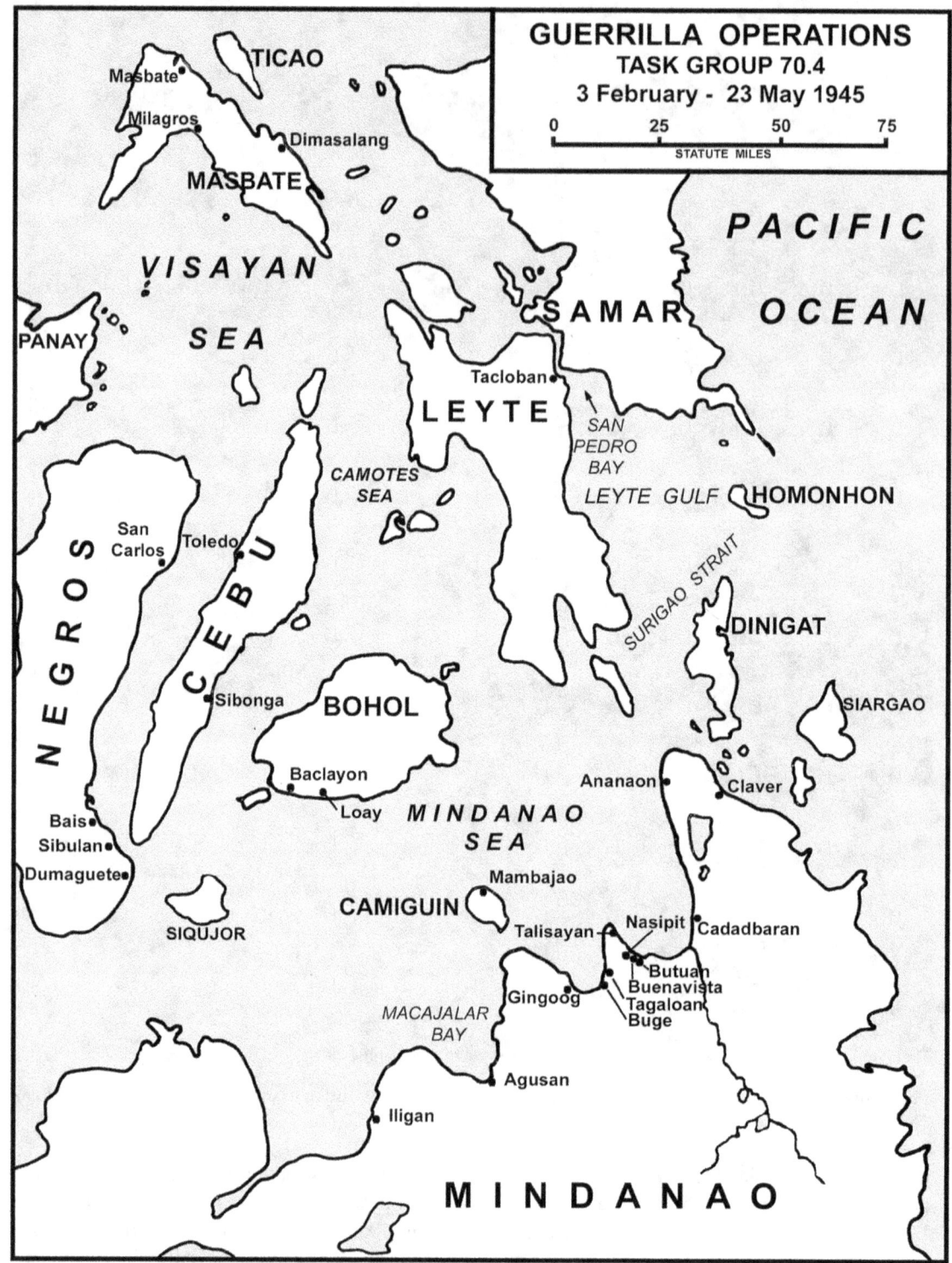

LCS(L)s *9*, *10*, and LCI(L)s *361*, and *363*, organized as Task Group 70.4, worked with Colonel Wendel W. Fertig's Philippine guerrilla forces in the area around Mindanao. They were successful in delivering supplies to the guerrilla fighters, as well as attacking Japanese positions in the area. The task group was under the command of Lieutenant Albert C. Eldridge.

proceeding to Nasipit, Mindanao, where they shelled Japanese positions, damaged two Japanese type A barges, and set a fuel dump afire. Their work for the mission completed, they returned to Tacloban on 10 April to prepare for their next mission.

Mission ten, from 14 to 20 April, involved the usual transportation of supplies and guerrillas. However, the attack on Nasipit, Mindanao, by guerrillas supported by the ships proved quite profitable. Captured in the attack were three machine guns, twenty rifles, two Class A barges, twenty drums of gasoline, fuel oil, food supplies, a truck and a car. Notable in the haul was a huge quantity of ammunition, including howitzer shells, anti-tank shells, and rifle ammunition. In all, it was the largest haul taken by the guerrillas with their support ships up to that time.[25]

Missions eleven (25–29 April), twelve (6–13 May), and thirteen (18–23 May 1945) involved the transport of guerrillas and supplies. The only action taken by the ships on mission eleven was the bombardment of Japanese positions at Baluarte, Tagaloan, and Buge on 28 April and Nasipit and Buenavista on 29 April. At that point, Japanese resistance on Mindanao and in the Visayas had diminished to where the services of Task Group 70.4 were no longer needed. The task group moved north and began operations near the Polillo Islands off the eastern coast of Luzon.

An indication of the effectiveness of the task group was demonstrated by a letter of commendation sent by Colonel Fertig to the Commanding General of the Eighth Army.

It read:

HEADQUARTERS TENTH MILITARY DISTRICT
Adv CP
APO 159

8 May 1945

SUBJECT: Letter of Commendation — Task Group 70.4
To: Commanding General. Eighth Army, APO 343

1. It is desired to make the activities of TG 70.4 commanded by Lieut. William [sic] Eldridge, a matter of record. They have landed approximately 600 tons of badly needed supplies in areas outside the operation of American troops. In addition, they have engaged in 4 amphibious operations. These operations were made against isolated Japanese garrisons. Guerrilla troops were loaded on the LCIs of the TG and landings made in each case under fire from the LCS units of the TG. Successful landings were made at Talisayan,(Misamis Oriental), Ananaon, (Surigao), Cabadbaran and Nasipit, (Agusan). In each case the enemy were driven from their positions and with the exception of Cabadbaran the enemy garrisons were annihilated. Large quantities of supplies, both ordnance and quartermaster, were captured. During the present operation, terminating approximately 13 May, troops will be landed at the vicinity of Butuan. This operation expects to eliminate remnants of Japanese garrison in Agusan. In addition to these operations they have shelled the coast of Tagoloan River to Cagayan on several occasions. Then activities in conjunction with guerrilla attacks forced the enemy to withdraw from the beaches at Macajalar Bay, allowing the American units to make an unopposed landing.

2. It is desired further that a copy of this letter be passed to the Commander, Seventh Fleet.

s/ Wendell W. Fertig
Colonel, CE
Commanding[26]

By 4 June 1945, Task Group 70.4 had established contact with the guerrilla forces at Infanta on Luzon. It was only a matter of time before the task group, operating among guerrilla forces, would come in contact with the Alamo Scouts of Major General Walter Krueger's Sixth Army. The Alamo Scouts had been formed late in 1943 and had begun their activities in New Guinea. By 1945 they were operating regularly in the Philippines, gathering information, conducting rescue operations, and other special missions. In June of 1945, they were assigned the task of locating General Tadashi Yamashita's headquarters on Luzon, as well as elements of the Japanese

Lieutenant Albert C. Eldridge (right), Commanding Officer of *LCS(L) 10*, receives the Legion of Merit from Vice Admiral T. C. Kincaid for his leadership of TG 70.4 in the Philippines. The Commanding Officer of *LCS(L) 9*, Lieutenant Donavan Ellis (not pictured), received the Bronze Star.

Army in various areas. In many cases the Alamo Scouts were brought in by submarine or PT boats but, on occasion, heavier firepower was needed. In a number of instances the ships assigned to carry them to their landing places were the four ships of Task Force 70.4. At that point, the original *LCI(L)s 361* and *363* had been replaced by *LCI(L)s 364* and *342*.

On 5 June the task group landed a team of Alamo Scouts under Lieutenant Woodrow E. Hobbs at Casiguran Bay, and 7 June landed them again further north at Palanan Bay. The area looked promising, so on 12 June the ships, the Alamo Scouts, and 200 guerrillas returned to

Palanan Bay and launched an attack. They successfully killed a number of Japanese troops aided by gunfire from the ships.[27]

From that time until 29 July 1945, the task group engaged in several other operations against the enemy, along with their constant companions, the Philippine guerrillas. Their final action was on 29 July when they bombarded Japanese held locations at Laguin Bay to the south of Infanta. Their next assignment was to be far to the south in Borneo, but the end of the war retired the task group. After visits to Manila and Tacloban, the ships headed for the states.

Chapter 7

Iwo Jima

Although the island of Iwo Jima had been Japanese territory since 1891, after the capture of Saipan and Tinian in July 1944, it had become increasingly problematic. Saipan and Tinian served as bases from which to launch B-29 raids against the Japanese mainland. Unfortunately, the aircraft had to pass by Iwo Jima going to the targets in Japan and on the return flight. This gave the Japanese an early warning system, as raids headed for the home islands could be detected.

Additionally, fighter aircraft stationed on Iwo Jima were in an excellent position to intercept B-29s both on the outgoing and return trips. As a result, Army Air Force missions gave the island a wide berth by requiring the bombers to carry more fuel and smaller payloads. The elimination of Iwo Jima as a functioning Japanese base was therefore desirable, and the Joint Chiefs of Staff began planning its capture in late 1944. In addition to eliminating the threat of the Japanese interfering with B-29 raids, the island could also be used as an emergency landing strip for aircraft damaged over Japan. It was also thought that long range fighters could be stationed there to accompany the B-29s to Japan.

The importance of Iwo Jima to the Americans was obvious to the Japanese and, on 27 May 1944, Lieutenant General Tadamichi Kurabayashi was given command of the 109th Division. The division had the responsibility of defending the Bonin Islands, known to the Japanese as the Ogasawara Islands. This group was considered a part of the Japanese home islands in that it was a part of metropolitan Tokyo and included Chichi Jima and Iwo Jima. Kurabayashi arrived on Iwo Jima between 8 and 10 June 1944. He correctly deduced that Iwo Jima would be targeted by the Americans because of its airfields. Accordingly, he set about bolstering the island's defenses.

Japanese strategy at the time called for the annihilation of enemy forces at water's edge to prevent a landing from gaining a foothold. Kurabayashi recognized that overwhelming naval gunfire and supporting air strikes would make such a defense impossible. He determined that an underground series of tunnels and interconnected bunkers would provide the best possible chance to defend the island. Guns and mortars in fortified positions were zeroed in on specific areas of the landing beaches so that once ashore, the invading force would be easy prey. By the time of the American landings, the Japanese force defending the island had grown to 21,000 men. It was not a part of Kurabayashi's strategy to drive the Americans away; he knew that he faced overwhelming military superiority. His strategy would be to slow the American advance and bleed them as much as possible. Once Iwo Jima fell, it would hasten and intensify the attacks on Japan.

Leading the U.S. Marine invasion force was Lieutenant General Holland M. Smith (CG of

Expeditionary Troops TF 56). Under Smith was Major General Harry Schmidt, Commanding General of the V Amphibious Corps. The 3rd, 4th, and 5th Marine Divisions were commanded by Major General Graves B. Erskine, Major General Clifton B. Cates, and Major General Keller E. Rockey, respectively.

The task facing the Marines was obvious and Major General Schmidt requested a ten day naval bombardment prior to the landing of the assault force. Having other responsibilities, the Navy allowed a three day bombardment period. The attack on Iwo Jima was assigned to Task Expeditionary Force 51 under Vice Admiral Richmond Kelly Turner. His force included nine battleships, eight heavy cruisers, five light cruisers, seven escort carriers and thirty-one destroyers. In addition to the larger warships, TF 51 also included an Amphibious Support Force under Rear Admiral W. H. P. Blandy. The amphibious gunboats were assigned to this force.

Task Units 52.5.1 (*LCI(G)s 450, 466, 469, 471, 473, 474, LCI(FF) 627*) under Commander Michael J. Malanaphy, and Task Unit 52.5.2 (*LCI(G)s 346, 348, 438, 441, 449, 457*) under Lieutenant Commander W. V. Nash, would be the first ships in action at Iwo Jima and the first ships to suffer under enemy fire. They had departed from Saipan on 13 February 1945 and arrived at

Practice for the invasion of Iwo Jima took place at various locations. Here a group of LCI(G)s practices rocket fire at Kahoolawe, Hawaii, on 17 January 1945. Commander Amphibious Forces Pacific — Commander Fifth Amphibious Force Serial 212, *General Action Report of COMPHIBSPAC—Capture of Iwo Jima,* Volume 2 of 2 Volumes, 23 March 1945.

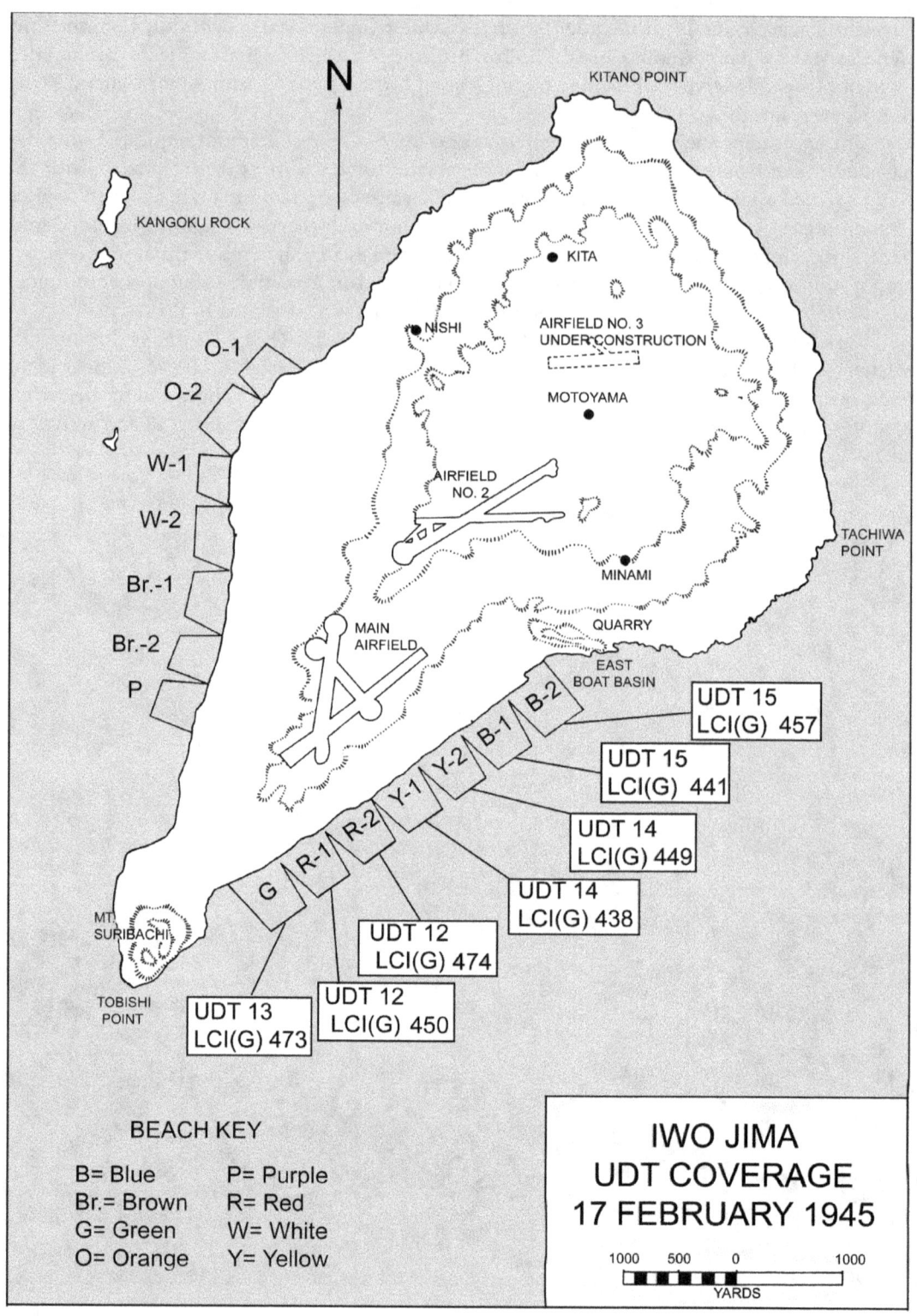

Gunboats covering UDT operations on 17 February 1945 came under heavy shore fire with the result that all seven of the original gunboats were put out of action, along with five of their relief gunboats. One of them, *LCI(G) 474,* was sunk.

Iwo Jima on 17 February. Their assignment was to cover Underwater Demolition Team activities along the beach. TU 52.5.1 was assigned to Red Beach One and TU 52.5.2 was assigned to Yellow Beach One.

The battle for Iwo Jima was costly in the extreme for the U.S. Marines, but it was also costly for the amphibious gunboats. The problem arose from a misinterpretation on the part of the Japanese defenders who mistakenly identified the LCI(G)s covering UDT operations as troop carriers.

The assault on Iwo Jima required reconnaissance of the landing areas prior to the actual assault. Marine Reconnaissance Units from the Scout and Sniper Platoons, 4th and 5th Divisions and VAC Amphibious Reconnaissance Battalion, FMFPAC and Underwater Demolition Teams 12, 13, 14, and 15 were assigned the task of reconnoitering the beaches and destroying obstacles. These teams of underwater warriors had been training in Hawaii and then moved to Ulithi for further training. Between 3 and 6 February 1945, the teams practiced and trained at Ulithi then headed for Saipan to rendezvous with other elements of the Iwo Jima assault force. On 17 February the UDTs on board *Bates APD 47* (UDT 12), *Barr APD 39* (UDT 13), *Bull APD 76* (UDT 14), and *Blessman APD 48* (UDT 15) arrived off Iwo Jima. Covering their operations was Fire-support Unit (TU 52.4.21) under Captain Hunter. This task unit was further divided into three sections, each containing two to three destroyers and three to four LCI(G)s. Fire-support Unit Able (TU 52.4.21) under Captain Hunter, had *Capps DD 550*, *Leutze DD 481*, *Henley DD 762*, and *LCI(G)s 450, 466, 473,* and *474*. Fire-support Unit Baker (TU 52.4.22) under Captain Conley, consisted of *Bryant DD 665* and *Twiggs DD 591*, along with *LCI(G)s 438, 449,* and *471*, while Fire-support Unit Charlie (TU 52.4.23) under Captain Martin, was made up of *Hall DD 583*, *Paul Hamilton DD 590* and *LCI(G)s 441, 457,* and *469*. In company with the three task units were *LCI(G)s 346* and *348*, which were held in reserve and *LCI(FF) 627* with Commander Michael J. Malanaphy aboard. Malanaphy had overall command of the gunboats.[1]

Commander Michael J. Malanaphy, shown here post-war as a Rear Admiral, was the commanding officer of LCI(G) Flotilla Three which covered the UDT at Iwo Jima. The ships under his command all were awarded Presidential Unit Citations. Malanaphy and the commanding officers of the gunboats under him were each awarded the Navy Cross. He went on to serve with distinction at Guam and Okinawa. Official U.S. Navy photograph.

The preferred landing beaches, Red, Yellow, Green, and Blue, were on the eastern side of the island, while Orange, White, Brown, and Purple beaches were on the west. The eastern beaches were due for reconnaissance and clearing in the morning, and the western beaches were scheduled for the afternoon. Seven of the LCI(G)s covered the morning operations with three held in reserve to replace them if necessary. The task units' destroyers maintained station 3,000 yards off the beach for supporting fire as needed. The assignments were as follows:

LCI(G)s 438, 474, and *450* move toward the beaches at Iwo Jima to cover UDT operations on 17 February 1945. During the coverage, all three ships were hit by Japanese shore batteries. *LCI(G) 474* was sunk and *438* and *450* sustained damage and casualties. NARA 80G 307117.

UDT Team	Beach	LCI(G) Support Ship	Relief LCI(G)
UDT 12	Red 1	LCI(G) 450	LCI(G) 466
	Red 2	LCI(G) 474	
UDT 13	Green	LCI(G) 473	
UDT 14	Yellow 1	LCI(G) 438	LCI(G) 471
	Yellow 2	LCI(G) 449	LCI(G) 469
UDT 15	Blue 1	LCI(G) 441	
	Blue 2	LCI(G) 457	

The destroyers and gunboats began moving into position about 0800 as *LCI(G)s 438, 441, 449, 450, 457, 473,* and *474(GF)* began their maneuvers. By 0920 they were five hundred yards off Mount Surabachi and heading north to a point 3,500 yards off the beaches. At 1030 they turned and headed for the shore, passing through the line of destroyers. The destroyers, now seaward of the gunboats, began firing on shore positions. At 1048 the LCI(G)s were about 2,000 yards off shore and began taking fire, which they immediately returned. At this point the UDT teams on board the LCP(R)s began to drop off their men for the swim in to the beaches. In spite of the heavy shore fire, the LCI(G)s headed for the thousand yard line in order to fire their rockets, but it was not to be. Between 1058 and 1105, all seven of the LCI(G)s were hit. At 1048,

Lieutenant Rufus Herring (far right) receives the Medal of Honor from Secretary of the Navy Forrestal. Photographs of Herring are almost non-existent and part of this original photograph was blacked out behind Herring's head for use in other publicity releases. Naval History and Heritage Command NH 104043.

both *LCI(G 449* and *474* were fired upon, but the incoming rounds were near misses. This changed within minutes. While covering UDT 14 on Yellow Beach 1, *LCI(G) 449* was hit by a shell on her bow, killing two men, blowing two overboard, and wounding two more. A few minutes later she took another incoming round on her port 40mm gun and then a third on the starboard side of her conning tower, killing and wounding a number of her crew.² The CO of the *449*, Lieutenant (jg) Rufus G. Herring, was severely injured by this shell. Herring was blown out of the conning tower and landed on the deck below. Enemy fire from the beach hit him again, but he propped himself up against some shell casings and continued commanding his ship. Eventually his strength ran out. With all of the other *449*'s officers wounded or killed, Ensign L. Bedell took command. With the able assistance of Boatswain's Mate Frank Blow, Bedell directed the ship back to safety. Bedell was awarded the Silver Star and Blow the Bronze Star for their actions.³ The highest award that day went to the CO of the ship, Lieutenant (jg) Rufus G. Herring, who received the Medal of Honor. His citation read:

> For conspicuous gallantry and intrepidity at the risk of his life above and beyond the call of duty as Commanding Officer of LCI(G) 449 operating as a unit of LCI(G) Group EIGHT during the pre-invasion attack on Iwo Jima on 17 February 1945. Boldly closing the strongly fortified shores under the devastating fire of Japanese coastal defense guns, Lieutenant (then Lieutenant, Junior Grade,)

LCI(G) 449 alongside *Terror CM 5* at Iwo Jima on 17 February 1945. Her commanding officer, Lieutenant (jg) Rufus G. Herring, was awarded the Medal of Honor and the ship was awarded the Navy Unit Commendation. Casualties are evident in the photograph. NH 65317.

Herring directed shattering barrages of 40-mm. and 20-mm. gunfire against hostile beaches until struck down by the enemy's savage counter fire which blasted the *449*'s heavy guns and whipped her decks into sheets of flame. Regaining consciousness despite profuse bleeding he was again critically wounded when a Japanese mortar crashed the conning station, instantly killing or fatally wounding most of the officers and leaving the ship wallowing without navigational control. Upon recovering the second time, Lieutenant Herring resolutely climbed down to the pilot house and, fighting against his rapidly waning strength, took over the helm, established communication with the engine

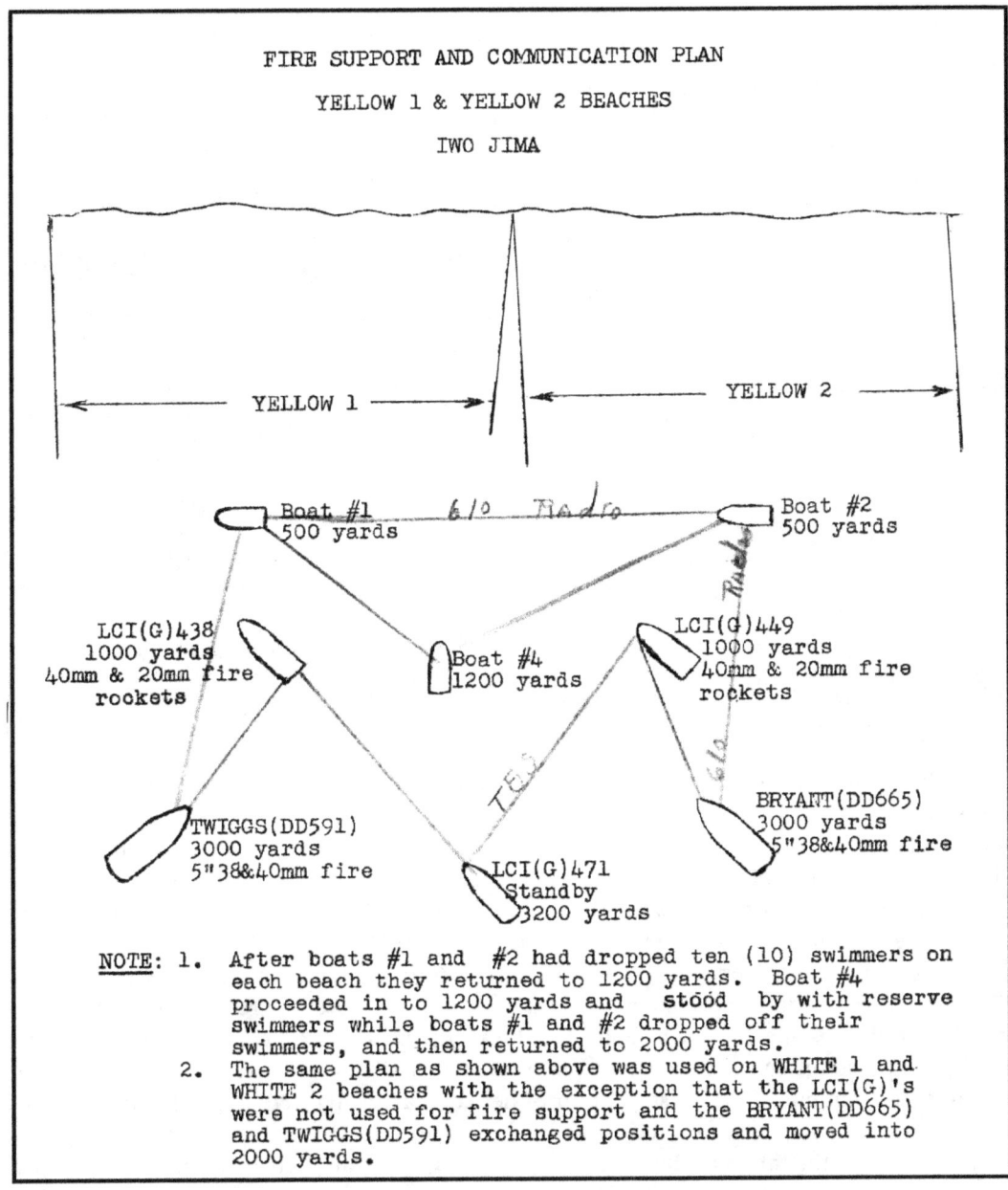

The fire support plan for Yellow Beaches 1 and 2 was similar to many UDT coverage assignments undertaken by the gunboats. Boats 1, 2, and 4 were LCVPs carrying UDT swimmers to their mission. Covering them with close-in fire support were *LCI(G)s 438* and *449*. To seaward were the destroyers *Twiggs* and *Bryant*, which lent heavier firepower to the coverage. *LCI(G) 471* stood by as a reserve gunboat in case it was needed. From Commander Underwater Demolition Team No. 14, Serial 02-45, *Action Report of UDT #14 in the Iwo Jima Operation—16th February to 1 March 1945*, 1 March 1945, Enclosure D.

room and carried on valiantly until relief could be obtained. When no longer able to stand, he propped himself against empty shell cases and rallied his men to the aid of the wounded; he maintained position on the firing line with his 20-mm. guns in action in the face of sustained enemy fire and conned his crippled ship to safety. His unwavering fortitude, aggressive perseverance and indomitable spirit against terrific odds reflect the highest credit upon Lieutenant Herring and uphold the highest traditions of the United States Naval Service.[4]

LCI(G) 474, hit by shore fire at Iwo Jima as she covered Underwater Demolition Team 12, had to be abandoned. With no hope of saving her, she was sunk by gunfire from *Capps DD 550*. Her Commanding Officer, Lieutenant (jg) Matthew J. Reichl, was awarded the Navy Cross and the ship was awarded the Navy Unit Commendation. NARA 80G 303818.

UDT 14 was assigned just south of *LCI(G) 449* to Yellow Beach 1, and *LCI(G) 438* drew the assignment to cover its operations. As she headed for her station, the commander of UDT 14 came aboard. As she neared her firing position and began her beach bombardment, she took a hit on her starboard waterline from a large shell estimated at 197mm. The area began to flood and the ship began to list to starboard. The Commander of UDT 14, Lieutenant A. B. Onderdonk, ordered the ship to retire as several mortar shells exploded nearby and small arms fire hit the ship. With her list, the ship could only make about four knots but made it to safety. *LCI(G) 471* was sent in to relieve the *438* and Onderdonk transferred over to the replacement.[5]

At about the same time that *LCI(G) 449* was hit, *LCI(G) 474*, covering UDT 12 at Red Beach 2, was also hit. Within the next five minutes she took a total of ten enemy shells. All of her guns were put out of commission, four of her compartments were flooded, and three fires blazed out of control. Ammunition clips for the 40mm and 20mm guns were ignited by the flames, adding to the carnage. Her most serious damage was caused by two shells which struck at her waterline on the port side causing instant flooding. These holes measured three to four feet in diameter. With the ship beginning to settle, her CO headed her back to *Capps* where her eighteen wounded men were transferred. The *474* then cast off from *Capps* and the destroyer moved away. At that point the gunboat was listing heavily to starboard and her CO, Lieutenant (jg) Matthew J. Reichl, gave the order to abandon ship. This was reinforced by the Commander Destroyer Squadron 46 who was on board *Capps*. The *LCI(G) 474* stayed afloat almost on its beam ends. At 1230 Reichl headed for his ship with four volunteers in a small boat to determine if there was any way to save her. As they approached the ship it rolled over, its bottom barely above the surface. With no hope for his ship, Reichl returned to *Capps* which sank the gunboat with 40mm shells at 1400. It was only 3,000 yards from the beach. The three crewmen killed in the action went down with the ship.[6]

Immediately to the south at Red Beach 1, *LCI(G) 450* was hit at 1112. Several large caliber

LCI(G) 441 comes alongside *Nevada BB 36* to transfer her wounded. She was hit by Japanese artillery at Iwo Jima on 17 February 1945. NARA 80G 307124.

LCI(G) 441 transfers her casualties to *Nevada BB 36* on 17 February 1945. NARA 80G 303786.

shells impacted her forecastle, disabling the bow gun and starting fires which threatened her forward magazine. It was flooded to save the ship, and she was ordered to leave her station to seek aid. She suffered six wounded.

In the midst of all of this, UDT operations had begun at about 1100. By that time the LCI(G)s were already in trouble, many having been hit by fire from shore batteries. Lieutenant (jg) Donald Murray, a member of the UDT, recalled: "The fire from shore was unmerciful. Bullets rained down on the swimmers. Eight inch shells were decimating the LCI(G)s."[7] *LCI(G)*s

441, 450, and *473* managed to get close enough to fire off their rockets before being hit. The others, damaged by shore fire, were unable to fire off complete salvos.

Beach reconnaissance fell to a combined force of Navy UDT and Marine Scouts and Raiders. The UDT members and Marine reconnaissance swimmers were scheduled to swim ashore, chart the bottom, look for mines and obstacles, and return to their pickup boat. On board the LCVP pickup boat, Marine reconnaissance members would run parallel to the shore photographing any items of interest, such as obstacles and enemy gun emplacements near shore. While the swimmers in the water dodged sniper fire, the Marines in the LCVP had other concerns. "The Japanese fired at them continually, using light mortars, machine guns, and rifle fire as well as the very devastating antiboat guns from their concealed positions. The close splashes and water plumes of the Japanese antiboat guns and mortars, sometimes bracketing their craft, gave everyone a great deal of concern."[8]

Ensign Frank Jirka, Jr., was a member of UDT 12 assigned to cover the Red beaches along with selected members of First Lieutenant Russell Corey's B Company, FMF Amphibious Reconnaissance Battalion. They had completed their mission and looked for their supporting LCI(G) to see if they could assist in identifying enemy targets. They searched for their ship but it was not there. *LCI(G) 466* had replaced it and was covering operations on the Green beaches. Along with a Marine captain and two other Marines, Jirka boarded the *LCI(G) 466*. He later recalled:

> We decided to go aboard and try to spot our gunfire from it. We came alongside and the four of us climbed aboard. I went up to the bridge, told them what I was there for and what team I represented. I was standing at the time, on the after port side of the bridge, but since the forward gun's smoke was obstructing my view, I moved to the forward starboard side. I no sooner moved over when our ship, which was around 1700 yards off the beach and slowly moving in, almost got hit.
>
> I said to the captain that it looks like we're getting in pretty close, when the next thing I knew I was flat on the deck, wounded. I tried to stand but was unable to do so. Since I was not suffering from any pain I looked down to see just why I was unable to stand. It was then that I noticed a pair of blown up feet at right angles to my body, without shoes or stockings. I thought surely those couldn't be mine for I was wearing shoes when I came aboard. Then I suddenly felt a painful drawing sensation and upon noticing carefully found that those mangled pieces of skin and bone were all that was left of my good nine and a half C's. I then crawled to the after end of the bridge, for the spot that I was standing on was no longer there. I asked for some morphine and gave myself a shot.[9]

LCI(G) 457, covering UDT 15 on Blue Beach 2, moved into her covering station 2,000 yards off the beach and began firing her 20mm and 40mm guns at targets along the shore and behind the east boat basin. At 1055 the Japanese began ranging in their mortars. Several fell about seventy yards ahead of the ship and the gunboat began evasive maneuvers. At 1101 the ship fired her ranging rockets but found them about 200 yards short. Two minutes later mortar fire bracketed the ship and one round exploded about a foot off the port side, opening a three by four foot hole and flooding her forward compartment. Machine gun fire raked the ship from bow to stern with a number of rounds striking the rocket launchers and disabling them. With a number of men wounded and most of her guns and rocket launchers out of commission, the ship was relieved by *LCI(G) 469* and her CO, Lieutenant (jg) Jerome J. O'Dowd, headed her to *Gilmer APD 11* to transfer casualties. She had suffered twenty-one wounded, twelve of whom were serious, with one who later died. *Gilmer* took them on board and the ship tied up to *Tennessee BB 43* to have her damage surveyed. With the prognosis indicating that she would remain afloat, she reported to *Terror CM5* for additional help pumping out her forward compartments.[10]

Just south of *LCI(G) 457*, *LCI(G) 441* was also covering UDT 15 on Blue Beach 1. At 1050 she opened fire on the shore area with 20mm and 40mm guns. A few minutes later an LCVP came alongside and two observers came aboard, one from UDT 15 and one from the Marines. The gunboat proceeded to within a thousand yards of the beach and began laying down covering fire for the UDT swimmers when she was hit in her galley area by a five inch shell. While her men battled the fires in the galley and surrounding area, she launched her rockets. As she turned to pull away from the beach, another shell struck her on the starboard side of the main deck. Within a few minutes her crew had the fires out and the ship zig-zagged back toward her station. As she maneuvered, small caliber machine gun fire splashed in the water, but no damage or casualties occurred. The *441* was able to continue firing on shore targets but, at 1125, her No. 1 40mm gun failed, and fifteen minutes later her No. 2 40mm also suffered a break-down. At 1143 a mortar shell struck the forecastle area abaft the No. 1 gun position and Commander Malanaphy ordered the ship to retire from the area. As her CO, Lieutenant (jg) Forrest W. Bell, gave the order for his ship to withdraw, it was hit by another shell on the starboard side of the gun deck, injuring a number of men and damaging her steering. The ship began to circle and at times was only 300 yards off the beach. A near miss by another shell sent water cascading over the decks and extinguished a fire in the aft part of the ship. At 1155 still another shell exploded on the ship a couple of feet above the water line. As they neared the terminal range of the shore batteries, two more shells fell just short of the transom and the gunboat made it into safe water. She tied up to *Nevada BB 36* and transferred her wounded men for treatment. The ship had survived, but she had six dead and twenty-seven wounded.[11]

At Green Beach, *LCI(G) 473* was covering the operations of UDT 13 when she came under fire at 1055. She was on station about 2,000 yards off the beach strafing suspected enemy emplacements when a five or six inch shell struck her starboard side on the main deck causing fifteen casualties. Another shell hit her gun deck, disrupting power to her port generator and switchboard and knocking out her steering. While under emergency steering from her stern station, she was hit by another shell in the same location and suffered additional casualties. The gunboat continued toward shore and launched her rockets at 1,000 yards. They struck the beach area about 200 yards inland. At this close range she was in great peril and, as she turned to move back out, she was struck by two five inch shells on her port waterline. The first opened a three by four foot hole and the second knocked out her engines. Adrift and in range of enemy guns, she was saved when *LCI(FF) 627* took her under tow and *LCI(G) 466* relieved her. The line parted, but she had enough headway to drift out of range of the shore fire. A number of shells struck the water about 100 yards behind her but she had escaped. She had managed to drift close enough to *Twiggs DD 591* and was able to transfer eleven of her seriously wounded men. *LCI(L) 627* again took her under tow and pulled her to safety.[12] She suffered thirty-one wounded and one dead. For *LCI(G) 473* the battle for Iwo Jima was over.

Shortly after noon, the LCI(G)s had all been pulled out of the action and spent the next few hours transferring wounded, burying their dead at sea, and making what repairs they could. Fortunately for them, the 455 foot minelayer *Terror CM5* had been assigned to the area as a repair and supply ship. As the gunboats became damaged, they headed to *Terror* for assistance. The first to tie up to her was *LCI(G) 449* which transferred seventeen dead and twenty wounded, two of whom died later that day. Emergency repairs were made to the ship and she was soon back in action. *LCI(G)s 438, 457, 469,* and *473* with *LCI(FF) 627* followed closely behind, transferring dead and wounded and receiving emergency repairs so that they could rejoin the action. By the end of the day, *Terror*'s crew had buried at sea those killed in action on the gunboats.[13]

February 17 had been costly for the ships. The combined death toll for the LCI(G)s was forty-seven, with three missing in action and presumed dead. Another 148 had been wounded in action. Casualties among three of the UDT teams during the beach action were not heavy. UDT 12 reported one missing and one wounded, UDT 13 had no casualties, and UDT 14 had one killed and two wounded. The most serious losses to the UDTs came at 2120 when UDT 15 was back aboard *Blessman* having lunch. A Japanese plane made an attack and its bomb pierced *Blessman*'s deck and exploded in the mess area. UDT 15 reported sixteen men dead, two missing, and twenty-three wounded.[14] With the gunboats essentially out of action, the UDT teams had to rely on fire from larger ships to cover them as they reconnoitered the western beaches in the afternoon. *Tuscaloosa CA 37*, *Arkansas BB 33*, *Texas BB 35*, and *Tennessee BB 43* supplied close fire support and the destroyers fired white phosphorus shells to mask the UDT movements.

The action of the LCI(G) gunboats was inspirational to everyone who watched. Captain B. Hall Hanlon, Commander Underwater Demolition Teams, Amphibious forces, U.S. Pacific Fleet reported:

> It is the opinion of this command that LCI(G) Flotilla THREE made Naval history and added a fine page to our Naval tradition during its support of the Underwater Demolition Teams on the morning of DOG minus TWO [17 February 1945] at IWO JIMA. This is not based alone on their original going in to the 1000 yard line on a very hazardous mission, but on the fact that these ships remained at their stations until either all guns were knocked out, fires were out of control, or the ship was sinking. Under those circumstances, and only under those, did they retire from the line, and then making such temporary repairs as were essential, they returned to the firing line.[15]

Bravery of this sort was not to go unnoticed. In addition to the Medal of Honor awarded to Lieutenant (jg) Rufus G. Herring, CO of the *LCI(G) 449*, the following commanding officers received the Navy Cross:

> Lieutenant Forrest W. Bell *LCI(G) 441*
> Lieutenant (jg) Wallace A. Brady *LCI(G) 450*
> Lieutenant Charles E. Fisher *LCI(G) 473*
> Lieutenant Gerald M. Connors *LCI(G) 469*
> Lieutenant (jg) Harry L. Gruver *LCI(G) 346*
> Lieutenant James J. Horovitz *LCI(G) 466*
> Commander Michael J. Malanaphy Comdr LCI(G) Flotilla Three on *LCI(FF) 627*
> Lieutenant Commander Willard V. Nash CTU 52.5.2 on *LCI(G) 457*
> Lieutenant (jg) Jerome J. O'Dowd CO *LCI(G) 457*
> Lieutenant (jg) Bernard J. Powers *LCI(G) 438*
> Lieutenant (jg) Matthew J. Reichl *LCI(G) 474*
> Lieutenant (jg) Alvin E. Rosenbloom *LCI(G) 348*
> Lieutenant (jg) Robert S. Hudgins *LCI(G) 471*

Navy Unit Commendations were awarded to LCI(G)s *346*, *348*, *438*, *441*, *449*, *450*, *457*, *466*, *469*, *471*, *473*, and *474*.

One of the Navy Cross recipients, Lieutenant (jg) Alvin E. Rosenbloom, CO of *LCI(G) 348*, assessed the situation in his action report of 9 March 1945:

> This ship [*LCI(G) 348*] was in excellent position, because it stood in so close to the line of departure, to observe the action against the other ships. It became obvious, after the first ten minutes, that the LCI's going in were sure to be hit; heavy splashes could be seen bracketing them, and the uncertain 40MM fire of the LCI's indicated they were unable to locate the source of the fire.
>
> Further, they were obviously being fired upon by guns of much heavier caliber than their own, some splashes indicating that the shell was at least a 5 inch, possibly larger.
>
> At 1100 yards, therefore, (the range of the 4.5 rockets we use), the LCI(G) would appear to be an ineffective weapon if used against a heavily defended beach; they were easy targets for the shore batteries and rocket and 40MM fire is no answer to medium and heavy caliber fire. A longer range rocket might possibly be a solution, since the Japs didn't open up until the LCI's were within 2000 yards, evidently supposing them to be troop transports.
>
> It is difficult to avoid the conclusion however, that the LCI(G)s, on a heavily defended beach, are vulnerable targets, with only the reluctance of the enemy commander to disclose the position of his shore batteries between the ship and heavy fire, the silencing of which the LCI(G) is in no way equipped.[16]

Summation of Battle Damage

Ship	Major Battle Damage	Wounded	Dead
LCI(G) 346	Light damage, need minor hull repairs	none reported	
LCI(G) 348	Light damage, need minor hull repairs	none reported	
LCI(G) 438	Moderate damage, parts available, Repairable and will return to duty	2	0
LCI(G) 441	Needs major rewiring, galley and refrigerator destroyed, Repairable and will return to duty	27	6
LCI(G) 449	Conn shot away, gyro and magnetic compasses destroyed, Control gear destroyed, communications gear destroyed, May be able to return to duty if parts can be obtained	20	17
LCI(G) 450	Foc's'le damage, rocket launchers and guns damaged, Repairable and will return to duty	6	0
LCI(G) 457	Damage to forward waterline on hull with interior flooding, Repairable and will return to duty	16	1
LCI(G) 466	Extensive hull damage, most guns destroyed, will require major hull repair	18	5*
LCI(G) 469	Some damage to engine room, many minor holes in hull, Repairable and will return to duty	7	0
LCI(G) 471	Foc'sle destroyed, well deck and ramp sponsons damaged, Repairable and will return to duty	6†	12
LCI(G) 473	Port quad and generators destroyed — to be parted out	30	0
LCI(G) 474	Sunk	16	3
LC(FF) 627	Minor hull damage, fully repairable and will return to duty	0	0

*Includes one man listed as missing
†Includes one man listed as a shock case

In all cases shown above, the ships suffered innumerable holes in their hulls of both a major and minor variety, requiring repair. Only major damage is listed with the prognosis for a ship's probability for return to service.[17]

Commander M. J. Malanaphy, Commander of LCI(G) Flotilla Three, in his report on the damage to the LCI Group 8 ships, noted that the battle damage suffered by the ships would need to be repaired quickly, as the ships were expected to participate in the invasion of Okinawa. Shortages of 40mm and 20mm guns, as well as conning tower equipment existed and this posed a major problem for the ships' repairs and readiness for Okinawa. In addition, work on LCI gunboats was always put off until larger ships were repaired, and this would work against their preparation for Okinawa. Malanaphy requested higher command to intercede in getting the needed repairs completed. As a last resort, he requested permission to cannibalize LCI(L)s for equipment as needed. Most of the ships went to Saipan for repairs, but the most seriously damaged ones had to go to Guam where repair facilities were more advanced.

Personnel problems were a major concern. Two hundred men were considered casualties, with another 200 considered to be suffering from battle shock and of no further use. Requests for replacements had fallen on deaf ears. Only eighteen enlisted men were sent when 150 had been requested.[18]

In several of the LCI(G) action reports, the commanding officers complained that the practice of painting large white hull numbers on the bows of the ships made them easy targets. The numerals stood out from the green camouflage and made a good focus for enemy gunners. This was disputed by higher authority which asserted that the main cause of devastation to the gunboats was by ranging buoys that the enemy had placed in the water. This enabled them to find the range of the LCI(G)s with ease. A possible problem with the camouflage was identified by Commander Malanaphy in his First Endorsement to the action report of *LCI(G) 450*. Malanaphy wrote "It is considered that the designs painted by some ships on the forward side of the conning station is an undesirable practice as it furnishes a point of aim at the most vital station in the ship."[19] As a result the practice was halted.

Praise from higher command and others was not long in coming. The following day Rear Admiral Harry W. Hill, CTF 53, sent this message to Malanaphy. "I regret to hear of your losses of many brave personnel and damage to your fine ships X The LCI(G)'s as usual are leading the way with boldness and bravery."[20]

The debacle of 17 February 1945 led to a number of recommendations for the use of the LCI(G) gunboats. In his report on the operations of Task Force 52 (Amphibious Support Force) at Iwo Jima, Rear Admiral W. H. P. Blandy (Commander Amphibious Group One) recommended "[t]hat LCI(G)'s be not employed in close support of UDT operations in heavily fortified areas until considerable reduction of the defenses has taken place."[21] Recommendations by Lieutenant Commander Willard V. Nash (Commander LCI(G) Group EIGHT—CTU 52.5.2) included the use of rockets with a longer range so that the gunboats could launch them while still out of range of shore batteries. Japanese buoys had been spotted in the water but were not taken into consideration. Later it was surmised that they were probably ranging markers that allowed the Japanese to effectively zero in on the gunboats.[22] The buoys were destroyed by LCI(G) and LCS(L) gunboats in the following two days.

The original plans for the invasion of the volcanic island included the use of the LCI(G)s and LCS(L)s in immediate support of the landings. The losses of 17 February made the inclusion of the LCI(G)s impossible. Of the twelve LCI(G)s that had covered the UDT on 17 February, all had been hit and damaged severely. With *LCI(G) 474* sunk and *441* and *473* under tow, the surviving LCI(G)s limped back to Saipan. Fortunately for the Marines about to land on the island, a new gunboat en route to the battle had remained unscathed. Twelve LCS(L)s from LCS(L) Flotilla Three were scheduled to arrive at the island just prior to the landing. Designated as Gunboat Support Unit Three under the command of Captain T. C. Aylward, it included *LCS(L)s 32–36* and *51*, along with flotilla flagship *LCI(FF) 988* (TU 52.5.3), and *LCS(L)s 31, 52–56*, with *LC(FF) 484* (TU 52.5.4). This variation of the LCS(L)s included a single 40mm gun mounted in the bow in addition to the two twin 40mm gun and four 20mm single guns. Ten Mark VII rocket launchers capable of launching salvos of 120 4.5 inch rockets were installed between the bow gun and the forward twin 40mm. Several .50 caliber machine guns rounded out the armament. Captain Walter Karig described the LCS(L)s as "looking something like a Fourth of July fireworks when all weapons were blazing."[23]

The LCS(L)s would not be acting alone. Also arriving the morning of the invasion was TU 52.6 Mortar Support Group with Lieutenant Commander S. J. Kelley on board *LCI(FF) 679*. It consisted of twenty-eight LCI(M)s divided into five units.

TU 52.6.1, Mortar Support Unit One—Lieutenant Commander William T. Dom
  LCI(M)s 630, 631(F), 632, 638, 756, and *1010*

TU 52.6.2 Mortar Support Unit Two—Lieutenant Frank Baumholz
  LCI(M)s 633(F), 757, 760, 1011, 1012, 1023

TU 52.6.3 Mortar Support Unit Three—Lieutenant Commander G. W. Hannett
  LCI(M)s 658–660, 754, 1056, 1057—*LCI(M) 1057* was in need of repair and had to remain at Saipan.

TU 52.6.4 Mortar Support Unit Four—Lieutenant Commander Harris Brown
  LCI(G)s 739–742, 975, 1058

TU 52.6.5 Mortar Gunboat Unit Five—Lieutenant Commander Connors
  LCI(G)s 351, 352, 354, 355(F), 356

Mortar gunboats were relatively new to the war. Many had been recently converted and still had their (G) designation. This was the case for many of the gunboats, as their physical changes were ahead of the administrative changes. It was not unusual for an LCI(G) to show up as a newly equipped mortar boat.

The mortar gunboats had their introduction at Peleliu and, from that point, a number were converted from LCI(L)s and some from previously converted gunboats. Since they were new, tactics had to be devised to utilize their capabilities to the maximum. Captain E. C. Rook, Commander Mortar Support Group for the invasion of Iwo Jima, had developed three fire plans for his group and trained and rehearsed them at Saipan prior to heading for Iwo Jima. A last minute medical illness befell the Captain, and he had to undergo an emergency operation at Saipan which put him out of the action. The plans that he developed were designated fire plans Able, Baker, and Charlie. They were described as:

(1) Plan Able is a means whereby a division or unit of LCI(G) mortars is enabled to deliver a sustained fire for a long period of time into a comparatively limited target area, capable of extension in depth and translation in deflection. It was believed to be best adopted for close supporting fire (flank protection) harassing and interdiction fire and through employment of its own established beacon to be a good plan for night firing....

(2) Plan Baker is a means whereby one or more mortar craft are enabled to fire a barrage having as much width as the number of ships provide, fixed or capable of extension in depth. It was assumed to be best adapted for progressive neutralization fire and close support fire over and beyond our own deployed forces....

(3) Plan Charlie includes independent or minor concentration fire on point targets or targets of opportunity for immediate or limited results. It might be used for harassing fire, counter-battery

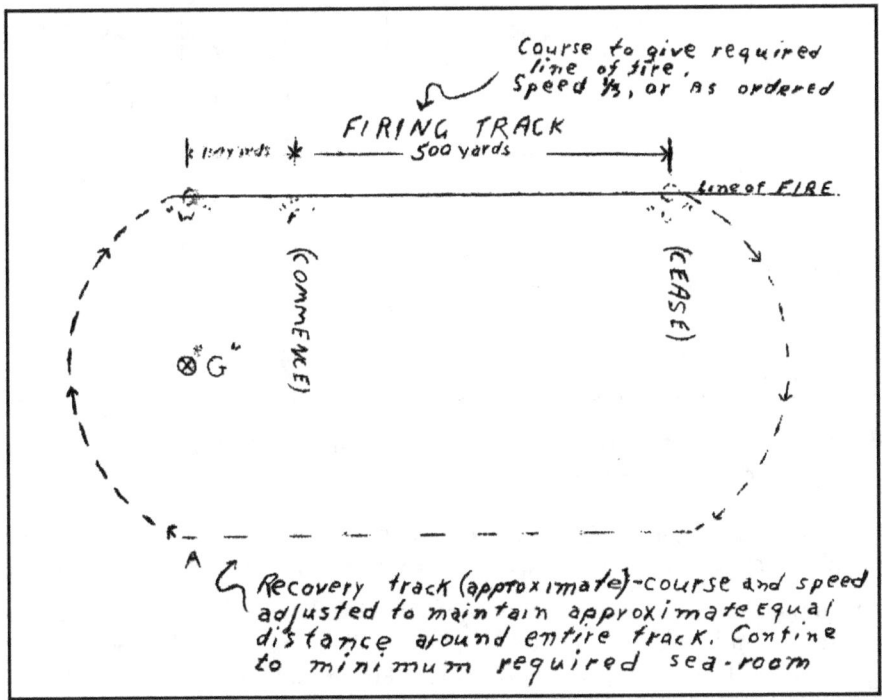

Mortar Plan Able. Prior to the assault on Iwo Jima, Captain E. C. Rook, Commander Mortar Support Group, had worked out three plans for the mortar ships to use and had the ships in his group rehearse them at Saipan. The three plans were assigned the names Able, Baker, and Charlie. Commander Task Unit 52.6.5 (Commander LCI(L) Group 67) No Serial, *Action Report—Invasion of Iwo Jima 18–26 February 1945*, No Date, Enclosure (A).

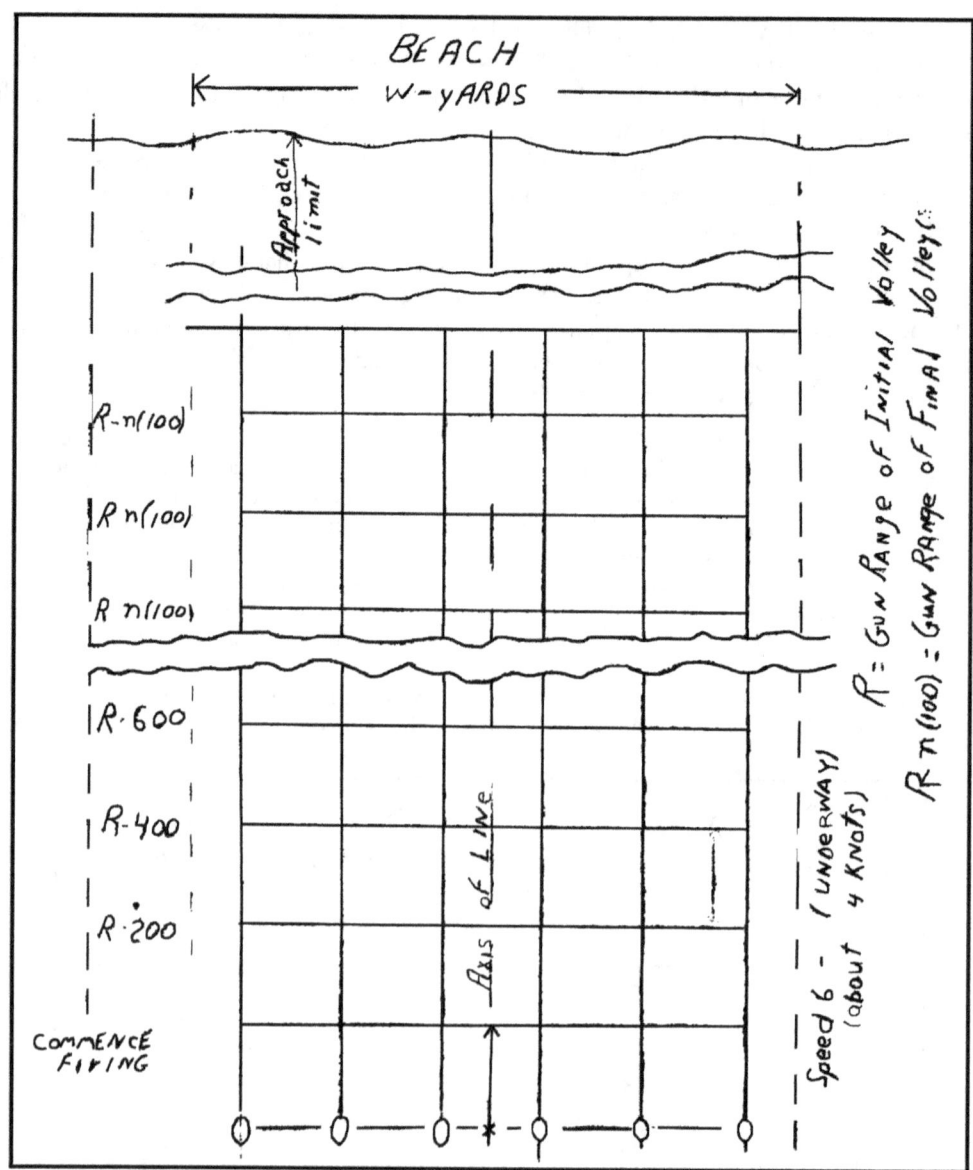

Mortar Plan Baker. Commander Task Unit 52.6.5 (Commander LCI(L) Group 67) No Serial, *Action Report—Invasion of Iwo Jima 18–26 February 1945,* No Date, Enclosure (B).

fire, interdiction fire, particularly where high trajectory is required. Plan Charlie may be conducted by single or several ships whose firing may or may not be coordinated depending on assignment.[24]

Although the plans reflected a great deal of thought, they were not always workable. After the demonstration landing at Okinawa on 1 April 1945 Lieutenant (jg) C. A. Schulz, Commanding Officer of *LCI(M) 1057,* reported that "Mortar Firing Plan 'Able' is not a workable plan if there is any swell or wind. Reference ship cannot hold proper positions and firing vessels waste too much time reorienting position,"[25] to which Lieutenant E. S. Thorn, Commanding Officer of *LCI(M) 975* added:

Plan Able of firing mortars is not considered effective and desirable by this command. The main feature of mortar fire is an effective barrage before the initial landing to paralyze and neutralize

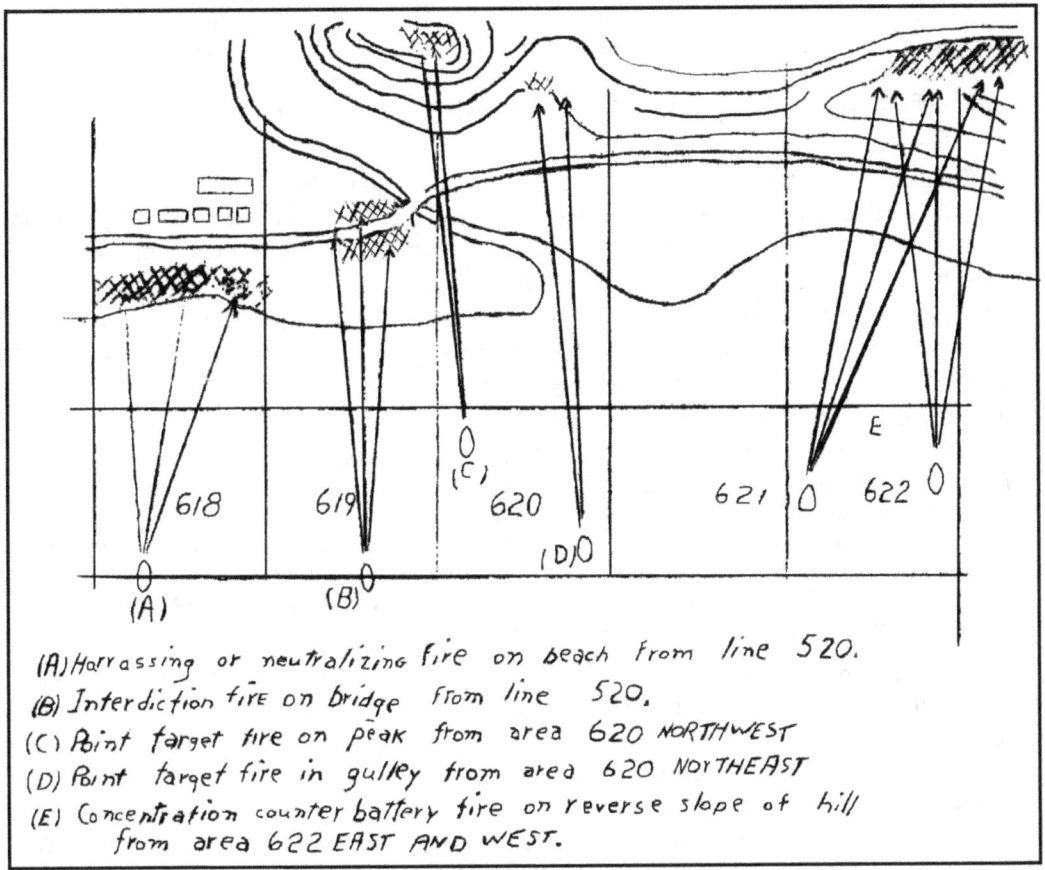

Mortar Plan Charlie. Commander Task Unit 52.6.5 (Commander LCI(L) Group 67) No Serial, *Action Report—Invasion of Iwo Jima 18–26 February 1945,* No Date, Enclosure (C).

enemy installations on the beach and surrounding flanks. The Plan Able has too many lapses of time between ships shelling the beach. Also the danger of putting the ship broadside to the beach at a close range. Plan Baker or Charlie would seem more effective and desirable for a pre-assault of the initial wave. Its effect of fire power can cover more area than Able Plan of fire.[26]

The mortar gunboats began their bombardment of inshore positions at about 0810 and ranged up and down the landing beaches. They finally arrived at a position to the north of Blue Beach 2 where they stood by for the next phase of their mission. *LCI(M) 633* reported that they employed Fire Plan Baker:

D Day H plus 25 [0925], When 2000 yards from the beach, slowed to 4 knots and commenced firing on course 325° T. This plan was to walk the shots 800 to 1000 yards. Stopped all engines and held position, when 1000 yards from beach; changed pattern of fire to range 3000 yards, 6 rounds per gun per minute using a dispersion in range. Fired in area between 000° T and 325° T. This plan of firing for the unit helped keep the enemy from attacking the landing forces. During this plan LCI(M) 633 received scattered machine gun and mortar fire from the enemy. One shell blew up part of our starboard raft and machine gun fire raked the ship. The ship's 40mm and 20mm return fire slowed the enemy fire.[27]

Mortar runs by various support groups continued throughout the day. Mortar Support Unit Five employed Fire Plan Able from 1953 to 0731 on the following morning. Typical of the amount of fire executed by the ships was that of *LCI(G) 352* which reported:

LCI(G) 352 made 54 runs around the bombardment track, expending 694 rounds of HE, 111 rounds of WP, and 100 rounds of DF mortar ammunition. As a result of the firing, several fires of a local nature were observed to be started in the target area. It was not possible to observe the effectiveness of most of the firing, however. Enemy fire was intermittent, consisting of occasional ineffective machine gun and mortar fire. No ships were hit.[28]

For the next several days and until the end of the campaign, the mortar gunboats provided support for the Marines ashore, responding to call fire requests to knock out enemy emplacements that were preventing the troop's advance. In addition, they kept the enemy off balance by providing harassing fire during the nighttime hours.

Ships do not always act alone and, in most cases, work better in consort with other vessels. LCI(M)s were excellent weapons but lacked the direct line firepower of other ships. Mortar units worked best when other ships provided covering fire. Lieutenant Commander William T. Dom, Commander of Mortar Support Unit One stated:

> It is the opinion of this officer that an LCS(L)(3) mounting a three inch gun would be the most effective type ship to support a mortar unit as this type is able to close the beach to the same distance as the mortar unit and thereby observe the enemy fire first hand. A DD such as the U.S.S. BRYANT, which rendered fire-support to this Unit on its third night firing mission, is the ideal fire-support ship as it contributes greatly to the morale of the men under fire when they know they are being supported by a DD. It is recognized however that all DDs may not be as aggressive as the BRYANT in supporting a mortar unit and an LCS(L)(3) could do the job.[29]

Among the greatest enemies of the fighting men both ashore and afloat were stress and fatigue. With a deadly adversary in front and around them, the fighting men had little chance for rest. Constant calls to general quarters, enemy fire or attacks, and the constant possibility of an air raid, kept men continually on edge. The plight of the Marines ashore was obvious, but on the ships there was little respite either. Years after the war ended, Charles Thomas, who served as a Gunner's Mate on board *LCS(L) 35* at Iwo Jima, recalled

> We try to sleep leaning or sitting against something whenever there is the opportunity, but our inexorable fatigue is more than beginning to reveal itself. The physical labor performed by our crew, especially the gunners and ammunition handlers, has been prodigious, not only on this day but in the days and weeks leading up to the invasion. The noise and smoke of continuous firing are finishing off our last energies…. Sleep deprivation over the past three days [19–21 February 1945], combined with the suspense and anxiety of our first invasion, has put every man near the limit of his endurance.[30]

For those above deck the strain was great, but at least they could see the

The new 5 inch spin-stabilized rockets made their first appearance on LCI gunboats at Iwo Jima. These photographs may be compared with ones showing the 4.5 inch fin-stabilized rocket. NARA 80G 312105.

Crewmen on board an LCI(G) load rockets just prior to the assault on Peleliu on 19 September 1944. The rockets shown are the original 4.5 inch fin-stabilized barrage rockets that were standard for most of the war. They were replaced by the 5 inch spin-stabilized rocket at Iwo Jima and Okinawa. NARA 80G 247558.

action and mentally prepare themselves. Those working below decks on the gunboats could only imagine the worst.

In addition to the mortar ships, Task Unit 52.7.1, consisting of *LCI(R)s 644, 651, 707, 708, 771, 772, 1029, 1030,* and *1077* and *LCI(G)s 80, 345,* and *437*, with Lieutenant Commander F. Thompson, Jr. on board the flagship *LCI(R) 707*, arrived early in the morning of 19 February. These ships all belonged to Flotilla 16 and had just undergone conversion at Hunter's Point, San Francisco. The new 5 inch spin-stabilized rockets carried a heavier payload and had a much longer range than the commonly used 4.5 inch barrage rockets. These were installed on the Flotilla 16 rocket gunboats. LCI(G)s and LCS(L)s carried the older 4.5 inch rockets. Overall control of the rocket gunboats was held by Commander Clarence E. Coffin who served as Commander Task Group 52.7. While other ships bombarded inland and covered the landing beaches, these rocket ships stationed themselves 2,500 yards off the northeastern beaches near Hanare Rock and kept up a constant fusillade of 5 inch rocket fire on enemy targets near Motoyama beginning at 0656 on 19 February and lasting throughout the day. Typical of the ammunition expended by each ship was that of *LCI(R) 644*. She reported firing 1,251 5 inch rockets, 176 rounds of 40mm, and 648 rounds of 20mm fire against the beaches.[31]

The naval bombardment of the beaches ceased at 0800 to allow a strike by Task Force 58 fighters and bombers to make their runs on the beaches and inland areas, including the slopes of Mount Surabachi. They were joined by fifteen B-24 Liberators which had flown in from the

Marianias. When the air strikes were completed, naval bombardment began again at 0825 and the LCS(L) gunboats formed up for the assault. LCI(M)s and LCI(R)s continued unleashing their missiles of death on the Japanese defenders.

The LCS(L)s were scheduled to make a total of two rocket runs on the beaches. The purpose of the rocket barrage was twofold. One involved the possibility that the Japanese had buried quantities of drums of gasoline at water's edge and just inland. *LCS(L) 31* reported:

> This initial salvo was intended to ignite any electrically wired gasoline drums which were believed to be arranged on the beaches' edge so as to set up a "wall of flame" ahead of our first assault wave just as it reached the beach. The tremendous rocket barrage almost perfectly placed over the questionable area produced no visible effect indicating that the "wall of flame" idea had been discarded and the gasoline drums removed sometime previously.[32]

The salvos of rockets moving from the shore line to a few hundred yards inland ensured that there would be no Japanese defenders left above ground to challenge the Marines as they landed. Twelve LCS(L)s each fired two salvos of 120 rockets on their initial runs. That made a total of 2,880 rockets to hit the landing beaches, the width of which was about 2,600 yards. This was in addition to the fire laid down by other ships and followed the earlier bombardment of the beaches and immediate areas by the LCI(M)s.

The LCS(L)s flew brightly colored pennants of either red, green, yellow, or blue from their masts as guides for the landing craft following them into the beaches. At the end of the rocket run, they turned and ran parallel to the beaches to deliver automatic weapons fire with their 20mm and 40mm guns before turning seaward. Enemy mortar and small arms fire was directed at them, but none of the ships were hit. By 0830 they were ready for their second run, again delivering a salvo of rockets against the shore. These rockets were judged to hit the beaches about one hundred yards inland from the water. Mortar and small arms fire again erupted from the shore and *LCS(L) 51* was hit, starting a small fire which was quickly extinguished.[33]

At this point, the LCS(L) line held station as the first wave of LCVPs and other landing craft passed through their line and headed for the shore. They continued firing over the heads of the Marines as the second boat wave passed through their lines and then turned and ran parallel to the beaches while firing on targets of opportunity.

LCS(L) 33 fired her second salvo at 0845 and almost immediately began taking fire from shore. Machine gun fire hit the ship and damaged a couple of her port rocket launchers. Moments later a mortar shell landed in the water only fifty feet off her bow. Since a wave of LVTs was passing by, she was unable to turn

Commander Clarence E. Coffin, Jr., Commander of TG 52.7, taking a break off Iwo Jima. Coffin's Task Group included the nine LCI(R)s and three LCI(G)s assigned to provide rocket support during the invasion of Iwo Jima. NARA 80G 305027.

LCI(R) 708 LCI Flotilla 1, TG 51.15.3 (Rocket Support Group) at Iwo Jima in D-Day 19 January 1945. This photograph shows the gun crew for the bow 40mm gun (R-L) Roberts S1/c on phones; A. Myhre, S1/c, pointer; Tommie Alexander S1/c 1st leader; H. V. Rowland, RDM 3/c; E. Ruglie S2/c. NARA 80G 305029.

as additional mortar rounds bracketed her port and starboard. Dye markers from the shells showed the Japanese that they were close to their target. The *33* backed her engines and maneuvered as much as possible to avoid being hit and also to avoid running into LVTs. Additional mortar rounds landed just where she had been minutes before, and for the next twenty minutes she maneuvered among the boat lanes until she was able to turn and move away from the beach. Two of her men were wounded by shrapnel in the attacks.

Landings on each of the designated beaches, listed from south to north, were made by:

Beach	*Battalion/Regiment*	*Division*	*Commanding Officer*
Green Beach	1/28*	5	LtCol Jackson B. Butterfield
	2/28	5	LtCol Chandler W. Johnson
Red Beach 1	2/27	5	Maj John A. Antonelli
Red Beach 2	1/27	5	LtCol John A. Butler
Yellow Beach 1	1/23	4	LtCol Ralph Haas
Yellow Beach 2	2/23	4	Maj Robert Davidson
Blue Beach 1	1/25	4	LtCol Hollis U. Mustain
Blue Beach 2†	3/25	4	LtCol James Taul

*Marine units are designated by battalion and regiment, thus 1/28 stands for 1st Battalion, 28th Marine Regiment.
†Original plans did not call for landings on Blue Beach 2, but the 3/25 inadvertently landed on the southern edge of the beach on D-Day.

The 3/27, under Lieutenant Colonel Donn J. Robertson, had initially been held back as regimental reserve. It landed at 1130 to assist the 2/27. The 3rd Marine Division had been held in reserve, and battalions were assigned as relief for units in the 4th and 5th Marine Divisions as needed. The 3rd Marine Division's 1/26, under Lieutenant Colonel Daniel C. Pollock, landed at 1500 to bolster 2/27, and additional 3rd Marine Divisions units followed over the next few days.

For the remainder of the day, the LCS(L)s cruised the areas adjacent to the landing beaches. From time to time groups of enemy soldiers were visible targets for their automatic weapons, and at other times they fired into any suspicious cave or enemy position they could identify. Marine observer teams reported on board and helped them direct their fire to enemy targets. Since the gunboats could get in close to shore, it was possible for them to spot enemy targets that the Marines ashore could not see. The gunboats eliminated a number of enemy soldiers while working with the observers.

The LCS(L)s also used themselves as bait. Working with destroyers or other larger ships, the gunboats cruised close to shore to draw fire from enemy gun emplacements. Once this took place, the LCS(L)s fired tracer ammunition back at the enemy gun to identify its location. Spotters on the destroyers then directed the fire of the heavier guns into these targets to eliminate them. *LCS(L)51* found herself with just such a mission as soon as she had completed covering for the landing craft waves on 19 January. From 0910 to 1030, with Marine spotter Second Lieutenant John J. Sweeney on board, she fired on pillboxes behind the boat basin. As they fired back, she aimed her tracers at them, and the cruiser *Vicksburg CL 86* demolished four of them.

Captain Theodore C. Aylward, Commander LCS(L) Flotilla Three. NARA 80 GK 2692.

The *51* claimed credit for two. Marines in the quarry area were being held up by heavy fire from Japanese mortars and other guns, and the *51* leveled automatic weapons fire on the area along with thirty-four of her rockets. The combined efforts of *LCS(L) 51* and *Vicksburg* helped to break up an enemy counterattack that was being organized. *Vicksburg* moved on at 1150 and Sweeney and the *51* began to work with *Paul Hamilton DD 590*. The gunboat withdrew from the area at 1330 to get a fresh supply of ammunition and then returned to the task. From 1530 until midnight she worked in conjunction with the destroyers. On this mission she ran in close to shore near the small boat area. According to her action report for the day her "strategy this time was to go in close to shore and draw fire. We would then answer with tracer and call DDs in. In this way quite a few positions were silenced."[34] Her destroyer partners during this period were *Fullam*

A row of LCS(L)s may be seen between the second and third waves of landing craft. After making rocket runs on the beach, the gunboats sat close inshore to fire over the heads of the Marines as they landed. NARA 80G 415308.

DD 474, Little DD 803, and *Shields DD 596.* Drawing enemy fire during the Iwo Jima campaign was a standard practice for the LCS(L)s and proved to be successful, particularly when they were teamed with larger ships. This type of fire support was most effective in the beginning of the campaign. Lieutenant Kenneth F. Machacek, CO of *LCS(L) 31* reported:

> Gunnery was most effective during the first two days of the action chiefly because of the enemy's lack of concealment of both themselves and their weapons in and around the base of Mount Surabachi. Twenty-five to one hundred of the enemy were definitely destroyed by this vessel's gunfire during these first two days. Rockets were able to reach into the ravines at the base of the mount to neutralize mortar emplacements and the close range enabled the forty and twenty millimeter batteries to keep the many caves and pill boxes silent during the early advances. Harassing fires both night and day kept the enemy guns down and hampered any attempts to counter-attack under cover of darkness…. Average range to all targets was about 1000 yards which made for nearly perfect visibility and as a result accurate, well controlled, most effective fire.[35]

Working in such close proximity to the beaches gave the sailors on board the gunboats an eye-opening view of the action. As *LCS(L) 33* worked close to the beach her CO, Lieutenant Frank C. Osterland, noted that "It was during one of these close-in operations that the full impact of what was happening on the island hit me. Not far back from the water's edge was a pile of what we could best identify as corpses in Marine uniforms. Bodies of dead Marines were stacked up like cordwood, awaiting an opportunity when they could be removed from the island."[36]

A line of LCS(L)s fires on Mount Suribachi, Iwo Jima, on 19 February 1945. NH 104146.

Once the initial waves of Marines had landed, the gunboats found themselves with a variety of duties. One of the most discouraging was that of salvage duty. Numerous landing craft littered the beach area where they had been struck and disabled by gunfire. This number grew constantly throughout the morning and afternoon of D-Day. At first, the idea of having them blown up by the UDT seemed feasible, but the nearness of the troops and other hazards that would be caused by the explosions soon indicated that this was not a good idea. Since they were able to get close to shore, it was thought that the gunboats would be able to attach cables to these wrecks and pull them off the beach. Unfortunately they were not suited for the duty. In many cases, their cables parted or their equipment just gave out. In addition, their flat bottoms, while useful for getting them in close to shore, made it difficult for them to keep course when pulling heavy objects. Time and again cables parted, ships collided with one other, screws were damaged, and very little was accomplished. Getting close to the beach presented numerous problems, not the least of which was running into submerged landing craft and vehicles that had sunk. The hulls of the LCS(L)s and LCIs were made of $\frac{3}{16}$ inch thick steel, which could easily be punctured by a collision. It was obvious that the ships were not suited for salvage duty. Lieutenant C. J. Boone, Commanding Officer of *LCS(L) 33* reported:

> It is believed we sustained more damage to our ship, through our salvage attempts, and from mooring alongside other ships, than we did from enemy effort. The forward frames of the ship are sprung, the stanchions below the 20mm gun tubs are broken, the starboard 20mm gun tub

LCS(L)s 34 and 36 approach the beach at Iwo Jima to fire on enemy positions on 19 February 1945. Official U.S. Navy photograph.

is completely free of outboard support, and is now shored up with 4x4 timbers. Bad dents all along each side of hull from towing and salvage attempts. Condition of bow below water line is unknown, from repeated beaching over sunken wrecks, but no leaks are noticeable.

We lost one anchor with approximately seventy fathoms of cable. Broke all our hawsers, and have about fifty feet of ¾" cable left, also burned out the clutch of our anchor winch.

It is strongly recommended that this type ship not be used for salvage duty. We are not equipped to do the job—and much embarrassment is felt on our part when called upon to do a job, for which we are not fitted.[37]

Resupply of the ships was usually accomplished by mooring alongside larger ships such as APAs and LSTs. This presented a great deal of danger to the smaller gunboats as they were continually battered against the sides of the larger ships by wave action. Lieutenant K. C. Huff, CO of *LCS(L) 35*, noted an additional cause of damage:

No damage was incurred from enemy fire. However, considerable damage was received while alongside of other vessels. This damage included 16 strained frames, four broken stanchions, bent gun tubs and shields, loosened water lines, two foot hole in bow, loss of all lines, during salvage work, near loss of the anchor during salvage work, damaged radar, damaged spare parts on mast, and cracked seams forward.[38]

To which Lieutenant H. D. Chickering, CO of *LCS(L) 51*, added:

We are definitely not designed to come alongside APAs, AOGs etc. for fuel, provisions, etc. Our construction is such that we batter ourselves to pieces even in a moderate sea, and logistics should be carried out from LCMs and similar smaller craft.[39]

Nighttime activities included a great deal of what was termed harassing fire. Mindful of the near proximity of American troops, the gunboats made sure that their rounds did not fall on friendly troops. During the first few days of the campaign, the LCS(L)s and LCI(R)s were used for call-fire. However, the nature of their rockets and automatic weapons fire was less useful as the fighting moved inland to areas that were not in their line of sight. It was at this point that the LCI(M)s came into greater use. Constant night firing, as well as daytime firing, was used to attack enemy targets that could not easily be seen. Fire to these targets was directed by Marine fire control teams on board the gunboats which coordinated with Marine units ashore. Nighttime harassing fire was useful in keeping the enemy off guard. Typical of the nighttime assignments was that of *LCI(M) 1056*. Her CO, Ensign C. L. Edman, reported that from 1930 on 26 February until 0630 the following morning, his ship was directed to deliver mortar fire on suspected enemy positions. By the end of the period they had fired 380 mortar rounds at the enemy, consisting of 308 rounds of high explosive and 78 white phosphorous.[40] Constant firing of the mortars and guns led to many malfunctions of equipment. The volume of fire delivered at enemy targets was more than equipment was designed for. Reports of bent mortar straps, broken tie rods, and broken firing pins were common.

In practice, the mortar gunboats frequently used plan A with one of their ships as a reference vessel. This vessel kept station at a particular point and the others cruised around it in a circle formation. As they reached a predetermined position relative to the reference vessel, the LCI(M) fired its mortar rounds while proceeding toward shore. This gave them the ability to "walk" the mortar rounds across a lengthy distance. At the end of their firing run, they circled around for another. During this time they used their 40mm and other guns against shore targets while preparing for the next firing of their mortars. The nearness to shore frequently caused problems for the reference ship in keeping its position, as wave action constantly worked against it. This was reported by Lieutenant J. C. Wilson, CO of *LCI(M) 1012*:

> There was quite a set off the beach from the swell and the reference ship had difficulty maintaining her position on the reference point. Visibility was poor most of the night. The continuous firing of star shells in this area helped us in keeping our formation. The moon being almost full also helped. We fired 520 rounds during the night and had the use of only one mortar for a large percentage of the time and only two for part of the time. The welded tie rods did not hold up. We went alongside a repair ship before firing again and got stronger ones made, having no further trouble on this score. Our shells appeared to be doing damage to the target area the extent of which we don't know. The return fire from shore was machine gun fire at long intervals. Again our secondary battery was a big help in keeping the fire down.
>
> 1610 Went alongside *ARS-34* to effect repairs to #2 and #3 Mortars. Stronger tie rods were secured and the back strap re-welded on both Mortars. While tied up to this repair ship our port side took an awful pounding due to the heavy swells banging the ships together. Six frames just aft of the conn were caved in 6 or 8 inches.[41]

The gunboats could deliver 20mm and 40mm gunfire at Japanese targets most any time. However, the use of rockets and mortars had to be interrupted when American fighters and bombers attacked the Japanese. Fear of hitting an aircraft with a rocket or mortar rounds was always a concern. Navy pilots had to worry about enemy fire. They did not need to dodge falling rockets and mortars launched by the gunboats. In spite of holding their rocket or mortar fire when their planes attacked enemy targets, mishaps did occur. On 19 February, a Kingfisher observation plane from one of the larger ships was observed flying low over the line of fire from the mortar gunboats. Shortly thereafter, it was observed spiraling downward minus its tail. It was thought that the observation plane was hit by a mortar round from *LCI(M) 638*. None of the ships in the unit had been warned of its approach. It hit the water 350 yards astern of *LCI(M) 756* which sent out a rescue boat. Unfortunately its crew did not survive the crash.[42]

Coordination of air and gunboat missions was considered desirable. On 27 February

LCI(M) 356 worked over enemy positions on the west side of Iwo Jima between air strikes. As a result of the experience, her CO, Lieutenant E. B. Wicklander, recommended that coordination of air strikes and gunboat attacks be stressed. In his action report of 7 March 1945 he stated:

> Enemy considered undivided attention to the air attack was more important. Mortar ship was free to lay its mortar fire without interruption, or opposition. It is suggested that the effect on the enemy was to distract their attention from the job of defending his position, even though well protected. Whether he attends his anti-aircraft job or fires at mortar ship, the other unit is left relatively free to operate.[43]

One of the tasks for which the LCS(L)s were well-suited was that of firefighting. On 22 February Japanese mortar fire managed to set fire to an American ammunition dump only forty yards off the beach. Innumerable cases of hand grenades, 5.0 rockets, and small arms ammunition were contained in the dump. However, the Marines desperately needed their ammunition, as the battle was only in its third day. *LCS(L)s 53* and *54* beached at 0155 and ran hoses from their Hale pumps and Johnson pumps over to the fire area and began to play water on it. A dazed and injured Marine stumbled from the area into their path and was taken aboard the *54* for medical aid. By 0230 the fires were under control, but exploding ordnance and fires were not their only problem. At 0255 a Japanese Betty dropped a stick of four small bombs only fifty yards from the ships but they were undamaged. By 0300 the fires were out and the LCS(L)s hauled themselves off the beach with their mission accomplished.[44]

By 26 February the need for so many fire support ships had diminished, and the LCS(L)s, and some of the other LCI gunboats departed for Saipan. Other gunboats would remain to assist the Marines ashore until 3 March 1945.

CHAPTER 8

The Liberation of Borneo

The island of Borneo is the second largest island in the East Indies, second only to New Guinea. Although it possessed raw materials in abundance, the most important of these were rubber and petroleum. Facilities for the production of petroleum and rubber were situated along the coast, with most of the interior inhabited only by indigenous peoples. Therefore the campaign to re-establish Allied control of the island focused on the perimeter of the island using amphibious assaults to provide access to the desired areas.

Earlier in the war the Japanese had taken over these areas from the Dutch and English for the purpose of obtaining raw materials unavailable in their home islands. Among them were Borneo's rubber and petroleum. The two centers of petroleum production, Balikpapan, on the Dutch-held southern part of the island, and the British-controlled areas of Brunei, Sarawak, Labuan, and North Borneo on the northwest coast, were prime targets of the Japanese and fell under their control early in 1942.

Where Borneo lay in the grand strategy was under consideration by the Joint Chiefs of Staff:

> The campaign that had led to the invasion of Luzon and was oriented northward toward Japan itself had resulted in the bypassing of the largest portions of the Netherlands East Indies. Although rich in resources for war, notably oil, rubber, and manganese, strategically the islands were of minor importance in the pattern set for the defeat of Japan. The Japanese depended upon them for vital supplies; but U.S forces did not need them sufficiently to warrant diverting resources to occupy any of the islands. At the beginning of February 1945, as the end of the major campaign in the Philippines came in sight, General MacArthur began to think of the desirability of seizing Borneo and acquiring its oil for use in the attack on Kyushu and Honshu. To the Joint Chiefs of Staff, then at Yalta, he reported that he was planning amphibious operations into Borneo that would be launched about 1 April 1945, using Australian troops.[1]

The liberation of Borneo had been put off by the Allied forces for several reasons, among them the overwhelming desire of General Douglas MacArthur to recapture the Philippines and the effectiveness of the U.S. Navy in cutting the Japanese supply lines. In addition, the island was far within the borders of the rapidly-expanding Japanese empire and a campaign in 1943 or 1944 was impractical. By 1945, little of the much-needed oil from Borneo was reaching the home islands of Japan thanks to an effective campaign by American submarines, surface ships, and aircraft. With success in the Philippines imminent, the attack on Borneo was planned. American forces had been committed to the taking of Okinawa, and the British desired to participate in that conquest as well. This fit in well with the planning of the Joint Chiefs of Staff who wanted the British to assume more responsibility for actions in the Southwest Pacific. They planned to transfer some of the area to British control. "The area transferred might be bounded by a line approximately from a point on the China coast between Indo-China and China southeastward through the Balabac Strait to the Equator and thence eastward."[2] This transfer would place Brunei Bay, Borneo, under their control and the British could use it as a home base. However, the British saw this as a move designed to keep them away from the eventual battle for Japan proper.

The battle for Borneo was fought by the Australians. In part this was a political move designed to assuage Australian feelings that they had been left out of the main part of the war. In his report to the Joint Chiefs of Staff, "General MacArthur reported that the Australians were becoming restive because their troops were not in action."[3] Not only were the Australians feeling left out, they wanted to be a part of the actual drive on Japan. Operations against bypassed groups of Japanese left behind in MacArthur's island-hopping campaign had given them the feeling that they were being relegated to what were basically insignificant duties. At the Australian War Cabinet meeting of 28 May 1945, it was noted that:

> There have been criticisms that the liquidation of by-passed Japanese forces is not by itself a worthwhile effort of our forces. The reasons for the non-participation in the Philippines campaigns have been made clear. But with American progress towards Japan, the operations against Borneo, the N. E. I. and Malaya, have assumed the nature of large-scale mopping-up campaigns. From the aspect of prestige, it is of greater importance to Australia to be associated with the drive to defeat Japan, though for reasons of British and Australian prestige, it would be desirable to have a token force in the recapture of Malaya, in order to avenge the defeat of 1941.[4]

Therefore Australian troops, aided by American, Australian, New Zealand, and Dutch Navy vessels, would take Borneo back from the Japanese. Involved in the assault on Borneo was the Australian Army's 1st Corps under Lieutenant General Sir Leslie Morshead, which consisted of the 7th and 9th Divisions. Support for the troops was supplied by the Royal Australian Air Force's 1st Tactical Air Force and the U.S. 13th Air Force. Elements of the Royal Australian Navy, elements from New Zealand's forces, and the U.S. Navy provided ships and gunfire-support. Originally six landings designated as Oboe I through VI were planned, but only three were used. Between 27 April and 20 July 1945, the Allied forces staged three operations: Oboe I, VI, and II. Oboe I, the landing at Tarakan, began on 1 May 1945. Oboe VI, the landing at British North Borneo, began on 10 June when Australian troops landed at Labuan Island in Brunei Bay. Oboe II took place on 1 July, with the Australians landing over 33,000 troops and support personnel at Balikpapan. In all cases the landing date was preceded by several days of minesweeping, UDT work, and naval and aerial bombardment of selected targets.

Major obstacles to the landings existed and included underwater beach obstructions. In addition, the Dutch, Americans, and finally the Japanese, had completed extensive mining operations off the beaches, and these had to be swept prior to any attempt to land troops. This stood in stark contrast to landing in the Philippines where such measures had not been taken by the Japanese. Underwater demolition teams and YMS minesweepers were in action several days prior to the actual invasion date, clearing mines and obstacles from the landing zones. YMSs would have to operate literally under the guns of the Japanese defenders, and several were sunk either by striking mines or being shelled by shore positions. LCPRs carrying UDT units operated close in to shore, covered by LCS(L)s and other fire-support craft. Their task was made even more difficult by errant aircraft bombing, poisonous sea snakes, and saltwater alligators. The frogmen operated within a few hundred yards of the beach and the gunboats were not far away, placing them in imminent peril from shore batteries. In Borneo, thirty-eight minesweepers from Mine Division 34 were used. Working in conjunction with the minesweepers were the LCS(L) gunboats.

Participating in the attack on Borneo were various elements of the amphibious gunboat

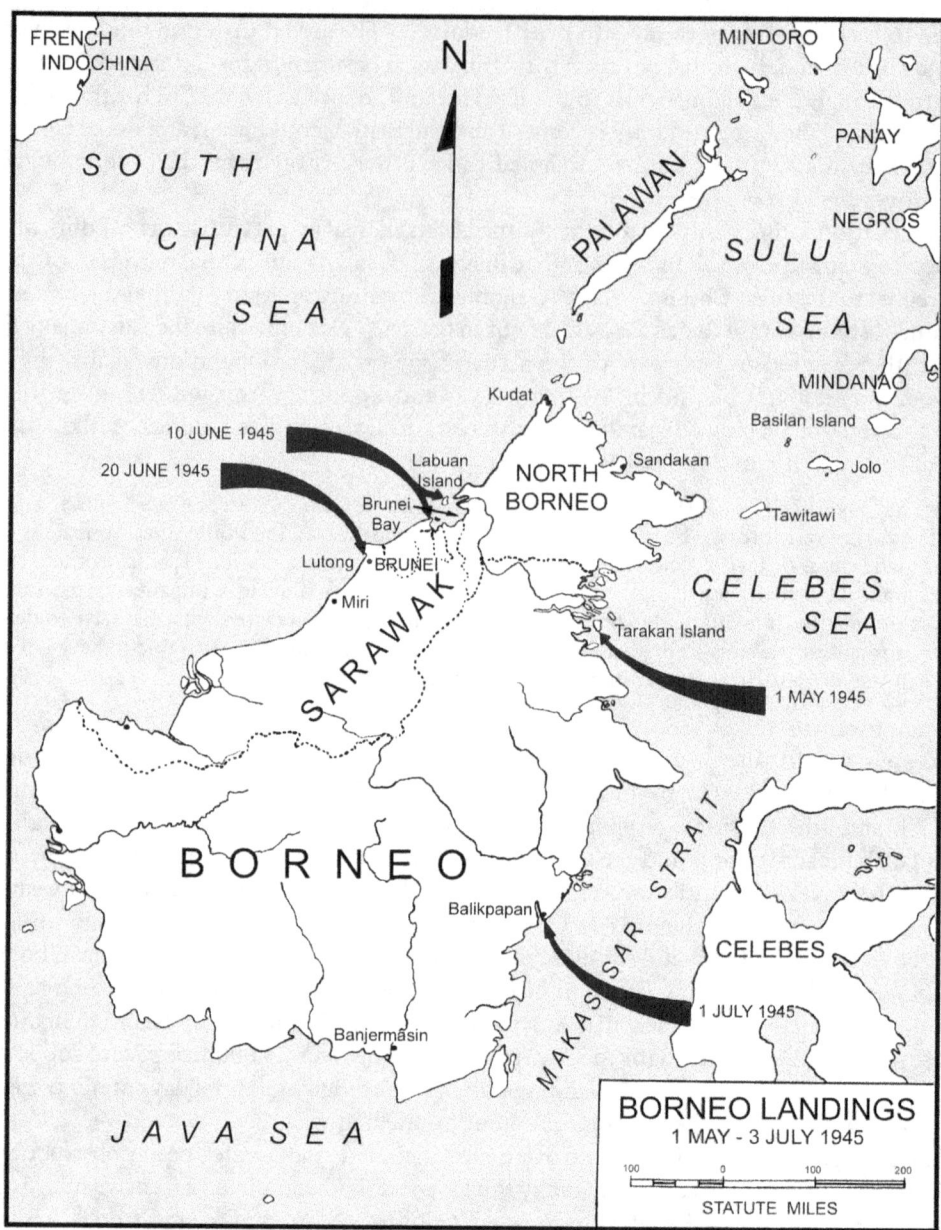

By mid–1944 the island of Borneo was under attack by Australian forces supported by the United States Navy and Army Air Forces. Numerous LCS(L)s and LCI gunboats were used in the four main assaults on the island. Adapted from OCE, GHQ, AFPAC (Historical).

units, including *LCS(L)s 8, 28–30, 41–48, 50, 58–60, LCI(R)s 31, 34, 71, 72, 74, 226, 230, 331, 337, 338, LCI(G)s 21–24, 59, 61, 64–70,* and *LCI(M)s 359, 362,* and *431.*

OBOE I

Tarakan Island is on the eastern coast of Borneo in the area previously under the control of the Dutch. It is approximately eleven miles wide and fifteen and one-half miles in length.

Rear Admiral F. B. Royal, Vice Admiral Daniel E. Barbey, and Rear Admiral A. G. Nobel on 26 March 1945. NARA 80G 328150.

The only access to the island was at the port of Lingkas which contained a pier used for docking tankers. Nearby beaches were of dubious value, heavily mined, and contained numerous obstacles constructed by the Japanese to discourage landings. However, the airfield at Tarakan was a prime target. If the island and its airfield could be captured, it would serve as a base for Allied aircraft in the campaigns in Borneo that would follow. Since it had been a Dutch possession, a contingent of Dutch troops accompanied the Australians in the landing. A Japanese garrison, estimated to be 2,300 strong, occupied the area. Defenses on the island were otherwise minimal, with only six coast defense gun emplacements.[5] Air support for the operation was supplied by the R.A.A.F.'s 1st Tactical Air Force and the U.S.'s 5th and 13th Air Forces. The air operations were under the command of Air Vice-Marshal Bostock.

The air attacks against Tarakan began on 12 April with P-38 Lightnings of the 13th Air Force staging a raid against enemy positions on south Tarakan. From then on until the invasion, regular flights of B-24s, B-25s, Lightnings, and Beaufighters made regular attacks on Japanese positions at Tarakan, making sure to eliminate the oil storage tanks and as many gun emplacements as possible.

Headquarters for planning the Tarakan campaign were on the island of Morotai. Once the plans had been finalized, the landing craft were run through their paces in a preliminary rehearsal which took place between 19 and 24 April. Larger ships from Rear Admiral R. S. Berkey's cruiser covering group headed south from Subic Bay, while minecraft and hydrographic ships set forth from Leyte. Still other ships, like *LCI(M) 359*, set out from diverse locations, such as Tawi Tawi

An LCI gunboat fires rockets at Tarakan. Official U.S. Navy photograph.

Not all of the days in the Pacific were filled with action. Here crew members on *LCS(L) 28* stand watch in their foul weather gear off Tarakan Island on 29 April 1945. Official U.S. Navy photograph.

8. The Liberation of Borneo

Australian engineers wade ashore on Red Beach at Tarakan to set explosives on 30 April 1945. NARA 80G 359858.

The Consolidated B-24L Liberator was used in the Pacific by both the Americans and the Royal Australian Air Force. This photograph was taken in 1944.

Australian troops of the 26 Australian Infantry Brigade, 9th Australian Army Infantry Division, wade ashore at Tarakan on 1 May 1945. The division was commanded by Brigadier David A. Whitehead. Rows of pilings designed to stop landing craft are visible just offshore. Australian engineers, using demolitions, blew gaps in the obstacles to allow landing. NARA 80G 259353.

RAAF Bristol Beaufighters 50 TU A19 MKI in training formation over Waga Waga, New South Wales, Australia.

Island, and headed for Borneo. On the way to Borneo, the *359* encountered two rafts with eight Japanese on board. They called for them to surrender, but two of the Japanese blew themselves up with hand grenades and the others appeared about to throw them at the ship. The enemy soldiers were cut down by .50 caliber gunfire from the gunboat. Only one survived. He threw up his arms while in the water and it was assumed that he wanted to surrender. He climbed aboard the raft. Men on board the gunboat kept a wary eye on him, and it was fortunate that they did. Once on the raft, he suddenly crouched down and began searching for something on the deck. Suspecting that he was looking for another grenade, the gunboat's crew opened fire and killed him.[6]

These varied elements of the attacking force rendezvoused off Tarakan on 27 April. A task group under Rear Admiral F. B. Royal arrived on 1 May to lead the landings. A predictable fatalism came over the gunboat crews and was demonstrated by EM 3/c Raymond J. Ross when he wrote: "Reports have it that the LCS's don't last long, many were said to have been sunk at Iwo Jima for they are the first to enter a battle zone along with mine sweepers to draw fire from the beach in order to find the strength of locations of the opposition. Will know all about it in a few days."[7] Ross was a bit mistaken about the identity and number of the ships lost at Iwo Jima; they were actually LCI(G)s and only one was sunk. But the comparison was close enough since both types of gunboats would always be in the hazardous first line of fire.

The actual assault on Tarakan began with minesweeping operations. Assigned to the chore was TU 78.1.5 Minesweeping Unit under Lieutenant Commander James R. Keefer. The task unit consisted of *Cofer APD 63*, which acted as the flagship, four minesweeping LCVPs, and ten *YMSs*. Their mission was to clear Tarakan's channels, approaches, anchorages, and landing beaches of mines. Numerous enemy minefields had been reported, and suicide boats and suicide swimmers were also suspected to be in the area. It was also known that the Japanese had shore batteries that could easily hit the small ships as they performed their hazardous work.

LCS(L)s *8, 28, 43, 44, 48*, and *50* were on hand to protect the minesweepers. The first day of sweeping, 27 April, was uneventful with the LCS(L)s destroying mines that had been cut loose. However, on 28 April, *YMS 329* hit a magnetic mine and suffered nineteen casualties. The severely damaged minesweeper was forced to retire from her assignment. A couple of days later, *YMS 51* set off another magnetic mine and sustained minor damage. Close calls were the order of the day. Robert C. Heim who served as BM 2/c on *LCS(L) 48* later wrote, "while following the minesweepers a mine came up off our bow — everyone ran aft for fear it would blow up. After it grazed the ship without going off it was shot out of the water with our 20mm and 40mm."[8] *Jenkins DD 447*, cruising in the area, also was damaged when she set off a contact mine. At 1530 on 2 May, the minesweepers took significant damage from the shore batteries at Cape Djoeata with *YMS 481* sunk and *YMSs 334* and *364* hit. *Cofer APD 62* and the LCS(L)s took the shore batteries under fire and put them out of commission. In addition, *YMS 363* detonated a mine during her operations and sustained damage as well.

Nearby Sadau Island was identified as a likely place to set up artillery batteries for bombardment of the beaches around Tarakan. *Philip DD 498* bombarded the landing area while LCS(L)s *48* and *50* made a rocket run on the beaches to cover the Australian landing, which took place around 0900. Following that, the LCS(L)s went to the aid of the Royal Australian Engineer Demolition Party which was landed near the Linkas area. Lieutenant (jg) Joseph E. Rhoads, who served as Engineering Officer on *LCS(L) 50*, described them as " a ruddy and zealous bunch."[9] They promptly set about blowing up the beach obstacles in preparation for the next day's landing as the gunboats provided covering fire. Small arms fire emanated from shore and placed the engineers in peril. The LCS(L), along with a nearby destroyer, took them under fire and put an end to the threat. The next task for the gunboats was a cruise along the south coast of Tarakan where they fired on several luggers and some shore installations.

The scheduled date for the landings on Tarakan was 1 May 1945. The 26th Australia Infantry Brigade was a part of the 9th Australia Infantry Division commanded by Brigadier David A. Whitehead. Landing on the beaches at Tarakan were 18,000 men, including 500 U.S. Army personnel and about 400 Dutch whose task would be to re-establish Dutch administration in the area.

Air support for the assault was provided by the 13th Air Force and the R.A.A.F., whose B-24 Liberators, B-25 Mitchells, and P-38 Lightnings bombed Japanese installations and provided close-in support over the beaches just prior to the landing. Aircraft from the Royal New Zealand Air Force and American aircraft also participated, but under the direction of the Australians. During the attack on Tarakan, the supporting aircraft flew off the fields on Morotai.

While the LCS(L)s were providing cover for the minesweepers and Australian engineers, other ships got underway from Morotai. Close Fire-Support Unit 78.1.3 under Commander D. H. Day, consisting of *LCS(L)s 8, 28, 43, 44, 48, 50, LCI(R)s 71, 72, 74, 338, LCI(M)s 359, 362, LCI(D)s 29,* and *228* headed for the assault.

On Peter Day (1 May 1945), the ships deployed at 0515 and began their first rocket run against the landing zone. Following the launching of their rockets, they fired on the beaches with their 3"/50 and 40mm guns and then circled back to await the landing of the Australian troops. Strong currents in the area pushed the landing craft to the right of their assigned location, and they had to do some hard last minute maneuvering to make it to the landing zone. In his action report of 1 May 1945 Lieutenant C. C. Henson, the Commanding Officer *LCI(R) 71,* recommended that the landing craft "be directed to follow the support craft and allow the support craft to determine the course for them, particularly when strong currents are present as was the situation during this assault. This will insure the troops the full effect of the fire-support offered by rocket ships."[10]

Australian and Dutch troops landed to light opposition and were soon in control of the island. The airfield had been seen as an important prize but it proved to be relatively worthless. It had fallen into disuse and had been damaged by the bombings and by naval ship fire. In addition, it was a wet area and would need much work before it could serve as a base for further campaigns.

The mortar ships had a role in the invasion as well. One suggestion for their improvement came from Lieutenant H. A. Peterson, CO of *LCI(M) 362.* He suggested:

> It is recommended if at all possible that the mortars be mounted on turntables with a 95 degree deflection to either side of ships center line. It has been found that due to the limited amount of deflection in these weapons this vessel is a menace to the wave guide line of support craft when assigned to accompany them in. Also that a set from the same direction as the flank assigned reduces the output. With turntables an effective broadside of at least two weapons could be obtained, it would also permit this type of vessel to anchor close-into the beach and provide more accurate support fire than could be obtained at present.[11]

OBOE VI

Although the initial assault on the Brunei Bay area was scheduled for 10 June 1945, preliminary air strikes were needed to reduce Japanese resistance in the area. The task was assigned to the 1st Tactical Air Force and the 13th Air Force. Two units of the 5th Air Force, the 90th and 380th Bomber Groups, were temporarily assigned to the 13th Air Force to bolster its striking power. In addition to bombing targets in the Brunei Bay area, they also flew missions against enemy emplacements at Balikpapan. Beaufighters of the Nos. 22 and 30 Squadrons R.A.A.F. were active on 3 June, bombing and strafing oil tanks at Bangsal and strafing and

A pair of LCS(L)s attack Japanese positions on the beach as they lead Australian landing craft in the assault on Borneo. Official U.S. Navy photograph.

bombing Brunei town. From that point on, both American and Australian air units conducted missions against the Japanese in preparation for the assault and in support of the troops once they landed.

The landings in and around Brunei Bay, including Labuan Island and Muara Island, were scheduled for 10 June. On that day there were three simultaneous landings at the north shore of Victoria Harbor, the east shore of Muara Island, and the north shore of Cape Polompong which lay to the east of Brunei Bluff.

The gunboats arrived in the area three days prior to the actual landings to assist in minesweeping and to cover UDT operations. While this had its usual share of risks, they could occur at strange times. Gilbert Nadeau, a signalman on *LCS(L) 45* later recalled:

> Our first night out, at approx. 9:00 PM, we were informed via the PA system that we had inadvertently sailed into a Jap minefield and were in it — like right now!! My ship was the #45. When the announcement was made I and another shipmate were seated "on the trough" in the head. My shipmate was a lean, lanky guy, wearing nothing by sea-bees shoes (rough leather, high topped, heavy soled shoes), undershorts and well-worn raggedy dungarees — which at that time were both down at his shoe tops. Suddenly we heard a loud metallic thump/clanging coming from under the ship towards the bow. My shipmate got real startled, cursed and said, "Shorty — do you think that's what I think it is??" I replied "cripes yes!! Sounds like we just run over a mine!!"
>
> Just about that time — and this time just about amidships (where we were still sitting in the head) — The metallic bump & scrapping & clanking happened again. This time my shipmate cursed, jumped straight up so fast he left his shoes, shorts & dungarees right there on the deck where his feet were — and flew out of the head & headed aft. Seeing this happen — jumping out of shoes, shorts & dungarees like a Mack Sennet cartoon — and heading aft bare naked I laughed so hard & so much I couldn't have run even if I had wanted to!! A minute or so later the banging, scraping, clanging sound came again — aft. We had definitely run over a mine!! A couple of minutes later my shipmate returned — nothing on, excited and visibly shaken. He took one look at me still seated on "the trough" and began yelling, "Geez Shorty!! Don't you know we just ran into a mine?? How come you're still here?? You a dummy or somethin'?? Weren't you scared?? Cripes!!" Still laughing like hell I answered, "Yeah I know it was a mine. No, I'm no dummy — you are running aft where the mine hit again and hell yes I was scared — That's why I just sat where I was!" And while I was still laughing he hopped back into his clothes & shoes, cussed me out again and stormed out raving![12]

Humorous incidents notwithstanding, the minesweeping process could also be deadly. The minesweeper *Salute AM 294* struck a mine on 8 June 1945 and suffered nine dead and thirty-seven wounded.

The frogmen of Underwater Demolition Team 11, which arrived at Brunei Bay aboard *Kline APD 120*, followed on the heels of the minesweepers. The team had trained at Leyte and Morotai. They departed Morotai for Brunei Bay on 2 June 1945 and arrived on 7 June.

At 0630 on 8 June, the seventy-seven men and thirteen officers of UDT 11 disembarked from *Kline* and boarded the support gunboats, *LCI(G)s 69* and *70* and *LCS(L)s 59* and *60*. Four LCP(R)s, used by the frogmen to infiltrate the beach, were taken in tow by the gunboats. At 1020 the gunboats were in position 1,000 yards off Brown Beach and began firing on shore targets. Adding to the conflagration ashore was the bombardment by *Phoenix CL 46* and *Conner DD 582*. At 1025 a flight of B-24s appeared and dropped their ordnance on the beach area. In regard to this, Lieutenant W. H. White, CO of *LCS(L) 60*, commented that "A perfect example of pin-point bombing was observed about R-10 when six B-24s laid bombs exactly along the dune line covering the entire 1200 yard beach."[13] Raymond J. Ross EM 3/c, on board *LCS(L) 60*, later wrote:

> We started for the beach along with mine sweepers over water which LCS 60 traversed time after time yesterday. To my chagrin, the sweeps picked up 8 contact mines. A little further on, they picked up more. LCIs proceeded to detonate them with rifle fire. When they went off, water and black smoke blew sky high. LCS 58, 59, 60, and two LCIs proceeded to within 1500 yards of the

beach when someone shouted, "There she comes," and the beach literally blew up in front of us. We were now broadside to the beach and the shells were dropping ahead of us about 400 yards to starboard. The first terrific blast was U.S. B-24s, two waves of six, dropping demolition bombs. The cruisers were far behind us getting the range on the beach. Cruisers *Alaska*, *Phoenix* and one other. We received the order to open fire and strafe the beach. Concentrating first on the shore line, then working back inland. Johnson and I put out several rounds and concentrated on a building about 1000 yards inland. We started a fire and then the whole sky was filled with trees, stone, mud and wood with flares and black smoke going in every direction. We had hit an ammunition dump. The boys said it was the best show of the day.[14]

The UDT men boarded their landing craft and headed for shore. By 1100 they were busy charting the beaches up to the high water mark. Shortly thereafter, at 1125, a flight of RAAF Beaufighters made a run on the area and bombed the enemy's positions. The UDT swimmers had finished their work and were headed back out to sea at 1135 when tragedy struck. Ross recalled that "two B-24s ... unleashed their bomb load while the swimmers were about 50 yards from the beach. The bombs missed the target and fell in the water among the demo squad. A column of water rose like Niagara in reverse. No demo squad could be seen. Soon heads began to bob around. The Higgins boats went in and picked up the men."[15] They were picked up only forty yards off shore, while the remainder of the team made it out to 300 yards where they were picked up. One man was reported missing and it was assumed that he had been killed by the force of the bombs.[16]

It was most important that neither bombs nor friendly gunfire fell in the water. The most obvious reason was to avoid injury to the frogmen. However, the UDT men needed to operate in water that was relatively clear. A bomb exploding in shallow water was sure to muddy the waters for a good distance around the impact area, making accurate visual observation of the bottom exceedingly difficult.

The landing at Labuan Island took place on 10 June 1945. Six squadrons of B-24 Liberators from the 13th Air Force and two from the Royal Australian Air Force preceded the assault with high-level bombing of the beaches and areas inland. Leading the assault were the gunboats, stationed about 200 yards apart in a line. They included, from left to right, *LCS(L) 58*, *LCI(R) 31*, *LCI(G) 70*, *LCS(L) 59*, *LCI(G) 69*, *LCI(R) 34*, and *LCS(L) 60*. At 0730 they began their run on the beach at a speed of eight knots. Their orders were:

> At about D-64.5 when 1100 yards from Brown Beach, LCS(L)s and LCI(R)s will commence firing ranging rockets. Upon hitting beach start salvoing rockets. The fire was to be distributed over a two minute period. At D-62.5 when range is 550 from beach come right and strafe with all automatic weapons. Reload rockets rapidly as we return to the line of departure.
>
> At Z-30, upon execution of ONE flag by PC, the first wave of LVT's will cross the line of departure, and proceed to the beach. A speed of 4 knots was to be maintained. At D-9 again salvo rocket on landing beach distributing them over a three minute period. Upon completion of firing stop all engines and lie to until the first four waves have passed. Upon their passage retire to a station on the starboard flank of boat lane waiting for call fire.[17]

Mortar fire was also used against the enemy with *LCI(M) 359* and others lending their firepower to the assault.

The landings at White and Red Beaches on Muara Island were almost simultaneous with the landings on Labuan Island. The water depth off White Beach was quite shallow, and in their pre-landing bombardment, the gunboats could not approach it directly from the front. Fortunately, the two beaches were at right angles to one another and met at Sapo Point. Covering fire for both could be attained by the ships approaching Red Beach. This was not an ideal situation and, by the end of the pre-landing fire, it was determined that while the gunboats had covered all of Red Beach, they were only able to cover about 70 percent of White Beach with rockets

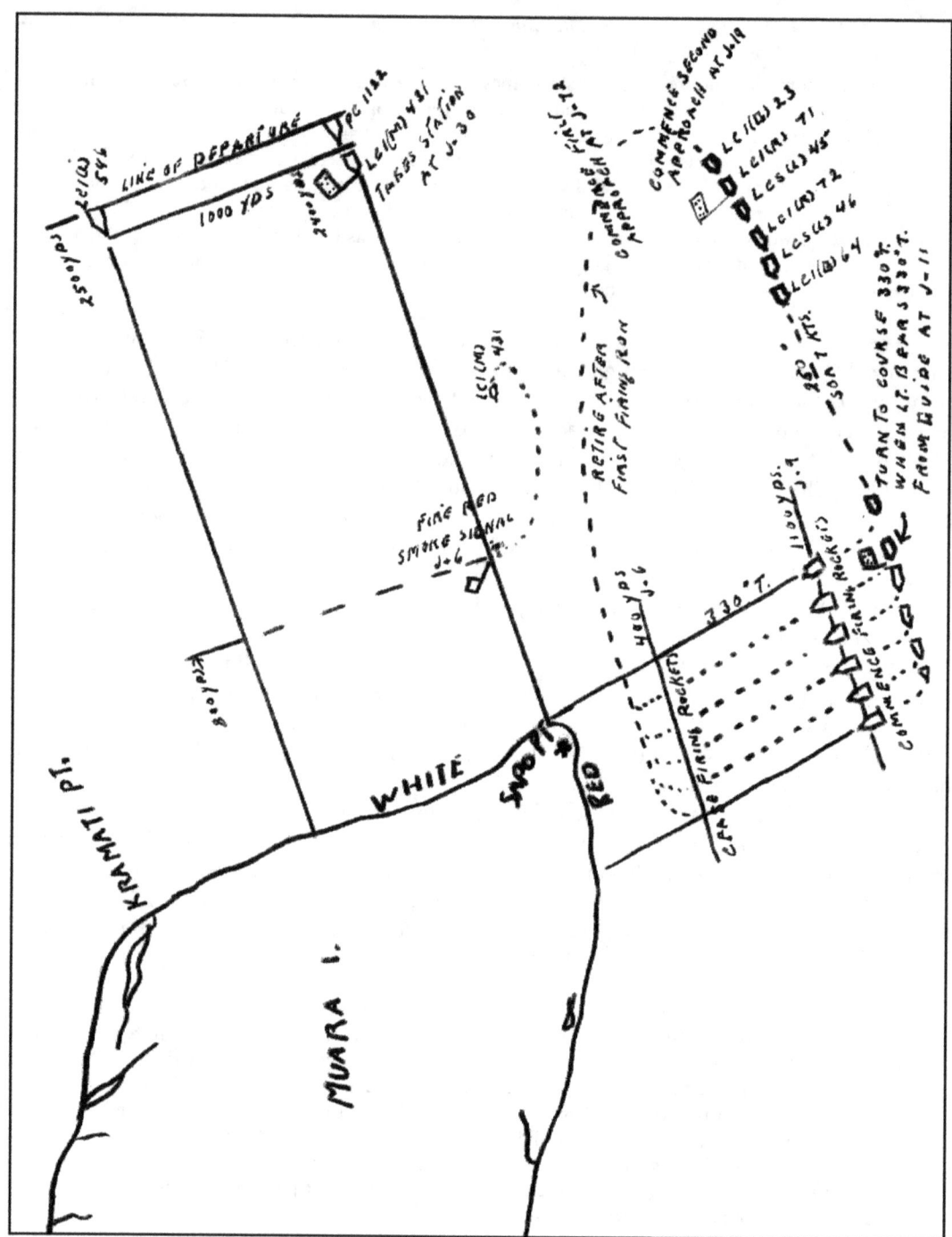

USS LCS(L)(3) 45 Serial 50, Action Report, U.S.S. LCS(L)(3) 45—Brunei Bay Operations, June 2 to June 12, 12 June 1945, Enclosure A.

and much less with gunfire. That left about 30 percent of the beach untouched. The rocket barrage was finished a full six minutes before the landing craft hit shore, making it necessary for the gunboats to cover the beaches with gunfire for an additional three minutes.

The ships of TU 78.1.38, which included *LCI(R)s 71, 72, LCI(G)s 23, 64,* and *LCS(L)s 45, 46* were involved in the 0905 assault on Red and White Beaches at Muara Island. Mortar fire was supplied by *LCI(M) 431.* Fortune was on the side of the troops on 10 June as they landed

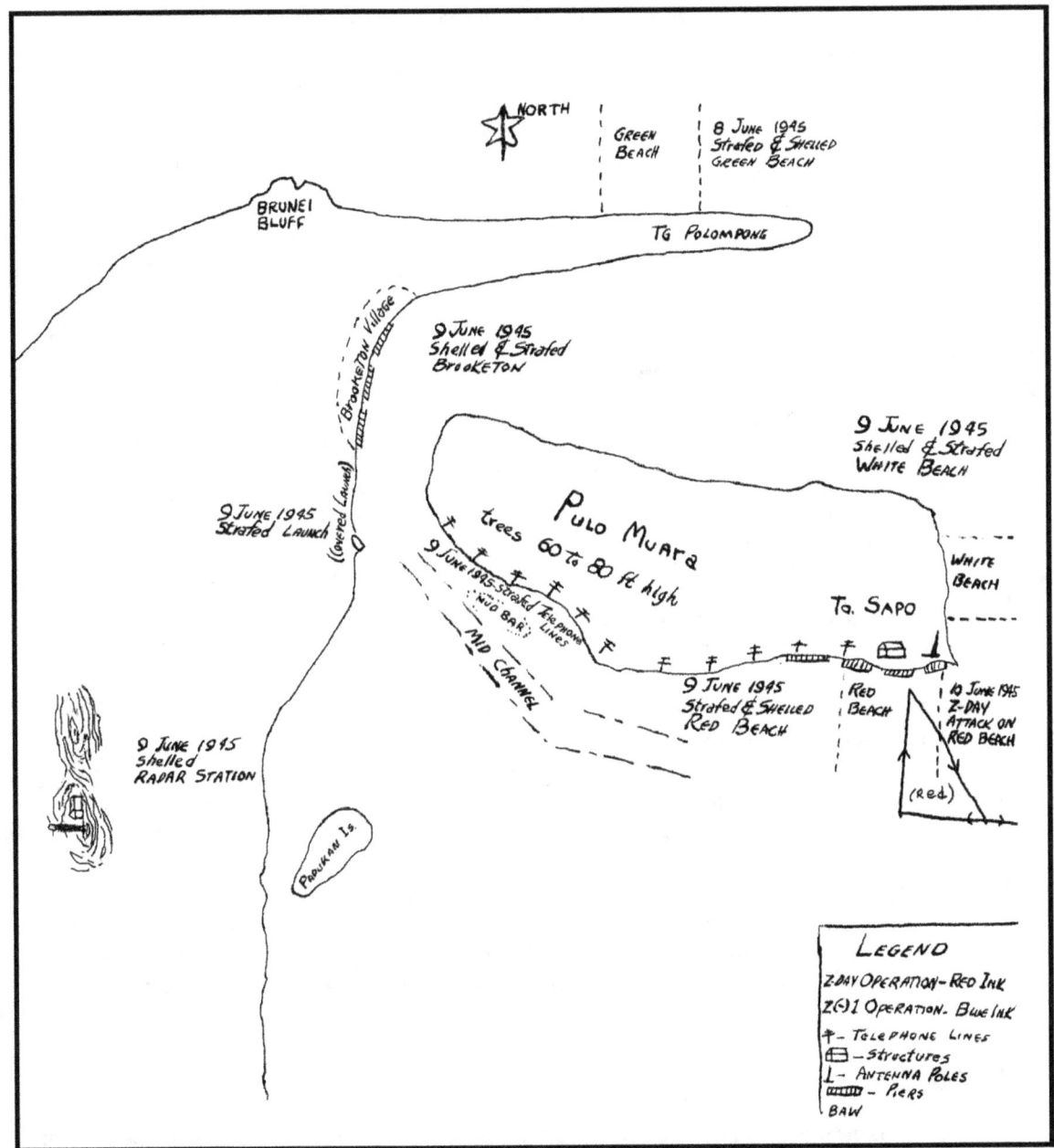

Between 8 and 10 June 1945, *LCI(G) 23* operated in Brunei Bay off the town of Brooketon. Her activities involved shelling and strafing various installations in the area, including telephone lines, a radar station, and various landing beaches. The chart above, taken from her action report, shows her activities during the period. U.S.S. *LCI(G) 23*, *Action Report, U.S.S. LCI(G) 23, OBOE-SIX (Brunei Bay, Borneo) Operation*, 12 June 1945, Enclosure (A).

on Muara Island with no opposition. At 1230 *LCS(L)*s *45* and *46* escorted Australian troops on board LVPs into Muara Harbor to land at Brooketon Town.

Green Beach was under the Brunei Bluff on the northwestern side of Brunei Bay. Attacking this area in preparation for the landings were the ships of TU 78.1.37 including *LCS(L)*s *42, 47, 48*, *LCI(G)*s *21, 22, 65, 68*, and *LCI(R)*s *72, 73, 74, 230*, and *338*. At 0905 six of the gunboats, *LCS(L)*s *42, 47*, *LCI(G)*s *65, 68*, and *LCI(R)*s *74* and *338*, were on line abreast and waiting 2,500 yards offshore. As the landing craft approached, they led them to the beaches. While larger ships

LCS(L) 45 fires on the beaches as landing craft head in to shore during the invasion of Brunei Bay, Borneo, on 10 June 1945. NARA 80 GK 5859.

bombarded the shore, the gunboats fired their automatic weapons. At 1,100 yards, the LCS(L)s and LCI(R)s let loose with their rockets. Once they had come within 500 yards of the beaches, the gunboats ceased firing and set off a red smoke flare to indicate the proximity of the landing craft to the shore. At that point the larger ships began to raise the level of their fire so that it impacted further inland. As the landing craft neared shore, the gunboats turned broadside to the beaches and raked them with automatic weapons fire. Following that, they took flank positions to the landing beach and awaited orders for fire support.

The target of the last landing in Oboe VI was in the Miri-Luotong area of Sarawak just to the west of Brunei Bay. This was a very important oil-producing area. The 2/15 Battalion of the 20th Brigade, 9th Australian Division, covered by gunboats, landed with no opposition.

OBOE II

Oboe II, the operation to take Balikpapan, was scheduled to begin on 1 July 1945. Balikpapan was an important oil refining and shipping area. This was to be the last amphibious landing against enemy forces in the war. Okinawa was declared subdued the following day on 2 July, and the battle for the Philippines was in its last stages. Landing on the beaches at Klandasan were Australian Army troops from the 7th Division, I Australian Corps under the command of Major General E. J. Milford. The invasion force numbered about 35,000 and faced Japanese forces estimated to be around 5,400, with another 1,100 Japanese workers who might be pressed into service. Additional assistance might come from 2,400 Indonesian and 1,000 Formosan workers working behind the lines to help the Japanese in moving supplies and equipment.

The assault on Balikpapan raised several concerns. First of all, the terrain of the area was ideal for defense. There was a narrow coastal plane, and within several hundred yards of the beach the land began to rise into a series of low, wooded hills whose elevation reached 700 feet. The Japanese had placed a number of pillboxes, tunnels, and other defensive features overlooking the landing beaches. In addition, it was estimated that at least eighteen coastal defense guns overlooked the landing beaches. Bolstering the larger guns were twenty-six heavy dual-purpose guns and another seventy-eight anti-aircraft guns. These could also be used against landing craft and troops as they approached the beaches. Behind the beaches the Japanese had constructed tank traps ten to fourteen feet wide. A primary concern was that they might flood them with oil and set them on fire, making a difficult barrier for tanks and troops to cross.[18] In order to prevent the Japanese from using the oil as a weapon, the oil storage tanks at Balikpapan were bombed into oblivion by Allied aircraft prior to the landings. Task Group 78.2 was assigned the task of attacking Japanese positions ashore. Included in the assault were a number of Australian Navy ships including *H.M.A.S.s Arunta, Shropshire, Hobart, Manoora, Westralia, Kanimbla, Gascoyne,* and *Warrego.* Rear Admiral A. G. Noble, Commander of Amphibious Group Eight, reported:

> From a gunnery standpoint the BALIKPAPAN operation presented a most difficult problem. Enemy defenses near to and in back of the beach were numerous, strong, and well placed. Typical Japanese defenses were present: tunneled guns, concrete pillboxes, caves, and revetted C/D and D/P guns, all of which required a direct hit or a very near miss to neutralize or destroy. There were many houses, shacks and similar structures on or near the beaches, which, while not appearing heavily fortified, were nevertheless potential machine gun and small arms emplacements, and which had to be destroyed or neutralized. In addition the beaches themselves formed part of a natural amphi-theatre with high ground in the background and on the flanks. Finally, the minesweeping situation, the long approach lane, and the presence of shoals in area PHILLIES severely restricted the movement of Fire-support Ships in this area, and deprived them of their maneuverability.[19]

Although the ships present had their work cut out for them, other tasks needed to be performed. In the water, a job for the UDT was present:

> To seaward the beaches along some fifteen miles of coast from Klandasan to Manggar were protected by a log barricade. At the Klandasan beach area this consisted of three lines of heavy wooden posts, set five feet apart, with five feet intervals between verticals. The center line was offset, and the posts were braced at the top with spiked double diagonal timbers. Apparently so placed to coincide with the surf line, the barricade was only about 10 to 15 yards off shore, and was thus within easy range of shore gunfire and Japanese snipers.[20]

In short, the Japanese were exceptionally well-prepared to resist any invasion force that attempted a landing. Still another problem lay just offshore. Since it was of such great strategic importance, the waters around the port had been heavily mined. In addition to mines laid by the Dutch before the war, it was suspected that the Japanese had mined the area as well. Allied forces had contributed to the plethora of mines by dropping magnetic and acoustic mines in the harbor. The task for the minesweepers was significant and placed them under the guns of the Japanese as they swept the area. Accompanying the minesweepers during their work were the gunboats which were also under attack.

Air support for the operation was supplied by several air units. The American 13th Air Force flew P-38 fighter aircraft from their base at Sanga Sanga Island in the Sulu Archipelago during minesweeping operations. The 13th Air Force and the Royal Australian Air Force flew B-24 and B-25 bombers from their bases on Morotai, Zamboanga, Tawitawi, and Palawan. These bombers were active during the entire operation bombing shore installations, and later, inland targets as the Australian Army moved forward against the enemy. As a backup, the American Navy supplied three escort carriers, *Suwannee CVE 27, Chenango CVE 28,* and *Gilbert Islands CVE 107.* On 3 July, squadrons from the carriers flew C. A. P. missions and attacked enemy positions.

Close-in fire support was rendered by the gunboats of Task Unit 78.2.8 under Commander D. H. Day on board his flagship *LCI(R) 230.* Included in this task unit were twenty-three support craft, including Day's flagship. In addition to *LCI(R) 230,* the TU was comprised of *LCI(R)s*

31, 34, 73, 226, 230, 331, 337, 338, LCI(G)s 21, 22, 24, 61, 66, 67, LCS(L)s 8, 28–30, 41, 43, 44, 48, and 50. Some of the support craft would be active on invasion day, while others would cover UDT and minesweeping operations. The LCI(R)s, LCS(L)s and some of the LCI(G)s had rockets among their armament, and the LCS(L)s and LCI(G)s packed additional firepower, as all of them mounted a 3"/50 gun in addition to their 20mm and 40mm guns.

One of the important assignments for the gunboats was the covering of Underwater Demolition Teams 11 and 18 as they explored and charted the Klandasan, Manggar, and Manggar-Ketjil landing beaches and blew up obstacles to the landing craft. UDT 11 arrived at Balikpapan on board *Kline APD 120* and UDT 18 on *Schmidt APD 76* on 24 June 1945. This assignment appeared to be much more difficult than the reconnaissance at Tarakan and Brunei Bay. Lieutenant L. A. States, the CO of UDT 11, noted:

> First intelligence indicated that the preferred and alternate beaches were heavily defended by concealed pillboxes and various other types of emplacements: that the beaches were protected by extensive and substantial man-made underwater obstacles; that these obstacles would prevent amphtracks or any other type of landing craft from reaching the beach and that the beaches, especially the preferred ones were heavily mined.[21]

By 1945 the Underwater Demolition Teams had perfected their techniques. They were carried to the target area on board larger ships such as the APDs, which also carried their rubber boats and LCPRs. Once the day of their operation arrived, they disembarked from the APD and went aboard a fire-support ship such as an LCS(L) or LCI(G). The fire-support ship took their boats in tow and headed in to the area of the beaches to be reconnoitered.

Equipment carried by the frogmen included a bathing suit, mask, swim fins, knife, webbed belt, mine detonators, and a plastic plate on which to record data. Neoprene wetsuits, popular with today's divers, were not in existence at the time. The best the men could do was cover their bodies with a heavy layer of grease to protect themselves from the cold. In tropical waters cold was not a problem, but in the chilly waters off the northern islands such as Okinawa, the temperature of the water was a problem. Water temperatures at Ulithi were reported to be around 85 degrees, but at Iwo Jima only 59 degrees.[22] In addition to the water temperature, other problems existed. Men might encounter sharks, stinging jellyfish, sharp coral, sea snakes and, in the more tropical areas, saltwater crocodiles.

After a period of covering gunfire, the LCPRs carrying the frogmen passed through the line of gunboats and headed to shore. At a distance of several hundred yards from shore, the LCPRs turned parallel to the beach and began to drop off swimmers while underway. A rubber boat was lashed alongside each LCPR. Swimmers went from the LCPR to the rubber boat and then rolled off the rubber boat into the water every 100 to 200 yards. "Flying Mattresses" were sometimes used. These were small rubber boats powered by electric motors. An officer would climb aboard one and head for shore. The swimmers would use them as guides so they did not get off course. The officer in the Flying Mattress made a great target, and many of the rubber boats were shot out from under them. Swimmers then headed for the beach carrying their slates and other equipment that would enable them to take notes on the conditions inshore. The depth of the water would be noted, as well as any reefs, coral heads, man-made obstructions, or mines. Once this information had been acquired, the swimmers headed back out to sea and waited in a line for the pick up. The LCPR, with the rubber boat lashed alongside, made a run past them. On board each of the rubber boats was a member of the team who held out a rope loop. As the LCPR passed by, the swimmer hooked his arm through the loop and was hauled aboard by the team member. He then climbed back up into the LCPR as the next swimmer was being picked up. The information from the first day was relayed up the chain of command. If no beach obstacles were present and no further information needed, the UDT swimmers were done. If not, they had to return for another day or two, carrying explosives inshore to dispose of obstacles.

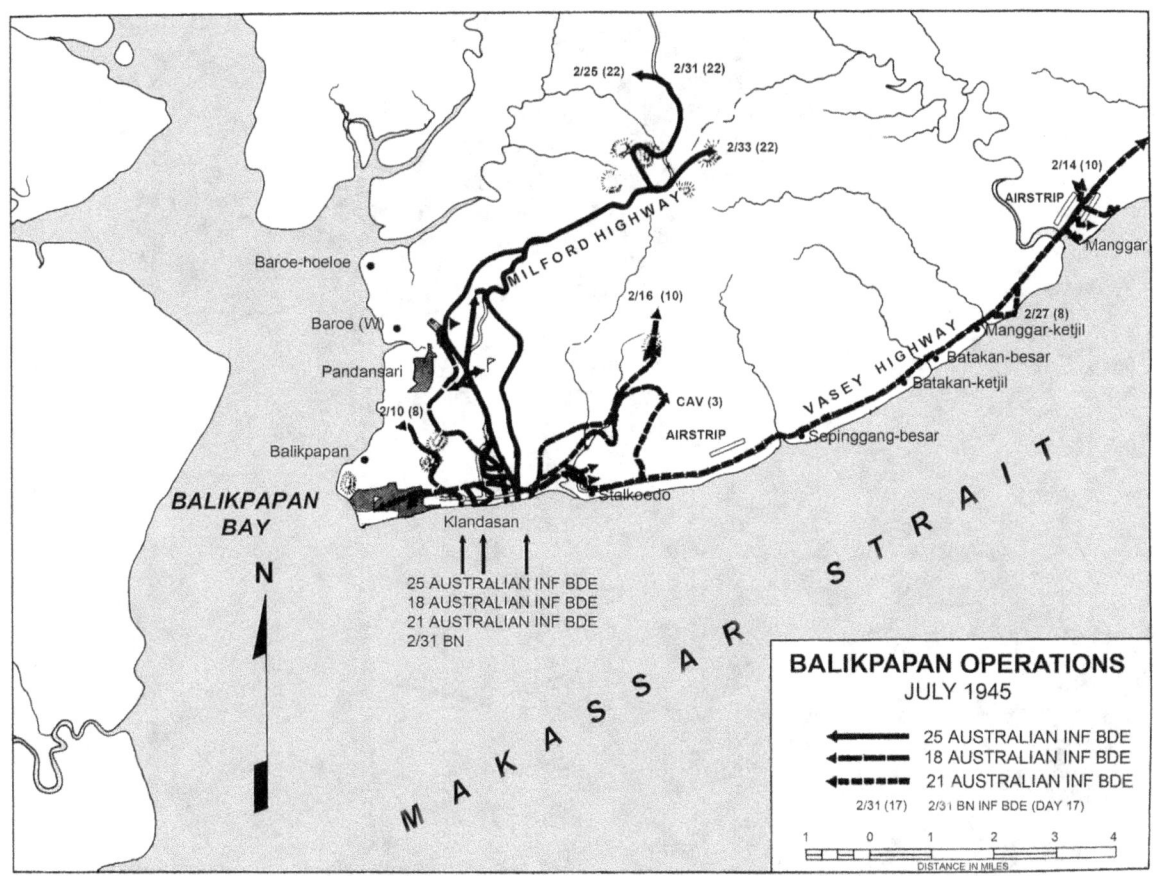

Balikpapan operations. Adapted from Major General Hugh J. Casey, Chief Engineer. Office of the Chief Engineer, General Headquarters Army Forces, Pacific. *Engineers in Theater Operations* (Washington, DC: U.S. Government Printing Office, 1947), p. 298.

Their missions usually lasted only an hour or two but the work was strenuous. Covering the UDT at Balikpapan were the ships of TU 72.2.93 which included *LCS(L)*s *8, 28–30, 41, 43, 44,* and *48.*

Reconnaissance of the landing beaches began at 0730 on 25 June with Underwater Demolition Teams leaving their mother ship for transit to the gunboats. UDT 11 was assigned to Green Beach at Manggar and UDT 18 to nearby Red and Yellow beaches at Klandasan. A flight of B-24s made a high level bombing run on the beach at 0730. Following that, a group of B-25s made a low level bombing and strafing attack followed by another high level attack by the B-24s. One of the B-25s was hit by enemy fire and crash-landed in the water between the gunboats and a nearby destroyer which picked up the survivors. The aircraft continued their attacks until after 0900. The gunboats attacked the shore with 3"/50 and automatic weapons fire. In the midst of this, at 0800, the LCPRs crossed the gunboat line and headed for shore.

One of the concerns of the close-in fire-support ships was a repeat of the tragedy at Iwo Jima when the Japanese mistakenly identified the LCI(G)s covering UDT operations as the beginning of the invasion. In his action report for the UDT coverage, Lieutenant J. M. Leggat, commanding officer of *LCS(L) 44*, noted that "LCS(L)s approached beach in an irregular manner, so as not to give the enemy impression of a landing mission."[23]

Although enemy aircraft attack was always a possibility, there were not that many air attacks

Rear Admiral Daniel E. Barbey (right) shakes hands with General Blamey. NARA 80G 328090.

on the ships. However, at 2030 on 25 June five bombers, identified as Bettys, attacked the ships off Balikpapan. They managed to drop some bombs in the area but none of the ships was hit. Three of the enemy aircraft were shot down by the combined fire of the ships in the task group.[24]

The following day, 26 June, the pattern was repeated with the swimmers entering the water at 0815. This time they brought explosives which were attached to many of the pilings that the enemy had set in the bottom to thwart landing craft. The explosives were set to go off at 1015, after the UDT men were safely back on board their boats. At the designated time the charges went off, blasting a 700 yard gap in the beach obstacles. The next day's action resulted in an additional 800 yards being cleared of obstacles and mines. Over the course of two days, the frogmen had removed about 2,300 pilings and cleared an area approximately 1,500 yards wide on the landing beaches.[25]

On the morning of 28 June, at 0730, *LCS(L)s 8, 28, 29, 41, 43*, and *44* once again took station to support UDT Teams 11 and 18 as they operated off the beaches. At 0945 machine gun fire erupted from shore emplacements and threatened the UDT operations. The LCS(L)s strafed the beaches and shelled them with their 3"/50 guns. Return fire from heavier shore batteries, estimated to be 75mm, began to zero in on the starboard side of the support ships' line. *LCS(L) 8* reported:

At 1018, our ship was taken directly under fire by an enemy battery, and at 1020, after several near misses, we received a hit through the base of the conn on the port side resulting in shrapnel wounds to one officer and two men. Evasive action was immediately taken and return fire directed at the enemy battery with no appreciable results. However, the enemy battery ceased firing and we returned to our station. At 1045 we were again taken directly under fire by the same battery and, after some near misses, received a second hit on the starboard side below the water line, knocking out one generator, the live shell lodging in its base.[26]

EM 3/c John C. Black, although wounded in the attack, nevertheless managed to plug the holes in the hull, preventing further damage to the ship. A third shell passed through the flag bag without causing any casualties. About the same time, *LCS(L) 41* also took hits from four shells, none of which caused serious damage. With the UDT teams recovered from their work, the gunboats headed for their anchorage at 1050. However, they soon found it under attack and had to move further out in the bay.

The initial landings at Balikpapan were scheduled for 1 July and included the Australian 18th and 21st Brigades of the I Corps. In addition, the 25th Brigade was scheduled to land on 2 July. Covering their landing was Commander Day's Task Unit 78.2.8. On board the gunboats, general quarters sounded at 0700. About that time the heavier ships began their bombardment of the beaches. To soften up the beaches for the landing, the LCI(R)s made two rocket runs, at 0744 and again at 0846. No enemy fire was directed at them on the first run and only minimal fire on the second. The first line of landing boats hit the beaches at 0855, only a few minutes after the second rocket barrage. Return fire from the defenders was sporadic and light, much of their strength having been diminished by the pre-invasion bombardment by the larger ships and the close support craft. No casualties were incurred by the Australians during their trip to the beach. "By nightfall 1 July, 10,500 troops (two brigades), 700 vehicles and 1950 tons of supplies had been landed and 7th Division had reached its F-Day phase line."[27] As they moved inland, resistance stiffened and the troops had a dangerous enemy to face as they fought their way into the hills. Their progress was steady and, by 22 July, the enemy was finished.

Americans love to celebrate their holidays, even when at war. Admiral Noble planned a special event for 4 July 1945. Participating in the celebration were the cruisers *Nashville CL 43* and *Phoenix CL 46*, along with the destroyers *Bell DD 587*, *Charrette DD 581*, *Burns DD 588*, *Connor DD 582*, and *Philip DD 498*. "Each ship fired 21 salvos; cruisers firing 21 six gun salvos and destroyers firing 21 five gun salvos into enemy troop and supply concentrations.[28] An enemy ammunition dump was hit in the barrage. Its explosion eliminated a number of Japanese troops in the area and put their force into disarray.

Although the action ashore was the main event, hazards still abounded off the coast. Suicide boats had been used in the Philippines and at Okinawa, but none had been encountered at Borneo. However, on the night of 3 July, radar on *LCS(L) 8* picked up a fast moving small boat heading for her. Gunners opened up with 40mm guns and, at a distance of 1,100 yards, the boat disappeared.[29] *LCI(G) 66* fell victim to a mine on 10 July. At 1826 she was on patrol off Balikpapan when she set off what was either a magnetic or an acoustic mine. Her engines and generators were knocked out, and the seams in her engine room and the after steering compartment were opened. She began taking on water and soon developed a list. *LCS(L) 30* came to her aid and, with the addition of her Hale pump, a Johnson pump, and handy billys, the flooding was brought under control. *LCS(L) 30* took her under tow and brought her alongside *Creon ARL 1* which supplied additional pumps and assisted her in making emergency repairs. One officer and three men were blown over the side in the explosion but were soon rescued. No serious casualties were suffered.[30]

The recapture of Borneo had involved the combined forces of the Australians and Americans and had proven successful. It was time to move on for the invasion of Japan.

Chapter 9

Okinawa

The gunboats had developed to fit certain needs as the war progressed. The first group of converted gunboats mounted 3"/50 guns to be used against Japanese barges and shore installations. As the situation changed, the use of them in island assaults was increased and they were fitted with 40mm guns and rockets. It became obvious that the guns and rockets could not reach enemy targets on the reverse slopes of hills and the installation of mortars on the ships became important. The limited range of the 4.5 inch fin-stabilized barrage rocket gave rise to the 5 inch spin-stabilized rocket which could reach further inland. The situation at Okinawa presented new problems that needed to be addressed. Whereas the initial assault and follow-up call-fire on targets close to shore had been an important use of the ships, at Okinawa things changed. There the gunboats performed in the initial assault but were challenged by suicide boats and kamikaze aircraft as soon as they were finished with the first phase of the operation. The radar picket line proved to be the most formidable challenge, and LCS(L)s mounting twin 40mm bow guns began to appear in greater numbers. The LCI(G)s, (M)s, and (R)s were utilized in anti–small boat patrols and in making smoke. Some of the LCI(R)s were fitted with radar jamming gear and were used to confuse enemy radar. They carried the additional designation of (RCM) which stood for Radar Counter Measures.

Operation Order A6-45 for the Amphibious Forces Pacific Fleet (Task Force 52), dated 16 March 1945, indicated the extent of gunboat participation. At Okinawa the Gunboat and Mortar Support Flotillas were designated as TG 52.9 under Vice Admiral Richmond Kelley Turner. The Task Group consisted of:

    (a) Force Flagship — ELDORADO — Captain Wallace   1 AGC

    (b) 52.9.1 *Picket Support Gunboats* — Captain Moosbrugger
        52.19.6 LCS Division SIX   6 LCS(L)
        52.19.7 LCS Division SEVEN   6 LCS(L)

    (c) 52.9.2 *Anti Small Craft Gunboats* — Commander Malanaphy
        LCI(FF) 637 (Flag Gunboat Support Unit ONE)   1 LCI(FF)
        52.17.1 Gunboat Support Division ONE 52.17.2   6 LCI(G)
        Gunboat Support Division TWO 52.17.3   6 LCI(G)
        Gunboat Support Division THREE 52.17.4   6 LCI(G)
        Gunboat Support Division FOUR 52.17.5   6 LCI(G)
        Gunboat Support Division FIVE 52.17.6   6 LCI(G)
        Gunboat Support Division SIX   6 LCI(G)

(d) 52.9.3 *Northern Support Gunboats*— Captain Rimer
    LCI(FF) 657 (Flag Mortar Support Flotilla)   1 LCI(FF)
    LCI(FF) 535 (Flag LSM(R) Group)   1 LCI(FF)
    52.19.3 LCS Division THREE   6 LCS(L)
    52.19.4 LCS Division FOUR   6 LCS(L)
    52.21.2 LSM(R) Unit TWO   6 LSM(R)
    52.24 Mortar Support Group TWO   21 LCI(M)

(e) 52.9.4 *Southern Support Gunboats*— Commander Balliere   LCI(FF)
    LCI(FF) 679 (Flag Mortar Support Group ONE)   1 LCI(FF)
    52.19.1 LCS Division ONE   6 LCS(L)
    52.19.2 LCS Division TWO   6 LCS(L)
    52.21.1 LSM(R) Unit ONE   6 LSM(R)
    52.23 Mortar Support Group ONE   24 LCI(M)

(f) 52.9.5 *Kerama Retto Gunboats*— Commander Montgomery   LCI(FF)
    LCI(FF) 782 (Flag Gunboat Support Unit TWO)   1 LCI(FF)
    52.18.1 Gunboat Support Division FOUR   6 LCI(G)
    52.18.2 Gunboat Support Division FIVE   6 LCI(G)
    52.20.3 RCM and Rocket Division THREE   5 LCI(R) (RCM)

(g) 52.9.6 *Reserve Gunboats*— Captain Aylward   LCI(FF)
    LCI(FF) 988 (Flag Gunboat Support Flotilla)   LCI(FF)
    370 (Flag RCM and Rocket Group) 52.20.1
    RCM and Rocket Division ONE 52.20.2   LCI(FF)
    RCM and Rocket Division TWO 52.20.4   LCI(FF)
    RCM and Rocket Division FOUR 52.20.5   6 LCI(R) (RCM)
    RCM and Rocket Division FIVE   6 LCI(R) (RCM)
                                                               6 LCI(R) (RCM)
                                                               6 LCI(R) (RCM)
    52.20.6 RCM and Rocket Division SIX   6 LCI(R) (RCM)
    52.19.5 LCS Division FIVE   6 LCS(L)[1]

It is interesting to note the composition of the assault force. In the beginning months of amphibious assaults in World War II, the pure gunboat types without rockets, and the later gunboat types with rockets, were the mainstay of the landing operation. By the invasion at Okinawa, the mortar ship had become the predominant assault craft with forty-five listed in the plan. The LCS(L) followed closely behind with forty-two in number. Thirty-six LCI(G)s and thirty-five LCI(R)s rounded out the total. The use of rockets, however, had not fallen by the wayside. LCS(L)s and LCI(G)s carried sufficient numbers to destroy enemy beach defenses as needed. The LCI(R)s participating in the landing on 1 April 1945 were used to cover areas adjacent to the landing beaches. In all, the plan called for the use of 170 of the amphibious gunboats for invasion day. In the days and weeks after 1 April, additional LCS(L)s would arrive from the States as would additional LCI conversions. Added to this mix was the new conversion of the LSM, the LSM(R), a special assault ship which could launch huge numbers of rockets at the enemy.

Prelude to Invasion

Okinawa was considered the final step toward the actual invasion of the home islands of Japan. Following immediately on the heels of the capture of Iwo Jima, the capture of Okinawa was of prime importance. As the forces of the Southwest Pacific Area under General Douglas MacArthur continued their campaign in the Philippines, the stage was set for the invasion of Okinawa. The Ryukyu chain of islands had been cut off from their resources to the south. The only defense available for Okinawa came from the home islands and from Japanese Army and Navy air units on Taiwan. Occupation of Okinawa and its surrounding islands would give the Allied forces a strong base from which to conduct operations against Japan proper. Several airfields already existed on the island, as well as excellent anchorages. The building of facilities to supply the assault on Kyushu was possible.

Taking Okinawa would be no small task; it would be the largest amphibious operation yet attempted in the Pacific. In order to capture the island the Navy would use:

> 1,213 ships, 564 carrier-based support aircraft and 451,866 ground troops, including both Army and Marine divisions. In addition this force was directly supported and covered by the Fast Carrier Force (82 ships, 919 aircraft) and the British Carrier Force (22 ships, 244 aircraft). Operations of the 21st Bomber Command of the United States Army Strategic Air Force and of the Far Eastern Air Force supported the invasion.[2]

For the Japanese, Okinawa was crucial and every resource that could be brought to bear was dedicated to holding the island. However, even the most die-hardened militarist knew that it was only a matter of time before the massive Allied forces arrayed against the Japanese on Okinawa would prevail. Their strategy was not to hold the island but to make the Americans pay so dearly for its capture that they would be discouraged from proceeding further toward Japan's home islands. Facing the American invaders was Japan's 32nd Army under the command of Lieutenant General Mitsuru Ushijima. Ushijima followed the strategy already employed by Lieutenant General Tadamichi Kurabayashi at Iwo Jima. Rather than opposing the landing on the beaches and exposing his troops to the massive firepower of the invasion fleet, he withdrew his forces to the southern part of the island where numerous ridges and hills would make the Americans pay heavily for every foot of the island taken.

The vast armada destined to attack Okinawa came from different areas of the Pacific. No one island or group of islands was sufficiently large enough to supply the number of troops, equipment, and supplies necessary for the attack. Loading troops, conducting rehearsals, acquiring supplies, and overall preparation was accomplished at a number of diverse areas, including Hawaii, Guadalcanal, Leyte, Ulithi, and Saipan.

The beginning of the invasion of the Ryukyu Islands began on 25 March 1945 as the Amphibious Support Force (TF52) and the Gunfire and Covering Force (TF54) arrived off Okinawa and began pounding the shore with naval gunfire. The UDT began its operations in the Kerama Rhetto islands off the southwest coast of Okinawa in prepara-

Vice Admiral Richmond Kelley Turner was Commander of Task Force 51, the Joint Expeditionary Force, during the invasion of Okinawa. Turner had served throughout the Pacific theater and was considered an expert on amphibious warfare. NARA 80G 302369.

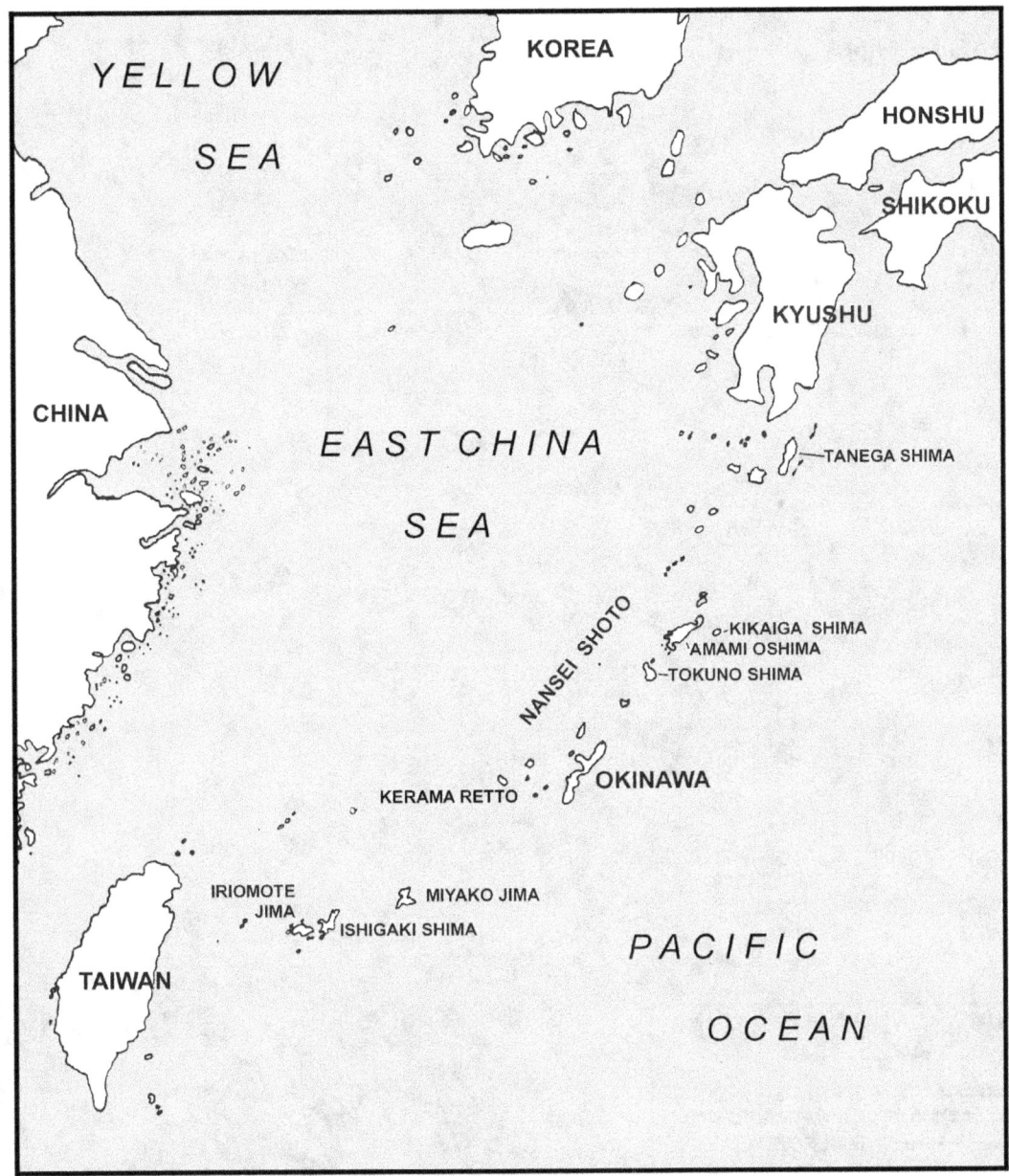

The invasion of Okinawa exposed the American fleet to Japanese air attacks from Kyushu and Taiwan.

tion for the invasion. Capture of these islands was deemed important as they would deny their use to the enemy and provide a location for ship repair, a seaplane base, and a sheltered anchorage. A bonus in the invasion was the capture and destruction of approximately 390 Japanese suicide boats. In addition, the islands had a number of sheltered harbors that would prove useful for ship repair.

Coordinating the efforts of the large number of converted gunboats and the newly launched LCS(L)s proved to be a sizeable administrative chore. The invasion of Okinawa was divided into a number of sectors, each of which required the use of particular types of gunboats.

The American forces had about a year and a half of experience using the gunboats in various

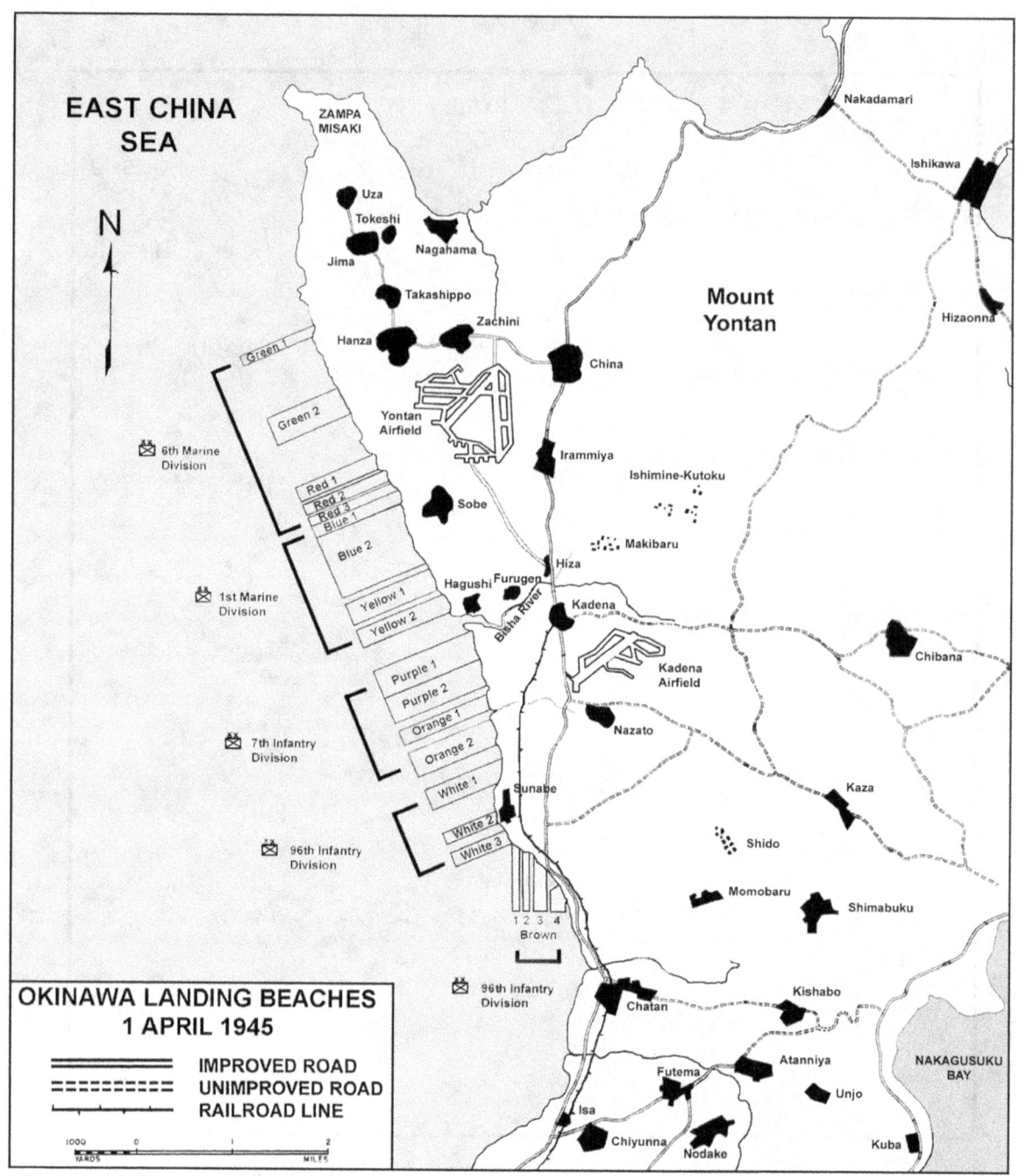

The 10th Army, consisting of both Army and Marine divisions, landed on Okinawa on 1 April 1945. Northern beaches were assigned to the Marines and the Army landed on the southern beaches.

configurations and in various roles. By the time of the invasion of Okinawa on 1 April 1945, they had learned how to put them to the most effective use. Vice Admiral Richmond K. Turner noted in his action report:

> LCI(G) and LCS(L), utilizing their 4.5" rockets and 40mm, preceded the leading wave utilizing the same tactics as in previous operations. A new procedure was instituted for LCI(M) who accompanied the leading wave toward the beach, commenced mortar fire at an intensive rate when approximately 1500 yards from shore, continued fire while closing to 700 yards, and then maintained fire

over the troops and landing craft until HOW plus 10. LCI(R) and LSM(R) were used from flank positions and covered towns and critical points with an intensive volume of 5" rocket fire. After HOW Hour, those craft had little employment as support craft, due to the rapid movement of troops and the tendency of the enemy to avoid shore areas. However, some specific tasks accomplished are detailed in subsequent paragraphs, and all of these types proved of great value as smokers, inshore screening and flak vessels, RCM ships, anti-suicide-boat pickets, and dispatch boats.[3]

UDT and Marine Reconnaissance

As usual, the initial landing on the enemy shores fell to the Marine Reconnaissance companies whose forays onto enemy beaches were always done under cover of darkness. Moving into the various beaches in the Keise Shima Islands on the night of 25-26 March were members of A Company VAC Reconnaissance Battalion under Captain Merwyn H. Silverthorn, Jr. Artillery installations were set up there to be used against enemy forces on southern Okinawa. For the next several days, Marine Reconnaissance companies surveyed virtually all of the landing beaches, locating enemy positions and installations.

The massive assault on the island of Okinawa, along with those against Kerama Retto and Ie Shima, required a more in-depth assessment of the beaches and the location of enemy forces than had been attempted before. Exploring the landing beaches and blowing up obstacles fell, as usual, to the men of the underwater demolition teams. Two sections of UDTs, carried on APDs, arrived off Okinawa. An additional APD served as the command ship and three APDs carried their reserve equipment. Overall command of the teams, designated as Task Group 52.11, was under Captain B. Hall Hanlon, with Rear Admiral W. H. P. Blandy, CTF 52, on board one of the APDs. The two groups consisted of:

Group ABLE

Gilmer (FF)	APD 11	Captain B. Hall Hanlon	
Bates	APD 47	UDT 12	LtComdr E. S. Hochuli
Barr	APD 39	UDT 13	LtComdr V. J. Moranz
Bull	APD 78	UDT 14	Lt A. B. Onderdonk
Knudson	APD 101	UDT 19	Lt G. T. Marion
Waters	APD 8	Reserve Equipment	

Group Baker

Loy	APD 56	UDT 4	LtComdr W. G. Carberry
Hopping	APD 51	UDT 7	LtComdr R. F. Burke
Kline	APD 120	UDT 11	Lt L. A. States
Herndon	APD 121	UDT 16	Lt E. A. Mitchell
Crosley	APD 87	UDT 17	Lt A. M. Downes
Bunch (GF)	APD 79	UDT 21	Lt E. P. Clayton
Griffin	APD 38	Reserve Equipment	
Reeves	APD 52	Reserve Equipment[4]	

The beaches in the islands of Kerama Retto were explored by UDT teams beginning on 25 March. Support for UDT operations was supplied by Task Unit 52.18.3 under Lieutenant Commander C. J. Starkus. It consisted of *LCI(G)s 366(GF), 372, 439, 440,* and *475.* Additional firepower was supplied by destroyers patrolling farther from the beaches. These included *Heywood L. Edwards DD 663* and *Preston DD 795.*

Underwater demolition teams operated at sea level or just a few feet above, if they were wading in shallow water. This made them particularly vulnerable to sniper fire. The gunboats covering them with 40mm and 20mm gunfire had to be extremely careful to keep their rounds out of the water, otherwise, the UDT swimmers might fall victim to friendly fire. Snipers firing on them from beach positions might be at an elevation of only ten to fifteen feet above sea level. Firing over the heads of the UDTs from a distance of several hundred yards required extreme care and excellent marksmanship. If the UDT was under fire from the enemy on the beaches, the gunboats had little choice. Fortunately, cases of friendly fire casualties were quite rare, a tribute to the marksmanship and training of the Navy's gunners.

UDT 12 explored the beaches at Yakabi Shima, Amuro Shima, and Zamami Shima on 25 March, while UDT 13 evaluated Tokashiki Jima and UDT 19 the beaches at Aka Shima, Geruma Shima, Hokaji Shima and Kuba Shima. The gunboats laid down covering fire, but there was no return fire and the swimmers returned safely. UDT 12 reported the presence of two Japanese luggers concealed near shore at Zamami Shima, and *LCI(G) 439* destroyed them with 40mm gunfire. Having determined which beaches had the best prospects and which were problematic, the 77th Infantry Division under Major General Andrew B. Bruce prepared to land.

Covering the landings on the various islands at Kerama Retto was Task Unit 51.1.16 under Captain T. W. Rimer. They were tasked to deliver close-in fire support for the landing of elements of the 77th Army Division. It consisted of:

> LCI Mortar Support Divisions Six and Eight
> LCI RCM and Rocket Division Three LCI
> Gunboat Divisions One, Three, Four, Five
> LSM(R) Units One and Two

Islands invaded on 26 March were Yakabi Shima, Zamami Shima, Aka Shima, Geruma Shima, and Hokaji Shima, as well as the first stage of the assault on Orange Beach at Tokashiki Shima. In general the landings on the various islands of the Kerama group were unopposed or lightly resisted. The heavy firepower of the gunboats and their accompanying destroyers quickly put an end to any enemy opposition. Gunboats were hard put to find suitable targets, releasing their standard rocket and mortar barrages on lightly defended or unoccupied beaches and then searching in vain for enemy targets. The mouths of caves and scattered huts became prime targets of opportunity, whether or not they were occupied.

Tokashiki Shima 27 March

The gunboats of Gunboat Support Unit 52.18.2, consisting of *LCI(G)s 465, 467, 472, 567, 568,* and *580,* spent that night on patrol and strafed Purple Beach on Tokashiki Shima the following day as Army troops landed. Mortar Division Six under Lieutenant H. M. Mattson, including *LCI(M)s 801–804,* fired mortars at Aware Town on Tokashiki Shima (Orange Beach Z-1). Mortar Support Division Eight TU 52.24.4 under Lieutenant J. A. Gage, along with *LCI(M)s 1055* and *1059,* fired mortars at Tokashiki Village and surrounding areas between 0835 and 0910. Some of the mortar gunboats had still not been outfitted with 40mm bow guns, so the best they could do was to strafe cave entrances and other shore targets with 20mm fire.

Commanding officers of these ships continually asked for the required 40mm guns, but apparently they were in short supply. In his endorsement of Lieutenant Gage's action report for the bombardment of Geruma Shima and Hokaji Shima, Commander A. R. Montgomery, CTG 52.18, noted that "This ship [LCI(M) 1059] being one of the first twelve (12) LCI(L)'s converted to LCI(M)'s and having operated continuously since has not been equipped with the authorized and much needed bow 40 MM gun."[5]

Some occasional mortar rounds fell near the ships but none were hit. Other large caliber

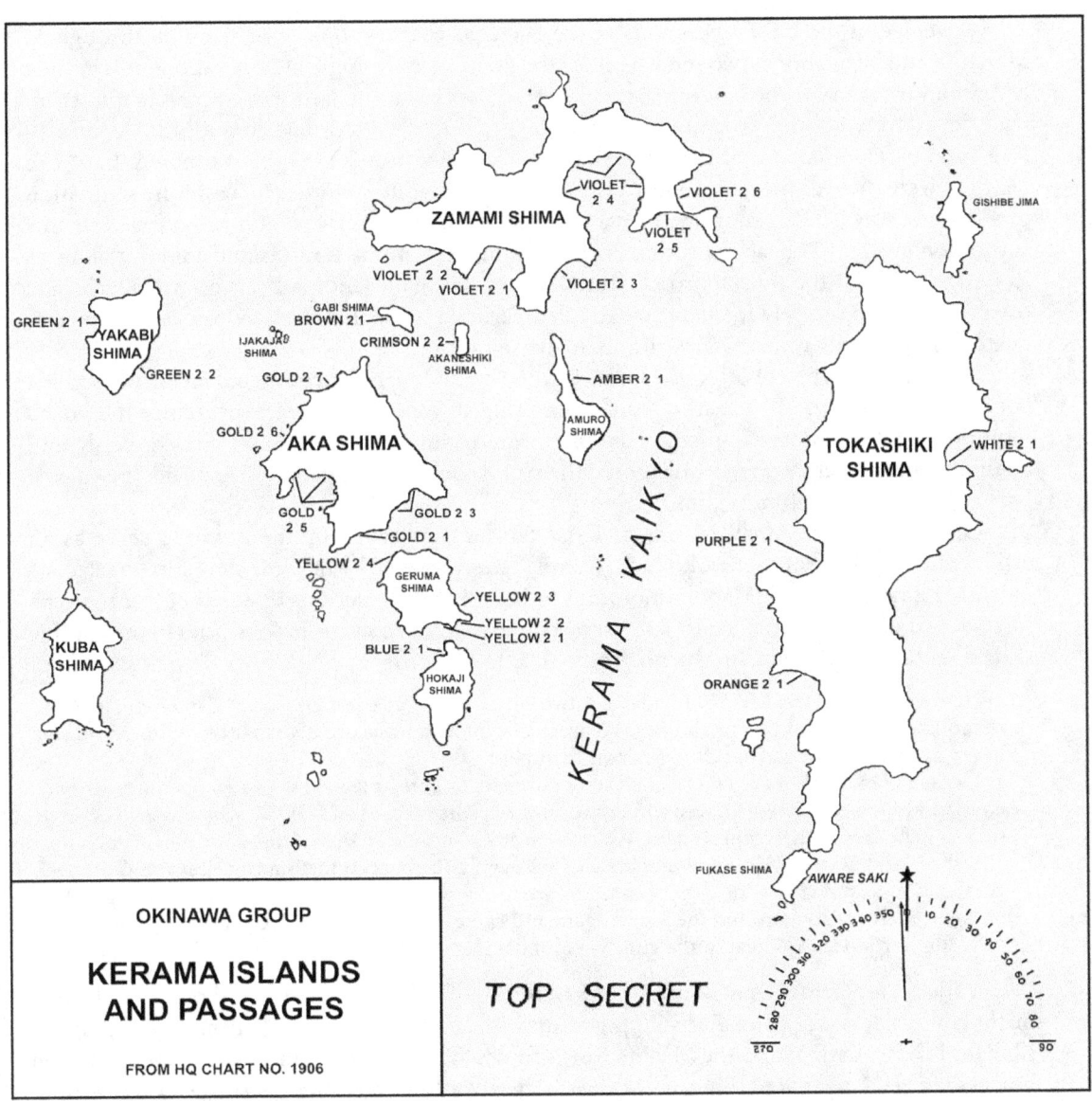

The plethora of islands in the Kerama Retto Group provided ample shelter for damaged ships and repair facilities, as well as a seaplane base during the assault on Okinawa. Its many landing beaches had to be surveyed by Navy UDTs and Marine Recon forces prior to landings. The Japanese word for island is *Shima*, but it is also read as *Jima*, depending on the word preceding it. Adapted from Commander Underwater Demolition Teams, Amphibious Forces, U.S. Pacific Fleet Serial 0028-45, *Action Report, RYUKYU ISLANDS Operations, 25 March–5 April 1945*, 4 April 1945, Enclosure (A).

shells hit the water near *LCI(M) 803*, but it was suspected that they were shells from American guns overshooting their targets on the island. Army troops indicated that: "rocket coverage was excellent and that gunfire (continued on their flanks after the waves had passed through the gunboat line) was accurate and comforting."[6]

Casualties incurred during the taking of the Kerama Retto islands included *LSM(R) 188*, with eleven dead, three missing and thirty-one injured by a kamikaze attack. *LCI(G) 560* suffered minor damage and two injuries when her mast was clipped by a kamikaze. *LCI(R) RCM 646* had two minor injuries from an encounter with a suicide boat.

Coverage of the UDT operations at the Hagushi beaches took place from 28 through 31 March. It had been almost two months since the LCI(G)s covering UDT operations at Iwo Jima had been mistaken for the landing force. The result was that the Japanese opened fire on them with devastating effects. To counter this problem, a new strategy had developed. Captain B. Hall Hanlon, Commander of the Underwater Demolition teams at Okinawa, noted that "The LCI(G)s were moved into position in a most irregular manner in order to avoid the suggestion of a landing wave. Their movement was checked by many observers, and in no case was this suggestion given."[7] The lack of serious resistance in the Kerama Retto Islands did not demonstrate the value of the new approach. In addition, the main landing beaches at Hagushi had been pounded so severely for such an extended period of time that the new tactics for the gunboats were probably unnecessary, although a wise precaution.

LCI(G) 451, on patrol off Keise Shima at 2250 on 27 March, encountered an enemy suicide boat with seven men aboard who were attempting to escape the area. Apparently the boat's motor was out of commission since the men were paddling. The gunboat circled warily and attempted to contact the men who ignored them and continued to paddle. They sank the suicide boat with 20mm and 40mm gunfire.

On 31 March the small islands of Keise Shima were taken by the Army to serve as an artillery base against southern Okinawa. They had been scouted by the FMF Amphibious Reconnaissance Battalion on 26 March and found to be lacking any serious opposition to American forces scheduled to land there. UDT 13 surveyed the beaches scouting for obstacles to the landing craft. Lieutenant (jg) Donald Murray from UDT 13 recalled:

> [W]e were assigned the Kiese Shima Island, two miles off the coast of Okinawa. It is a long, low island like an atoll and had small trees. We were to explore and secure it so that the Army could put heavy artillery ashore for the Okinawa bombardment.
>
> I was in command of the LCP(R) and ten swimmers to enter a lagoon with two openings around an island in the center. We arrived under the gunfire protection of an LCI(G), which was liberally spraying the area with 40mm rounds. We came around and the LCP(R) dropped our men and circled the island, waiting for the swimmers and zigzagging the boat so that mortar fire would be inaccurate. The most men lost in UDT operations are in the small boats with mortar fire landing right on them.... We roared around the island again and came alongside the LCI(G) just after one of its own 40mm rounds exploded in the gun. We found a messy gun tub.[8]

Underwater Demolition Team surveys of the landing beaches at Hagushi reflected the two major landing areas. The Northern Support Gunboats, under Captain T. W. Rimer, were responsible for beaches assigned to the Marine Corps forces. These were, from north to south, the ten beaches labeled Green, Red, Blue, and Yellow. They would be reconnoitered by UDTs 7, 16, and 17. The Southern Support Gunboats covered UDTs 4, 11, and 21 on the southern beaches, Purple, White, Orange, and Brown, which were scheduled for assault by the Army. The Southern Support Gunboats were under the command of Commander L. B. Bailliere.

UDT swimmers at the Okinawa invasion beaches came under fire constantly from snipers ashore. Caves near the shore and numerous burial tombs in the area gave them the advantage of cover. The tombs were only about 150 yards beyond the seawall which gave the snipers a good position from which to fire on the UDT men. Gunboats and destroyers assigned to each sector spent a good deal of their time on station firing into these positions, as all along the beach the UDT was taking heavy sniper fire.

Obstacles discovered by the UDTs had to be destroyed. On the northern beaches, one to

Opposite: The first wave of landing craft approaches the beach at Okinawa on 1 April 1945. Smoke drifts from support landing craft which have just fired a salvo of rockets at the beach. *USS Yorktown CV 10 Serial 0205 17 May 1945 Actions Air Support for and Support of Occupation of Okinawa from 14 March to 11 May 1945.*

9. *Okinawa*

four rows of wooden posts, six to eight feet high, had been set in the coral reef. Approximately 1,725 of the posts barred easy passage to the beaches and had to be blown up in order for the landing craft to get to shore. The southern landing beaches were barred by another 1,200 posts, also requiring destruction by the UDTs. Once having destroyed the posts and charted the bottom, members of the various Underwater Demolition Teams stayed aboard the PCs and SCs off the beaches on invasion day to assist in guiding the landing craft to shore.

Additional danger for the ships and the UDTs came from the air. *LCI(G) 560,* a part of TU 52.17.1, was assigned to cover operations of UDT 17 at Green Beach on the morning of 29 April. As she cruised the area she came under attack at 0615 by a combination of three Nates and a Val. The three Nates made a run on her and she shot down two with her 20mm guns. One of the planes clipped her conning tower but only one man was injured.

Invasion Day—1 April 1945

The landing beaches themselves had ample attention from numerous gunboats, including LCI(G)s, LCI(M)s, and LCS(L)s. A total of eighty-one gunboats directly supported the landings

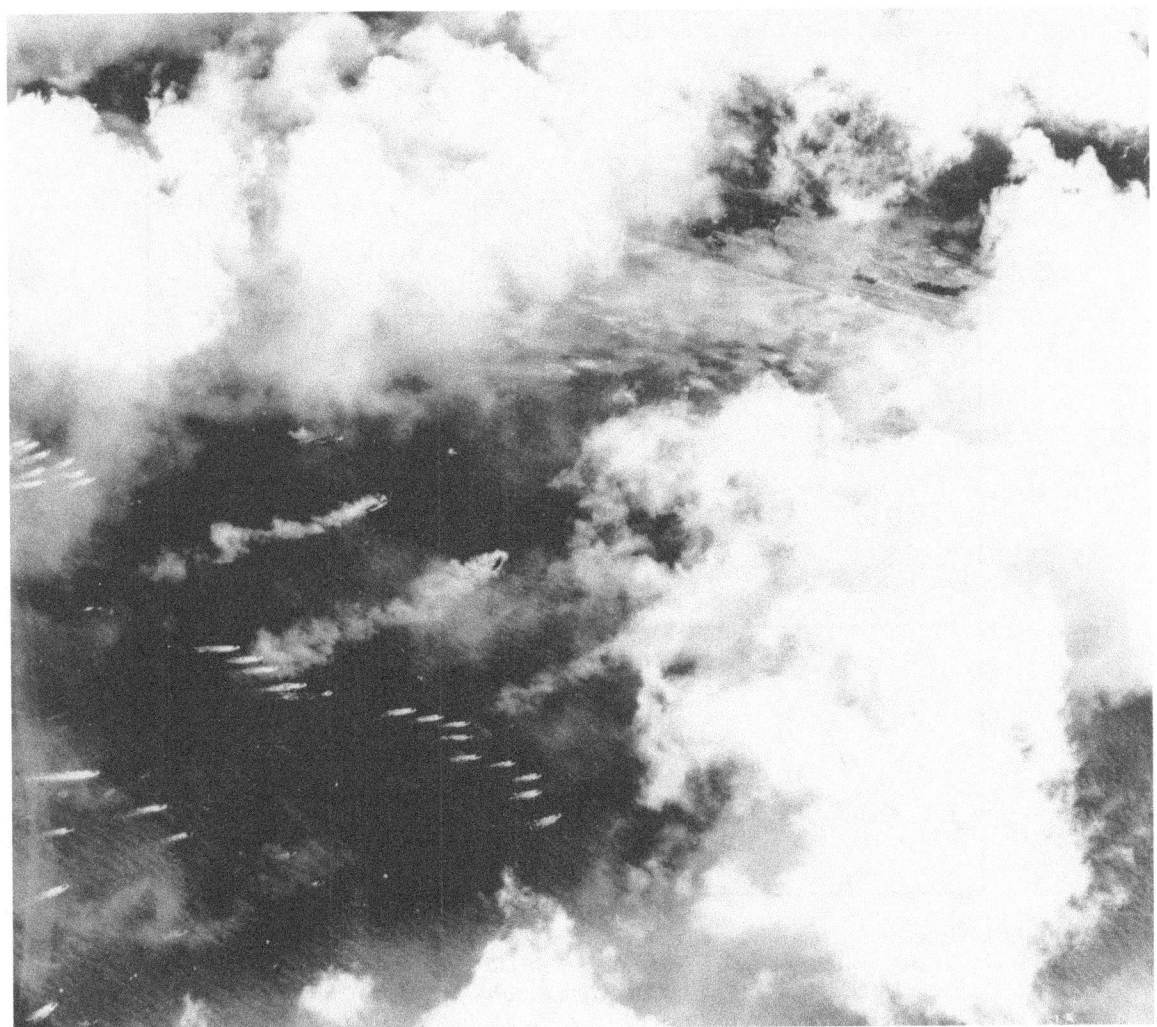

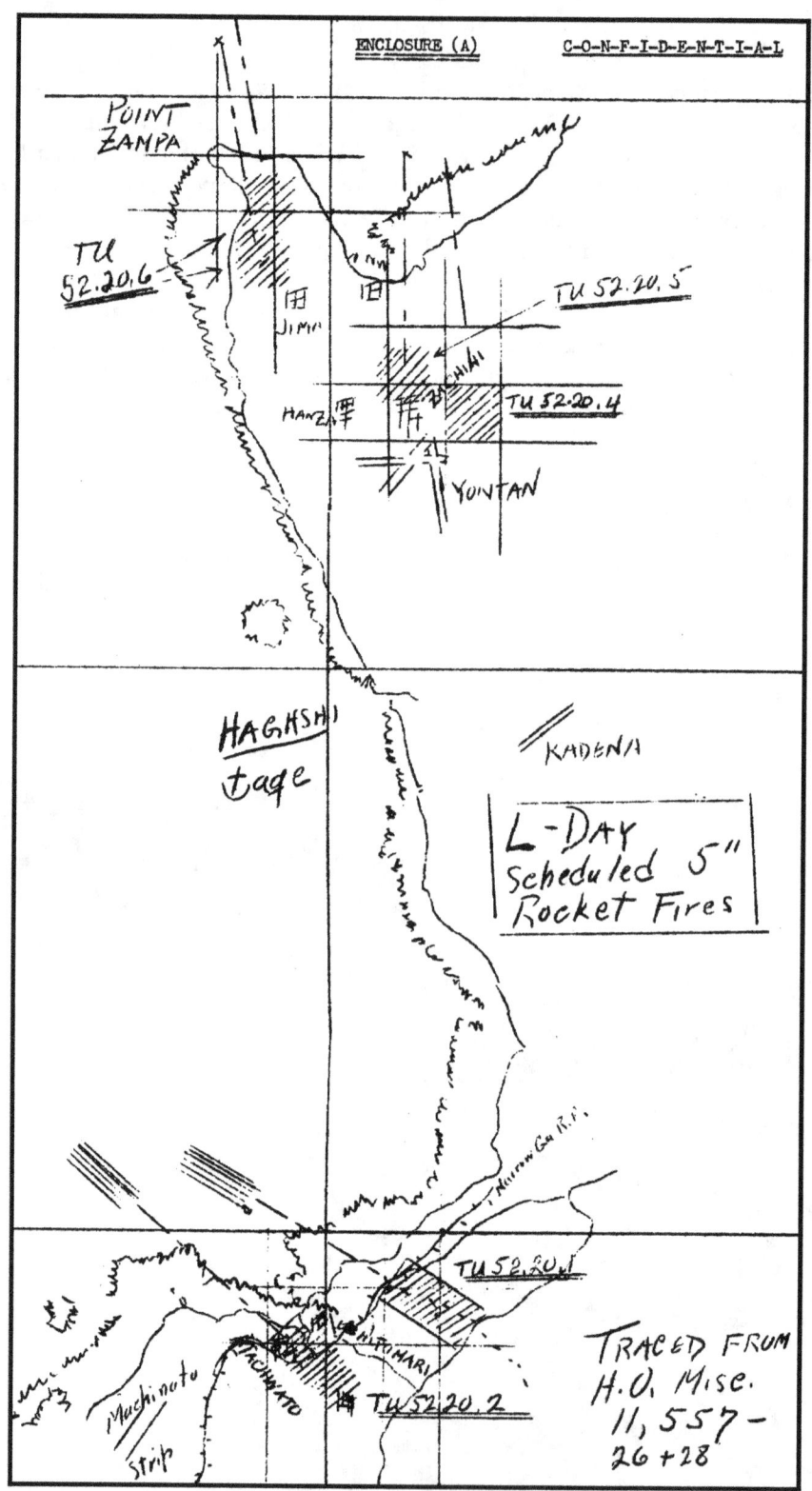

While the landings at the Hagushi beaches were underway it was necessary to prevent enemy movement on the flanks. LCI(R)s with the new five inch spin stabilized rockets, along with LSM(R)s, were used for this task. Commander LCI Flotilla 16 Serial 35, *Action Report—Invasion of the Okinawa Group Liu Chius, 26 March to 21 June 1945*, 15 July 1945, Enclosures (A) Fire Support Missions.

LCI(G) 1030 (center) and *LCI(G) 1078* (right) fire rockets at Okinawa on 1 April 1945. NARA 80G 312105.

on the twenty-one beaches at Hagushi. One of the concerns during the landing was the possibility that enemy troops might be brought into the area from north and south of the landing zone. To counter this, a combination of LSM(R)s, LCI(R)s, and LCI(M)s were used to supply heavy supporting fire on both the northern and southern flanks.

To the north of the Marine landing beaches, Green, Red, Blue, and Yellow, these ships delivered rocket and mortar fire on the areas around Zampa Misaki and the areas just to its south. The towns of Uza, Tokeshi, Jima, Takashippo, and Hanza, on Zampa Misaki were fired upon by TU 52.20.6 under Lieutenant Commander P. W. Howard. Ships under Howard were *LCI(R)s 647–649* and *762(F)–764*. Lieutenant Commander A. F. Eckelmeyer's TU 52.20.5, consisting of *LCI(R)s 704, 705, 1024, 1026, 1068(F),* and *1069*, joined in the attack.

These two divisions targeted the area from the beach to about 1,700 yards south of the town of Nagahama, including the town itself. In order to get closer to their target, the two divisions headed north around Zampa Misaki and approached the town of Nagahama on a heading of 178° true, heading almost due south toward the beach at Nagahama.[9] Targets were spread to the east near the foothills of Mount Yontan and westward toward the towns of Zachini and Hanza. Accompanying them on this northern foray were the ships of TU 52.20.4 under Lieutenant Commander H. T. McKnight. They included *LCI(R)s 643(F), 648, 706, 763,* and *764*. These towns were all interconnected by a highway that led into the northern end of Yontan Airfield. TU 52.21.2, LSM(R) Unit Two, included *LSM(R)s 194* and *196–199*. Their longer range rockets saturated the flanks on the northern end of the landing beaches.

The dividing line between the northern and southern attack areas was the Bisha River. Beaches Purple, White, Orange, and Brown were assaulted by the Army while their southern flanks were

LCS(L)s 12, 13, 14, 15, and *16* prepare to shell Yellow Beach during the Okinawa invasion 1 April 1945. Official U.S. Navy photograph.

covered by LCI(R)s, LSM(R)s, and LCI(M)s which delivered their barrages near Machinato Airfield and adjoining areas, as well as the towns of Kakazu, Itchitomari, and Uchitomari. Of particular interest in this area were the Route 1 highway and a rail line that ran along the coast. These could provide ready access to the landing zone by Japanese forces attempting to get to the area.

Adding their firepower to the southern flank was LSM(R) Unit One (TU 52.21.1), which included *LSM(R)s 189–193* and *195*. Overall command of the two LSM(R) units was held by Lieutenant Commander J. H. Fulweiler. The newly converted LSMs targeted the heavily defended village of Gusukuma which lay just to the north of Machinato Airfield and about a mile inland.

LCI RCM and Rocket Division One under Lieutenant Commander F. Thompson, Jr., consisted of *LCI(R)s 644(F), 650, 707, 771, 772,* and *1077*. In operation just to their south was LCI RCM and Rocket Division Two commanded by Lieutenant Commander J. W. Sullivan. It included *LCI(R)s 651(F), 708, 1028–1030,* and *1078*. At 0955, after the last rocket run on its targets, *LCI(R) 644* set off a mine as she retired from her run. The explosion took place approximately thirty feet off the ship's port beam. Shrapnel from the mine landed on the deck of the gunboat, wounding Lieutenant Robert E. Sweeney, Jr. as he climbed the ladder to the conning tower. Sweeney served as the communications officer for LCI(R) Group Sixty-Three. He was transferred to *LST(H) 929* and later to *Barnstable APA 93* for treatment.

Although the invasion of the Kerama Retto islands had taken place several days before, the main event at Okinawa centered on landing the troops on the beaches at Hagushi. Scheduled to land there was the Tenth Army, comprised of units of both the Army and the Marine Corps. Overall command of the ground forces was held by Lieutenant General Simon B. Buckner. Included in the landing forces were:

Tenth Army

Lieutenant General Simon Bolivar Buckner, Jr.—Commanding Officer

III Amphibious Corps—Major General Roy S. Geiger (Northern Attack Force)
1st Marine Division (1st, 5th, 7th, 11th Marines)—Major General Pedro A. Del Valle
6th Marine Division (2nd, 6th, 8th, 10th Marines)—Major General Lemuel Shepherd, Jr.
2nd Marine Division (4th, 15th, 22nd, 29th Marines)—Major General Thomas E. Watson†
XXIV Corps—Lieutenant General John R. Hodge (Southern Attack Force)
7th Infantry Division (17th, 32nd, 184th Infantry)—Major General Archibald V. Arnold
27th Infantry Division* (105th, 106th, 165th Infantry)—Major General George W. Griner, Jr.
77th Infantry Division (305th, 306th, 307th Infantry)—Major General Andrew B. Bruce
96th Infantry Division (381st, 382nd, 383rd Infantry)—Major General James L. Bradley
81st Infantry Division (321st, 322nd, 323rd Infantry)—Major General Paul J. Mueller*

*Held in reserve at New Caledonia.
†Held as floating reserve.

April 1 dawned with pleasant conditions for the invasion. Light east winds played over a calm sea. Visibility in the landing area was unlimited until the smoke from numerous rockets, mortars, and shells blanketed the landing zone and made it difficult to see the target areas.

The landing zones for the American assault were centered in the area between the two airfields of Yontan and Kadena. Dividing the assigned areas was the Bisha River. The Marine's III Amphibious Corps, consisting of the 1st and 6th Marine Divisions, landed on the beaches north of the river, and the Army's XXIV Corps landed on the beaches to the south. Held as a floating reserve was the Marine's 2nd Division, while the Army kept their 81st Infantry Division in reserve at New Caledonia. The gunboats assigned to the Northern Attack Force covered the Marine's landings, while those of the Southern Attack Force covered the Army's landings.

LCS(L)s 11–16, of LCS Division Three, were assigned to provide rocket and gunfire for the Marines landing on Yellow Beach One. Scattered mortar fire came near some of the ships but none were hit.

The gunboats of Mortar Support Division Six under Lieutenant H. M. Mattson included *LCI(M)s 801–806*. They fired on targets beyond Red Beaches 1, 2, and 3, which included Yontan Airfield and Toya Town. Mattson reported that "During the firing the entire beach area appeared as one continuous explosion and coverage was excellent."[10] This was the situation on most of the beaches. The combined rocket and mortar fire from the ships raised so much smoke and debris that an exact accounting of the effect was difficult to determine. All that could be assured was that any enemy forces on or near the beaches were probably killed in the initial bombardment. Delivering longer range fire power were *LSM(R)s 194–199* which targeted Takashippo Village about a mile inland and a mile north of Yontan Airfield.

Not all danger was on the receiving end of the gunboats' missiles. On board *LCI(M) 807*, which was assigned to bombard Blue Beach 2, along with Mortar Division Seven *LCI(M)s 808-810(F), 1088,* and *1089,* a mortar shell exploded prematurely on the foc'sle deck about 0821, during the assault phase of the operation. It was thought that the mortar barrel had become overheated from the rate of fire. The explosion set off four cans of 40mm ammunition which had been stored nearby, compounding the effect. Eleven men were blown overboard. As a result of the explosion four men were killed and another eight suffered serious wounds. Shrapnel blanketed the forward end of the ship and an additional thirteen men suffered minor wounds. The explosion blew a two foot diameter hole in the foc'sle deck and caused general damage to equipment in the area.[12] The men who had been blown overboard were picked up by small boats from *LST 949* and *LCI(M) 809*. In his endorsement of the action report on the incident by *LCI(M) 807*, the Commanding Officer of Flotilla Fourteen, Captain Theodore W. Rimer, noted:

"The 4.2 mortar casualty described in this action report was probably due to a premature burst. Many units were supplied with some of the M3 fuzed ammunition. This type was disposed of and segregated as units were resupplied."[12] As she left the firing line, *LCI(M) 1089* passed close to the stern of *Idaho BB 42*. A salvo from the battleship's gun battery "tore hinges off the wooden door to the conn, scattered charts and papers over the deck of the pilot house, and made the men on the welldeck, firing mortars, feel that their clothes were being torn off. The concussion caused the radar to behave strangely for a few minutes."[13]

Orange Beaches One and Two were the landing sites for the Army units. Covering them were the mortar gunboats of Mortar Division One (TU 52.23.1) under Lieutenant Commander W. T. Dom. They included *LCI(M)*s *630–632, 638, 756,* and *1010*. Thirty-five minutes before the assigned landing time, the mortar gunboats moved into position and headed for the beaches at five knots. At a distance of 3,200 yards from shore, they began firing their mortars and continued their fire as they moved toward shore, marching the mortar rounds inland from the beach. Rocket ships nearby fired off their second salvos, marking the time for all units to cease fire. Two days later on 3 April, on board *LCI(R) 648*, Charles Lamson S 2/c wrote to his mother: "I presume you know by now rockets is our specialty—well we fired the damned things all day and certainly dug up the hillside...."[14] Joe Dumenigo, a storekeeper on board *LCI(G) 568*, had the position of pointer on the forward 40mm gun during general quarters. The destruction wrought upon the beach areas by their rocket salvos had him spellbound. Sixty-seven years after the end of the war he still recalled that "it looked like an inferno when the rockets went off."[15]

As the LVTs approached the beaches an air strike passed through the area, strafing and bombing targets of opportunity. The gunboats continued their fire as the LVTs landed on the beaches. The mortar gunboats, having the greatest range, continued firing for an hour after the landings.

On the southern flank of the landing zone was Brown Beach 4. The ships of LCS(L) Group Nine covered the landing of the 96th Infantry Division there. They included *LCS(L)*s *24, 37–40,* and *57* under the overall command of Lieutenant B. A. Thirkield. The ships made their initial rocket run at 0805. However, before they could get into range to launch their rockets, they came upon the reef which at Brown Beach 4 was about 1,200 yards off the beach. With the LVTs close behind them, they had no time to search for breaks in the reef and had to use 20mm and 40mm gunfire to suppress enemy emplacements on the beach. Following their aborted rocket runs, they turned south to engage targets of opportunity near the towns of Kue and Chatan, raking the area with 20mm and 40mm gunfire. Later in the morning, after the troops had landed, they were able to work their way through breaks in the reef and launch rockets at various targets inshore. Thirkield recommended that the gunboats be given a greater lead time so that they could effectively find breaks in the reef that would allow them to get within rocket range.

To distract the enemy from giving its full attention to the landings at Hagushi on the western side of the island, a fake or "demonstration" landing was scheduled on the southeastern tip of Okinawa to coincide with the real landings at Hagushi. Leading the assault waves in to the diversionary landing were a variety of LCI gunboats, including LCS(L) Divisions 1, 6, and 7, along with Mortar Divisions 4 and 5, and Gunboat Support Division 1. The gunboats had trained for the demonstration at Saipan under Lieutenant Commander McFadden in mid–March. None of the LCI(R)s were used for the demonstration. Underwater Demolition Teams had also worked over the beaches in the days preceding the diversionary landing, blowing up obstacles to make it seem as though the invasion at that point was real.

The ships of the diversionary force were about fifteen miles from the landing site at 0555 when they came under aerial attack. One kamikaze was shot down but a second managed to get through the hail of gunfire and crash into *LST 884*. Explosions and fires broke out on the LST and the order was given to abandon ship. Three hundred Marines and the crew were taken off the ship. *ATR-80* and *Van Valkenburgh DD 656* attempted to put out the fires but called in the LCS(L)s to fight them. *LCS(L)s 115, 116, 118,* and *119* moved into position and played their fire hoses on the flames. Firefighting teams from each of the gunboats boarded the LST and fought the fires in the midst of exploding ammunition and gasoline. The battle raged for four hours before the fires were finally out. A quantity of the water used to fight the fires went down into the LST's hold, and by the end of the ordeal she had a ten degree list. The gunboats then had to pump her out, but they had saved her. Unfortunately, the ground swell continually pounded the gunboats against the LST's sides and they looked much the worse for their ordeal after being battered for over four hours.

The rest of the diversionary force moved into position at 0830 on 1 April and began their assault. LCS(L)s made their strafing runs on the beaches without encountering any return fire, and the LCI(M)s sent their barrages of mortar rounds at the beach. The troop carriers followed them in closely, but at a distance of only a few hundred yards off the beaches, they all turned and headed back to sea. They repeated the diversionary landing the following day and, once having distracted the Japanese, the ships all headed on to other duties around the island. Some joined the forces at Hagushi and others went to patrol and screening stations. Many of the LCS(L)s were assigned to the radar picket stations.

The Campaign Continues

Kamikazes began to step up their operations. On 2 April, *LCI(G)s 465* and *568* were on patrol off Motobu Peninsula. They were sent in search of a downed pilot around 1820 when they were attacked by a Japanese plane identified in the action reports as either a Tony or a Judy. The aircraft were picked up visually with binoculars at a distance of five miles and the ships were ready for them. The gunboats were at general quarters when the plane crash-dived into the after part of *LCI(G) 568*'s gun deck. As the plane approached, it was hit by 20mm fire and knocked off course. It strafed the ship on its way in, but the combination of the ship's gunfire and its movement caused it to miss the conn and fall short, hitting the gun deck and 20mm guns with its port wing. The crash destroyed two 20mm guns and killed one man. Three other men were injured, one seriously. Another plane attempted to crash into *LCI(G) 465* but undershot its target and crashed into the sea.[16]

The LCI hulls had their advantages and disadvantages. With their flat bottoms and no keel area, they were difficult to maneuver. They rolled in any kind of rough water and pounded their way through the seas. In all, they were not a comfortable ride. However, on 3 April the shoal draft of *LCI(R) 763* saved her from sure destruction. She was on a screening station off western Okinawa at 0240 when a Frances headed toward *LCI(R) 648* which was underway near her. The plane was driven off by the ship's gunfire and veered toward *LCI(R) 763* dropping its torpedo. The pilot's aim was true and the torpedo headed right for the port beam of the rocket gunboat. It passed underneath the ship, traveled a short distance, and exploded. The ship was shaken but not damaged, and there were no casualties. Her shoal draft had saved her from sure destruction.[17]

Suicide boats were a constant threat in the area, and gunboats were sent in search of their lairs. On 5 April, four LCS(L)s of TU 52.19.5, *LCS(L)s 24, 37, 39,* and *40*, with the commander of the task unit, Lieutenant Commander B. A. Thirkield on board *LCS(L) 24*, rendezvoused with Commander Bailliere in his flagship *LC(FF) 679*. They headed south to the area between Naha Airfield and the southern tip of Okinawa to search out and destroy suspected suicide boat bases. Foul weather dominated the area with rain, fifteen knot winds, and rough seas, making it unlikely that any of the small enemy boats would be on the water. Visibility was limited to one to four thousand yards, and it did not seem likely that the mission would be a success. The poor visibility made inshore navigation difficult due to the presence of reefs that threatened to ground any vessel that got too close. Bailliere requested that the mission be relocated but received no response. He then set about pursuing his mission. At 0815 the gunboats made a run parallel to the reef about 1,000 yards off shore, but found nothing of interest save a floating mine. *LC(FF) 679* took it under fire and exploded it. A second run at 0915 was more successful. Cave openings presented themselves to the sea, and the LCS(L)s fired into them and hit other targets of opportunity in the area. Men were seen pulling a boat into a cave, and the LCS(L)s poured some heavy fire into it. Two additional runs were completed and the gunboats returned to the anchorage.[18]

On 7 April, Mortar Division Six, *LCI(M)s 801–806,* was sent north from Hagushi to Nago Wan to assist the Marines around Motobu Peninsula. They shelled the beach near the town of Yabu and, on the following day, the beach west of the town of Awa. Call-fire was not requested until 9 April when a company of Marines needed support. On 12 April *LCI(M)s 801, 802,* and *805* were sent to assist some Marines trapped in a ravine on the northwestern tip of Motobu Peninsula. Mortar fire was out of the question and 40mm fire was attempted. However, reefs in the area prevented the gunboats from getting within range. A destroyer was called in and, with her larger guns, was able to fire into the requested target area. The gunboats were sent back to Hagushi for smoke details.

Okinawan civilians and Japanese Army personnel attempted to escape from the Marines in large numbers during the night of 9-10 April. Gunboats of LCI(R) Group Forty-Six reported intercepting and destroying at least twenty small boats with automatic weapons fire. One of the boats contained three men, three women, and fourteen children. They were taken aboard *LCI(R) 1070* and put ashore safely on Hanaee Shima.

Tsugen Shima

Tsugen Shima lies off the southeast coast of Okinawa at the entrance to Nakagusuku Wan. It is nearly the central island in a string of islands that stretch across the mouth of the bay. As the fighting progressed southward on the main island of Okinawa, seizure of the eastern islands became important as they guarded the entrance to Nakagusuku Wan. The Marine's FMFPac Amphibious Reconnaissance Battalion scouted the island on 6 April, paddling their rubber boats into the island at 0200. Unfortunately they encountered four civilians, two of whom escaped to warn the Japanese troops stationed there. The result was a fire fight which gave a good indication that the Japanese on the island were well-equipped and ready to resist. Having determined that the enemy was on the island in force, the Marine recon companies withdrew under heavy fire. Their losses were two dead and eight wounded. Reconnaissance of the other islands at the mouth of Nakagusuku Wan was completed during the next day, and it became obvious that Tsugen Shima would soon be the scene of the fighting. No enemy forces were found on Kutaka Shima to the south or the other islands to the immediate north. The condition of the landing beaches at Tsugen Shima was checked by the Underwater Demolition Teams and found to be clear of any problems.[19]

At 0650 cruisers and destroyers began shelling the beach. The mortar gunboats began their firing at 0800 until 0828 on the northwest, south, and southwest sides of the island. Some ships reported small arms fire and mortar fire directed at them but none were hit.

April 10 was the scheduled day for the invasion. Assigned to capture the island was the Third Battalion, 105th Regimental Combat Team of the Army's 27th Infantry Division. Their landing was relatively unopposed but, once ashore, they faced stiff resistance from the Japanese who were well-hidden in bunkers and blockhouses. Two other battalions were held in reserve. All 234 members of the Japanese force were killed, and the 3/105 suffered eleven dead and eighty wounded. By 1530 on 11 April the fighting was over.

The gunboats of TU 52.24.3, under Lieutenant Commander R. F. Hunnicutt, were assigned to provide covering fire for the landing and call-fire if needed. They included *LCI(M)s 808– 810(GF) 1088,* and *1089.* They were not needed for the initial landing but stood by on the west side of island. They fired on some targets at 1156, then stood by for screening duties.

Ie Shima

To the northwest of Okinawa is the island of Ie Shima. Separated from Okinawa by about three and one half miles, the island would prove useful as a radar site and for its airfields. The Japanese had determined that it would be difficult to defend and began to destroy the infrastructure, particularly the airfield. The island was extensively mined as a precaution against American invaders, and fortifications were constructed that would enable the defenders to resist the American invasion. The Japanese defenses were in caves and tombs and not visible to aerial observation, leaving the Americans to believe that the island was poorly defended. Shelling of the island by American ships began on 25 March and continued up until landing day. Scheduled to land on 16 April were elements of the 77th Army Infantry Division. From 1 through 10 April and again from 13 to 15 April, the island was subjected to continued air attacks by carrier aircraft.

UDTs 4, 17, and 21 surveyed the beaches in preparation for the assault. FMF Marine Reconnaissance Units had already landed and found the enemy defenses. The UDTs noted that enemy measures against them were primarily sniper rifle and machine gun fire. To make it more difficult to see them, the UDT members had painted themselves with aluminum camouflage paint to lessen their visibility. Covering the work of UDTs were the gunboats of TU 57.18.1 under Lieutenant Commander Robinson, including *LCI(G)s, 373(F),452, 454, 462, 465, 467, 472, 561, 567, 568, 580* and *751. LCI(G) 452* reported placing two 40mm shells in the entrance door to a block house on shore. Fires were started by the shelling from the gunboats and enemy snipers were kept down by their gunfire. By 1050 all the swimmers had been recovered and the gunboats ceased fire and left the immediate area.

The following day, 14 April, the crew of *LCI(G) 452* reported an unusual incident involving a Japanese soldier on shore:

> At about 0915 a rather peculiar incident occurred one which had never occurred to us or to anyone else so far as we knew. A Jap strolled nonchalantly out on the upper edge of the beach, stood around for a few moments and sat down; by this time the Executive Officer had pointed him out to our number three 40 mm gun crew. After a couple of close straddles he stood up and making no effort to duck or protect himself, just stood there. After a few more rounds, he was hit in the middle by a 40 mm projectile which blew him to bits. We noticed what was left of him as we left the beach.[20]

Participating in the assault on Ie Shima on 16 April were Lieutenant Commander C. F. Robinson's Gunboat Support Division Four which included *LCI(G)s 373(F), 451, 454, 461, 561, 751,* and Lieutenant Gilberty's Gunboat Support Division Five which consisted of *LCI(G)s 452, 465, 467, 567,* and *568.* Rocket fire notwithstanding, the majority of the gunboats at Ie Shima carried mortars. Four mortar task units delivered mortar fire during and after the assault. They were:

TU 51.21.25	Lieutenant Commander Harris Brown	LCI(M)s 356, 739(F)-741, 975
TU 51.21.27	Lieutenant Commander R. E. Hunnicutt	LCI(M)s 807–810, 1088, 1089
TU 51.21.28	Lieutenant J. E. Gage	LCL(M)s 755, 1055, 1059(F)
TU 51.21.29	Lieutenant (jg) Frederick J. Geiger	LCI(M)s 742(F), 805, 806

Supporting the gunboats offshore was the destroyer *Heywood L. Edwards DD 663*.

The landing at Ie Shima went well. Apparently the ships' fire kept most of the snipers at bay. Once the assault was completed, the ships retired to their anchorage at Nago Wan. In the early evening, enemy artillery from the north shore of Motobu Peninsula took them under fire and they had to move further offshore. Several shells fell in the area near the *561* but did not hit her.

Once she had finished her rocket run, *LCI(G) 452* had to back down full in order to avoid running up on a reef. *LCI(G) 568* was not so fortunate, but her grounding was brief; she was pulled off promptly. As she was stuck on the reef, a 5 inch shell from an American destroyer hit the water about one hundred yards off her bow. The explosion dented her forward splinter shield but there were no injuries. A number of fuel tanks on shore were hit and buildings were demolished by mortar fire.

Concerns were raised over the late landing of the LVTs. They had been ordered to proceed to the beach at top speed, which was four knots. The gunboats, ahead of them by 300 yards, were supposed to adjust their speed so as to keep the correct interval. A four knot speed for the flat bottomed gunboats made it difficult for them to maintain position. As a result, the LVTs lagged a bit too far behind to make effective use of the rocket salvos. By the time they reached shore, the best support the gunboats could manage was 40mm fire. There was concern that the Japanese might have time to exit their fox holes and bunkers and put up a more effective resistance. Fortunately, the Japanese had elected not to defend the beaches but to resist farther inland.[21]

Preparatory bombing of the island by two battleships, four cruisers and seven destroyers began the invasion day fireworks. Following that, the rocket and mortar gunboats did their part and continued until the LVTs were safely ashore. Once the troops of the 77th Infantry Division had been safely landed, the gunboats remained in the area to supply anti-aircraft protection for the ships that were unloading. Enemy aircraft appeared in the afternoon, and *LCI(G) 561* shot down a Zeke which was about to attack the anchorage.

Landing on Ie Shima was the 77th Infantry Division, which was covered by fire support from the gunboats and destroyers. The American forces faced light opposition as they landed. The Japanese had determined to fortify ridges on the island and conducted their defense away from the beaches. Once having landed, the American forces encountered difficult opposition and the island was not secured for six days. During that time the Japanese suffered 4,706 dead and 149 taken prisoner. As usual, civilian workers and others had been pressed into service and most died during the battle. American losses were 172 dead, 902 wounded, and forty-six missing in action.

Once the island was secured, repair of the airfields was undertaken. On 20 April, ground elements of the Army Air Force's 318th Fighter Group arrived, and on 13 May the first P-47N Thunderbolts arrived on the island. They would be used for long range attacks against Kyushu and Korea, as well as local combat air patrols.

Small groups of Japanese remained on the island and many attempted to escape by using rafts and small boats to get across to the mainland. To prevent their escape the channel was under continual patrol. On 22 April *LCI(M)s 802* and *803* were on patrol in the channel at 2320 when they spotted a raft with seven Japanese soldiers on board. Intending to capture the Japanese, *LCI(G) 803* fired ten rounds of .30 caliber fire across the side of the raft. As she approached the raft, the Japanese indicated that they would surrender and threw their weapons overboard.

The Japanese were told to remove their clothing prior to being brought on board the gunboat. A search of their clothing revealed hand grenades which were thrown overboard. Their clothing and knapsacks were soaked in a bucket. A further search of the raft revealed eighteen hand grenades which were dropped into the ocean. The other materials removed from the Japanese included clothing, money, knives, and other personal items, all of which were dried and turned over to Commander LCI Mortar Support Flotilla along with the prisoners.

LCI(G) 802 headed toward *803* to assist and soon found a couple of rafts to investigate. Each of them contained five Japanese. Since there was no additional need to take prisoners, the *802* opened fire on the rafts and killed the Japanese soldiers. At 0221 *LCI(G) 802* spotted another raft with six Japanese and opened fire, killing at least three. The rafts were towed to shore where additional hand grenades were found between the floorboards.[22]

The islands of Kerama Retto, although under American control, could still be dangerous since scattered elements of the Japanese Army existed in some areas. In the evening of 18 April an LCVT had been driven ashore by thirty knot winds and heavy swells on the north shore of Zamami Shima. It soon came under machine gun fire and two of the five men on the LCVT were wounded. *LCI(R) 770* was sent to aid them. Sea conditions caused the rocket gunboat to ground on a reef only 200 yards off shore as she moved in to assist. She was able to suppress the enemy fire with her guns and the following morning sent her small boat in to the shore to rescue the men. The two wounded men were removed first and the remaining three men taken back on a second trip. In spite of her efforts to get off the reef, she was unsuccessful. She sent out for help from a tug and was soon pulled free of the reef with no damage to her hull.[23]

Diversionary Landing 19 April

The Tenth Army continued to make progress to the south. To divert the enemy's attention, a feint was made on southern Okinawa in the vicinity the village of Oshima. Under the overall command of Commander M. J. Malanaphy (CTU 52.23.4), in *LC(FF) 627,* were a number of gunboats. Malanaphy's command consisted of: Gunboat Support Divisions Two and Three, LSM(R) Unit Two, and Mortar Support Groups One and Two. The mortar gunboats utilized mortar fire plan Baker and the ships opened fire at 0625. They fired for twenty minutes before departing the area. Additional coverage of the area was provided by American aircraft which bombed and strafed the area.

With the initial landings at Hagushi completed, the gunboats turned to a variety of duties, including smoke-making, anti–small craft patrol, anti-aircraft fire, call-fire, and shore bombardment as the fighting moved south. Involved in the shore bombardment were a variety of LCI(M)s, (R)s and (G)s, along with some LCS(L)s. However, the majority of the LCS(L)s were assigned to radar picket duty stations since all of them had at least two twin 40mm guns and some mounted three.

As the fighting moved south on Okinawa, there were few places safe from the guns of the American fleet. Areas close to shore were attacked by the gunboats and LSMRs, while those targets further inland fell under the guns of the destroyers, cruisers, and battleships. The reverse slopes of ridges and hills could be attacked by mortar fire near shore, and those targets further inland fell victim to aerial bombing and strafing. In short, there were few places that the Japanese could feel safe. The only thing that saved them was the hilly topography of the area and extensive underground tunnels they had constructed.

Two of the gunboats operating in Nakagusuka Bay on 4 May were *LCI(R)s 651* and *763.* Their primary duty in the area was making smoke during the night, but they were given the

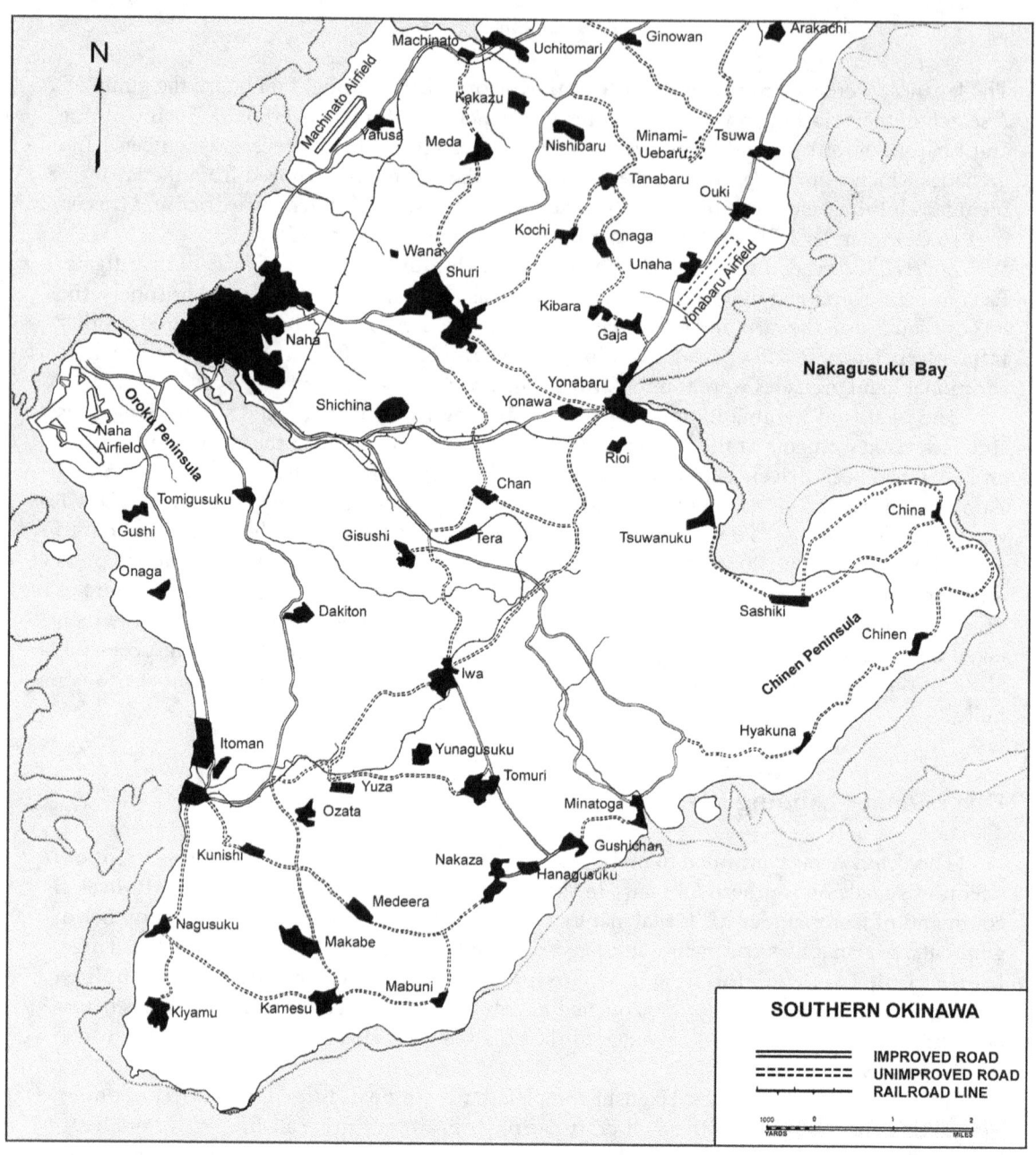

After the initial landing at the Hagushi beachhead on 1 April 1945, the bulk of the fighting moved to the southern part of Okinawa. LCI gunboats were continually called upon to supply rocket, mortar, and automatic weapons fire on targets close to the shoreline in support of Army and Marine forces moving south. As the Japanese were pressed into the southernmost areas of the island, they became ready targets for the gunboats.

additional assignment to patrol for targets of opportunity on the beach between China Point and Baten-ko. The coastline in that area extends westward for a mile and a half. Shore access was prevented by a reef which extended seaward 200–600 yards. Toward one end was a seawall and a flat stretch of beach. Pulled up on shore was an assortment of twenty-five to thirty boats. These were not military vessels but were probably native fishing boats. However, any boat could be of use to the Japanese, if even to supplement their rations with fresh fish. From 1055 to 1900, the two ships, backed up by the destroyer *Hall DD 583*, cruised the area between Chinen Point and Yonabaru firing their 20mm and 40mm guns at small boats on the beach, fuel dumps, and caves where they suspected enemy presence.

The fusillade from the ships started large fires in the grass just off the beach, and within a short time, four grass huts in the area were burned down. Moving on down the beach, the rocket ship fired on and burned down three more huts near Yonabaru, hitting a dozen large drums of fuel and two large boats, all of which were left in flames. As they neared Yonabaru, the ships were bracketed by mortar fire; *LCI(R) 651* sustained minor damage and suffered one crewman wounded.

Smoke-screening was a tedious and unglamorous undertaking but most welcome to the ships being covered. On 4 May *LCI(M) 356* was sent to a reef off Kouri Shima, arriving at 2335. *PGM 17* had run up on the reef and was solidly grounded. The fleet tug *Tawakoni ATF 114* was attempting to pull her off. For the next two days, the LCI(M) anchored upwind from the tug and PGM, covering them with smoke whenever there was an air alert. By 6 May increasing air raids threatened the three ships and they were strafed by a Betty at 0426 on 6 May. *PGM 17* continued to be pushed further on to the reef and had to be abandoned. Her men were transferred to the tug along with sensitive materials, and *LCI(M) 356* remained in the area to make sure that the Japanese on the island could not get to the PGM. Later in the day she was relieved of the duty by *LCI(M) 975* and returned to Ie Shima. *LCI(M)s 356, 740,* and *975* took turns patrolling nearby for the next few weeks.

While diversionary assaults were useful, the gunboats frequently supplied bombardment of enemy positions ahead of advancing American forces. From 14 to 15 May and again on 19, 22, and 23 May, LCI RCM and Rocket Support Division Five (Lieutenant Commander A F. Eckelmeyer) with *LCI(R)s 704, 705, 785, 1024, 1026,* and *1068,* and mortar gunboats from Mortar Support Division Seven (Lieutenant Commander R. E. Hunnicutt) with *LCI(M)s 807–810(F), 1088,* and *1089,* were assigned fire-support duties for the 6th Marine Division as it attacked enemy emplacements around the city of Naha. Navigating the entrance to the harbor at Naha was of concern, as the break in the reefs provided only a narrow channel into the bay. The LCI(M)s delivered their mortar fire on the city of Naha while the LCI(R)s fired on enemy positions on Yahara Ridge and Orokumura. *LCI(M) 808* ran aground on the southern tip of Kanna Se around 1600 but managed to get off in short order.

Once again problems in the construction of the mortar boxes arose. *LCI(M) 1089* reported that the high rate of fire caused one of her mortar boxes to break, and the other two were close to breaking. The need for stronger boxes and water cooling jackets on the mortars was again suggested. *LCI(M) 1089*'s mortar box had already been repaired but not with the required hardwood. The only material available in the area was soft wood which quickly proved to be inadequate.[24]

The following day, Mortar Support Division Two, consisting of *LCI(M)s 632, 633(F), 1010–1012,* and *1023* under the command of Lieutenant Commander S. J. Kelley, was relieved of its smoke-making duties at Hagushi and sent into action. Using mortar fire plan Charlie, the ships supported the 6th Marine Division and bombarded areas of Naha and its airfield from 0827 until 1642. Observed on shore at the airport was the hulk of an enemy plane and a hangar, both of which had been worked over by aircraft and fire from the larger ships. At times it was difficult to find a target that had not been hit; the accumulated gunfire to that date having been extensive. The primary purpose of the fire was to suppress enemy action in front of the advancing troops. After each mortar barrage, the ships used their automatic weapons to fire on targets of opportunity, including buildings, cave entrances, and suspected enemy positions. Since the mortar gunboats were the newest of the conversions used at Okinawa, this led to problems as neither the infantry forces ashore, the Naval Liaison Officers (NLO) or Shore Fire Control (SFC) officers were familiar with its operations and limits. After much confusion on 15 May between Lieutenant Commander Kelley and the NLOs he noted:

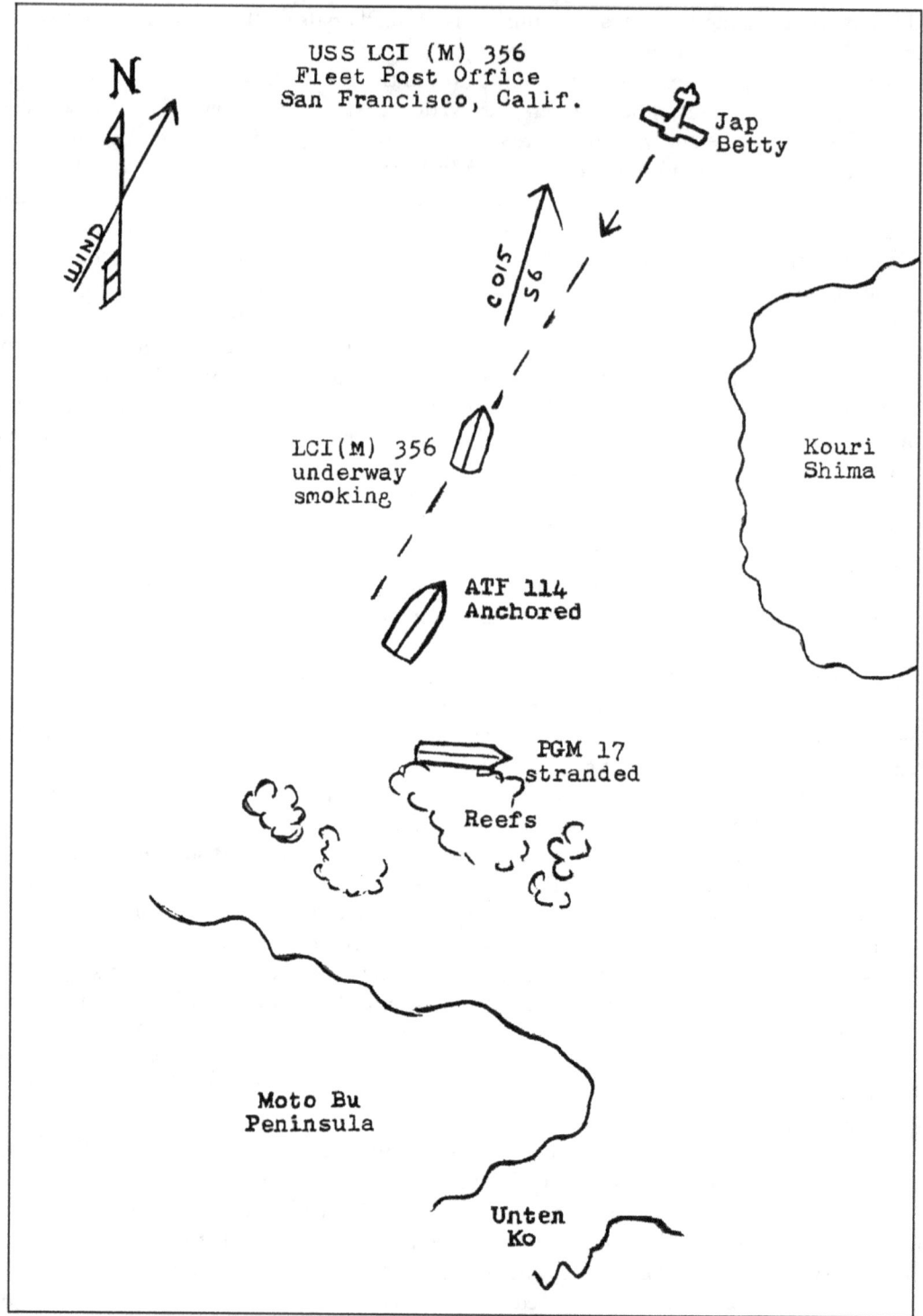

On 4 May 1945 *PGM 17* was grounded on a reef off Motobu Peninsula. *Tawakoni ATF 14* went to her aid and *LCI(M) 356* covered the operation. The ships were strafed by a Japanese Betty bomber on 6 May. LCI gunboats patrolled the area for several weeks, keeping the Japanese from gaining access to the ship. *USS LCI(M) 356* Serial 1286, *Anti-Aircraft Action and Operation Report, Kouri Shima, 4 to 15 May 1945*, 27 May 1945, Enclosure (B).

It is felt that there is much room for improvement in the knowledge and understanding of NLO's and SFC parties in the ability, characteristics, limitations, and standard tactical procedures of LCI mortar craft. It has been difficult at times for the Division Commander to know what it is that the NLO wants due to this limitation. In short, we don't seem to speak the same language. Examination of Enclosure (A) will show that the NLO with which this command worked with on 15 May 1945 had:
(a) No knowledge of class patterns.
(b) No appreciation of how long it takes to move a division from the standby area to the position from which to fire.
(c) No knowledge of "reference point" as used for the various plans of fire.
(d) No appreciation of navigational problems. Witness the location of numerous reefs in vicinity of area from which fire was delivered into NAHA town.
(e) No knowledge of safety margins in regard to own troops.
(f) No appreciation of ammunition allowances.[25]

Apparently the mortar ships had run through their allotment of ammunition for the mission and were reluctant to exceed the total in spite of the urging of the NLO that additional mortar fire be unleashed on the targets. Kelley further noted that the NLO was not on board his ship but on board *LCI(R) 1068* with the Commander of the RCM and Rocket Division Five.

Mortar Support Division Three, including *LCI(M)s 351–356,* were reassigned from the smoke and patrol duties at Hagushi anchorage and sent south to attack targets in and around Naha. They targeted the seawall around Naha Airfield, artillery positions near the airport and harbor, and the harbor and city itself. As with all of the gunboats supplying rocket and mortar fire in the area, they made ample use of their 20mm and 40mm guns against targets of opportunity once their mortar run had been completed. A new assignment was given to the division on 17 May. The 6th Marine Division was concerned with enemy forces slowing their advance and identified seven targets for them. They supplied mortar fire for the Marines and then retired from their position. The Marines needed their assistance again on 18 May, identifying two targets for the mortar gunboats. From about 0907 to approximately 1120, the mortar gunboats poured mortar fire on both. However, at 1120, they were called away from their mortar bombardment duties to aid *Longshaw DD 559* which had run onto a reef in the area, fallen under the guns of the Japanese Army ashore, and was on fire. They aided in picking up survivors and spent several hours patrolling the area looking for additional men in the water. Attempts to come alongside the destroyer to help with firefighting were made, with *LCI(G) 356* managing to secure lines. Other gunboats of the division made the attempt as well, but the flat bottomed LCI hulls made maneuvering difficult. The gunboats eventually cast off as there was no further assistance that could be given to *Longshaw.*

The gunboats returned to the Hagushi area for a few days of making smoke, but were back off Naha from 19 to 23 May. Their mission was to support the advance of the Army's 7th Division as it made its way southward in the Naha area. Rocket and mortar assaults were made on Naha and also on the eastern side of the island at Yonabaru. Participating in these support missions were LCI RCM and Rocket Divisions One, Two, Four, Five, and Six, along with Mortar Support Division One.

LCI(M) 353 was operating off Ie Shima on 25 May when she found herself in the middle of an air raid. At 0800 the ships in the area received a flash red-control green air raid signal indicating that enemy aircraft were in the area. As she went to general quarters, a Japanese twin-engine bomber crashed into the water about 300 yards off her bow. Other enemy planes swarmed overhead, many out of range of the gunboat's 40mm gun. A few miles away *Spectacle AM 305* was hit by a kamikaze, killing twenty-nine of her men and wounding six. *LCI(M) 353* headed toward her to render assistance. *LSM 135* also came to the scene and no sooner arrived when she was crashed by an enemy bomber. Firefighting on the ship was impossible as her water mains had been broken in the attack. She began to list to starboard, and leaking oil set the water around her ablaze. Her commanding officer, Lieutenant H. L. Derby, Jr., and ten of the crew were killed, with another ten wounded. She was abandoned and drifted on to a nearby reef, a complete loss. Gunners on *LCI(M) 353* spotted a Japanese Tony diving on a nearby destroyer escort, the *William C. Cole DE 641*. The Tony overshot the DE and headed for *LCI(M) 353*. The mortar gunboat took it under fire with its 20mm guns and scored a number of hits. The plane flew over the gunboat and headed away, bursting into flame a few minutes later. It crashed into the sea. *LCI(M) 353* patrolled the area picking up survivors from *LSM 135* and *Spectacle*, in addition to three men from *William C. Cole* who inexplicably wound up in the water during the attacks.

Iheya Shima

The invasion of Iheya Shima, originally scheduled for 1 June 1945, was postponed until 3 June. Assigned to fire support for the invasion was Lieutenant Commander A. H. Connors' TU 31.25.42 which consisted of *LCI(M)s 351–356*, and Lieutenant Commander R. F. Hunnicutt's TU 31.25.43 comprised of *LCI(M)s 807–810(GF) 1088*, and *1089*. At 0955 the ships took their fire-support stations and began to prepare for the assault. They followed plan Charlie and began

LCS(L)s 95, 91, 68, and *124* lead the attack on Blue Beaches 1 and 2 at Aguni Island, 9 June 1945. NARA 80G 274357.

LCS(L) 124 fires at Japanese positions on Aguni Shima as she leads landing craft to shore. NARA RG 19 LCS(L) (3) 124.

their mortar bombardment at 1028. Occasional pauses in the firing took place as American aircraft bombed and strafed targets ashore. It was difficult to determine the effect of the bombardment since there were no enemy positions observable and no return fire was encountered. The 2nd Marine Division landed. A typhoon was predicted for the region and the mortar division headed for Nago Wan to ride it out, returning the following day to resume screening and smoke-laying duties which ended on 6 June.

Aguni Shima was taken on 9 June 1945. Connors' TU 31.25.42 provided mortar fire support beginning at 0542. After about twenty minutes of fire on the shore area, it was determined that there was no enemy resistance and the troops were given the go ahead to land. The gunboats remained in the area for two days, providing smoke cover and anti-aircraft protection.

The End of the Campaign for Okinawa

The deadly fighting on Okinawa had continued into May and June. By that time the Japanese had been pushed to the far southern extreme of Okinawa, and many of their units were near the shoreline in range of the rocket ships and mortar gunboats.

Early activity in the fire-support region saw numerous Japanese soldiers killed by gunfire, rockets, and mortars. June 2 found *LCI(R) 769* patrolling along the southeast coast of Okinawa near the southernmost tip of the island. Numerous targets of opportunity were on display, including pill boxes, cave openings, and occasional enemy activity. On occasion an explosion indicated that they had hit an ammunition dump. Some suspected enemy positions in the hills were observed, and *LCI(R)s 646* and *769* fired rocket salvos into the forward slopes at Sakibaru Saki.

On 3 June *LCI(R) 647* hit an ammo dump, causing a small explosion. Shortly thereafter, one of her rocket salvos landed in the middle of about fifty Japanese soldiers near Gushtokan,

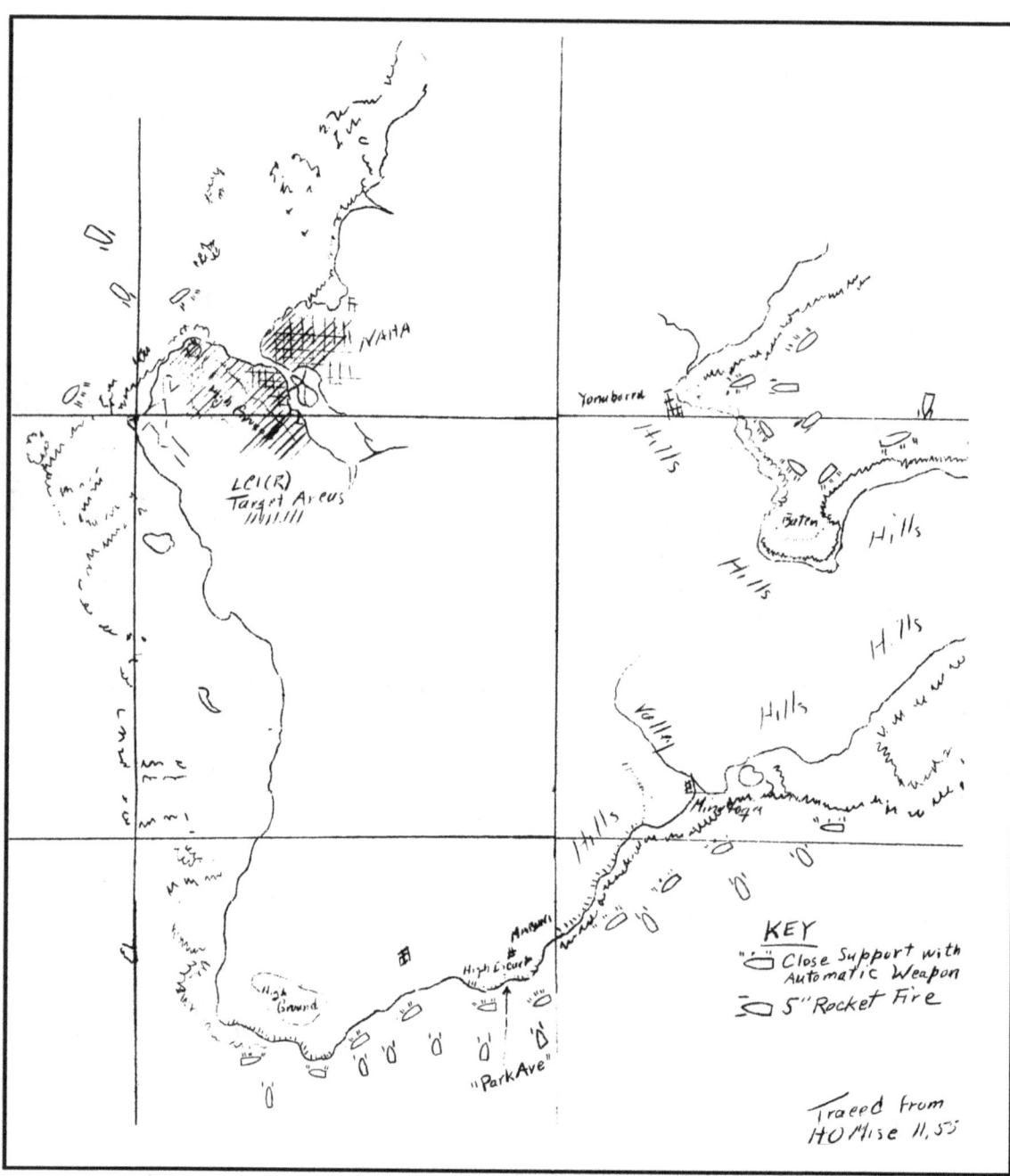

By the end of the Okinawa campaign, the Japanese forces had been pushed to the far southern end of the island. There they fell victim to constant raids by gunboats and destroyers operating just off shore. LCI gunboats were constantly firing in support of advancing American troops. Commander LCI Flotilla 16 Serial 35, *Action Report—Invasion of the Okinawa Group Liu Chius, 26 March to 21 June 1945*, 15 July 1945, Enclosures (A) Fire Support Missions.

killing most of them. LCI(R)s *647*, *764*, and *770* cruised the area with no shortage of targets, using 40mm and 20mm fire in addition to their rockets.

LCI(R)s *643*, *645*, *647*, *762*, and *770* patrolled off the southern tip of Okinawa on 5 June. On board *649* was an Army recon party to help them spot targets. The Japanese had positioned a six inch naval gun in a cave overlooking the plateau south of Gushtokan which was preventing Army advances in the area. Call-fire was requested to eliminate the threat. The gunboats fired on the cave with 40mm guns, receiving heavy mortar and small arms fire in return. When the smoke had cleared, it appeared that the gun had been destroyed and the Army unit made its advance.

The following day the gunboats continued their cooperation with the Army. A spotter plane from the cruiser *Tuscaloosa CA 37* directed their rocket fire against targets near Mabuni and Komesu. Return fire from the Japanese was heavy. They recognized the severe threat from the gunboats but were unable to hit any of them. The spotter plane pilot radioed back that the gunboats were on target, and the Army radioed their great appreciation for the assistance. Reports from Army units began to filter back to the naval command indicating that the support of the gunboats was extremely valuable. Just knowing that heavy firepower was only a call away gave the Army and Marine units ashore a psychological boost. That sort of benefit was impossible to quantify, but it was invaluable.

As the fighting moved to the southern end of Okinawa and reached its final stage, it was not uncommon for enemy troops to attempt to escape from the area. Numerous individuals and small groups of men were captured as they attempted to swim away from the beaches or escape using small boats and canoes. Patrolling offshore to prevent their escape were the gunboats, many of which either captured or killed them. *LCI(G) 567* reported capturing seven Okinawans at 2300 on 9 June. They were attempting to escape the area near Naha in a small boat. The boat was sunk with .50 caliber machine gun fire. Several hours later, at 0300 on 10 June, another boat with five Okinawans was sighted. Five more prisoners were added to the group and the boat was sunk. On 11 June an intermittent radar blip gave away the position of still another swimmer near the reef at Naha. The gunboat followed him for a half hour trying to get him to accept the life ring they were throwing. He finally consented, was pulled aboard, and added to the prisoner tally. Lieutenant K. C. Flory, CO of *LCI(G) 567*, recommended that cargo nets be used to aid in picking up prisoners. Also, it was found useful to keep a spotlight shining in their eyes to prevent the use of any weapons they might have. He further recommended that the gunboats be issued Japanese phrasebooks giving them the ability to communicate orders to those being picked up.[26]

On 6 June, *LCI(R) 769* patrolled the southeast coast of Okinawa firing on numerous pill boxes and suspected enemy installations. At 1640 her lookouts spotted what appeared to be a Japanese command post at Mabuni-dake and hit it with a rocket salvo. A few days later, on 9 June, the rocket gunboat was back in the same location. This time she discovered two camouflaged twenty-five foot dugouts on the beach and destroyed them with 40mm fire. Japanese small arms fire erupted from some of the caves in the area and the ship was hit by a number of rounds. However, .30 caliber rifle bullets had little impact on the steel hull and topsides. The gunboat turned toward shore and ran in close to the beach firing her guns into every cave opening visible. That ended the enemy small arms fire.

There was no dearth of targets in the southern part of Okinawa. On 10 June Lieutenant Commander H. T. McKnight led his fire-support group (TU 52.20.4) in a mission against the towns of Mabuni, Ibaru, and Komesu. They maneuvered in close to shore and strafed various targets. Some of their rounds hit a small ammo dump resulting in a large explosion. Enemy mortar fire was directed at the ships but none were hit.[27] *LCI(R) 1028* had the closest call when she was narrowly missed by a mortar round which hit the water only fifteen feet off her starboard beam. Having overheated their guns with constant firing, the gunboats retreated to a position 5,000 yards from shore to let them cool. After an hour they had cooled sufficiently and the rocket ships headed inshore once again. This time they caught about forty enemy troops moving through the area and cut them down with ten minutes of 20mm and 40mm fire. Thirty minutes later a half dozen more enemy troops were observed near a cornfield and killed by gunfire from the ships.

The land on the southernmost area of Okinawa is hilly with cliffs along the seashore. To the west of the town of Mabuni, a path ran up the bluffs and over the top. This was a busy area. *LCI(R) 647* reported:

> A great deal of activity was observed on this particular path, which ran almost straight up the bluff and disappeared through a V-shaped notch on the top. Path became so popular we dubbed it "Park Ave." Women were frequently observed carrying food and supplies down the path, disappearing behind large rocks at bottom of path. Believed that this large rock housed an Army activity of importance for our consistent bagging of enemy troops along path did not seem to discourage traffic. Dawn and dusk sweeps proved extremely effective. Caught many troops by surprise as they strolled up the hill in plain sight.[28]

Between 10 and 20 June, numerous Japanese soldiers were killed while transiting the path or crossing the notch at the top. It was obvious that a number of enemy troops were in the area, and mortar and rocket fire was aimed at the reverse sides of the bluffs. The forward bluffs facing the sea were covered with foliage and this made it difficult to spot enemy soldiers. From time to time soldiers were seen with foliage attached to themselves in an attempt at camouflage.

Five and six inch Japanese guns were located in some of the caves near the water, and ships reported being taken under fire by them from time to time. On a number of occasions mortar fire from shore bracketed the gunboats, but none were hit. Small arms fire also emanated from areas of dense foliage on shore and it was difficult to find the source. In all cases, the suspect area was blanketed with 20mm and 40mm fire with unknown results.

A particularly severe attack occurred on 18 June when the area seemed strangely quiet. No enemy soldiers were seen and no fire was directed at the ships. The enemy was lying in wait. The ships were struck with a shower of machine gun and rifle fire from the shore. None of the gunboats were damaged and there were no personnel casualties. Twenty and 40mm fire from the ships soon put an end to the ambush.

The Japanese at the southern end of the island were nearing their final efforts. Under fire from American troops ashore and from ships afloat, they were also subject to air attacks. On 13 June, observers on *LCI(R) 769* watched as sixty F4U Corsairs hit the Japanese in the southern area with rockets and napalm. The napalm in this instance was not as useful as it might have been against other targets; it could not penetrate the cave entrances. Napalm in the hills did not work particularly well, as there was nothing to set afire in the area. It had already been destroyed by naval gunfire, shore based artillery, and previous air strikes.[29]

Japanese soldiers, as well as civilians, continued to flee the onslaught of Army and Marine forces at the southern end of Okinawa. On 16 June *LCI(R) 650* was firing on caves in the cliffs overlooking ARA Point and Chiyan Point when her lookouts spotted ten people on the beach waving white flags. The gunboats put out a request to the Army to cease fire in the area so that the ten could be picked up. The Flotilla Commander attempted to communicate with them using Chinese, but they could not understand the language. Fortunately the CO of *LCI(R) 762*, Lieutenant (jg) E. E. Kelley, did speak their language. Using his Japanese skills, he convinced one of them to swim out to the ship. An Army interpreter was on board and learned that there were a number of civilians in the area, as well as some troops, who wished to surrender. The location of Japanese headquarters near Mabuni was learned through the interrogation.[30]

Twiggs DD 591 was on patrol off the southern end of Okinawa when she was torpedoed and then crashed by a Jill at 2030. The torpedo caused her No. 2 magazine to explode. The plane circled around and crashed into the destroyer, finishing the job. *Twiggs* went under as *LCS(L) 14* and *LCI(R) 650* tried to close on the ship to assist in firefighting, but they were driven off by the intense fires. Both gunboats patrolled the area picking up survivors.

LCI(R) 1077, operating as a part of RCM and Rocket Division One, was tasked with the mission of encouraging Japanese soldiers and Okinawan civilians to surrender. Her CO, Lieutenant G. N. Armstrong, reported:

> On 17 June we were assigned to work with 1st Lt. Kwiecinski of the Army in trying to obtain a mass surrender. We remained in this capacity until 22 June. We had a Japanese interpreter and a Japanese soldier aboard; their job was to talk to the people in the caves. A loudspeaker system was installed. As this was the first big scale attempt, no knowledge of the outcome could be seen. We met with no appreciable success the first two days; but the remaining days brought a complete change. Hundreds poured out of the caves and began walking to American lines as we talked to them. When asked why they surrendered, many answered, "American ship promise we would not be harmed if we surrendered." The take included many soldiers as well as civilians. Our mission was a success and we received a "Job Well Done" from the Army.[31]

LCI(M)s 807–809, 1088, and *1089* (TU 32.24.3) operated from Hagushi anchorage and steamed to the southernmost area of Okinawa to provide fire support for the 1st Marine Division on 17 and 18 June. Arriving at the scene, the mortar gunboats found that the target area was already being worked over by larger ships and aircraft. The enemy was positioned on a series of ridges in the area, and the ships directed mortar fire on these areas which were to the north of the town of Komesu. Marine spotters requested that specific targets be destroyed and the ships were selective in their fire support. Headquarters 1st Marine Division reported that the mortar fire was on target and that the ships had provided significant assistance.

At the same time Mortar Division Six, under Lieutenant Young Davis, was supporting the Army's 7th Division in the southern area. They targeted the area south of the village of Ibaru and the beach south of Mabuni from the water to 400 yards inland. North of Mabuni village lay a ridge with Japanese positions. Using mortars and 40mm shell fire, the mortar gunboats worked over the area both days before returning to Hagushi each night. Included in Mortar Division Six were *LCI(M)s 801–806*. On 17 June, machine gun fire from shore fell near the ships but they suffered no damage. A mishap occurred on *LCI(M) 806* during the firing when a flash from one of the mortars set off powder rings in the number 3 ready box. The flash covered the entire well deck, causing three men to go over the side to escape the fire. Fortunately, the men suffered only minor burns and were soon hauled back on board.

With the fighting on Okinawa nearing its conclusion, more and more Okinawan civilians and Japanese soldiers began to surrender to the gunboats operating inshore. On 19 June, the end was near:

> At 1520, LCI(R)s 762 and 1069 closed the beach east of ARA SAKI to investigate a large movement in that area. As they closed the "big parade" started. Civilians and troops appearing from behind cover when it was seen that the LCI(R)s were not firing. Troops stacked their arms and joined the procession moving northeast along the surrender route. There was no apparent control of the mob.
> At 1640 it was seen that our troops had broken through the beach, and at dusk 7th Division announced that there were no longer any front lines.[32]

Lessons Learned and Recommendations

The campaign for Okinawa had seen the use of the gunboats in their various configurations on a grand scale. Commanders of the various task groups and units were justifiably proud of their accomplishments. They were equally distressed at the use to which some of the ships had been put. In particular, the ships were little understood by the infantry forces ashore. They appreciated their firepower in the initial assault, but failed to recognize that they could continue to supply fire support as the troops advanced on the enemy. In areas where the fighting moved far inland, they could not be used, however, as long as the fighting was near the shoreline, rocket, mortar, and automatic weapons fire could be supplied by the gunboats.

Captain Clarence E. Coffin, Jr., who served as the Commander of LCI Flotilla Sixteen, was particularly appalled at the misuse of the rocket ships under his command after the initial assault on Okinawa on 1 April 1945. Coffin's experience with the ships in combat was significant; he had also commanded LCI(R) units at Iwo Jima. In his *Action Report—Invasion of the Okinawa Group Liu Chius, 26 March to 21 June 1945,* he stated:

> In view of the excellent performance of the LCI(R)s on fire-support duties during the latter part of May and during June it is strongly recommended that they be used primarily for close fire-support and not put to uses that completely ignore their tremendous fire power. It is well understood that it is necessary to use some LCI types for press duties, dispatch boats, etc; but it is felt that an LCI type with less fire power could be used, or if none are available, that these onerous duties could be spread out among all LCI types so that none would be completely lost to combatant duties. This Group was particularly hard hit as all 36 LCI(R)s were assigned to miscellaneous duties ranging from barracks for LCT officers to dispatch boats. For about two weeks after L-Day there was no concerted effort to reduce or consolidate this miscellaneous employment of LCI(R)s; but on the contrary, units to which they were assigned made a great effort to keep them busy enough to claim their retention. Once an LCI type is assigned a unit it is extremely difficult to obtain their permanent release.[33]

Continued lobbying by the officers in charge of LCI(R) units resulted in their increased use. In March and April, Coffin's ships, excluding invasion day, had engaged in only nineteen fire-support missions. By mid–May their use had increased, thanks to this pressure. Seventy-five fire-support missions were completed, primarily in the last half of May. As enemy forces were driven to the coastal areas in southern Okinawa, the ships were engaged in 145 fire-support missions from 1 to 21 June.

Part of the problem in the lack of use for the ships had to do with basic education. Many of the ground commanders were just unfamiliar with them, and concerns were voiced over the possibility of rockets falling short. This was not a real problem, and the greater accuracy of the newer spin-stabilized rockets made it a non-issue. More knowledge of the ship's capabilities by ground commanders would have led to their increased use earlier in the campaign and saved American lives.

It was noted by the commanding officers of other types of gunboats that the rocket ships were particularly suited for call-fire after the initial invasion. The new spin-stabilized rockets had a longer range than mortars[34] and were more useful as many targets were inland. Lieutenant John E. Farrar, commanding officer of *LCI(M) 1010,* noted:

> The range of the rocket [spin-stabilized] is greater than the mortar. This additional range would eliminate possibilities of endangering the lives of troops on the beaches.
>
> The rate of fire would be greater and more continuous because of a lower maximum ordinate. The danger of hitting low flying planes would not be as great.
>
> Additional armament of the rocket ship, including twin and single mount 40's would permit greater effective firing power, better adapted for close-in firing and call fire. It must be remembered that the return fire from the assault beaching area was practically negligible, but with stiffer opposition it is felt doubtful whether the mortar ship would have proved to have been the "right" ship for the "right job."[35]

Interestingly enough, Farrar's description of the "right" ship fitted the newer LCS(L)s which had fired 4.5 inch barrage rockets at the beaches alongside the LCI(M)s. An upgrade to the new 5 inch spin-stabilized rockets would make the LCS(L)s even more potent. This was not attempted and the LCS(L)s finished the war with their original rocket armament.

Trying to hit the enemy suicide boats at night was difficult unless the ship's 40mm guns were equipped with telescopic sights. Experiments with putting Mark 77 sights on *LCI(G) 442*'s 40mm gun proved to give excellent results. This gave gunners on the 40mms the advantage of sighting in on suicide boats at a greater distance from the ship and destroying them before they could get so close that the gun could not depress sufficiently to destroy them.[36]

By the end of the campaign for Okinawa, most of the LCI(R)s had replaced their original 4.5 inch fin-stabilized rockets with 5 inch spin-stabilized rockets which had a greater range and better accuracy. SO-1 Radar was only installed on one ship in each division. Coffin recommended that every third ship be so equipped.

Small ships such as the LCI(R)s, LCI(M)s, LCI(G)s, and LCS(L)s had limited storage facilities and could not store specialty foods and other items. Coffin recommended that some system be devised to replenish fresh provisions, fruit juices, and other perishable items. Larger ships frequently took the more desirable supplies before the smaller ships could get in their requisitions. Life on the gunboats was not like life on the larger ships. There were no movies, recreational areas, or large storage space. This writer has had the opportunity to investigate virtually every compartment and space on the *LCS(L) 102,* currently a floating museum at Mare Island, California, and can attest to the fact that space is extremely limited. So much so, that it is nothing short of amazing that such a ship could perform the tasks required of it.

The ships suffered from maintenance problems as well. Paint was in short supply in the war zone, and many of the ships had rust in various places. Acquiring paint to remedy the situation was often extremely difficult; the commanding officer of a destroyer or other large ship usually was able to acquire paint and maintenance supplies, whereas the Lieutenant (jg) commanding a gunboat would not be so fortunate. Coffin noted that:

> Adverse comment has been made about the rusty "Tramp Steamer" appearance of many of the landing craft. 98% of the officers and men are proud of their ships and resent the unseamanlike appearance; but the landing craft are again among those left out when paint is issued. Practically every pot of paint used by this Flotilla at staging areas and the objective was begged or traded for.[37]

Many of the gunboats wore out their automatic weapons gun barrels and their engines constantly needed repairs. Spare parts were in short supply. With so many of the gunboats operating at Okinawa, Coffin felt that sufficient spares should be placed on ARLs.

The LCS(L)s had standard armament, with the exception of the bow gun. Mounted there on the ships sent to the southern areas was a 3"/50, which proved very useful against barge traffic and shore targets in the Philippines, Iwo Jima, and Borneo. Most of the ships sent to Okinawa were supposed to be equipped with a twin 40mm bow gun, however, many of the first ships to arrive at Okinawa were fitted with an "interim" 40mm single. Wiring and controls were installed for the twin 40mm, but shortages of the twin led to many of the ships being equipped with the single 40mm. Since most of the LCS(L)s served on the radar picket stations and their major concern was enemy aircraft, a third twin 40mm gun would have been preferred by all of their commanding officers.

Radar on the LCS(L)s was insufficient to pick up all but low flying planes. Although it was useful for detecting suicide boats, the assignment of many LCS(L)s to the radar picket lines left them at a distinct disadvantage for the task. By the end of the first month, experiments were under way to install improved radar units on some of the LCS(L)s. However, by the time conclusions had been reached on their use, the war was nearly over. Had they been scheduled for radar improvements, they might have had new radar installed by the time of the planned invasion of Japan.

LCI(M)s were also in need of some changes. Constant firing of the mortars damaged the beds and support frameworks for the weapon. Numerous repairs had to be made on site, and the problem became so extreme that some mortar gunboat COs requested that welding equipment be a standard part of their assigned equipment.

Chapter 10

Screening the Fleet

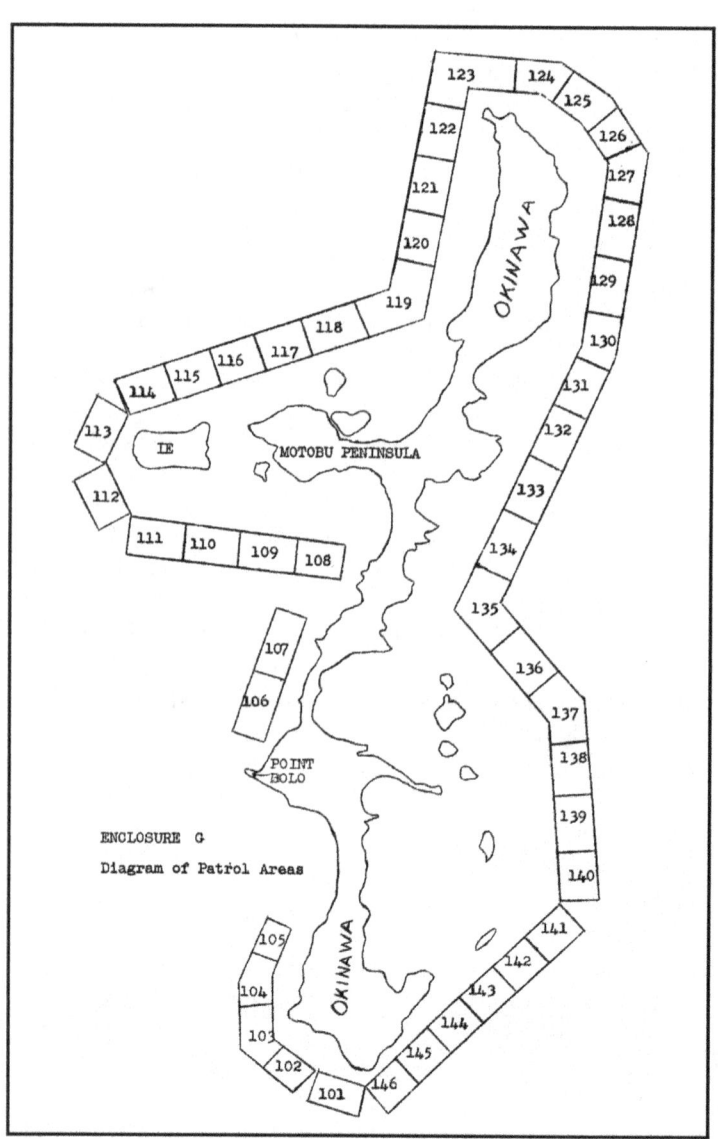

ENCLOSURE G
Diagram of Patrol Areas

Once the initial landings had been completed, the mundane tasks of patrolling, screening, and making smoke became the primary occupation of most of the gunboats. They were assigned to protect the ships in the anchorages. Anti-small craft patrol was usually described as "fly-catching," but the sailors soon named it "skunk patrol." However, they saw more action during air attacks. In the immediate waters around Okinawa, forty-six inner screening patrol stations had been designated. Each was approximately two miles long and one mile wide. They were designed to give maximum protection to the fleet and prevent attacks by suicide boats and the escape of the Japanese troops as the action

In order to provide security for American ships anchored at Hagushi and in Nakagusuku Bay, it was necessary to set up a ring of screening stations around the island. They were patrolled by LCS(L)s and LCI gunboats. Destroyers patrolled to seaward of the stations for additional support. Commander Task Unit 52.17.1 (Commander LCI Group 16) Serial 031, *Action Report, Anti Small Craft Screen, Okinawa, 1 April thru 8 April 1945*, 29 April 1945, Enclosure (G).

moved to the southern areas of Okinawa. They were numbered from 101 through 146. Screen number 101 was at the southernmost tip of Okinawa and the screen numbers ran in a clockwise pattern around the island, ending again at the southernmost tip with station 146, just to the east of station 101.

The anti–small craft gunboats patrolling the southeastern and southwestern areas were designated as TU 52.9.2 under Commander Michael Malanaphy on *LC(FF) 627*. TU 59.9.2 consisted of four task units of six LCI(G)s each. On 12 May the Task Unit was modified. At that point command shifted to Commander Eikel on *LC(FF) 627* who commanded six LCI(G) divisions of from five to six LCI(G)s each. From time to time, LCS(L)s, LCI(M)s, or LCI(L)s were used to supplement the LCI(G)s on a temporary basis.

On 9 April it became apparent that more protection from the suicide boats was needed in the Hagushi anchorage. LCS(L)s from TG 52.19, under the direct tactical command of CTU 32.19.3, were assigned to the task. Seven new stations were added in two lines, running approximately from east to west and were to the south and west of the anchorage. The new stations were designated as X2 through X8. An additional and unnumbered station was positioned near the grounded and destroyed hulk of *Longshaw* to prevent enemy boarding. As the fighting progressed southward, some of the inner screening stations were abandoned, particularly on the eastern and southeastern side of the island, including stations 135–142. By mid–April, these were no longer deemed necessary.

Suicide Boats

Two *Shinyo* Squadrons, Numbers 22 and 42, were assigned to the defense of Okinawa. They were based at Chinen and Yonabaru respectively. Both bases were in the southeast part of Okinawa, and these small vessels frequently attacked American ships in Nakagusuku Bay. In early attacks on the island, prior to its invasion, many of the boats were destroyed by air raids. By 1 April, only about fifty to sixty boats were operational. Other boats were stationed in the islands of Kerama Retto. Zamami Shima was home to the 1st Surface Raiding Squadron, while the 2nd Surface Raiding Squadron was based on Aka Shima. The 3rd Surface Raiding Squadron made its home base on Takashi Shima.

By comparison, the Imperial Japanese Army's suicide boats were more numerous. Assigned to the Okinawa area were eight suicide boat regiments, Numbers 1, 2, 3, 4, 26, 27, 28, and 29. Suicide Boat Regiments Numbers 1, 2, 3, and 4 were based on several islands of the Kerama Retto group.[1] Although they launched some attacks prior to 1 April, they were captured early in the campaign so that use of them was denied to the Japanese. Other units continued to attack American shipping where possible, but vigilant LCS(L) and LCI(G) gunboats, assigned to combat them, destroyed many. The effectiveness of the gunboats was evident in the fact that they destroyed seventy-one of the suicide boats between 1 April and 17 May 1945.

Fly-catching also involved patrolling the inshore waters to prevent the Japanese from mounting counter-landings behind American troops. Although barge traffic was not seen very much at Okinawa due to the pre-invasion bombardment and constant air attacks, it was still possible to infiltrate behind the American lines using all manner of small craft.

It was usual to begin "fly-catching" patrols around 1600 each day, and the gunboats were accompanied by destroyers and a cruiser which stood a bit farther off shore. If enemy small craft were spotted by the gunboats, they could call for assistance. This might take the form of additional gunfire, spotting the small boats using their searchlights, or firing star shells to illuminate the area. Vice Admiral Turner reported:

A Marine stands guard near a *Shinyo* found on Aka Jima, Kerama Retto. These *Shinyo* were hidden in caves and then transported to the water on trailers. The trailer can be seen under the nearest *Shinyo*. Official USMC photograph.

The effectiveness of the program is best illustrated by the fact that only four counter-landings were accomplished out of the many attempted, and on those four only a small portion of the enemy boats succeeded in getting through the patrol. Only one suicide type boat succeeded in reaching the transport area on each coast. "Fly-catcher" ships also performed the additional tasks of dusk and dawn harassment of NAHA, ITOMAN, and YONABARU airfields, to prevent enemy planes from taking off and landing.[2]

The rivers and streams on Okinawa leading to the bays and oceans provided excellent cover for the suicide boats. Along the small rivers numerous hiding places had been constructed. They were difficult to spot from the air, and at night the suicide boats were launched and sent out to attack American ships. Foliage along the shore provided cover for the boats as well. Large clumps of marsh grass made it difficult to spot the boats from seaward, however, gunboats frequently fired on suspected locations with positive results.

The first encounter by gunboats with a Japanese suicide boat at Okinawa came on 29 March 1945 when *LCI(G) 558* was attacked by a Japanese Army *Maru-re*. The *558* was patrolling station P-9 which was off the western coast of Okinawa. At 0300 a small boat was reported heading for the gunboat about 1,000 yards away. Lookouts had seen the boat although it had not been picked up on radar. The ship opened fire with her #1 and #5 40mm guns, forcing the approaching boat to alter course. It then made its final run on the bow of the gunboat. The gunboat's speed was only eight knots, but the *Maru-re* was doing at least twenty. *LCI(G) 558*'s starboard .50 caliber

The *Maru-re*, used by the Japanese Army, was easy to distinguish from the Japanese Navy's *Shinyo*. The presence of the racks behind the driver was the primary indicator. Two depth charges were mounted on the racks to be released next to an American ship. This captured *Maru-re* is shown being tested by American personnel on 9 April 1945, shortly after its capture at Kerama Retto. Official U.S. Navy photograph.

machine gun then took the boat under fire as the OOD ordered full left rudder and flank speed. The maneuver prevented the boat from successfully dropping its depth charges next to the ship. It struck a glancing blow and headed aft. As it veered away it was taken under fire by the #7 and #2 20mm guns, which scored a number of hits on it. The suicide boat disappeared from sight about fifty yards behind the gunboat and its depth charges went off as it sank, shaking the gunboat, but not causing any damage. At 0409 another small boat was sighted at a range of 1,100 yards and the gunboat turned to engage it, but it fled the area. Twenty minutes later a third suicide boat was spotted at a distance of 1,400 yards, and the *558* fired some 40mm rounds in its direction. The *Maru-re* dropped its depth charges and fled. What was most alarming for the gunboat's crew was that none of the small suicide boats had registered on the ship's radar.[3] Nearby, *LCI(G) 452* spotted its first *Maru-re* at 0330 and drove it off with automatic weapons fire.

LCI(R) 646 had been held in reserve during the landings at Kerama Retto and was on patrol off Tokashiki Shima. At sunrise, the gunboat was about to head back to her anchorage when she spotted three small boats and fired a shot across the bow of one. It failed to respond and the gunboat opened up with her 40mm guns. One turned toward her to make a run and was destroyed by 40mm and 20mm fire. She gave chase to the other two boats which had headed toward shore. A nearby destroyer also took them under fire and they disappeared from sight, apparently sunk. A nearby APD sent men ashore to search for survivors and took two men prisoner.[4]

The first gunboat to fall victim to the suicide boats at Okinawa was *LCI(G) 82*. On 3 April

Japanese suicide boats were well-hidden to prevent discovery and destruction. This is a typical boat revetment discovered along the banks of the Bisha River at Okinawa. COMPHIBSPAC Serial 01400, *Photographic Report—Okinawa Operation L-Day 1 April 1945,* Volume 3 of 3 Volumes, 25 July 1945.

1945, she was operating as a part of Gunboat Division Six, patrolling station 137 on the eastern coast of Okinawa as part of the inner screen. *LCI(G) 347* patrolled a station to her south and *LCI(G) 79* was on patrol to her north. *Tracy DM 19* was further offshore to provide heavier firepower for the three gunboats should the need arise.

Late in the evening, about 2030, ships to her south fired on a plane which subsequently crashed into the water near her. No one saw the plane crash but they heard the engine until it hit the water. A search of the area revealed that the plane was still floating in the water, and the gunboat circled it to investigate. It proved to be a Kate torpedo plane and the gunboat fired about fifty rounds of 20mm into it and sank it. Shortly thereafter they sighted a life raft with three Japanese aboard. As they approached the raft, it was obvious that one of the men had a grenade, and the three were killed by .30 caliber machine gun and small arms fire from the gunboat. Two bodies were picked up and searched for anything of intelligence value before being returned to the sea.

At 0125 the following morning, lookouts on *LCI(G) 82* spotted a *Maru-re* making a run on the ship and took it under fire. They were not able to stop it. Only the gunner manning the .30 caliber machine gun on the conning tower managed to get off some shots. The 40mm and 20mm guns were unable to fire due to mechanical and personnel problems. The boat swerved

The Japanese made every attempt to hide their suicide boats from American aircraft and gunboats. This Japanese Navy *Shinyo*, hidden in a cave on Tokashiki Shima in the Kerama Retto Islands, was part of the 3rd Surface Raiding Battalion. COMPHIBSPAC Serial 01400, *Photographic Report—Okinawa Operation L-Day 1 April 1945,* Volume 3 of 3 Volumes, July 25, 1945.

right against the ship and dropped its depth charges. In his action report her Commanding Officer, Lieutenant (jg) Theodore Arnow, described what happened:

> The boat approached rapidly, turned, and crashed into the ship on the port side just forward of the conning tower. A double explosion resulted, tearing a large hole in the side of the ship. This opening covered most of number two compartment (which was used as a petty officer's sleeping quarters) and extended into number three compartment (which was used for crew's sleeping quarters). The explosion knocked out all the ship's lights and the ship immediately heeled to starboard. Number two and three compartments started to fill with water and within five minutes of the attack flames were shooting out of number two compartment, through the hatch and through holes in the deck. A hose was rigged but there was no water pressure.... The life rafts were launched and filled with the wounded. The fire enveloped the forward section of the ship and started to spread aft. Ammunition began to explode forward and the ship was abandoned approximately fifteen minutes after the attack.[5]

With his men accounted for and safely on *Tracy* and *LCI(G) 347,* the commanding officer donned oxygen breathing equipment and re-boarded his ship. He found her to be a smoldering wreck. The blast had torn a hole on her port side that was about twenty feet long and she was listing thirty-five degrees to starboard. "The ship was almost completely split in half forward of the conning tower and the deck over number two compartment was completely shattered."[6]

Arnow departed knowing that nothing could be done to save her. *LCI(G) 725* managed to get a line on the *82* but had a difficult time keeping her off the reef, as she only had one engine operational herself. Finally the salvage vessel *Gear ARS 34* arrived and took over the tow, but the swells proved too much for the hulk. At 1415 she broke in two, rolled over, and went under. She was the first gunboat victim of a suicide boat at Okinawa. Her casualties were one dead and nine wounded.

Between 2 and 3 April, *LCI(G)s 465, 559,* and *751* experienced air attacks at screening stations 116 and 117. Civilians attempting to escape from the fighting frequently took to the sea. On 4 April *LCI(G) 559* spotted a small boat and went to investigate. It contained nine civilians, eight men and one woman. They were taken prisoner and their boat was destroyed. The prisoners were transferred to *Purdy DD 734*. One could never be sure of the true status of such people. It would not be unusual for Japanese soldiers to hide among civilians to cause damage or just to escape.

Although the ships were on screen to thwart the suicide boat attacks, other targets soon came to their attention. On 14 April at 1900, *LCI(G) 442*'s lookouts spotted enemy movement ashore just north of Naha and moved in to attack the enemy. Her guns hit a number of trucks accompanied by troops moving along a shore road. Large explosions shook the area as a number of the trucks erupted in balls of fire.[7]

Overnight from 15 to 16 April, *LCI(G) 659* had her first experience with suicide boats. She was on patrol off the southwestern coast of Okinawa near the town of Naha when a cruiser spotted a suicide boat and took it under fire at 2335. As the boat attempted its escape from the cruiser, it came between it and the gunboat. The cruiser immediately ceased fire. As the suicide boat came within 300 yards, the *659* opened fire. The pilot of the boat, realizing that he could not escape, changed course and made a run on the gunboat. It concentrated its guns on the approaching craft, setting the suicide boat afire with its 20mm and .50 caliber guns, causing it to explode and sink. It was believed that the boat had a crew of two but no bodies were found. A few hours later, at 0218, the gunboat spotted another suicide boat at a distance of 250 yards and took it under fire. It took evasive action to escape the illumination of the ship's spotlight, but it disappeared from sight, apparently sunk by the ship's gunfire. Lieutenant (jg) Thomas A. Cooke CO of *LCI(G) 659*, in his action report for the events, noted the tactics of the suicide boats. He wrote: "The small boat used by the enemy in this action was propelled by an inboard engine which sounded not unlike that of an old Chevrolet. It makes considerable noise and provides a method of detecting the approach of the boat if it is not otherwise already observed, being heard distinctly at 20 yards."[8] He further noted that because of the noisy engine he felt that the boats traveled at a slow speed until the target vessel was identified, then switched to a high speed run. This was an accurate assessment, as the boats usually proceeded at a slow pace to avoid detection and to save fuel. In addition to the noise from the engine, the wake left by the boats was visible when they were at high speed.

While on screening duty, the gunboats never knew what they might encounter. On 18 April at 0130, *LCI(G) 754* was on patrol station 104 when her lookouts sighted a small blinker light off Naha. Marine Second Lieutenant Charles A. Engman of VMF 543 had been flying off the field at Kadena and had run into engine problems. He made a water landing in the area and had been adrift in his life raft for approximately four hours. The crew fished him out of the water and transported him to *El Dorado AGC-11* which returned him to his squadron.

Although suicide boats were frequently encountered, other means of water-born attack were used by the Japanese. At 0128 on 23 April, *LCI(G)s 802* and *803* were patrolling off Ie Shima when they encountered several rafts with Japanese soldiers on board. The *803* captured one raft and took aboard seven prisoners. After they were secured, the gunboat illuminated the raft with its searchlight and found that it had about twenty hand grenades on board. At that point the order was given to the ships to fire on any rafts and not take prisoners. A short while later, *LCI(G) 802* sighted a four by eight foot raft with seven Japanese soldiers aboard at a distance of one hundred yards, and a slightly smaller raft about fifty yards off the ship. Hand grenades were wired together on the rafts in an attempt to cause damage to the ships and they were taken under fire. All of the Japanese were killed and the rafts sunk. At 0212 another four by eight foot raft was spotted and taken under fire. The six Japanese on board were killed by gunfire, three of whom were swimming toward the ship to throw hand grenades.

The events of 27 April 1945 involving the *LCI(R) 763*'s experience with a suicide boat seemed to indicate that the Japanese were beginning to run out of their standard boat types and were pressing other types of craft into service that might be useful as suicide boats. A large number of both Army and Navy suicide boats had been captured by that date, and their construction and design was well-known. However, the boat used to attack *LCI(R) 763* that evening had a different configuration. Apparently, it had completed an attack on a nearby destroyer. Since that was the case, it was probably an Army *Maru-re* with depth charges on the stern, however, no mounting racks for the depth charges were seen:

> The opinions of several men who saw the small boat agree on the following description (refer encl. (A): the boat was approximately 18 feet in length, 6 feet in width, and 2 feet of freeboard; it was gray in color with a red disk and white numbers painted on the side; it had a small superstructure forward of midships; one man was located forward and one aft in a cockpit located abaft the superstructure; the engines sounded powerful and owing to the strong odor of gasoline after its sinking, it probably used such fuel.[9]

The *763*, having been alerted to the presence of the boat, spotted it about 0500 and closed on it. Some maneuvering and evasive action was taken by the suicide boat and, at one point, it attempted to crash into the stern of the LCI(R). The gunboat took evasive action and fired on it with Thompson machine guns and other small arms. It was finally sunk by 20mm fire. The two man crew managed to escape before the boat sank and were killed by small arms fire. The body of one was taken aboard.

April 28 proved to be an active date for the gunboat-suicide boat battles. The suicide boat encounters began at 0013. *LCI(G) 347* was off the southern coast of Okinawa. She had escaped an air attack only fifty-five minutes before when her lookouts spotted the wake of a suicide boat off her port side. She took it under fire with her #2 40mm gun and her two port side .50 caliber machine guns. The boat went dead in the water about thirty yards off the ship's port bow. They fired on it again, causing it to explode. The concussion from the explosion temporarily knocked out the ship's power but it was quickly restored.

A short while later at 0227, in Nakagusuku Wan off China Saki, a *Maru-re* managed to sneak in close to *LCS(L) 37* and drop its depth charges alongside the port side of the ship. The

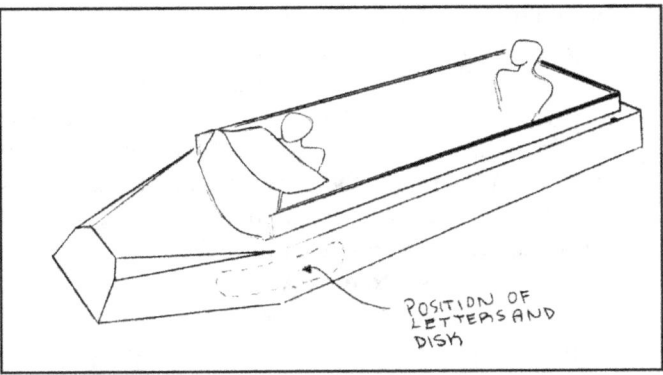

As the battle for Okinawa wore on and the bulk of the available suicide boats were destroyed, the Japanese employed whatever was available in order to complete their missions against American shipping. The sketch above is of an eighteen foot boat with an approximate six foot beam. That was used in an attack on the *LCI(R) 763* on 27 April 1945. Reports indicate that it was painted grey with a red disk and white numbers on the side. *USS LCI(R) 763* Serial 24, *Action Report—27 April 1945*, 27 April 1945, Enclosure (A).

gunboat immediately took it under fire and sank it. Several of her crew were injured, her engines were knocked out, and her rudder was jammed. She was towed back to safety by *LCS(L) 38*. *LCI(R) 648* picked up one of her men who had been blown overboard by the explosion. After a complete inspection it was found that her main engines were beyond repair. In a message to his commanding officers Commander L. M. Bailliere, CTU 52.9.4 Southern Support Gunboats, warned about the dangers in the Nakagusuku Bay area: "THIS AREA IS INFESTED WITH SUICIDE BOATS. KNOCK OUT EVERYTHING THAT LOOKS AS THOUGH IT MAY CONCEAL ANY SMALL BOATS. BE AGGRESSIVE."[10]

That same evening, *LCS(L) 84* was on "skunk patrol" in the Hagushi anchorage. During the night two suicide boats appeared, probably coming from hidden bases in the Bisha Gawa (Bisha River). Although the two boats were eventually sunk, it was not by any of the ship's guns. The two had managed to get so close that the LCS(L)s guns could not depress sufficiently to hit them. Men lined the rails of the gunboat and hit the suicide boats with fire from carbines and rifles. One sank but the other exploded. Part of the problem in detecting the suicide boats was that the smoke in the anchorage made it hard to see them. In the case of the two boats that approached *LCS(L) 84*, it was only when they were very close that the crew was able to spot them.

LCS(L) 84 was a part of Group 11 under Lieutenant Commander Clifford E. Montgomery. Group 11 was a part of Flotilla 4 under the command of Captain Neill Phillips. When he learned of the problem with the suicide boats he took action. After consultation with Montgomery, he sent for Lieutenant (jg) Ray Perkins who was serving on the *84*. Perkins had known Captain Phillips from serving on his staff at the ATB Solomons. Phillips gave him the following order:

> Tomorrow morning at 0700 hours an M-boat will come alongside the "84." You are to get aboard and go into the beach. There you are to find someone who can issue you 50 fifty-caliber, air-cooled machine guns. Put them in the M-boat and bring them back here to the "84." Send me a signal when you get back and I will give you instructions for issuing them to our ships.[11]

The following morning the M-boat arrived as ordered and Perkins headed for shore. A small mountain of supplies lay in front of him, but the possibility of finding the guns was remote, as many of the boxes were not labeled. To make matters worse, there was no one around to help him find them. Perkins finally located a Marine Major at the side of the supply dump standing next to a 4 × 4 truck. He asked the Major for assistance but, after careful consideration, the Major made a counter-offer. He would get the needed machine guns for Perkins, but Perkins would have to help him drive to the northern end of the island to deliver mail since his driver had been shot the day before. With little choice in the matter, Perkins agreed and took the wheel as the Major manned the machine gun on top of the vehicle.

After a bumpy ride over a rough trail punctuated with potholes, the truck arrived at its destination. The Major made his delivery, picked up outgoing mail, and obtained some C-rations for the two of them. After a quick meal they were on their way back to Hagushi. When they arrived at the supply dump, the Major located the .50 caliber machine guns. They were in boxes about a foot square and five feet long. As the Major watched, Perkins loaded fifty of the unmarked boxes into the rear of the truck. The Major then drove him back to the beach.

The M-boat was waiting off shore and Perkins waved to the Coxswain to come in. Fortunately, the Coxswain had brought along a seaman to assist Perkins in loading the guns on the boat. The Coxswain had to stay at the wheel to keep the boat from broaching in the surf. Perkins thanked the Major for his help, whereupon the Major left.

Once alongside *LCS(L) 84*, the crew unloaded the M-boat and placed the gun boxes on the deck. Lieutenant Commander Montgomery was at the rail and informed Perkins that Captain Phillips wanted to speak to him immediately. Phillips wanted to know why the task took so long. After listening to Perkins' explanation, he ordered him to open each of the boxes and record the serial numbers of the guns. During the following two days each of the LCS(L)s of Flotilla Four came alongside the *84* and each was given two of the guns. In this manner they would be better-prepared to combat the suicide boats. The issuing of the guns began at 0800 the following day. The Flotilla Four LCS(L)s had arrived at Okinawa with three .50 caliber guns and now mounted five.

With no space below to work on the guns, the crew had to open all of the boxes on deck, record the numbers on the outside of the boxes, and then repack them. The guns were distributed on schedule, official records kept, and the LCS(L) in Flotilla Four had additional firepower with which to combat the suicide boats.[12]

A few days went by and, on 1 May, the *84* encountered a dugout canoe with four Japanese on board. They kept their guns trained on the dugout and persuaded one of the Japanese to take his clothes off and swim to the ship. Once he was taken into custody, the others surrendered. The dugout was hoisted on board and destroyed with an axe and the four prisoners transferred to a prison ship.

On 3 May at 0004, *LCI(R) 708* was on patrol near Kutaka Island when she picked up two blips on her radar. She headed in their direction to cut them off and prevent them from escaping behind the island. By 0200 she had one in sight and requested illumination from *Wichita CA 45* which was nearby. Star shells lit up the night and the gunboat opened up with all of her automatic weapons, but the suicide boat ducked behind the reefs. As she moved in to fire on the suicide boat, her 40mm gun jammed and she was then fired upon by a gun on the island. Fortunately it missed. The suicide boat made full speed to the north where it fell victim to an LCS(L). The second suicide boat had avoided the rocket gunboat and tried to sneak by astern of her, only to be spotted and destroyed by another LCS(L). Gunners on *Wichita*, eager to assist, lit up the entire area with star shells. The light blinded the gunners and they were unable to spot the guns on the island.

LCS(L) 40 encountered an enemy swimmer at 0608 on 4 May. The gunboat was on patrol with others in Nakagusuku Wan. It had destroyed a suicide boat earlier in the morning and a second had been sunk by her fire and fire from *LCS(L) 24*. The swimmer was spotted 600 yards off Chinen Misaki. When the gunboat approached him and tried to pick him up, he took a hand grenade out of his shirt and tried to throw it at the crew. Ever alert for treachery, the crew killed him with small arms fire before he could throw the grenade. They reported that the man had been in full uniform with a life jacket but no helmet. As they approached him he had requested help in English, but it was only a ruse.

A half hour later a second swimmer was spotted 1,600 yards east of Yonabaru. Having experienced the treachery of the first swimmer, they killed him with small arms fire from a distance of 300 yards. The following day, at 1412, the ship fired on small boats beached in Yonabaru Wan and destroyed them. Several days later, at 0025 on 13 May, the gunboat and *LC(FF) 536* approached a small boat off Chinen Misaki. The men on board capsized it and dove in the water. They were eventually found and dispatched with 20mm and 40mm gunfire.

The ship and its group continued on small craft patrol in Nakagusuka Wan for the remainder of the month. They fired on numerous targets on the beaches which they suspected concealed suicide boat positions. They also captured a half dozen more swimmers.

Task Unit 52.19.3, consisting of *LCS(L)s 19, 53, 82, 83, 84, 86,* and *111*, were on anti–small craft patrol on a line from east to west of the Hagushi beaches during the evening of 12–13 May. The anchorage at Hagushi was a prime target for the suicide boats, and continual vigilance was necessary to keep them from getting into the transport area. About 2330 on the 12th, the line was approached by seven suicide boats. The ships requested star shell illumination and searchlight illumination from nearby larger ships. However, the combination of smoke in the anchorage and the light from the star shells made visibility difficult. Finally, *LCS(L) 82* spotted one suicide boat dead in the water about seventy-five yards from her starboard bow. Her commanding officer ordered flank speed and left hard rudder. This combination caused the ship to heel and made it easier for the guns to fire on the suicide boat. They took the boat under fire and it headed for the ship. The flash from the gunboat's 40mm guns temporarily blinded the gunners and they lost track of the suicide boat in the dark, the problem compounded by smoke from the anchorage and also from her own guns. The suicide boat passed only fifteen feet from the bow, turned out to starboard, and then headed back directly toward the starboard quarter of the ship. It passed behind the ship, all the while under fire from the gunboat's aft 20mm and 40mm guns. In the confusion, three men went over the side and had to be rescued. It was next spotted at a range of 800 yards and taken under fire. The suicide boat maneuvered to avoid the gunfire but eventually was hit and sunk.

Reports on the incidents were sent up the chain of command with appropriate recommendations. Based on the action reports, Lieutenant Commander E. C. Thomas, CTU 52.19.3, noted the need for larger searchlights on the gunboats as they sought to find and destroy the suicide boats. In his first endorsement to the action report of *LCS(L) 19* he stated:

> It is noted that an arc light is of great assistance in carrying out anti small craft patrol at night. This is illustrated in this action as evidenced by the fact that it was possible to pick up the first suicide boat by means of the DM25's arc light at considerably greater range than the second boat was picked up by the blinker light of the LCS(L) #19. In view of this, it is recommended that a 24" arc light be installed on all LCS(L)'s.[13]

The close proximity of the ship to the suicide boat had allowed the crew to get a good look at the boat. They described it as "about twenty feet long, with a large, open cockpit in which four (4) men sat upright. It lay low in the water, was muddy brown topsides, and made speed estimated during the chase at about fifteen (15) knots."[14] Once again, the Japanese had pressed into service a non-standard boat for use in the suicide attacks. Whether or not this was a *Shinyo* or *Maru-re* was not clear, but the method of attack and the absence of depth charges on the stern led observers to believe it was a Navy *Shinyo*.

In mid–May, reports came in about suspected suicide boat locations on the beaches along the southwest shore of Kutaka Shima in Nagagusuku Wan, and on 15 May *LCS(L) 113* was ordered to investigate. Hidden in the foliage along the shore of the beach were several small boats concealed in the palmetto bushes, and the ship took them under fire, destroying three. Enemy troops were seen attempting to move a fourth boat to cover and were taken under fire. There was no further movement, and it was not clear if the troops had moved their boat to safety or if they were killed by gunfire. The search took place from 0800 to 1135.

The Japanese had committed a variety of weapons to combat the Americans at Okinawa. Kamikaze aircraft, suicide boats, flying bombs, and suicide swimmers had been encountered, along with conventional air attacks. Also committed to the struggle were submarines, many of the midget variety. They were assumed to be in the Okinawa area, an assumption that was confirmed on 21 May.

LCS(L) 68 spotted two wakes at 2125 on 21 May. She turned to run parallel to the wakes and requested illumination from *Bobolink AM 20*. She lost sight of the wake at 2148, and shortly thereafter, sighted three wakes crossing her fantail. She identified them as three midget submarines. She turned hard to starboard and took them under fire. *LCS(L)s 69, 93,* and *95* were called to the scene and the cruiser *Vincennes CL 64* was also alerted. The subs submerged, and reappeared a short while later near *LCS(L) 124*, and then disappeared again. No further sightings were made in the area, and it appeared that the midget subs had withdrawn. *Riddle DE 185* remained in the area, depth charges ready to launch if the subs returned.[15]

By June, most of the suicide boats had been destroyed. Sporadic attacks by remnants of the suicide boat forces were undertaken using whatever means they could to get out to the American ships. Some were in dugouts, others on rafts, and still others swam out only to be picked off by gunboat fire. Remaining members of the suicide boat units either joined Army units or made a last ditch effort to cause problems for the fleet.

In many cases the Japanese, having been compressed into a small area in the southern part of Okinawa, made attempts to swim off the main island to smaller islands offshore. On 3 June at 0025 *LCI(G) 751*, patrolling on station 141, reported several capsized boats in her area with about twenty to twenty-five swimmers in the water. *LCI(G) 558* joined her in taking prisoners. Between the two gunboats six prisoners were taken, with the others either drowning, committing suicide, or being killed. The boats were found to contain rifles, grenades, and provisions for the men. Some of the captured men had goggles and grenades on them.[16]

Task Unit 32.19.12, consisting of *LCS(L)s 61, 62, 65, 81, 82*, and *90*, under the command of Lieutenant Commander B. D. Voegelin on board *LC(FF) 786*, patrolled in Nakagusuku Wan on 5 June. At 2230 *LCS(L) 62* made radar contact with a suspected suicide boat at 800 yards. Star shells from nearby ships were requested, and the illumination from them revealed a twenty foot dugout canoe with six enemy combatants aboard. They were dressed in breech cloths and two had goggles. A tarpaulin in the boat covered what appeared to be a substantial cargo. At 2245 the gunboat was ordered to take the men prisoner, but their commands via bullhorn went unheeded. Seeing no alternative, the gunboat took the dugout under fire, at which time the six men went overboard. The gunboat secured its larger guns and relied on small arms fire from the crew to dispatch the men in the water. Five were killed and the sixth was persuaded to surrender after .50 caliber machine gun fire splashed all around him. He was taken aboard at 1130 and was about to be tied up when he jumped overboard and swam back to the dugout. His refusal to return to the ship made it impossible to pick him up, and the canoe and man were run over by the gunboat which dropped an anti-tank mine for good measure. This was not successful and the man appeared to be unhurt. *LCS(L) 81*, which had joined in the action, ran him over. No trace of him was found after that. Subsequent inspection of the remains of the dugout revealed Navy uniforms and equipment leading to the assumption that they were Navy personnel attempting to escape from Okinawa.

Lieutenant Commander R. S. Rickabaugh, CO of Task Unit 51.17.1, determined that certain tactics against the suicide boats were more effective than others. The ships under his command, *LCI(G)s 452, 467, 558, 559, 560*, and *751* had ample experience with the suicide boats during the first week of the Okinawa campaign. He felt that the .50 caliber machine gun was the most effective weapon to be employed. In his action report for the task unit dated 29 April, he stated that:

> A 50 caliber gun was the most effective weapon used against the suicide boat. Twice the oncoming boat was driven from his intended course by the steady stream of 50 caliber fire and when the boat finally hit the side of the ship it was a glancing blow which apparently did not release the depth charges and it was necessary to release them by hand inasmuch as the explosion of the charge did not occur until about 50 yards astern of the ship.
>
> The large volume of fire possible and the ability to depress the 50 caliber gun well below the horizontal and along the side of the ship provides protection which is not available from any other type gun on board and its installation on board all LCI(G)s is strongly recommended with two mounts on the bow, two on the gun deck just forward of the 20MM mounts, and two on the fantail.[17]

Rickabaugh further noted that the use of tracer rounds and sealed beam searchlights at night had the effect of momentarily blinding the crew and obscuring the target. Tracer rounds from the 40mm guns were particularly bright. On hazy or foggy nights, the searchlights might be reflected by the haze and cause difficulties in seeing the target. Rickabaugh concluded that the ships were better off not using the lights at all.

On a number of occasions, observers on the gunboats remarked that the suicide boats did not seem particularly aggressive. Although never proven, it was suspected that when enemy troop movements were undertaken at night, a standard practice would be to send a couple of suicide boats out into the bay. This would detract the gunboats from discovering and firing on enemy troops ashore. Chasing after the suicide boats would put them farther out to sea or out of positions from which they could fire on enemy troop movements. In his *Action Report of Task Unit 51.2.9 From 25 March 1945 to 15 May 1945*, Lieutenant Commander James F. McFadden, who served as Commander of LCI(G) Group Seven, noted:

> Except for the boat which suicided into LCI(G) 82, the enemy boats were not aggressive. This lends credence to the theory that contacts made on the western side of Okinawa were deliberately brought about by the enemy as a diversion to keep our gunboats and illumination away from points close-inshore where movements of troops along the coast could be accomplished. There is no information on hand now, however, which substantiates this theory. Without this theory, the lack of aggressiveness by the so called suicide boats is difficult to explain. On two occasions the LCI(G) 725 could have been hit by suiciders had they really been bent on their mission.[18]

Japanese soldiers continued their efforts to escape the carnage ashore. They usually ran afoul of the gunboats on the inner screen. Early in the morning of 1 June, a Japanese Army sergeant took a small native boat and attempted to escape by sea. He was soon picked up by *LCI(G) 558*. Two days later, on 3 June, twenty to twenty-five Japanese attempted to escape at screening station 142. They were intercepted by *LCI(G)s 558* and *751*. Six of the enemy were captured and taken on board the gunboats; the others were killed trying to escape.[19]

The Air Attacks

At Okinawa, the Japanese committed large numbers of aircraft to conventional and kamikaze missions. These attacks came in numbers not previously experienced by the American forces and they were hard put to combat them. Numerous ships were attacked and many were hit by the kamikazes but, in the end, the American Navy prevailed. It is doubtful that any of the gunboats operating around Okinawa did not have the opportunity to fire on enemy aircraft. Many of the engagements were of a minor nature, with gunboats firing on and driving off attacking aircraft. Ships were not usually alone, and an enemy airplane flying near any one was sure to draw fire from several. The list of "sure" kills paled in comparison the list of aircraft reported as shot down by the combined fire of several ships. An exhaustive list could be compiled but would seem greatly repetitious. The incidents detailed below are representative of the anti-aircraft action experienced by the screening ships.

LCI(R) 1078 was patrolling the anti-aircraft screen about ten miles from Aguni Shima during the evening of 1-2 April. During the day she had participated in a fire assignment covering the initial invasion at Hagushi. At 0540 on 2 April she went to general quarters with the report of enemy aircraft in the area. A Hamp had targeted a minesweeper operating near her, which nearly ran her over as it maneuvered to escape the air attack. Her gunners observed the Hamp making its run on the minesweeper and took it under fire as it passed near the gunboat at a height of only sixty-five feet off the water. Shells from one of her 20mm guns hit the plane in the cockpit area at a distance of one hundred yards. It turned into the gunboat in an attempted suicide run and its engine was hit by additional 20mm fire, causing it to crash into the sea only fifty yards off the ship's port beam. It was a close call for the gunboat and the minesweeper, but both escaped the attack with no damage.[20]

From 1 to 3 April, *LCI(G)s 465* and *568* were on patrol at screening stations 117 and 116 respectively, just to the north of Motobu Peninsula. At 1836 on 2 April, they observed an F6F Hellcat shot down three miles behind them. They changed course and headed toward the crash site with the hope of rescuing the downed pilot. A Japanese fighter plane, either a Zeke or Oscar, made a run on the ships and was shot down off the port beam of *465*. Within minutes another plane dove on and strafed the *568*. It was also shot down by the combined fire of the two gunboats. However, the *568* had sustained wounded men and headed for *Wilson DD 408*, which was nearby. The destroyer took her wounded aboard and brought them to a hospital ship. *LCI(G) 568* had to head back to Kerama Retto for repairs and *465* continued on patrol. She was joined by *LC(FF) 627* which then accompanied her on patrols.

The following morning, at 0400, the two ships were approached by another enemy plane. Fire from the *465* set her ablaze and *LC(FF) 627* finished her off. The plane crashed near *LC(FF) 627* in a great ball of fire. At mid-day, *LCI(G) 559* replaced *LC(FF) 627*. Later that day, at 1820, the ships were approached by another enemy fighter which dove on *LCI(G) 465*. The plane was hit by 20mm and .50 caliber gunfire and crashed fifty feet off the gunboat's port beam. It was surmised that the pilot had been killed by the gunfire and lost control of the plane, causing it to pass over the ship prior to crashing. Disturbing to the CO of *LCI(G) 465* was that both her bow 40mm and starboard 40mm had jammed along with her aft port 20mm gun. This seriously reduced her firepower to the point where she had to return to Kerama Retto for repairs.[21]

The first of the *Kikusui* raids began on 6 April and, although a number of the enemy aircraft fell victim to the radar picket ships and the combat air patrols, many still made it through to the anchorage at Hagushi. Patrolling near some LSTs anchored south of Zampa Misaki off Black Beach, were *LCI(R)s 651* and *1029*. Two Vals were seen in the area lining up for their runs on the LSTs. Both were shot down by the combined fire of the two rocket ships.

On 8 April, *LCI(G) 567* was on anti–small boat patrol north of Ie Shima when she came under attack by a Val at 1835. The enemy plane was spotted at a distance of 3,000 yards off the port beam and heading past the ship. It turned in toward her and made a run. Lieutenant K. C. Flory, the CO, gave the order to turn the ship in order to take the aircraft on its beam and allow both forward and aft 40mm guns to fire. Gunfire from the smaller guns, 20mm and .50 caliber, was withheld until the plane came into range at about 1,000 yards. The Val was hit by a number of rounds from the ship but managed to pass by, bank to its left, and dive on the starboard quarter of the gunboat. The 20mm and .50 caliber guns hit the plane's greenhouse and killed the pilot. The kamikaze's wing hit the water twenty yards off the ship and it crashed only a few yards from the bow. A huge column of water went into the air and the ship was covered with pieces of the plane and other debris. The hard turn to port had saved the ship from a sure disaster.

The following day, 10 April, another Val attacked the ship at 0700 in the same area. The attack was sudden and the ship was not able to effectively fire on it. It passed over the fantail of *LCI(G) 567*, turned hard to its port, and crashed in the water only twenty yards off the port bow. The bomb carried by the plane exploded but the gunboat was not damaged. It was almost a repeat of the previous day's action and once again, the hard turn to port had saved her.

Landing on the stern of the ship was a mascot doll and its letter, which was retrieved by the ship's crew.[22] Mascot dolls were frequently carried by kamikaze pilots and a few were recovered after the crash of a kamikaze. The letter, written by Japanese schoolgirl Tsuko Miwachi, read:

> Even the hearing of this name arouses a deep emotion. Of the acts of the American and British devils, attacking and surrounding on all sides our Army, poor in material resources at this time of fierce decision in the war. We are raging at the unspeakable destruction. We also as students and laborers give help to the men. With a clear mind, daily to be able to rush forth to the destruction of the American ... is happiness. Of the spirit of the SPECIAL ATTACK FORCE, not stopping till it strikes! In this is the thought of the Gods I believe. I believe it is the lofty state of mind which will make an eternal future of great righteousness for the Emperor's sake. Ah, this time, thinking, "if I

were only a boy." I grow more envious; when I think of making a mascot to send to the men of the SPECIAL ATTACK FORCE I am filled with a great happiness. With this mascot the fierce spirit which will crumble the enemy ships into small pieces boils passionately, positively attack! Can you bear defeat? The foolish rascals of America and Britain! I am in a mood to shout these things aloud. Since I made the "mascot" in this spirit, it is doubtless unskillful, but please sink the enemy ships together with the "mascot." This is my greatest request.

Soon the mascot will take off gaily with the SPECIAL ATTACK FORCE. What will this be but the greatest happiness? Though I myself am not in the attack, my spirit will be serving as a member of the SPECIAL ATTACK FORCE.

Be of good health. I pray for great war results.[23]

The strain caused by the suicide boats and planes was beginning to tell on the crews of the gunboats. Lieutenant K. C. Flory reported:

Suicide attacks are hard on morale because of the suddenness with which they develop, (Requiring constant condition one or two watches and intense air-look-out alertness when on outlying patrol), and because of the apparent impossibility of stopping the planes. The plain fact that in a period of two weeks (in our flotilla alone) the Nips paid around fifteen planes in order to get one mast, a 20mm gun, and two men, should be widely publicized, and if possible gunboats patrolling popular "suicide resorts" during the day should be relieved of Q-boat patrol occasionally during the night, since standing a tight condition two watch both day and night is in itself wearing on the nerves.[24]

Also included in Flory's recommendations was the addition of a half-dozen twin .50 caliber guns to amplify close-in fire support.

LCI(G) 407 was struck by a kamikaze on 16 April while on patrol at station 136 on the eastern side of Okinawa. At about 0930, her lookouts sighted a Val flying low over the island of Taka Hanare. Its southeasterly flight path seemed to be taking it away from the ship which was heading directly north. However, the plane circled back and picked up altitude. The Val turned and flew a parallel course off the starboard quarter of the ship, and as it approached a position off the starboard beam of the gunboat, it banked and headed directly toward the ship. It was hit by a number of 40mm shells but kept coming. It crashed into the starboard ramp near the forecastle. Fortunately there was no explosion on board the ship. Apparently the bomb carried by the aircraft exploded harmlessly in the water. One man received a cut over his eye, but the gun tub shielded the others from any shrapnel from the bomb's explosion and the impact of the plane. As a result of the plane's impact, there was a four foot hole in the hull below the starboard ramp, along with some attendant damage to bulkheads and wiring in the area. "Most of the body of the pilot was found in the boatswain's locker. It had dropped there after being thrown from the plane through the forecastle hatch."[25]

The gunboat was once again under attack on 27 April when she was patrolling on station 104 just west of Naha. As she headed north in her patrol area during the night, she spotted a Kate heading south on her starboard bow. It turned in and made a run on her but was hit by a number of her 20mm shells as it passed over the ship's stern. It crashed off her starboard quarter.

LCI(R) 770 was on patrol in the Kerama Retto islands when she came under attack on 28 April. She was anchored and engaged in making smoke to cover the various ships in the area between Hokaji Shima and Tokashiki Shima. At 0051 a Val came out of the south and made a run on her. It dropped a bomb which glanced off the ship and exploded in the water nearby. Some minor damage to the ship occurred but there was no major damage; it had been a close call.

May was a busy time for Mortar Support Division Six under Lieutenant H. M. Mattson, which consisted of *LCI(M)s 801* to *806* inclusive. Their assignment during May was to patrol the south side of Ie Shima during the day, screening ships against air attacks, and escorting cargo ships to the Hagushi anchorage. At night they made smoke for the ships in the area.

On 6 May, at 0830, an incoming Dinah made its attack on the anchorage with the assembled

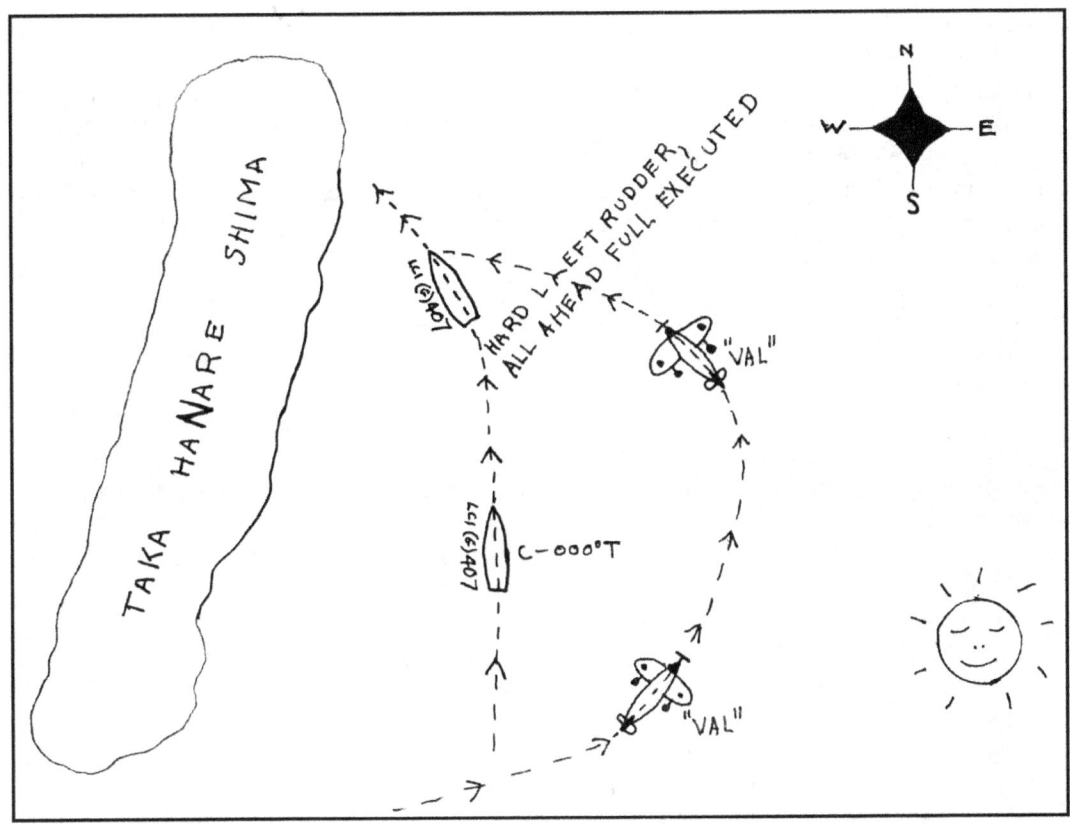

LCI(G) 407 narrowly escaped serious damage when she was crashed by a Val on 16 April 1945 at Okinawa. She was screening the eastern side of Okinawa near Taka Hanare Island when she came under attack. *USS LCI(G) 407 No Serial, **Anti-Aircraft Action Report,** 16 April 1945, Enclosure (B).*

ships opening fire. The plane flew out of range, circled around, and came back heading for *Panamint AGC 13* in a crash dive. All ships in the area, including *LCI(M) 804*, opened fire and the plane passed over the command ship, crashing 700 yards past her. A crash into *Panamint* would have created many problems, as she was the amphibious force flagship for the Northern Attack Force with Rear Admiral L. F. Reifsnider and his staff on board.

Panamint became a target again on 11 May when three Japanese Jills made an attempt to crash her. At 0900 the first of the planes dropped its bombs on a destroyer at Hagushi and then headed for *Panamint*. *LCI(M) 804* and other ships in the anchorage opened fire. By the time it reached *Panamint*, it was an uncontrolled ball of fire. It passed closely over her, hitting the cargo ship *M. S. Tjisadane*, killing four of her crew and wounding nine. A second plane headed toward the amphibious force command ship and was taken under fire. A 5 inch shell from a destroyer disintegrated it. The third plane made the same run soon after and ran into a blanket of automatic gunfire from the screening ships. It veered off smoking and was chased by four Corsairs which finished it off.[26]

On 18 May *LCI(M)s 739, 741*, and *1058* were screening for the Merchant Marine ship *S. S. Cornelius Vanderbilt* which was anchored off Ie Shima. At 1920, the ships anchored near *Vanderbilt* went to general quarters with the approach of enemy aircraft. The first kamikaze, a Zeke, was taken under fire at 1927, and the combined fire of the three ships brought it crashing into the sea off *Vanderbilt*'s starboard bow. Ten minutes later, a second Zeke was sighted diving on *Vanderbilt* from an altitude of about 1,000 feet. It too met its fate after the combined gunfire from all three ships hit it. It crashed into the water near *LCI(M) 1058.* At 1947, an Oscar was seen diving on *Vanderbilt.* It was also shot down, crashing close astern *LCI(M) 739* which was given credit for shooting it down. A Japanese torpedo plane, possibly a Kate, came in low at 2010. It crossed the bow of *LCI(M) 1058* and launched a torpedo at *Vanderbilt,* which fortunately missed. Gunfire from the ships hit the plane and it went down past the anchorage. By this time, the gunboats had engaged their smoke making equipment and the freighter was fairly well covered. Another plane dropped a stick of twelve bombs nearby but was unable to hit the merchant ship. Only a few days passed before *Vanderbilt* was again under attack. On 20 May, at 1834, a Zeke came in from the north in an apparent crash dive. Gunfire from *LCI(M) 741* tore into the plane and it crashed into the sea between her and *Vanderbilt.* Six minutes later an Oscar appeared to be diving on *Vanderbilt,* but fire from *LCI(M) 741* drove it off. It aimed for another part of the transport area but went down in flames.

LCI(M) 804 was making smoke for the ships anchored at Ie Shima at 2200 on 18 May when an enemy plane came through the haze and dropped a torpedo which hit *LST 808.* Fire from the gunboat was directed at the plane but it flew out of range and escaped. Fortunately, there was only one man wounded on the LST, but she was out of the war. Tugs towed her to a nearby reef where she sat for two days until, on 20 May, a kamikaze crashed her bridge and set her on fire. By the time the fires were put out, she was unsalvageable. The same attack included two other kamikazes, and both were shot down by the gunboats and other ships in the area.

On 24 May, *LCI(R) 651* anchored near four merchant ships and *Winston AKA 94* in Nakagusuku Bay. Her mission was to cover the ships with smoke. At 2043 the ships were warned that enemy aircraft were in the vicinity and they went to general quarters. Several hours of waiting went by before a single engine torpedo bomber appeared out of the haze and dropped a torpedo which hit *S. S. William D. Allison* amidships. *LCI(R) 651* got underway, and within a half hour, she was moored to the port side of the merchant ship. Three men had died and a number were wounded. *LC(FF) 536* and *LCI(R) 772* came alongside bringing doctors to aid the wounded, and *Tawakoni ATF 114* stood by to render assistance as needed. Also on the merchant ship were 190 members of the 12th Naval Construction Battalion who were there to help in unloading supplies that they needed. *LCI(R) 651* took them off the merchant ship and prepared to deliver them ashore.

S. S. William D. Allison, with several gunboats and a tug moored to her, made a good target. At 0645 a Zeke made a run on the ships, dropped two bombs, then banked around to crash the ship. It went down under the combined gunfire of the ships, which at this point included *LCS(L) 23.* It crashed in the water only fifty feet astern of *Allison.* Its pilot, apparently uninjured in the crash, made it out of his plane and attempted to swim away. He was killed by 20mm fire from the gunboats. By 0900 the merchant ship was no longer in need of assistance and the gunboats pulled away. *LCI(R) 651* delivered the Seabees to the causeway at Brown Beach.[27]

LCI(M) 741 continued her screening duties in the Ie Shima area. She was making smoke at 0040 on 25 May when her lookouts spotted a plane diving on her. *LCI(M) 742,* cruising behind her, took the plane under fire as well. It passed over the port side of *LCI(M) 739* and crashed into the water close astern. *LCI(M) 740* was caught in the explosion and suffered damage and crew casualties. Later, at 0808, *LCI(M) 741* fired on a plane making a suicide dive on a merchant ship in the Ie Shima anchorage. Fire from the *741* hit the plane causing it to go off course and only partially hit the merchant ship. It crashed into the water on the other side. Fortunately its bombs did not explode.

Many of the newly converted mortar ships lacked a 40mm bow gun. Although they were supposed to have them, shortages of the 40mms meant that they still had only 20mm bow guns with which to protect themselves. On 27 May *LCI(M) 1058* was anchored off Kouri Shima when she came under attack by a single Val at 0815. When it came in range at about 1,500 yards, it was taken under fire and hit by several 20mm shells. At a range of about 800 yards it turned off and went after a nearby destroyer escort, which shot it down. The addition of a 40mm gun to its armament would have been welcomed by the crew of the LCI(M). Another Val circled the ship at 0918, staying at the extreme range of its guns for several minutes before making its run. It was hit by 20mm, .50 caliber, and .30 caliber fire from the ship, veered off course, and crashed twenty-five feet off the ship's bow. The gunboat's CO, Lieutenant (jg) R. B. Purdy, reported that "It is the opinion of this command that the purpose of the circling plane ... was two-fold: (1) To try to get our gunners to open fire at maximum range, thereby having empty magazines when he started his dive; (2) To observe ship to see which, bow or stern, had the greatest fire power to oppose him in dive."[28]

On 28 May at 0755, a Nick made a crash dive on *Brown Victory* which was anchored at Ie Shima. The LCI gunboats, including *LCI(M) 741*, hit the Nick and it went off course. It clipped the after mast of the Victory ship and broke in two. Pieces of the plane fell in the water and its bombs exploded, killing four men and injuring sixteen more. It was a close call as *Brown Victory* was carrying 1,000 tons of gas and trucks. A successful crash on the ship would have been a disaster.

The following day, gunboats anchored off Tsuken Shima came under attack at 0733. Anchored there were several LCI(R)s from Group Forty-Seven and the degaussing vessel *YDG 10*. Two Oscars were spotted heading for the ships in the anchorage. *LCI(R) 648* had just gotten underway. Fire from the ships at anchor caused one of the Oscars to veer off and make a run on the *648*. All of the anchored gunboats and the *648* opened fire on the plane and hit it with numerous shells. It overshot the *648* and hit the water only fifteen yards from *YDG 10*. Its two bombs exploded covering the ships with a wall of water and debris, but there was no damage to the ships and no casualties. It had been a close call.

Analysis of the American tactics for combating the kamikazes at night was given by Lieutenant H. M. Mattson in the *War Diary for LCI(L) Flotilla Fourteen*:

> Under present enemy air suicide tactics, it is highly recommended that ships under smoke coverage at night definitely do not open fire and ships outside of smoke screen only if solution is very good. Enemy suicide planes will home on the tracers every time.
>
> 20MM gunfire will rarely stop a suicide plane from accomplishing its mission as it has to be literally dismantled in the air.
>
> Antiaircraft screen should be stationed sufficiently far from ships under protection to allow hits to have effect on damaged aircraft.[29]

Chapter 11

The Radar Picket Line

One of the most hazardous duties faced by the LCS(L) gunboats at Okinawa was duty on the infamous radar picket stations.[1] As plans for the invasion of the island were drawn up, it was obvious to the planners that the invasion fleet would face significant attacks by aircraft flying from the home islands of Japan, as well as from Japanese bases on Taiwan. Early detection of these incoming raids was imperative, and the Navy set up a ring of radar picket stations around the island to warn the fleet of approaching enemy aircraft. These stations were set at distances of from eighteen to ninety-five miles from the point of land known as Point Bolo or Zampa Misaki, a part of the island which was just north of the Hagushi invasion beaches at the tip of Motobu Peninsula. Various stations were patrolled from 24 March to 13 August 1945. Stations 6, 8, and 13 were never used. As time went on, the Japanese identified the locations of the stations and it was necessary to move some of them, resulting in an "A" variation.

Radar Picket Stations and Dates of Operation
24 March–13 August 1945

Radar Picket Station	Dates of Operation
1	1 April–6 May (night station for RP #15, 2 June–17 July)
2	1 April–6 May
3	1 April–6 May
4	1 April–4 May
5	24 March, 28 March, 6 May–23 June
6*	
7	1 April–21 May
8*	
9	24, 26, 28–31 March–1 April, 29 April–1 July
9A	2–19 July, 21 July–1 August, 3–13 August
10	1 April–6 May
11	Used as a night station for RP #11A, 2–16 June
11A	21 May–16 June
12	1 April–6 May
13*	
14	1 April–6 May
15	1 April, 6 May–21 May
15A	21 May–17 July

306

16	6–8 May
16A	9 May–1 July

*These stations were not put into use during the campaign for Okinawa.[2]

A destroyer, equipped with specialized radar and a fighter director team on each of the radar picket stations, was constantly on watch. To aid and support the radar picket destroyer, additional destroyers (DD), high speed minesweepers (DMS), light minelayers (DM), landing ship medium, rockets, (LSM(R))s, patrol motor gunboats (PGM)s, and landing crafts support, large (LCS(L))s were assigned. By the end of the campaign for Okinawa, eighty-eight of the LCS(L)s served on the seventeen radar picket stations used at Okinawa.

LCS(L)s, rather than the converted LCI(L) gunboats, were put to use there since the LCS(L)s carried at least two twin 40mm guns, with some mounting a third twin 40mm in the bow.

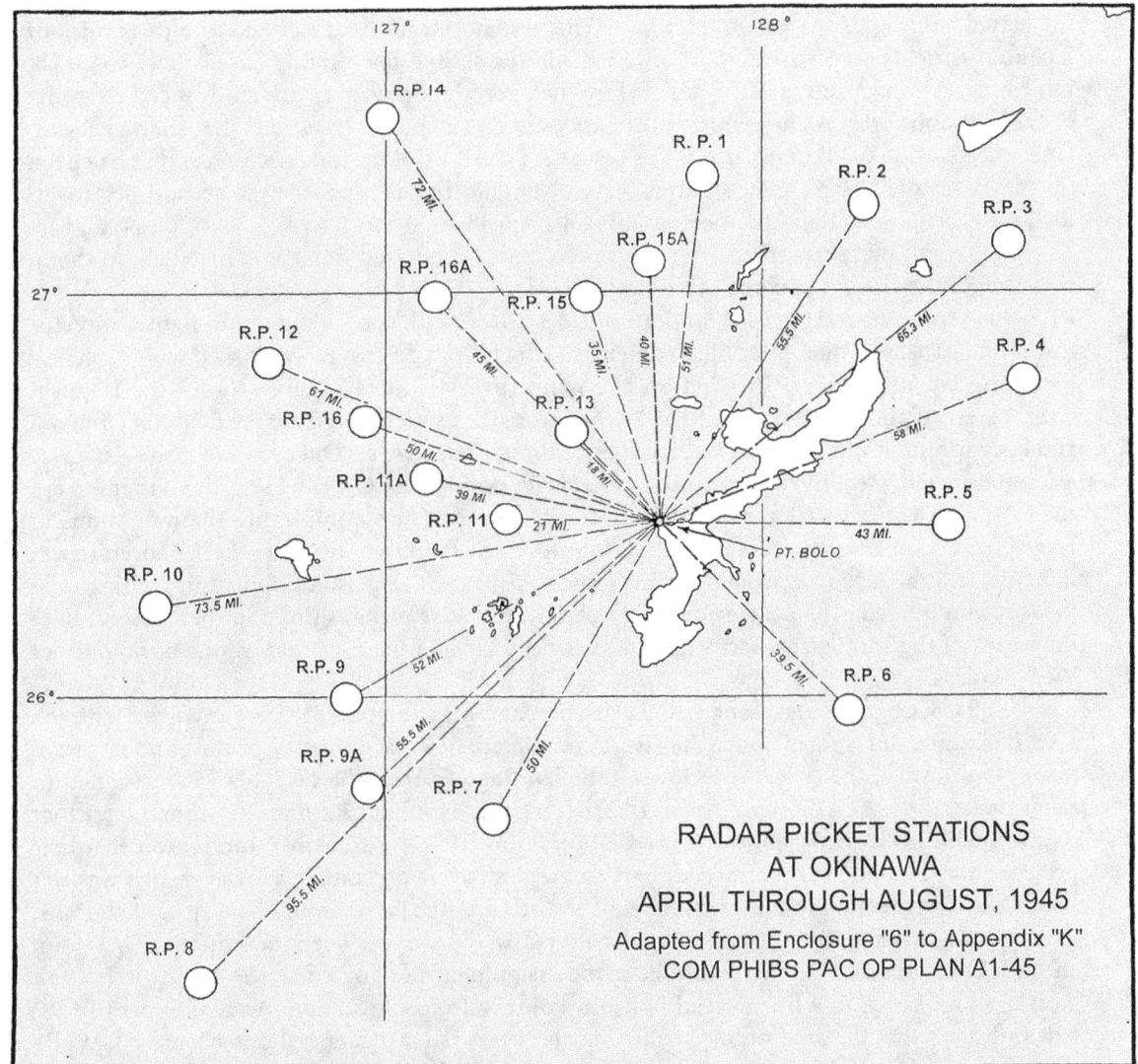

One of the screens created for the invasion of Okinawa involved setting up a ring of radar picket stations around the island to detect Japanese aircraft flying from Kyushu and Taiwan to attack the invasion fleet. Eighty-eight of the LCS(L)s joined the destroyers and LSM(R)s in patrolling the stations.

These had proven more useful in anti-aircraft action than the single 40mm guns or the 3"/50 mounted on some LCI(G)s. LCS(L)s with 3"/50 bow guns were not employed in great numbers at Okinawa, but they saw much action in the Philippines and Borneo. This reflected an adaptation to the enemy situation. Where the Japanese barge was a great threat in the southwest Pacific, aircraft had become the prime concern at Okinawa.. This resulted in the latest LCS(L)s mounting a third twin 40mm gun in the bow to combat them.

Once the initial assault phase on Okinawa had been completed, the LCS(L)s began to appear on the radar picket stations. The majority of the LCI(G)s, (M)s, and (R)s were used for call fire, suicide boat patrol, making smoke, and other tasks that made best use of their particular armament. In almost all cases the gunboats were tasked with making smoke at the Hagushi anchorage once they had come off their patrols, whether they were on the radar picket lines or any other type of patrol or assignment.

Radar picket stations #5 and #9 became operational on 24 March 1945, eight days prior to the actual landing of troops on Okinawa. This was necessary because the close proximity of Japanese airfields on Kyushu and Taiwan made it possible for aircraft based there to attack minesweepers operating in the waters before the operation, as well as other advanced elements of the invasion force. At first only destroyers were on the picket lines, but that soon changed. Once the invasion of Okinawa had taken place on 1 April 1945, the lone destroyers that had been operating on the radar picket stations were given additional support by a second destroyer. Radar picket stations that became operable on 1 April were RPs #1, 2, 3, 4, 7, 10, 12, 14, and 15. As time passed, outlying islands were captured and shore based radar was installed on them, resulting in the closing of some of the stations.

On each of the radar picket stations one destroyer, with special radar and fighter director teams on board, was the center of the defensive effort. That destroyer was tasked with detecting incoming Japanese aircraft headed for the main invasion force in and around the Hagushi anchorage. A flight of Combat Air Patrol (CAP) from the carriers and from the fields on Okinawa and later Ie Shima was attached to each fighter director destroyer. Once the incoming Japanese aircraft were detected, the fighter director destroyer notified the CAP and sent them to intercept the enemy. Through that means many were prevented from completing their missions at Hagushi. It soon became evident that getting through the large number of CAP aircraft was difficult, and the Japanese airmen began to pick the nearest targets of opportunity which were the ships on the radar picket stations. As a result, the radar picket ships and their escorts bore the brunt of the kamikaze attacks in what has been labeled the most hazardous naval duty of World War II.

The LCS(L) gunboats, along with their companion LCI gunboats, were involved with the 1 April landings at Hagushi. Once they were completed, new assignments for the gunboats were made. On 2 April, the first day following the landings, four of the LCS(L)s were assigned to radar picket duty. At 0755 on 2 April, *LCS(L)s 62* and *64* joined *Bush* on RP #1 and later that day, at 0650, *LCS(L)s 84* and *87* joined *Bennion* on RP #2. Ostensibly, the reason for their presence was to lend anti-aircraft support to the destroyers on station. However, this was not the case at first. Feeling that there were gaps in the coverage between the radar picket stations, the Navy determined that the gunboats should patrol the area between the stations. Therefore, an LCS(L) assigned to RP #2, would have the assignment designated as RP #2R or #2L when located in reference to a line extending from Point Bolo to the station. An assignment to RP #2R indicated that the area to be patrolled lay between radar picket stations #2 and #3. While this may have given additional aircraft spotting capabilities overall, it did not lend support to the destroyer operating directly on the radar picket station. If it came under attack, a relatively slow LCS(L) would not be able to get near enough to the destroyer to render effective anti-aircraft support.

During the time that the radar picket stations at Okinawa were manned, a total of 206 ships served on them. The eighty-eight LCS(L)s serving on the radar picket stations comprised the largest number among the types. By the end of the Okinawa campaign, it was not uncommon to see three destroyer types[3] and four LCS(L)s on a picket station.

The relatively small size and maneuverability of the LCS(L)s made them hard targets to hit. While forty-two of the 101 destroyer types (DD, DM, DMS) were struck by kamikazes, only thirteen of the LCS(L)s were crashed by the Japanese planes. The worst hit on the radar picket stations were the larger, slower, and poorly gunned LSMRs, with five of the eleven being hit.

Although the LCS(L)s were continually on the picket lines from 2 April through 13 August 1945, their most daunting experience was the series of ten massed air attacks known as *Kikusui* 1 through 10, collectively known as the *Ten Go* campaign. The first of these raids took place from 6 to 7 April and saw a total of 699 aircraft from Kyushu and Taiwan attacking the American forces at Okinawa. Of this number 355 were kamikazes. The ordeal of all ships at Okinawa was linked to the air attacks, but the ships on the radar picket lines bore the brunt of their savagery. As time wore on and the resources of the Japanese declined, successive raids saw fewer and fewer aircraft. By *Kikusui* 10, which ran from 21 to 22 June, the Japanese sent out only ninety aircraft. Part of this decline in the numbers had to do with declining resources which led the Japanese to save aircraft for what they saw as the coming invasion of Japan. Another factor was the realization that Okinawa was a lost cause.

Although there had been a few scattered attacks on the radar picket ships in the first few days, the bulk of the attacks began with the first of the *Kikusui* raids on 6 April. American intelligence had picked up Japanese planning for large scale air attacks, but they were not sure how large they would be. Elements of the 1st, 3rd, 5th, 10th, and 13th Air Fleets from the Imperial Japanese Navy and the 3rd and 8th Air Armies were involved. The attacks were scheduled to begin around 0400 on 21 June 1945.

On that day, Radar Picket Station #1 was patrolled by *Bush DD 529* and *LCS(L)s 62* and *64*. Unfortunately, *LCS(L) 62* was ordered to leave the station to patrol elsewhere, leaving *Bush* and *64* alone to face the oncoming swarms of Japanese aircraft. Radar picket station #1 was directly in line between southern Japan and Okinawa. Any aircraft flying toward Okinawa would be sure to pass over or close by RP #1. In time it would come to be considered the "hottest" of the radar picket stations. Immediately east of RP #1 were RPs #2 and 3. Ships serving on these three radar picket stations would see the most action at Okinawa. On patrol at RP #2 was *Colhoun DD 801*, while RP #3 was patrolled by *Cassin Young DD 793* and *LCS(L)s 109* and *110*. These six ships would face the deadliest onslaught of Japanese aircraft to be launched at Okinawa.

Japanese aircraft began to appear near RP #1 about 0245, and most passed by when taken under fire. Apparently they were after choicer targets at Hagushi. One dove at *Bush*, was taken under fire, and apparently shot down by the destroyer as observers saw it hit the water about ten miles away. At this point, and during the night, the ships were basically alone. There was no possibility of Combat Air Patrol aircraft coming to their rescue. Combat Air Patrols usually began at sunrise and lasted until dark. Carriers were reluctant to show landing lights at night for fear of drawing enemy aircraft.

Colhoun, on RP #2, was attacked eleven times between 0247 and 0600. Fortunately, none of the aircraft were able to hit their target, and *Colhoun* remained unscathed throughout the night. At dawn the Combat Air Patrol arrived and shot down one plane at 0830. Other carrier aircraft from *San Jacinto CVL 30*, *Bennington CV 20*, *Belleau Wood CVL 24*, *Hornet CV 12*, and *Anzio CVE 57*, as well as Marine Corsairs from Kadena and Yontan air fields on Okinawa joined in the gigantic air battle. Generally, the escort or "jeep" carriers (CVEs) carried FM2 Wildcats, while the larger carriers primarily had F4F Hellcats. Marine squadrons flew F4U Corsairs from the fields on Okinawa. One or two of the carriers had Corsair squadrons flown by both Marine and Navy pilots. Facing them were a variety of Japanese Army and Navy aircraft from the latest model fighters, such as the Jack and Tony, to old wood and cloth biplane trainers.

Even the great numbers of American fighters were not enough to stem the onslaught of Japanese aircraft bent on crashing into American ships. By late in the day on 6 April an estimated forty to fifty Japanese aircraft were attacking *Bush* on RP #1 and a dozen were after *Cassin Young* at RP #3. *Colhoun* left RP #2 and went to the aid of *Bush* which was crashed by a kamikaze at 1515. At that point, *LCS(L) 64*, patrolling to the east on RP#1R, was unaware that *Bush* had been hit. *Bush* began to flood rapidly and took a ten degree list to port.

Overhead, the Combat Air Patrol was taking its toll of Japanese aircraft, but there were just too many. Pilots from *Belleau Wood*'s VF-30 reported that their Hellcats had shot down forty-six of the enemy planes. However, that still left numerous Japanese aircraft over the picket ships. Other Combat Air Patrol planes scrambled off their carriers, located the air battle, and joined in. Sooner or later they ran out of ammunition or were low on fuel and had to return to their carriers, leaving the picket ships to fend for themselves. As *Colhoun* arrived on the scene, she noted that *Bush* was down by the stern and on fire. *LCS(L) 64* arrived shortly thereafter and began taking men off the sinking destroyer. *Bush* ordered her to clear away in the face of a new attack, and the gunboat maneuvered nearby to keep some semblance of protection for herself and the stricken *Bush* which was soon crashed by another kamikaze. *Colhoun* was next, taking a kamikaze crash on her main deck. Shortly thereafter, another crashed into her starboard side. It was common for kamikazes to carry a bomb or two which they released just prior to crashing into an American ship. This maximized damage. The bomb in this case exploded and broke the keel of *Colhoun*, inflicting a mortal wound on the destroyer. A third kamikaze came in from the starboard bow and crashed into the superstructure, spreading flaming gasoline across the deck. Its bomb careened off the deck and exploded in the water just behind the destroyer, holing its hull. *Colhoun* was finished. Still another kamikaze aimed for *Colhoun*, overshot, and headed for *Bush* for a successful crash into her side. Two more kamikaze strikes between 1730 and 1945 finished *Bush*. At 1830 she began to break up and sank around 1845. The seas were heavy at that point and many men were in the water. Fortunately, a number of ships had been sent to her aid, including *LCS(L)s 24, 36, 37, 40, 64, PCE(R) 855*, and *Pakana ATF 108*. It was not unusual for the gunboats to be survivors in the aftermath of an attack and the ships, generally known as the "Mighty Midgets," also gained the nickname "the pallbearers," as they frequently had to pick up the remains after an attack.

LCS(L) 64, near the two destroyers to render anti-aircraft support, also came under attack. At 1725 two Zekes flew by and she turned her guns on them as one turned in to attack her. Executing a turn to port, she brought all her guns to bear on the kamikaze and shot it down only twenty feet off her starboard quarter. Some ships preferred to meet attacks head-on so as to minimize their target area. The LCS(L)s preferred method of firing at an enemy to the front was to turn 45° toward the enemy, allowing both her forward and aft 40mm guns to bear on the target.

Meanwhile, *Colhoun*'s crew fought to save her but to no avail. Still another kamikaze crashed into her at 1800 and soon after, the decision was made to abandon ship. At 2015 *LCS(L) 84* came alongside *Colhoun* and took off 217 enlisted men and eleven officers. *LCS(L) 87* rescued another fifty-six. It was not clear how long it would take *Colhoun* to go under and so, at 2355, *Cassin Young* was ordered to sink her with gunfire.

The two gunboats still patrolling on RP #3, *LCS(L)s 109* and *110*, also saw their share of the action. At 0515 lookouts on *LCS(L) 109* saw a twin-engine Sally heading for her. Gunfire from the ship hit the plane when it was 800 yards out and turned it away. A short while later *LCS(L) 110* shot down a Judy as it passed over her. With no destroyer to support, the two gunboats were ordered back to the Nago Wan anchorage.

Radar Picket Station #4 was patrolled by *Bennett DD 473* and *LCS((L)s 111* and *114*. The station came under attack around 1540 when two Vals attacked her. The destroyer accounted for one of the aircraft, and the Hellcats flying Combat Air Patrol for her got the other. CAP Hellcats accounted for another five, and the destroyer shot down one more. *LCS(L) 39* drove off a Zeke at 1813 after taking it under fire. *Bennett* was moved to RP #2 and the gunboats headed for RP #1, arriving there at 1940 to assist in the search for survivors.

Hudson DD 475 and *LCS(L)s 115* and *116* patrolled RP station #10. The ships came under attack at 1215 and 1702 but, in both cases, drove off the attacking aircraft. At 1829 a twin-engine Betty bomber approached the station and was taken under fire by both *Hudson* and *LCS(L) 115*. The gunboat was credited with the kill. Their brief presence and performance on the radar picket stations had not gone unnoticed. Commander Task Force Fifty-One wrote that "The gunboat types proved valuable additions by their AA armament, and by the fact that they are a difficult target to hit."[4] With praise like that it was to be expected that the gunboats would see a great deal of action on the radar picket stations.

Although *Kikusui* 1 was scheduled to last into 7 April, the Navy brass was unaware of that fact and decided to send some of the ships back. In all, nineteen ships were on patrol on 6 April, but at the end of the day four gunboats were sent back, leaving only fifteen on station overnight. The following day additional ships were sent out, including three LSMRs, which would prove to be extremely vulnerable to attack. A total of twenty-two ships faced the Japanese onslaught on 7 April.

Several days elapsed filled with actual and threatened attacks on the radar picket stations. On 12 April, RP #1 was patrolled by *Cassin Young DD 793*, *Purdy DD 734*, and *LCS(L)s 33, 57, 114*, and *115*. Although the day was clear and the seas calm, the air above the picket station was not.

The first incoming Japanese air raid was picked up on radar at 1112. The fighter director ship, *Cassin Young*, controlled a CAP of three divisions of Corsairs from VF-10 on *Intrepid CV 11*. When the incoming raid was spotted, she vectored the Corsairs to intercept them. The enemy aircraft were fifteen in number, a combination of Nates and Vals. Twelve of them were shot down by the CAP. Wildcats from *Petroff Bay CVE 80* joined in the battle which now included Zekes and Oscars. The battle continued throughout the afternoon as the enemy began to zero in on the picket ships. At 1430 *Purdy*'s lookouts observed a Val approaching on her starboard quarter. It was shot down by the combined fire of *Purdy* and *LCS(L) 114*. Several more enemy aircraft were shot down by *Purdy* and the CAP. At 1500 a Val made it through the combined fire of *Purdy* and *LCS(L) 114*, striking the water only twenty feet from the destroyer. It bounced off the water and into *Purdy*'s side where its bomb went through her hull and exploded, severely damaging the ship. With thirteen dead and fifty-eight wounded, her CO, Commander Frank L. Johnson, headed her back to the anchorage.

As *Purdy* and *LCS(L) 114* were under attack, so was *LCS(L) 57*. At 1347 eight enemy aircraft were spotted off her starboard beam and one made a run on her. It was shot down fifty yards from the gunboat after dropping a bomb which missed. Another Japanese airman decided to try his luck with the gunboat and made a strafing run on the ship. Fire from the gunboat's forward twin 40mm gun killed the pilot but his plane kept coming. It struck the forward 40mm gun tub, careened off, and hit the water twenty-five yards to port of the ship. This left the gunboat with much less ability to defend itself. At 1352 three Nates attacked her. The first two were shot down but the third, also hit, exploded only ten feet off her port quarter, blowing an eight foot hole in her side and disabling her aft 40mm twin. With only a single 40mm bow gun, four 20mm guns, and a few .50 caliber machine guns left, the gunboat was in dire straits. She began to take on water and soon had a ten degree list to starboard. *LCS(L) 33* came to her aid, picking up men who had been blown into the water. The attacks continued; at 1420 a CAP fighter chased another Nate toward the *57*. The enemy plane was hit by fire from the ship and the CAP fighter but still managed to crash into the bow of the *57*, disabling her 40mm bow gun. Recognizing that her situation on the picket station was hopeless, her CO, Lieutenant Harry L. Smith, requested permission to leave the station and head back to the anchorage before his ship sank.

Meanwhile, *LCS(L) 33* was also under attack. At 1500 two Vals attacked her simultaneously, one from port and one from starboard. Her gunners shot down the Val on the port side, but the Val attacking from the starboard side crashed into the gunboat amidships and exploded. The force of the crash broke the gunboat's fire mains and she was unable to fight the ensuing fires. Her power was out and her Johnson pumps were on fire. She took a list thirty-five degrees to port.

MoMM 3/c John D. Meader was on duty in the engine room when the *33* was hit. He later wrote:

> Suddenly there was a loud noise, even with ear plugs in your ears, something had exploded. The ship just seemed to bounce, like standing on a diving board and someone else jumps on it too. The lights went out, the acid smell of fuel began to enter the engine room, it was a different smell than the manifolds. This must have lasted for about 10 seconds and the backup battery powered lites came on: two battle lanterns. The place looked eerie at least scary. We waited, the phones were dead, the ship started to list badly to port....
>
> Suddenly the red warning lite on the aft bulkhead started to flash. This was the signal to abandon ship. I know we just stood for a second or two and looked at each other. We were going at "Flank Speed." We had many discussions about this, we should reduce the speed to one-third, so as to be able to get to safety. However no signal came to reduce speed, it was leaning to Port badly, so up we went topside.
>
> Once up there we started forward, just a couple of steps, fire seemed every place forward, lots of black smoke.[5]

Meader and the other men from the engine room made it off safely. After a couple of hours in the water, he was picked up by *LCS(L) 51*, the last survivor of the *33* to be rescued.

Her CO, Lieutenant (jg) Frank C. Osterland, was in the conning tower when the kamikaze hit. He later wrote:

> A third plane dove down along the ship's starboard side and leveled off just above the wave tops. It struck Dolly Three (*LCS(L) 33*) full force, forward of amidships. There was a terrific crash and gasoline was sprayed over the ship. Fires immediately engulfed much of the superstructure.
>
> Many of the crew topside were temporarily rendered unconscious by the concussion. The Captain was thrown violently against the conning tower and suffered a broken vertebra. The mortally wounded ship began to list in the water and go out of control. All engines were shut down. Below decks in what would very quickly become a steel coffin, we were deafened by gunfire and tossed about by the wildly maneuvering ship. Then came a terrific crash when the plane struck and suddenly, for me, there was only darkness, stillness, and emptiness. I was lying on the deck of the radio/radar room which was my Dolly Three battle station. I had apparently been thrown off my feet, unconscious, under the radar console and against the bulkhead. There was a deep dent in my helmet that hadn't been there before, and I knew that I'd received a hard blow to my head and that my nose was bleeding.[6]

Dazed and injured, Osterland could hear his officers giving the command to abandon ship. As he crawled out of the radio room and onto the deck he was able to see how badly his ship was damaged. Many of the crew were already in the water and Osterland dove in to assist them. As they tried to keep together in the water, the ship's magazines began to explode. An hour later the survivors were picked up by *LCS(L) 115*. Three men were missing and presumed dead. *LCS(L) 33* was a smoldering hulk and *Purdy* was ordered to sink her. Two rounds from the destroyer's five inch gun put her under.

LCS(L) 115 was the most fortunate of the ships at RP #1 that day. On her way to pick up survivors from *LCS(L) 33*, she came under attack at 1427 when a Val tried to crash her, strafing her decks on the way in. Three men were wounded in the strafing attack, but the ship maneuvered quickly and the plane overshot her, crashing into the water only twenty-five feet off her port side. Thirty minutes later another Val made an attempt to crash her but, once again, the ship's maneuvering left the Val to crash one hundred feet off the port beam. She continued on her way and picked survivors from the water.

LCS(L) 114 was the only ship to get through the attack unscathed. Her gunfire supplemented that of the destroyers and other gunboats in successfully shooting down a number of enemy aircraft. In his action report on the battle at RP #1, Commander Frank L. Johnson, noted: "One shipboard enlisted observer who kept a tally of the 'splashes' made by friendly fighters, surface ships including LCS type, and by suicide hits, stated that he counted a total of 22 splashes during the 86 minute air action. It is believed that at least 20 and probably about 25–30 Japanese planes were destroyed in the above action."[7]

Radar Picket Station #1 continued to be one of the most hazardous assignments. On 16 April three ships on patrol there, *Laffey DD 724*, *LCS(L)s 51* and *116*, saw heavy action. Attacks on the ships began at 0827, with *Laffey* as the prime target. Four Vals attacked the destroyer, two from each side. The destroyer shot one down and another fell under fire from *Laffey* and *LCS(L) 51*. From that point on *Laffey* was subjected to a series of attacks, successfully shooting down a number of Japanese aircraft, but sustaining kamikaze crashes from eight planes and bombs from three others.

In the early attacks, the Japanese focus had been destroyers, but the gunboats were soon under attack also. At 0815 a Val selected *LCS(L) 51* as its target and came in on its starboard beam, only to be met by fire from every gun that could train on it. The Val went down in flames 300 yards off the ship. A half hour later the gunboat shot down a Val heading for *Laffey* and the plane crashed in the water. Still another Val attacked her from the port side and was shot down. A fifth Val made its crash dive at 1010, coming in from the port side of the gunboat. Gunners

LCS(L) 33 was active in the battle for Iwo Jima where she provided support for the landing craft and call-fire against enemy targets. While patrolling on Radar Picket Station #1 at Okinawa on 12 April 1945, she was crashed by a kamikaze and sunk. NARA 80GK 2681.

LCS(L) 57 at Kerama Retto after sustaining damage in a kamikaze attack while on radar picket duty. NARA 80G 330114.

Mate 3/c Frances F. Ryers, manning his 20mm gun, faced the incoming Val. Ryers had run out of ammunition but stayed at his post as the enemy plane headed directly toward him. "You could really get a good look at the pilot … he was sitting straight up in there, holding on to his joy stick, and he looked like he was just staring at me." Ryers "just stared back."[8] The Val was shot down by another gunner only twenty-five feet from the side of the ship. Its engine was propelled forward after the crash and imbedded itself in the side of the gunboat's hull. Shortly thereafter, the gunboat spotted a Zeke flying across its bow heading for *Laffey* and shot it down. Her score for the day was six enemy aircraft destroyed. She headed toward *Laffey* to assist with firefighting and rescuing survivors. At 1150 she was sent back to the anchorage to deliver the wounded. For her actions that day she was awarded the Presidential Unit Citation.

LCS(L) 116 took on three Vals that approached her at 0905. Two were driven off by her gunfire, but the third crashed into her stern and exploded, putting her twin 40mm mount out of action. Eleven men died and nine were wounded in the attack. Two more Vals tried to crash the ship and both were shot down by the gunboat. Her damage was such that she had to be towed back to the anchorage.

Opposite, top: The engine from a Japanese Val kamikaze plane was embedded in the side of *LCS(L) 51* after it was shot down by the ship at Radar Picket Station #1 on 16 April 1945. NARA 80G 359030. *Bottom:* The engine from the Japanese Val that crashed into the side of *LCS(L) 51* on 16 April 1945 protrudes into the ship's crew mess area. Official U.S. Navy photograph.

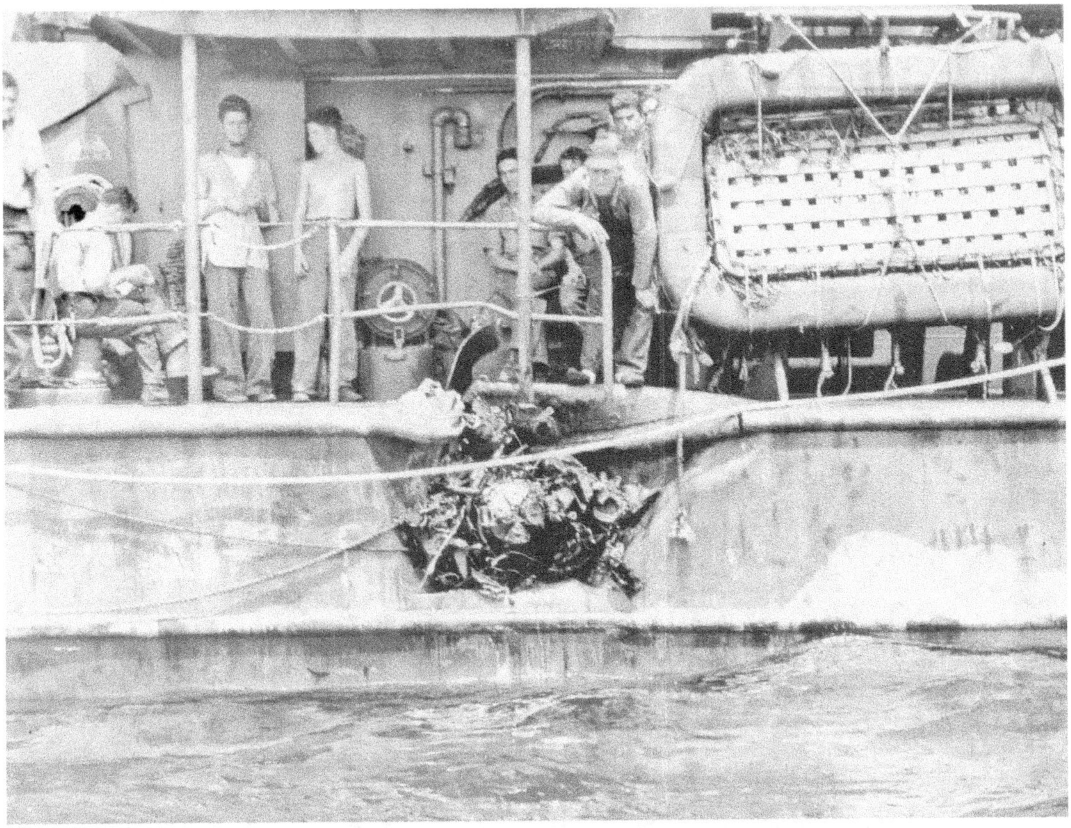

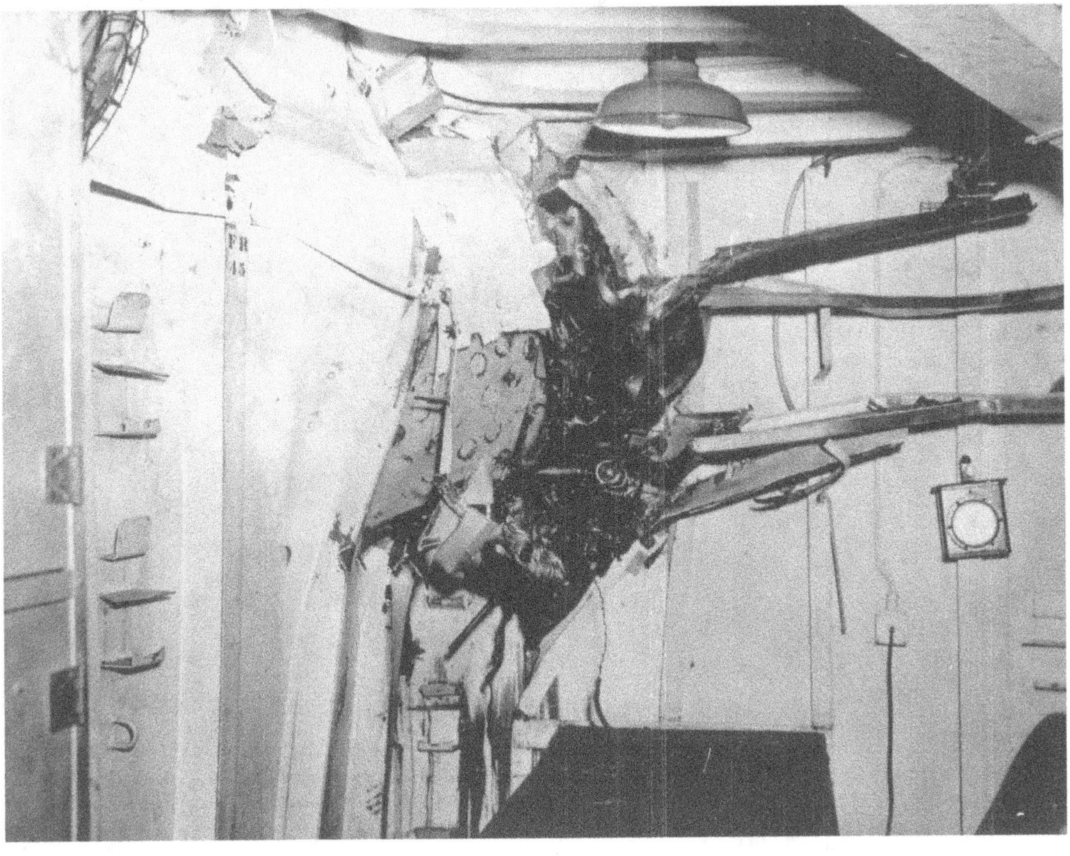

Top: *LCS(L) 116* was on patrol at Radar Picket Station #1 on 16 April 1945 when she was hit by a kamikaze. In addition to damage to her aft gun tub, she suffered twelve dead and twelve wounded. NARA 80G 342580. *Bottom:* The Aichi D3A Type 199 carrier bomber was frequently used in attacks on American ships at Okinawa. It carried the Allied code name "Val."

Days and weeks elapsed with the kamikazes coming in droves. Although the massed raids of the *Kikusui* campaign saw the largest number of Japanese aircraft attacks, the time between them was filled with sporadic attacks on American ships. Lieutenant H. D. Chickering, commanding officer of *LCS(L) 51*, later wrote: "The raids seemed ceaseless, our guns were always manned and the gunners literally slept at them. As Captain I seldom left the bridge. For a week, we fired on, or reported, dozens of raids, and lost count very quickly. The radio reported continuous fighting, hits and sinking on all stations."[9]

Kikusui #4 was scheduled to run from 25 to 29 April 1945, but inclement weather delayed the start until the 27th. Patrolling Radar Picket Station #1 on 28 April were *Aaron Ward DM 34*, *Mustin DD 413*, *LCS(L) 11* and *LSM(R) 191*. *LCS(L) 61* was on patrol two-thirds of the way to the station, a practice designed to give additional coverage for the anchorage. At 0023 and 0030 several Japanese aircraft passed by the station. They were too distant to attack the ships directly on the station, but one peeled off and made a run on *LCS(L) 61* from dead ahead. The pilot's aim was off and it passed over the ship before its gunners could fire on it. The best they could manage were a few parting shots from the aft twin 40mm. Throughout the night enemy aircraft attacked the station and were driven off or shot down by the ships. At the station, *Ward* shot down three aircraft and possibly a fourth.

At 1100 on 28 April *Aaron Ward* was relieved by *Bennion DD 662* and *Mustin DD 413*. *LCS(L) 61* was brought in to the station where it joined with the two destroyers and *LCS(L) 23*, which had relieved *LCS(L) 11*.

That evening, about 2200, the two gunboats were cruising on RP #1 about three miles to starboard of the destroyers when they came under attack. A third LCS(L), number *31*, had joined the station during the day. The three were cruising in a line which was one of the formations used by the gunboats while on RP Duty. *LCS(L) 31* was in the lead, followed by *61*, with *23* bringing up the rear. *The War Diary of LCS(L) 61* describes the action:

> Roger Peter One had been alerted for a good part of the night and the DD's had taken bogies under fire several times. It was an active night all over the Picket Line and we had been at Red & Green for a long period. Our private bogie had not been reported to us by any source until our own Radarman, A. H. Bleiler, RdM2/c, picked him up and tracked him in. LCS 61 was second ship in a column of three and the bogie was closing from ahead, from right to left and at an angle of about 201 to the axis. The lookouts and fire control man sighted him visually while he was still on the starboard side of the column and started tracking. Fire was not opened until he cleared the ship ahead. The number 2 40MM gun with Larry Fabroni, FC 2/c, at the director was right on from the first shot. As soon as he realized he was being fired on the Jap turned in toward the 61 but he was much, much too late. We had him on fire and he fell within 100 yds. on our port beam. 18 rounds of 40MM ammunition were expended. And that was that. The OTC investigating the wreckage, discovering two bodies. Just as easy as falling off a log. We had visions of our take running into the dozens. We were soon to be disillusioned, but our first conquest gave us a world of confidence. Bring on the bogies. We were ready and waiting for them.[10]

*LCS(L)*s *61* and *31* shared the credit for the plane which was identified in action reports as a Myrt.

*LCS(L)*s' firefighting abilities were put to the test on 3 May 1945. Three of the gunboats, *LCS(L)*s *13*, *16*, and *61* were on patrol at RP #7 when word was received that the escort carrier *Sangamon CVE 26* had been hit by a kamikaze. At 1920, a Nick with a bomb had crashed in the middle of her flight deck starting a raging fire which was out of control. The close proximity of the radar picket station to the carrier meant that the gunboats could be of assistance, so they were sent to her aid. As they approached, they could see aircraft being jettisoned in order to keep them from exploding. *Hudson DD 475*, which had been nearby, was already on the scene playing water on the fire with her hoses. The three gunboats came alongside and began to fight the fires with their equipment. *LCS(L) 13* had her mast broken as ammo on the carrier's deck went off. *LCS(L) 61* was nearly hit by a Hellcat, as *Sangamon*'s crewmen jettisoned it over the side. Ammunition and star shells exploded around the gunboats as they fought the fires. In time the fires were under control and *Sangamon* was able to continue on her own. The three gunboats headed back to radar picket duty. Apparently their work had been exemplary. *Hudson* sent the following message:

> THE SUPPORT SHIPS OF ROGER PETER SEVEN ARE TO BE CONGRATULATED FOR A SUPERB JOB LAST NIGHT X YOU WERE CERTAINLY RESPONSIBLE TO A LARGE DEGREE IN SAVING THE CARRIER X REQUEST DUNGEON SIX SUBMIT NAMES OF ALL COMMANDING OFFICERS INCLUDING DUNGEON THREE AND ALBERT FOURTEEN.[11]

The commanding officers of the three gunboats, Lieutenants Homer O. White, Jr. *(16)*, James W. Kelley *(61)*, and Lieutenant (jg) Billy R. Hart *(13)* were awarded the Silver Star for their actions in assisting the carrier.

Meanwhile, on Radar Picket Station #10, *Aaron Ward DM 34*, *Little DD 803*, *LCS(L)s 14, 25, 83*, and *LSM(R) 195* were on patrol. At 1883 incoming enemy aircraft were detected and the ships went to general quarters. The two Japanese Vals managed to slip by the four Hellcats on patrol and close in on the ships. *Ward* shot one down 100 yards to starboard. It disintegrated and its engine, propeller, and part of the wing landed on the *Ward*'s deck. The second Val was hit by her gunfire and crashed into the water 1,200 yards to port. While *Ward*'s gunners were concentrating on the Vals, a Zeke with a bomb attacked from port. Although it was hit by the ship's fire it managed to crash into the ship, killing and wounding a number of men. *Ward* began taking on water and circled to port, her rudder jammed by the explosion. However, her guns were still operable and she fired on and turned away other attackers.

The gunboats, which had been stationed five miles south of *Ward*, went to her aid along with *Shannon DM 25*, which had been on patrol nearby. *Aaron Ward* underwent another attack which began at 1859. She managed to shoot down a Betty and two Vals before a third Val made it through the hail of gunfire to crash into her main deck. Its bomb, released just prior to the crash, exploded and holed the minelayer. *Ward* went dead in the water and, within minutes, was crashed by another Val and then a Zeke. She had been hit by five kamikazes but was still afloat. Her gunners had shot down four of the enemy planes.

By this time the LCS(L)s were on the scene. *LCS(L) 14* shot down another kamikaze as it made its run on the minelayer. The gunboats came aside, taking off wounded and helping fight fires. It was *Little*'s turn next. An estimated eighteen to twenty-four enemy aircraft circled over the ships, lining up for their attacks. Between 1843 and 1845 *Little* was struck by four kamikazes, the last of which broke her keel. At 1851 her CO, Commander Madison Hall, Jr. ordered his crew off the ship, and a few minutes later she went to the bottom.

LSM(R) 195 had been on her way to aid the ships but lost an engine, causing her to fall behind the LCS(L)s. Once separated from the other ships she was a lone target. With only a single 40mm gun to protect herself, she was basically helpless. Within a short space of time she was struck by only one kamikaze. However, the impact of the crash broke her water mains and started fires in her midship and forward magazines. Without the ability to fight the fires she was finished. Her CO gave the order to abandon ship at 1920, and fifteen minutes later she went under. Left on the picket station were three LCS(L)s and *Aaron Ward* which was dead in the water.

The kamikazes began to target the gunboats. At 1909 one made a run on *LCS(L) 25* and was shot down by the combined fire from the *25* and *LCS(L) 14*. As it crashed into the water its engine broke loose, ricocheted off the water, and broke the mast off *LCS(L) 25*. Other parts of the plane hit the gunboat's deck, killing one man, wounding eight, and knocking two overboard. Two more Japanese planes made a run on *LCS(L) 83*. Her maneuvers caused the planes to miss and both crashed into the water. As the *83* headed for the sinking ships, still another plane came at her from astern. Her gunners faced down the plane's gunfire and shot it down behind her. The gunboat had arrived in the area where *Little* sank and began picking up survivors. As she rescued survivors, an Oscar made a run on her. Her gunners poured out a blanket of fire and killed the pilot, causing the plane to miss her. She continued to pick up survivors from *Little* and *Aaron Ward*. In his action report for the day, the CO of *LCS(L) 83*, Lieutenant James M. Faddis, related the courageous acts of his crew during the battle:

> They had previous to that day seen the LCS 15 sunk by a suicide plane. They had seen several suicide dives on Destroyers. They had seen the LSM 195 hit and burning. They had seen the DD and DM hit repeatedly. The chances of stopping the suicide attacks seemed remote yet while picking up survivors they were calm, stood to their guns and poured out a murderous fire. The men on number one 40, with the plane barely 50 feet away, were loading and firing unceasingly. Neither noise nor smoke nor confusion bothered the men. They stuck to their guns and fired like demons.[12]

Radar Picket Station 1 was patrolled by *Morrison DD 560*, *Ingraham DD 694*, *LSM(R) 194* and *LCS(L)s 21, 23,* and *31* from 3 to 4 May. By the end of the day on 4 May, *Morrison* and *LSM(R) 194* would be sunk and *Ingraham* and *LCS(L) 31* would be damaged in kamikaze attacks. Early in the morning, about 0715, the radar picket station came under attack by an estimated thirty-five to fifty enemy aircraft. The first ship attacked was *Morrison*, which controlled the nearby CAP. Because of the size of the raid, the destroyer radioed for additional assistance. Within a short time, the combat air patrol numbered forty-eight Hellcats and Corsairs. *Morrison* shot down three attacking enemy planes. She suffered her first kamikaze hit at 0825 as a Zeke crashed into her forward stack. This was followed by a second Zeke crashing into her main deck near the No. 3 5 inch gun. Seven twin-float biplanes attacked the ship and two made it through to crash into the destroyer. Within minutes *Morrison* was down by the stern and sinking. She rolled over and went down stern first at 0840 shortly after her commanding officer, Commander James R. Hansen, gave the order to abandon ship. She lost 159 crewmen and suffered 102 injured. *LSM(R) 194* sustained a crash into her stern by a Val about the same time that *Morrison* was sunk. The explosion blew up her boiler and split her seams. She went down within a half hour. Her casualties were thirteen dead and twenty-three wounded. As *LCS(L) 21* raced to her aid, the LSM(R)s magazine exploded underwater, damaging the gunboat by opening some of her seams and knocking out her gyro compass. *Ingraham* was hit by a Zeke which struck her waterline about 0830. Its bomb penetrated the destroyer's hull near the waterline, and the resultant explosion tore a hole in the port side of her hull thirty feet long. Prior to being hit, *Ingraham's* gunners had shot down eight enemy planes, including Vals and Zekes. Her crew set about saving their ship which limped back to Ie Shima for repairs. Her dead numbered fourteen and her wounded thirty-seven.

As the larger ships were under attack, the LCS(L)s were heavily engaged in fighting off kamikazes which were attacking the destroyers and the LSM(R), as well as themselves. *LCS(L) 21* shot down three enemy aircraft and hit the Val that crashed into *LSM(R) 194*, but it still managed its crash into the rocket ship. She patrolled the area, picking up 187 men from *Morrison* and another fifty from *LSM(R) 194*. Her decks packed to the rails with survivors, the *21* was barely able to fight off additional kamikazes as they came within range. *LCS(L) 23*, patrolling nearby, shot down four enemy aircraft and was credited with an assist on three additional enemy planes.

On board *LCS(L) 31*, Gunners Mate 1/c Thomas Lee watched the action surrounding his ship. As the most experienced gunnery man on the ship, he was stationed on deck just forward of the conning tower. The ship's gunnery officer, Lieutenant (jg) Laurance McKenna, had assigned him as the trouble shooter for the guns. If there was a problem with any of the ship's guns, McKenna contacted Lee by phone and sent him to solve the problem.

At 0822 a Zeke dove on the gunboat from the ship's port beam. It was hit by 40mm fire at a range of about 2,000 yards, diverting its path sufficiently to miss the conning tower. It splashed into the sea fifty feet off the starboard beam of the *31*. A problem had arisen with one of the ship's guns and Lee was sent aft by McKenna to clear a jam on gun No. 7. This saved his life, as moments later another Zeke roared in from the gunboat's port bow and, in spite of being hit numerous times, crashed into the deck just forward of the conning tower where Lee had been standing. The pointer for the twin 40mm gun dove out of the director's tub and narrowly escaped death. He survived with a gash on his foot from the Zeke's propeller.[13] The port wing of the plane crashed into the twin 40mm gun, and its starboard wing tore a two by six foot hole in the conning tower. With its wings ripped off, the fuselage of the plane continued on, destroying the starboard 20mm gun before exploding just off the ship's starboard beam. Five men were killed in this attack and another three injured. Within minutes another Zeke was sighted off the port beam and shot down with the one remaining 40mm gun. At 0837 a Val made an apparent suicide run on the gunboat from her port beam. This time a burst from the 20mm and 40mm gun hit the plane as it was about 500 yards from the ship. Damage to the plane caused it to swerve and pass closely over the aft twin 40mm gun. It left a trail of gasoline and debris on the ship before plunging into the sea off the ship's starboard quarter. Two men were killed in this attack and three were injured. One man was reported blown over the side and Lee, who had been in the area near the 40mm gun tub, was reported over the side as well. He immediately contacted the conn via headphones, and the gunnery officer was surprised to hear his voice, having been told he was blown overboard in the attack. With only one 20mm gun and a single 40mm gun left, the ship was in no condition to continue fighting. A Zeke approached from the port quarter heading for *Ingraham* and was shot down by 20mm fire from the *31*. The plane crashed into the water twenty-five yards off the ship's port quarter. At 0855, the aft twin 40mm gun had one barrel operational, just in time to shoot down a sixth Japanese plane coming in on the ship from astern. With no further attacks occurring, the Commanding Officer of *LCS(L) 31*, Lieutenant Kenneth F. Machacek, led his ship through the area to pick up a few survivors from the sunken ships. She headed for the Hagushi anchorage and repairs. Both of her twin 40mm guns and two of her 20mms were destroyed or damaged beyond repair.[14] Her accomplishments for the day would be recognized. For her actions on 4 May 1945, *LCS(L) 31* was awarded the Presidential Unit Citation.

The greatest air-sea battle at the radar picket stations took place at RP #15 from 10 to 11 May 1945. Patrolling there were *Evans DD 552*, *Hugh W. Hadley DD 774*, *LCS(L)s 82, 83, 84* and *LSM(R) 193*. Overnight between 10 and 11 May, enemy aircraft were constantly in the area, but at 0740 on 11 May, the action escalated. Flying CAP over the station were twelve American aircraft, but they would be greatly outnumbered by the attacking Japanese planes. Virtually the entire Japanese *Kikusui #6* raid was headed in their direction. *Hadley's* radar indicated a total of 156 aircraft approaching the ships and they went to general quarters. She finished the day having shot down twenty-three enemy aircraft in spite of having been hit by a *Baka* bomb, a bomb hit aft, and two kamikazes. All but her damage control parties were ordered off the ship, and these fifty men fought fires and kept her afloat until help arrived. She survived the encounter and was towed back to safety by the tug *Avoyel ATF 150*.

Evans was also severely mauled by the raids, with her engineering spaces flooded by four kamikaze hits. She was dead in the water but still fought back. By the end of her ordeal she had shot down fourteen enemy aircraft. The destroyer was unable to move and had to be towed back to safety. She suffered thirty-two killed and twenty-seven wounded in the attacks. Both destroyers were awarded the Presidential Unit Citation.

As the destroyers came under attack, the gunboats closed their positions to aid in fighting the kamikazes. *LCS(L) 82* assisted in shooting down a Tony as it dove on *Evans* at 0845. Fourteen minutes later *LSM(R) 193* shot down a Kate as it was about to dive on her. *LCS(L) 83* spotted a Hamp making a run on her from head on and shot it down at 0910. With *Evans* dead in the water, support from the gunboats was crucial. *LCS(L) 83* fired on and drove off two more aircraft that were attempting to crash into her. The LSM(R) drove two off and then shot down a Hamp at 0912. Three more aircraft approached the gunboats and the LSM(R)'s gunners shot one down, and the LCS(L)s combined their fire power to send the other two down in flames. *LCS(L) 84* tried to assist *Evans* as her crew fought the fires. As she aided the stricken destroyer, she came under attack and shot down a Zeke at 0900. The Zeke crashed close aboard and showered the forward decks of the gunboat with water and flaming gasoline. The near miss blew one man overboard and wounded another. Within the next fifteen minutes her gunners shot down a Zeke and a Tojo.

The air battle raged overhead and many aircraft were shot down by the CAP, but there were just too many. In spite of their valiant action and the destruction of a number of enemy planes, many still managed to get through.

LCS(L) 82 was also in the thick of the fighting. At 0910 an Oscar dove on her and was disintegrated by her gunfire while it was almost directly overhead. Her CO, Lieutenant Peter G. Beierl, ordered flank speed, and the debris from the aircraft showered down just aft the ship. The *82* then went to the aid of *Evans* and tied up on her starboard side. Another plane attacked as she was tied up to *Evans* and she shot it down 200 yards away. *LCS(L) 84* tied up to *Evans'* port side and began pumping her out as she was taking on water. Two Corsairs, following closely on the tail of a Zeke, passed over her fantail. The *84* shot the Zeke down and it crashed in the water 200 yards off the ships.

Had it not been for the presence of the gunboats, it is likely that the two destroyers would have been sunk. *LCS(L) 82* had shot down three enemy aircraft and assisted in the destruction of two more. For her actions that day she was awarded the Navy Unit Commendation and her CO, Lieutenant Peter G. Beierl, was awarded the Bronze Star. *LCS(L) 83* also was awarded the Navy Unit Commendation. In all, the support gunboats had performed admirably and justified their presence on the radar picket stations.

It would seem logical that the duty performed by the picket ships was appreciated by all, and measures taken to ensure that they were given as much support as possible. This did not always occur. *LCS(L) 82*, after a harrowing experience on the picket line, went back to the Hagushi area for supplies and skunk patrol. On 20 May, her commanding officer received word to head back to the radar picket station. He notified the SOPA that his ship was short of ammunition and was ordered to an ammunition ship to get more. William J. Ross SM 3/c on the *82* reported:

> By the time we got underway and located the AE, it was a little after 1600. We signaled by blinker for permission to come alongside, but could get no response. We had to come in close enough for the Captain to use the bull horn to request them to handle our lines. However, the answer came back that they were a union ship — no work after 5PM!
>
> As I have said, the Captain was a quiet man, but not now. He backed the ship off, and I believe, considered putting a couple of shots across their bow. Finally, we lowered our dinghy and sent a couple of men over to handle our own lines.
>
> To show they weren't all bad, the union men did show us where the ammunition was stored — about three decks below. Due to union rules, however, they refused to operate their winches. We had to manhandle our ammunition up to the main deck and then, to the 82.[15]

Radar picket station #5 was patrolled by *Braine DD 630*, *Anthony DD 515*, and *LCS(L)s 13, 82, 86*, and *123* on 26 May. The CAP shot down two Tojos at 0830 and *Braine* fired on and destroyed a Betty with an *Oka* before the piloted bomb could be released by the mother ship. The following morning foul weather closed in. The eight Army P-47 Thunderbolts on CAP asked permission to return to their base on Ie Shima as flying conditions were difficult. No sooner had they departed the radar picket station than the ships went to general quarters at 0737. A Val headed toward *LCS(L) 123* from dead ahead and was hit repeatedly by her forward twin 40mm guns. Apparently discouraged, the pilot turned off and headed toward *Anthony* but it crashed before it got much farther. *LCS(L) 123* had claimed her first kill for the day. From that point on, *Braine* and *Anthony* suffered a series of Japanese air attacks, with *Braine* getting crashed by two kamikazes at 0745. *Braine* was aflame and the gunboats went to her aid. *LCS(L) 86* turned away an incoming attacker with her gunfire and it headed for *Anthony*. Fire from *LCS(L)s 82, 86,* and *123* struck the plane and it crashed before it could get to the destroyer.

Braine was out of control. Fires on her deck effectively divided the ship into three sections and the men in each could not communicate with those in the other sections. Her steering had been damaged, and she nearly ran into *LCS(L) 123* which had come to her aid. Men began jumping off the ship and were rescued by the gunboats. However, not all made it safely. Sharks swarmed through the waters, and men on the gunboats fired rifles at them to drive them away. *LCS(L) 82* gunners shot a number of them and rescued some men who had been mauled by the sharks. John Rooney, who served as a radioman on board *LCS(L) 82*, wrote: "We recovered one who had not made it, hanging pale and lifeless in his Mae West, a leg torn away, the other arm gone, gutted by the sharks.... We machine-gunned the sharks. In their mindless savagery they started tearing each other apart, this time turning the ocean crimson with their own blood."[16]

Anthony, which had been damaged by a kamikaze's near miss, tied up to *Braine* and began to assist in firefighting as the gunboats picked up the rest of the survivors. That having been done, the gunboats turned their firefighting capabilities loose and went to the assistance of the two destroyers. *LCS(L) 123* managed to get a boarding party on *Braine* by 0957 and the fires were eventually brought under control. On board *Braine*, sixty-seven were dead and 103 wounded.

Anthony began the task of towing her back to the anchorage. The gunboats remained on station and were there when the destroyers, *William D. Porter DD 579* and *Massey DD 778* reported on station.

Ammen DD 527, Boyd DD 544, and *LCS(L)s 52, 55, 56,* and *61* were on patrol at RP #15A on 27 May. Late in the day *Ammen* detected four enemy aircraft heading toward the station and sent the CAP after them. The four planes escaped the CAP and were not seen again.

Unfortunately, the CAP usually had to return to base at dusk, leaving the picket ships without any air cover. At 1918 the CAP was departing, and an hour later the first of the Japanese planes made their appearance. Between 2028 and 2047 the destroyers detected two Japanese aircraft and their gunfire drove them off. Still another enemy plane was detected at 2221 and the destroyers and gunboats all fired on it. As it approached the ships it passed over *LCS(L) 61*, which scored a number of hits on the plane. It targeted *LCS(L) 52*, but fire from both ships shot it down. Its bomb exploded only twenty yards off the starboard quarter of the *52*. A bomb going off that close to a ship was sure to cause damage. *LCS(L) 52* had nine men and one officer killed, with another officer wounded. *LCS(L) 61* closed on the ship and drove off another attacker.

It became imperative for *LCS(L) 52* to go back to the anchorage for repair and to transfer wounded. *LCS(L) 61* was ordered to escort her. As they headed back to Hagushi they came under attack again. *LCS(L) 61* was in the lead with the *52* behind her. A twin-engine Betty bomber approached the ships from astern and the *52* fired on it. The bomber passed over the *52* and made straight for *LCS(L) 61* which, at this point, had taken it under fire as well. On board the *61*, CO Lieutenant Jim Kelley watched the approaching Betty, knowing that the large bomber would surely sink his small gunboat if it were to crash her. Apparently that was what the Betty intended to do. On fire after having been hit by both ships, it headed directly for the conn of the *61*. Kelley coolly watched as the Japanese bomber headed for his ship. At the last moment he called down to Quartermaster Bob Rielly, who was on the wheel, to give the ship hard left rudder. Rielly spun the wheel and the *61* listed severely as she made the rapid turn at flank speed. Many members of the crew thought that they had been hit and that the ship was sinking. The Japanese bomber passed by the ship, missing it by only a few feet. It crashed in the water about twenty feet off the starboard bow. Parts of the plane bounced off the water and landed on the ship's deck and she was showered with gasoline. Scraping noises could be heard as the ship brushed by the remains of the plane. *LCS(L) 61* would live to fight again.[17] It was the fifth kamikaze shot down by the gunboat.

Radar picket station #11A was active from 3 to 5 June. Patrolling there on 3 June were *Robert H. Smith DM 23*, *Thomas E. Fraser DM 24*, *Cassin Young DD 793*, and *LCS(L)s 16, 54, 83*, and *84*. On 3 June between 0215 and 0358, enemy aircraft approached the ships but turned away before the destroyers could engage them. Later that day the LCS(L)s, cruising three miles eastward of the destroyers, were not so fortunate. At 1330 a Zeke was spotted between breaks in the clouds, and minutes later it dove on *LCS(L) 54*. Both *LCS(L) 54* and *16* took it under fire, causing it to change course and head for *16*. It splashed in the water only fifty feet from the gunboat's port side. *LCS(L) 16* was credited with shooting the plane down and *54* was recorded as having made the assist. Several other aircraft approached the gunboats during the next hour but were turned away by their gunfire.

On patrol on 10 June 1945 at RP Station #15A were *William D. Porter DD 579*, *Aulick DD 569*, *Cogswell DD 651*, and *LCS(L)s 18, 86, 94*, and *122*. A total of ten aircraft were overhead. Two Corsairs from the radar picket patrol on Okinawa were assigned to provide direct cover for the ships on station, while two divisions of Corsairs from VMF-212 at Awase, Okinawa, and VMF-314 on Ie Shima flew regular CAP. The pilots from VMF-314 spotted a Val approaching the ships but had to turn away from the interception as the destroyers put up a wall of anti-aircraft fire. *Aulick* and *Porter* had already spotted the enemy plane and taken defensive action. Unfortunately it was not enough. Although they shot the plane down, it crashed so close to *Porter*'s stern that its bomb exploded under the ship. It was almost the same as being mined. No damage to the ship was apparent, but the underwater explosion of the bomb lifted her stern and opened *Porter*'s hull seams. She later reported:

> The plane struck the water close aboard to port, abreast the after engine room. There was a single, violent but almost silent explosion, which seemed to lift the ship bodily and drop it again in a quick movement. The Commanding Officer who had been asleep in the sea cabin was awakened by the explosion, and coming out on the bridge was informed by the Officer of the Deck that the ship had been struck by a Val. It is not known whether the explosive was carried within the plane or in a bomb which might have been released, but it is believed that the explosion occurred nearly directly under the ship, under the after engine room or slightly aft of it. All the events of this paragraph occurred within a space of seconds. Pertinent to the failure of any ship in company to make radar contact on this plane until it had closed to 7000 yards, and to the failure of this ship to make radar contact at all was a later report from one of the LCS's which had recovered parts of the plane, that paper and wood appeared to have been used extensively in its construction.[18]

Porter had been mortally wounded. In a short time it became evident that she could not be saved. Her stern area was filling rapidly with water and it was just a matter of time before she went under. As *Aulick* and *Cogswell* circled her providing anti-aircraft support, the gunboats tied up to her sides and began to aid in pumping her out, but it was a losing battle. Commander C. M. Keyes, the CO of *Porter*, gave the order to abandon ship. He was the last man off, departing his ship at 1113, and stepping aboard *LCS(L) 86*. As the gunboats left the side of the destroyer, it pointed its bow skyward and sank stern first.

Radar picket station #15A continued to be a hot spot for air raids. On 11 June it was patrolled by *Ammen DD 527*, *Aulick DD 569*, and *LCS(L)s 19, 86, 94*, and *122*. Some early morning action at 0730 took place with the CAP shooting down an enemy plane north of the station. Later in

LCS(L) 122, her decks filled with survivors from the destroyer **William D. Porter DD 579**, stands by the sinking ship. *Porter* was struck by a kamikaze at Radar Picket Station #15A on 10 June 1945. On patrol with her that day were the destroyers **Aulick DD 569** and **Cogswell DD 611**, along with *LCS(L)s* **18, 86, 94, and 122**. The four gunboats were instrumental in aiding the destroyer and rescuing its survivors. *Porter* sank later that day with sixty-one of her men listed as wounded.

the day, at 1845, an incoming raid of six Vals was picked up forty miles north of the station and the CAP was vectored to intercept it. The CAP shot down two Vals, but three others escaped their attention and made it to the station. At 1901 the gunboats took the three Vals under fire, shooting one down between *LCS(L)s 86* and *122*. Another Val made a run on the ships and, in spite of being hit by *Aulick* and *LCS(L) 122*, it crashed into the base of the conning tower on *122* after missing *LCS(L) 86* by only ten feet.

The Commanding Officer, Lieutenant Richard M. McCool, was knocked unconscious. Eleven of his crew were killed in the attack and another twenty-nine wounded, including McCool. He later wrote:

> For the second plane, I had ordered "hard right rudder" to make the pilot have to try to adjust his run after it had begun, but I doubt that it had time to be effective. This plane, I believe a so-called VAL bomber with fixed landing gear, hit us at the base of the conning tower with the closest part of the plane about 6–8 feet from me. I believe that I actually made out the face of the pilot before he hit, but that may be my imagination. The bomb (or naval projectile) apparently exploded a split second after impact having gone through the radio shack and the passageway, exiting on the port side. Probably the cylindrical structure of the pilot house is what saved my life.[19]

Fires from the crash burned a number of men, causing twenty-three to jump over the side to escape the flames, but others were still below in the burning ship. *LCS(L)s 19* and *94* tied up to the ship and each other and began working to assist survivors and to check the condition of the *122*. By that time McCool had regained consciousness and took charge, saving his ship. After ensuring that his crew was being taken care of, he was taken off the ship badly wounded. His Executive Officer, Lieutenant R. K. Bruns, took command. For McCool the war was over.

The commanding officer of *LCS(L) 86*, Lieutenant (jg) H. N. Houston, went on board the *122* and put one of his officers, Ensign Warren, in charge of his own ship. *LCS(L) 86* began the arduous task of towing the *122* to Hagushi. Wounded survivors from the ship were on *LCS(L) 94*, which took them directly back for aid. *LCS(L) 19* stood by for assistance if needed. As they reached the transport area, a tug met them and took over the tow.

The commanding officers of the gunboats were all relatively new to command and many acted with extreme courage. At Iwo Jima, the actions of Lieutenant (jg) Rufus Herring, CO of *LCI(G) 449*, were so outstanding that he was awarded the Medal of Honor, the nation's highest award. Then, at Okinawa, Lieutenant Richard M. McCool received the same award. It was the war's second Medal of Honor award to a gunboat's Commanding Officer. The Medal of Honor citation for Lieutenant Richard M. McCool reads:

> For conspicuous gallantry and intrepidity at the risk of his life above and beyond the call of duty as commanding officer of the U.S.S. LCS(L) 3 122 during operations against enemy Japanese forces in the Ryukyu chain, 10 and 11 June 1945. Sharply vigilant during hostile air raids against Allied ships on radar picket duty off Okinawa on 10 June, Lt. McCool aided materially in evacuating all survivors from a sinking destroyer which had sustained mortal damage under the devastating attacks. When his own craft was attacked simultaneously by 2 of the enemy's suicide squadron in the evening of 1 June, he instantly hurled the full power of his gun batteries against the lunging aircraft,

Lieutenant Richard M. McCool receiving the Medal of Honor from President Harry Truman. McCool's ship, *LCS(L) 122*, was struck by a Val kamikaze plane while on Radar Picket Station #15A on 11 June 1945. McCool was severely wounded but was able to continue in command of his ship, saving it and a number of his crew. Official U.S. Navy photograph courtesy Captain Richard M. McCool USN (Ret.).

The wheel of the Val kamikaze plane that crashed into the conning tower of *LCS(L) 122* may be seen on the lower right. The *122* was on Radar Picket Station #15A when she was hit. Official U.S. Navy photograph courtesy Captain Richard M. McCool USN (Ret.).

shooting down the first and damaging the second before it crashed his station in the conning tower and engulfed the immediate area in a mass of flames. Although suffering from shrapnel wounds and painful burns, he rallied his concussion-shocked crew and initiated vigorous firefighting measures and then proceeded to the rescue of several trapped in a blazing compartment, subsequently carrying 1 man to safety despite the excruciating pain of additional severe burns. Unmindful of all personal danger, he continued his efforts without respite until aid arrived from other ships and he was evacuated. By his staunch leadership, capable direction, and indomitable determination throughout the crisis, Lt. McCool saved the lives of many who otherwise might have perished and contributed materially to the saving of his ship for further combat service. His valiant spirit of self-sacrifice in the face of extreme peril sustains and enhances the highest traditions of the U.S. Naval Service.[20]

The Yokosuka K5Y biplane was a Navy trainer. Its Allied code name was "Willow." Toward the end of the war the trainers came into use as kamikazes. Their slow speed made them maneuverable and their wood and fabric construction made it hard to pick them up on radar. Willows attacking the American ships at Okinawa were flown from Japanese naval airfields on Taiwan.

McCool spent the rest of the war in the hospital but went on to a successful career in the Navy, retiring with the rank of Captain.

Attacks on the radar picket stations continued nearly until the end of the war. As more land-based radar stations came into use, the number of picket stations diminished significantly. Between 29 and 30 July, Radar Picket Station #9A was patrolled by *Callaghan DD 792, Pritchett DD 561, Cassin Young DD 793,* and *LCS(L)s 125, 129,* and *130.* Although a significant amount of firepower patrolled the station, it would not be sufficient to prevent the last sinking of the war. The last ship sunk on radar picket duty at Okinawa was *Callaghan.* A single Japanese plane approached the station at 0030 and was taken under fire by *Pritchett* and *Callaghan,* but they failed to stop it. It crashed into *Callaghan's* main deck aft. Its 250 lb. bomb penetrated her deck and exploded below in the aft engine room. Although ships frequently suffered stronger attacks, it was always a matter of luck as to whether they survived. An important factor was whether or not the ship's firefighting apparatus was damaged or destroyed. In the case of *Callaghan* it was. With her crews unable to stop the fires, it was only a few minutes until flames reached the upper handling room of the number 3 gun and caused a massive explosion. The blast tore a hole in the hull, virtually dooming the ship. Within minutes she was listing fifteen degrees to starboard and was down by the stern. The commanding officer of *LCS(L) 125,* Lieutenant Howell C. Cobb, moored his ship to *Callaghan's* port side and began to fight the fires. Lieutenant William H. File, Jr., CO of *LCS(L) 130,* brought his ship close along the port side and also began firefighting, while *LCS(L) 129,* under Lieutenant Louis A. Brennan, circled the area rescuing survivors. With the threat of other approaching enemy aircraft, the LCS(L)s moved away from the destroyer to aid in anti-aircraft activity. An incoming plane fell under the guns of *LCS(L) 130* and hit the water near *Pritchett*.

The fires on *Callaghan* diminished somewhat but her ammunition began to cook off, causing increasing danger to the men on board and the nearby gunboats. Between 0200 and 0205 she was abandoned and sank at 0234, stern first. Lieutenant Cobb reported:

> Passed close aboard the Callaghan and she was settling slowly by the stern. At 0234 the Callaghan sank by the stern with depth charges going off a short time later. At this time we were about a mile away and we received a substantial concussion from charges. It is thought that anyone still in the water within a half mile could not have survived this explosion. As far as we know there were no more men taken from the water afterward.[21]

The work of the gunboats had been important, even though they were not able to save the ship. For their actions Lieutenant William File (*130*) was awarded the Silver Star and Lieutenants Howell C. Cobb (*125*) and Louis A. Brennan (*129*) were awarded the Bronze Star.

Toward the end of the war, the Japanese had resorted to using biplane trainers as kamikazes. The aircraft were not very fast but were quite maneuverable. Their wood and fabric construction made it extremely hard for the ships to pick them up on radar. The aircraft that attacked the ships at RP #9A on 30 July 1945 were apparently Navy Willow trainers which flew from bases on Taiwan.

As early as 17 May, it was obvious that the picket ships had taken substantial losses, but that they had also performed their task exceptionally well. Vice Admiral Richmond K. Turner wrote:

> The picket system operated efficiently. While eight and nine picket stations were filled, raids were detected at an average distance of 72 miles from the reference point at PT. BOLO, which was a few miles North of the main transport area and close to KADENA and YONTAN airfields. Only seven percent of all raids approached within 50 miles of PT. BOLO undetected; less than one percent approached within thirty miles undetected.[22]

The battle for the radar picket stations had taken its toll. Men had been subjected to constant calls to general quarters, making any semblance of rest impossible. Numerous ships had been hit by kamikazes or attacked by aircraft or suicide boats. Lieutenant Howell D. Chickering, Commanding Officer of *LCS(L) 51*, would later write:

> For all practical purposes, the war ended for me shortly after this final episode at Okinawa [sinking of *Callaghan*]. The island was secured by our armed forces, and all picket ships were called in. We were boarded by a Navy medical crew for examination, and I was ordered to the hospital ship Solace, or maybe it was Comfort — I forget.
>
> I had lost 40 pounds, 85% of the hearing in my left ear, had blast concussion, advanced anorexia — loss of appetite, and couldn't sleep without Nembutol. Along with other picket Captains, combat fatigue had finally caught up with me, and we were sent back home for rest and recuperation, via ship and plane, stopping at Tinian, Hawaii, San Francisco and, for me, the Naval Hospital in Philadelphia.[23]

Chickering's ship had performed exemplary service. For her actions on 16 April at Radar Picket Station #1, she was awarded the Presidential Unit Citation, and Chickering was awarded the Navy Cross.

Chapter 12

War's End and Post-War

What Might Have Been

The events surrounding the dropping of the atomic bombs on Japan and the ending of the war have been covered exhaustively in numerous books and articles. It is not the purpose of this work to delve into President Harry S. Truman's motives in the final months of World War II. However, it is informative to assess the role of the LCS(L) and LCI gunboats had the invasion of Japan actually taken place.

By 1945, the value of the amphibious gunboats had been recognized and continuing conversions were ordered. This became particularly noteworthy during the invasion of Okinawa, and numerous conversions of ships into rocket and mortar versions were under way in the final months of the war. That they would have been in the first wave of any assault on Japan proper was a foregone conclusion. A cursory look at any amphibious assault plan indicated that the LCI gunboats and the LCS(L)s were the first line of attack in any landing.

A directory of amphibious vessels, including the LCI gunboats and the LCS(L)s, was put forth by the Amphibious Forces, U.S. Pacific Fleet on 15 May 1945 and listed sixty-six LCI(G)s, fifty-five LCI(M)s, thirty-four LCI(R)s, and ninety-nine LCS(L)s. This gave the Amphibious Forces a total of 254 amphibious gunboats available for the landings in Japan as of 15 May.[1] Some additional gunboats were still on patrol around various bypassed islands but would probably have to remain on duty there to keep the Japanese troops under control. An additional forty-four LCI(FF)s were available to act as flotilla flagships. Other ships were en route to Okinawa even as the list was published. Back in the States numerous other LCI(L)s were being converted to bolster the numbers. Orders for new LCS(L)s had not been promulgated and the *LCS(L) 108* was the last of the class, having been launched at Commercial Iron Works in Portland, Oregon on 10 March 1945.[2]

Although the end of the war was only months away, there was no way that the Americans could know that. The launch of *LCS(L) 108* signaled the end of the run of 130 LCS(L)s, but it was also possible that more might be ordered. Conversion of LCI(L)s continued with a number not finished until after the war ended. Some, in the beginning stages of conversion, were cancelled. Continued changes in the armament and configuration of the converted gunboats was obvious. The final conversions had morphed into quasi-LCS(L)s mounting director controlled twin 40mm guns, as well as 20mm and .50 cal. machine guns. This last change reflected the need for additional anti-aircraft capability since the Japanese air attacks had escalated as the Allied forces approached the home islands of Japan. Lacking on these final versions of the converted gunboats were the Mk. 7 rocket launchers carried by all LCS(L)s and most of the LCI(G)s. Had

As the war neared its final stages and modification of the LCI gunboats progressed, various changes took place. *LCI(G) 538*, shown here off Jacksonville, Florida, was one of the last conversions of the war, having been converted after LCS(L) gunboats had been placed in service. She closely approximates the LCS(L) in both her armament and profile. NARA 19 LCM LCI (G) 538.

the war continued, additional LCS(L)s might have been ordered and other LCI(L)s converted. How many additional gunboats might have been available for the invasion of Japan is open to speculation. Since the invasion of Kyushu would have seen some of the gunboats lost, it is possible that more might have been converted or produced.

During the war gunboat service had been hazardous with the ships subjected to attack from air, land, and sea. Their small size, maneuverability, and heavy armament had weighed in their favor. However, they had paid a toll. Statistics compiled after the war indicated that the LCS(L)s had a Rate of Ship Casualties calculated at .986. This was compared to the average of .56 for the combined ships serving in the Pacific Theater. No separate statistics were formulated for the LCI gunboats, but LCI(L)s overall had a rate of .66. Of the seventy-six ship types listed in the report, the only ships with higher rates than the LCS(L)s were: Patrol Craft YP (11.830); Ocean Tugs Old ATO (9.004); Patrol Gunboats PG (7.727); Fuel Oil Barges YO (5.218); Mine Layers CM (3.621); Ocean Tugs AT (2.635); Submarines SS (1.894); Heavy Cruisers CA (1.678); High-Speed Transports APD (1.116); and Submarine Tenders AS (1.075). These were ships heavily engaged in combat activities, hazardous assignments, or simply unequipped to defend themselves properly.[3]

Typhoon Ida

The war had ended, but the forces of nature were always perilous. Typhoon Ida roared through Okinawa on 15–16 September 1945, causing significant damage to ships in the area.

LCI(G) 67 was anchored in Nakagusuku Bay in seven fathoms of water on 15 September. There had been no warnings of a typhoon, and her commanding officer, Lieutenant (jg) G. L. Burris, had gone ashore at 1320 leaving Ensign Thomas F. Lerch as the O.O.D. At 2130 Lerch received a notice that a storm was heading in his direction and he took the necessary precautions to ready the ship for heavy weather. All loose gear was secured, and he inspected the ship and its anchor cable as the wind began to pick up. At 0530 on 16 September, the full force of the typhoon was on the ship. Buffeted by high winds and seas, the ship's anchor cable parted about six feet from the eye and she began to drift towards a nearby reef. Lerch had the engines started and the anchor cable pulled in, but the force of the wind and waves was too much. *LCI(G) 67* was pushed onto the reef at 0540, where she took a fifteen degree list to starboard. Within five minutes the list had increased to twenty-five degrees. Calls were sent out to the SOPA but no response was received. At 0900 the ship finally made contact with the salvage vessel *Extricate ARS 16* which was standing by. However, the force of the waves and the close proximity to the reef made it impossible for her to help and she was called away to assist another vessel. At 0955 a large swell lifted the ship off the reef and set her on shore where her list was only ten degrees. Still another swell at 1015 moved her further inland and put her on an even keel. She was safe on shore, but her hull had sustained damage from being pounded against the reef. At 1120 her CO, Lieutenant (jg) Burris, was able to return to his beached ship. The sudden escalation of waves and wind had prevented his return during the storm. *LCI(G) 67* remained high and dry for the next several months. On 31 December 1945, her commissioning pennant was lowered and she was officially decommissioned from the United States Navy. She was eventually scrapped.

LCI(R) 230 chose to ride out the storm with other ships of Group Twenty in Nago Bay. At 0029 on 16 September her anchor began to drag and she had to get underway. By 0400 the storm

LCI(G) 67 hard aground at Baten Ko on Nakagusuku Bay, Okinawa. She was driven ashore on 16 October 1945 when the area was hit by a typhoon. It was not possible to pull her off and she was officially decommissioned on 31 December 1945. Official U.S. Navy photograph.

LCI(R) 337 (center) and *LCI(G) 463* (right) were driven ashore in Nakagusuku Bay, Okinawa, during Typhoon Louise. Official U.S. Navy photograph.

was at its height with waves of twenty feet and winds estimated at fifty knots. The confines of the bay made it difficult for ships to maneuver and many were either dragging anchor or underway. At 0420 she scraped up against *LCI(L) 965* and then had to dodge an LCS(L) which was heading for her port bow. Her CO ordered her starboard engines to full power, but the wind and waves turned her so that her bow was again against *LCI(L) 965*. Another contact with the LCI was made and the *230* scraped her bow against the anchored ship before clearing it. Fortunately, there was no damage to either ship.

In spite of competent ship handling, circumstances were beyond the control of the ship and its crew. It was maneuvering between two anchored ships at 0452 when it spotted a disabled LCI heading in its direction from off its port bow. Engines were backed at two-thirds to help clear the ships but the wind and waves were too powerful. *LCI(R) 230* found her bow passing over the anchor line from *LCI(L)776* and had to stop her engines to avoid fouling her screws. Within seconds her port side collided with *LCI(L) 776*'s port stern corner. The result was a three by four foot hole in the LCI(R)'s side which caused flooding in her A205L compartment. The amount of water entering the ship was too much for the temporary shoring that had been put in place, and the gunboat was in danger of sinking. To save his ship her commanding officer, Ensign J. H. Brown, Jr., decided to beach her. *LCI(R) 230* headed for the beach at two-thirds speed. When it came time to drop her stern anchor, it would not drop and the gunboat had to beach without it at 0533. Within minutes strong waves pushed her stern around and she broached. It was high tide and the ship was able to kedge her anchor out and pull herself off after the storm had passed. No injuries had been reported and the ship survived a close call.[4]

Another Group Twenty ship, *LCI(R) 337,* found herself in a difficult situation. Her commanding officer, Lieutenant (jg) Wilferd H. Baum, had brought her to *Coronis ARL-10* in Nakagusuku Wan for numerous repairs. Her port quad engines were not running and her starboard quad could only make 380 RPMs. A new pitch control shaft had just been installed and had yet to be adjusted, so her ability to put to sea to avoid the storm was non-existent. She was anchored next to the repair ship and began dragging her anchor at 0436. Her engines were started and she regained her berth. At 1010 her stern anchor cable parted and the ship was at the mercy of the storm. Once again her engines were started and the ship maneuvered about the harbor, barely avoiding collisions with other ships in the area. Finally, with no other prospect in sight, her CO decided to run her ashore next to the auxiliary floating dry dock *AFD-13* which had been beached earlier. The gunboat tied up to the dry dock with the expectation that she would be safe, however, that was soon found to be in error. At 1303 the mooring lines parted and the waves pulled the dry dock off the beach, leaving the gunboat on its own. A barge used for living quarters for the crew of the dry dock was adrift and pounded the side of the gunboat as it sat on the beach. Lines from the barge fouled the gunboat's propellers and she was damaged. At 1510 mooring lines were run from the gunboat up to another barge that lay beached so that the gunboat would not be pulled out to sea. The remainder of her anchor line was passed ashore and secured to the barge as well. The sleeping quarters below had been damaged by the pounding, and the Executive Officer with six of the crewmen went ashore to find shelter for the remainder of the storm.

The following morning a survey of the gunboat was made which revealed five large holes and a smaller one in the ship's hull. Bent frames, submerged engines and other machines, along with general flooding throughout the ship had occurred. The pounding against the coral reef beneath her had bent both of her drive shafts and practically destroyed her twin screws and three skegs. Her rocket racks had sustained severe damage and the 20mm gun on her starboard side aft was destroyed. All manner of equipment, both personal and official, had washed out of the many holes in the ship.[5] She was one more victim of the storm.

Typhoon Louise

Less than a month passed before the next typhoon hit the fleet at Okinawa. Navy observers had identified its beginnings north of Rota in the Marianas Islands on 4 October 1945 and predicted that it would head toward mainland China north of Taiwan. However, storms are not always predictable. This one, named Typhoon Louise, turned north heading directly for Okinawa. The main anchorage for the ships by that time was Nakagusuku Bay, also known as Buckner Bay after the death of Army Lieutenant General Simon B. Buckner during the battle for the island. The bay was large and fairly protected from most minor storms, however, the magnitude of this storm was too great and would result in damage to numerous ships and shore installations.

Forecasts for this storm predicted sustained winds of sixty knots, gusting to ninety in the waters around Okinawa. The Commander In Chief, Pacific Fleet and Pacific Ocean Areas, later reported:

> "Louise," however, failed to conform to pattern, and that evening, as it reached 25° N (directly south of Okinawa) it slowed to six knots and greatly increased in intensity. As a result, the storm which struck in the afternoon of the 9th has seldom been paralleled in fury and violence; the worst storm at Okinawa since our landings in April.
>
> The sudden shift of the storm 12 hours before its expected maximum, from a predicted path 150 miles west of Okinawa to an actual path that brought the center of the storm less than 15 miles east of Okinawa's southeast coast, caught many craft in the supposedly safe shelter of Buckner Bay [Nakagusuku Bay] without time to put to sea far enough to clear the storm. The ninth of October found

the Bay jammed with ships ranging in size from Victory ships to LCV(P)s. All units, both afloat and ashore, were hurriedly battening down and securing for the storm.[6]

The actual intensity of the storm, measured at its peak on 9 October at 1600, revealed sustained winds of 100 knots with gusts to 120. Seas measuring thirty to thirty-five feet were recorded in the bay, causing many ships to drag anchor or part anchor lines. The power of most of the smaller vessels was insufficient to maneuver under those conditions and a number were driven ashore.

The storm passed but the damage to the American fleet was severe. Had the war not ended and the storm struck earlier, it would have had a significant impact on any invasion campaign against the main islands of Japan. CinCPacPOA reported:

> A total of 12 ships were sunk, 222 grounded, and 32 damaged beyond the ability of ships' companies to repair. ComServDiv 104 under Commodore T. J. Keliher, was assigned to the salvage work. By 19 November, 79 ships had been refloated, and 132 were under repair. The remaining 53 badly damaged vessels still afloat had been, or were being, decommissioned, stripped, and abandoned. On 14 November, ComServPac, (Vice Admiral W. W. Smith) inspected the damage, and decided that only 10 ships were worth complete salvage, out of some 90 ships with major work to be done on them. This decision was made chiefly because similar types of ships were rapidly being decommissioned in the United States, and the cost of salvage would have been excessive for unneeded ships.[7]

Among the ships deemed unworthy of salvage were a number of LCI(L)s, LCI(FF)s and LCI gunboats.

Gunboats to China and Korea

The ending of hostilities was not the end of action for the amphibious gunboats. Numerous tasks had to be performed in the aftermath of the war, including the repatriation of Japanese forces to their homeland, the clearing of minefields, and covering the landing of American forces in various locales in Japan, Korea, and China.

From 27 September to 3 October 1945, Task Unit 78.1.7 operated in conjunction with the landing of the 1st Marine Division at Tientsin in North China. The task unit, under the command of Captain Rae E. Arison, consisted of *LCS(L)s 27–29, 44, 46, 47* and *LCI(L) 778* along with Mortar Support Division Six under Lieutenant H. M. Mattson, which included *LCI(M)s 801–806*.

Their primary mission was to furnish fire support for the landing of the Marines at Taku Bay, Tientsin, but their services were not needed and the Marines landed without incident. The gunboats remained in the area, covering the transit of LSMs up the Hai Ho River to the Russian Bund, where they stood by as the ships unloaded supplies. Swift river currents made anchoring difficult and the narrow river had numerous sand bars, causing some of the ships to run aground. Their mission was completed by 3 October and the gunboats withdrew.[8]

Mattson's Mortar Support Division Six headed for Tsingtao to support Marine landings on 10 October and returned to Taku Bay on 15 October. Several of the ships were assigned to accompany the Kailan Mining Administration as they recovered a dredge that had been taken by the communists. Routine patrols and the transport of sailors from the larger ships on liberty runs occupied the ships until the end of November. Then they prepared to return to the States.

As the battle for Okinawa commenced, numerous gunboats began to arrive on the scene. Many were new conversions of existing LCI(L)s, and others were the newly designed LCS(L)s. A surplus of these vessels, along with the need to give their crews some rest and relaxation from the battle scene, saw a number of them sent south to Leyte and other locations in the Philippines. There they would gather their strength for the final assault on the home islands of Japan.

Fortunately this never came to be. They were in the Philippines when word came that the war had ended. Many were sent stateside and others retained in the Far East for a variety of duties. The first of the assignments was the occupation of Japan, and gunboats not headed for the States headed north to Kyushu, Tokyo Bay, and other locations in Japan. There they assisted in covering the landing of troops, served as troop carriers, mail carriers, minesweeper escorts, and any other duty that the Navy brass desired. In all, 354 ships were slated to join the occupation force, including *LCI(G)s 438, 441, 450, 457, 458, 469, 726, 752, LCI(R)s 647, 649, 762, 763, 785, 1024, 1026, 1068–1070,* and *LCS(L)s 3, 61–69, 81–87, 89, 90, 92–95, 114, 115, 117–119,* and *121–124*.[9] Acting as liberty boats for the battleships and other large ships was a common task. As many as 150 sailors could be carried on the decks of one of the gunboats. Upon landing, the MPs would search the men for contraband that might be sold on the black market. Once this had been accomplished, the MPs left the docks, leaving the gunboat crews free reign to wander about on shore without being searched.

Clearing Minefields

As hostilities ended, a serious problem remained in the waters around the Japanese-held islands and, in particular, around the home islands. During the war, the Japanese had placed mines in a number of areas in order to thwart attacks by American warships. In addition, the Allied forces had mined Japanese waters to jeopardize their supply lines. The war had ended, but not the danger from the mines which had no ability to distinguish friend from foe. One of the tasks for the Allied forces was the sweeping and destruction of mines in numerous areas. It was common practice for minesweepers to be accompanied by several gunboats.

The standard minesweeping procedures used during the war continued. Minesweepers cut mines loose from the sea floor, the mine surfaced, and was taken under fire by the gunboats. In many cases regular rifle fire was used, but .50 caliber, 20mm and 40mm guns might also be used. Peter Elliot claimed that in the twenty minesweeping operations in and around Japan, a total of 11,200 mines were cleared.[10]

The only positive note about the post-war minesweeping activities was that there were no enemy gun emplacements on shore to fire on the minesweepers and gunboats as they pursued the task. The purpose of the minesweeping had also changed. Instead of clearing an area for invasion, it was now necessary to clear the waters around Japan so the Allied forces could be supplied and some normalcy returned to Japanese shipping. Supplies were desperately needed in Japan, and importing many of them was necessary. Japanese minesweepers were also put into use to clear the waterways.

The hazards of minesweeping continued. Charles Thomas, Gunner's Mate 2/c on *LCS(L) 35,* wrote:

> After several more days of sweeping, during which the 35 destroys two additional mines, we again head back to Kiirun. Back in harbor, when the 35 ties up alongside the 56, only inches separate the two vessels. Almost at once we sense a pall hanging over the 56. "Okie" Yost greets a big man who is obviously taking a break from his duties in the engine room. The big man in the grease stained dungarees slowly strolls along the deck of the 56 smoking a cigarette. Yost quickly determines the reason for our feelings of foreboding.
>
> "One of our guys got killed a couple of weeks back," the man from the 56 says. "What the hell happened?" Yost exclaims "Who was it?"
>
> "Gunners Mate named John Cooper." The crewman from the 56 says tersely. "Damn mine cut him right in two."
>
> "Cut in two! Jesus Christ!"
>
> "Yes, the skipper pulled in a little too close when the sweepers cut a mine. John was in the port

Crewmen on board *LCI(L) 88* fire on mines in Kii Suido Strait, Japan, on 13 February 1946. This was a common task for all LCI(L)s, LCS(L)s, and LCI gunboats during the war and in the post-war period. Official U.S. Coast Guard photograph NARA RG 26-G.

twenty gun tub in the waist waiting for the guys with the rifles to give up. All of a sudden the sonovabitch really went off."

"Go On," Yost says.

"John was standing in the gun tub leaning over the edge and watching. He would have been firing at it himself in another minute. Just then one of the guys hit it in the right place with a rifle bullet. When it went up, a big piece of flying steel cut John completely in two. The top half fell over the side — we never did find that part, and his legs scooted across the deck. His guts went all over the gun tub."[11]

Cooper's remains were stitched into a canvas bag, weighted down, and buried at sea. He had been due to return home to his wife shortly after the accident that caused his death.

China Duty

LCS(L) 27 and the LCS(L) Group One ships were stationed at Subic Bay in the Philippines undergoing training for the invasion of Japan when the war ended. LCS(L) Group One ships included *LCS(L)s 8–10, 27–30, 48,* and *50*. They were ordered to Jinsen (Inchon), Korea, in September where they did routine patrol and mine destruction. In October their assignment changed and they were ordered to Taku Bay, China, to cover the occupation by the 3rd Marine Division.

The Marines had already landed and were being shipped by train upriver to Tientsin. Their landing had been covered by LCI(M)s from Mortar Support Division Six. The gunboats headed up the Hai Ho River to cover them if needed. Tientsin was still in the hands of the Japanese who were awaiting repatriation. LSTs were in the process of repatriating them from the city and bringing them back to Japan. It was not unusual for the ships to go from Jinsen to Tientsin, or Shanghai and back. The areas were close enough so that they could easily make the trip if their duties were needed, primarily for minesweeping.

A major complication for the gunboats were the throngs of well-wishing Chinese who packed the river banks. Once at Tsientsin the docks were so crowded with onlookers that the ships had difficulty tying up. The city proved to be a good liberty port, with the gunboat sailors taking advantage of the opportunity. Unfortunately, not all were careful with their liaisons and came down with venereal disease.[12] Sailors on some ships were particularly careless. D. Reid Ross, who served as Gunnery Officer on *LCS(L) 58*, reported that "During the two months we were in Shanghai one third of the ship's crew contracted venereal disease, despite the fact that they couldn't leave the ship without being given a prophylactic. Fortunately a Navy hospital ship was tied up immediately behind us, where a steady stream of our crewmen received treatment."[13] By December 1945 the ships were on their way home.

LCS(L) Flotilla Three Group Seven ships had been in Wakayama, Japan, performing a number of routine duties when they received word that they were being reassigned. On 24 October 1945 they left Wakayama and headed for Nagoya in company with six LSTs, five LSMs and an LCI(L). They were to land occupation troops there and perform additional duties as needed. This assignment lasted only about two weeks and, on 13 November, they departed for Jinsen, Korea. Included in the group were *LCS(L)s 31, 34, 51, 52, 54,* and *57,* along with *LC(FF) 484.* They arrived in Jinsen on 19 November and came under the command of Captain Rae E. Arison who was serving as Commander Task Group 71.3.

Problems for the ships working around Jinsen included swift currents and high tidal falls. Once the ships had arrived, they were sent out on various tasks, most of which involved mine sweeping. Although previous practice had the gunboats working with minesweepers, this time they were on their own. Their task was to spot the mines and explode them wherever they could be found. Frank N. Farmer who served on *LCS(L) 34* noted: "Equipment aboard was totally inadequate for this type of assignment. Lookouts stationed at various positions on the ship served as the only method of mine detection."[14] The mine total for the ships was not great, but every one destroyed eliminated a threat to other ships.

Finally on 10 December 1945 *LCS(L) 34* and her companion ships received orders to head home. As Farmer later wrote:

> But the days and months ahead were destined to be trying ones. Experienced personnel had left or were leaving at each step. Engines and other machines, built for but one operation, began to tell the strain of two major operations and a completed tour of the Orient. Each port found more work to be accomplished and less time; by inexperienced men and each period underway brought to light new difficulties to be reckoned with.[15]

The ships made it to Saipan for Christmas. From there they headed for Eniwetok, Pearl Harbor, and finally San Pedro, California, which they reached on 3 February 1946. While a number of the sailors were transferred off the ships in California, many remained on for the final voyage from San Pedro to the Panama Canal and then up to New Orleans where the ships were prepared for decommissioning. Once ready to be moth-balled, they were sailed to Green Cove Springs, Florida, to be part of the Reserve Fleet. On 6 May *LCS(L) 34* arrived at her final destination. For her the war was over.

LCS(L) 78 and the Group Seven ships left Okinawa on 17 November heading for Jinsen, Korea, where they arrived on 21 November. The few weeks on duty at Jinsen passed slowly with

The high tidal range at Jinsen (Inchon), Korea, made it possible for ships to examine their bottoms and do repair work when the tide went out. *LCS(L) 44* is shown grounded at Jinsen, Korea, in the fall of 1945. Courtesy Kenneth J. DeBoer.

everyone anxious to head for the States as soon as possible. It was not a desirable place for the gunboat sailors. Merl L. Riggs, who served on *LCS(L) 78*, wrote: "Jinsen is a hell hole and I wouldn't wish it on a dog to be stationed there. There is a treacherous tide that makes anchoring very difficult."[16] Here and there men with enough accumulated points were transferred off the ships and sent home for discharge.

U.S. Forces Assigned to China

The Commander of Task Force 73, Commander Yangtze Patrol Force, was Rear Admiral C. Turner Joy. His Cruiser Group (TG 73.1.1) consisted of two light cruisers, *Nashville CL 43* and *St. Louis CL 49*, and two destroyers, *Waller DD 466* and *Philip DD 498*. The remainder of Task Force 73 was made up of six AMs, eighteen YMSs, six DDs, one AOG, two PCs, two AGs, one APD, fifty LCI(L)s, six PCs, and seven PGMs. Within a short period of time, the force was bolstered by the arrival of a number of gunboats, including LCI(G)s and LCS(L)s:

> Superimposed on the above was an additional outfit from Rear Admiral Bertram Rodger's Seventh Amphibious Force, which had shotgun responsibility for lifting Nationalist troops and equipment downriver, setting to rights the scrambled or missing navigational aids, marking wrecks, and transporting United Nations Relief and Rehabilitation Agency (UNRRA) supplies and personnel upriver. The "relief supplies" would be food and medical supplies that had been stockpiled for Operation Olympic, the invasion of Japan.[17]

Captain R. C. ("Zeke") Pedin controlled the area from Shanghai to Nanking, a distance of 210 miles, while Captain Clarence E. Coffin controlled the area from Nanking to Chungking which was 1,115 miles in length. Coffin operated out of Hankow through August 1946 as CTG 78.2. His last mission was to transport a U.S. trained artillery regiment to Nanking in July 1946.

One of the interests that the United States had in regard to China was access to the interior

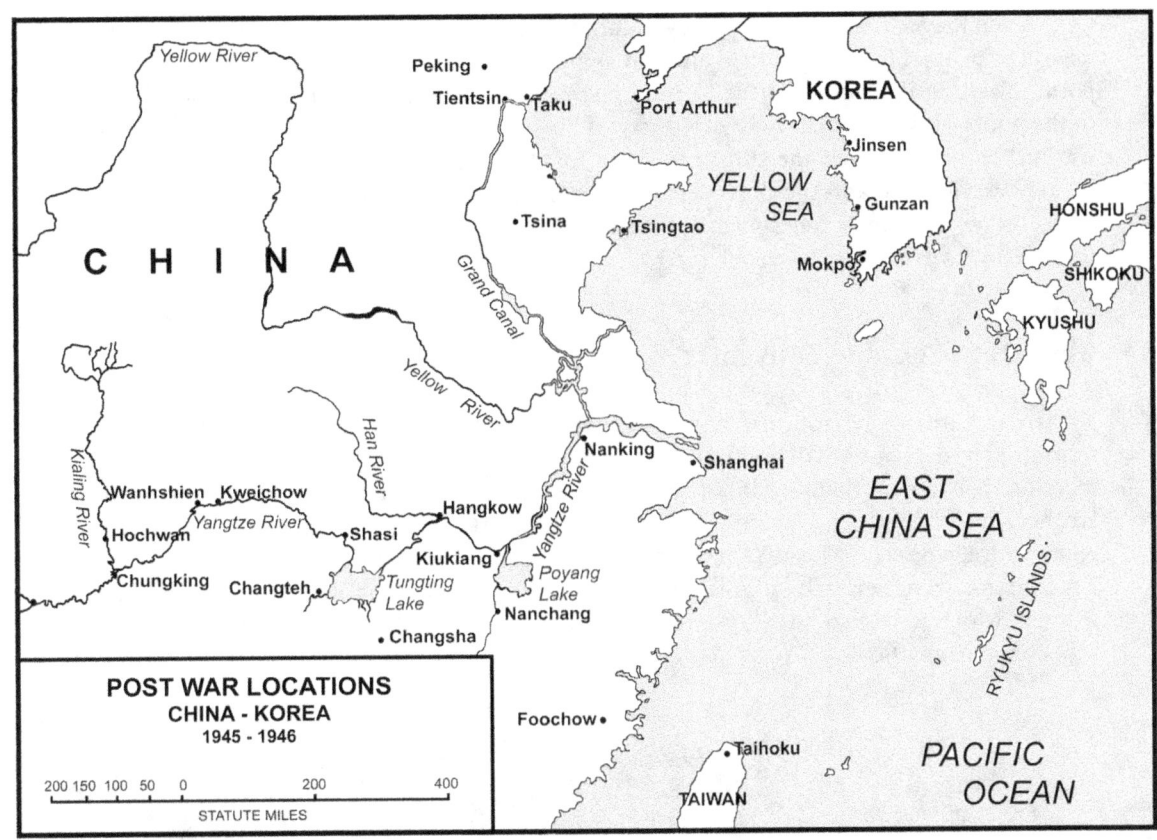

The end of the war did not mean the end of duty for the LCS(L)s and LCI gunboats. There were numerous tasks to be undertaken in China and Korea including mine destruction, the landing of Marine forces in China and Korea, and the repatriation of Japanese forces.

by transiting up the Yangtze River. The Commander Yangtze Patrol Force determined that a survey of the river was in order. *John Blish*, a Coast and Geodetic Survey Vessel, was sent up the river from Shanghai inland as far as Hankow which lay approximately 650 miles upstream. Assigned to provide security for the survey ship were *LCS(L) 75* and *PC 1134*.

The ships, operating as TG 73.6, departed Shanghai on 19 November 1945 when they left the Wangpoo River and entered the Yangtze. William B. Bell, who served as Communications Officer aboard the *LCS(L) 75*, recalled:

> There was a strong feeling of apprehension as we left Shanghai and entered the Yangtze. What we knew was that on the north side of the river were massed upwards of 90,000 Japanese soldiers with full artillery who had not yet surrendered to anyone. This was within days of the peace signing on the Missouri in Tokyo harbor. And while the Japanese Army remained under excellent discipline they were only now being sent out in open railroad cars for repatriation to Japan. I will say that they showed admirable restraint in not firing, for example, a 150mm Howitzer at us. Of this they were perfectly capable, and it would have spoiled our trip right away. We saw them as only a vast Army which was completely obedient to its leaders and at no time did they do anything to threaten us.[18]

As the small fleet progressed up the river, they had greater problems with which to be concerned. Nationalist control of many areas had dwindled, only to be replaced by Communist control. The journey was uneventful and the ships reached Nanking. Progress up the river was slow. The current ran at four to six knots in many places, and the ships had to use the full power of their engines to make any significant progress.

When they reached Hangkow they found the city in relatively good condition, but it seemed devoid of people. It had been held alternately by the Japanese, the Nationalists, and was, at that point, awaiting the arrival of the Communist forces. At Hangkow a local warlord paid a visit to the gunboat with about twenty to thirty of his men. It was a cordial visit but ended with the warlord demanding that the ships accede to his demands for weapons and ammunition. The "order" was ignored and the ships departed for Shanghai, their mission completed.[19] As a result of the survey mission, a *Book of Sailing Instructions* for the Yangtze was published and distributed to American vessels transiting the river.

Bumboats, Sex, and Souvenirs

In any area away from the immediate war zone, bum boats would appear. This was the term used to describe small boats manned by local natives who came out to trade for anything of value. For sale on the bum boats were various goods and services ranging from local fruit, alcohol, craft items, pets, Japanese left-over equipment, or women. Enterprising natives were ready to trade or sell basically anything they could to obtain American dollars or equipment. Trade items were generally allowed with the exception of alcohol, which was banned, and women, which were also not allowed. This prohibition did not prevent crewmen from making other arrangements.

At any location away from the immediate war zone, natives in local small craft swarmed around the gunboats attempting to sell or barter whatever they could to support themselves. The native boats were referred to as "bum boats" and were a common sight. Here sailors on a group of LCS(L)s tied up at port in Tsingtao, China, shortly after the war, barter with Chinese. The photograph was taken from the conning tower of *LCS(L) 48*. Courtesy Robert Amick, *LCS(L) 48*.

In areas where liberty ashore was permitted it was the usual practice to allow only half the crew off the ship at a time. Port and Starboard sections divided the liberty time allotted. It would not be prudent to leave the ship basically unoccupied or unprotected from thieves or bandits in a foreign country, particularly where there was little or no authority in control.

Where shore liberty was granted, sailors headed for bars and looked for women. Pimps were ready to oblige and it was not difficult to find prostitutes in any port town. Penicillin, recently developed, managed to stop most cases of venereal disease. It was administered by the Pharmacist's Mate on board the gunboats. However, some cases were not cured so easily and it was not uncommon for men to be transferred to hospital ships for treatment.

Shanghai was typical of the liberty ports, and Raymond J. Ross reported that "Bum boats filled every available position alongside [*LCS(L) 60*] to sell their wares. Mostly junk jewelry and novelties. Many of the crew tried their watches at $2.00 to $5.00. Most of them turned out to be poor potatoes.... Shanghai is perhaps the most corrupt city in the world. Lots of fun on liberty here."[20] Shanghai turned out to be a good liberty port. There was relative order in the streets and numerous businesses were anxious to relieve the American sailors of their money. Good food, entertainment, and women were available for any who wished to pay the price. Most of the prices were relatively inexpensive, even for an enlisted man's pay.

LCS(L) 35 had similar experiences with the Shanghai bum boats. Charles Thomas recalled:

> On these particular "bum boats" the principal sales items were liquor and women: "Whisky for good time sailor! Best Scotch! Hay and Hay!" Other boats follow with the other principal item of trade. "Nice young Hong Kong school girl, Joe!" the boatmen call enticingly. Other boats offer all manner of services and trinkets: barbers, garbage collectors, dentists (how about a gold tooth sailor?), picture post cards, pornographic pictures, photos of the city, books, Chinese lacquer work, and hand-made silks. Several of the boatmen hawk cigarette lighters that turn out to be cheap copies of a Ronson, an expensive American cigarette lighter. These "Ronsons," however, are stamped with the word "RANSON," underlined by extending the line from the "R" beneath the word in the trademark style of the Ronson.[21]

Tientsin was not much different. Enterprising pimps worked out arrangements with sailors. When *LCS(L) 27* anchored in the river on a dark night in October 1945, she was soon serviced by the locals. Harry G. Meister, Engineering Officer on *LCS(L)27* recalled: "On the trip down the river we encountered darkness and had to anchor in the river. A sampan had come alongside with a whore. A number of the crew were lined up on the bow when someone yelled, 'The Skipper.' With that, one guy grabbed her feet and another her arms and threw her overboard."[22] It is not clear if the sampan returned in the following days. Bum boats also brought women to *LCS(L) 35*, where they were taken on board and serviced a number of the crew in the gun tubs and aft steering room.[23] Throughout the harbor this became a common occurrence unless the officers were on hand to put a stop to it. The smaller ships, such as the gunboats, were able to obtain the services of the prostitutes in this manner as their freeboard was not that high. Larger ships had a more difficult time bringing women aboard.

Almost as much as desiring women and alcohol, both of which were impossible to obtain in the war zone, the men longed for a good meal. Months of powdered milk and mashed potatoes, canned spam and other poor substitutes for food had left them with a desire for something much better, and the liberty ports obliged. Raymond J. Ross from *LCS(L) 60*, recalled:" Councilman and I went on liberty together. Shopped. Ate three dinners: Jimmy's, Barcelona Club and Army chow. Met Sgt. Appert of Milwaukee at Army P.X. on Joffre Ave. Had Schlitz and Budweiser beer. 10¢ per can — best deal in Shanghai."[24]

While on board their ships the sailors were well protected from disease. Their immunity inoculations for various diseases found in the Far East protected them in most cases. Once the war was over and the sailors began to move ashore, any number of problems with disease arose.

Dysentery was endemic in the Philippines and China. In some cases men swam off the gunboats close to the beach. One crew swam in water near the outlet of a local river that was contaminated by heavy concentrations of sewage from villages along the shore. Many of them contracted dysentery. One could never feel safe in foreign lands where poor sanitation was the norm.

No matter where the gunboats landed, there were always the homeless and hungry. Many of these were children who had been abandoned or orphaned during the war. It was difficult to see so much misery knowing that little could be done to help. Any scraps left over from the meals were given to the people nearby who were begging for food. Most sailors did what they could, but there were always a few who refused to help.

Duty in China, Taiwan, and Japan was made difficult by the continual transfer of men. Many of them had accumulated enough points and were rotated back to the States for discharge. Some others were transferred to ships which were in need of their particular skills. Replacing them were new men from the States, many of whom were unfamiliar with the LCI gunboats and had to be retrained. Where the ships had been finely-tuned fighting machines during the war, now the crews were less confident. Men left ships and friends behind with little remorse. It was time to move on.

Disposition of the Gunboats

With the end of World War II, the need for the amphibious gunboats by the United States Navy came to an end. Other ships and craft would be developed and put to use in Korea and later in Vietnam. The LCI conversions were not seen as worthy of preservation, but the LCS(L)s survived longer. LCI gunboat conversions were sold off in the few years following the end of the war. Most were scrapped and a few were kept as fishing vessels. The LCS(L) fleet fared better. Of the 130 built in 1944 and 1945, 123 survived the war. Five had been sunk in action, one grounded and declared a total loss, and one damaged beyond repair. From 1946 to 1947 seventeen were sold off for use as commercial fishing boats or for scrap. By 1948, there were still 106 on the Navy's list, some of which were in use as training vessels.

One of the LCS(L) gunboats, *LCS(L) 39*, had been sold as surplus to Martin B. Dahl of Seattle, Washington, in October 1947. It was destined for use in the fishing fleet and passed through several owners. Finally, she was used as a fish processing barge in the salmon fishing industry in Bristol Bay, Alaska, in the 1970s. Peter Benoit worked on her in the 1970s and became curious about her history. He discovered that she was the former *LCS(L) 39* which, at that point, had been renamed the *Maren I*. Fortunately, Benoit was able to make a sketch of her which has survived. It showed the changes made to the former gunboat. By 2001 the ship was in a poor state of repair. She struck a submerged object and sank near Dutch Harbor, Alaska. She was subsequently refloated but in such poor shape that she was towed out to sea and sunk in 5,400 feet of water about twenty miles off Unalaska.

Benoit reported that there were a number of ships used in the fishing industry in Alaska in the 1970s to 1980s that obviously had LCI hulls. How many were former LCS(L)s or LCI gunboats is unknown.

In the late 1940s, the vessels formerly designated as landing craft were re-designated as landing ships. Thus the Landing Craft Support Large LCS(L) became the Landing Ship Support Large (LSSL).

Surplus ships were of interest to the allies of the United States. Throughout the world it became necessary for the United States to rebuild foreign fleets that had been decimated during World War II. The growing threat of communism made it imperative that America's allies be well-prepared.

LCS(L) 39 is shown in her original World War II configuration. Official U.S. Navy photograph.

Loans to Foreign Navies

Number of LCS(L) Ships	Country Receiving Loan	Date(s) of Loan
56	Japan	1953–63
9	France	1950–52
8	South Vietnam	1954–57
6	Italy	1951
5	Ryukyu Islands	1952
2	Greece	1957, 1958
1	Thailand	1966
7	Philippines	1975
4	South Korea	1952
5	Taiwan	1954, 1957[25]

The majority of surplus LSSLs were sent to Japan to be used in coastal patrol and defense. This transfer took place under the Charter Party Agreement which took effect on 27 December 1952. Over the next few years, fifty-six of the ships were loaned to Japan. Most were not in good condition and refitting them was costly. Between 1958 and 1977, the ships were returned to the United States as they were no longer needed by the Japanese. Some were then transferred to Taiwan, Thailand, Philippines, and South Vietnam. Many of the remaining LSSLs had outlived their usefulness and were used for target practice by the U.S. Navy. They were sunk in an area about eighty miles south-southeast of Tokyo. The rest were sold off as surplus. Most of the ships remaining in foreign service had been struck from their naval files by the 1980s and scrapped. The sole exception was *LCS(L) 102*, which continued in Thai service until 2007 when it was transferred to the National Association of USS LCS(L) 1–130 for use as a floating museum at Mare Island, California.

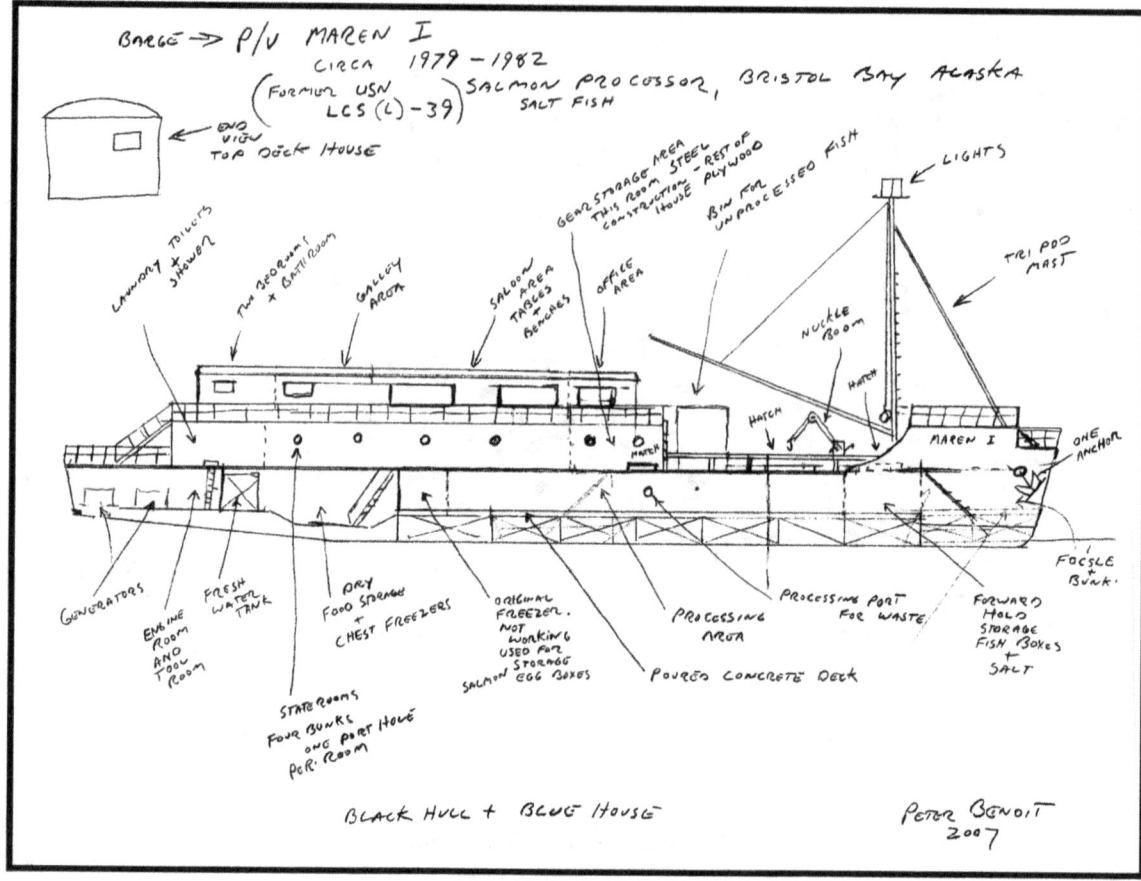

This sketch of former *LCS(L) 39* in Alaska in the late 1970s shows her reconfigured for use in the fishing industry. She was known at that point as *Maren I*. The ship was finally towed out to sea and sunk in 2001. Sketch by Peter Benoit, courtesy of the artist.

France and Vietnam

Many of the unconverted LCI(L)s were loaned to foreign navies but, of the gunboat types, only the LCS(L)s were deemed suitable for further use. They served in the maritime forces of the Ryukyus, Korea, Greece, Italy, Japan, the Philippines, Thailand, France, South Vietnam, and Taiwan. Transfer of the ships was affected under the authority of the Mutual Defense Assistance Program and the Security Assistance Program. Many of the ships served in the navies in several countries. For example, *LCS(L) 9* was transferred to France in 1950 under the MDAP and renamed the *Hallebarde*. After several years of service in French Indochina, she was transferred back to the United States in 1955 and then transferred to Japan in 1956 where she was renamed *Asagano*. In 1965, she was transferred to South Vietnam and renamed *Doan Ngoc Tang (HQ 228)*. When South Vietnam fell in 1975, she escaped to the Philippines carrying refugees from the communist takeover. At that point she was transferred to the Philippine Navy and renamed *La Union (LLF 50)*. She eventually was decommissioned and used for parts until her scrapping in the mid–1980s. Not all of the LCS(L)s served in this manner, but many did serve under more than one foreign flag.

The Mutual Defense Assistance Program was created in 1949 in an attempt to bolster America's allies against the spreading threat of Communism. European countries faced with the threat of Russian expansion led America to transfer the gunboats to some of her allies. NATO signatories, Italy and France, were among the first to receive LCS(L)s. On 25 July 1951, *LSSLs 34, 38, 62–64,* and *118* were transferred to Italy where they were used for coastal patrol.

The most significant use of the LSSLs took place in Vietnam, first under the French and later under the South Vietnamese. The takeover of French Indochina by the Japanese during the war had broken the French hold in the area. Once the Japanese departed, a power vacuum was created, giving an opportunity for Vietnamese Communist forces to take control of the northern part of the country. To the north, the Chinese Communist forces under Mao Tse-tung had finally defeated the Kuomintang forces of Chiang Kai-Shek and driven them off the mainland to their last refuge on Taiwan. The government of North Vietnam, headed by Ho Chi Minh, was formally recognized by the newly-formed government of the People's Republic of China. The French, making an effort to regain control of their colonies in Southeast Asia, called on the United States for aid and support. The growing expansion of Communism in the area made Indochina and the halt of Communist expansion a first priority. The Mutual Defense Assistance Act, which had set up the MDAP, had originally provided support for Western Europe. The new threat in Indochina provided the impetus for an additional $75 million for efforts in the Far East, aimed in particular at French needs which were estimated at $100 million for 1951. The French set about compiling military equipment lists for their efforts in North Vietnam, and the Bao Dai government in South Vietnam did likewise. Having been burned by Chiang Kai-Shek's corrupt Kuomintang, the American government was reluctant to hand anything to the Bao Dai government in Saigon and decided to funnel their aid through the French.

LSSL Ships to France and Vietnam

LSSL	1st French No.	2nd French No.	French Name	Vietnamese Name & No.
2	1	9021	Arbalete	No Than HQ 225 — taken out of service in 1956 and sold to Taiwan for scrap in 1957 — the name and number was then assigned to the newly transferred *Framee* (ex *105*)
4	2	9022	Arquebuse	Linh Kiem HQ 226 — renamed *Le Trong Dam* in 1970
9	3	9023	Hallebarde	Doan Ngoc Tang HQ 228
10	4	9024	Javeline	Le Van Binh HQ 227
28	5	9025	Pertuisane	
35	—	—	Etendard	
65	—	—	Oriflamme	
80	6	9026	Rapiere	
96	—	—	—	Nguyen Ngoc Long HQ 230
101	—	—	—	Luu Phu Tho HQ 229
105	—	—	Framee	Transferred to VN in March, 1956 and named *No Than HQ 225* renamed *Nguyen Van Tru* in 1970
129	—	—	—	Nguyen Duc Bong HQ 231[26]

As French power began to wane in Vietnam and the Vietnamese gained their independence, some of the ships were transferred to the newly-formed South Vietnamese Navy. The first of these transfers took place in 1954 with the transfer of *LSSL 2*. *LSSLs 4* and *105* were transferred in 1955 and 1956. In 1965 and 1966, in order to bolster South Vietnam's abilities, the U.S. trans-

LSSL 80, showing the French hull number 6, is shown patrolling on the Day River in North Vietnam, circa 1951.

A Vietnamese crew mans the 3"/50 bow gun on a French LSSL, circa 1950s. Courtesy of the Naval History and Heritage Command.

Transfer of LSSLs and PFs in Yokosuka on 14 January 1953. At the top (not in order) are *LSSLs 57* (*Kiku*), *104* (*Ran*), *107* (*Yuri*) and *130* (*Hagi*). Within the next few years Japan received an additional fifty-two of the ships. Official U.S. Navy photograph.

LSSLs HQ225 (ex *105*) and *HQ226* (ex *4*) dock at Phnom Penh, Cambodia, in June of 1970. Army Signal Corps photograph.

Doan Ngoc Tang HQ 228 (ex *LSSL 9*), under the command of Lieutenant Hong Vo Duong, arrives at Subic Bay, Philippine Islands, with refugees on 5 May 1975. Her anti-rocket screens may be seen around the conning tower. A small boat with Vietnamese refugees is tied up in the foreground. Official U.S. Navy photograph.

ferred *LSSLs 9, 10, 96, 101,* and *129.* Some of these ships had originally been transferred to Japan and then returned to U.S. possession.

Communist activity in Cambodia prompted the U.S. and South Vietnamese governments to exert a presence in Cambodia and *Linh Kiem HQ 226* (ex *4*) and *No Than HQ 225* (ex *105*) were sent up river to Phnom Penh, Cambodia, to assist anti-communist forces. From 1970 through April 1975, the LSSLs were used to escort supply ships up the Mekong River to Phnom Penh. In that month the Khmer Rouge finally won their struggle and the Cambodian government fell, ending the supply runs.

The government of South Vietnam fell soon after. Escaping from Vietnam in 1975 were the remaining gunboats *LSSLs 9, 96, 101,* and *129.* They headed for the Philippines heavily laden with refugees. However, while they were en route, the government of the Philippines officially recognized the new communist government of Vietnam which demanded the return of the LSSLs and other ships that had escaped their grasp. Quick negotiations between the American and Philippine governments took place, with the former South Vietnamese Navy ships being transferred back to United States' possession in the middle of the ocean. An American officer was put on board each ship. Ammunition was dumped overboard, and the flag of the South Vietnamese Navy was lowered and the American flag was raised. The fleet of ships were once again American. They entered Philippine waters safe from the communists. The gunboats and some other ships were eventually transferred into the Philippine Navy. The LCS(L)s, which had been developed during World War II, were only in action for little over a half year. However, their combat role in Vietnamese waters had spanned twenty-five years under the French and later the Vietnamese navies. None had ever fallen into the hands of the enemy. Although the duration of their wartime experience in Indochina was great, only twelve of the 130 LSSL ships actually served there.

Japan

In the wake of World War II, it had been necessary to keep some elements of the Imperial Japanese Navy active. Their assistance was needed in the clearing of minefields left over from the war, as well as general coastal patrol. With the outbreak of the Korean War, the American Navy in the Far East was focused on the new adversary. Accordingly, the Japanese forces were needed to patrol their own waters in the wake of a diminishing American naval presence there.

The Mutual Security Act between the United States and Japan did not allow for assistance to the Japanese. To remedy this problem, the Charter Party Agreement was passed by the legislatures of both countries and took effect on 27 December 1952. Under this agreement patrol frigates and LSSLs could be loaned to Japan for a period of five years, renewable for an additional five years.

The largest number of LSSLs loaned to a foreign Navy were sent to the newly-formed Japanese Maritime Self-Defense Force. It seems odd that a ship designed to combat the Japanese would eventually be given to them, but the expansion of communism in the Far East made it necessary to keep our former enemies armed in the face of communist expansion. As a result, fifty-six of the ships were taken out of mothballs and sent to Japan. The condition of many of them was poor, and numerous repairs had to be made before they were serviceable.

Typical of the problems were the defects in *LSSL 67.* Lieutenant J. H. Sims took command of the newly re-commissioned gunboat in 1952. Problems with the ship were in evidence, and it had to be taken to Charleston Naval Shipyard in South Carolina for repairs. From there the ship headed for Japan, but it had to stop for additional repairs in the Canal Zone, Long Beach,

California, and Pearl Harbor. Sims noted six pages of deficiencies including leaking rudder posts, defective engine gears, inoperable guns, and dirty fuel tanks.[27]

Taking the LSSLs to Japan involved the use of "ferry crews." These were regular U.S. Navy personnel temporarily assigned to the duty. In January 1952, Chief Bosun's Mate Paul W. Boblette found himself assigned to the ferry crews at Astoria. The ferry crews were charged with the task of activating fifty-three LSSLs at Astoria before their transfer to Japan. Boblette observed:

> Before me were 53 hulks, sitting alongside the piers. They were stripped; they were rusty; they were foul bottomed; they were a real mess. Slowly our crew began to trickle aboard. There were 5 snipes, 1 electrician's mate, 1 Chief Quartermaster, 6 deck hands (four of whom were seaman seconds with hash marks), 2 radiomen, 1 first class motor machinist and 2 cooks. The skipper was a reserve lieutenant and the exec was a reserve JG. We enlisted would fill all the department head slots and do the work.[28]

Where the original ship's complement was sixty-five men and six officers, the ships ferried to Japan had only two officers and nineteen enlisted men. Preparing the ships for the voyage to Japan was labor-intensive and required a number of spare parts. Many were delivered but of questionable use. The weather in Astoria proved uncooperative with constant rain preventing proper painting of the ships. About half had to await repainting until they reached Long Beach, California.

The shakedown cruise to Long Beach revealed the poor condition of the gunboats. Leaking hoses, generator power, electrical problems, and nonfunctioning radar were among the difficulties the gunboats faced. Many of these problems were supposed to be addressed either in Long Beach, San Diego, or Pearl Harbor.

From Pearl Harbor, Hawaii, the ships headed to Midway Island, then on to Yokosuka, Japan. By that time many of the shortcomings of the reactivation process had surfaced. *LCS(L) 83* made it into port with only one engine operable. Once they arrived in Yokosuka, they were relegated to back areas of the harbor. Japanese sailors boarded the ships and basically stripped off virtually anything that could be taken. Boblette reported that the fifty-three million dollars the United States had spent on refurbishing the ships had been a waste as only a few were in operation the following year.[29]

Ships transferred to Japan were *LSSLs 3, 10, 12–14, 18, 20, 22, 24, 25, 27, 52, 57, 58, 60, 67, 68, 72, 74–85, 87–90, 94, 96, 98, 100–104, 106, 107, 109–111, 114–116, 118–120, 126, 129* and *130*.[30] In the Japan Maritime Self-Defense Force they were designated as the *Yuri* Class.

The U.S.–Japan Mutual Defense Assistance Agreement of 1954 re-assigned the ships. However, the need for them decreased, and between 1958 and 1959, twenty-seven of the ships were returned. By 1977 all of the ships had been remanded to U.S. custody. Many were in poor condition and suitable only for target practice, while others were sold for scrap.

Korea, Greece, Taiwan, Thailand, Ryukyus

The division of Korea into North and South at the end of World War II made it necessary for the U.S. to bolster the small nation's defenses. The U.S. sent thirty ships to Korea, among them four LSSLs, the *54, 77, 86,* and *91*. They remained on active duty until the early 1960s, at which time they were decommissioned.

Greece joined NATO in 1952 and received two of the LSSLs, the *35* and *65* in 1957 and 1958 respectively. The ships were used for coastal patrol until they were scrapped in 1976.

Taiwan was the recipient of *LSSLs 56, 81,* and *95*. They were transferred to them in 1954 after having served in the Japanese Maritime Self-Defense Force. Two ships formerly used by the French, the *LSSLs 2* and *28*, were given to Taiwan for parts. Of the ships transferred to Taiwan, *LSSLs 81* and *95* were on the active list until stricken in 1971.

Nakha (ex *LSSL 102*) is the last of the World War II gunboats. This photograph of her was taken at the entrance to Songkhla Navy Base in Thailand on 31 January 1997 while she was a part of the Royal Thai Navy. While in the Royal Thai Navy she was used for coastal patrol against pirates and smugglers. In 2007 she was transferred to the National Association of USS LCS(L) 1-130, which maintains her as a floating museum at Mare Island, California. Photograph courtesy NavPic Holland.

The last major battle of the war had taken place on and around the island of Okinawa. In its aftermath the island was virtually destroyed and a large percentage of its population killed by both Japanese and American fire. Little of the administration of the island was in operation, and the Americans had to extend themselves in getting it back to some semblance of normalcy. In order to keep the coasts secure, *LSSLs 54, 56, 81, 95,* and *105* were loaned to the Ryukyuan Coast Guard between 1952 and 1954 and then transferred to other countries.

Only one ship was transferred to the Royal Thai Navy, the *LSSL 102*. She was originally transferred to Japan in 1953 and renamed the *Himawari* and then brought back to the United States in the mid–1960s. After that she was transferred to Thailand in 1966 and remained a part of her Navy as the *Nakha* until 2007.

Her duty in the Thai Navy included coastal patrols between the border of Cambodia and Thailand. At other times she served as a protection ship for the King and Queen of Thailand as they vacationed at Jlai Kangwol Palace, Hua Hin. The coastal palace had been built in 1927 and still serves as a summer palace for the king. Cruising off shore while the monarch was in residence, the gunboat was ably-equipped to ward off any terrorist who might wish to attack the king and queen. The Thais had added mortars to her armament and removed the barrage rocket launchers.

Adaptation and Change

The amphibious gunboats were a small but important part of the war effort. Their development and use corresponded to changes in the enemy's tactics and strategies. After the ascendancy of American power rendered the transport of men and supplies in larger ships too hazardous, the Japanese began to transport them in barges. To answer this new threat, the Americans armed LCI(L)s with new weapons and converted them into LCI(G) gunboats. The first series of these gunboats mounted 3"/50 guns to combat the barges. The ease with which the troop carriers could be converted led to their use in amphibious assaults with another generation of the ships armed with 40mm guns and rockets. As the effect of the gunboats in amphibious assaults became evident, the Japanese adapted their tactics and began to move away from the shoreline. This necessitated the development of the mortar gunboats and longer range rockets that could reach enemy positions as far as 5,000 yards inland. As the American forces began to close in on the home islands, the Japanese began to escalate their air attacks in order to knock out the ships that caused their land forces such great losses. The newly developed LCS(L) gunboats arrived on the scene with twin 40mm guns, and many of those arriving for the conquest of Okinawa had a third twin 40mm in the bow. Other LCI(L)s being converted at the builders' yards were also outfitted with the twin 40mm guns. This would allow them to combat the increase of kamikaze attacks against the American fleet which was preparing to invade Japan.

The adaptations of tactics and weapons on both sides gave evidence to the Darwinian aspect of war, with the stronger American forces ultimately winning out. Adaptation and change was only one element of the victory for the Americans, but it was an important one. The amphibious gunboats were only one aspect of this change and adaptation, but they stand as a notable example of how it worked.

Change for the gunboats did not end in 1945. LCS(L)s, newly designated as LSSLs, would continue in service in Vietnam, first with the French and later with the South Vietnamese Navy. The first adaptation came with the change in the bow gun. Of the LSSLs sent to Vietnam, *LSSLs 2, 4, 9, 10, 28, 35, 65, 80, 96, 101,* and *105,* the majority mounted the preferred 3"/50 bow gun. *LSSLs 35* and *65* mounted the interim 40mm single 40mm gun, and *96, 101,* and *105* the twin 40mm. While the 40mm guns were acceptable for shore bombardment during an assault and anti-aircraft defense, they were not as good for close quarters combat on Vietnam's rivers. The French and Vietnamese Navies changed the bow guns to the 3"/50, which was more useful against enemy positions defended by concrete structures. These included buildings and houses that were used for machine gun nests and other gun emplacements.

One of the hazards of close combat on the rivers and bays of Vietnam was the danger from snipers. The Viet Minh and Viet Cong had found that sniper fire directed against the gun crews was a good way to combat the LSSLs. They were eager to pick off the gun crews and personnel on the conning towers. To protect them, additional armor was mounted on each gun. Rockets and grenades were frequently launched at the conning towers of the ships from hiding places in the jungle. To thwart these attacks, screening was erected around the conning towers to deflect the rockets and rocket propelled grenades. These adaptations are visible in the photographs of the Vietnamese Navy ships in this book.

The rocket launchers mounted aft the bow gun were useful in beach assaults but were not of much use in Vietnam. The rocket launchers were removed and replaced with mortars, a far more useful weapon for the situation in Vietnam.

The Last Gunboat

November 10, 2007, was an overcast, drizzly day at Mare Island, California. However, it did not seem to matter to the two hundred or so assembled witnesses to the transfer ceremony. Dr. William J. Mason, a Professor Emeritus at San Francisco State University, surveyed the crowd. In addition to the officers, board, and members of the National Association of USS LCS(L) 1–130 and their guests, the Royal Thai Navy had sent Rear Admiral Surasak Rounroengrom and a number of his staff to the ceremony. Representing the official arm of the United States government was Rear Admiral Mark W. Balmert. Former Secretary of the Navy John Lehman (1981–1987) was the guest speaker. Lehman's father had served as the commanding officer of *LCS(L) 18* during World War II. His brother Dr. Christopher M. Lehman, who served as Special Assistant to President Reagan for National Security Affairs from 1983 through 1985, was also in attendance. Both men had been actively involved in the quest to regain possession of the *LCS(L) 102*. For Mason, this was the culmination of many years' work by him and others who had preceded him since the formation of the association in 1989. At its inception, the members had set as one of their goals the retrieval of an LCS(L) to serve as a floating museum in the United States.

Also present at the ceremony was Richard L. Jones who had served as the commanding officer of *LCS(L) 102* at Okinawa. Jones was a Lieutenant at that time and had previously been commanding officer of *LCI(G) 345* during the assault of Guam. His gunboat was covering UDT operations on 18 July 1944 when it came under fire from shore batteries. Jones and two enlisted men on the ship were wounded by shrapnel and transferred off the ship. After recovering from his wounds, Jones was assigned command of the new *LCS(L) 102*. He was awarded the Purple Heart for his wounds at Guam, and his ship, *LCI(G) 345*, was awarded the Navy Unit Commendation.

The actual ceremony at Mare Island was a re-enactment of the official turnover ceremony that had taken place on 22 May 2007 in Sattahip, Thailand.

LCS(L) 102 Returns

Efforts for the return of the *LCS(L) 102* had some early success in the mid–1990s when Congress passed Public Law 104-201 in 1996. Section 1025 of the law read:
Section 1025 Sense of Congress Concerning USS LCS 102 (LSSL 102)

> It is the sense of Congress that the Secretary of Defense should use existing authority in law to seek the expeditious return, upon completion of service, of the former LCS 102 (LSSL 102) from the Government of Thailand in order for the ship to be transferred to the United States Shipbuilding Museum in Quincy, Massachusetts.[31]

By 1999, progress toward retrieving the *LCS(L) 102* had been made. *The National Defense Authorization Act for Fiscal Year 2000* contained a relevant Amendment (No. 511) which authorized the transfer of a *Cyclone* Class patrol ship to Thailand. It was understood that the transfer would basically be a trade for the *102*.

Negotiations for the acquisition of the *LCS(L) 102* continued throughout the remaining years of the 1990s. The return of the ship looked promising until 11 September 2001 with the terrorist attack on the twin towers in New York City and the Pentagon in Washington, D.C. As a result of these attacks, the thirteen *Cyclone* Class high-speed patrol craft were taken out of mothballs and transferred to the Coast Guard for use as coastal security craft. Gone was the bargaining chip that would have seen a *Cyclone* Class patrol ship traded for the *LCS(L) 102*.

This put a damper on the prospect of retrieving the gunboat from the Thai Navy. However, at the same time, another possibility presented itself. Another LCS(L) was found still afloat on the West Coast of the United States.

A number of the gunboats had been sold to fishing companies in Seattle, Washington. Among those were *LCS(L)s 44, 50,* and *51. LCS(L)s 39–43, 45–48,* and *66* were sold to individuals in Seattle, Washington, and were probably destined for the fishing fleets as well. *LCS(L) 50* had been sold to the Copper River Packing Company in Seattle on 8 October 1947. It had then been converted for use as a fishing boat and apparently passed through several owners. Researcher Ron MacKay, historian for the LSM/LSMR Association, had spotted her tied up at a pier in Seattle in 1995. Renamed the *Seabird*, she was in poor condition. Her guns and other military hardware had been removed and her conning tower cut off. Other modifications made her look very unlike a gunboat, but the hull and other features were still there, although she was rusting badly. Photographs of the ship were displayed at the LCS(L) Association's convention in Virginia Beach in 2002.

The gunboat had been converted for use as a fishing vessel and was owned by New Hope Marine, Inc. of Seattle. In addition to her conning tower, many of her interior bulkheads had been removed and cranes had been installed on her deck, along with additional modifications. She would need work, but she was basically sound. It was rumored that the original conning tower was available and being used as a child's playground in someone's backyard. Further investigation indicated that it was not an LCS(L) conning tower, but that of an LCI(L). The owners were willing to sell the LCS(L) to the Association for $30,000 but were open to offers.

With the possibility of obtaining an LCS(L) closer to home and also available immediately, the Association set forth to produce a feasibility study. Chaired by Dr. William J. Mason, the *LCS(L)(3) 50* Renovation Committee consisted of Medal of Honor recipient Richard M. McCool, former commanding officer of *LCS(L) 122*, Ray McDade, Felix Muldoon, Keith Reid, and Frank Simpson.

It soon became obvious that the ship was in need of much work. The committee suggested to the owners that they donate it to the Association in return for a tax write-off, which they eventually agreed to. An intensive survey indicated that approximately $500,000 would be needed to bring the ship back to its World War II configuration. The primary cost would be for refurbishment of the ship by professional ship building yards. Outfitting the ship would not be that expensive since many of the parts such as bunks, galley equipment and other ship's furniture was available for free from the Suisun Bay Reserve Fleet in Benicia, California. Items that would be difficult to acquire were 40mm and 3"/50 guns, as there seemed to be no source available for them.[32]

Another problem did arise. The possibility of retrieving the *LCS(L) 102* still existed. Over the years, much political contact had been made with various members of the United States' government, and support had been given as evidenced by the bills already passed in the House and Senate, and the agreement to transfer a *Cyclone* Class ship as a trade. It was feared that if the Association were then to cast aside the possibility of regaining the *LCS(L) 102*,

Mrs. E. Nofke, daughter of the Leading Cupola Tender at Commercial Iron Works, Portland, Oregon, breaks a bottle of champagne against the hull of *LCS(L) 102* as part of the launching ceremony. In the later years of the war so many ships were being launched that virtually anyone with a connection to the Navy could arrange to christen one. Official U.S. Navy photograph.

LCS(L) 102, shown at Mare Island, California, on November 10, 2007. She had returned to the U.S. only a few weeks before from service in the Royal Thai Navy and still carries the hull number *751* and the name *Nakha* (Sea Serpent). The changes from her original configuration including the bow gun, enclosed conn, and hawse pipe are evident here.

political support would be lost. This support might be needed in the future to find a location for the ship and other political considerations that might be needed by the Association.

As a result of the study, a comparative analysis of the two ships was formulated. As they were considering the possibility of obtaining *Seabird*, word came that the Government of Thailand had informed the United States that they were prepared to return the *HTMS Nakha* (ex *LCS(L) 102*) to the United States as a gesture of friendship between the two navies. This was the turning point in the process and, as a result, *Seabird* would stay in Seattle to slowly rust away or be scrapped.

The official transfer of the *102* took place in Thailand on 22 May 2007. For several months prior to that date, the ship had been disarmed for transfer with her gun barrels plugged. Admiral Sathiraphan Kaelyanon, Commander in Chief of the Royal Thai Navy, signed the vessel over to Captain Walter B. Watson Jr., U.S. Naval Attaché and Dr. William J. Mason, who represented the National Association of USS LCS(L) 1–130.

The gunboat was towed to Hong Kong and placed on board a transport ship owned by National Air Cargo, which had become interested in assisting the veteran's association. It arrived in San Francisco Bay in September of 2007, and work began to prepare the ship for its American ceremony. Able volunteers from the area have continued to maintain and improve the condition of the ship.

A tribute to their work was obtained on 22 January 2010 when the United States Department of State granted the Association's request to convert the *102* from a stationary museum to a mobile museum offering cruises in the San Francisco Bay area.

Glossary

The terms and abbreviations below are by no means exhaustive, but I have listed those found within this work. Generally they follow OPNAV 29-P1000, which is the *Glossary of U.S. Naval Abbreviations 1940–1946*. Current usage in the U.S. Navy may vary from this format. Within the time period there were also numerous variations on usage. For instance, OPNAV 29-P1000 lists ComdgOf as the correct abbreviation for commanding officer. However, it was usually entered as CO in most of the official action reports and other documents. In all likelihood these variations reflected the training of the yeoman writing the report and his immediate superior. The exigencies of war did not always permit perfect editing.

Adm Admiral
AH Hospital Ship
AK Cargo Ship Auxiliary (cargo ship of any kind operated by the Navy)
AKA Cargo Ship Attack
AM Minesweeper
AO Oiler or Fuel Tanker
AP Transport operated by the Navy
APA Transport, Attack
APD Transport, High Speed
ARD Auxiliary Repair Dock (Floating Drydock)
ARG Repair Ship, Internal Combustion Engine
ARL Repair Ship — Landing Craft
ARS Salvage Vessel
ATB Amphibious Training Base
ATR Ocean Tug — Rescue
BB Battleship
Betty Allied code name for the Japanese Mitsubishi G4M1 Navy Type 1 Attack Bomber
BLT Battalion Landing Team
Bum Boat Slang term for small native boats that approached Navy ships looking to sell or trade various items.
BuShips Bureau of Ships
CA Heavy Cruiser
CAP Combat Air Patrol
CAPT Captain
Captain's Mast A form of non-judicial punishment in which the Commanding Officer of a ship studies and disposes of an infraction of the rules in his command.
CL Light Cruiser
Col Colonel
Comdg Commanding
ComdGen Commanding General
ComdgOf or **CO** Commanding Officer
Comdr Commander
ComO Communications Officer
Como Commodore
CTF Commander Task Force
CTG Commander Task Group
CTU Commander Task Unit
CV Aircraft Carrier
CVB Aircraft Carrier — Large
CVE Aircraft Carrier — Escort
CVL Aircraft Carrier — Light
DD Destroyer
DE Destroyer Escort
DM Light Minelayer
DMS High Speed Minesweeper
DUKW Heavy Amphibious Tank
Ens Ensign
(F) This designation after a ship's number indicates that it is the Flagship for the unit
(FF) This designation after a ship's number indicates that it is the Flotilla Flagship with the Flotilla Commander on board. This was a special LCI(L) set up with extra communications equipment. It did not carry troops for landings.
FS Army Freight and Supply Ship
(GF) This designation after a ship's number indicates that it is the Group Flagship.

Hamp Allied code name for the Japanese Mitsubishi A6M3, Navy Type 0 Carrier Fighter Model 32. This was a variation of the Zeke.
Handy Billy A water pump designed for a variety of uses on board ships, including fire fighting and pumping out water in the hold
Higgins Boat see LCP(L)
Jill Allied code name for the Japanese Nakajima B6N, Navy Carrier Attack Bomber
Jima see Shima
Judy Allied code name for the Japanese Yokosuka D4Y, Navy Carrier Bomber
Kate Allied code name for the Japanese Nakajima B5N, Navy Type 97 Carrier Attack Bomber
Kawa or Gawa Japanese term for river, ex. Bisha Gawa is Bisha River
LCC Landing Craft Control
LC(F) Landing Craft (Flak)
LC(FF) Landing Craft (Flotilla Flagship)
LCG Landing Craft Guns
LCG(L) Landing Craft Guns (Large)
LCG(M) Landing Craft Guns (Medium)
LCI(A) Landing Craft Infantry (Ammunition); ammunition carrier
LCI(D) Landing Craft Infantry (Demolition); carried UDT units
LCI(G) Landing Craft Infantry (Guns)
LCI(L) Landing Craft Infantry (Large)
LCI(M) Landing Craft Infantry (Mortars)
LCI(R) Landing Craft Infantry (Rockets)
LCI(RCM) Landing Craft Infantry (RadarCounter Measures)
LCM Landing Craft Mechanized, also (G) and (R) versions— Guns and Rockets
LCP(L) Landing Craft Personnel (Large)
LCP(R) Landing Craft, Personnel (Ramp)
LCS(L) Landing Craft Support (Large); also LCS(L)(3) Landing Craft Support Large Mark 3
LCS(M) Landing Craft Support (Medium)
LCS(S) Landing Craft Support (Small)
LCT Landing Craft Tank
LCT(R) Landing Craft Tank (Rockets)
LCVP Landing Craft Vehicle and Personnel
Lily Allied code name for the Kawasaki Ki-48, Army Type 99 twin-engine Light Bomber
LSIL Landing Ship Infantry Large; redesignation for LCI(L) after 1949
LSM Landing Ship Medium
LSM(R) Landing Ship Medium (Rockets)
LSSL Landing Ship Support Large; redesignation for LCS(L) after 1949
LST Landing Ship Tank
Lt Lieutenant
LtCol Lieutenant Colonel
LtCom or LtComdr Lieutenant Commander
LtGen Lieutenant General
Lt (jg) Lieutenant (Junior Grade)

LV Landing Vehicle
LVT Landing Vehicle Tracked
Maj Major
MajGen Major General
Mighty Midget Nickname for the LCS(L), also "Pall Bearers," "Small Boys," "Spit Kits"
Misaki Japanese term for Cape
MTB Motor Torpedo Boat; see also PT
Myrt Allied code name for the Japanese Nakajima C6N, Navy Carrier Reconnaissance Plane
Nate Allied code name for the Japanese Nakajima Ki-27, Army Type 97 Fighter
Nick Allied code name for the Japanese Kawasaki Ki-45, Army Type 2 Two-seat Fighter
Oscar Allied code name for the Japanese Nakajima Ki-43, Army Type 1 Fighter
PBR Patrol Boat River
PC Submarine Chaser; see also SC
PCE Patrol Craft Escort
PCS Patrol Craft Sweeper
PGM Motor Gunboat
Plank Owner A member of the crew who joined the ship when it was commissioned.
Point Bolo Cape north of Hagushi beaches; see Zampa Misaki
PT Motor Torpedo Boat
RADM Rear Admiral
RCT Regimental Combat Team
RP Radar Picket Station
Rufe Allied code name for the Japanese Nakajima A6M2-N, Navy Type 2 Fighter Seaplane
Sally Allied code name for the Japanese Mitsubishi Ki-21, Army Type 97 Heavy Bomber
SC Sub-Chaser
Shima Japanese word for island; see also Jima
SOPA Senior Officer Present Afloat
TF Task Force
TG Task Group
Tony Allied code name for the Japanese Kawasaki Ki-61, Army Type 3 Fighter
TU Task Unit
UDT Underwater Demolition Team
VADM Vice Admiral
Val Allied code name for the Japanese Aichi D3A, Navy Type 99 Carrier Bomber
Wan Japanese for Bay
Willow Allied code name for the Japanese Yokosuka K5Y, Navy Type 95 Intermediate Trainer
Woofus Landing craft such as an LSM fitted with rockets
YMS Motor Minesweeper
YOG Gasoline Barge
Zampa Misaki Cape north of the Hagushi beaches, also referred to as Point Bolo
Zeke Allied code name for the Japanese Mitsubishi A6-M fighter, also known as the Zero

Appendix I: LCI Gunboat Flotillas and Commanding Officers as of 15 May 1945

LCI Flotilla Three
Comdr R. Eikel Jr., Com LCI Flotilla Three

Group 1
LtComdr J. F. McFadden

Division 13		Division 14	
LCI(G) 77	Lt (jg) R. W. Clark	LCI(G) 452	Lt (jg) R. O. Croskey
LCI(G) 78	Lt (jg) R. O. Rogers	LCI(G) 453	Lt (jg) J.W. Baikie
LCI(G) 79	Lt (jg) J. E. Lewis	LCI(G) 454	Lt (jg) H. Rosenburg
LCI(G) 81	Lt (jg) D. A. Parsons	LCI(G) 455	Lt (jg) G. J. Sullivan
LCI(G) 347	Lt W. F. Sorsby	LCI(G) 725	Lt R. A. Gustafson

Group 8
LtComdr W. V. Nash

Division 15		Division 16	
LCI(G) 438	Lt (jg) B. J. Powers	LCI(G) 441	Lt (jg) F. W. Bell
LCI(G) 450	Lt (jg) W. A. Brady	LCI(G) 457 (GF)	Lt (jg) J. J. O'Dowd
LCI(G) 469	Lt (jg) G. M. Connors	LCI(G) 458	Lt (jg) J. D. Templeton
LCI(G) 471	Lt (jg) R. S. Hudgins	LCI(G) 752	Lt (jg) R. Sullivan
LCI(G) 473	Ens E. W. Burden	LCI (G)**	
LCI(G) 726	Lt (jg) H. J. Barnum Jr.	LCI(G)**	

Group 9
LtComdr C. J. Starkus

Division 17		Division 18	
LCI(G) 365	Ens J. L. Mills	LCI(G) 80 (RCM)	Lt (jg) T. A. Bird
LCI(G) 366 (GF)	Lt H. J. Garibaldi	LCI(G) 345 (RCM)	Lt (jg) H. M. Smith
LCI(G) 407	Lt (jg) J. D. McEnroe	LCI(G) 346	Lt (jg) H. T. Coller
LCI(G) 439	Lt (jg) H. A. Mullins	LCI(G) 348	Lt (jg) A. E. Rosenbloom
LCI(G) 440	Lt (jg) V. Grace	LCI(G) 437(RCM)	Lt(jg) W. B. Watkins Jr.
LCI(G) 475	Lt C. W. Hartness	LCI(G) 449	Lt (jg) J. J. Mittleman

LCI Flotilla Six
Comdr A. R. Montgomery, Com LCI Flotilla Six

Group 16
LtComdr R. S. Rickabaugh

Division 31		Division 32	
LCI(G) 558 (GF)	Lt (jg) H. S. Lewis	LCI 422(G)	Lt P. A. Crowl
LCI(G) 559	Lt (jg) J. M. Horner	LCI(G) 442	Lt (jg) F. B. Clark
LCI(G) 560	Lt (jg) C. J. Mackres	LCI(G) 565	Lt G. J. Headley
LCI(G) 561	Ens K. D. Mann	LCI(G) 567	Lt K. C. Flory
LCI(G) 751	Lt H. D. Frick	LCI(G) 568	Lt H. H. Brown
LCI(G)**		LCI(G) 580	Lt E. S. Smith

Group 17
LtComdr C. F. Robinson

Division 33		Division 34	
LCI(G) 372	Lt W. P. Hendricks	LCI(G) 451	Lt (jg) C. E. Orr
LCI(G) 373	Lt (jg) M. P. Mills	LCI(G) 462	Lt (jg) D. G. Griggs
LCI(G) 406	Lt B. G. Brown	LCI(G) 464	Lt R. Taurman
LCI(G) 461	Lt (jg) O. M. Taylor	LCI(G) 465	Lt (jg) J. S. Nicholls III
LCI(G) 466	Lt (jg) J. J. Horovitz	LCI(G) 566	Lt (jg) G. W. Hartland
LCI(G) 467	Lt (jg) W. R. Taylor	LCI(G) 472	Lt A. H. Rudge

Group 18
LtComdr E. L. Yates

Division 35		Division 36	
LCI 397(G) (GF)		LCI(G) 404	Lt (jg) S. S. Politano
LCI(G) 460	Lt (jg) C. J. Baker	LCI(G) 405	Lt (jg) A. C. Timmons
LCI(G) 463	Lt (jg) M. F. Sheldon	LCI(G) 456	Lt (jg) E. M. Clark
LCI(G) 470	Lt (jg) W. M. Welsh	LCI(G) 729	Lt (jg) M. H. Fischer
LCI(G) 727	Lt (jg) H. H. Upton	LCI(G) 730	Comdr M. B. Brown
LCI(G) 728	Lt (jg) E. R. Seaver		

LCI Flotilla Fourteen
CAPT W. Rimer, Com LCI Flotilla Fourteen

Group 40
LtComdr H. Brown

Division 79		Division 80	
LCI(M) 739 (GF)	Lt (jg) C. W. Rhodes	LCI(M) 975	Lt E. S. Thorn
LCI(M) 740	Lt (jg) L. A. Gates	LCI(M) 1055	Lt R. R. Dean
LCI(M) 741	Lt R. M. Laird	LCI(M) 1056	Ens C. L. Eldman
LCI(M) 742	Lt (jg) F. J. Geiger	LCI(M) 1057	Lt (jg) C. A. Schulz
LCI(M) 1059	Lt J. A. Gage	LCI(M) 1058	Lt (jg) R. B. Purdy
LCI(M)**		LCI(M)**	

Group 41
LtComdr R. F. Hunnicutt

Division 81		Division 82	
LCI (M) 801**		LCI(M) 807	Lt (jg) H. G. Murphy
LCI(M) 802**		LCI(M) 808	Lt (jg) B. C. Walter
LCI(M) 803**		LCI(M) 809**	
LCI(M) 804 (FF)	Lt (jg) W. M. Shumard	LCI(M) 810	Lt (jg) W. T. Osborne
LCI(M) 805	Lt (jg) Y. Davis	LCI(M) 1088**	
LCI(M) 806	Lt (jg) W. H. Cochenour	LCI(M) 1089	Lt (jg) B. L. Brenneman

Group 42
LtComdr A. H. Connors

Division 83		Division 84	
LCI(M) 658	Lt (jg) E. E. Ward	LCI(M) 351	Lt D. C. Meek
LCI(M) 659	Lt (jg) T. A. Cooke	LCI(M) 352	Lt P. B. Sadtler
LCI(M) 660 (GF)	Lt (jg) P. P. Marvin	LCI(M) 353	Lt J. M. Nicholson
LCI(M) 754	Lt (jg) L. A. West	LCI(M) 354	Lt L. G. Payne
LCI(M) 755	Lt (jg) W. E. Bowser	LCI(M) 355	Lt (jg) A. V. Cole
LCI(M) (to be assigned)		LCI(M) 356	Lt E. B. Wicklander

LCI Flotilla Sixteen
Comdr C. E. Coffin, Com LCI Flotilla Sixteen

Group 46
LtComdr A. F. Eckelmeyer

Division 91		Division 92	
LCI(R) 785	Lt (jg) J. W. Mudge	LCI (R) 643	Lt (jg) R. W. Sauer
LCI(R) 1024	Lt E. J. Ritz	LCI(R) 644	Lt (jg) C. J. Smith Jr.
LCI(R) 1026	Lt (jg) J. H. Bartley	LCI(R) 645	Lt (jg) F. X. Wright
LCI(R) 1068	Lt F. W. Budke Jr.	LCI(R) 646	Lt (jg) P. W. Ahlstedt
LCI(R) 1069	Lt J. A. Wagner	LCI(R) 769	Lt (jg) D. K. Hobert
LCI(R) 1070	Lt E. J. Lukas	LCI(R) 770	Lt (jg) V. E. Strickland

LCI Group 47
LtComdr H. T. McKnight, Com LCI Group 47

Division 93		Division 94	
LCI(R) 647	Ens W. T. Wilroy	LCI(R) 704	Lt (jg) M. Leavitt
LCI(R) 648 (GF)	Lt (jg) R. W. Harma	LCI(R) 705	Lt F. R. Moran
LCI(R) 649	Lt J. M. Rogers	LCI(R) 706	Lt (jg) F. S. Staley
LCI(R) 762 (FF)	Lt (jg) E. E. Kelley	LCI(R) 765	Lt B. B. Swegle
LCI(R) 763	Lt H. H. Goff	LCI(R) 766	Lt (jg) J. L. Turner
LCI(R) 764	Lt A. C. Shoemake	LCI(R) 767	Lt (jg) J. A. Larson

Group 48
LtComdr F. Thompson Jr.

Division 95		Division 96	
LCI(R) 642 (GF)	Lt (jg) E. A. Rollins	LCI(R) 651	Lt J. W. Sullivan
LCI(R) 650	Lt W. G. Bagley	LCI(R) 708	Lt (jg) W. E. Davis
LCI(R) 707	Lt (jg) H. N. Karanemont	LCI(R) 1028	Lt (jg) B. A. Lowrance
LCI(R) 771	Lt H. W. Campbell	LCI(R) 1029	Lt (jg) J. H. Lusk
LCI(R) 772	Lt (jg) W. K. McDaniel	LCI(R) 1030	Lt (jg) F. J. Niess
LCI(R) 1077	Lt G. N. Armstrong	LCI(R) 1078	Lt W. H. Lewis

LCI Flotilla Twenty-One
Comdr L. B. Balliere, Com LCI Flotilla Twenty-One

LCI Group 61
LtComdr W. T. Dom

Division 121		Division 122	
LCI(M) 630 (GF)	Lt (jg) J. J. Gasiorek	LCI(M) 632	Lt (jg) W. C. O'Donnell, Jr.
LCI(M) 631	Lt G. P. Hamilton	LCI(M) 633	Lt F. C. Baumholtz
LCI(M) 638	Lt (jg) K. L. Bush	LCI(M) 1010	Lt J. E. Farrar
LCI(M) 756	Lt (jg) M. C. Wunsch	LCI(M) 1011	Lt C. M. Adams
LCI(M) 757	Lt E.Z. Winkleman	LCI(M) 1012	Lt J. C. Wilson
LCI(M) 760	Lt (jg) M. O. Gipe	LCI(M) 1023	Lt H. K. Meister

Group 62
Lt W. P. Eckel

Division 123	Division 124
LCI(M) 582**	LCI(M) 595**
LCI(M) 588**	LCI(M) 664**
LCI(M) 594 (GF)**	LCI(M) 670**
LCI(M) 596**	LCI(M) 673**
LCI(M) 669**	LCI(M) 674**
LCI(M) 952**	LCI(M) 951**

**Some LCI gunboats were assigned to groups while still under conversion. In some cases a commanding officer had not been assigned to the ship.

Based on Commander, Administrative Command Amphibious Forces U.S. Pacific Fleet. *Directory of Amphibious Type Vessels and Commanding Officers.* (Amphibious Forces U.S. Pacific Fleet.) 15 May 1945, pp. 43–49.

Appendix II: Building and Conversion Locations

LCI(L) Builders

Albina Engine and Machine Works, Portland, OR: *LCI(L)s 1014–1018, 1023, 1024, 1026, 1028–1030**
Brown Shipbuilding Company, Houston, TX: *LCI(L)s 337, 338, 340–342, 345–348*
Commercial Iron Works, Portland, OR: *LCI(L)s 725–730, 732, 739–742, 744–749, 751–757, 760, 762–767, 769–776*
Consolidated Steel Corporation, Orange, TX: *LCI(L)s 61, 64–74, 77–82, 948, 951–959, 961, 962, 964, 974, 975, 1010–1012*
Defoe Shipbuilding Company, Bay City, MI: *LCI(L)s 1055–1060, 1068–1070, 1077, 1078, 1088, 1089*
Federal Ship Building and Dry Dock Company, Port Newark, NJ: *LCI(L)s 191, 192, 194–196*
George Lawley & Sons, Neponset, MA: *LCI(L)s 220, 224–226, 230, 231, 233–237, 351–356, 359, 362, 365, 366, 372, 373, 396–398, 401, 403–408, 412–415, 417–422, 658–660, 664, 669, 670, 673, 674, 704–708*
New Jersey Shipbuilding Corporation, Barber (Perth Amboy), NJ: *LCI(L)s 428, 431, 437–442, 449–475, 506, 514, 516, 517, 528, 538–544, 546–548, 556–561, 563–568, 570–580, 582, 588, 594–596, 630–633, 638, 642–651, 785, 801–810*
New York Shipbuilding Corporation, Camden, NJ: *LCI(L)s 17–19, 21–24, 31, 34, 36, 41–43, 45, 46*

The ships listed above underwent conversion to gunboats after their initial construction as LCI(L)s. Other LCI(L)s were produced by each of these yards but since they were not converted to gunboats, they are not listed above.

LCI(L) Conversion Locations

Espiritu Santo, New Hebrides: *LCI(G)s 61, 64, 65, 66*
George Lawley & Sons, Neponsett, MA: *LCI(G)s 401, 403, 408, 412–415, 428*
Jacksonville, FL: *LCI(G)s 506, 538–541, 556*
Manus Island: *LCI(M)s 366, 372, 373, 461, 464, 465, 467, 472–475, LCI(R)s 366, 372, 373, 439, 440, 451, 461, 462, 464, 465, 467, 472, 475*
Milne Bay, New Guinea: *LCI(R)s 31, 34, 73, 74, 224–226, 230, 331, 337, 338, 340–342*
Mios Woendi, Schouten Islands: *LCI(M)s 359, 362, 431, 658, 659, 754, 755, 974, 975, 1055*
Noumea, New Caledonia: *LCI(G)s 21–24, 67–70*
Pearl Harbor, Hawaii: *LCI(G)s 77–80, 345–348, 365, 366, 437–442, 704–706, 739–742, 1056–1059, LCI(M)s 653, 727, 728, 729, 756, 757, 760, 1011, 1012, 1023, 1024, 1068–1070, 1088, 1089, LCI(R)s 639, 640, 643, 645–649, 704–706, 761–766, 784, 785, 787, 992, 996, 997, 1062*
Portsmouth, VA: *LCI(G)s 422, 442, 558–561, 565–567, 568, 580, 751*
San Diego, Naval Repair Base, CA: *LCI(G)s 81, 82, 191, 192, 194, 345, 346, 348, 398, 404–407, 417–421,*

449–453, 455, 457, 558, 727–730, 751, 752, 948, LCI(M)s 396, 397, 449–453, 455, 465, 467, 468–475, 516, 542, 582, 588, 594–596, 633, 727, 728, 729, 739, 740, 742, 756, 1011, 1012, LCI(R)s 639, 640, 706, 761, 765, 766, 784, 785, 768, 787, 992

San Francisco—Hunter's Point: LCI(R)s 642, 644, 650, 651, 707, 708, 771, 772, 1028, 1029, 1030, 1077, 1078

San Francisco—Treasure Island: LCI(G)s 41, LCI(R) 1078

San Pedro, CA (General): LCI(G)s 196, 220, 233, 754, LCI(M)s 630–633, 638, 801–810, 1010

Craig Shipbuilding Company: LCI(M)s 351–354, 803

Harbor Boat Building, Terminal Island: LCI(M)s 355, 356, 456

Standard Shipbuilding Company: LCI(G)s 454, 458–461

West Coast Shipbuilding Company, Terminal Island: LCI(G)s 462, 463, 725, 726

West Coast Yards (General): LCI(G)s 42–46, 195, 234, 422, 466, 514, 517, 528, 566, 570–579, 751

A number of the gunboats underwent two conversions, from a (G) configuration to an (R) or (M). They are listed at the location where each change took place. Thus, an individual ship may be listed twice. Some ships are not listed as their conversion locations are unavailable. Numerous small yards in southern California converted ships and they are identified wherever possible. Many of the shipyards existing in 1944–1945 were in the area between San Diego and Long Beach, California.

Conversions were made in a single yard or in a combination of yards. For instance, LCI(L)s of Group Sixty-Three received their rocket launchers and guns at the U.S. Naval Drydocks, Hunter's Point, San Francisco. Once the new weapons had been installed, the ships went to several yards in the San Francisco area for further work. The second part of the conversion involved modifying interior spaces to rocket storage compartments. In the San Francisco area, this work was performed by United Engineering, San Francisco; Bethlehem Steel, San Francisco; Moore's East Yard, Oakland; Hurley's Marine Works, Oakland; General Engineering, Alameda; and United Engineering, Alameda.

LCS(L) Builders

Albina Engine and Machine Works, Portland, OR: LCS(L)s 48–78
Commercial Iron Works, Portland, OR: LCS(L)s 26–47, 79–108
George Lawley & Sons, Neponset, MA: LCS(L)s 1–25, 109–130

The first LCS(L), *LCS(L) 1*, was launched by the Lawley yard on 15 May 1944. The last built there was *LCS(L) 130*, launched on 15 December 1944. Albina launched her first, *LCS(L) 48*, on 7 July 1944, and Commercial launched *LCS(L) 26* on 13 August 1944. The last LCS(L) built was *LCS(L) 108*, launched by Commercial on 10 March 1945. None of the LCS(L)s underwent conversion as they were purpose-built as gunboats from the beginning.

Appendix III:
LCS(L) Flotillas and Commanding Officers as of 15 May 1945

LCS(L) FLOTILLA ONE
CAPT R. E. Arison, Com LCS(L) Flotilla One

Group 1
Lt W. I. Hunt, *LCS(L) 30**

Division 1		Division 2	
LCS(L) 7	Lt Franklin L. Elder	LCS(L) 26	Lt Herbert Chernin
LCS(L) 8	Lt R. T. Daniel	LCS(L) 27	Lt (jg) J. M. Bledesoe Jr.
LCS(L) 9	Lt D. R. Ellis	LCS(L) 28	Lt R. H. Bost
LCS(L) 10	Lt A. C. Eldridge	LCS(L) 29	Lt J. Pierrepont
LCS(L) 48	Lt D. E. Widel	LCS(L) 30	Lt C. H. Sanders
LCS(L) 49	Lt H. W. Smith		
LCS(L) 50	Lt B. T. Clark		

Group 2
Lt M. C. Fitzgerald, *LCS(L) 42*

Division 3		Division 4	
LCS(L) 41	Lt (jg) A.P. Marincovich	LCS(L) 46	Lt W. P. McCarthy
LCS(L) 42	Lt R. S. Sondree	LCS(L) 47	Lt F. R. Butler
LCS(L) 43	Lt W. A. Moore	LCS(L) 59	Lt N. L. Claxton
LCS(L) 44	Lt J. M. Leggat	LCS(L) 60	Lt W. H. White
LCS(L) 45	Lt E. M. Lang	LCS(L) 79	Lt J. D. Fleming
LCS(L) 58	Lt D. Gregory	LCS(L) 80	Lt T. C. Lynch

LCS(L) FLOTILLA THREE
CAPT T. C. Aylward, Com LCS(L) Flotilla Three
LC(FF) 988

Group 7
LtComdr E. P. Stone, *LC(FF) 484*

Division 13		Division 14	
LCS(L) 32	Lt J. M. Evans	LCS(L) 53	Lt M. F. Steldt
LCS(L) 33	Lt C. J. Boone	LCS(L) 54	Lt J. Synan
			Lt J. P. Murphy**

Division 13		Division 14	
LCS(L) 34	Lt J. B. Seely		
LCS(L) 35	Lt K. C. Huff	LCS(L) 55	Lt A. B. Cooper
LCS(L) 36	Lt J. Sansone	LCS(L) 56	Lt (jg) H. M. Scherling
LCS(L) 51	Lt H. D. Chickering	LCS(L) 57	Lt H. L. Smith
LCS(L) 52	Lt J. O. Harper	LCS(L) 31	Lt K. F. Machacek

Group 8
LtComdr E. C. Thomas, LCS(L) 12

Division 15		Division 16	
LCS(L) 11	Lt M. E. White	LCS(L) 18	Lt J. F. Lehman
LCS(L) 12	Lt G. J. O'Hare		Ens A. O. Hungerford
LCS(L) 13	Lt (jg) B. R. Hart	LCS(L) 19	Lt F. Woods III
LCS(L) 14	Lt (jg) J. R. Todd	LCS(L) 20	Lt L. R. Hof
LCS(L) 15	Lt N. H. Brower	LCS(L) 21	Lt J. C. Geib
LCS(L) 16	Lt H. O. White Jr.	LCS(L) 22	Lt B. G. Brewster
LCS(L) 17	Lt (jg) J. M. Sharpe		

Group 9
Lt B. A. Thirkield, LCS(L) 24

Division 17		Division 18	
LCS(L) 23	Lt W. D. Wilson	LCS(L) 40	Lt (jg) T. T. Hollen
LCS(L) 24	Lt W. A. Russell	LCS(L) 109	Lt (jg) M. L. Smith
LCS(L) 25	Lt J. M. Willette	LCS(L) 110	Lt (jg) H. W. Blose
LCS(L) 37	Lt S. M. Brickhouse	LCS(L) 111	Lt L. E. Culp
LCS(L) 38	Lt J. C. Smith	LCS(L) 112	Lt A. H. LaMotte
LCS(L) 39	Lt R. A. Anderson	LCS(L) 113	Lt T. H. Smith

LCS(L) FLOTILLA FOUR
Comdr N. Phillips, Com LCS(L) Flotilla Four
LC(FF) 1082

Group 10
LtComdr J. A. Dodson, LC(FF) 1079

Division 19		Division 20	
LCS(L) 114	Lt G. W. Mefferd	LCS(L) 120	Lt F. H. Lamartin Jr.
LCS(L) 115	Lt A. P. Gliemke	LCS(L) 121	Lt W. C. Lewis
LCS(L) 116	Lt A. J. Wierzbicki	LCS(L) 122	Lt R. M. McCool
LCS(L) 117	Lt E. R. Stanford Jr.	LCS(L) 123	Lt D. A. Oliver Jr.
LCS(L) 118	Lt P. F. Gilmore Jr.	LCS(L) 124	Lt D. Ward

Group 11
LtComdr C. E. Montgomery, LC(FF) 367

Division 21		Division 22	
LCS(L) 61	Lt J. M. Kelley	LCS(L) 83	Lt J. M. Faddis
LCS(L) 62	Lt E. F. Greenleaf	LCS(L) 84	Lt J. A. Noye
LCS(L) 63	Lt W. E. Pfau	LCS(L) 85	Lt C. E. Randall
LCS(L) 64	Lt C. W. Fogg	LCS(L) 86	Lt (jg) H. N. Houston
LCS(L) 81	Lt C. C. Lockwood	LCS(L) 87	Lt H. N. Martin
LCS(L) 82	Lt P. O. Beierl	LCS(L) 88	Lt C. L. Bigos
			Lt (jg) M. V. Sellis

Group 12
LtComdr B. D. Vogelin, LC(FF) 789

Division 23		Division 24	
LCS(L) 65	Lt T. B. Bannister	LCS(L) 90	Lt W. N. Birt
LCS(L) 66	Lt (jg) E. M. Eakin	LCS(L) 91	Lt S. A. McCray

Division 23		*Division 24*	
LCS(L) 67	Lt J. R. Bullock	LCS(L) 92	Lt J. J. Cardamone
LCS(L) 68	Lt M. G. Loessig	LCS(L) 93	Lt C. F. Botright
LCS(L) 69	Lt F. W. Harlow	LCS(L) 94	Lt J. L. Cronk
LCS(L) 89	Lt J. A. Kidston	LCS(L) 95	Lt D. Bowerman

LCS(L) Flotilla Five
CAPT J. M. McIsaac, Com Flotilla Five
LCS(L) 96

Group 12
LtComdr R. L. Jackson, LCS(L) 96

Division 25		*Division 26*	
LCS(L) 96	Lt O. K. Franklin	LCS(L) 125	Lt H. C. Cobb
LCS(L) 97	Lt R. H. Woodside	LCS(L) 126	Lt R. S. Gunn
LCS(L) 98	Lt J. C. Price	LCS(L) 127	Lt J. N. Kelly
LCS(L) 99	Lt O. L. Miles	LCS(L) 128	Lt J. B. Myers
LCS(L) 100	Lt F. J. Dimenna	LCS(L) 129	Lt L. A. Brennan
LCS(L) 101	Lt G. C. Ferris	LCS(L) 130	Lt W. H. File Jr.

Group 14
LtComdr K. E. Curley, LCS(L) 72

Division 27		*Division 28*	
LCS(L) 70	Lt R. J. Liechti	LCS(L) 102	Lt R. L. Jones
	Lt G. E. Hart Jr.	LCS(L) 103	Lt R. K. Crawford
LCS(L) 71	Lt R. B. Brokaw	LCS(L) 104	Lt F. M. Adams
LCS(L) 72	Lt F. R. Jaeger	LCS(L) 105	Lt G. W. Smith
	Lt (jg) H. R. Schwartz	LCS(L) 106	Lt H. W. Griswold
LCS(L) 73	Lt P. S. Carlton	LCS(L) 107	Lt (jg) G. S. Brown
LCS(L) 74	Lt H. J. Wittman		Lt (jg) D. A. Glover
LCS(L) 75	Lt R. B. Rivel		

Group 15
LtComdr H. Heine, LCS(L) 108

Division 29		*Division 30*	
LCS(L) 2	Lt J. B. Whitmore U	LCS(L) 108	Lt R. E. Hone
LCS(L) 3	Lt T. J. Ryan		Lt H. W. Chanidas
LCS(L) 4	Lt E. W. Welch Jr.		
LCS(L) 76	Lt B H. Eklund		
LCS(L) 77	Lt R. C. Shannon		
LCS(L) 78	Lt T. N. Fortson		

LCS(L) Ships Permanently Assigned to Training in the United States

LCS(L) 1	Lt W. K. Townsend	LCS(L) 5	Lt J. Kendall
	Lt (jg) L. H. Bishkin		Lt (jg) R. H. Kistler
	Lt (jg) L. T. Kermon	LCS(L) 6	Lt (jg) E. S. Wright

*Flotilla and Group Commanders were supposed to direct their units from ships designed for that purpose and designated as Landing Craft — Flotilla Flagship or LC(FF). In some cases, these specialized ships were not available and the Flotilla or Group Commander was aboard one of the LCS(L)s.

**Some ships had more than one Commanding Officer. As they became eligible for transfer their ship was turned over to a new Commanding Officer for the duration of its service life. In other cases, the original Commanding Officer was killed or disabled in the line of duty. The list above is based primarily on the source shown which lists the Commanding Officers as of 4 May 1945. Where multiple names are listed, as in the case of the training ships, alternate sources were used.

Based primarily on: Commander Amphibious Forces, U.S. Pacific Fleet. LCS(L)(3) FLOTILLAS, *AMPHIBIOUS FORCES, PACIFIC FLEET — Organization of*, 4 May 1945.

Appendix IV: LCI(G), LCI(M), LCI(R), and LCS(L) Ships Damaged or Lost in World War II

Ship	Date	Location	Cause	Dead	Wounded
LCI(G) 468*	6/17/44	Saipan	Air Attack	15	3
LCI(G) 459*	9/19/44	West Caroline Is. (Guam)	Mine	0	0
LCI(G) 70	1/5/45	Philippines	Kamikaze	6	9
LCI(G) 404	1/8/45	Palau Is.	Suicide Swimmers	0	0
LCI(G) 365	1/10/45	Philippines	Suicide Boat	0	4
LCI(M) 974*	1/10/45	Luzon, PI	Suicide Boat	0	30+
LCI(G) 365	1/10/45	Philippines	Suicide Boat	0	4
LCI(G) 82*	4/4/45	Okinawa	Suicide Boat	8	11
LCS(L) 7*	2/14/45	Mariveles, PI	Suicide Boat	2+	—
LCS(L) 26*	2/14/45	Mariveles, PI	Suicide Boat	25**	8
LCS(L) 27	2/14/45	Mariveles, PI	Suicide Boat	2	23
LCS(L) 49*	2/14/45	Mariveles, PI	Suicide Boat	24	22
LCI(G) 457	2/17/45	Iwo Jima	Shore Batteries	1	21
LCI(G) 474*	2/17/45	Iwo Jima	Shore Batteries	3	18
LCS(L) 127*	3/5/45	California	Grounded and Destroyed during training	0	0
LCI(G) 558	3/29/45	Okinawa	Suicide Boat	0	0
LCI(G) 560	3/29/45	Okinawa	Kamikaze	0	1
LCI(G) 82	4/4/45	Okinawa	Suicide Boat	8	11
LCS(L) 36	4/9/45	Okinawa	Kamikaze	0	5
LCS(L) 33*	4/12/45	Okinawa	Kamikaze	4	29
LCS(L) 57	4/12/45	Okinawa	Air Attack	2	6
LCI(G) 407	4/16/45	Okinawa	Kamikaze	0	1
LCS(L) 51	4/16/45	Okinawa	Kamikaze	0	0
LCS(L) 116	4/16/45	Okinawa	Kamikaze	12	12
LCS(L) 15*	4/22/45	Okinawa	Kamikaze	15	11
LCS(L) 37	4/28/45	Okinawa	Suicide Boat	0	3
LCI(G) 580	4/28/45	Okinawa	Kamikaze	0	6
LCS(L) 37	4/29/45	Okinawa	Suicide Boat	0	4
LCS(L) 31	5/4/45	Okinawa	Kamikaze	5	2
LCS(L) 25	5/4/45	Okinawa	Kamikaze	1	8
LCS(L) 84	5/11/45	Okinawa	Kamikaze	0	1

LCI(G), LCI(M), LCI(R), and LCS(L) Ships Damaged or Lost in World War II

Ship	Date	Location	Cause	Dead	Wounded
LCS(L) 88	5/11/45	Okinawa	Kamikaze	7	9
LCS(L) 119	5/27/45	Okinawa	Kamikaze	12	6
LCS(L) 52	5/27/45	Okinawa	Kamikaze	1	10
LCS(L) 61	5/27/45	Okinawa	Kamikaze	0	1
LCS(L) 119	5/28/45	Okinawa	Kamikaze	14	18
LCS(L) 122	6/11/45	Okinawa	Kamikaze	11	29

The list above indicates that, of the LCI gunboat variants, twenty-two LCS(L)s, fourteen LCI(G)s and one LCI(M) suffered war damage or loss in attacks. The large number of LCS(L) ships lost may be explained by the fact that four were hit in Mariveles Harbor, PI, during a single suicide boat attack. At Okinawa, many of the LCS(L) ships were assigned the hazardous duty of serving as support gunboats on the radar picket stations. There they were under frequent air attack and suffered greatly.

*Ships noted were sunk; this was through various means, including friendly fire after they were damaged beyond repair and deemed a hazard to navigation.

**The death statistic shown here is based on official ship's Muster Roles, identified graves in the Manila American Cemetery, Manila, Philippines Islands, as well as those identified as being buried in the United States. The casualty toll for LCS(L) 26 was developed by Professor Philip M. Anderson.

Appendix V: Awards

Presidential Unit Citation

Criteria: The unit must have clearly rendered itself conspicuous by action of a character comparable to that which would merit the award of a Navy Cross to an individual. The performance of duty in carrying out a mission under the ordinary hazards of war, or participation in extended periods of combat duty, or in a large number of combat missions, does not in itself justify the award which is designed to recognize specific acts of heroism on the part of the unit acting as a team. An award will not be made to a large unit for actions of one or more of its component parts unless such large unit performed as a total team in a manner justifying the award.

Ship	Date	Location
LCI(G) 70	5–10 November 1943	Bougainville Landings
	5–9 January 1945	Lingayen Landings
LCI Flotilla Three, LCI(G) Group 8	17 February 1945	Iwo Jima, Volcano Islands
LCI(G) 346 LCI(G) 466		
LCI(G) 348 LCI(G) 469		
LCI(G) 438 LCI(G) 471		
LCI(G) 441 LCI(G) 473		
LCI(G) 450 LCI(G) 474		
LCI(G) 457 LCI(FF) 627		
LCS(L) 31	4 May 1945	Okinawa
LCS(L) 51	16 April 1945	Okinawa
LCS(L) 57	16 April 1945	Okinawa

Navy Unit Commendation

Criteria: The unit must have performed service as a unit of a character comparable to that which would merit the award of a Silver Star Medal or a Legion of Merit to an individual. Normal performance of duty under the ordinary hazards of war, or participation in extended periods of duty or in a large number of combat missions does not in itself justify the award.

Ship	Date	Location
LCI(G) 64	24–29 October 1944	Leyte Landings
	15 December 1944	Mindoro Assault
	3–9 January 1945	Lingayen Operation
LCI(G) Flotilla 3, Amphibious Forces Pacific Fleet	31 January–28 July 1944	Kwajalein and Eniwetok Atolls in the Marshall Islands and Saipan, Guam, and Tinian in the Marianas
LCI(G) 77 LCI(G) 80		
LCI(G) 78 LCI(G) 81		
LCI(G) 79 LCI(G) 82		

Ship		Date	Location
LCI(G) 345	*LCI(G) 451*		
LCI(G) 346	*LCI(G) 452*		
LCI(G) 347	*LCI(G) 453*		
LCI(G) 348	*LCI(G) 454*		
LCI(G) 365	*LCI(G) 455*		
LCI(G) 366	*LCI(G) 456*		
LCI(G) 371	*LCI(G) 457*		
LCI(G) 372	*LCI(G) 458*		
LCI(G) 373	*LCI(G) 459*		
LCI(G) 437	*LCI(G) 460*		
LCI(G) 438	*LCI(G) 461*		
LCI(G) 439	*LCI(G) 462*		
LCI(G) 440	*LCI(G) 463*		
LCI(G) 441	*LCI(G) 470*		
LCI(G) 442	*LCI(G) 725*		
LCI(G) 449	*LCI(G) 726*		
LCI(G) 450			
LCI(M) 356		18 May 1945	Okinawa
LCI(R) 31		18 May–22 September 1944	Western New Guinea
		20 October–12 November 1944	Leyte Landing
		7 December 1944	Ormoc Landing
		9 January 1945	Lingayen Landing
		7 June 1945	Borneo Operation
LCI(R) 34		22 April–30 July 19445	Western New Guinea Operation
		15 December 1944, 9 January–2 February 1945	Luzon
		7 June 1945–1 July 1945	Borneo Operation
LCI(R) 73		22 April–22 September 1944	Western New Guinea
		20–27 October 1944	Leyte Landing
		7 December 1944	Ormoc Landing
		9 January 1945	Lingayen Landing
LCI(R) 338		2–7 July 1944	Western New Guinea Operation
		4 September 1943	Eastern New Guinea Operation
		20–26 October 1944	Leyte Landings
		13–15 December 1944	Mindoro Landings
		9 January 1945	Lingayen Landings
		15–16 February 1945	Capture of Manila and Corregidor
LCI(R) 464		17 June–21 July 1944	Marianas Campaign
		20–24 October 1944	Leyte Landings
		6–10 January 1945	Lingayen Landings
		26 March 1944–6 April 1945	Okinawa Campaign
LCI(R) 659		19–23 October 1944	Leyte Landing
		7–18 January 1945	Lingayen Landings
		19 February–3 March 1945	Capture of Iwo Jima
		16 April 1945–14 June 1945	Okinawa Campaign
LCS(L) 21		4 May 1945	Okinawa Jima Area
LCS(L) 32		19–26 February 1945	Capture of Iwo Jima
		1 April–17 June 9145	Okinawa Operation
LCS(L) 82		11 May 1945	Okinawa
LCS(L)83		3 and 11 May 1945	Okinawa, Ryukyu Islands
LCS(L) 84		11 May 1945	Okinawa, Ryukyu Islands
LCS(L) 86		18 April–21 June 1945	Okinawa Operation
LCS(L) 118		1 April–6 June 1945	Okinawa, Ryukyu Islands
LCS(L) 122		10 and 11 June 1945	Okinawa Campaign*

*Department of the Navy. *Navy and Marine Corps Awards Manual* NAVPERS 15,790 (Rev. 1953), pp. 11–26a.

Notes

Chapter 1

1. Samuel Eliot Morison, *Breaking the Bismarcks Barrier 22 July 1942–1 May 1944* (Edison, NJ: Castle Books, 1950), p. 62.
2. Commanding General Fifth Amphibious Corps, Serial 00334, *Naval Gunfire Support, Tarawa, Recommendations On*, 20 January 1944, p. 643.
3. Gerald Rawling, *Cinderella Operation: The Battle for Walcheren 1944* (London: Cassell, 1980), p. 74.
4. Ibid., p. 74.
5. *The Chief of the Bureau of Ships, to The Vice Chief of Naval Operations*, letter of 7 July 1943, p. 6.
6. I am aware that this information is in conflict with the work of other historians. Samuel Eliot Morison (*Breaking the Bismarcks Barrier*, p. 294) states that the first two LCI(L)s converted were the 24 and 68. Norman Friedman (*U.S. Amphibious Ships and Craft*, p. 233) states that LCI(L)s 22, 24, 68, and 69 had been converted by August 1943. My assertion is based on the *United States Pacific Fleet, Service Squadron, South Pacific Force, Force Maintenance Serial M-0252* letter from the Force Maintenance Officer (Captain R. T. Cowdrey) to the COs of *LCI(L)s 21, 22, 23* and *70* dated 11 October 1943. This letter describes stability adjustments for the ships that were under conversion at that time. In addition, ship movements and comments identifying the exact dates of conversions are found in the *War Diary of LCI(L) Flotilla Five* and the *War Diary of LCI(L) Group Fourteen*, as well as the individual ships' war diaries.
7. *United States Pacific Fleet Service Squadron, South Pacific Force, Force Maintenance Serial M-0252*, 11 October 1943, Enclosure (B).
8. Louis V. Plant, Signalman 1/c, *LCI(G) 24, Memories of World War II* (typescript, 2000), p. 22.
9. Ibid., p. 22.
10. *Chief of Naval Operations to Chief of the Bureau of Ordnance*, letter of 24 March 1944.
11. John E. Burchard, ed., *Rockets Guns and Targets: Rockets, Target Information, Erosion Information, and Hypervelocity Guns Developed during World War II by the Office of Scientific Research and Development* (Boston: Little, Brown, 1948), pp. 118–119.
12. Ibid., pp. 120–122.
13. Karl C. Dod, *United States Army in World War II The Corps of Engineers: The War Against Japan* (Washington, D.C.: Office of the Chief of Military History United States Army, 1966), p. 273.
14. Hugh. J. Casey, Major General, *Engineers of the Southwest Pacific 1941–1945. Engineers in Theater Operations* (Washington, D.C.: Government Printing Office, 1947), p. 117.
15. Burchard, pp. 128–129.
16. Vice Admiral Daniel E. Barbey, *MacArthur's Amphibious Navy: Seventh Amphibious Force Operations 1943–1945* (Annapolis: Naval Institute Press, 1969), p. 112.
17. *LCI(R) 73, Deck Log,* March 31 to April 18, 1943.
18. *USS LCI(G) 451 Serial 0126, Action Report of Beach Assault on Lingayen Gulf Luzon Island in the Philippines*, 15 January 1945, p. 3.
19. *USS LCI(G) 440 Serial 052, U.S.S. LCI(G) 440— Action Report of LINGAYEN Operation*, 15 January 1945, p. 1.
20. *USS LCI(G) 407 Serial — None, Action Report, Lingayen Operation, Luzon, P. I. 9 January 1945*, 20 January 1945, p. 2.
21. *USS LCI(G) 373 Serial 02-45. Initial Invasion Lingayen, Luzon Island, Philippines, Action Report of, 14 January 1945*, 2nd Endorsement, 30 January 1945, p. 1.
22. Chief of the Bureau of Ordnance to the Coordinator of Research and Development, letter of 14 December 1943.
23. Leo P. Brophy, Wyndham D. Miles and Rexmond C. Cochrane, *United States Army in World War II The Technical Services, The Chemical Warfare Service: From Laboratory to Field* (Washington, D.C.: Center of Military History, United States Army, 1988), p. 137.
24. Colonel George F. Unmacht Chemical Officer, C.P.A, letter of 24 April 1944, to Brigadier General Alden H. Waitt, Chemical Warfare Service, Washington, D.C.
25. Ibid.
26. Paul Lund and Harry Ludlam, *The War of the Landing Craft* (London: W. Foulsham & Co., 1976), pp. 92–104.
27. Colonel G. F. Unmacht, CWS USA, "Chemical Mortar Boats in the Pacific Ocean Area," *Military Review* (November 1946): 16.
28. *Departure Report, USS LCI 741*, 28 January 1945, p. 1.
29. *USS LCI(M) 739, War Diary*, July-September 1944.
30. Commander Task Unit 79.6.21—Commander LCI(L) Group 17 Serial 114, *Action Report*, 4 November 1944, p. 4.
31. *USS LCI(M) 638 Serial — None. Action and Operation Report, Okinawa Jima, Period from 1st April to 10 April 1945, Submittal of*, 14 April 1945, p. 7.
32. Unmacht, 17–18.
33. *USS LCI(L) #24 (G), Action Report — 25 January 1944. MAVAVIA VILLAGE, EMPRESS AUGUSTA BAY,*

BOUGAINVILLE— SOLOMON ISLANDS, 10 February 1944, p. 5.
34. Commander Task Unit 52.23.2 (Commander LCI Group 55) Serial 040, *Action Report— Nansei Shoto, Okinawa, Operation —1 May to 31 May 1945*, 6 June 1945, p. 4.
35. Commander LCI(M) Group 18 (Temporary Commander Task Unit 79.7.3) Serial 051, *Action Report, Invasion of Philippines, Island of Leyte*, 23 October 1944, pp. 6–7.
36. *LCI(L) 659*, Serial-None, *Action Report*, 1 November 1944, p. 4.
37. *The Chief of the Bureau of Ships, to the Vice Chief of Naval Operations*, letter of July 7, 1943.
38. *World War II History of the Supervisor of Shipbuilding, USN Portland, Oregon* (circa 1946), IV-6.
39. *SupShip, USN, Quincy, OinC. to George Lawley & Son's Corp*, letter of 15 May 1944.
40. *Monthly War Diary of LCS(L) (3) 61, 81, 82, 83*, 1 April 1945.
41. *The Chief of the Bureau of Ordnance to Commander Amphibious Training Command, U.S. Atlantic Fleet, Supervisor of Shipbuilding, Portland, Supervisor of Shipbuilding, Quincy. (OinC, George Lawley & Son Corp., Neponset, Mass.)*, letter of 14 August 1944.
42. Thomas Lee, GM 1/c, *LCS(L) 31*, interview of 26 September 2011.
43. Thomas Ryan, *LCS(L) 81*, interview of 21 February 2004.
44. Jim Mallin, QM 3/c, *LCS 117*, interview, 21 October 2011.
45. *Supervisory Cost Inspector, Thirteenth Naval District to Chief of the Bureau of Supplies and Accounts (Cost Inspection Service), Navy Department, Washington, D.C.*, letter of 31 October 1944.
46. *World War II History of the Supervisor of Shipbuilding USN Portland, Oregon.* VI—5.
47. Ibid., VI—5.
48. Ibid., VI—5.

Chapter 2

1. Vaughn E. Hampton, "Amphibious Ships with No Names," http://www.geocities.com/Heartland/Plains/5850/hampton.html, pp. 3–8.
2. Navy Department, *History of the Navy's Bases in World War II, History of the Bureau of Yards and Docks and the Civil Engineer Corps 1940–1946. Vol. I* (Washington, D.C.: Government Printing Office, 1947), p. 261.
3. John Rooney, *Mighty Midget U.S.S. LCS 82* (Phoenixville, PA: self-published, 2001), p. 2.
4. Hulbert Footner, "Simple Life of Solomons Becomes a Thing of the Past as Result of War," *The* [Baltimore] *Sun*, 17 January 1943: 20+.
5. Alberta Woodburn, "Is This 'Solomons' Anymore?" *Calvert Independent* (Barstow, MD), 10 June 1943.
6. Rooney, p. 1.
7. John H. Morrill, *The Cincinnati* (Wytheville, VA: self-published, 1994), pp. vii-2.
8. *The Beachmaster Final Edition 36*, U.S.N.A.T.B. (Solomons, MD: February 1945).
9. *Allied Landing Craft of World War Two* (Annapolis, MD: Naval Institute Press, 1989), pp. 45–47.
10. Edgar De Coursey, MM 2/c, *LCS(L) 61*, interview of 25 August 1995.
11. Joseph Staigar, *LCS(L) 61*, Diary and Collected Papers.
12. Robin L. Rielly, *Kamikaze Patrol: The LCS(L)(3)61 at War* (Toms River, NJ: self-published, 1996), pp. 36–40.

13. Charles Thomas, *Dolly Five* (Chester, VA: Harrowgate Press, 1996), pp. 365–366.
14. Robert F. Rielly, QM 2/c, *LCS(L) 61*, interview, 20 September 2001.
15. Louis V. Plant, Staff Signalman, Flotilla 3, *A Brief History of LCS 55*, Typescript, 2000, p. 20.
16. Samuel Eliot Morison, *The Struggle for Guadalcanal August 1942–February 1943* (Edison, NJ: Castle Books, 2001), p. 269.
17. United States Strategic Bombing Survey (Pacific) Naval Analysis Division, *The Campaigns of the Pacific War* (Washington, D.C.: Government Printing Office, 1946), p. 175.
18. Robert Leckie, *Strong Men Armed: The United States Marines vs. Japan* (New York: Da Capo Press, 1997), p. 240.
19. Military Intelligence Service, War Department, *Tactical and Technical Trends* No. 43, 27 January 1944, p. 10.
20. "Japanese Barges," *U.S. Army-Navy Journal of Recognition* (March 1944): 40.
21. Military Intelligence Service, War Department, *Tactical and Technical Trends* No. 43, 27 January 1944, p. 13.
22. Peter Schrijvers, *Bloody Pacific American Soldiers at War with Japan* (New York: Palgrave Macmillan, 2010), p. 119.
23. Masahiro Kawai, Lieutenant Colonel, *The Operations of the Suicide-Boat Regiment in Okinawa Their Battle Results and the Countermeasures Taken by the U.S. Forces* (National Institute for Defense Studies, Undated), p. 2.
24. Ibid.
25. Soemu Toyoda, Admiral, "Combined Fleet Ultrasecret Dispatch 041213," *The Campaigns of the Pacific War* (Washington, D.C.: United States Strategic Bombing Survey (Pacific) Naval Analysis Division, 1946), p. 233.
26. Kawai, p. 2.
27. Robin L. Rielly, *Kamikazes, Corsairs, and Picket Ships: Okinawa 1945* (Philadelphia: Casemate, 2008), pp. 351–352.
28. Robert Wisner, *LCS(L) 37*, interview, 15 August, 2001.

Chapter 3

1. GHQ SWPA Warning Instructions 2, 6 May 43, in GHQ SWPA G-3 Jnl 6 May 43, cited in John Miller, Jr., *Cartwheel: The Reduction of Rabaul* (Washington, D.C.: Office of the Chief of Military History — Department of the Army, 1959), p. 26.
2. Grace Person Hayes, *The History of the Joint Chiefs of Staff in World War II— The War Against Japan* (Annapolis, MD: Naval Institute Press, 1982), p. 425.
3. John Miller, Jr. *Cartwheel: The Reduction of Rabaul* (Washington, D.C.: Office of the Chief of Military History — Department of the Army, 1959), p. 235.
4. *War Diary Commander LCI(L) Group Fourteen 1 September 1943–30 September 1943*, p. 8.
5. Charles R. Ports, "My Life as an LCI Gunboat Sailor," *The Elsie Item* No. 56 (June 2006): 20.
6. *USS LCI(L) 23 Action Report; Support of Landing, Treasury Islands, 27 October 1943*, p. 3.
7. *USS LCI(L) 23 Action Report, Support of Landing, Treasury Islands, 27 October 1943*, Second Endorsement, 24 November 1943.
8. Samuel Eliot Morison, *History of United States Naval Operations in World War II, Breaking the Bismarcks Barrier 22 July 1942–1 May 1944* (Edison, NJ: Castle Books, 2001), pp. 316–328.
9. *USS LCI(L) 2*, No Serial, *Action Report: Empress Augusta Bay, Bougainville Islands, 29 November 194*, 3 December 1943, Second Endorsement.

10. USS LCI(L) 24 (G), No Serial, *Action Report — Night of 25, February 1944, MOTUPENA Pt. — GAZELE HARBOR AREA, BOUGAINVILLE — SOLOMON ISLANDS*, 26 February 1944, pp. 1–3.

11. USS LCI(G) #69, No Serial, *War Diary and Log, Month of May 1943*, 29 May to 31 May 1944.

12. Commander LCI(G) Group 13. Serial 121. *LCI Gunboat Operations of 1–4 July 1944*. 7 July 1944, pp. 1–2.

13. Captain Walter Karig, Lieutenant Commander Russell L. Harris, and Lieutenant Commander Frank A. Manson, *Battle Report: The End of an Empire* (New York: Rinehart and Company, 1948), pp. 50–52.

14. Daniel E. Barbey, Vice Admiral, *MacArthur's Amphibious Navy: Seventh Amphibious Force Operations 1943–1945* (Annapolis: United States Naval Institute, 1969), p. 119.

15. "Yanks Use Rockets Against Japs," *The Deseret News* (Salt Lake City), January 16, 1944: p. 2.

16. Barbey, pp. 144–157.

17. *War Diary Commander LCI Group 45*, September 1945, p. 3.

18. Commander Task Group 78.14, Serial 1073/08, *Action Report — Mapia Islands and Asia Islands Operation*, 27 November 1944, p. 1.

19. Commander Task Group 78.14, Serial 1073/08, *Action Report — Mapia Islands and Asia Islands*, 27 November 1944.

20. Henry I. Shaw, Jr., and Major Douglas T. Kane, USMC, *History of U.S. Marine Corps Operations in World War II, Volume II, Isolation of Rabaul* (Historical Branch, G-3, Headquarters, U.S. Marine Corps, 1963), p. 538.

Chapter 4

1. Samuel Eliot Morison, *History of United States Naval Operations in World War II, Volume VII, Aleutians, Gilberts and Marshalls June 1942-April 1944* (Edison, NJ: Castle Books, 2001), p. 70.

2. Vaughn. E. Hampton, *Amphibious Ships with No Names*, http://www.Geocities.com/Heartland/Plains/5850/Hampton.html, pp. 4–5.

3. Dominick C. Maurone, USS LCI Stories, "Dominick C. Maurone *LCI 440*," USS Landing Craft Infantry National Association, pp. 4–6. http://www.usslci.com/maurone/maurone1.htm.

4. Commander LCI Group 8, Flotilla Three, Serial 15, *War Diary, submission of*, 10 March 1944, p. 24.

5. Commander Eniwetok Expeditionary Group (Commander Task Group FIFTY ONE POINT ELEVEN — Commander Group TWO, FIFTH Amphibious Force), *ENIWETOK Operations — Report of*, 7 March 1944, Enclosure (A), p. 76.

6. Ibid., Enclosure (A), p. 78.

7. Commander LCI Group 8, Flotilla Three, Serial 15, *War Diary, submission of*, 10 March 1944, pp. 18–19.

8. Commander LCI Group 9, *War Diary 7–14 March 1944*, pp. 1–6.

9. Commander Amphibious Forces, Pacific (Commander Joint Expeditionary Force) Serial 00704, *Report of Amphibious Operations for the Capture of the Marianas Islands: Operation*, 25 August 1944, p. 6.

10. Wyatt Blassingame, *The U.S. Frogmen of World War II* (New York: Random House, 1964), p. 77.

11. Commanding General, Fifth Amphibious Corps (Commander Task Group 56.1), Serial 0024A, *Northern Troops and Landing Force Operations Report, Forager Phase I (Saipan)*, 12 August 1944, Enclosure (I), p. 6.

12. USS LCI(G) 458 Serial 1025-1, *Marianas Operation, Saipan — Action Report of LCI(G) 458*, 25 October 1944, Enclosure (A), Part 1.

13. Ibid., Enclosure (A), p. 5.

14. USS LCI(G) 452 No Serial, *USS LCI(G) 452 — Action Report*, no date. p. 2.

15. Commander LCI(L) Flotilla 3, Serial 050-44, *Engagement Between Enemy Troop Barges and LCI(G)'s of Flotilla Three*, 26 June 1944, p. 1.

16. Commander Task Force FIFTY TWO (Commander Group TWO, Amphibious Forces U.S. Pacific Fleet), Serial 0232, *Capture of TINIAN — Report of*, 24 August 1944, Enclosure (A), pp. 65–66.

17. USS LCI(G) 453, Serial 063, *Action Report (Delayed), Marianas Campaign*, 11 October 1944, p. 4.

18. Commander LCI(G) Group 8, Serial 025, *Action Report of LCI(G) Group Eight, Division Sixteen*, 10 August 1944, p. 62.

19. United States Strategic Bombing Survey (Pacific) Naval Analysis Division, *The Campaigns of the Pacific War* (Washington, D.C.: Government Printing Office, 1946), pp. 219–220.

20. USS LCI(G) 468, Serial None, *Action Report*, 28 June 1944, p. 1.

21. Commander Task Force 53 (Commander Amphibious Forces, Pacific Group 3) Serial 00224, *Report of Amphibious Operations for the Capture of Guam*, 10 August 1944, pp. 8–9.

22. Officer in Charge UDT #3 Serial 00229, *Underwater Demolition Team #3 — Operation Report of*, 18 August 1944.

23. USS LCI(G) 469, No Serial, *Action Report on the Assault on the Island of Guam*, 30 July 1944, p. 2.

24. The Commander, LCI(G) Group 37, No Serial, *Action report for period 21 July to 31 July 1944*, 1 August 1944, p. 2.

25. USS LCI(G) 469, No Serial, *Action Report on encounter with enemy gunfire at Guam*, 1 August 1944, p. 1.

26. USS LCI(G) 466, Serial — None, *Action Report of September 1944*, 5 October 1944, p. 2.

27. Headquarters, Third Marines, Third Marine Division, FMF, in the Field, *Special Action Report Number Two*, 12 September 1944, Annex "B," p. 1.

28. Commander LCI(L) Flotilla Thirteen Group 37, *War Diary 1 July to 30 September 1945*.

29. Headquarters, Third Marines, Third Marine Division, FMF, in the Field, *Special Action Report Number Two*, 12 September 1944, Annex "B," p. 2.

30. U.S.S. LCI(G) 471, No Serial, *Action Report on Capture of One Hundred Jap Prisoners by LCI(G) 471*, 30 September 1944, p. 6.

31. Commanding Officer, Underwater Demolition Team Four, *Beaches Violet ONE and Violet TWO, Reconnaissance report of*, 19 October 1944, p. 4.

32. United States Strategic Bombing Survey (Pacific) Naval Analysis Division, *The Campaigns of the Pacific War* (Washington, D.C.: Government Printing Office, 1946), p. 220.

33. Robert Leckie, *Helmet for My Pillow: From Parris Island to the Pacific* (New York: Bantam, 2010), p. 278.

34. USS LCI(M) 739, *War Diary September 1944*, 15–20 September 1944, p. 7.

35. USS LCI(G) 453, Serial 068, *Action Report, PALAU Operation*, 15 November 1944, p. 2.

36. U.S.S. LCI(G) 458, Serial 1101, *Palau Campaign, Peleliu — Action Report of LCI(G) 458 for*, 1 November 1944, pp. 4–5.

37. Commander LCI Group 9, *War Diary 4 September through 30 September 1944, inclusive*, Enclosure (A), pp. 3–7.

38. John H. Morrill, *The Cincinnati* (Wytheville, VA: self-published, 1994), pp. 126–127.
39. Ibid., pp. 175–177.
40. Dick Arnold, *LCI(G) 730*, "Dick Arnold's Peleliu Memories," http://www.home.sprvnet.com/~kier/arnold.htm, pp. 1–2.
41. Robert F. Heath, *With the Black Cat USS LCI Flotilla 13* (Chico, CA: The Technical Education Press, 2003), p. 67.
42. *USS LCI(G) 397*, Serial 38, *Action Report — Submission of*, 9 March 1945, p. 2.
43. *USS LCI(G) 405*, No Serial, *Action Report — Report of Action Morning of 24 December 1944*, 15 February 1945, pp. 1–2.
44. *USS LCI(L) 732*, Serial 58, *Enemy Action — Report of*, 27 February 1945, pp. 1–2.
45. Morrill, p. 194.
46. Commander LCI(L) Flotilla THIRTEEN (U.S.S. *LCI(G) 730*, Flagship), *War Diary for April 1945*, 2 May 1945, p. 8.
47. LCI(L) Flotilla Thirteen, Serial 0627, *War Diary for August 1945*, 1 September 1945, p.4.

Chapter 5

1. Grace Person Hayes., *The History of the Joint Chiefs of Staff in World War II: The War Against Japan* (Annapolis: Naval Institute Press, 1982), p. 604.
2. Ibid., p. 605.
3. *USS LCI(G) 451*, Serial — None, *War Diary and Action Report*, 28 October 1944, p. 1.
4. Samuel Eliot Morison, *History of United States Naval Operations in World War II, Vol. XII, Leyte June 1944–January 1944* (Edison, NJ: Castle Books, 2001), p. 120.
5. Commander Task Unit 78.3.5, No Serial, *Action Report — Central Philippines — Panaon Attack Group*, 30 November 1944, pp. 1–3.
6. M. Hamlon Cannon, *United States Army I World War II The War in the Pacific: Leyte: The Return to the Philippines* (Washington, D.C.: Center of Military History United States Army, 1996), p. 65.
7. Edward H. Laylin, Lieutenant (jg), Commanding Officer of *LCI(L) 1064*, letter of 11 November 1944.
8. Joseph A. Dumenigo, *LCI(G) 568*, interview, 17 February 2011.
9. *USS LCI(G) 72*, Serial 027, *Action Report — LEYTE Operation*, 1 November, 1944, p. 5.
10. Commander Task Force 78 (Commander Seventh Amphibious Force), Serial 00911, *Leyte Operations — Report On*, 10 November 1944, p. 13.
11. Underwater Demolition Team 10, Serial 02, *Action Report, Assault Landings at Leyte Island, P.I.* 24 October 1944, p. 9.
12. U. D. T. #9, No Serial, *C. O., U. D. T. #9 Action Report, Leyte Operation*, 3 November 1944, p. 4.
13. Commander Task Group 79.1 (Commander Amphibious Group 3), Serial 454, *Report of Task Group 79.1 Participation in Amphibious Operations for the Capture of Leyte, P.I.*, 26 October 1944, p. 10B.
14. *USS LCI(M) 660*, No Serial, *Action Report of 20 to 24 October 1944*, 31 October 1944, p. 4.
15. Ibid., p. 8.
16. Commander LCI(M) Group 18 (Temporary Commander Task Unit 79.7.3), Serial 051, *Action Report, Invasion of Philippines, Island of Leyte*, 23 October 1944, p. 1.
17. Lieutenant Steward W. Hellman, "Leyte Landing," in S. E. Smith, ed., *The United States Navy in World War II* (New York: William Morrow, 1966), pp. 836–837.
18. Commander LCI(L) Flotilla 6, Serial 132, *Action Report — Submission of*, 14 November 1944, p.4
19. *USS LCI(L) 372*, Serial 078, *Action Report 3-44; Beach Assault on Leyte Island*, 21 October 1944, p. 4.
20. Ibid., p. 5.
21. *USS LCI(G) 422*, Serial — None, *Action Report Covering Operation of This Vessel 20 October, 1944.*, Undated, pp. 1–3.
22. *USS LCI(G) 475*, Serial None, *Action Report*, no date, pp. 1–2.
23. *USS LCI(G) 568*, No Serial, *Action Report*, no date, p. 2.
24. *USS LCI(G) 462*, No Serial, *Action Report of USS LCI(G) 462 During Assault on Leyte Island, Philippines*, 24 October 1944, p. 1.
25. "LCI Memories … A Lucky Japanese Dive-Bomber Spoils the Day for *LCI(G) #23*," *USS Landing Craft Infantry National Association*, undated, pp. 1–2, http://usslci com/html_L2/stories/divebomber.html
26. *USS LCI(G) 752*, Serial 131, *War Damage, Report of*, 5 November 1944.
27. *U.S.S. LCI(G) 340*, No Serial, *Action Report — LEYTE Operation*, 28 October 1944, pp. 6–7.
28. *USS LCI(G) 342*, Serial-None, *Action Report San Pedro Bay, Central Philippines*, 31 October 1945, p. 1.
29. Commander Task Unit 78.1.8 (Commander LCI(R) Group 20) Serial 160, *Action Reports, Task Unit 78.1.8, Leyte Operation (20 Oct. to 20th Nov.) — Information Additional to*, 20 November 1944, pp. 4–6.
30. Commander Task Group 78.2 (Seventh Amphibious Force Group 8) Serial 098, *Anti-Aircraft Action Report — Leyte Operation, Forwarding Of*, 4 December 1944, pp. 22–24.
31. *USS LCI(G) 558*, Serial None, *Action Report, Anti-Aircraft*, 18 January 1945, pp. 1–2.
32. *USS LCI(G) 558*, Serial None, *Action Report*, 10 December 1944.
33. Ibid.
34. Robin L. Rielly, *Kamikaze Attacks of World War II* (Jefferson, NC: McFarland, 2010), p. 109.
35. Commander LCI Group 20, Serial 178, *Action Report — Mindoro Operations, 15 December 1944*, 19 December 1944, Enclosure (B), p. 2.
36. Robert Ross Smith, *United States Army in World War II: The War in the Pacific: Triumph in the Philippines* (Washington, D.C.: Center of Military History United States Army, 1991), p. 95.
37. Commander Task Force 78 (Commander Task Group 7.1) (Commander Seventh Amphibious Force), Serial 0071, *Report of the Lingayen Operation — San Fabian Attack Force*, 12 February 1945, p. 3.
38. Commander Task Unit 79.7.1 (Commander LCI(G) Group 16), Serial 017, *Action Report for Luzon Operation on 24 December 1944 to 23 January 1945*, 4 February 1945, pp. 4–5.
39. *USS LCI(G) 559*, No Serial, *Action Report, Support of Hydrographic Survey Group, and Lingayen Beach Assault*, no date, p. 4.
40. *USS LCI(G) 558*, No Serial, *Action Report*, 22 January 1945, p. 2.
41. Ibid.
42. Arden Lee Hunt, *The Journal of Arden Lee Hunt*, *LCI 226*, USS Landing Craft Infantry National Association, pp. 14–15, http://www.usslci.com/html/lci226.htm.
43. Smith, p. 76.
44. *USS LCI(G) 365*, Serial None, *Action Report, Submission of*, 12 January 1945, p. 3.

45. *USS LCI(G) 559*, No Serial, *Action Report, Support of Hydrographic Survey Group, and Lingayen Beach Assault*, no date, p. 3.
46. *War Diary of Task Force Thirty-One Third Fleet and Task Force Seventy-Nine, Seventh Fleet. 1 January to 31 January 1945*, Enclosure (H), p. 3.
47. *USS LCI(G) 560*, No Serial, *Action Report*, 25 January 1945, p. 5.
48. Commander Task Unit 79.8.1 (Commander LCI(M) Group 17), Serial 010, *Action Report*, 18 January 1945, pp. 1–9.

Chapter 6

1. Commander Task Unit 78.2.6, No Serial, *Action Report — Mike Six Operation — Nasugbu — Southern Luzon — January 31–February 2, 1945*, 9 February 1945, Part I, p. 5.
2. Claude Haddock, S 1/c, *LCS(L) 49*, interview of 24 July 2008.
3. Harry G. Meister, Lieutenant Commander USNR. *USS LCS(L) 3-27, A WWII Amphibious Landing Craft Support Vessel* (Vancouver, WA: Typescript, 2002), pp. 16–17.
4. L. Richard Rhame, Lieutenant (jg), LCS(L) Flotilla One, *Mariveles Bay — 15 February 1945*, Typescript, January 1988, p. 2.
5. Arden Lee Hunt, *The Journal of Arden Lee Hunt, LCI 226*, USS Landing Craft Infantry National Association, pp. 19–20, http://www.usslci.com/html/lci226.htm
6. Commander Task Force SEVENTY-EIGHT (Commander SEVENTH Amphibious Forces), Serial: 0907, Action Reports, *MARIVELES — CORREGIDOR Operation, 12–15 February 1945*, 12 April 1945, p. 1.
7. Gordon L. Rottman, *World War II Pacific Island Guide: A Geo-Military Study* (Westport, CT: Greenwood Press, 2002), p. 308.
8. *USS LCI(R) 341*, Serial — None, *Action Report — Cebu City Area, Cebu Island*, 28 March 1945, p. 3.
9. Commander Task Unit 78.2.6, Serial None, *Action Report — Victor-Two Operation — Cebu City Philippine Islands, 26–28 March 1945*, 31 March 1945, p. 3.
10. Commander Task Group 78.2, Serial 0145, *Action Report — Malabang-Parang-Cotabato Mindanao Operation*, 22 May 1945, p. 1.
11. Ibid., p. 12.
12. Commander Task Unit 78.2.12 (Commander LCS Flotilla 1), Serial 051, *Action Reports of PGMs 4 and 6 and LCI(G) 61 — Pulangi River, Mindanao Operation*, 9 May 1945.
13. Kenneth R. Krayer ETCS, *On a Ship with No Name: The U.S.S. LCSL(L)(3) 28 in World War Two* (Erie, PA: self-published, circa 1990s), p. 39.
14. Commander Task Unit 78.1.31, Serial 05, *Action Report — Zamboanga Peninsula Operation*. 15 March 1945, pp. 1–3.
15. Commander Task Unit 78.1.3, Serial 014, *Action Report — Zamboanga Operation*, 16 March 1945, p. 3.
16. *USS LCS(L) 43*, No Serial, *Action Report*, 19 March 1945, p. 1.
17. Commander Task Group 70.4, Serial None, no date, *Summary of Missions to Supply Guerrilla Forces*, p. 1.
18. Albert C. Eldridge, Lieutenant, CO *LCS(L) 10*, *The Mighty Ten* (History of the *LCS(L) 10*), Typescript, undated, p. 3.
19. Ibid., pp. 3–4.
20. Commander Task Group 70.4, Serial None, no date, *Summary of Missions to Supply Guerrilla Forces*, pp. 2–3.
21. Ibid., pp. 3–4.
22. Frank P. Muth, *History of the LCS(L) 9*, Typescript, undated, p. 8.
23. Commander Task Group 70.4, Serial None, no date, *Summary of Missions to Supply Guerrilla Forces*, pp. 4–5.
24. Krayer, p. 42.
25. Commander Task Group 70.4, Serial None, no date, *Summary of Missions to Supply Guerrilla Forces*, p. 8.
26. Eldridge, p. 9.
27. Larry Alexander, *Shadows in the Jungle: The Alamo Scouts Behind Japanese Lines in World War II* (New York: NAL Caliber, 2010), pp. 293–294

Chapter 7

1. Commander LCI(G) Group 8 (Commander Task Unit 52.5.2) Serial 0035-45, *Action of LCI(G) Group Eight in the Iwo Jima Campaign From 17 February to 20 February 1945 — Report of*, 30 March 1945, pp. 2–3.
2. *Deck Log LCI(G) 449*, 17 February 1945, p. 20.
3. Dennis Blocker, "The Firey Ordeal of *LCI(G) 449* at Iwo Jima," *The Elsie Item*, USS Landing Craft Infantry, National Association, Blythewood, SC, Issue #60 (July 2007): 19–23.
4. U.S. Navy, *Medal of Honor 1861–1949 — The Navy*, Washington, D.C.: Government Printing Office, 1949.
5. *USS LCI(G) 438*, Serial 220, *Action Report — Assault on Iwo Jima, Volcano Islands, 17–21 February 1945*, 1 March 1945, pp. 3–4.
6. *USS LCI(G) 474* No Serial, *Action Report — Assault on Iwo Jima, 17 February 1945*, 17 February 1945, pp. 1–3.
7. Lieutenant (jg) Donald Murray quoted in Chet Cunningham, *The Frogmen of World War II* (New York: Pocket Star Books, 2005), p. 263.
8. Bruce F. Meyers, *Swift, Silent, and Deadly — Marine Amphibious Reconnaissance in the Pacific, 1942–1945* (Annapolis: Naval Institute Press, 2004), p. 106.
9. Frank Jirka, Lieutenant (jg),UDT 12, speech at Great Lakes Naval Hospital, Chicago, IL, circa 1946.
10. *USS LCI(G) 457* Serial — None, *Action Report*, 27 February 1945, pp. 3–5.
11. *USS LCI(G) 441*. Serial — None, *Action Report, Assault on Iwo Jima, Volcanoes, February 17 to 19, 1945*, 6 March 1945, pp. 3–5.
12. *USS LCI(G) 473* Serial 14-45, *Action Report on Invasion of Iwo Jima*, 1 March 1945, pp. 1–2.
13. *USS Terror CM5* Serial 0107, *Action Report*, 2 March 1945, pp. 1–2.
14. Commander Underwater Demolition Team 15, No Serial, *Action Report — Beach Reconnaissance, Iwo Jima Island*, 10 March 1945, pp. 5–6.
15. Commander LCI(G) Flotilla 3 (Commander Task Unit 52.5.1), Serial 005-44, *Action Report — Assault of Iwo Jima, Volcano Islands, 17–19 February 1945*, 24 February 1945, 1st Endorsement, 24 February 1945.
16. *USS LCI(G) 348*, Serial-None, *Action Report, Underwater Demolition Support on Iwo Jima, Feb. 17, 1945*, 9 March 1945, pp. 2–3.
17. Commander LCI(G) Flotilla 3 (Commander Task Unit 52.5.1) Serial 005-44, *Action Report — Assault of Iwo Jima, Volcano Islands, 17–19 February 1945*, 24 February 1945, Enclosures A and B.
18. Commander LCI(G) Flotilla Three, Serial 003. *Detachment Operation*, 22 February 1945, p. 6.
19. *USS LCI(G) 450, Serial None. Action Report, Forwarding of*, 24 February 1945, First Endorsement, 22 March 1945, p. 1.
20. Commander LCI(G) Group 8 (Commander Task

Unit 52.5.2) Serial 0035-45, *Action of LCI(G) Group Eight in the Iwo Jima Campaign, From 17 February to 20 February 1945 — Report of,* 30 March 1945, p. 9.

21. Commander Task Force 52 (Amphibious Support Force), (Rear Admiral W. H. P. Blandy, USN, Commander Amphibious Group One, *U.S.S. Estes,* Flagship), Serial 009, *Operations of Task Force 52 in the Iwo Jima Campaign from 10 February to 0600(K) 19 February, at which time CTF 51 assumed title CTF 52 according to Plan; Report of,* 22 February 1945, p. C-9.

22. Commander LCI(G) Group 8 (Commander Task Unit 52.5.2). Serial 0035-45, *Action of LCI(G) Group "Eight in the Iwo Jima Campaign, From 17 February to 20 February 1945 — Report of,* 30 March 1945, p. 9.

23. Captain Walter Karig, *Battle Report: Victory in the Pacific* (New York: Rinehart and Company, 1949), p. 261.

24. Commander Task Unit 52.6.5 (Commander LCI(L) Group 67), No Serial, *Action Report — Invasion of Iwo Jima 18–26 February 1945,* no date, p. 2.

25. *USS LCI(M) 1057* Serial None, *Action Report of Okinawa Operation, 1–10 April 1945,* 11 April 1945, p. 3.

26. *USS LCI(M) 975* Serial 003, *Action Report of Okinawa Operation,* 2 April 1945, pp. 2–3.

27. *USS LCI(M) 633,* No Serial, *Action and Operation Report — Iwo Jima — Volcano Islands,* 1 March 1945, p. 2.

28. Commander Task Unit 52.6.5, (Commander LCI(L) Group 67), No Serial, *Action Report — Invasion of Iwo Jima 18–26 February 1945,* no date, Enclosure (E), p. 2.

29. Commander Task Unit 52.6.1, (Commander LCI(L) Group 61), Serial AR 1-45, *Action Report — Amphibious Assault on Iwo Jima — 15 February 1945 to 2 March 1945,* 5 March 1945, p. 11.

30. Charles Thomas, *Dolly Five: A Memoir of the Pacific War* (Chester, VA: Harrowgate Press, 1996), pp. 135, 145.

31. *USS LCI(R) 644,* No Serial, *Action Report — Invasion of Iwo Jima — 15 February–2 March 1945,* 5 March 1945, p. 3.

32. *LCS(L) 31,* No Serial. *Action Report; Capture and Occupation of Iwo Jima, 19 February–8 March 1945,* 10 March 1945, p. 1.

33. *LCS(L)(3) 51,* No Serial, *Report of Action of USS LCS(L)(3) 51 Against IWO JIMA,* 19 February through 26 February 1945, Undated, p. 2.

34. Commander Task Group 52.5 (Commander LCS(L) Flotilla 3), Serial 027, *Action Report — Invasion of Iwo Jima — 19–26 February 1945,* 10 March 1945, Enclosure (G), p. 2.

35. *USS LCS(L) 31,* No Serial, *Action Report; Capture and Occupation of Iwo Jima, 19 February–8 March 1945,* 10 March 1945, pp. 4–5.

36. Frank C. Osterland, LCDR USNR, *Dolly Three,* Typescript, 28 August 28 1993, p. 6.

37. *USS LCS(L) 33,* No Serial, *Action Report U.S.S. LCS(L) (3) 33,* 10 March 1945, p. 11.

38. Commander Task Group 52.5 (Commander LCS(L) Flotilla 3), Serial 027, *Action Report — Invasion of Iwo Jima — 19–26 February 1945,* 10 March 1945, Enclosure (C), p. 11.

39. Commander Task Group 52.5 (Commander LCS(L) Flotilla 3), Serial 027, *Action Report — Invasion of Iwo Jima — 19–26 February 1945,* 10 March 1945, Enclosure (E), pp. 4–5.

40. *USS LCI(M) 1056,* Serial None, *Action Report,* 5 March 1945, p. 2.

41. *USS LCI(M) 1012,* Serial 008, *Action and Operation Report, Iwo Jima,* 28 February 1945, p. 5.

42. *USS LCI(G) 756,* Serial 1, *Action Report — Iwo Jima,* 3 March 1945, p. 4.

43. *USS LCI(M) 356,* Serial 1252, *Action and Operation Report, Iwo Jima, 27 February 1945, D Plus 8,* 7 March 1945, Enclosure (C).

44. *USS LCS(L) 54,* No Serial. *Action Report: Assault and Capture of Iwo Jima, 19 February–8 March 1945,* 14 March 1945, p. 2.

Chapter 8

1. Grace Person Hayes, Lieutenant, *The History of the Joint Chiefs of Staff in World War II, The War Against Japan* (Annapolis: Naval Institute Press, 1982), p. 695.

2. Ibid., p. 697.

3. Ibid., p. 696.

4. George Odgers, *Air War Against Japan, 1943–1945* (Canberra: Australian War Memorial, 1968), p. 434.

5. Samuel Eliot Morison, *The Liberation of the Philippines: Luzon, Mindanao, the Visayas 1944–1945* (Edison, NJ: Castle Books, 2001), p. 259.

6. *USS LCI(M) 359* Serial 7, *Action Report of Encounter with an Enemy Raft Containing Eight Japanese,* 26 April 1945, 27 April 1945, p. 2.

7. Raymond J. Ross, EM 3/c, *LCS(L) 60,* Typescript, March 1945, p. 5.

8. Robert C. Heim, BM 2/c, *LCS(L) 48,* Typescript, July 1989, p. 2.

9. Joseph E. Rhoads, Lieutenant (jg), *LCS(L) 50, The Birth and Life of our Ship the USS LCS(L)(3) 50,* Typescript, circa 1945, p. 4.

10. *USS LCI(R) 71* No Serial, *Action Report, U.S.S. LCI (R) 71 — Tarakan Island, Borneo Operation,* 1 May 1945, p. 2.

11. *U.S.S. LCI(M) 362,* No Serial, *Action Report, Tarakan Island,* 2 May 1945, p. 2.

12. Gilbert D. Nadeau, *LCS(L) 45* letter to Richard Rhame, National Association of USS LCS(L) 1–130, 9 March 1990.

13. *USS LCS(L) 60,* Serial 0055, *Action Report, U.S.S. LCS(L)(3) 60 — BRUNEI BAY Operation,* 10 June 1945, p. 4.

14. Raymond J. Ross, EM 3c, *LCS(L) 60, History of LCS(L) 60,* Typescript, 1991, p. 8.

15. Ross, p. 8.

16. Commander Underwater Demolition Team No. 11, Serial 0008, *Action Report,* 10 June 1945, pp. 1–4.

17. *USS LCI(R) 34* Serial 0023, *Action Report, U.S.S. LCI (R) 34 — Labuan Island, Brunei Area Borneo Period — 7 June 1945 to 12 June 1945,* 13 June 1945, p. 1–2.

18. Gavin Long, *Australia in the War of 1939–1945: The Final Campaigns* (Canberra: Australian War Memorial, 1963), pp. 502–503.

19. Commander Task Group 78.2 (Commander Amphibious Group EIGHT, SEVENTH Fleet), Serial No. 0235, *Action Report — BALIKPAPAN-MANGGAR-BORNEO June 15–July 6, 1945,* 14 August 1945, p. V-1.

20. G. Hermon Gill, *Royal Australian Navy, 1942–1945* (Canberra: Australian War Memorial, 1968), p. 648.

21. Commander Underwater Demolition Team 11, *Action Report C.T.U. 78.2.11— 25 June to 1 July 1945 Operation OBOE TWO,* 2 July 1945, p. 2.

22. Marvin Cooper, *The Men from Fort Pierce,* quoted in U.S. Naval Special Warfare Archives, http://www.navy frogmen.com/team13.html, p. 6.

23. *U.S.S. LCS (L (3) 44, Action Report, U.S.S. LCS(L) (3) 44 — Balikpapan Operation (June 24-July 2),* 2 July 1945, p. 1.

24. *U.S.S. LCS(L)(3) 28,* Serial 46-45, *Action Report U.S.S. LCS(L)(3) 28 — Balikpapan Operation,* 1 July 1945, 2 July 1945, p. 1.

25. Commanding Officer, Underwater Demolition Team No, 18. Serial 0001, *Action Report*, 2 July 1945, pp. 1–5.
26. *LCS(L) 8* Serial 020, *Action Report, Balikpapan Operation (Including Demolition Operations Prior to "F" day)*, 2 July 1945, pp. 1–2.
27. Samuel Eliot Morison, *The Liberation of the Philippines: Luzon, Mindanao, The Visayas 1944–1945* (Edison, NJ: Castle Books, 2001), p. 274.
28. Commander Task Group 78.2 (Commander Amphibious Group EIGHT, SEVENTH Fleet), Serial No. 0235, *Action Report — BALIKPAPAN-MANGGAR-BORNEO June 15-July 6, 1945*, 14 August 1945, p. V-14.
29. *LCS(L) 8*, *Ship's History*, circa 1945, p. 8.
30. *USS LCI(G) 66*, No Serial, *Action Report, U.S.S. LCI(G) 66 — Balikpapan Screening Operation, 10 July 1945*, 14 July 1945, pp. 1–2.

Chapter 9

1. Amphibious Forces Pacific Fleet, (Task Force 52), Serial 000166, *Operation Order A6-45*, 16 March 1945, pp. 1–2.
2. United States Strategic Bombing Survey (Pacific) Naval Analysis Division, *The Campaigns of the Pacific War* (Washington, D.C.: Government Printing Office, 1946), p. 324.
3. Commander Amphibious Forces U.S. Pacific Fleet (Commander Task Force FIFTY-ONE and Joint Expeditionary Force) Serial 01400, *General Action Report, Capture of OKINAWA GUNTO, Phases I and II, 17 February 1945 to 17 May 1945 — Submission of*, 25 July 1945, (V) (C)-7.
4. Commander Underwater Demolition Teams, Amphibious Forces, U.S. Pacific Fleet, Serial 0028-45, *Action Report, RYUKYU ISLANDS Operations, 25 March–5 April, 1945*, 4 April 1945, p. 1-1.
5. Commander A. R. Montgomery, Commander Task Group 52.18, First Endorsement to CTU 52.24.4 conf., letters dated 9 April 1945, 26 April 1945.
6. *USS LCI(G) 567* Serial — None. *Action Report for Okinawa Gunto, Phases One and Two, March 26–June 25, 1945*, 15 July 1945, p. 4.
7. Commander Task Group 52.11 (Commander Underwater Demolition Teams, Amphibious Force Pacific) Serial 0028-45, *Action Report, Ryukyu Islands Operations, 25 March–5 April 1945*, 4 April 1945, p. 5.
8. Lieutenant (jg) Donald Murray UDT 13 quoted in Chet Cunningham, *The Frogmen of World War II: An Oral History of the U.S. Navy's Underwater Demolition Units* (New York: Pocket Books, 2005), pp. 267–268.
9. *USS LCI(R) 1026*, Serial 165, *Action Report for Period 21 March to 1 May 1945*, 1 May 1945, p. 1.
10. Commander LCI Group 14, Serial 04, *Action Report — Okinawa Operation, 1 April to 15 April 1945*, 20 April 1945, p. 1.
11. Commander LCI Flotilla 14 (Commander Task Group 52.24), Serial 0566, *Action Report — Okinawa Shima — 1 April 1945*, 7 May 1945, p. 5.
12. *USS LCI(M) 807*, Serial 143, *Action Report at Okinawa Shima 1 April 1945*, 29 May 1945. Second Endorsement, 15 July 1945.
13. *U.S.S. LCI(G) 1089*, Serial 1-45, *Action Report, Western Haguchi Beach, Okinawa Jima*, 5 April 1945, p. 5.
14. Charles J. Lamson, S 2/c, *U.S.S. LCI(R) 648*, letter to Mrs. Charles W. Lamson, 3 April 1945.
15. Joseph A. Dumenigo, *LCI(G) 568*, interview of 17 January 2011.
16. *USS LCI(G) 568*, Serial 5-45, *Anti-aircraft Action Report by USS LCI(G) 568*, 7 April 1945, p. 2.
17. LCI(R) Group 47, *War Diary*, 1–30 April 1945, p. 3.
18. Commander Task Group 52.23, (Commander LCI Flotilla 21), Serial 0001, *Action Report, Invasion of Okinawa Jima, Nansei Shoto Group, 25 March through 10 April 1945*, 10 April 1945, p. 7.
19. Benis M. Frank and Henry I. Shaw, Jr., *Victory and Occupation, Vol. V, History of the U.S. Marine Corps Operations in World War II* (Washington, D.C.: Historical Branch, G-3 Division, Headquarters, U.S. Marine Corps, 1968), pp. 162–164.
20. *USS LCI(G) 452* Serial 141, *LCI(G) 452 Action Report*, no date, p. 3.
21. *USS LCI(G) 567* Serial — None, *Action Report for Okinawa Gunto, Phases One and Two, March 26–June 25 1945*, 15 July 1945, p. 4.
22. Commander LCI(L) Group Fourteen — Third Amphibious Force, *War Diary 1–30 April 1945*, Enclosure (B), p. 1.
23. *USS LCI(R) 770*, Serial None, *Action Report — Okinawa Operation 1 April–22 June 1945*, no date, p. 25.
24. *USS LCI(M) 1089*, Serial 4045, *Action Report, Naha, Okinawa Jima, Attack on*, 18 May 1945, pp. 3–4.
25. Commander Task Unit 52.23.2 (Commander LCI Group 55) Serial 040, *Action Report — Nansei Shoto, Okinawa, Operation — 1 May to 31 May 1945*, 6 June 1945, pp. 4–5.
26. *USS LCI(G) 567* Serial — None, *Action Report for Okinawa Gunto, Phases One and Two, March 26–June 25 1945*, 15 July 1945, pp. 8–9.
27. *USS LCI(R) 1028*, Serial — None, *General Action Report, Okinawa, 1 April 1945–27 June 1945*, 28 June 1945, pp. 4–5.
28. *USS LCI(R) 647*, Serial 205, *General Action Report for the Capture of Okinawa Gunto, from 21 May to 22 June 1945*, 29 June 1945, p. 4.
29. *U.S.S. LCI(R) 769*, Serial None, *General Action Report, 28 March–30 June 1945*, no date, p. 3.
30. Commander LCI Flotilla 16, Serial 35, *Action Report — Invasion of the Okinawa Group Liu Chius, 26 March to 21 June 1945*, 15 July 1945, pp. 21–22.
31. *USS LCI(R) 1077*, No Serial, *Report of Capture of Okinawa Gunto — Phase 2 — 18 May 1945 to 21 June 1945*, 29 June 1945, p. 6.
32. Commander LCI Flotilla 16, Serial 35, *Action Report — Invasion of the Okinawa Group Liu Chius, 26 March to 21 June 1945*, 15 July 1945, p. 23.
33. Ibid., p. 35.
34. Prior to the invasion of Okinawa, most LCI(R)s carried the 4.5 inch fin-stabilized barrage rocket. It had a tested range of 1,000–1,100 yards. The newly developed 5 inch spin-stabilized rocket began to replace it. The new spin-stabilized barrage rocket had a range of approximately 5,000 yards. Commander Clarence Coffin's LCI(R) ships were the first fitted with the new rockets and were used at Iwo Jima. Coffin continually lobbied for the conversion of all LCI(R)s to the new spin-stabilized rocket. For more detailed information see Chapter XXIII of John E. Burchard, ed., *Rockets, Guns and Targets* (Boston: Little, Brown, 1948).
35. *USS LCI(G) 1010*, Serial 10, *Action Report, Invasion of Okinawa*, 10 April 1945, p. 7.
36. Commander LCI Flotilla 3 (Commander Task Unit 52.9.2) Serial 069-45, *Action Report, Anti-Small Craft Gunboats, Okinawa, 1 April to 14 June 1945*, 28 August 1945, p. 19.
37. Commander LCI Flotilla 16/ Serial 35, *Action Report — Invasion of the Okinawa Group Liu Chius, 26 March to 21 June 1945*, 15 July 1945, p. 33.

Chapter 10

1. Robin L. Rielly, *Kamikaze Attacks of World War II* (Jefferson, NC: McFarland, 2010), p. 80.
2. Commander Amphibious Forces U.S. Pacific Fleet (Commander Task Force FIFTY-ONE and Joint Expeditionary Force) Serial 01400, *General Action Report, Capture of OKINAWA GUNTO, Phases I and II, 17 February 1945 to 17 May 1945 — Submission of*, 25 July 1945, (V) (C)-16.
3. USS LCI(G) 558, No Serial, *Report of Capture of Okinawa Gunto, Phases 1 and 2*, 21 July 1945, pp. 2–3.
4. USS LCI(R) 646, Serial 60, *Action Report — Invasion of Okinawa, 26 March to 30 April 1945*, 11 May 1945, p. 14.
5. USS LCI(G) 82, Serial — None, *Action Report of USS LCI(G) 82 for 3–4 April 1945*, 14 April 1945, pp. 2–3.
6. USS LCI(G) 82, Serial — None, *Action Report of USS LCI(G) 82 for 3–4 April 1945*, 14 April 1945, p. 3.
7. Commander LCI Flotilla 3 (Commander Task Unit 52.9.2), Serial 069-45, *Action Report, Anti-Small Craft Gunboats, Okinawa, 1 April to 14 June 1945*, 28 August 1945, p. 6.
8. USS LCI(G) 659, Serial — None, *Action Report, Report of Action Night of 15 and 16 April 1945*, 19 April 1945, p. 4.
9. USS LCI(R) 763, Serial No. 24, *Action Report — 27 April 1945*, 27 April 1945, p. 2.
10. Commander LCI Group 47, *War Diary*, 1–30 April 1945, p. 6.
11. B. Raymond Perkins, *Mission Ashore*, Typescript, no date, p. 4.
12. Ibid., pp. 4–10.
13. USS LCS(L)(3) #19, Serial #0-4, *Action Report, 18 May 1945, First Endorsement to*, 21 May 1945, p. 1.
14. U.S.S. LCS(L) (3) 82, Serial None, *Action Report, USS LCS(L)(3) 82, of 12–13 May 1945*, Enclosure (A), p. 3.
15. LCI Flotilla 3, *War Diary*, 1–31 May 1945, p. 6.
16. Commander LCI Flotilla 3 (Commander Task Unit 52.9.2). Serial 069-45, *Action Report, Anti-Small Craft Gunboats, Okinawa, 1 April to 14 June 1945*, 28 August 1945, p. 14.
17. Commander Task Unit 51.17.1 (Commander LCI Group 16) Serial 031, *Action Report, Anti Small Craft Screen, Okinawa, 1 April Thru 8 April 1945*, 29 April 1945, p. 11.
18. Commander LCI(G) Group 7, Serial 081-45, *Action Report of Task Unit 51.2.9 From 25 March 1945 to 15 May 1945*, 3 June 1945, p. 7.
19. Commander LCI Group 16, Serial 046, *Report of Capture of Okinawa Gunto, Phases 1 and 2*, 30 June 1945, p. 12.
20. USS LCI(R) 1078, No Serial, *USS LCI(R) 1078 — Anti-Aircraft Action Report*, 8 April 1945, p. 2.
21. USS LCI(G) 465, Serial — None, *Action Report on Screening Station 117*, 7 April 1945, pp. 1–3.
22. USS LCI(G) 567 Serial — None, *Action Report for Okinawa Gunto, Phases One and Two, March 26–June 25 1945*, 15 July 1945, p. 7.
23. Commander Fifth Amphibious Force, *Translation of a Japanese Letter*, 11 June 1945.
24. USS LCI(G) 567 Serial — None, *Action Report for Okinawa Gunto, Phases One and Two, March 26–June 25 1945*, p. 7.
25. USS LCI(G) 407, No Serial, *Anti-Aircraft Action Report*, 16 April 1945, pp. 2–3.
26. Commander LCI(L) Group Fourteen Third Amphibious Force. *War Diary 1 May 1945 to 1 June 1945*, Enclosure (A), p. 1.
27. Commander RCM and Rocket Division Two, Serial 024, *Report of Capture of Okinawa Gunto, Phases 1 and 2, 1 April to 21 June 1945*, no date, Enclosure (K), pp. 1–2.
28. USS LCI(M) 1058, Serial — None, *Action Report — Special Anti-Aircraft*, 30 April 1945, p. 2.
29. Commander LCI(L) Flotilla Fourteen, *War Diary 1 May 1945 to 1 June 1945*, Enclosure (A), p. 2.

Chapter 11

1. The events surrounding the battles at the radar picket stations at Okinawa are extremely detailed and lengthy. For practical purposes I have only mentioned some of the highlights which concern the gunboats in this chapter. For the complete story of the events at the radar picket stations and the involvement of the LCS(L) gunboats, see my work *Kamikazes, Corsairs, and Picket Ships: Okinawa, 1945* (Philadelphia: Casemate, 2008).
2. Robin L. Rielly, *Kamikazes, Corsairs, and Picket Ships: Okinawa, 1945* (Philadelphia: Casemate, 2008), p. 7.
3. The term "destroyer types" is meant to include the DM and DMS, as well as the DD, as they were converted from destroyers and had similar hulls and armament.
4. Commander Task Force Fifty-One, Commander Amphibious Forces U.S. Pacific Fleet, *Report on Okinawa Gunto Operation from 17 February to 17 May 1945*, Page (II) — p. 17.
5. John D. (Evans) Meader. MoMM 3/c, LCS(L) 33, *USS LCS 33 Recollections of Ship's Sinking April 12, 1945*, pp. 4–5.
6. Frank C. Osterland, Lieutenant Commander, *Dolly Three*, Typescript, 28 August 1993, pp. 10–11.
7. USS Purdy DD 734 Serial 024, *Action Report*, 20 April 1945, p. 10.
8. John R. Henry, "Out Stares Jap Pilot After Ammo Runs Out," *Honolulu Advertiser*, 27 April 1945.
9. H. D. Chickering, Lieutenant, CO, LCS(L) 51, *World War II*, Typescript, undated, p. 32.
10. Powell Pierpont, Lieutenant (jg), XO, LCS(L) 61, *The War History of the LCS(L) 61*, p. 4.
11. DD475 Dispatch, 5 June, 1945.
12. U.S.S. LCS(L) 83, Serial 02-45, *Anti-Aircraft Action Report of 3 May 1945*.
13. Thomas Lee, GM 1/c, LCS(L) 31, interview, 26 September 2011.
14. USS LCS(L) 31, Serial 31/A 12-1, *Action Report (4 May 1945)*, 9 May 1945, pp. 1–3.
15. William J. Ross, SMC 3/c, LCS(L) 82, *Ammo from a Civilian Manned Ship*, Typescript, undated, p. 1.
16. John Rooney, *Mighty Midget U.S.S. LCS 82* (PA: self-published 1990), p. 140.
17. Robert F. Rielly, QM 2/c, LCS(L) 61, interview of 20 May 2001.
18. U.S.S. *William D. Porter (DD 579)*, Serial 00236, *Action Report of 18 June 1945*, pp. 2–3.
19. Richard M. McCool, Captain (Ret), CO USS LCS(L) 122, letter to the author with narrative, 23 May 1997.
20. *Committee on Veteran's Affairs, U.S. Senate, Medal of Honor Recipients: 1863–1973* (Washington, D.C.: Government Printing Office), 1973.
21. U.S.S. LCS(L) (3) 125, Serial 37, *Action Report, Submission of*, 1 August 1945, p. 3.
22. Commander Amphibious Forces U.S. Pacific Fleet (Commander Task Force FIFTY-ONE and Joint Expeditionary Force) Serial 01400, *General Action Report, Capture of OKINAWA GUNTO, Phases I and II, 17 February 1945 to 17 May 1945 — Submission of*, 25 July 1945, (V) (D)-6.
23. Howell D. Chickering, Lieutenant, CO LCS(L) 51, *World War II*, Typescript, circa 1990s, p. 36.

Chapter 12

1. Commander, Administrative Command, Amphibious Forces, U.S. Pacific Fleet, *Directory of Amphibious Type Vessels and Commanding Officers,* (Amphibious Forces U.S. Pacific Fleet), 15 May 1945, pp. V-VIII.

2. Robin L. Rielly, *Mighty Midgets at War: The Saga of the LCS(L) Ships From Iwo Jima to Vietnam* (Central Point, OR: Hellgate Press, 2000), pp. 258–261.

3. C. G. Blood, Report 90-16, *Shipboard and Ground Troop Casualty Rates Among Navy and Marine Corps Personnel During World War II Operations* (San Diego: Naval Health Research Center — Medical Decisions Support Department, 1990), pp. 3, 29.

4. USS *LCI(R) — 230,* Serial 210, *Typoon Damage,* 17 September 1945, pp. 1–3.

5. USS *LCI(R) 337,* Serial None, *Typhoon Damage, 16 September 1945,* 1 October 1945, pp. 1–3.

6. Commander in Chief, Pacific Fleet and Pacific Ocean Areas, *Report on the Surrender and Occupation of Japan,* Annex A.

7. Ibid.

8. Commander Task Unit 78.1.7 (Commander LCS Flotilla 1) Serial 0110, *Taku Tientsin Operation Report, Task Unit 78.1.7, Beleager Operation — 27 September to 3 October 1945,* 3 October 1945.

9. "List of Allied Warships Closing in on Jap Isles," *NY Daily News,* 27 August 1945: 42.

10. Peter Elliot, *Allied Minesweeping in World War 2,*(Annapolis: Naval Institute Press, 1979), p. 177.

11. Charles Thomas, *Dolly Five: A Memoir of the Pacific War* (Chester, VA: Harrowgate Press, 1996), pp. 346–347.

12. Harry G. Meister, Engineering Officer, *LCS(L) 27, USS LCS(L)(3) 27 A WWII Amphibious Landing Craft Support Vessel,* Typescript, 2002, pp. 23–24.

13. D. Reid Ross., *The World War II Saga of LCS 58,* Typescript, 2011, p. 18.

14. Frank N. Farmer, *LCS(L) 34, History of the U.S.S. LCS(L) (3) 34,* Typescript, September 1989, pp. 16–17.

15. Ibid., p. 17.

16. Merl L. Riggs, *LCS(L) 78,* "Diary of My Experiences Aboard The *LCS(L)(3) 78,*" Typescript, circa 1940s, p. 1.

17. Kemp Tolley, Rear Admiral, *Yangtze Patrol: The U.S. Navy in China* (Annapolis: Naval Institute Press, 1971), p. 294.

18. William B. Bell, *LCS(L) 75,* "A Report of a Yangtze Cruise in November, 1945," Typescript, circa 1990s, p. 2.

19. Ibid., pp. 3–5

20. Ross, pp. 20–21.

21. Charles Thomas, *Dolly Five: A Memoir of the Pacific War* (Chester, VA: Harrowgate Press, 1996), p. 313.

22. Harry G. Meister, Engineering Officer, *LCS(L) 27, USS LCS(L)(3) 27 A WWII Amphibious Landing Craft Support Vessel,* Typescript, 2002, p. 24.

23. Charles Thomas, *Dolly Five: A Memoir of the Pacific War* (Chester, VA: Harrowgate Press, 1996), p. 315.

24. Ross, p. 221.

25. Robin L. Rielly, *Mighty Midgets at War: The Saga of the LCS(L) Ships from Iwo Jima to Vietnam* (Central Point, OR: Hellgate Press, 2000), p. 208.

26. Ibid., p. 232.

27. Officer in Charge *LSSL 67* to Commander, Florida Group, Atlantic Reserve Fleet, 16 July 1953.

28. Paul W. Boblette, BMC, *LCS(L) 83,* "Six Months on a Spit Kit," Typescript, 1989, p. 1.

29. Ibid., pp. 3–6.

30. Commander, Naval Sea Systems Command, *Security Assistance Program Ships and Craft Summary,* 1 October 1992.

31. United States Public Law 104-201 Section 1025.

32. The National Association of USS LCS(L) (3) 1–130, "*Feasibility Study for Acquiring and Restoring the Seabird to the Original USS LCS(L) (3) 50,*" 2002.

Bibliography

The majority of primary source materials for this book are located at the National Archives and Records Administration in College Park, Maryland. Additional materials were obtained at the Naval History and Heritage Command based at the Washington Navy Yard in Washington, D.C. Other materials relating to my topic were found in the United States Army Military History Institute at Carlisle, Pennsylvania; the Library of Congress in Washington, D.C.; the Alexander Library at Rutgers University, New Brunswick, New Jersey; and the Firestone Library of Princeton University in Princeton, New Jersey.

Records located in the National Archives come primarily from four record groups: 19, 24, 38, and 80, although other record groups occasionally led to additional material. I have listed the materials in each group for those wishing to pursue the topic further. Specific reports in each category are listed in the notes for each chapter. It should be noted that there is an inconsistency in the way in which many of the official reports are listed, particularly in the notes. Navy action reports, for instance, may show the ship's number written as USS or U.S.S. The ship's number may or may not be in parentheses, and the date of a report sometimes contains a comma between the month and year. In addition, some sections of the title may be in capital letters while in similar reports they are not. Many variations in style appear in official ship documents. Inconsistencies in the note and bibliographic entries contained in the text are found in the originals. I have not made changes for the sake of consistency.

The majority of photographs come from either the National Archives or the Naval History and Heritage Command. These are identified as either NARA or NH in the photo caption, followed by additional file numbers. Other photographs were obtained from various sources, and those loaned for this work show credit to the individual supplying the photograph.

Primary Sources

National Archives and Records Administration, College Park, Maryland

RG 19: Records of the Bureau of Ships. For the LCT, LCI(G), LCI(M), LCI(R), LCS(S) and LCS(L) ships. This group contains various written records of plans, correspondence, and other information relevant to the design, construction, or conversion of the ships.

RG 24: List of Logbooks of U.S. Navy Ships, Stations, and Miscellaneous Units, 1801–1947. Ship Logs for the LCI(G), LCI(L), LCI(M), LCI(R), LCS(L), and various other ships mentioned in the text. Log entries for specific ships and dates are cited in the end notes to each chapter.

RG 38: Records of the Chief of Naval Operations—Records Relating to Naval Activity During World War II. Action Reports and War Diaries for the LCI(G), LCI(L), LCI(M), LCI(R), LCS(L), and various other ships; COMINCH, Task Force, Task Group, Task Unit Action Reports, Fleet Marine Force, Various Dates. Specific reports and dates are cited in the end notes to each chapter.

RG 80: General Records of the Department of the Navy 1798–1947. Amphibious Forces U.S. Pacific Fleet, *Directory of Amphibious Type Vessels and Commanding Officers,* 15 May 1945.

Official Histories and Other Government Publications

Administrative Division, Second Demobilization Bureau. Serial 2057. *Japanese Naval Vessels at the End of War.* April 25, 1947.

Allied Translator and Interpreter Section Southwest Pacific Area. *A.T.I.S. Publication No. 1. Japanese Military Conventional Signs & Abbreviations.* 4 March 1943.

_____. *Wartime Translations of Seized Japanese Documents. Allied Translator and Interpreter Section Reports, 1942–1946.*

Australia in the War of 1939–1945. Five Series, 22 Volumes. Canberra: Australian War Memorial, circa 1960s.

    Dexter, David. Series 1 (Army) Volume VI. *The New Guinea Offensives.* Canberra: Australian War Memorial, 1961.

    Gill, G. Hermon. Series Two (Navy) Volume II. *Royal Australian Navy 1942–1945.* Canberra: Australian War Memorial, 1968.

    Long, Gavin. Series 1 (Army) Volume VII. *Australia in the War of 1939–1945: The Final Campaigns.* Canberra: Australian War Memorial, 1963.

    Odgers, George. Series 3 (Air) Volume II. *Air War Against Japan, 1943–1945.* Canberra: Australian War Memorial, 1968.

The Beachmaster Final Edition 36. U.S.N.A.T.B. Solomons, MD: February 1945.

Blood, C. G. Report No. 90–16. *Shipboard and Ground Troop Casualty Rates Among Navy and Marine Corps Personnel During World War II Operations.* San Diego: Naval Health Research Center, Medical Decisions Support Department, 1990.

Bureau of Ships, Navy Department. NAVSHIPS 250–011. *Ships' Data U.S. Naval Vessels Vol. II Mine Vessels (Less CM & DM) Patrol Vessels, Landing Ships and Craft.* April 15, 1945. Washington, D.C.: Government Printing Office, 1946.

Casey, Major General Hugh J. *Airfield and Base Development: Engineers of the Southwest Pacific, 1941–1945, Volume VI.* Reports of Operations United States Army Forces in the Far East, Southwest Pacific Area, Army Forces, Pacific. Office of the Chief Engineer, General Headquarters, Army Forces Pacific. Washington, D.C.: Government, 1951.

_____. *Amphibian Engineer Operations: Engineers of the Southwest Pacific, 1941–1945, Volume IV.* Reports of Operations United States Army Forces in the Far East, Southwest Pacific Area, Army Forces, Pacific. Office of the Chief Engineer, General Headquarters, Army Forces Pacific. Washington, D.C.: Government. Printing Office, 1959.

_____. *Engineers in Theater Operations: Engineers of the Southwest Pacific, 1941–1945, Volume I.* Reports of Operations United States Army Forces in the Far East, Southwest Pacific Area, Army Forces, Pacific. Office of the Chief Engineer, General Headquarters, Army Forces Pacific. Washington: Government. Printing Office, 1947.

Commander Naval Sea Systems Command. *Security Assistance Program Ships and Craft Summary,* 1 October 1992.

Congressional Record—Proceedings and Debates of the 106th Congress, First Session. Thursday, May 27, 1999. Amendment No. 445.

Craven, Weseley F., and James Lea Cate, eds. *The Army Air Forces in World War II: Vol. V. The Pacific: Matterhorn to Nagasaki June 1944 to August 1945.* Washington, D.C.: Office of Air Force History, 1953.

Department of the Navy. *Navy and Marine Corps Awards Manual.* NAVPERS 15,790 (Rev, 1953), 1953.

Dictionary of American Naval Fighting Ships. Nine Volumes. Office of the Chief of Naval Operations. Washington, D.C.: Naval History Division, 1959–1991.

Dyer, George C. *The Amphibians Came to Conquer: The Story of Admiral Richmond Kelly Turner, Vol. I & II.* Washington D.C.: Department of the Navy, 1969.

Foreign Histories Division, Assistant Chief of Staff G-2/3, Headquarters, U.S. Army, Japan. Japanese Monograph Series: circa 1960s.

    Japanese Monograph #6. Philippines Operation Record Army Phase III Defense Operations (June 1944–August 1945).

    Japanese Monograph #7. Philippines Operations Record Army Phase III Defense Operations (January–August 1945).

    Japanese Monograph #8. Philippines Operations Record Army Phase III Defense Operations (December 1944–August 1945).

    Japanese Monograph #12. Philippines Air Operations Record Army Air Force Phase III Defense Operations (August 1944–February 1945).

    Japanese Monograph #53. 3rd Army Operations in Okinawa Army Defense Operations 1943–1945).

    Japanese Monograph #83. Okinawa Area Naval Operations Naval Air Force Defense Operations (January–June 1945).

    Japanese Monograph #135. Okinawa Operations Record Army Defense Operations (March–June 1945).

General Staff, Supreme Commander for the Allied Powers. *Reports of General MacArthur. Japanese Operations in the Southwest Pacific Area Vol. II — Part II.* Facsimile Reprint, 1994.

_____. *Reports of General MacArthur. MacArthur in Japan: The Occupation: Military Phase Volume I Supplement.* Facsimile Reprint, 1994.

_____. *Reports of General MacArthur. The Campaigns of MacArthur in the Pacific Volume I.* Facsimile Reprint, 1994.

Glossary of U.S. Naval Abbreviations 1940–1946 OPNAV 29-P1000. Fifth Edition. Washington, D.C.: Office of Naval Records and History, 1949.

Handbook on Japanese Military Forces. War Department Technical Manual TM-E30–480 October 1944–September 1945. Washington, D.C.: Government Printing Office, 1944.

History of U.S. Marine Corps Operations in World War II.

    Frank, Benis M., and Henry I. Shaw, Jr. *History of U.S. Marine Corps Operations in World War II Vol. V Victory and Occupation.* Historical Branch, G-3 Division, Headquarters, U.S. Marine Corps. Washington, D.C.: Government Printing Office, 1968.

    Garand, George W., and Truman R. Strobridge. *History of U.S. Marine Corps Operations in World War II Volume IV Western Pacific Operations.* Historical Branch, G-3 Division, Headquarters, U.S. Marine Corps. Washington, D.C.: Government Printing Office, 1971.

Shaw, Henry I., Jr., and Major Douglas T. Kane. USMC. *History of U.S. Marine Corps Operations in World War II Vol. II Isolation of Rabaul*. Historical Branch, G-3 Division, Headquarters, U.S. Marine Corps. Washington, D.C.: Government Printing Office, 1963.

Hough, Major Frank O. *The Assault on Peleliu*. Historical Division Headquarters U.S. Marine Corps, 1950.

King, Ernest J. *U.S. Navy at War 1941–1945*. Washington, D.C.: United States Navy Department, 1946.

Military History Section, Special Staff, General Headquarters, Far East Command. *The Imperial Japanese Navy in World War II: A Graphic Presentation of the Japanese Naval Organization and List of Combatant and Non-Combatant Vessels Lost or Damaged in the War*. Tokyo: 1952.

Military Intelligence Service, War Department. *Japanese Defense Against Amphibious Operations*. Special Series No. 29. Washington, D.C.: February 1945.

_____. *Tactical and Technical Trends, 1942–45*. Various dates and issues.

Office of Naval Records and History, Office of the Chief of Naval Operations Navy Department. OPNAV 29-P1000. *Glossary of U.S. Naval Abbreviations 1940–1946*. Washington, D.C.: 1949.

ONI 208-J Supplement No. 2. *Far-Eastern Small Craft*. Division of Naval Intelligence. March 1945.

ONI 225 J. *Japanese Landing Operations and Equipment*. Division of Naval Intelligence. 21 May 1943.

Recognition Journal. War Department. Volumes 1 through 24 — Various dates and issues, September 1943 through August 1945.

Soldiers Guide to the Japanese Army. Special Series No. 27. Washington, D.C.: War Department, Military Intelligence Service. 15 November 1944.

Supervisor of Shipbuilding, USN, Portland, Oregon. *World War II History of the Supervisor of Shipbuilding, Portland, Oregon*. Portland, OR: Undated (circa 1946).

The U.S. Army Campaigns of World War II. Washington, D.C.: U.S. Army Center of Military History. circa 1995.

    Anderson, Charles R. *Leyte*. The U.S. Army Campaigns of World War II Series. Washington, D.C.: Center of Military History United States Army, Undated.

    Fisch, Arnold G., Jr. *Ryukyus*. The U.S. Army Campaigns of World War II Series. Washington, D.C.: Center of Military History United States Army, Undated.

    Hirrell, Leo. *Bismarck Archipelago*. The U.S. Army Campaigns of World War II Series. Washington, D.C.: Center of Military History United States Army, Undated.

    Lofgren, Stephen J. *Southern Philippines*. The U.S. Army Campaigns of World War II Series. Washington, D.C.: Center of Military History United States Army, Undated.

    Newell, Clayton R. Lt. Col. *Central Pacific*. The U.S. Army Campaigns of World War II Series. Washington, D.C.: Center of Military History United States Army, Undated.

The United States Strategic Bombing Survey Naval Analysis Division. Washington, D.C.: Government Printing Office.

    Air Campaigns of the Pacific War. 1947.

    The Campaigns of the Pacific War. 1946.

    The Fifth Air Force in the War Against Japan. 1947.

    Interrogations of Japanese Officials Volume I. 1945.

    Interrogations of Japanese Officials Volume II. 1945.

    Japanese Air Power. 1946.

    The Seventh and Eleventh Air Forces in the War Against Japan. 1947.

    Summary Report (Pacific War). 1946.

United States Army in World War II.

    Appleman, Roy E., James M. Burns, Russell A. Gugeler, and John Stevens. *Okinawa: The Last Battle*. Washington, D.C.: Center of Military History, United States Army, 1984.

    Brophy, Leo P., Wyndham D. Miles and Rexmond C. Cochrane. *The Chemical Warfare Service: from Laboratory to Field*. Washington, D.C.: Center of Military History, United States Army, 1988.

    Cannon, M. Hanlon. *Leyte: The Return to the Philippines*. Washington, D.C.: Center of Military History, United States Army, 1996.

    Crowl, Philip A. *The War in the Pacific: Campaign in the Marianas*. Washington, D.C.: Center of Military History, United States Army, 1960.

    Crowl, Philip A., and Edmund G. Love. *The War in the Pacific: Seizure of the Gilberts and Marshalls*. Washington, D.C.: Center of Military History, United States Army, 1993.

    Dod, Carl C. *Technical Services, the Corps of Engineers, The War Against Japan*. Washington, D.C.: Office of the Chief of Military History, United States Army, 1966.

    Kleber, Brooks E., and Dale Birdsell. *The Chemical Warfare Service: Chemicals in Combat*. Washington, D.C.: Office of the Chief of Military History, United States Army, 1966.

    Miller, John, Jr. *The War in the Pacific — Cartwheel: The Reduction of Rabaul*. Washington, D.C.: Office of the Chief of Military History, Department of the Army, 1959.

    _____. *The War in the Pacific — Guadalcanal: The First Offensive*. Washington, D.C.: Center of Military History, The United States Army, 1995.

    Morton, Louis. *The Fall of the Philippines*. Washington, D.C.: Center of Military History, United States Army, 1985.

    _____. *Strategy and Command: The First Two Years*. Washington, D.C.: Center of Military History, United States Army, 1989.

    Smith, Robert Ross. *The Approach to the Philippines*. Washington, D.C.: Office of the Chief of Military History, United States Army, 1953.

    _____. *Triumph in the Philippines*. Washington, D.C.: Center of Military History, United States Army, 1991.

U.S. Navy. *Medal of Honor 1861–1949 — The Navy*. Washington, D.C.: Government Printing Office, 1949.

War Department Technical Manual TM 9-394. *4.5-Inch Rocket Material for Ground Use*. War Department. 7 February 1945.

Interviews, Diaries, Correspondence, Memoirs

Alberti, Frank. Engineering Officer, *LCS(L) 106*. "Plank Owners Survive 3 Shots in the Head." Circa 1946.

Amick, Robert. *LCS(L) 48. LCS(L) 48: A Souvenir Photo Booklet.* Typescript, circa 1990s.

Anderson, Philip M. "Disposition of *LCS(L) 26* Crew." July 2012.

Arnold, Dick. *LCI(G) 730.* "Dick Arnold's Peleliu Memories." http://www.home.sprvnet.com/~kier/arnold.htm, pp. 1–2.

Augustad, Robert. S 2/c, *LCS(L) 50.* Interview. 22 October 2011.

Ball, Donald L. *LCS(L) 85.* Interview. 18 September 2002.

Barnby, Frank. *LCS(L) 13.* Collected papers and photographs.

Baumler, Raymond. *LCS 14.* Letter of 4 March 2003.

Bell, Dean . *LCS(L) 26.* Interview. 11 August 2007.

Bell, William B. *LCS(L) 75.* "A Report of a Yangtze Cruise in November, 1945." Typescript, circa 1990s.

Boblette, Paul W. BMC, *LCS(L) 83.* "Six Months on a Spit Kit." Typescript, 1989.

Bors, Fred F. BM 2/c, *LCS(L) 28.* Correspondence. 1995.

Blanton, Earl. *LCS(L) 118.* Interview. 19 September 2002.

Blyth, Robert. *LCS(L) 61.* Interview. 25 August 1995.

Burgess, Harold H. *LCS(L) 61.* Interview. 25 August 1995.

Burroughs, Spencer. Engineering Officer, *LCS(L) 52.* Memoirs, Correspondence, Memorabilia edited by Geoffrey Burroughs and Norma Vines.

Cardwell, John H. *LCS(L) 61.* Collected papers.

Chickering, Howell D. Lieutenant, Commanding Officer, *LCS(L) 51.* "World War II." Circa 1990s.

Christman, William R. *LCS(L) 95.* Letter of 9 April 2003.

Curley, K. E. Lieutenant Commander, *LC(FF) 368. Shanghai to Hankow.* Typscript, undated.

Davis, Franklin M., Sr. *LCS(L) 61.* Interview. 25 August 1995.

Davis, James. QM 2/c, *LCS(L) 112.* "The USS LCS(L)(3) #112: a history." Typescript, 1997.

Desmond, Ed. Cook 3/c, *LCS(L) 128.* Interview. 19 October 2011.

Domenigo, Joseph A. *LCI(G) 568.* Interview. 17 January 2011.

Eldridge, Albert C. Lieutenant, Commanding Officer, *LCS(L) 10.* Letter to L. Richard Rhame of 6 April 1990.

Farmer, Frank N. *LCS(L) 34. History of the U.S.S. LCS(L)(3) 34.* Typescript, 1989.

Hampton, Vaughn E. *LCI(G) 450.* Memoirs. http://www.geocities.com/Heartland/Plains/5850/hampton.html

Hannah, Russ. Signalman 3/c, *LCS(L) 129.* "The Okinawa Diary of Russ Hannah, Signalman USN." Circa 1990s.

Harkins, Jack MM 2/c, *LCS(L) 88.* Interview. 19 October 2011.

Heinecke, G. Edward. Lieutenant (jg), Executive Officer, *LCS(L) 3.* Interview. 22 July 2012.

Howell, Linda. Letter to Ray Baumler, 27 March 1992.

Hunt, Arden Lee. *The Journal of Arden Lee Hunt, LCI 226.* USS Landing Craft Infantry National Association, pp. 14–15. http:// www.usslci.com/html/lci226.htm.

International News Service Press Release 153.

Katz, Lawrence S. *LCS(L) 61.* Diary, Interview. 25 August 1995.

Kaup, Harold. *LCS(L) 15.* Interview. 29 September 1996.

Kelley, James W. Lieutenant, Commanding Officer, *LCS(L) 61.* Interview. 18 December 1995.

Lake, Roy Eugene. S 1/c, *LCS(L) 56 & LC(FF) 988. World War II Memoirs January 1944 — May 20, 1946.*

Lambert, Roy, Jr. Ship's Historian, *LCS(L) 33. History of LCS(L) 33.* Typescript, 1990.

Laylin, Edward J. Lieutenant (jg), Commanding Officer, *LCI(L) 1064 .* Letter. 11 November 1944.

Lee, Thomas. GM 1/c, *LCS(L) 31.* Interview. 25 September 2011.

Mallin, James. QM 3/c, *LCS(L) 117.* Interview. 21 October 2011.

Martin, Arthur R. *LCS(L) 88.* "A History of USS LCS(L) 88 with Emphasis on May 11, 1945." Circa 1990.

Mason, William. Yeoman 2/c, *LCS(L) 85.* Interviews. 28 August 2010 and 20 October 2011.

Maurone, Dominick C. *LCI(G) 440.* Memoirs. USS Landing Craft Infantry National Association. USS LCI Stories. http://www.usslci.com/maurone/maurone1.htm.

McCool, Captain Richard M., USN (Ret). CO, *USS LCS(L) 122.* Interview. 21 May 1997. Letter to the author with narrative. 23 May 1997.

Meader, John D. (Evans). MoMM 3/c, *LCS(L) 33. USS LCS 33 Recollections of Ships Sinking April 12, 1945,* pp. 4–5.

Meister, Harry G. Lieutenant (jg). Engineering Officer, *LCS(L) 27.* Typescript, circa 1990s.

Miller, James. *LCI(G) 568. My Service in World War II.* Personal diary, circa 1945.

Miller, Jim (Revo). SK 2/c, *LCI(G) 568. A Cruise That We Will Never Forget.* Typescript, 1998.

Morrisson, Paul E. Jr. GM 3/c, *LCS(L) 91.* Memoirs.

Moulton, Franklin. *LCS(L) 25.* Collected papers and photographs.

Nadeau, Gil. *LCS(L) 45.* Interviews. 28 August 2010 and 22 October 2011.

Osterland, Frank C. Lieutenant (jg), *LCS(L) 35. Dolly Three.* Typescript, 1992.

Pederson, Marvin. Letter to the editor of LCS Association newsletter. Undated.

Peterson, Phillip E. *LCS(L) 23.* Collected papers and photographs.

Plant, Louis V. *LCI(G) 24. Memories of World War II.* Typescript, 2000.

Prunty, Jonathan G. GM 1/c, *LCS(L) 65. My Days in the U.S. Navy 1944 to 1946.* Typescript, 1998.

Rhoads, Joseph E. Lieutenant (jg). *LCS(L) 50. The Birth and Life of Our Ship the USS LCS(L)(3) 50.* Typescript, circa 1945, p. 4.

Rielly, Robert F. QM 2/c, *LCS(L) 61.* Interview, 20 September 2001.

Rielly, Robert F. QM 3/c, and Lawrence S. Katz, RM 3/c., *LCS(L) 61.* "Life Aboard a Landing Craft." Typescript, 1945.

Riggs, Merl. L. *LCS(L) 78. Diary of My Experiences aboard the LCS(L) (3) 78.* Typescript, circa 1940s.

Robinson, Ed. Letter to Lester O. Willard. 10 January 1991.

Rooney, John. *Sailor.* Interview with Julian Becton, CO of *Laffey.*

Ross, D. Reid. *The World War II Saga of LCS 58.* By the author, 2012.

Ross, Raymond J. EM 3/c, *LCS(L) 60.* Memoirs, 1991.

Ross, William J. SM 3/c, *LCS(L) 82.* Memoirs.

Ryan, Thomas. *LCS(L) 81.* Video Interview. Broadcast 20 May 2011 on Channel 24, Monterey, California.

Schuldenrein, Morris. Fire Controlman, *LCS(L) 36.* Memoirs, circa 1990s.

Schulman, Woody, ET 2/c, and Bill Keiser, GM 2/c, LCS(L) 75. "The First American Battle with the Chinese Commmunists Just After the End of World War II." Typescript, circa 1990.

Scott, Eugene W. Radioman, LCS(L)14. *Experiences of a Sailor in World War Two and the Korean War.* Typescript, circa 1990.

Selfridge, Allen. LCS(L) 67. Collected papers and photographs.

Sellis, Mark. Lieutenant (jg). Executive Officer, LCS(L) 61. Interview. 25 August 1995.

Sprague, Robert. LCS(L) 38. Letter. 29 September 2002.

Squire, William. LCS(L)20. Diary.

Staigar, Joseph. LCS(L) 61. Interview. 14 July 1995.

Tolmas, Harold. LCS(L) 54. Letter. 5 December 2002.

Topping, William S. Gunnery Officer, LCS(L) 63. *I Remember.* Typescript, circa 1990.

Wackenhut, Norman H. Communications, Supply Officer, LCS(L) 91. "The Unsung Heroes." Typescript, circa 1990.

West, Oscar Jr. Gunners Mate, *U.S.S. Barber APD 57.* Letter to Thomas English, 18 August 1992.

Wiram, Gordon H. LCS(L) 64. Letter to Ray Baumler, 13 April 1991.

Wisner, Robert. LCS(L) 37. Interview. 15 August 2001.

Secondary Sources

Books, Journals, Newsletters

Alexander, Joseph H. *Storm Landings Epic Amphibious Battles in the Central Pacific.* Annapolis: Naval Institute Press, 1997.

Alexander, Larry. *Shadows in the Jungle: The Alamo Scouts Behind Japanese Lines in World War II.* New York: NAL Caliber, 2010.

Astor, Gerald. *Operation Iceberg: The Invasion and Conquest of Okinawa in World War II.* New York: Donald I. Fine, 1995.

Auer, James E. *The Postwar Rearmament of Japanese Maritime Forces, 1945–1971.* New York: Praeger, 1973.

Baker, A.D., III. *Allied Landing Craft of World War Two.* Annapolis: Naval Institute Press, 1985.

Ball, Donald L. *Fighting Amphibs: The LCS(L) in World War II.* Williamsburg, VA: Mill Neck Publications, 1997.

Barbey, Daniel E., Vice Admiral, USN. *MacArthur's Amphibious Navy: Seventh Amphibious Force Operations 1943–1945.* Annapolis: Naval Institute Press, 1969.

Becton, F. Julian. *The Ship That Would Not Die.* Missoula, MT: Pictorial Histories Publishing, 1980.

Bertoch, Marvin J. *The Little Ships.* Salt Lake City, UT: self-published, 1989.

Blassingame, Wyatt. *The U.S. Frogmen of World War II.* New York: Random House, 1964.

Blore, Trevor, Lieutenant Commander. *Commissioned Barges: The Story of the Landing Craft.* London: Hutchinson & Co. Ltd. Circa 1940s.

Brooks, Victor. *Hell is Upon Us. D-Day in the Pacific June–August 1944.* Cambridge, MA: DaCapo Press, 2005.

Brossard, Maurice Raymond de. *Dinassaut.* Paris: Editions France-Empire, 1952.

Bull, Peter. *To Sea in a Sieve.* London: Peter Davies, 1956.

Burchard, John E., ed. *Rockets, Guns & Targets: Rockets, Target Information, Erosion Information, & Hypervelocity Guns Developed During World War II by the Office of Scientific Research & Development.* Boston: Little, Brown, 1948.

Cable, James. *Gunboat Diplomacy, 1919–1991: Political Applications of Limited Naval Force.* New York: St. Martin's, 1994.

Cleary, Thomas. *The Japanese Art of War: Understanding the Culture of Strategy.* Boston: Shambhala, 2005.

Condon, Don. *Combat the War With Japan.* New York: Dell, 1962.

Controvich, James T. *The Central Pacific Campaign, 1943–1944: A Bibliography.* Westport, CT: Greenwood, 1990.

Cook, Haruko Taya, and Theodore F. Cook. *Japan at War: An Oral History.* New York: The New Press, 1992.

Costello, John. *The Pacific War 1941–1945.* New York: Atlantic Communications, 1981.

Craig, William. *The Fall of Japan.* New York: The Dial Press, 1967.

Croizat, Victor H. *Vietnam River Warfare 1945–1975.* New York: Blandford Press, 1986.

Cunningham, Chet. *The Frogmen of World War II.* New York: Pocket Star Books, 2005.

Denfeld, D. Colt. *Hold the Marianas: The Japanese Defense of the Mariana Islands.* Shippensburg, PA: White Mane Publishing, 1997.

Dissette, Edward, and Hans Christian Adamson. *Guerrilla Submarines.* New York: Bantam, 1980.

Dolloz, Jacques. *The War in Indo-China 1945–54.* Trans. Josephine Bacon. Savage, MD: Barnes and Noble, 1990.

Drea, Edward J. *In the Service of the Emperor: Essays on the Imperial Japanese Army.* Lincoln: University of Nebraska Press, 2003.

———. *MacArthur's ULTRA: Codebreaking and the War Against Japan, 1942–1945.* Lawrence: University Press of Kansas, 1992.

Edgerton, Robert B. *Warriors of the Rising Sun: A History of the Japanese Military.* New York: W.W. Norton, 1997.

Edwards, Norman L. *The Times in My Life: 5 Years Old–60 Years Old.* Victoria, BC: Trafford, 2006.

Eldridge, Albert C., Lt. *The Mighty 10* (History of LCS(L) 10). Typescript, undated.

Eliot, Peter. *Allied Minesweeping in World War 2.* Annapolis: Naval Institute Press, 1979.

Evans, David C., ed. *The Japanese Navy in World War II.* Annapolis: Naval Institute Press, 1986.

Fahey, James C. *The Ships and Aircraft of the United States Fleet Victory Edition.* Annapolis: Naval Institute Press, 1977.

Ford, Ken. *Dieppe 1942.* Westport, CT: Praeger, 2004.

Forty, George. *Japanese Army Handbook 1939–1945.* Phoenix Mill, Great Britain: Sutton Publishing, 2002.

Foster, Simon. *Okinawa 1945 Final Assault on the Empire.* London: Arms and Armour Press, 1994.

Frank, Benis M. *Okinawa: The Great Island Battle.* New York: Talisman/Parrish Books, 1978.

Frank, Richard B. *Downfall: The End of the Imperial Japanese Empire.* New York: Penguin, 2001.

Friedman, Norman. *U.S. Amphibious Ships and Craft.* Annapolis: Naval Institute Press, 2002.

Fuller, Richard. *Shokan: Hirohito's Samurai.* London: Arms & Armour Press, 1992.

Gailey, Harry A. *Bougainville 1943–1945: The Forgotten*

Campaign. Lexington: The University Press of Kentucky, 1991.

Gibney, Frank B., ed. *The Japanese Remember the Pacific War*. Armonk, NY: An Eastgate Book, 1995.

Goldstein, Donald M., and Katherine V. Dillon. *The Pacific War Papers*. Washington, D.C.: Potomac Books, 2004.

Gregory, Barry. *Vietnam Coastal and Riverine Forces Handbook*. Wellingborough, Northamptonshire, England: Patrick Stephens, 1988.

Guillot, L. E., Lieutenant (jg). *How Did We Ever Win the War?* Dallas, TX: self-published, circa 1990.

Hanson, Mike. *Yangtze Patrol: American Naval Forces in China—A Selected, Partially-Annotated Bibliography*. Dudley Knox Library, Naval Postgraduate School, 1998.

Hayashi, Saburo, in collaboration with Alvin D. Coox. *Kogun: The Japanese Army in the Pacific War*. Quantico, VA: The Marine Corps Association, 1959.

Hayes, Grace Person, Lieutenant. *The History of the Joint Chiefs of Staff in World War II: The War Against Japan*. Annapolis: Naval Institute Press, 1982.

Heath, Robert F., with LeRoy A. Olson. *With the Black Cat USS LCI Flotilla 13*. Chico, CA: The Technical Education Press, 2003.

Hellman, Lieutenant Steward W. "Leyte Landing." In S. E. Smith, ed., *The United States Navy in World War II*. New York: William Morrow, 1966: pp. 835–838.

Ienaga, Saburo. *The Pacific War, 1931–1945: A Critical Perspective on Japan's Role in World War II*. New York: Pantheon, 1978.

Iritani, Toshio. *Group Psychology of the Japanese in Wartime*. New York: Kegan Paul International, 1991.

Ito, Masanori, with Roger Pineau. *The End of the Imperial Japanese Navy*. New York: W. W. Norton, 1962.

Jirka, Frank, Lieutenant (jg). Speech to Ceska Beseda, Association of Croatian Czechs. Circa mid to late 1940s.

Kaijo Jietai 25 Nenshi/Henshu Kaijo Jietai 25 — Nenshi Hensan Iinkai. [Maritime Self-Defense Forces: 25 Year History] Tokyo: Boeicho Kaijo Bakuryao Kanbu, 1981.

Kakehashi, Kumiko. *So Sad to Fall in Battle: An Account of War Based on General Tadamichi Kuribayashi's Letters from Iwo Jima*. New York: Ballantine, 2007.

Karig, Captain Walter, Lieutnenant Commander Russell L. Harris, and Lieutenant Commander Frank A. Manson. *Battle Report: The End of an Empire*. New York: Rinehart and Company, 1948.

_____. *Battle Report: Victory in the Pacific*. New York: Rinehart and Company, 1949.

Krayer, Kenneth R. *On a Ship with No Name: The U.S.S. LCSL(L)(3) 28 in World War Two*. Erie, PA: self-published, circa 1990s.

LCS(L) Landing Craft Support (Large). Paducah, KY: Turner Publishing, 1995.

Leary, William M., ed. *We Shall Return: MacArthur's Commanders and the Defeat of Japan*. Lexington: University Press of Kentucky, 1988.

Leckie, Robert. *Helmet for My Pillow: From Parris Island to the Pacific*. New York: Bantam Books, 2010.

_____. *Strong Men Armed: The United States Marines vs. Japan*. New York: DaCapo Press, 1962.

Lewin, Ronald. *The American Magic: Codes, Ciphers and the Defeat of Japan*. New York: Farrar Straus Giroux, 1982.

Lorelli, John. *To Foreign Shores: U.S. Amphibious Operations in World War II*. Annapolis: Naval Institute Press, 1995.

Lory, Hillis. *Japan's Military Masters: The Army in Japanese Life*. New York: Viking, 1943.

Lund, Paul, and Harry Ludlam. *War of the Landing Craft*. London: W. Foulsham & Co., 1976.

Marshall, S. L. A. *Island Victory: The Battle of Kwajalein Atoll*. Lincoln: University of Nebraska Press, 2001.

Mason, William. *U.S.S. LCS(L)(3) 86: "The Mighty Midget."* San Francisco: self-published, 1993.

McKee, William L. *The Amphibians Are Coming!* Santa Barbara, CA: BMC Publications, 2000.

Meyers, Bruce F. *Swift, Silent, and Deadly: Marine Amphibious Reconnaissance in the Pacific, 1942–1945*. Annapolis: Naval Institute Press, 2004.

Michel, Jacques, Capitaine. *La Marine Francaise En Indochine de 1939 a 1955*. [The French Navy in Indochina 1939 to 1955] Vol. I, Jan. 1950 to April 1953. Paris: Marine Nationale, Etat-major de la Marine, Service Historique, 1972–1977.

_____. *La Marine Francaise En Indochine de 1939 a 1955*. [The French Navy in Indochina 1939 to 1955] Vol. V, April 1953 to May 1956. Paris: Marine Nationale, Etat-major de la Marine, Service Historique, 1972–1977.

Mordai, Jacaues. *Marine Indochine* [*Indochina Navy*]. Trans. Normal L. Williams and A.W. Atkinson. Paris: Le Livre Contemporain—Aimont-Dumont, 1953.

Morison, Samuel Eliot. *History of United States Naval Operations in World War II. Volume III, The Rising Sun in the Pacific 1931–April 1942*. Edison, NJ: Castle Books, 2001.

_____. *History of United States Naval Operations in World War II. Volume V, The Struggle for Guadalcanal August 1942–February 1943*. Edison, NJ: Castle Books, 2001.

_____. *History of United States Naval Operations in World War II. Volume VII, Aleutians, Gilberts and Marshalls June 1942–April 1944*. Edison, NJ: Castle Books, 2001.

_____. *History of United States Naval Operations in World War II. Volume VIII, New Guinea and the Marianas March 1944–August 1944*. Edison, NJ: Castle Books, 2001.

_____. *History of United States Naval Operations in World War II. Volume XII, Leyte June 1944–January 1945*. Edison, NJ: Castle Books, 2001.

_____. *History of United States Naval Operations in World War II. Volume XIII, The Liberation of the Philippines Luzon, Mindanao, the Visayas 1944–1945*. Edison, NJ: Castle Books, 2001.

_____. *History of United States Naval Operations in World War II. Volume XIV, Victory in the Pacific 1945*. Edison, NJ: Castle Books, 2001.

Morrill, John H. *The Cincinnati*. Wytheville, VA: self-published, 1994.

Moskin, J. Robert. *The U.S. Marine Corps Story*. New York: McGraw-Hill, 1982.

National Association of U.S.S. LCS(L) 1–130 *Newsletter*. Various dates and issues. 1998–2010.

Neillands, Robin. *The Dieppe Raid: The Story of the Disastrous 1942 Expedition*. London: Arum Press Limited, 2005.

Newcomb, Richard F. *Iwo Jima*. New York: Holt, Rinehart and Winston, 1965.

Peattie, Mark R. *Ishiwara Kanji and Japan's Confrontation with the West*. Princeton: Princeton University Press, 1975.

_____. *Nan'yo: The Rise and Fall of the Japanese in Micronesia, 1885–1945*. Honolulu: University of Hawaii Press, 1988.

Prados, John. *Combined Fleet Decoded: The Secret History of American Intelligence and the Japanese Navy in World War II*. Annapolis: Naval Institute Press, 1995.

Rawling, Gerald. *Cinderella Operation: The Battle for Walcheren 1944*. London: Cassell, 1980.

Rielly, Robin L. *Kamikaze Attacks of World War II: A Complete History of Japanese Suicide Strikes on American Ships by Aircraft and Other Means*. Jefferson, NC: McFarland, 2010.

_____. *Kamikazes, Corsairs, and Picket Ships: Okinawa 1945*. Philadelphia: Casemate, 2008.

_____. *Mighty Midgets at War: The Saga of the LCS(L) Ships from Iwo Jima to Vietnam*. Central Point, OR: Hellgate Press, 2000.

Rooney, John. *Mighty Midget U.S.S. LCS 82*. PA: self-published, 2000.

Rottman, Gordon L. *U.S. Marine Corps World War II Order of Battle*. Westport, CT: Greenwood, 2002.

_____. *World War II Pacific Island Guide: A Geo-military Study*. Westport, CT: Greenwood, 2002.

Russell, Scott. *Operation Forager: The Battle for Saipan*. Saipan: Division of Historic Preservation, 1994.

Schrijvers, Peter. *Bloody Pacific: American Soldiers at War With Japan*. London: Palgrave Macmillan, 2010.

Smith, Kearney. *Aboard LCS 11 in World War II: A Memoir by Lawrence B. Smith*. Philadelphia: XLibris, 2011.

Smith, S. E., ed. *The United States Navy in World War II*. New York: William Morrow, 1966.

Stone, Robert P. *USS LCS(L)(3) 20 A Mighty Midget*. Self-published, 2002.

Taylor, Robert A. *World War II in Fort Pierce*. Charleston, SC: Arcadia, 1999.

Thomas, Charles. *Dolly Five: A Memoir of the Pacific War*. Chester, VA: Harrowgate Press, 1996.

Tolley, Kemp. *Yangtze Patrol: The U.S. Navy in China*. Annapolis: Naval Institute Press, 1984.

A Translation from the French: Lessons of the War in Indochina Volume 2. Trans. V.H. Croizat. Santa Monica, CA: The Rand Corporation, 1967.

Ugaki, Matome, Vice Admiral. *Fading Victory: The Diary of Admiral Matome Ugaki 1941–1945*. Trans. Masataka Chihaya. Pittsburgh: University of Pittsburgh Press, 1991.

U.S.S. Landing Craft, Infantry, National Association, Inc. *The Elsie Item Newsletter*. Various dates and issues.

USS LCI "Landing Craft Infantry" Volume I. Paducah, KY: Turner Publishing Company, 1993.

USS LCI "Landing Craft Infantry" Volume II. Paducah, KY: Turner Publishing Company, 1995.

Wollard, James K. *History of USS LCI(G) 345: An Amphibious Ship Serving in the Pacific Theater in World War II*. San Marcos, CA: self-published, 1995.

Articles

Blocker, Dennis. "The Fiery Ordeal of *LCI(G) 449* at Iwo Jima." *The Elsie Item*. USS Landing Craft Infantry, National Association, Inc. Blythewood, SC, Issue #60 (July 2007): 19–23.

"Chronique Des Forces Maritimes D'Extreme-Orient" [Chronicles of the Naval Forces in the Far East]. *La Revue Maritime*. Editions of November 1953: 1407–1411; June 1954: 803–806; July 1954: 1071–1078; January 1955: 105–109.

"Chronique Des Forces Maritimes D'Extreme-Orient" [Chronicles of the Naval Forces in the Far East]. *La Revue Maritime*. Editions of March, April, May, July, August, September, and October 1953; March, April, May, August, and Christmas 1954; January 1955.

"Chronique de la Marine Militaire Française" [Chronicles of the French Military Navy]. *La Revue Maritime*. (October 1952): 1315–1324.

Connery, Robert H., and Paul T. David. "The Mutual Defense Assistance Program." *The American Political Science Review*. Vol. XLV, No. 2 (June 1951): 321–347.

Gin, Ooi Keat. "Prelude to Invasion: Covert Operations Before the Re-Occupation of Northwest Borneo, 1944–45." *Journal of Australian War Memorial*, Oct. 2002.

Foley, Kevin. "The Work We Did Was Unbelievable." *The Stars and Stripes*. Washington: D.C.: 3–9 October 1994: 20.

Footner, Hulbert. "Simple Life of Solomons Becomes a Thing of the Past as Result of War." *The* [Baltimore] *Sun*, 17 January 1943: 20+.

Friedman, Norman. "Amphibious Fire Support." *Warship Vol. IV*. London: Conway Maritime Press, 1980: 199–205.

Henry, John R. "Out Stares Jap Pilot After Ammo Runs Out." *Honolulu Advertiser*. April 27, 1945.

Hough, Major Frank. "End on Saipan." *Combat Pacific Theater World War II*. Don Condon, ed. New York: Dell, 1958: 253–276.

Julien-Binard, Louis. "Souvenirs de Nam-Dinh mars 1954" [Memories of Nam-Dinh March 1954]. *La Revue Maritime*, Special Edition Noel, 1956: 1583–1607.

Kawai, Lieutenant Colonel Masahiro. *The Operations of the Suicide-Boat Regiment in Okinawa: Their Battle Result and the Countermeasures Taken by the U.S. Forces*. National Institute for Defense Studies. Undated.

Lofgren, Stephen. J. ed. "Diary of First Lieutenant Sugihara Kinru: Iwo Jima, January-February 1945." *The Journal of Military History* Vol. 59, No. 1 (January 1995). Lexington, VA: George C. Marshall Library, Virginia Military Institute, 1995: 97–133.

McClintock, Robert. "The River War in Indochina." *United States Naval Institute Proceedings*, December 1954: 1303–1311.

"Mighty Midget Goes Home: Royal Thai Navy Bids Fond Farewell to the HTMS *Nakha (LCS 102)*." *Pattaya Mail*— Vol. XV No. 22. June 1–7, 2007: 1–6.

Morris, Frank D. "Bazooka Boats." *Collier's*. 11 November 1944: 21, 83.

Ortoli, P. "La Marine Française en Indochine" [The French Navy in Indochina]. *La Revue Maritime* (October 1952): 1497–1505.

Payne, Alan. "British Landing Craft of WWII." *Naval Historical Review 1971*. Garden Island, N.S.W., Australia: 33, 35, 37, 39.

Ports, Charles R. "My Life as an LCI Gunboat Sailor." *The Elsie Item*, No. 56 (June 2006). Blythewood, SC: 19–22.

Schloesing, P. "Un Example de Collaboration Interarmes Yen-Cu-Ha" [An Example of Interservice Cooperation Yen-Cu-Ha]. *La Revue Maritime* (October 1951): 1326–1332.

Schonenberg, John J., Jr., Captain FA. "The Rocket Field Artillery Battalion." *The Field Artillery Journal.* September 1945: 515–522.

Seino, Hideo, Commander, Imperial Japanese Navy. "Japan and Her Maritime Defense." Annapolis: *U.S. Naval Institute Proceedings Naval Review 1971*: 98–121.

Unmacht, Colonel G. F. "Chemical Mortar Boats in the Pacific Ocean Area." *Military Review* Vol. XXVI No. 8 (November 1946): 15–19.

U.S. Office of Naval Intelligence. "The Dinassaut Units of Indochina." *The ONI Review, Secret Supplement,* Autumn 1952: 26–34.

"Veteran of Okinawa Invasion Puts in at T. I. for Repairs." *The Masthead.* 22 September 1945. Treasure Island, San Francisco, CA: 1, 12.

Wells, W. C. "The Riverine Force in Action, 1966–1967." *Riverine Warfare: Vietnam. A Collection of Writings.* Naval History Division, Office of Chief of Naval Operations. Washington, D.C.: Government Printing Office, 1972.

Woodburn, Alberta. "Is This 'Solomons' Anymore?" *Calvert Independent.* Barstow, MD: 10 June 1943.

Wright, Burton III. "Mortar Support from the Sea." *CML Army Chemical Review,* July 2000.

"Yanks Use Rockets Against Japs." *The Deseret News.* 16 January 1944. Salt Lake City, UT: 2.

Internet Sources

Australia's War 1939–1945. http://www.ww2australia.gov.au/lastbattles/landings.html.

Brown, J. F. Lieutenant (jg). CO *LCI(M) 974.* Department of the Navy—Navy Historical Center Oral History—http://history.navy.mil/faqs/faq87-3q.htm.

Commander Chick Parsons and the Japanese. http://www.us-japandialogueonpows.org/Parsons.htm.

D-Day—524 LCA Flotilla. Combined Operations http://www.combinedops.com.

Dick Arnold's *Peleliu Memories.* http://home.sprvnet.com/~kier/arnold.htm.

Hampton, Vaughn E. *Amphibious Ships with No Names.* http://www.geocities.com/Heartland/Plains/5850/hampton.html.

Mortar Gunboats. http://www.4point2.org/gunboats.htm, http://www.NavSource.Org.

National Association of U.S.S. LCS(L) 1–130. Mighty Midgets.Org.

Naval History and Heritage Command. Navy Historical Center, Washington: D.C.. Oral History—Luzon Operation, Lingayen Gulf Landing, 4–18 January 1945. *Recollections of Lt. (jg) J. F. Brown, CO LCI(M) 974.* http://www.history.navy.mil/faqs/faq87-3q.htm.

To the Blue Sky's End Miracle of Kamikaze. http://www.warbirds.jp/senri/19english/english.html.

Underwater Demolition Team Histories WWII UDT Team http://users.frii.com/archives/UST3.html.

U.S. Naval Special Warfare Archives. http://www.navyfrogmen.com.

US Navy Landing Craft Tank (Rocket). Combined Operations. http//www.combinedops.com.

USS Landing Craft Infantry National Association. http://www.usslci.com/html.

Index

Numbers in ***bold italics*** indicate pages with photographs. Many of the LCI(L) gunboats were converted to (G), (M), and (R) variants. In some cases they underwent two changes. In order to avoid confusion in the index, they are listed as LCI, along with their hull number.

Aaron Ward DM 34 317, 318
Abbot DD 629 185, 194
Achilles ARL 41 157, 159
Adams, Lt. C.M. 361
Adams, Lt. Frank M. 48, 367
Admiralty Islands 94
Adroit AM 82 78
AFD 13 333
African-Americans 58–59
Agano 84
AGC 9 152
Ahlstedt, Lt. (jg) P.W. 361
Airsols 82
Alamo Scouts 205, 206
Alaska CB 1 247
Albina Engine and Machine Works 33, ***36***, 37, ***39***, ***40***, ***41***, ***42***, 50, 363, 364
Alexander, S 1/c Tommy 229
Alexander Majors 159
Allen, Mrs. A. ***40***
Aloe AN 6 118
American Army Air Force Units: Air Forces (1st Tactical Air Force) 244; (5th Air Force) 82, 96, 165, 239–243, (13th Air Force) 165, 193–194, 237, 239, 244, 247, 251; Groups (8th Fighter Group) ***163***; (30th Bomber Group) 244; (49th Air Group) 148; (90th Bomber Group) 244; (318th Fighter Group) 274; Squadrons (9th Fighter Squadron) 148; (36th Fighter Squadron) ***163***; (475th Fighter Squadron) 148
American Army Units: Armies (6th Army) 94; (8th Army) 189; (10th Army) 260, 268–269, 275; Battalions (88th Chemical Mortar Battalion) 26; Brigades (Second Engineer Special Brigade) 16, ***17***, 19; Corps (I Corps) 169, 171; (VII Amphibious Corps) 96; (X Corps) 146, 188, 189; (XI Corps) 175; (XIV Corps) 169, 171, 173; (XXIV Corps) 146, 150, 269; Divisions (Americal Division) 186, ***187***; (1st Cavalry Division) 148; (6th Infantry Division) 164, 169; (7th Cavalry Division) 156; (7th Infantry Division) 150, 152, 269; (11th Airborne Division) 175; (24th Infantry Division) 161, 183, 188– 190; (27th Infantry Division) 103, 117, 269, 272; (31st Infantry Division) 96, 188–189; (37th Infantry Division) 164, 169 173; (40th Infantry Division) 164, 169, 173, 185, 193; (41st Infantry Division) 193, 194, 195; (43rd Infantry Division) 164, 169, 171; (77th Infantry Division) 118, 146, 160, 262, 269, 273–274; (81st Infantry Division) 129, 135, 269; (96th Infantry Division) 150, 269; Forces (VII Amphibious Force) 13, 21; Regiments (5th Cavalry Regiment) 148; (7th Cavalry Regiment) 148; (12th Cavalry Regiment) 148; (17th Infantry Regiment) 152, 269; (19th Infantry Regiment) 189; (21st Infantry Regiment) 147, 190; (32nd Infantry Regiment) 96, 152, 269; (105th Infantry Regiment) 103, 269, 272; (106th Infantry Regiment 269; (111th Infantry Regiment) 26; (124th Infantry Regiment) 96; (126th Infantry Regiment) 96; (132nd Infantry Regiment) 88; (155th Infantry Regiment) 96; (162nd Infantry Regiment) 193, 195; (165th Infantry Regiment 269; (167th Infantry Regiment 96; (184th Infantry Regiment) 152, 269; (305th Infantry Regiment) 269; (306th Infantry Regiment) 269; (307th Infantry Regiment) 269; (321st Infantry Regiment) 269; (322nd Infantry Regiment) 269; (323rd Infantry Regiment) 269; (381st Infantry Regiment) 152, 269; (382nd Infantry Regiment) 152, 269; (383rd Infantry Regiment) 152, 269; (503rd Parachute Regiment) 161, ***184***; (553rd Engineer, Boat and Shore Regiment) 189; Regimental Combat Teams (103rd Regimental Combat Team) 169; (108th Regimental Combat Team) 192; (112th U.S. Cavalry Regimental Combat Team) 93; (129th Regimental Combat Team) 173; (151st Regimental Combat Team) 178; (160th Regimental Combat Team) 173; (162nd Regimental Combat Team) 193; (165th Regimental Combat Team) 103; (169th Regimental Combat Team) 169; (185th Regimental Combat Team) 173–174; (321st Regimental Combat Team) 135; (322nd Regimental Combat Team) 135
American Marine Corps Ground Units: Battalions (FMFPac Amphibious Reconnaissance Battalion) 218, 264, 272; (1st Marine Parachute Battalion) 87; (2nd Marine Parachute Battalion) 79; (3rd Marine Raider Battalion) 87; (V Phib Corps Artillery) 122; (VAC Reconnaissance Battalion) 117, 261; Brigades (1st Marine Provisional Brigade) 110; Corps (III Amphibious Corps) 110, 269; (V Amphibious Corps) 110, 209; Divisions ((1st Marine Division) 77, 93, 129–130, 269, 285, 334; (2nd Marine Division) 77, 110, 117, 269; (3rd Marine Division) 110, 118, 122, 209, 220, 336; (4th Marine Division) 110, 117, 209, 220; (5th Marine Division) 209, 220; (6th Marine Division) 269, 277, 279; (22nd Marine Pac Howitzer Division) 123; Platoons (Scout and Sniper Platoon) 211; Regiments (1st Marine Regiment) 269; (2nd Marine Regiment) 269; (4th Marine Regiment) 269; (5th Marine Regiment) 269; (6th Marine Regiment) 269; (7th Marine Regiment) 269; (8th Marine Regiment) 269; (15th Marine Regiment) 269; (22nd Marine Regiment) 106, 109, 269; (23rd Marine Regiment) 229; (25th Marine Regiment) 229; (26th Marine Regiment) 230; (27th Marine Regiment) 229–230; (28th Marine Regiment) 229; (29th Marine Regiment) 269
American Marine Corps Air Units: Groups (Marine Air Group 12) 194, 199; (Marine Air Group 14) 194; (Marine Air Group 32) 194; Squadrons (VMF 543) 294
American Navy Units: Battalions (121st Naval Construction Battalion) 304; Corps (VII Amphibious Corps) 175; Divisions (Mine Division 34) 237; Forces (Fifth Amphibious Force) 12; *see also* individual ship listings

INDEX

Amick, Robert 13
Amick DE 168 141
Ammen DD 527 322
Amory, LtCol Robert 189, 190
Amphibious Training Bases: Coronado (San Diego), CA 45; Florida Island, Solomon Islands *10*, 12, 78; Fort Pierce, FL *19*, 34, 45, 50; Galveston TX 50; Little Creek, VA 45; Morro Bay, CA 50; Ocracoke, NC 50; Panama City, FL 50; Solomons, MD 16, 34–35, 45–*46*, *47*–48, 50
Anderson, Lt R.A. 366
Anthony DD 515 321, 322
Antonelli, Maj John A. 229
Anzio CVE 57 309
Apache ATF 67 120
Appalachian AGC 1 155
Arawe 19, 77, 92–94
Arison, CAPT Rae E. 178, 181, 188–*189*, 191, 194, 197, 334, 337, 365
Arkansas BB 33 220
ARL 3 118
Armstrong, Lt G.N. 285, 361
Arnold, MajGen Archibald V. 269
Arnold, QM 2/c Dick 137
Arnold, MajGen William H. 186
Arnow, Lt (jg) Theodore 293
Ashburne, Captain Lord 100
Asia Islands 100; Igi Island 100
Atago 84
ATR 80 271
Auge, Lt John F. 121
Augustus Thomas 156
Aulick DD 569 147, 323–324
Australian Air Forces: Royal Australian Air Force 247, 251; Royal Australian Air Force 1st Tactical Air Force 237, 239
Australian Army Forces: Brigades (18th Infantry Brigade) 255; (20th Infantry Brigade) 250; (21st Infantry Brigade) 255; (26th Infantry Brigade) 242; Corps (1st Corps) 237, 250, 255; Divisions (7th Division) 237, 250, 255; (9th Australian Army Infantry Division) 237, 242, 244, 250; Regiments (167th Infantry Regiment)
Australian Navy Ships: *Ariadne* 100; *Arunta* 251; *Australia* 93, 147; *Gascoyne* 251; *Hobart* 186, 251; *Kanimbla* 251; *Manoora* 251; *Shropshire* 93, 147, 251; *Warrego* 251; *Westralia* 251
auxiliary motor minesweepers (YMS): *YMS 6* 193; *YMS 8* 193; *YMS 9* 193; *YMS 46* 193; *YMS 50* 193; *YMS 52* 193; *YMS 68* 193; *YMS 71* 193; *YMS 329* 243; *YMS 334* 243; *YMS 340* 193; *YMS 363* 243; *YMS 364* 243; *YMS 365* 193; *YMS 481* 193, 243
Avoyel ATF 150 320
Aylward, CAPT T.C. 222, *230*, 257, 367

Bagley, Lt W.G. 361
Baikie, Lt (jg) J.W. 354
Baka bomb 320
Baker, Lt (jg) C.J. 360
Balliere, Comdr L.B. 257, 264, 271, 272, 296, 361
Balmert, RADM Mark W. 353
The Baltimore Sun 47
Bannister, Lt T.B. 366
Bao Dai government 345
Barber DE 161 34
Barbey, VADM Daniel E. 21–22, 93, 96, 147, 250, 169, 182, *239*, *254*
barges (Japanese) 7, 12, *60*–*65*, 88–90, 126, 130, 133, 186, 199, 205

Barnstable APA 93 268
Barnum, Lt (jg) H.J., Jr. 359
Barr APD 39 211, 261
Bartley, Lt (jg) J.H. 361
Basilan Island 193, 195
Bates APD 47 211, 261
Battle of Empress Augusta Bay 84
Battle of the Bismarck Sea 7, 60
Battle of the Philippine Sea 118
Battle off Samar 149
Baum, Lt (jg) Wilferd H. 333
Baumholz, Lt Frank 222, 361
Bedell, Ens L. 213
Beierl, Lt Peter G. 321, 366
Beightler, MajGen R.S. 169
Belknap APD 34 166
Bell, S 2/c Dean 180
Bell, Lt (jg) Forrest W. 219–220, 359
Bell, Lt (jg) William B. 339
Bell DD 587 255
Belleau Wood CVL 24 309–310
Benjamin Ide Wheeler 157
Bennett DD 473 311
Bennington CV 20 309
Bennion DD 662 308, 317
Benoit, Peter 342, 344
Berkey, RADM R.S. 96, 147, 186, 194, 239
Berlin, Ens Theodore 85
Berter, S 1/c Fred *54*
Bethlehem Steel, San Francisco 364
Biak Island 99, 145
Bigos, Lt C.L. 366
Bird, Lt (jg) T.A. 359
Birt, Lt W.N. 366
Bishkin, Lt (jg) Leo H. 367
Bismarck Archipelago 77
Black, EM 3/c John C. 255
Blamey, Gen *254*
Blanchard, LtComdr Theodore 104, 109, 112, 115, 120–121
Blandy, RAdm William H.P. 22, 24, 135, 209, 222, 261
Bledesoe, Lt (jg) J.M., Jr. 365
Bleiler, RdM 2/c A.H. 317
Blessman APD 48 166, 211, 219
Blose, Lt (jg) H.W. 366
Blow, Bosun's Mate Frank 213
Boblette, Chief Bosun's Mate Paul W. 350
Bobolink AM 20 298
Bohol Island 145, 186, 187, 199
Boise CL 47 147, 194–195
Boone, Lt C.J. 232, 367
Borneo 196; Oboe I 237–244; Oboe II 237, 250–255; Oboe III 237; Oboe IV 237; Oboe V 237; Oboe VI 237, 244–250
Bost, Lt R.H. 187, 365
Bostock, Air Vice Marshal 239
Botright, Lt C.F. 367
Bougainville Island 12–13, 73, 175, 77, 82–83, 85, 90, 92, 95, 111
Bowerman, Lt D. 367
Bowser, Lt (jg) W.E. 361
Boyd DD 544 322
Bradley, MajGen James L. 150, 269
Brady, Lt (jg) Wallace A. 220, 359
Braine DD 630 321–322
Brennan, Lt Louis A. 327–328, 367
Brennerman, Lt (jg) B.L. 360
Brewster, Lt B.G. 366
Bricker, S 2/c James 131
Brickhouse, Lt S.M. 366
Brokaw, Lt R.B. 367
Brower, Lt N.H. 366
Brown, Lt B.G. 360
Brown, Lt (jg) G.S. 367
Brown, LtComdr Harris 222, 274, 360
Brown, Lt H.H. 360
Brown, Ens J.H. 332

Brown, Comdr M.B. 140, 360
Brown, VADM Wilson 16
Brown Shipbuilding Company 36, 363
Brown Victory 305
Bruce, MajGen Andrew B. 118, 160, 262, 269
Brunei 236, 249–250
Bruns, Lt (jg) R.K. 324
Brush, MajGen Rapp 169, 185
Bryant DD 665 211, 215, 226
Buckner, LtGen Simon B. 268–269, 333
Budke, Lt W., Jr. 361
Buka Island 75, 82–84, 88
Bull APD 76 166, 211, 261
Bullock, Lt J.R. 367
bum boats 340–342
Buna, New Guinea 93
Bunch APD 79 261
Burden, Ens E.W. 359
Bureau of Ordnance 22
Bureau of Ships 11
Burgin, Gen 24
Burke, LtComdr R.F. 261
Burns DD 588 255
Burris, Lt (jg) G.L. 331
Bush, Lt (jg) Kenneth L. 26, 31
Bush DD 529 308–310
Butler, Lt F.R. 365
Butler, LtCol John A. 229
Butterfield, LtCol Jackson B. 229

Cable ARS 19 157
Caldwell DD 605 100
Calicoan Island 146
California BB 44 150
California Institute of Technology 16–17, 19, 24
Callaghan DD 792 109, 327–328
The Calvert Independent 47
Cambodia, use of gunboats in *348*–349
camouflage 43–44
Campbell, Lt H.W. 361
Canton, China 64
Cape Gloucester 19, 21, 77, 92–94
Cape Torokina 82–85, 88
Capps DD 550 211, 216
Carabao Island 183
Carberry, LtComdr W.G. 261
Carbury, Lt W.G. 125
Cardamone, Lt J.J. 367
Carlson, LtCol Evans F. 8
Carlton, Lt James C. 138
Carlton, Lt P.S. 367
Caroline Islands 103
Casablanca 16
Cassin Young DD 793 309–311, 323, 327
Cataisan Point, Leyte, PI 148, *150*
Cates, MajGen Clifton B. 209
Cebu Island 145, 186, 199; Cebu City 186–187, 199
Chanidas, Lt H.W. 367
Chaote, LtComdr A.O., Jr. 151
Charleston Naval Shipyard 349
Charrette DD 581 255
Charter Party Agreement 343, 349
Chase, MajGen 178
Chemical Warfare Service 24, 27
Chenango CVE 28 251
Chernin, Lt Herbert 365
Chiang, Kai-Shek 345
Chickasaw ATF 83 156
Chickering, Lt H.D. 233, 317, 328, 366
Choiseul Island 75, 77–78, 81, 92
Clark, Lt B.T. 365
Clark, Lt (jg) E.M. 360
Clark, Lt (jg) F.B. 360
Clark, Lt (jg) R.W. 359
Claxton, Lt N.L. 365

Claxton DD 571 177
Clayton, Lt E.P. 261
Clemson APD 31 120, 166
Cleveland CL 55 185, 188
Cobb, Lt Howell C. 88, 327–328, 367
Cochenour, Lt (jg) W.H. 360
Cofer APD 63 243
Coffin, CAPT Clarence E., Jr. 24, 227–**228**, 286, 338, 361
Cogswell DD 651 323–324
Cole, Lt (jg) A.V. 361
Cole, Lt (jg) Francis W., Jr. 114, 131
Colhoun DD 801 309–310
Coller, Lt (jg) H.T. 359
Colombia CL 56 174
Columbus, Joe BM 1/c 59
Commercial Iron Works 33, **34, 35**, 36–37, 42, 50, 130, 363–364
commissioning ceremonies 39–43
Conflict AM 85 78
Conley, CAPT 211
Connor DD 582 246, 255
Connors, LtComdr A.H. 222, 280–281, 361
Connors, Lt Gerald M. 220, 359
Conolly, RADM R.L. 104, 118, 151
Consolidated Steel Corporation 36, 363
Conway DD 507 188
Cony DD 508 78, 189
Cooke, Lt (jg) Thomas A. 32, 294, 361
Cooper, Lt A.B. 366
Cooper, John 335–336
Copper River Packing Company 354
Coral Sea CVB 43 103
Corey, Lt Russell 1st 218
Cornelius Vanderbilt 303–304
Coronis ARL 10 333
Corregidor CVE 58 103
Corregidor Island 103, **182**
Cowdrey, CAPT Roy T. **12**
Craig Shipbuilding Company **364**
Crawford, Lt R.K. 367
Creon ARL 1 255
crew duties 51–53
Crist, Lt T.C. 120
Cronk, Lt J.L. 367
Croskey, Lt (jg) R.O. 359
Crosley APD 87 261
Crowl, Lt P.A. 360
Culp, Lt L.E. 366
Cunningham, BrigGen 93
Curley, LtComdr K.E. 367
Cyclone class 353–354

Dahl, Martin B. 342
Daniel, Lt R.T. 367
Daring AM 87 78
Davidson, Maj Robert 229
Davies, S 1/c Arthur L. 131
Davis, LtComdr N. Burt 162
Davis, Lt (jg) W.E. 361
Davis, Lt Young 285, 360
Day, Comdr Dwight H. 21, **22**, 176–178, 185–187, 244, 251, 255
Dean, Lt R.R. 360
DeCoursey, MoMM Edgar 51
Defoe Shipbuilding Company 36, 363
Del Valle, MajGen Pedro A. 269
Denver CL 58 84, 147, 185, 188
Derby, Lt H.L., Jr. 280
Dewey DD 349 120
Dickerson APD 21 166
Dimenna, Lt F.J. 367
Dinagat Island 146
Dodson, LtComdr J.A. 363
Doe, MajGen Jens E. 193
Dom, LtComdr William T. 222, 226, 270, 361

Donato, Maj 200, **201**
Doster, StM 2/c Robert 58
Downes, Lt A.M. 261
Dray, Lt (jg) J.F. 149
DUKW 16, **17**, 19, 21, 93, 106
Dulag, Luzon 146, 160; airfield 152
Dumenigo, Storekeeper Joe 149, 270
Dunckel, BGen William C. 161
Duong, Lt Hang Vo 348

Eakin, Lt (jg) E.M. 366
Eaton, LtComdr J.B., Jr. 151
Eaton DD 510 188–189
Eckel, Lt W.P. 362
Eckelmeyer, LtComdr A.F. 267, 277, 361
Edman, Ens C.L. 234
Eikel, LtComdr Robert 112, 129, 132, 289, 359
Eklund, Lt B.H. 367
Elder, Lt Franklin L. 179, 367
Eldman, Ens C.L. 360
El Dorado AGC 11 294
Eldridge, Lt Albert C. 196, 198, 204, **206**, 365
Elkton Plan 73
Elliot, Peter 335
Ellis, Lt Donovan R. 197, 206, 365
Emirau Island 91
Empress Augusta Bay 77, 82, 88
Engman, 2nd Lt Charles A. 294
Eniwetok Atoll 103, 106, **107, 108**; Camellia Island 106; Canna Island 106; Engebi Island 106; Parry Island 106; Ruunitto Island 107
Enterprise CV 6 61
Erskine, MajGen Graves B. 209
Espiritu Santo Island 62, 90, 363
Evans, Lt J.M. 365
Evans DD 552 320–321
Extricate ARS 16 331

Fabroni, FC 2/c Larry 317
Faddis, Lt James M. 319, 363
Fagan, Maj Richard 87
Farmer, Frank N. 337
Farrar, Lt John E. 286, 361
Fechteler, RADM William M. 96, 147, 175
Federal Ship Building and Dry Dock Company 36, **37, 38**, 363
Ferris, Lt G.C. 367
Fertig, Col Wendell W. 198–199, 204–205
File, Lt William H., Jr. 327–328, 367
fin-stabilized rocket **10, 19, 23**, 22–23, 301, 304; *see also* rocket development
firefighting **46**, 51, **71–72**; Iwo Jima 225; Okinawa 317–318, 325–328; Philippines 157–159, **179**
Fischer, Lt (jg) M.H. 360
Fisher, Lt Charles E. 220
Fitzgerald, Lt M.C. 365
Fleming, Lt J.D. 365
Fletcher DD 445 185, 194
Flory, Lt K.C. 283, 301–302, 360
Flusser DD 368 191–193
Fogg, Lt C.W. 363
Foote DD 511 84
Forrestal, SecNav 213
Fort, RADM George H. 78
Fort Pikit, Mindanao 189–191
Fortson, Lt T.N. 367
Franklin, Lt O.K. 367
Fremont APA 44 135, 160
French Indochina, use of gunboats in 345–346
French Navy, Vietnam 343–**346**; LSSL 2 Arbalete 345; LSSL 4 Arquebuse 345, **348**; LSSL 9 Hallebarde 344, 345; **348**; LSSL 10 Javeline 345; LSSL 28 Pertu-

isane 345; LSSL 35 Etendard 345; LSSL 65 Oriflamme 345; LSSL 80 Rapiere 345–**346**; LSSL 105 Framee 345, **348**
Frey, Lt (jg) H.W. 85–86
Frick, Lt H.D. 360
Friedman, Norman 372n6
FS 225 192
Fullam DD 474 87, 135, 230
Fulweiler, LtComdr J.H. 268

Gage, Lt J.A. 262, 274, 360
Gambier Bay CVE 73 157
Garibaldi, Lt H.J. 359
Gasiorek, Lt (jg) J.J. 361
Gates, Lt (jg) L.A. 360
Gazelle Harbor, Bougainville 89–90
G.E. Badger APD 126 166
Gear ARS 34 294
Geib, Lt J.C. 366
Geiger, Lt (jg) Frederick J. 274, 360
Geiger, MajGen Roy S. 87, 118, 269
General Engineering, Alameda, CA 364
George Lawley & Sons Shipyard 29–**30**, 31–33, 37, 50, 197, 363–364
Gilbert Islands 103, 110, 126, 251
Gilbert Islands CVE 107 251
Giliberty, Lt Frank R. 146, 173, 273
Gilmer APD 11 218, 261
Gilmore, Lt P.F., Jr. 363
Gingoog, Mindanao **202, 203**
Gipe, Lt (jg) M.O. 361
Gliemke, Lt A.P. 366
Glover, Lt (jg) D.A. 367
Godbout, Lt H.F. 100
Goff, Lt H.H. 361
Gooding, Lt E.W. 115
Goto, Maj Ushio 135
Grace, Lt (jg) V. 359
Great Lakes Naval Training Center 45
Greece, loan of gunboats to 343, 350
Green Cove Springs, FL 337
Greenleaf, Lt E.F. 363
Gregory, Lt D. 365
Griffin APD 38 261
Griffis, Earl O., Sr. *PC 1129* 176
Griggs, Lt (jg) D.G. 360
Griner, MajGen George W., Jr. 269
Griswold, Lt H.W. 367
Griswold, MajGen O.W. 169
Gruver, Lt (jg) Harry L. 220
Guadalcanal Island 7, 60–62, 73, 75, 78, 130
gunboat development, Royal Navy 8–10
gunboat tactics 1–2, 4
Gunn, Lt R.S. 367
Gustafson, Lt R.A. 359

Haas, LtCol Ralph 229
Haddock, S 1/c Claude 180
Haguro 84
Hall, Lt Charles A.U.S. 160
Hall, MajGen C.P. 175
Hall, Comdr Madison, Jr. 318
Hall DD 583 211, 276
Halmahera Island 95, 98, 145
Halsey, Adm William 12
Hamilton, Lt G.P. 361
Hampton, Vaughn E. 45
Hanlon, CAPT B. Hall 220, 261, 264
Hannett, Lt Comdr G.W. 153, 173–174, 222
Hansen, Comdr James R. 319
Harbor Boat Building 364
Harlow, Lt F.W. 367
Harma, Lt (jg) R.W. 361
Harned, Lt (jg) W.L. 170
Harper, Lt J.O. 363
Hart, Lt (jg) Billy R. 318, 363
Hart, Lt G.E., Jr. 367

Hartland, Lt (jg) G.W. 360
Hartness, Lt Carlton W. 155, Lt 359
Hatsukaze 84
Hayashi 2nd 171
Hazlewood DD 531 130
Headley, Lt G.J. 360
Heath, Robert F. 138
Heim, BM 2/c Robert C. 243
Heine, LtComdr H., Jr. 48, 367
Hellman, Lt Stewart W. 152
Hemingway, CAPT 147
Hendricks, Lt W.P. 154, 360
Henley DD 762 211
Henson, Lt C.C. 244
Herndon APD 121 261
Herring, Lt (jg) Rufus G. *213*, 214, 220, 325
Heywood L. Edwards DD 663 261, 274
Hidatsa ATF 102 172
Hill, RADM Harry W. 109, 222
Himawari 351
Himelright, Lt (jg) Paul C. 178
Hobbs, Lt Woodrow E. 206
Hobert, Lt (jg) D.K. 361
Hochuli, LtComdr E.S. 261
Hoctor, Lt (jg) John M. 172
Hodge, LtGen John R. 269
Hof, Lt L.R. 366
Hoffman, BGen Hugh F. 148
Hogland, Lt Edgar D. 191–192
Hollandia, New Guinea 110, 175, 197
Hollen, Lt (jg) T.T. 363
Holly AN 19 118
Holmes, LtComdr A.M. 166, 170
Homonhon Island 146–147, 160
Hone, Lt R.E. 367
Honolulu CL 48 121
Hoover, SM 3/c Harold 159
Hopping APD 51 261
Horner, Lt (jg) J.M. 167, 360
Hornet CV 12 309
Horovitz, Lt James J. 220, 360
Houston, Lt (jg) H.N. 325, 363
Howard, LtComdr P.W. 267
Howard DMS 7 191
Hudgins, Lt (jg) Robert S. 220, 359
Hudson DD 475 311, 317
Huff, Lt K.C. 233, 263
Hugh W. Hadley DD 774 320
Humboldt Bay, New Guinea 35, 175
Humphries APD 12 166
Hungerford, Ens A.O. 363
Hunnicutt, LtComdr R.F. 273–274, 277, 280, 360
Hunt, SM Arden Lee 170
Hunt, Lt W.I. 365
Hunter, CAPT 211
Hunter's Point, San Francisco 24, 227, 364
Hurley's Marine Works 364
Hyakutake, Gen Seikichi 77
Hynes, Lt (jg) James A. 311

Idaho BB 42 270
Ingraham DD 694 319–320
Inoue, LtGen Sadae 126, 140–*141*
Intrepid CV 11 311
Italy, loan of gunboats to 345
Iwabuchi, RADM Sanji 164
Iwo Jima 27, 111, 126, 130

Jackson, LtComdr R.L. 367
Jaeger, Lt F.R. 367
Japan, loan of gunboats to 343, *347*, 349–350
Japan Maritime Self-Defense Force 350
Japanese Army Air Units: (3rd Air Army) 309; (4th Air Army) 163–164

Japanese Army Ground Units: Armies (2nd Army) 95; (8th Army) 164, 309; (17th Army) 77; (31st Army) 112; (32nd Army) 258; Battalions (19th Liaison Boat Battalion) 176; Brigades (38th Independent Mixed Brigade) 77; Divisions (2nd Division) 95; (6th Division) 77; (29th Division) 115, 118; (32nd Division) 95; (105th Division) 164; (109th Division) 208; Groups (Kembu Group) 163; (Shimbu Group) 163–164; (Shobu Group) 163; Miscellaneous Units (Manila Defense Force) 164; (1st Field Base Unit) 95; (1st Raiding Group, 2nd Mobile Infantry, 39th Infantry) 163; (2nd Provisional Raiding Unit) 95; (6th Expeditionary Force) 118; (10th Expeditionary Unit) 95; (26th Special Base Force) 95; (87th Garrison Force) 77; Regiments (Suicide Boat Regiment 1) 289; (Suicide Boat Regiment 2) 289; (Suicide Boat Regiment 3) 289; (Suicide Boat Regiment 4) 289; (Suicide Boat Regiment 26) 289; (Suicide Boat Regiment 27) 289; (Suicide Boat Regiment 28) 289; (Suicide Boat Regiment 29) 289; (2nd Infantry Regiment) 129; (50th Infantry Regiment) 115
Japanese Navy Air Units: (1st Air Fleet) 309; (3rd Air Fleet) 309; (5th Air Fleet) 309; (10th Air Fleet) 309; (13th Air Fleet) 309
Japanese Navy Sea Units: 5th Cruiser Division 83; 8th Fleet 77, 84; Miscellaneous Units (6th Sasebo Special Naval Landing Force) 77; (7th Kure Landing Force) 77; Squadrons (*Shinyo* Squadron) 22, 42; (1st Surface Raiding Squadron) 289; (2nd Surface Raiding Squadron) 289; (3rd Surface Raiding Squadron) 289; (9th *Shinyo-tai* Unit) 179, 182; (12th *Shinyo-tai* Unit) 77
Japanese surrender to gunboats 124–125
Jenkins DD 447 185, 194, 243
Jeremiah M. Daily 159
Jinsen (Inchon), Korea 337–338
Jirka, Lt (jg) Frank, Jr. 218
John Blish 339
Johns, Lt A.U.S. James 160
Johnson, LtCol Chandler W. 229
Johnson, Comdr Frank L. 313
Johnston DD 557 157
Joint Chiefs of Staff 143, 145, 236, 237
Jones, Lt Richard L. 353, 367
Joy, RADM C. Turner 338

Kaelyanon, Adm Sathiraphan 356
Kakuta, VADM Kakuji 115
Kanda, LtGen Masatane 77
Kane APD 18 120
Karanemont, Lt (jg) H.N. 361
Karig, CAPT Walter 222
Kavieng, New Ireland 75
Kawashima, Maj Takenobu 95
Keefe, Lt (jg) Joseph J. 93
Keefer, LtComdr James R. 243
Keise Shima 264
Keliher, Commodore T.J. 334
Kelley, Lt (jg) E.E. 284, 361
Kelley, Lt James W. 318, 322
Kelley, Lt J.M. 363
Kelley, LtComdr S.J. 27, 222, 277, 279
Kelly, Lt J.N. 367
Kendal, Lt Joe 367
Kennedy, Lt (jg) Thomas F., Jr. 104
Kenney, LtGen George C. 63, 84
Kephart APD 61 161

Kerama Retto 261–*263*, 268, 275, 289–291, 293, 301–302, 314; Aka Shima 262, *290*; Amuro Shima 262; Geruma Shima 262; Hokaji Shima 262, 302; Kuba Shima 262; Tokashiki Shima 262–265, 291, 293, 301; Yakabi Shima 262; Zamami Shima 262
Kermon, Lt (jg) L.T. 367
Key DE 348 191–192
Keyes, Comdr C.M. 323
Kidston, Lt J.A. 152
Kikusui raids 301, 309, 317
Kimura, RADM Masatomi 63
Kincaid, VADM T.C. 198, *206*
King, Adm Ernest 73, 145
Kiriwina Island 77
Kistler, Lt (jg) R.H. 367
Kline APD 120 246, 252, 261
Knox APA 46 152
Knudson APD 101 261
Koga, Fleet Adm Mineichi 83
Korea, loan of gunboats to *36*
Korean "comfort women" 124
Krayer, RT 2/c Kenneth 193, 200–201
Krueger, MajGen Walter 205
Krulak, LtCol Victor H. 79
Kuribayashi, LtGen Tadamichi 129, 208, 258
Kutaka Shima 322
Kwajalein Atoll 104–106, 109, 118; Ebeye Island 104, 106; Ennubirr Island 104; Ennubuj Island 105; Ennylabagen Island 104; Gugegwe Island 105; Loi Island 106; Roi-Namur Islands 105
Kwiecinski, 1st Lt 285

Labiranan Head, Leyte Island *153*–154, *156*
Labuan Island 236–237, 246–247
Lae Atoll 7, 16, 62, 77, 109
Laffey DD 724 167, 313–314
Laird, Lt R.M. 360
Lamartin, Lt F.H., Jr. 366
LaMotte, Lt A.H. 363
Lamson, S 2/c Charles J. 270
Lamson DD 367 161
Lang, Lt E.M. 365
Larson, Lt (jg) J.A. 361
Lawrence, Risley Lt *LCS(L) 27* 180
Laylin, Lt (jg) Edward H. 148
LCF 8
LCF (Mark 3) 8
LC(FF) 41 195
LC(FF) 367 366
LC(FF) 484 222, 337, 365
LC(FF) 536 297, 304
LC(FF) 627 209, 211, 219–221, 275, 289, 301, 330
LC(FF) 651 364
LC(FF) 679 222, 271–272
LC(FF) 707 364
LC(FF) 708 364
LC(FF) 771 364
LC(FF) 772 364
LC(FF) 786 299
LC(FF) 789 366
LC(FF) 988 222, 365
LC(FF) 1079 366
LC(FF) 1082 366
LCG(L) 8, 9
LCG(L) 15 9
LCG(L) 16 9
LCG(M) 9
LCI 17 363
LCI 18 363
LCI 19 363
LCI 21 8, 12–13, 78, 87, 89, 90–91, 189, 191–192, 238, 249, 252, 363

Index

LCI 22 8, 14, 78–81, 87–89, 189, 192, 238, 249, 252, 363
LCI 23 8, 12, 78–81, 88–89, 192, 238, 249, 252, 363
LCI 24 12, 27, 78, 80, 82, 88–91, 189, 191, 238, 252, 263
LCI 29 244
LCI 31 21, 93, 147, 160–161, 169, 238, 247, 252, 363, 371
LCI 34 21, l93, 157–158, 162, 176, 238, 247, 252, 363, 371
LCI 36 363
LCI 41 364
LCI 42 363, 364
LCI 43 363, 364
LCI 45 363
LCI 46 363
LCI 59 238
LCI 61 13, 78, 189–191, 238, 252, 363
LCI 64 13, 96, 162, 166, 168, 170, 238, 248, 363, 370
LCI 65 13, 96, *98*, 166, 238, 249, 363
LCI 66 13, 90, 92, 189, *190*–191, 238, 252, l255, 363
LCI 67 12–13, 78, 89, 199, 238, 252, *331*, 363
LCI 68 12–13, 88–89, 96, 147, 162, 166, 168, 238, 249, 363
LCI 69 12, 13, *56*, *58*, 78, 89–90, 96, 98, 162, 166, 170, 238, 246,-247, 363
LCI 70 8, 12, 13, 78, 81–82, 84–*86*, 87, 89–90, 96, l98, 147, 162, 168, 238, 246–247, 363, 368, 370
LCI 71 148–149 156–158, 160–161, 185, 238, 244, 248, 363
LCI 72 148–149, 156, 1568, 169, 185, 189, 238, 244, 248–249, 363
LCI 73 148, 160–161, 169, 176–177, 249, 252, 363, 371
LCI 74 148, 158, 176, 185, 189, 238, 244, 249, 363
LCI 77 13, 112, 117, 129, *133*, 359, 363, 370
LCI 78 13, 112, 129, 359, 363, 370
LCI 79 13, 78, 112, 114–115, 129–130, 147, 359, 363, 370
LCI 80 13, 112, 227, 359, 363, 370
LCI 81 13, 115, 129, 359, 363, 370
LCI 82 13, 68, 112, 129, 132, 291, 292, 363, 368, 370
LCI 88 336
LCI 191 363
LCI 192 31
LCI 193 363
LCI 194 363
LCI 195 363, 364
LCI 196 363, 364
LCI 220 367
LCI 222 78, 80, 334
LCI 224 363
LCI 225 170, 178, 183, 185–186, 193–194, 363
LCI 226 170, 178, 182–183, 189, 191, 193, 195, 238, 363
LCI 227 193
LCI 228 162, 193, 244
LCI 230 162, 170, 185–187, 238, 249, 251, 331–332, 363
LCI 231 363
LCI 233 363–364
LCI 234 363–364
LCI 235 363
LCI 236 363
LCI 237 363
LCI 267 183
LCI 315 *37*, *38*
LCI 330 78
LCI 331 149, 156, 160–161, 169, 176, 185–186 238, 252

LCI 334 78
LCI 336 78
LCI 337 156, 158 162, 170, 178, 189, 193, 195, 238, 252, *332*, 333, 363
LCI 338 158, 162, 170 178, 183, 189, 238, 244, 249, 252, 363, 371
LCI 340 157–158, 178, 183, 186, 189, 193, 194, 363
LCI 341 157, 158, 170, 178, 1896, 189, 193–194, 363
LCI 342 147, 158, 160, 162, 169–170, 185–186, 189, 206, 363
LCI 345 13, 109, 112, 115, 120, 227, 353, 359, 363, 371
LCI 346 13, 112, 120, 209, 220–221, 359, 363, 370–371
LCI 347 13, *15*, 112, 129, 292–293, 295, 359, 363, 371
LCI 348 13, 120–121, 209, 220–221, 359, 363, 370–371
LCI 351 148, 222, 279–280, 361, 363–364
LCI 352 222, 225, 279–280, 361, 363–364
LCI 353 219, 280, 361, 363, 364
LCI 354 222, 279–280, 361, 363–364
LCI 355 222, 279–280, 361, 363–364
LCI 356 222, 235, 274, 277, 277–280, 361, 363–364, 371
LCI 357 157
LCI 359 169, 176, 185, 238–239, 244, 247, 363
LCI 361 194, 196, *203*–204, 206
LCI 362 169, 176, 185, 193–195, 238, 244, 363
LCI 363 196, *202*–204, 206
LCI 364 206
LCI 365 13, l04–108, 121–122, 152, 172, 359, 363, 368, 370
LCI 366 13, 121–122, 145, 150, 173, 261, 359, 363, 371
LCI 371 115, 371
LCI 372 112, 145, 154, 173, 261, 360, 363, 371
LCI 373 21, 100, 112, 145, 173, 273, 360, 363, 371
LCI 396 129, 135, 139, 141, 363, 364
LCI 397 129, 135, 138, 360, 363, 364
LCI 398 363
LCI 401 363
LCI 403 363
LCI 404 129, 135–136, 139, 360, 363, 368
LCI 405 129, 135–136, 138–139, 360, 363
LCI 406 129, 133, 135, 141, 360, 363
LCI 407 21, 100, 152, 176, 302–303, 359, 363, 368
LCI 408 *30*, 363
LCI 412 363
LCI 413 363
LCI 414 29, *30*, 363
LCI 415 363
LCI 417 363
LCI 418 363
LCI 419 363
LCI 420 363
LCI 421 363
LCI 422 152, 155, 168, 360–364
LCI 429 196
LCI 431 169–170, 176, 185, 193–195, 238, 248, 363
LCI 432 194
LCI 437 13, 121–123, 227, 359, 363, 371
LCI 438 13, 104–105, 109, 112, 120, 209–*212*, 215, 219, 220–221, 335, 359, 363, 370, 371
LCI 439 13, 100, 104–105, 121–122, 145, 150, 173, 261–262, 359, 363, 371
LCI 440 13, 21, 104–108, 112, 121–122, 145, 150, 173, 261, 359, 363, 371

LCI 441 13, 104–106, 109, 120, 209–212, 217–222, 235, 359, 363, 370–371
LCI 442 13, 104–106, 109, 121–123, 152, 166, 172, *176*–177, 286, 360, 363, 371
LCI 449 13, 112, 120, 209–*214*, 215–216, 221, 325, 359, 363–364, 371
LCI 450 13, 45, 104, 121–122, 209–*212*, 216, 218, 220–222, 335, 359, 363–364, 370–371
LCI 451 13, 21, 112, 114–115, 150, 173, 264, 360, 363–364, 371
LCI 452 13, 112, 115, 129, 131, 273–274, 291, 299, 359, 363–364, 371
LCI 453 13, 21, 112, 117, 129–130, 359, 363–364, 371
LCI 454 112, 129, 273, 359, 363–364, 371
LCI 455 13, 112, 120, 129, 359, 363–364, 371
LCI 456 112, 115, 129, *132*–133, 140, 360, 363–364, 371
LCI 457 13, 112, 117, 209–212, 218–221, 335, 359, 363–364, 368, 370–371
LCI 458 112, 114–115, 120, 129 131, 152, 335, 359, 363–364, 371
LCI 459 112, 129, 131, 152, 363–364, 371
LCI 460 112, 115, 129, 152, 360, 363–364, 371
LCI 461 100, 112, 145, 150, 152, 154, 173, 274, 360, 363–364, 371
LCI 462 100, 112, 145, 150, 153–154, 172–173, 360, 363–364, 371
LCI 463 112, 129, 332, 360, 363–364, 371
LCI 464 121, 123, 145, 150, 153–154, 173, 360, 363, 371
LCI 465 121–123, 145, 173, 262, 271, 294, 300–301, 360, 363–364
LCI 466 121–124, 209, 211–212, 218–221, 360, 363–364, 370
LCI 467 100, 121–123, 145, 150, 173, 262, 299, 360, 363–364
LCI 468 118, 363–364, 368
LCI 469 120–124, 209, 211–212, 218–221, 335, 359, 363–364, 370
LCI 470 112, 129, 363–364, 371
LCI 471 120–124, 209, 211–212, 220–221, 359, 363–364, 370
LCI 472 120–123, 145, 150, 167, 267, 360, 363–364
LCI 473 120–123, 209–212, 218–222, 359, 363–364, 370
LCI 474 121–123, 209–*212*, 213, *216*, 220–222, 363–364, 368, 370
LCI 475 121–122, 145, 150, 155, 173, 261, 359, 363–364
LCI 506 363
LCI 514 363–364
LCI 516 364
LCI 517 363–364
LCI 528 363–364
LCI 538 *330*, 363–364
LCI 539 363
LCI 540 363
LCI 541 363
LCI 542 363–364
LCI 543 363
LCI 544 363
LCI 550 141
LCI 556 363
LCI 557 363
LCI 558 68, 158–159, 166, 168, 172, 177, 290, 299, 360, 363, 368
LCI 559 159, 166–168, 294, 299, 301, 360, 363, 368
LCI 560 159, 166, 168, 173, 265, 299, 360, 363, 368
LCI 561 176, 273–274, 360, 363
LCI 564 152, 166
LCI 565 152, 173, 360

Index

LCI 566 141, 360, 364
LCI 567 100, 152, 166, 173, 262, 283, 360
LCI 568 100, 149, 152, 155, 166, 173, 262, 270–271, 274, 300–301, 360
LCI 569 48
LCI 570 363–364
LCI 571 363–364
LCI 572 363–364
LCI 573 363–364
LCI 574 363–364
LCI 575 363–364
LCI 576 363–364
LCI 577 363–364
LCI 578 363–364
LCI 579 363–364
LCI 580 **43**, 100, 152–153, 166, 173, 176, 262, 360, 363–364, 368
LCI 582 362–364
LCI 588 362–364
LCI 592 48
LCI 594 362–364
LCI 595 363–364
LCI 596 363–364
LCI 630 222, 269, 361, 364
LCI 631 222, 269, 361, 363–364
LCI 632 222, 269, 277, 361, 363–364
LCI 633 222, 225, 277, 361, 363–364
LCI 638 22, 222, 234, 269, 361, 363–364
LCI 639 364
LCI 640 364
LCI 642 361–363
LCI 643 267, 282, 361, 363
LCI 644 227, 268, 361, 363
LCI 645 282, 361, 363
LCI 646 281, 291, 361, 363
LCI 647 267, 281–282, 335, 361, 363
LCI 648 267, 271, 305, 361, 363
LCI 649 267, 282, 335, 361, 363
LCI 650 268, 284, 361, 363
LCI 651 227, 275, 277, 304, 361, 363
LCI 658 150, 153, 173–174, 222, 361, 363
LCI 659 32, 150, 153, 173, 222, 294, 361, 363, 371
LCI 660 150, 151, 153, 173, 222, 361, 363
LCI 664 362–363
LCI 669 362–363
LCI 670 362–363
LCI 673 362–363
LCI 674 362, 364
LCI 676 152, 166
LCI 704 267, 277, 361, 364
LCI 705 267, 277, 361, 364
LCI 706 267, 361, 364
LCI 707 227, 268, 361, 364
LCI 708 **22**, 227, **229**, 268, 297, 361, 364
LCI 725 112, 129, 335, 359, 363–364, 371
LCI 726 112, 129, 335, 359, 363–364, 371
LCI 727 129, 135, 360, 363–364
LCI 728 129, 135, 139, 360, 363–364
LCI 729 129, 135, 138–139, 141, 360, 363–364
LCI 730 129, 135, 137, 139, 141, 360, 363–364
LCI 731 141
LCI 732 139, 141, 363
LCI 733 140–141
LCI 734 141
LCI 735 141
LCI 736 141
LCI 737 141
LCI 739 25, 26, 129–130, 135, 222, 274, 303–304, 360, 363–364
LCI 740 25, 129, 135, 222, 274, 304, 360, 363–364
LCI 741 25, 129–130, 135, 222, 274, 303–305, 360, 363
LCI 742 25, 129–130, 135, 222, 274, 304, 360, 363–364
LCI 744 363
LCI 745 363
LCI 746 363
LCI 747 363
LCI 748 363
LCI 749 363
LCI 751 152, 159, 166, 168, 176, 273, 294, 299–300, 360, 363–364
LCI 752 151, 157, 335, 359, 363–364
LCI 754 111, 150, 153, 173, 222, 294, 361, 363–364
LCI 755 173, 176, 274, 361, 363
LCI 756 222, 269, 361, 363–364
LCI 757 222, 361, 363
LCI 760 222, 361, 363
LCI 761 364
LCI 762 267, 282, 285, 335, 361, 363
LCI 763 267, 271, 275, 295, 335, 361, 363
LCI 764 267, 282, 361, 363
LCI 765 361, 363–364
LCI 766 361, 363–364
LCI 767 361, 363
LCI 768 364
LCI 769 281, 283–284, 361, 363
LCI 770 275, 282, 302, 365, 363
LCI 771 227, 268, 361, 363
LCI 772 227, 268, 304, 361, 363
LCI 773 363
LCI 774 363
LCI 775 363
LCI 776 332, 363
LCI 778 175, 189, 334
LCI 785 277, 335, 361, 363–364
LCI 787 364
LCI 801 262, 272, 285, 302, 334, 360, 363–364
LCI 802 262, 272, 274–275, 285, 294, 302, 334, 360, 363–364
LCI 803 **29**, 262–263, 272, 274–275, 285, 294, 302, 334, 360, 363–364
LCI 804 262, 272, 285, 302–304, 334, 360, 363–364
LCI 805 272, 274, 285, 302, 334, 360, 363–364
LCI 806 272, 274, 285, 302, 334, 360, 363–364
LCI 807 269, 274, 277, 280, 285, 360, 363–364
LCI 808 269, 273–274, 277, 280, 285, 360, 363–364
LCI 809 269, 273–274, 277, 280, 285, 360, 363–364
LCI 810 269, 273, 274, 277, 280, 360, 363–364
LCI 820 141
LCI 821 141
LCI 866 141
LCI 867 141
LCI 868 141
LCI 869 141, 142
LCI 870 141, 142
LCI 871 141, 142
LCI 872 141
LCI 874 141
LCI 875 141, 142
LCI 948 363–364
LCI 951 362–363
LCI 952 362–363
LCI 953 363
LCI 954 363
LCI 955 363
LCI 956 363
LCI 957 363
LCI 958 363
LCI 959 363
LCI 961 363
LCI 964 363
LCI 965 332
LCI 973 141
LCI 974 68, 171–172, 363, 368
LCI 975 152, 173–174, 222, 274, 277, 360, 363
LCI 991 141
LCI 992 364
LCI 1003 48
LCI 1010 222, 270, 277, 286, 361, 363–364
LCI 1011 222, 277, 363–364
LCI 1012 222, 234, 277, 361, 363–364
LCI 1013 **38**, 39
LCI 1014 363
LCI 1015 363
LCI 1016 363
LCI 1017 363
LCI 1018 363
LCI 1023 222, 361, 363
LCI 1024 267, 277, 335, 361, 363
LCI 1026 267, 277, 334, 364
LCI 1028 268, 283, 361, 364
LCI 1029 227, 268, 361, 364
LCI 1030 227, **267**, 268, 361, 364
LCI 1032 39
LCI 1055 152, 262, 274, 360, 363
LCI 1056 152, 158, 222, 234, 360, 363
LCI 1057 222, 360, 363
LCI 1058 159, 222, 303–304, 360, 363
LCI 1059 159, 262, 274, 360, 363
LCI 1060 363
LCI 1064 148
LCI 1066 141
LCI 1068 267, 277, 335, 361, 363
LCI 1069 267, 285, 335, 361, 363
LCI 1070 335, 361, 363
LCI 1073 141
LCI 1074 **201**
LCI 1077 227, 268, 285, 361, 363–364
LCI 1078 **267**, 300, 361, 363–364
LCI 1088 269, 273, 274, 277, 280, 285, 360, 363
LCI 1089 269–270, 273–274, 277, 280, 285, 360, 363
LCI Flotilla 3 211, 221, 359–360
LCI Flotilla 5 12, 90
LCI Flotilla 6 360
LCI Flotilla 13 48, 130, 137, 140, 142
LCI Flotilla 14 25, 129, 130, 173, 305, 360–361
LCI Flotilla 16 24, 227, 286, 361
LCI Flotilla 21 361–362
LCI(G) 10
LCI Group 1 359
LCI Group 7 112
LCI Group 8 112, 115, 117, 213, 221, 359
LCI Group 9 112, 114, 129, 132, 359
LCI Group 10 129
LCI Group 13 12
LCI Group 16 360
LCI Group 17 360
LCI Group 18 152, 360
LCI Group 19 138
LCI Group 39 129
LCI Group 40 130, 360
LCI Group 41 360
LCI Group 42 361
LCI Group 46 361
LCI Group 47 361
LCI Group 48 361
LCI Group 61 361
LCI Group 62 362
LCM(R) **10**
LCS(L) 1 33, 50, 364, 367
LCS(L) 2 33, 50, 345, 352, 364, 367
LCS(L) 3 33, 50, 345, 350, 364, 367
LCS(L) 4 33, 150, 345, **348**–349, 352, 364, 367
LCS(L) 5 33, 50, 364, 367
LCS(L) 6 33, 150, 364, 367

Index

LCS(L) 7 33, 35, 68, 178–179, 182, 364, 368
LCS(L) 8 *14*, 33, 35, 178, 183, ***184***, 238, 243–244, 252–255, 336, 364–365
LCS(L) 9 27, 33, 35, 175, ***196***, ***197–201***, 202–207, 336, 344–345, ***348***–349, 354, 364–365
LCS(L) 10 27, l33, l35, 175, 196–***200***, 201–***202***, 203–***206***, 336, 345, 349–350, 354, 364, 365
LCS(L) 11 33, 317, 364, 366
LCS(L) 12 33, ***268***, 360, 364, 366
LCS(L) 13 33, ***268***, 317–318, 321, 350, 364, 366
LCS(L) 14 33, ***268***, 284, 318, 350, 364, 366
LCS(L) 15 33, ***268***, 317–318, 323, 364, 366
LCS(L) 16 33, ***268***, 317, 323, 364, 366
LCS(L) 17 33, 364, 366
LCS(L) 18 33, 323–324, 350, 353, 364, 366
LCS(L) 19 33, 297–298, 323–325, 364, 366
LCS(L) 20 33, 350, 364, 366
LCS(L) 21 33, 319, 364, 366, 371
LCS(L) 22 33, 350, 364, 366
LCS(L) 23 33, 304, 317, 319, 364, 366
LCS(L) 24 33, 270–271, 310, 350, 364, 366
LCS(L) 25 33, 34, 318, 350, 364, 366, 368
LCS(L) 26 33, 34–***35***, 68, 175, 178, 180, 364, 365, 368
LCS(L) 27 33, 35, 68, 175, 178, 180, 182, 334, 336, 341, 350, 354–365, 368
LCS(L) 28 33, 35, ***69***, 175, 185–189, 193, 195, 200, 238, 239–***240***, 243–244, 252–254, 334, 336, 345, 350, 354, 365–365
LCS(L) 29 33, 35, 175, 185–189, 193, 195, 200, 238, 252–254, 334, 336, 364–365
LCS(L) 30 33, 35, 175, 185–187, 193, 195, 238, 252–253, 255, 336, 364–365
LCS(L) 31 33–35, 222, 228, 231, 319–320, 337, 364, 366, 368, 370
LCS(L) 32 33, 222, 364–365, 371
LCS(L) 33 33, 222, 228–229, 232, 311–***313***, 364–365, 368
LCS(L) 34 33, 70, 222, ***233***, 337, 345, 364, 366
LCS(L) 35 ***14–15***, 33, 58, 70, 222, 226, 233, 335, 341, 345, 354, 364, 366
LCS(L) 36 33, 70, 222–***233***, 310, 364, 366, 368
LCS(L) 37 33, 270–271, 295, 310, 364, 366, 368
LCS(L) 38 33, 270, 296, 364, 366
LCS(L) 39 33, 270–271, 342, ***343-344***, 353, 364, 366
LCS(L) 40 33, 270–271, 310, 353, 364, 366
LCS(L) 41 33, 193, 195, 238, 252–255, 353, 364–365
LCS(L) 42 33, 193, 195, 238, 249, 353, 364–365
LCS(L) 43 33, 189, 193, 195, 238, 243–244, 252–254, 353, 364–365
LCS(L) 44 33, 238, 243–244, 252–254, 339, 353, 364–365
LCS(L) 45 33, 238, 246, 248, ***250***, ***338***, 353, 364
LCS(L) 46 33, 238, 248, 339, 353, 364–365
LCS(L) 47 33, 238, 249, 339, 353, 364–365
LCS(L) 48 *13*, 35, ***39***, ***40***, ***41***, ***42***, 175, 178–179, 181–183, 238, 243–244, 249, 252–253, 336, ***340***, 353, 364–365
LCS(L) 49 33, 35, 68, 175, 178, 180, 182, 364–365, 368

LCS(L) 50 33, 35–***36***, 175, 185–186, 189, 193, 195, 238, 248, 252, 336, 353–354, 364–365
LCS(L) 51 22, 222, 228, 230, 233, 312–***315***, 317, 328, 337, 353, 364, 366, 368, 370
LCS(L) 52 33, 222, 322, 337, 350, 364, 366, 369
LCS(L) 53 222, 235, 297, 364, 365
LCS(L) 54 33, 222, 235, 323, 337, 350–351, 364–365
LCS(L) 55 33, 222, 322, 364, 366
LCS(L) 56 33, 222, 322, 335, 350–351, 364, 366
LCS(L) 57 33, 270, 311–312, ***314***, 337, ***347***, 350, 364, 366, 368, 370
LCS(L) 58 33, 44, 238, 247, 337, 350, 364–365
LCS(L) 59 33, 238, 246–247, 364–365
LCS(L) 60 33, 238, 246–247, 341, 350, 364–365
LCS(L) 61 33, 51, ***54***–55, 58, 299, 317–318, 322–323, 335, 364, 366, 369
LCS(L) 62 33, 299, 308–309, 335, 345, 364, 366
LCS(L) 63 33, 335, 345, 364, 366
LCS(L) 64 33, 308–310, 335, 345, 364, 366
LCS(L) 65 33, 299, 335, 345, 352, 364, 366
LCS(L) 66 33, 335, 353, 364, 366
LCS(L) 67 33, 335, 349–350, 364, 367
LCS(L) 68 33, ***280***, 298, 335, 350, 364, 367
LCS(L) 69 33, 48, 246, 298, 335, 364, 367
LCS(L) 70 33, 246, 364, 367
LCS(L) 71 33, ***72***, 364, 367
LCS(L) 72 33, 350, 364, 367
LCS(L) 73 33, 364, 367
LCS(L) 74 33, 350, 364, 367
LCS(L) 75 33, 339, 350, 364, 367
LCS(L) 76 33, 350, 364, 367
LCS(L) 77 33, 36, 350, 364, 367
LCS(L) 78 33, 337–338, 350, 364, 367
LCS(L) 79 33, 193, 350, 364–365
LCS(L) 80 33, 193, 345–***346***, 350, 352, 364–365
LCS(L) 81 33, 35, 299, 335, 350–351, 364, 366
LCS(L) 82 33, 47, 297, 299, 320–322, 335, 350, 364, 366, 371
LCS(L) 83 33, 297, 318–321, 323, 335, 350, 364, 366, 371
LCS(L) 84 33, 296–297, 308, 320, 323, 335, 350, 364, 366, 368, 371
LCS(L) 85 33, 335, 350, 364, 366
LCS(L) 86 33, 294, 321–325, 335, 350, 364, 366, 371
LCS(L) 87 33, 308, 310, 335, 350, 364, 366
LCS(L) 88 33, 350, 364, 366, 369
LCS(L) 89 33, 335, 350, 364, 367
LCS(L) 90 33, 299, 335, 350, 364, 366
LCS(L) 91 33, 36, ***42***, ***280***, 350, 364, 366
LCS(L) 92 33, 335, 364, 367
LCS(L) 93 33, 298, 335, 364, 367
LCS(L) 94 33, 323, 326, 335, 350, 364, 367
LCS(L) 95 33, 280, 298, 335, 350, 361, 364, 367
LCS(L) 96 33, 345, 349–350, 352, 364, 367
LCS(L) 97 33, 364, 367
LCS(L) 98 33, 350, 364, 367
LCS(L) 99 33, 364, 367
LCS(L) 100 33, 350, 364, 367
LCS(L) 101 33, 345, 349–350, 356, 364, 367
LCS(L) 102 5, 33, 287, 343, 350, ***351***, 353–***354***, ***355***, 364, 367

LCS(L) 103 33, 350, 364, 367
LCS(L) 104 33, 48, ***347***–348, 350, 364, 367
LCS(L) 105 33, 345, 349, 351, 356, 364, 367
LCS(L) 106 33, 350, 364, 367
LCS(L) 107 33, ***347***, 350, 364, 367
LCS(L) 108 33, 329, 364, 367
LCS(L) 109 33, 309–310, 350, 364, 366
LCS(L) 110 33, 309–310, 350, 364, 366
LCS(L) 111 33, 297, 311, 350, 364, 366
LCS(L) 112 33, 364, 366
LCS(L) 113 33, 298, 364, 366
LCS(L) 114 33, 311, 313, 335, 350, 364, 366
LCS(L) 115 33, 271, 311–312, 335, 350, 364, 366
LCS(L) 116 33, 271, 311, 313–***316***, 350, 364, 366, 368
LCS(L) 117 33, 35, 335, 364, 366
LCS(L) 118 33, 271, 335, 345, 350, 364, 366, 371
LCS(L) 119 33, 271, 335, 350, 364, 368–369
LCS(L) 120 33, 350, 364, 366
LCS(L) 121 33, 335, 364, 366
LCS(L) 122 33, 323, ***324***, 325, ***326***, 335, 354, 364, 366, 369, 371
LCS(L) 123 33, 321–322, 335, 364, 366
LCS(L) 124 33, ***280–281***, 298, 335, 364, 366
LCS(L) 125 33, 327–328, 364, 367
LCS(L) 126 33, 350, 364, 367
LCS(L) 127 33, 364, 367, 368
LCS(L) 128 33, 364, 367
LCS(L) 129 33, 325, 328, 345, 349–350, 364, 367
LCS(L) 130 33, 325, 328, ***347***, 350, 364, 367
LCS(L) Flotilla One 175, 181, 189, 365
LCS(L) Flotilla Three 230, 337, 365
LCS(L) Flotilla Four 297, 366–367
LCS(L) Flotilla Five 367
LCS(L) Group 1 365
LCS(L) Group 2 365
LCS(L) Group 7 365
LCS(L) Group 8 366
LCS(L) Group 9 366
LCS(L) Group 10 366
LCS(L) Group 11 366
LCS(L) Group 12 366, 367
LCS(L) Group 14 367
LCS(L) Group 15 367
LCS(M) 10
LCS(S) 10, 11
LCT(R) 8, 9
LCT(2) 9
LCT(3) 8, 9
LCT(5) 10, 11
LCV(P) 10
Leavitt, Lt (jg) M. 361
Leckie, Robert Pvt USMC 130
Lee, GM 1/c Thomas 35, 319
Legaspi, Luzon Island 164, 187
Leggat, Lt J.M. 253, 365
Lehman, Dr. Christopher M. 353
Lehman, Lt J.F. 363
Lehman, SecNav John 353
Leland E. Thomas DE 420 193
Lerch, Ens Thomas F. 331
Leutze DD 498 171, 211
Lewis, Lt (jg) Harold S. 180, 360
Lewis, Lt (jg) J.E. 359
Lewis, Lt W.C. 363
Lewis, Lt W.H. 361
Leyte Gulf 145, ***146***
Leyte Island 94, 145, 147, 153
Liddle APD 60 161

Liechti, Lt R.J. 367
Lindemann, LtComdr M.J. 129
Lingayen, Luzon Island 145
Lingayen Gulf, PI 21, 68, 163–174
Liscome Bay CVE 56 103
Little DD 803 231, 318–319
Lockwood, Lt C.C. 366
Loessig, Lt M.G. 367
Long Beach, CA 350
Long Beach Naval Shipyard *31*
Longshaw DD 559 279, 289
Los Negros Island 94
Lough DE 586 176
Lowrance, Lt (jg) B.A. 361
Loy APD 56 261
LSM 135 335
LSM 169 178
LSM 318 161
LSM(R) 188 335
LSM(R) 189 268
LSM(R) 190 268
LSM(R) 191 268, 317
LSM(R) 192 268
LSM(R) 193 268, 320
LSM(R) 194 319
LSM(R) 195 268, 318
LST (H) 929
LST 226 157
LST 399 80–81
LST 453 21
LST 610 172
LST 667 179
LST 737 161
LST 808 304
LST 884 271
LST 925 172
LST 949 269
LST 1028 172
Lukas, Lt E.J. 361
Lusk, Lt (jg) J.H. 361
Luzon Island 124, 145, 161, 163, 164
Lynch, Lt T.C. 365

Maalaea Bay, Maui, Hawaii 104
MacArthur, Gen Douglas 7, 73, 77, 94–95, 102–103, 110, 143, 145, 186, 198, 236–237, 258
Machacek, Lt Kenneth F. 231, 320, 363
MacKay, Ron 354
Mackres, Lt (jg) Charles J. 173, 360
Mahan DD 364 161
Makin Atoll 103; Butaritari Island 103
Malabang, Mindanao, PI 188–189
Malanaphy, Comdr Michael J. 112, 209, *211*, 219–222, 256, 275, 289
Mallin, QM 3/c Jim 35
Mann, Ens K.D. 360
Manus Island 94, 145, 363; Seeadler Harbor 21, 94
Mapia Islands 99; Bras Island 100; Finaldo Island 100; Pegun Island 100
Mare Island 352–353, 355
Maren I 342, **344**
Mariana Islands 67, 110, 117–119, 126, 228; Guam 67, 118, *119*, 120–123, 125, 142; Saipan *54*, 67, 103, 110, 112–*113*, 115, 121, 125, 165, 208–209, 223, 235; Tinian 67, 110, 112, 115–*116*, 117, 125, 208
Marincovich, Lt (jg) A.P. 365
Marine Reconnaissance 1, 4; units 68–69
Marion, Lt G.T. 261
Mariveles Harbor, Luzon Island 13–14, 173, 179, 181, 183
Mark 7 rocket launcher *18*, *19*, *20*
Marshall, George C. Gen 73
Marshall, Paul Maj 203
Marshall Islands 103, 105, 110, 126

Martin, CAPT 211
Martin, MajGen Clarence A. 189
Martin, Lt H.N. 363
Maru-re 67–**68**, 171–172, 176, 290, **291**–292, 295, 298
Marvin, Lt (jg) Philip P. 151, 361
Maryland BB 46 147
Masbate Island 145, 199–**201**
mascot dolls 302
Mason, Prof.William J. 352, 354, 356
Massey DD 778 322
Matsueda, Lt Yoshihisa 179
Matthew P. Deady 159
Mattson, Lt H.M. 262, 269, 302, 305, 335
Maurone, Dominick C. 107
Maya 84
Mayo, Lt (jg) George D. 118
McCaleb, LtComdr William R. 121
McCarthy, Lt W.P. 365
McCloud, StM 1/c Huram 58
McCool, Lt Richard M. 324–**325**, 326–327, 354, 363
McCray, Lt S.A. 363
McDade, Ray 354
McDaniel, Lt (jg) W.K. 361
McEnroe, Lt (jg) John D. 21, 359
McFadden, LtComdr James F. 112, 129, 270, 300, 359
McIsaac, CAPT J.M. 367
McKee DD 575 106
McKenna, Lt (jg) Laurance 319
McKnight, LtComdr H.T. 267, 283, 361
Meader, MoMM 3/c John D. 312
Medal of Honor 214, 325
Meek, Lt D.C. 361
Mefferd, Lt G.W. 363
Meister, Lt (jg) Harry G. 180, 341
Meister, Lt H.K. 361
Merrill, RADM A. Stanton 82, 84
Miles, Lt O.L. 367
Milford, MajGen E.J. 250
Mills, Ens J.L. 359
Mills, Lt (jg) M.P. 360
Milne Bay, New Guinea 363
Mindanao Island 95, 145, 188–193, 196, 200, 205
Mindoro Island, taking of 161–163, 165, 185
Minneapolis CA 36 120
Mios Woendi Island 363
Mississippi BB 41 103, 147
Mitchell, Lt E.A. 261
Mittleman, Lt J.J. 359
Miwachi, Tsuko 301
Montgomery, Comdr A.R. 257, 262, 360
Montgomery, LtComdr Clifford E. 296, 363
Montpelier CL 57 84, 188
Moore, Lt W.A. 365
Moore's East Yard 364
Moosbrugger, CAPT Frederick 256
Moran, Lt (jg) F.R. 361
Moranz, LtComdr V.J. 261
Morison, Samuel Eliot 7, 103
Morotai Island 13, 95, 98–**99**, 100, 165, 188, 251; Cape Gorango 98; Cape Sopi 98; Posi Posi 98
Morrill, Comdr John H. 48, 135, 137, 140
Morrisey, Lt (jg) Thomas J. 93
Morrison DD 560 319
Morshead, LtGen Sir Leslie 237
mortar development, shipboard 24–32
mortar gunboat fire plans 223–226
motor gunboats (PGM): *PGM 4* 189–191; *PGM 5* 189–190; *PGM 6* 189–191; *PGM 8* 189–191; *PGM 17* 277–278
M.S. Tjisadane 303
MTB Motor Torpedo Boat *see* PT Boat
Muara Island, Borneo 246–249

Mucchi, Col H.A. 147
Mudge, Lt (jg) J.W. 361
Mueller, MajGen Paul J. 129, 137
Muldoon, Felix 354
Mullinnix, RADM H.M. 103
Mullins, Lt (jg) H.A. 359
Murphy, Lt (jg) H.G. 360
Murphy, Lt J.P. 365
Murray, Lt (jg) Donald 217, 264
Mustain, LtCol Hollis U. 229
Mustin DD 413 **31**, 317
Muth, Frank P. 199
Mutual Defense Assistance Agreement 344, 350
Mutual Security Act 349
Myers, Lt J.B. 367
Myhre, S 1/c A. **229**

Nadeau, SM Gilbert 246
Nail, Lt (jg) **190**
Nakagawa, Col Kunio 129, 135, 140–141
Nakajima, Lt (jg) Kenjiro 179, 182
Nakha 351; *see also LCS(L) 102*
Nash, LtComdr Willard V. 209, 220, 222, 359
Nashville CL 43 93, 255, 338
Nasugbu, Luzon 145, 173
National Air Cargo 356
National Association of USS LCS(L) 1–130 343
National Defense Authorization Act for Fiscal Year 2000 353
National Defense Research Committee 16, 22
Negros Island 145, 161, 185–186, 199
Nevada BB 36 217, 219
New Britain Island 13, 73, 90, 92–93
New Georgia Island 73, 77
New Guinea Island 7, 17, 65, 73, 75, 92, 102, 110
New Hebrides Islands 21
New Ireland Island 83, 90–92, 101
New Jersey Shipbuilding Corporation 37, 363
New York Shipbuilding Corporation 37, 363
New Zealand Army Forces: 3rd New Zealand Division 89; 14th Brigade Group 89
Newport Naval Training Center 45
Nicholas DD 449 194
Nicholls, Lt (jg) J.S., III 360
Nicholson, Lt J.M. 361
Niess, Lt (jg) F.J. 361
Niitsuma, 2nd Class PO Junzo 124–125
Nimitz, Adm Chester W. 7, 143, 145
Noble, RADM Albert G. **22**, 188, **239**, 251, 255
Noemfoor Island 94
Noffke, Mrs. E. 354
Norfolk Naval Training Center 45
North Platte canteen 48, **49**, 50
North Vietnam, use of gunboats in 345–**346**
Noshiro 84
Noumea, New Caledonia 12, 363
Noye, Lt J.A. 363

Oak Hill LSD 7 45
Oak Ridge ARD 19 160
O'Bannon DD 450 185
O'Donnell, Lt (jg) W.C., Jr. 361
O'Dowd, Lt (jg) Jerome J. 218, 220, 359
officer duties 50–51
Ogata, Col Kiyochi 115
O'Hare, Lt G.J. 363
Oie, LtCol Satyoshi 187
Okinawa 69, 130, 143

Index

Oliver, Lt D.A., Jr. 363
Omori, Adm Sentaro 83–84
Onderdonk, Lt A.B. 216, 261
O'Neal, Lt **190**
Ormoc, Leyte Island 160, 161
Orr, Lt (jg) E.E. 360
Osborn, Lt (jg) W.T. 360
Osterland, Lt Frank C. 231, 312
Overton APD 23 166
Oya, CAPT Goichi 115
Oyamada, LtComdr Shoichi 179

Pakana ATF 108 310
Palau Islands 100, 103, 126, 127, 141, 142, 165; Angaur Island 126–127, 130, 136; Babelthuap Island 126–127, 137, 140; Denges Passage *127*; Eil Malk Island 138; Garameyaosu 139; Gorokottan Island 130, 133; Kossol Passage *127*, 137–138; Koror Island 126; Ngargersiul Island 130, 133; Peleliu Island 21, 27, 94, 111, 126, **128–131**, 133, **134**, **136**, 137, 140–141; Schonian Harbor *127*, 137, 138, 140; Urukthapel 139; Yoo Passage *127*
Palawan Island 145, 184, 251
Palo, Leyte Island 146
Panamint AGC 13 303
Panaon Island 147
Panay Island, PI 145, 161, 185–186
Panichi, S 1/c Peter **54**
Parang, Mindanao Island 188–189
Parsons, Comdr Charles "Chick" 198
Parsons, Lt (jg) D.A. 359
Patrick, MajGen E.D. 169
patrol craft: *PC 14* 157; *PC 111* 157; *PC 625* 157; *PC 1078* **11**; *PC 1122* 100, 147; *PC 1129* 176; *PC 1133* 147, 179; *PCE 852* 157; *PCE(R) 855* 310; *PCS 10* 11
Paul Hamilton DD 590 211, 230
Payne, Lt L.G. 361
Pearl Harbor, Hawaii 13, 25, 28, 34, 103, 109–110, 123, 142, 172, 350, 363
Pedin, CAPT R.C. "Zeke" 338
Pennsylvania BB 38 150
Perkins, Lt (jg) Ray 296–297
Persons, MajGen John C. 96
Peterson, Lt H.A. 244
Petroff Bay CVE 80 **31**
Pfau, Lt W.E. 363
Philip DD 498 171, 243, 255, 338
Philippine Islands **144**
Philippine Guerrilla Forces 196–**201**, **202**, **203**, 205–207; 110th Guerrilla Division 203
Philippine Operations 145; King II 145; Love III 145; Mike I 145; Mike VI 145; Victor I 145; Victor II 145, 186–188; Victor III 145; Victor IV 145; Victor V 145, 188–193
Philippines, loan of gunboats to 343–344, 349
Phillips, CAPT Neill 296, 363
Phnom Penh, Cambodia: gunboats in **348–349**
Phoenix CL 46 93, 147, 194, 246, 255
Pierpont, Lt (jg) Powell 379
Pierrepont, Lt J. 365
Plant, Signalman 1/c Louis V. 13, 59
Politano, Lt (jg) S.S. 360
Polloc Harbor, Mindanao 188–189
Pollock, LtCol Daniel C. 230
Port Sual, Luzon Island 171
Ports, Charles R. 81
Powers, Lt (jg) Bernard J. 220, 359
Preston DD 795 261
Price, Lt J.C. 367
Princeton CV 37 84

Pritchett DD 561 327
PT boat 7; *PT 106* 192; *PT 167* 84; *PT 187* 87; *PT 245* 89; *PT 249* 89; *PT 251* 89; *PT 332* 191; *PT 334* 191; *PT 335* 192; *PT 336* 191; *PT 340* 191; *PT 341* 192; *PT 342* 191; *PT 343* 191–192; PT Squadron 24 191
Public Law 104–201 353
Puerta Princessa, Palawan Island 184
Purdy, Lt (jg) R.B. 305, 360
Purdy DD 734 294, 311–312
Puruata Island 82–83, 87–88

Rabaul 7, **60**, 62, 73, 75, 82–84, 91
Rabenstein, Lt L. Howard 121–122
radar picket stations **307**
Randall, Lt C.E. 363
Rann, Lt (jg) J.R. 132
Rathburne APD 25 166
Reed, SM 3/c Eugene 160
Reeves, RADM John W. 137
Reeves APD 52 261
Reichl, Lt (jg) Matthew J. 216, 220
Reid, Keith 354
Reifsnider, RADM L.F. 303
Rendova Island 77
Requisite AM 109 109
Rhame, Lt (jg) L. Richard 181
Rhodes, Lt (jg) C.W. 360
Rice, S 2/c Albert L. 131
Richardson, Gen 354
Rickabaugh, LtComdr Robert S. 152, 168, 299, 360
Riddle DE 185 298
Rielly, Robert QM 2/c 322–323
Rigel AR 11 21
Riggs, Merl L. 338
Riggs, RADM R.S. 185
Rimer, CAPT Theodore W. 21, 173, 257, 262, 269, 360
Ringold DD 500 98
Ritz, Lt E.J. 361
Rivel, Lt R.B. 367
Robert H. Smith DM 23 323
Roberts, S 1/c **229**
Robertson, LtCol Donn J. 230
Robinson, LtComdr Carl F. 152, 273, 360
Robinson DD 562 171–172, 195
rocket development 16–24
rocket launcher **10**, **17**, **18**, **19**, **20**
Rockey, MajGen Keller E. 209
Rodgers, RADM Bertram 338
Roesti, Lt (jg) Homer R. **165**, 166
Rogers, BGen Ford O. **141**
Rogers, Lt J.M. 361
Rogers, Lt (jg) R.O. 359
Rollins, Lt (jg) E.A. 361
Rook, CAPT E.C. 223
Rooney, YN John 47, 322
Roosevelt, President Franklin D. 145
Rosenbloom, Lt (jg) Alvin E. 220, 359
Rosenburg, Lt (jg) H. 359
Ross, Lt (jg) D. Reid 337
Ross, EM 3/c Raymond J. 243, 246, 341
Ross, SMC 3/c William J. 321
Rounroengrom, RADM Surasak 353
Rowland, RdM 3/c H.V. **229**
Royal, RADM Forrest B. 150, 194, **239**, 243
Royal Thai Navy 343–344, **351**, 353, 356
Rudge, Lt A.H. 360
Rugle, S 2/c E. **229**
Rupertus, MajGen William H. 93, 129
Russell, Lt W.A. 363
Russell DD 414 177
Ryan, Thomas 35
Ryan, Lt T.J. 367
Ryers, GM 3/c Frances F. 314

Ryukyuan Coast Guard, loan of gunboats to 343

Sadtler, Lt P.B. 361
Saidor, New Guinea 77, 94
St. Lo CVE 63 148
St. Louis CL 49 120, 338
Saito, LtGen Yoshitsugu 112
Salamaua, New Guinea 16
Salute AM 294 246
Samar Island 145, 160
Samejima, VADM Tomoshige 77, 83
San Antonio, Zambales, Luzon 35
San Diego Naval Repair Base 363
San Diego Naval Training Center 45
San Jacinto CVL 30 309
San Jose, Leyte Island 153
Sanders, Lt C.H. 365
Sands APD 13 166
Sanga Sanga Island 196
Sangamon CVE 26 317–318
San Pedro, California **29**, 364
Sansone, Lt Joseph 363
Saratoga CV 3 84
Sarawak 236, 250
Sasebo, Japan **72**
Sauer, Lt (jg) R.W. 361
Saufley DD 465 78, 195
Schenck 122
Scherling, Lt (jg) H.M. 363
Schmidt, MajGen Harry 209
Schmidt APD 76 252
Schroeder DD 501 120
Schulz, Lt (jg) C.A. 224, 360
Schwartz, Lt (jg) H.R. 367
Seabird 354–355; *see also LCS(L) 50*
Seaver, Lt (jg) E.R. 360
Seely, Lt J.B. 363
Sellis, Lt (jg) Mark V. 363
Sendai 84
Shannon, Lt R.C. 367
Shannon DM 25 318
Sharpe, Lt (jg) J.M. 363
Shaw, Henry I., Jr. 93
Shaw DD 373 100
Sheldon, Lt (jg) M.F. 360
Shepherd, MajGen Lemuel C., Jr. 118, 269
Sherman, RADM Frederick C. 82
Shields DD 596 231
Shigemitsu, MajGen Kiyoshi 118
Shinyo **66**–68, 179–**181**, **182**, **290**–291, 293, 298
ship transfers, post war 342–351
Shoemake, Lt A.C. 361
Shortland Islands 77, 81–82, 92
Shoup Col David M. 8
Shumard, Lt (jg) W.M. 360
Sibert, MajGen Franklin C. 189
Sigourney DD 643 147, 189
Sigsbee DD 502 120
Silverthorn, CAPT Merwyn H., Jr. 261
Simpson, Frank 354
Sims, Lt J.H. 349–350
Skinner, Maj R.H. 152
Smith, LtCol A.U.S. 160
Smith, Lt (jg) C.J., Jr. 361
Smith, Lt E.S. 360
Smith, Lt G.W. 367
Smith, Lt Harry L. 312, 363
Smith, Lt Harry W. 180, 365
Smith, Lt (jg) H.M. 359
Smith, LtGen Holland M. 110, 114, 208
Smith, Lt J.C. 363
Smith, Lt (jg) M.L. 363
Smith, CAPT R.H. 194
Smith, Lt T.H. 363
Smith, VADM W.W. 334
Solomon Islands 7, 63, 77, 83, 102

Sondree, Lt R.R. 365
Sonoma ATO 12 156
Sorsby, Lt W.F. 359
South Vietnam, use of gunboats in 344–349
Spectacle AM 305 279–280
Spence DD 512 84
Spencer USCG 186
spin-stabilized rocket *22*–*23*, ***226***–***227***, 256, 286–287
Sprague, CAPT Albert T. 186
Sprague, RADM Thomas L. 148
Spruance, Adm Raymond A. 145
Staigar, S 2/c Joseph 53
Staley, Lt (jg) F.S. 361
Standard Shipbuilding Company 364
Stanford, Lt E.R., Jr. 363
Starkus, LtComdr C.J. 100, 261, 359
States, Lt L.A. 261
Steldt, Lt M.F. 365
Stembel DD 644 120
Stevens DD 479 189
Stone, LtComdr E.P. 59, 365
Strickland, Lt (jg) V.E. 361
Struble, RADM Arthur D. 147, 160, 162, 185
submarine chaser: *SC 10* 11; *SC 726* 160–161; *SC 731* 160
suicide boats 4, 65–68; *see also Maru-re*; *Shinyo*
suicide swimmers: Okinawa 297; Peleliu 137–140
Suisun Bay Reserve Fleet 354
Sullivan, Lt (jg) G.J. 359
Sullivan, LtComdr J.W. 268, 361
Sullivan, Lt (jg) R. 359
Sulu Archipelago 196
Suluan Island 145, 147
Sumner AGS 5 167
Surigao Strait 146–147
Suwanee CVE 27 251
Suzuki, LtGen Yoshiaburo 67
Sweeney, 2nd Lt John J. 230
Sweeney, Lt Robert E. 268
Swegle, Lt B.B. 361
Swift, MajGen I.P. 169
Swing, MajGen J.M. 175
Synan, Lt J. 365

Tacloban, Leyte Island 146–150, 198, Lt 200
Tada, Col Tokuchi ***141***
Tahara 2nd 171
Taiwan 143, 161–163; loan of gunboats to 343, 350
Takahashi, CAPT Isao 171
Takao 84
Takashina, LtGen Takeshi 118
Takeda, RADM Isamu 77
Tarakan Island ***69***, 237–239, 243, 252
Tarawa Atoll 8, 103
Tauali, New Britain 19
Taul, LtCol James 229
Taurman, Lt R. 360
Tawakoni ATF 114 277–278, 304
Taylor, Lt (jg) Olin 89
Taylor, Lt (jg) O.M. 360
Taylor, Lt (jg) W.R. 360
Taylor DD 468 194
Templeton, Lt (jg) J.D. 359
Ten-Go Campaign 309
Tennessee BB 43 150, 218, 220
Terminal Island, CA 364
Terror CM 5 214, 218–219
Terry, Lt (jg) John H. 59, 130
Terry DD 513 59, 130
Teshima, LtGen Fujisaro 95
Texas BB 35 220

Thailand, loan of gunboat to 350–351, 353, 355–356
Thirkield, Lt B.A. 81, 270–271, 363
Thomas, GM 2/c Charles R. 14–15, 226, 335, 341
Thomas, Comdr Edwin C. 47, 298
Thomas E. Fraser DM 24 323
Thomas Nelson 159
Thompson, LtComdr F., Jr. 227, 268, 361
Thorn, Lt E.S. 224, 360
Tientsin, China 337, 341
Timmons, Lt (jg) A.C. 360
Todd, Lt (jg) J.R. 363
Toem, New Guinea 94
Tojo Cabinet 126
Townsend, Lt (jg) W.B. 139
Townsend, Lt William K. 367
Toyoda, Adm Soemu 67
Tracy DM 19 292–293
Treasure Island, CA 364
Treasury Islands 5, 12, 75, 77, ***79***, 81, 83, 189, 105; Blanche Harbor 77–78, 80; Mono Island 75, 77–78, ***79***, ***80***–81; Stirling Island 75, 77–78
Truk Atoll 83, 103
Truman, President Harry S. ***325***, 329
Tsingtao, China 334
Tsukada, MajGen Rikichi 163
Turnage, MajGen Alan 118
Turner, Lt (jg) J.L. 361
Turner, Adm Richmond Kelley 8, 103–105, ***110***–112, 145, 209, 256, ***258***, 260
Tuscaloosa CA 37 220, 283
Twiggs DD 591 211, 215, 284
Typhoon Ida 330–333
Typhoon Louise 333–334

Underwater Demolition Teams: equipment 252; UDT 3 120, 150; UDT 5 150, 166; UDT 6 120, 150; UDT 7 261, 264; UDT 8 150, 166; UDT 9 150–151, 166; UDT 10 150–151; UDT 11 246, 252–254, 261; UDT 12 210–212, 216, 218–219, 261–262; UDT 13 210–212, 219, 261–262, 264; UDT 14 166, 210–213, 216, 261; UDT 15 166, 210–212, 218–219, 264; UDT 16 261, 264; UDT 17 261, 264, 273; UDT 18 252–254; UDT 19 261; UDT 21 261, 264, 273
Uemura 2nd 171
United Engineering, Alameda, CA 117, 126
U.S.–Japan Mutual Defense Assistance Agreement 350
United States Strategic Bombing Survey 117, 126
Unmacht, Col George F. 24, ***27***
Upton, Lt (jg) H.H. 360
Ushijima, LtGen Mitsuru 258
USS Landing Craft Support Museum 5

Van Valkenburgh DD 656 271
Vanderpool, Maj 176
Vella Lavella Island 77
Vicksburg CL 86 230
Vietnamese Navy (South): *Doan Ngoc Tang HQ 228* (ex *LSSL 35*) 344–345, ***348***; *Le Trong Damn HQ 226* or *Linh Kiem HQ 226* (ex *LSSL 4*) 345; ***348***–349; *Le Van Binh HQ 227* (ex *LSSL 10*) 345; *Luu Phu Tho HQ 229* (ex *LSSL 101*) 345; *Nguyen Duc Bong HQ 231* (ex *LSSL 129*) 345; *Nguyen Ngoc Long HQ 230* (ex *LSSL 96*) 345; *Nguyen Van Tru HQ 225* (ex *LSSL 105*) 345, ***348***–349; *No Than HQ 225* (ex *LSSL 2*) 345
Vincennes CL 64 298

Visaya Islands 126, 185
Voegelin, LtComdr B.D. 299, 263
Vogelkop Peninsula, New Guinea 145

Wadke Island 94, 145
Wagner, Lt J.A. 361
Waitt, BGen Alden H. 24
Wake Island 103
Wallace, CAPT 256
Waller DD 466 78, 195, 338
Walter, Lt (jg) B.C. 360
War Hawk AP 168 172
Ward, Lt D. 363
Ward, Lt (jg) E.E. 361
Ward APD 16 161
Warren, Ens 325
Wasatch AGC 90 189
Waters APD 8 261
Watkins, Lt (jg) W.B., Jr. 359
Watson, MajGen Thomas E. 269
Watson, CAPT Walter B., Jr. 356
Welch, Lt E.W., Jr. 367
Welsh, Lt (jg) W.M. 360
West, Lt (jg) L.A. 361
West Coast Shipbuilding Company 364
West Virginia BB 48 147, 167
Wewak, New Guinea 75
Weyler, RADM G.L. 147
Whalon, GM 3/c R.T. 87
White, Lt Homer O., Jr. 318, 363
White, Lt M.E. 363
White, Lt W.H. 246, 365
Whitehead, BGen David A. 242, 244
Whitmore, Lt J.B. 367
Wichita CA 45 120, 297
Wicklander, Lt E.B. 235
Wicks, S 1/c Stanley ***54***
Widel, Lt D.E. 365
Wierzblickli, Lt A.J. 363
Wilkinson, VADM Theodore S. 81, 87, 150, 169, 172–173
Willette, Lt J.M. 365
William C. Cole DE 641 280
William D. Allison 304
William D. Porter DD 579 322–***324***
Willmarth DE 638 100
Wilroy, Ens W.T. 361
Wilson, Lt J.C. 234, 361
Wilson, Lt W.D. 363
Wilson DD 408 301
Wing, MajGen L.F. 169
Winkleman, Lt E.Z. 361
Winston AKA 94 304
Wisner, Lt (jg) Robert 71
Wittman, Lt H.J. 367
Woodburn, Alberta 47
Woodlark Island 77
Woodruff, MajGen Roscoe B. 189
Woods, Lt F., III 363
Woodside, Lt R.H. 367
Wotho Atoll 109–110
Wright, Lt (jg) Edward S. 367
Wright, Lt (jg) F.X. 361
Wunsch, Lt (jg) M.C. 361

Yamashita, Gen Tadashi 205
Yamashita, Gen Tomoyuki 163
Yangtze Patrol Force 338–340
Yap Island 126
Yates, LtComdr E.L. 129, 360
YDG 10 305
Yokoyama, LtGen Shizuo 163–164
Young DD 580 189
Yuri Class 350

Zamboanga, Mindanao Island 145, 193–196, 200, 251
Zampa Misaki 267, 306

www.ingramcontent.com/pod-product-compliance
Lightning Source LLC
Chambersburg PA
CBHW080802020526
44114CB00046B/2729